Anticipating Total War

THE GERMAN AND AMERICAN EXPERIENCES, 1871–1914

The essays in *Anticipating Total War: The German and American Experiences, 1871–1914* explore the discourse on war in Germany and the United States between 1871 and 1914 – in the era bounded by the midcentury wars in Europe and North America and World War I. The concept of "total war," which was prefigured in aspects of the earlier conflicts and realized in 1914, provides the analytical focus. The essays reveal vigorous discussions of warfare in several forums – among soldiers, statesmen, women's groups, and educators – on both sides of the Atlantic. Predictions of long, cataclysmic wars were not uncommon in these discussions, while the involvement of German and American soldiers in colonial warfare suggested that future combat would not spare civilians. Despite these "anticipations of total war," virtually no one foresaw the practical implications in planning for war in the early twentieth century.

Manfred F. Boemeke is the director of the press, United Nations University Press, Tokyo.

Roger Chickering is a professor of history at Georgetown University.

Stig Förster is a professor of modern history at the Universität Bern.

PUBLICATIONS OF THE GERMAN HISTORICAL INSTITUTE

The German Historical Institute is a center for advanced study and research whose purpose is to provide a permanent basis for scholarly cooperation among historians from the Federal Republic of Germany and the United States. The Institute conducts, promotes, and supports research into both American and German political, social, economic, and cultural history, into transatlantic migration, especially in the nineteenth and twentieth centuries, and into the history of international relations, with special emphasis on the roles played by the United States and Germany.

Recent books in the series

Anticipating Total War

THE GERMAN AND AMERICAN EXPERIENCES,
1871–1914

Edited by

MANFRED F. BOEMEKE
ROGER CHICKERING
and
STIG FÖRSTER

GERMAN HISTORICAL INSTITUTE
Washington, D.C.
and
 CAMBRIDGE
UNIVERSITY PRESS

PUBLISHED BY THE PRESS SYNDICATE OF THE UNIVERSITY OF CAMBRIDGE
The Pitt Building, Trumpington Street, Cambridge, United Kingdom

CAMBRIDGE UNIVERSITY PRESS
The Edinburgh Building, Cambridge CB2 2RU, UK   http://www.cup.cam.ac.uk
40 West 20th Street, New York, NY 10011-4211, USA   http://www.cup.org
10 Stamford Road, Oakleigh, Melbourne 3166, Australia

© German Historical Institute 1999

First published 1999

Printed in the United States of America

Typeface Bembo 11/13 pt.   *System* QuarkXPress®   [BB]

*A catalog record for this book is available from
the British Library.*

Library of Congress Cataloging-in-Publication Data
Anticipating total war : the German and American experiences,
1871–1914 / edited by Manfred F. Boemeke, Roger Chickering, and Stig
Förster.
p.   cm. – (Publications of the German Historical Institute)
Includes bibliographical references and index.
ISBN 0-521-62294-8
1. Germany – Military policy.   2. Nationalism – United States.
3. Nationalism – Germany.   4. Culture conflict.   5. United States –
Military policy.   6. War and society – United States.   7. War and
society – Germany.   I. Boemeke, Manfred F. (Manfred Franz)
II. Chickering, Roger, 1942–   .   III. Förster, Stig.   IV. Series.
UA710.A76   1999
355′.033043′09034 – dc21   98-36611
                                                                CIP

hardback 0-521-62294-8

Contents

vii

Contributors

Volker R. Berghahn is a professor of history at Columbia University.

John Whiteclay Chambers II is a professor of history at Rutgers, The State University of New Jersey.

Roger Chickering is a professor of history at Georgetown University.

Sabine Dabringhaus is a research fellow at the Institute for East Asian Studies at the University of Munich.

Gerald D. Feldman is a professor of history at the University of California at Berkeley.

Stig Förster is a professor of history at Bern University, Switzerland.

Gangolf Hübinger is a professor of history at the European University Viadrina, Frankfurt an der Oder.

Alfred Kelly is a professor of history at Hamilton College.

Paul A. C. Koistinen is a professor of history at California State University, Northridge.

Raimund Lammersdorf is a research fellow at the German Historical Institute, Washington, D.C.

Derek S. Linton is a professor of history at Hobart and William Smith College.

David I. MacLeod is a professor of history at Central Michigan University.

Glenn Anthony May is a professor of history at the University of Oregon.

Jean H. Quataert is a professor of history at the State University of New York at Binghamton.

Thomas Rohkrämer is a lecturer in history at the University of Lancaster.

Irmgard Steinisch is a professor of history at York University, Toronto.

David F. Trask is a retired historian living in Locust Grove, Virginia.

Trutz von Trotha is a professor of sociology at the University of Siegen.

Robert M. Utley is a professor of history at Utah State University.

Bruce White is a professor of history at the University of Toronto in Mississauga.

Introduction

ROGER CHICKERING AND STIG FÖRSTER

The chapters in this book were the focus of deliberations at a conference that convened in Augsburg in July 1994. This meeting was the second in a projected series of five conferences on "The United States and Germany in the Age of Total War, 1860–1945." The design of the series is to survey the effects of new forms of warfare – and the new requirements of preparing for them – on these two countries, whose social structures, political institutions, and cultural traditions displayed significant differences during the period in question. The object is accordingly a comparative analysis of war and society – to study the massive impact of changes in technology and social organization on the conduct of war, as well as the impact of warfare on broader social, political, and cultural developments in the two lands.

The first conference in the series met in Washington, D.C., in April 1992, to examine the American Civil War and the midcentury wars of German unification in this light.[1] Here the deliberations laid bare the difficulties of comparison, for these campaigns appeared to have little in common beyond their contemporaneity. The German wars proceeded with a dispatch that not only kept the German casualty figures low but also limited the dislocations visited by mobilization on the home front, if one can even speak of a German "home front" during these conflicts. The American war, by contrast, provided many more plausible anticipations of the comprehensive kind of warfare that became known in the next century as "total war." It was far longer, more extensive geographically, and more costly, and it involved civilians directly to a far greater degree as providers of moral and material support to the soldiers and as immediate victims of military operations. However, analysis of the American Civil War also drew attention to features of the German wars that seemed to betray the

---

1 Stig Förster and Jörg Nagler, eds., *On the Road to Total War: The American Civil War and the German Wars of Unification, 1861–1871* (New York, 1997).

1

operation of forces, both on and off the battlefield, that subsequently drove the prodigious aggrandizement of warfare in the twentieth century. Tactical operations during these campaigns confirmed on a small scale the lessons from the other side of the Atlantic, where modern weaponry had frustrated offensive maneuver and the quest for the "decisive battle." Like the American Civil War, the war of 1870–1 also showed signs of becoming a *Volkskrieg,* a war that involved entire peoples. During the later phases of the Franco-German conflict, French civilians swelled the category of combatants, as the Germans directed their artillery on Paris and appeals from the French republican government for a new *levée en masse* ate away at operational distinctions between soldiers and civilians.

The second conference addressed the era bounded by the end of the midcentury wars and the outbreak of World War I, the great conflict that gave birth to the idea of total war. Framed as a question, "Anticipating Total War?" the theme of this conference was whether the experiences of war at midcentury figured in the subsequent anticipation and planning of warfare in Germany and the United States – and whether anyone anticipated warfare in the dimensions that it assumed after 1914. The first conference suggested a number of areas in which this question ought to be posed. Beyond analyzing the thinking of the soldiers and civilian planners who were professionally charged with anticipating warfare, it seemed important to investigate the attitudes of the figures who guided politics and diplomacy, as well as the calculations of business leaders about the likely economic impact of modern warfare. The study of popular attitudes toward war in this era recommended a survey of leading social and cultural groups, such as churches, veterans organizations, and other influential voluntary associations. Finally, it seemed essential to investigate possible portents of total war in several episodes of colonial warfare at the turn of the twentieth century that involved the soldiers of Germany or the United States.

The theoretical underpinnings of this venture are explored at more length in the book's two initial chapters. To anticipate the findings of the subsequent chapters, which constitute the heart of the book, the answer to the question posed was in most cases "no." The chapters reveal that discussion of war was ubiquitous in both countries. Apocalyptic visions were not uncommon, but many were tainted by association with pacifists or other marginal groups. Despite the extraordinary accuracy of some of them, these prophecies were remarkable for their extravagance or rhetorical abstraction; and regardless of who embraced them, they resulted in little reflection on the implications of protracted warfare and less in the way of practical planning. As a consequence, the course of events after the summer of 1914 surprised virtually everyone. Bellicose nationalism and aggressive enthusiasm about the benefits of warfare, which could be found in abundance on both sides of the ocean, provided little guidance as to the face of combat and mobilization in 1914. This generalization applies alike to Germany, where anticipations of war filtered through institutions and traditions that supported the militarization of society, and to the United States, where despite the direct legacy of the Civil War, military institutions and traditions were much more inchoate. In both countries, if for different reasons, the "lessons" of the American conflict paled in the eyes of most observers, as the German wars of unification suggested a more inviting – and deceptive – precedent for thinking about the next war.

The essays by Roger Chickering (Chapter 1) and Irmgard Steinisch (Chapter 2), which make up Part One, are designed to provide bearings for the investigations that follow. The discussions during the first conference suggested the wisdom of examining the idea of total war more systematically. Chickering's chapter surveys the history of this concept, whose utility, he argues, has suffered in the extravagance with which some observers have employed it. Chickering pleads for more sober use of the concept, principally as an "ideal type" or developmental model of warfare's extension along a number of axes, the most critical of which was the "systematic, calculated incorporation of civilians into the category of participants." Steinisch then explores some of the central parameters of comparison between Germany and the United States. Both countries, she argues, confronted problems born of rapid capitalist industrialization, the growth of imperial ambitions, and the currency of exceptionalist ideologies. Nonetheless, significant contrasts in institutions and traditions, as well as Germany's more immediate involvement in great-power rivalries, affected the way in which "matters of war" – such as militarism, navalism, imperialism, social Darwinism, and pacifism – were debated in the two lands.

The chapters in Part Two examine how the debate over war in both Germany and the United States was interwoven into economic and social issues, particularly into questions of social integration and social control. In exploring the economic foundations of military planning in the two countries, Paul A. C. Koistinen (Chapter 3) and Gerald D. Feldman (Chapter 4) suggest that most economic elites failed to foresee a conflict that would require extended mobilization or the coordinated planning of military and economic affairs. Koistinen concludes that the professionalization of the U.S. military – a growing awareness of the managerial, technological, economic, and broader political imperatives of modern warfare – advanced significantly further in the navy than the army during this epoch. Feldman examines the case of the German industrialist Hugo Stinnes, whose aggressive expansionism during World War I seemed to epitomize the marriage of war and industrial profit. However, during the prewar era, Feldman insists, neither Stinnes nor other leading German businessmen gave much thought to war, which they feared would only disrupt their pursuit of profit. "The great industrialists and the great bankers," Feldman concludes, "showed very little interest in preparing for war."

In other areas, discussions about war and preparations for war were impossible to divorce from questions of social power. Bruce White (Chapter 5) surveys the impact of military issues, from imperial expansion to intervention in World War I, on ethnic and racial relationships in the United States and Canada. He argues that debate over these issues fostered a growing intolerance of ethnic diversity in the United States, the conviction that minority allegiances could not be reconciled with patriotism. That attitudes toward ethnic minorities remained more tolerant in Canada was due to several factors, White suggests, including the nature and timing of immigration from eastern and southern Europe. Debates over war and peace also bore centrally on issues of social power that were garbed in confessional tension, as Gangolf Hübinger's essay (Chapter 6) on the German churches reveals. He notes the "asymmetry" between the Catholic and Protestant discourses on war. The enthusiasm with which several strains of German Protestantism embraced militarism and radical nationalism contrasted with the reservation of German Catholics, whose reluctance to wear these ideological emblems of "Germanness" corresponded to the stigma Catholics bore as second-class citizens in Imperial Germany.

Because war figured so large in the definition of patriotism and civic orthodoxy in Germany and the United States, it bore centrally on debates about the socialization of young people. The essays by David I. MacLeod (Chapter 7) and Derek S. Linton (Chapter 8) investigate the different circumstances in which this debate took place, although both authors conclude that in neither country did premilitary training anticipate the kind of war that came in 1914. In the United States, argues MacLeod, the direct effort to train boys and young men in military skills and attitudes fell primarily under the auspices of the ROTC, but it was "limited and mostly ineffective." More effective, he contends, was the "indirect" campaign that took place in the realm of youth groups, such as the Boy Scouts, and in organized team sports such as American football, where the virtues of aggressiveness, manly competition, and teamwork guided the agenda. Here the effort to inculcate patriotism and attitudes that were "effectively premilitary" provided training in a "metaphorical language," in which ethnic conscripts from the lower classes could one day converse with white upper- and middle-class officers. The "relative optimism" that MacLeod notes in these American efforts was absent in Germany, where, as Linton shows, class tensions, particularly middle-class anxieties about the success of socialist youth groups, drove the militarization of youth work. In his examination of the Pfadfinder and the Jungdeutschlandbund, Linton notes the centrality of premilitary training, war games, and the virtues of collective solidarity.

The systematic militarization of attitudes in Imperial Germany is also the theme of the essays by Thomas Rohkrämer (Chapter 9) and Jean H. Quataert (Chapter 10), which conclude Part Two. On the strength of his survey of veterans' associations, Rohkrämer argues that a significant segment of the German population was prepared for a "major war," if not the one that broke out in 1914. Of particular importance, he argues, was the intergenerational shift that occurred in these organizations, as veterans of the wars of unification ceased to make up the bulk of the membership. The place of these old soldiers, whose thinking about war reflected a sense of pride in their own achievement, went instead to reservists who had never seen action and who, to compensate for this lack, indulged in a general glorification of war. The radicalization of German militarism, Rohkrämer concludes, "resulted from the way in which [German] society dealt with [the] memories" of its earlier wars. Quataert draws attention to another dimension of the problem, which she calls the "gender war culture." She points out that understanding the popular acceptance of war requires attention to the gendering of the ideology of war. Women participated in this ideology because it provided them a public place – as care-givers to the male warriors. "The female sphere of care," she writes, "supported and authorized the emergence of a coordinated infrastructure of institutionalized civilian war-preparedness outside the usual military machinery." No less than the premilitary training of youth, though, the rituals practiced in this gender war culture "reinforced power hierarchies and inequalities while they affirmed as well notions of community and solidarity."

The focus of the chapters in Part Three is cultural. They deal directly with representations of war, the images that informed several levels of discourse on the character of future warfare, and the role of this discourse in the framing of national identities and policies. The chapters also provide direct documentation for the wide gulf that separated public expectations from the reality of combat. In a broad-ranging survey of the leading national magazines in the American market, John Whiteclay Chambers II (Chapter 11) controverts the proposition that acceptance of war was less widespread or enthusiastic in the American "public dialogue about the future of war" than it was in the German. The American discourse was both comprehensive and "extraordinarily inaccurate," as most participants reject-ed the idea that the American Civil War was a harbinger of future con-flicts. Alfred Kelly's essay (Chapter 12) on the myth of the "Great and Glo-rious War of 1870–1" suggests why the memory of midcentury German triumphs nurtured images of war that were as compelling as they were ob-solete. He demonstrates not only how this memory systematically misrep-resented the experiences of the soldiers who fought in it but also how the myth was constructed and why it was persuasive. Volker R. Berghahn (Chapter 13) takes up a related problem, namely, the vital connection be-tween war preparations and images of national identity in Imperial Ger-many. In his analysis of *Rüstungsnationalismus,* or armaments nationalism, he argues that constructing a German battle fleet was based initially on an "inclusive" construction of national identity that accommodated Catholics and industrial workers. A shift in armaments policy in 1906, however, be-trayed the belief among German leaders that a European war was now im-minent, and it encouraged a new "exclusive" definition of the national community as it added urgency to the German arms buildup. The catego-ry of "the other" henceforth applied not only to potential foreign enemies but also to the German "critics of vigorous war preparations."

Whether they were associated with martial skills or caregiving, opti-mism or anxiety, heroic individualism or teamwork, images of war were common currency in Germany and the United States. In describing sce-narios of conflict, they provided points of reference, however fantastic, that united veterans, young people, women, journalists, and churchmen in the popular discourse on "military matters." These images also were the central concern, if not an obsession, of strategists and military planners in both countries, whose charge was to translate images into operational reality. As the next two chapters show, the professional "military imagination" drew on the same cultural inventory that provisioned the popular imagination. David F. Trask (Chapter 14) surveys the torpor into which American secu-rity policy fell in the aftermath of the Civil War, when war meant policing frontiers in the continental West or the new pockets of American empire in the Caribbean and Pacific. These frontier adventures encouraged neither the armed forces nor the strategic thinking appropriate to the challenge that the outbreak of European war signaled to American security in 1914. Woodrow Wilson, Trask suggests, accepted the challenge; and by the time the United States entered World War I in 1917, the president had presided over a "revolutionary revision of the nation's cardinal national security policies." Stig Förster (Chapter 15) then offers the book's most significant challenge to the proposition that planners failed to foresee a long war. He reexamines a belief that has long been orthodox in the historiography of World War I, namely, that the scenario for war laid out in the Schlieffen Plan represented a "recipe for victory" and that the German army entered the war confident of a quick triumph. Förster shows that many of the officers who led this army into war, from Helmuth von Moltke on down, had a (more) sober appreciation of the risks that they were about to undertake. They entertained anxious images of the impending conflict, which some of them expected to last for years. If, however, these soldiers anticipated something approaching a "total" war, they did little to avert it, nor did they undertake any serious planning for long-term mobilization; and, in the moment of crisis, they pressed civilian leaders to pursue policies that promised, as Förster notes, to turn dreams into nightmares.

Finally, civilian leaders were themselves prey to fantasies when they contemplated war. In his analysis of the views of Theodore Roosevelt, Raimund Lammersdorf (Chapter 16) emphasizes the social Darwinist and racial motifs in the philosophy of this "most prominent militarist in American history." In Roosevelt's eyes, Lammersdorf points out, war represented the "highest and noblest achievement" to which a man could aspire. The American president's brief intervention on behalf of European peace during the Moroccan crisis of 1905–6 represented no departure from this principled embrace of warfare, but rather his fear lest the "higher" races of Europe fight with one another instead of spreading civilization, by conquest if need be, to the rest of the globe.

Statesmen and soldiers might be pardoned their illusions about the war into which they were wandering, insofar as their most immediate impressions of combat were drawn from "small" wars in Africa and Asia. Because these contests involved vast disparities of force, they required only minor exertions of modern armies and seemed to offer little guidance to their leaders. To judge from the concluding chapters in Part Four, however, the impressions conventionally drawn from colonial warfare are misleading. These chapters are devoted to several episodes in which German or American troops saw action, and they suggest that these small wars paved the transition between the people's wars of the nineteenth century and the total wars of the twentieth. Robert M. Utley (Chapter 17) examines the conflicts on the American Indian frontier. He rejects the suggestion that American Indians were objects of genocidal policies; in fact, he argues, the tribes fell victim to forces that were more economic, political, cultural, and psychological than military. Nonetheless, aspects of the conflict did anticipate "total" features of later wars, particularly the targeting of civilian infra-

structures by warriors on both sides. The purpose, Utley writes of the
army's strategy, "was not only to kill the enemy but also to destroy food,
clothing, shelter, and transportation and cast everyone destitute on a hostile
land to endure climatic extremes and psychological stress." Trutz von
Trotha (Chapter 18) looks at the behavior of German troops in Africa,
where he detects a similar tendency. In pursuing an "unlimited war of pacification" against indigenous peoples, he argues, the Germans recognized
no distinction between soldiers and civilian populations. He concludes that
"in the strategy of exposing entire populations to certain death by hunger
and thirst, unlimited wars of pacification are radicalized to the limit and
take on the genocidal trait of total war." In a careful analysis of the United
States' "ugly little war" in the Philippines, Glenn Anthony May (Chapter
19) takes these observations further. He points out that that the "fragile
barrier separating soldiers from civilians was definitely breached," particularly in the operations of the U.S. Army in southwest Luzon. In herding
civilians into "zones of concentration" in order to contain the guerrilla
campaign, the American forces consciously courted demographic disaster
and anticipated "the World War II practice of bombing cities." In fact, May
argues, "what came to be called 'total war' was colonial warfare writ large."
Finally, Sabine Dabringhaus's account (Chapter 20) of the German expedition to China in the wake of the Boxer uprising features the same whole-
sale violence against both civilians and soldiers. The so-called cleansing of
towns and villages, she writes, "extended warfare into purely civilian areas
and cost more lives than in open battles." No more than in the other instances of colonial war, however, did this savagery reflect a set plan to wage
total war against the Chinese. Like Utley, Trotha, and May, Dabringhaus
underscores instead the ideological violence, the dehumanization of Chinese, Hereros, Filipinos, and Sioux, which ratified the indiscriminate physical violence that Caucasian troops visited upon peoples of color.

The chapters in this book invite similar conclusions. Although expectations of war were widespread in Germany and the United States, most
were blind. The great majority of observers overlooked or disregarded the
manifold forces that were transforming warfare into a protracted, comprehensive, and ruinous ordeal in which civilians were no less essential than
soldiers to the outcome, and the very foundations of society were put at
risk. Most soldiers and statesmen were no less unprepared for these developments than were the populaces they led. Plans to harness industry, commerce, or morale in support of a long war were nowhere in place; only delayed entry into the war spared the United States the grim surprises that
greeted the European belligerents in 1914.

These conclusions harbor important interpretive ramifications for the war that came in 1914. There were no realistic plans to fight it. The first total war of the twentieth century was from the start a titanic exercise in improvisation. The mobilization of armed forces, economies, and societies proceeded everywhere with no prior design, no precedent, and no clear goals save for the play of contingency and institutional and cultural constraints. At the risk of slighting longer-term continuities, World War I might well be portrayed as the great disjuncture in the "narrative" of total war. In all events, these are among the problems to be addressed in the third installment of this series, whose theme will be the Great War.

PART ONE

Germany, the United States, and Total War

I

Total War

The Use and Abuse of a Concept

ROGER CHICKERING

Military history has largely escaped the methodological assaults that have been launched in the name of the "linguistic turn." The decentering of the historical subject, the constitutive function of language, and the discursive construction of meaning have unsettled the history of class, gender, and ethnicity to a much greater extent than they have the history of the battle-field. This state of affairs appears to vindicate Gordon Craig's long-standing complaint about the disdain with which social and cultural historians have regarded military history, although recent studies of industrial war's impact on relations of class and gender have betrayed significant traces of the new methodologies in the history of the home front.[1] But battlefield operations are evidently secure. Here questions of meaning and significance are resolved in troop movements, casualties incurred, or objectives seized – terms that seem, methodologically at least, unproblematic.

The security is deceptive. In even its most basic operational varieties, the history of military affairs is as much wedded to language and the discursive construction of meaning as is any other genre of historical writing. Here it suffices to note that modern military history has been governed for the better part of the twentieth century by a "master narrative." It is emplotted in the concept of total war.

---

1 Gordon Craig, "Political History," *Daedalus* 100 (spring 1971): 324. See Bernd Hüppauf, "Experiences of Modern Warfare and the Crisis of Representation," *New German Critique* 59 (1993): 41–76; Young-Sun Hong, "The Contradictions of Modernization in the German Welfare State: Gender and the Politics of Welfare Reform in First World War Germany," *Social History* 17 (1992): 251–70; Margaret Randolf Higonnet et al., eds., *Behind the Lines: Gender and the Two World Wars* (New Haven, Conn., 1987); Jean Bethke Elshtain, *Women and War* (New York, 1987); Jean Bethke Elshtain and Sheila Tobias, eds., *Women, Militarism, and War: Essays in History, Politics, and Social Theory* (Savage, Md., 1990); Sandra M. Gilbert and Susan Gubar, *No Man's Land: The Place of the Woman Writer in the Twentieth Century,* vol. 1: *The War of the Words* (New Haven, Conn., 1988).

13

The narrative informs all the standard histories of modern warfare.[2] It begins in 1792, when the armies of republican France, backed by the mobilized citizenry at home, revolutionized combat by virtue of their sheer numbers and the intensity of their commitment to the cause they were serving. The French Revolution thus foretold developments during the next two centuries, the growth in both intensity and expanse that marked the modernization of warfare en route to totality.[3] After the great political upheaval had laid the moral foundations of total war in the nation-in-arms, the industrial revolution provided its material bases after the middle of the nineteenth century.[4] Railways and telegraphy made possible the movement and management of mass armies, while factory production ensured the supply and equipment of these armies with modern weapons. The American Civil War occupies a pivotal place in the narrative of total war.[5] This great conflict demonstrated for the first time that the modern tools of war were encouraging strategic stalemate, that the prolongation of combat required the general mobilization of economy and society, and that the theater of operations was extending to civilians, whose labor and moral support were indispensable for the continuation of military action. During the last decades of the nineteenth century, industrialization and the modernization of armed forces throughout Europe laid the groundwork for wars that were to recapitulate the dynamics of the American Civil War but to dwarf it in scale.

The plot culminates in the "Century of Total War."[6] In World War I, the purview of conflict became global. At the same time, improvements in military technology, particularly advances in artillery and rapid-fire infantry weapons, created a strategic stalemate in the central theater of combat, which was so paralyzing that it remanded the decision at arms to the home front. Victory fell accordingly to the belligerent powers that best mobilized

---

2 See, e.g., J. F. C. Fuller, *A Military History of the Western World,* 3 vols. (New York, 1956); John U. Nef, *War and Human Progress: An Essay on the Rise of Industrial Civilization* (Cambridge, Mass., 1950); Theodore Ropp, *War in the Modern World* (New York, 1962); Henri Bernard, *Guerre totale et guerre révolutionnaire,* 2 vols. (Brussels, 1965–6); Richard A. Preston et al., *Men in Arms: A History of Warfare and Its Interrelationships with Western Society,* 5th ed. (Fort Worth, Tex., 1991); Hew Strachan, *European Armies and the Conduct of War* (London, 1983); Geoffrey Best, *War and Society in Revolutionary Europe, 1770–1870* (New York, 1986); Brian Bond, *War and Society in Europe, 1870–1970* (New York, 1986).
3 See Eric J. Hobsbawm, *The Age of Revolution* (New York, 1964), 101–25.
4 See Daniel Pick, *War Machine: The Rationalization of Slaughter in the Modern Age* (New Haven, Conn., 1993).
5 This theme is explored in Stig Förster and Jörg Nagler, eds., *On the Road to Total War: The American Civil War and the German Wars of Unification, 1861–1871* (New York, 1997), which presents the proceedings of the first in this series of conferences on "total war."
6 Raymond Aron, *The Century of Total War* (Boston, 1955).

all of their resources, human and material, and best withstood the efforts of the other side to carry the war to their civilian populations via blockades, submarines, and sporadic strategic bombing. Whatever distinctions remained between the military and civilian sectors then vanished inexorably in the second, quintessential total war of this century.[7] Despite the restoration of operational mobility in armored warfare between 1939 and 1945, this conflict was, by virtually all indices, more vast than even its immediate predecessor; and it featured the calculated and systematic annihilation of civilians, both from the air and in the death camps.

Despite the fact that this narrative portrays increasing levels of violence, death, and destruction, its structure is romantic.[8] The narrative subject is war, whose growth and fulfillment provide the central element of the plot. The theme is the *Selbstbehauptung des Krieges* (the self-assertion of war), and it culminates in the self-transcendence of war in Auschwitz and Hiroshima – in a destructive achievement so consummate that it defies historical representation – whereupon the narrative falls into foreboding silence.[9] The narrative's structure provides, in addition, its own dynamic and constraint. Modern war, writes Raymond Aron, has an "irrepressible dynamism," so that "national wars naturally tend to expand into total wars."[10] The modernization of warfare, the transition from Valmy to Hiroshima, thus proceeds with an inherent and ineluctable logic. The world wars of the twentieth century represent a "natural progression from earlier conflicts"; Hiroshima brings "a logical conclusion to a century of industrialized warfare."[11]

The narrative is underlain by philosophical assumptions drawn from several German sources. Total war, the telos of the narrative, represents in a common reading the realization of what Clausewitz called "absolute war," its liberation from the restraints that the Prussian philosopher himself identified in calculations of policy and the "friction" of combat.[12] In a variation on this theme, total war represents an ideal type of the sort that Max We-

---

7 Gordon Wright, *The Ordeal of Total War, 1939–1945* (New York, 1968); Peter Calvocoressi and Guy Wint, *Total War* (New York, 1972).

8 Hayden White, *Metahistory: The Historical Imagination in Nineteenth-Century Europe* (Baltimore, 1973); Hayden White, *The Content of the Form: Narrative Discourse and Historical Representation* (Baltimore, 1987).

9 Saul Friedlander, ed., *Probing the Limits of Representation: Nazism and the "Final Solution"* (Cambridge, Mass., 1992).

10 Aron, *Century of Total War,* 19, 39.

11 Ian F. W. Beckett, "Total War," in Clive Emsley et al., eds., *War, Peace and Social Change in Twentieth-Century Europe* (Milton Keynes, 1989), 31; Martin Shaw, *Dialectics of War: An Essay in the Social Theory of Total War and Peace* (London, 1988), 38.

12 Thomas Powers and Ruthven Tremain, *Total War: What It Is, How It Got That Way* (New York, 1988), 10; Preston, *Men in Arms,* 238.

ber envisaged. The phenomenon can never be fully realized; it poses instead the absolute toward which the development of warfare is tending. This is evidently the status of the term in the study of James Turner Johnson, whose eclectic employment of the philosophical sources is not atypical. Clausewitz, he notes, "in defining his concept of 'absolute war,' grasped well the nature of the ideal type of total war."[13]

Whatever the uncertainties over the ontology of total war, consensus reigns, at least implicitly, on the characteristics that define it. Total war is distinguished by its unprecedented intensity and extent. Theaters of operation span the globe; the scale of battle is practically limitless. Total war is fought heedless of the restraints of morality, custom, or international law, for the combatants are inspired by hatreds born of modern ideologies. Total war requires the mobilization not only of armed forces but also of whole populations. The civilians who labor on the home front are accordingly no less essential to the war effort than are the soldiers, nor are they less vulnerable to attack. The war aims and political goals of the belligerents are unlimited in total war, which accordingly ends only in the destruction or collapse of one side.[14]

The master narrative of total war has had enormous appeal to military historians in the second half of the twentieth century, for it has provided a coherent structure and a compelling heuristic framework to address aspects of warfare that have left an enduring imprint on our own world. It also has inspired enough bombast, confusion, misinterpretation, and historical myopia to invite the question whether it ought to be rethought and its central element, the concept of total war, be jettisoned. To anticipate, the remarks that follow culminate in a proposal that the concept be retained but that historians henceforth attend more to its manifold hazards and limitations.

Even a cursory glance at the history of the concept of total war suggests the wisdom of skepticism and caution in employing it. The honor of paternity appears to belong to the French leadership during World War I. Georges Clemenceau used the term *la guerre intégrale* to describe his intentions upon taking office in November 1917.[15] In the aftermath of the same conflict, Erich Ludendorff reflected on his own recent experiences and elaborated the concept *Der totale Krieg* into a systematic theory of war

---

13 James Turner Johnson, *Just War Tradition and the Restraint of War: A Moral and Historical Inquiry* (Princeton, N.J., 1981), 267.
14 The list can be found in numerous variations. See Qunicy Wright, *A Study of War* (Chicago, 1964), 303–13; Johnson, *Just War Tradition,* 228; Beckett, "Total War," 31–6.
15 Marc Ferro, *The Great War, 1914–1918* (London, 1973), 199.

and society. He argued that the titanic dimensions and all-pervasiveness of warfare in the modern era demanded the ruthless mobilization of all society's material and moral resources, and that this great effort required a military dictatorship.[16] The concept of total war was likewise attractive to the Italian theorist of air power, Giulio Douhet, who concluded that bombing civilians on the home front offered the only prospect of resolving the paralysis of modern land warfare.[17] By the outbreak of World War II, the term was in general use on both sides of the conflict, whose propaganda in turn assured the popular acceptance of the concept of total war.

The idea of total war has historically meant different things to different people. The men who contrived and popularized the concept were without exception pursuing specific, often conflicting agendas. Clemenceau's embrace of total war signaled his government's determination to assert civilian control over the war effort, whereas Ludendorff's use of the same term reflected not only his own frustrations with civilian interference in the affairs of the third Supreme Command ("civilian control" is too strong a term for the German case) but also his vision of a government free of all civilian interference in any phase of war. That the concept was of great service to Douhet and the other advocates of strategic air power during their interservice battles in the 1920s and 1930s needs no elaboration. Participants in the interagency battles of World War II found the concept serviceable, too. Goebbels's famous "total war speech" in February 1943 staked out a claim in a bureaucratic struggle for control of the civilian war effort in Germany; it also rehearsed a formula employed to similar ends on the other side.[18]

"Total" is a powerful word. Its connotations are foreign to compromise, qualification, or nuance. When soldiers, politicians, and bureaucrats invoked the idea of total war for partisan purposes in times of duress, they indulged the rhetorical excess that was inherent in the concept from the beginning. When historians subsequently did the same, they offered testimony to the power of the word, if not, as the proponents of the linguistic turn contend, to the power of all language to constitute meaning. The

16 Erich Ludendorff, *Meine Kriegserinnerungen 1914–1918* (Berlin, 1919); *Der totale Krieg* (Munich, 1935); cf. Hans Speier, "Ludendorff: The German Concept of Total War," in Edward Meade Earle, ed., *Makers of Modern Strategy: Military Thought from Machiavelli to Hitler* (New York, 1966), 306–21; Edmund Szcot, *Die deutsche Doktrin des totalen Krieges von der Machtübernahme Hitlers bis zum Ausbruch des zweiten Weltkrieges* (Vienna, 1946); Hans-Ulrich Wehler, "'Absoluter' und 'totaler' Krieg: Von Clausewitz zu Ludendorff," *Politische Vierteljahresschrift* 10(1969): 220–48.
17 Claudio Segré, "Giulio Douhet: Strategist, Theorist, Prophet?" *Journal of Strategic Studies* 15 (1992): 351–66; Edward Warner, "Douhet, Mitchell, Seversky: Theories of Air Warfare," in Earle, ed., *Makers of Modern Strategy*, 485–503.
18 Dietrich Orlow, *A History of the Nazi Party: 1933–1945* (Pittsburgh, 1973), 463–4; cf. John Burnham, *Total War: The Economic Theory of a War Economy* (Boston, 1943).

scholars are legion who have fallen prey to what Stig Förster and Jörg Nagler have called the "almost inflationary use of the term total war."[19] One
historian, who is distinguished enough to weather citation here, has recently written of "modern total war," in which "politicians and generals organized the total and material resources of a mass industrial society for war
and turned them to the total destruction of the resources, as well as the social and political system of another society."[20] This characterization claims
to describe the American Civil War, but its terms are so extravagant that
no war yet fought has fulfilled them.

Use of the concept of total war entails other rhetorical pitfalls, and
scholars have had to employ contrivances to sustain their metaphors. In an
influential article, Ian Beckett explained that warfare became "increasingly
more total" during the nineteenth century, although another scholar has
suggested that totality is not total, that it has phases, and that in the contemporary world, "total war becomes less total."[21] Still another writer has
claimed that during the Franco-Prussian War, total war was "partially in
place," and Raymond Aron has noted of the next European conflict that
"total war, for four years, limited itself to the trenches."[22]

As if to concede the rhetorical exhaustion of "total war," writers have
resorted to alternatives. Clausewitzian purists can appeal directly to "absolute war." Aron, perhaps uneasy over the capacity of total war to limit itself, preferred the term "hyperbolic war" to describe the combat of the
twentieth century.[23] Johnson has attempted to distinguish among varieties
of total war, which he categorizes as "holy," "national," and "ideological"
wars.[24] The systems theorists are less interested in the character of combat
than they are in its impact on world politics, but they commonly write of
"general," "hegemonic," or "systemic" wars, any of which can be "total."[25]

The rhetorical disarray reflects a grave flaw in a narrative organized
around the concept of total war. The narrative repeatedly misrepresents the
history of warfare during the past two centuries, for its heuristic constraints

19 See Förster and Nagler's introduction to *On the Road to Total War,* 13.
20 Edward Hagerman, "Union Generalship, Political Leadership, and Total War Strategy," in Förster
    and Nagler, eds., *On the Road to Total War,* 141. A similar view of the Civil War informs Hagerman's
    highly praised study, *The American Civil War and the Origins of Modern Warfare: Ideas, Organization, and
    Field Command* (Bloomington, Ind., 1988).
21 Beckett, "Total War," 28; Shaw, *Dialectics of War,* 44.
22 Stéphane Adoin-Rouzeau, "French Opinion in 1870–71 and the Emergence of Total War," in
    Förster and Nagler, eds., *On the Road to Total War,* 410. Aron, *Century of Total War,* 21.
23 Aron, *Century of Total War,* 20–1.   24 Johnson, *Just War Tradition,* 228.
25 William R. Thompson, *On Global War: Historical-Structural Approaches to World Politics* (Columbia,
    S.C., 1988), 100–11. For a review of some of this literature, see Jack S. Levy, "Theories of Gener-
    al War," *World Politics* 37 (1985): 344–74.

elide varieties of military experience that violate the developmental patterns it prescribes. Mark E. Neeley Jr. has recently challenged historians of the American Civil War for their uncritical embrace of total war as a central interpretive category.[26] To regard the Civil War as the first historical instance of total war, he argues, is to confuse the rhetoric with the reality of war and to overlook the powerful restraints, both material and moral, under which soldiers and politicians on both sides – including the crown witnesses, Philip Sheridan and William Tecumseh Sherman – prosecuted this conflict. Neeley's charges have brought a spirited response, and the debate over the "total" character of the Civil War has been salutary.[27] By emphasizing how much the term "total" obscures Nazi mobilization for war, Alan Milward has stimulated another salutary debate.[28] Countless other shibboleths, which the total war narrative has made staples of modern military history, cry out for critical examination. Napoleonic warfare was similar in fundamental respects to the style of fighting that it purportedly supplanted.[29] Global conflict has hardly been unique to the twentieth century.[30] Restraints of many kinds survived in the combat of the twentieth century.[31] Belligerent countries responded in fundamentally different ways to the challenges of warfare in the modern period. Even during the massive conflicts of our own century, the everyday life of most participants, men, women, and children, was a great deal more "normal" than the extravagant terms of total war imply. Mundane concerns of life and love, the pursuit of wealth, power, social mobility, and recreation, remained the most time-consuming occupations.

And in a fundamental respect, the distinction between the home and fighting fronts never disappeared entirely. Military historians must attend to the work of historians of gender. War, as Jean Quataert has recently emphasized, is a "gendering activity," and the distinctions between male and female roles in war, the "ideological division between men's and women's

26 Mark E. Neeley Jr., "Was the Civil War a Total War?" *Civil War History* 37 (1991): 5–28, and reprinted in Förster and Nagler, eds., *On the Road to Total War*, 29–51. cf. John B. Walters, "General William T. Sherman and Total War," *Journal of Southern History* 14 (1948): 447–80.

27 See James M. McPherson, "From Limited War to Total War in America," in Förster and Nagler, eds., *On the Road to Total War*, 295–310. James M. McPherson, *Battle Cry of Freedom: The Civil War Era* (New York, 1988).

28 Alan Milward, *The German Economy at War* (London, 1965); cf. R. J. Overy, "Hitler's War and the German Economy: A Reinterpretation," *Economic History Review* 35 (1982): 272–91.

29 See Arthur Ferrill, *The Origins of War: From the Stone Age to Alexander the Great* (London, 1985).

30 See Stig Förster, "Der Weltkrieg 1792–1815: Bewaffnete Konflikte und Revolutionen in der Weltgesellschaft," in Jost Dülffer, ed., *Kriegsbereitschaft und Friedensordnung in Deutschland 1800–1814*, special issue of *Jahrbuch für historische Friedensforschung*, no. 3 (1994): 17–38; Imanuel Geiss, *Der lange Weg in die Katastrophe: Die Vorgeschichte des Ersten Weltkriegs 1815–1914* (Munich, 1990).

31 Geoffrey Best, *Humanity in Warfare* (New York, 1980), 217–18.

worlds," have survived the purported breakdown of the separation between civilians and soldiers in the total wars of this century.[32] Whether in the home, in industry, as nurses, or even in the armed forces, the role of women has remained the support of men, who fight. Because their gender roles have also prescribed their vulnerability, women have enjoyed a degree of ideological exemption (admittedly diminishing) from the direct violence of warfare. In the guerrilla campaigns in Missouri during the Civil War, fighters on both sides usually drew the line at harming (white) women and children.[33] And even the most cheerful proponents of "city busting" in World War II professed some occasional public regret that women and children were incidental victims of their strategy.[34]

Another of the great shibboleths of total war is objectionable on additional grounds. Portraying total war as the military analogue of social, economic, and political modernization attracts to the one concept all the charges of teleology, determinism, schematic thinking, and regional bias that have attached to the other. The link between modernization and total war of any description also defies much of the empirical evidence. Economic historians have pointed out, for example, that the mobilization of the economy in the Confederacy during the Civil War was by most measures far more complete than the mobilization of the economy in the more industrially advanced Union.[35] This discrepancy matched another, also noted by historians of the American Civil War, in the theaters of operation. By all accounts, the most brutal combat of this war took place in the western theater, particularly in Missouri, where the atrocities visited by the two sides on each other had nothing whatsoever to do with modernization; it corresponded instead to the salience here of irregular warfare, which has universally provoked a brutal response.[36] It is also noteworthy that the soldiers most associated with the Union's "total war" against the South, including Sheridan, Sherman, and Ulysses Grant, saw action in this

---

32 Jean H. Quataert, "German Patriotic Women's Work in War and Peace Time, 1864–90," in Förster and Nagler, eds., *On the Road to Total War,* 449–77.

33 Michael Fellman, "At the Nihilist Edge: Reflections on Guerrilla Warfare During the American Civil War," in Förster and Nagler, eds., *On the Road to Total War,* 519–40. Michael Fellman, *Inside War: The Guerrilla Conflict in Missouri During the American Civil War* (New York, 1990).

34 See Charles Messenger, *"Bomber" Harris and the Strategic Bombing Offensive, 1939–1945* (New York, 1984), 25–6; Uri Bialer, "'Humanization' of Air Warfare in British Foreign Policy on the Eve of the Second World War," *Journal of Contemporary History* 13 (1978): 79–86.

35 Stanley L. Engerman and J. Matthew Gallman, "The Civil War Economy: A Modern View," in Förster and Nagler, eds., *On the Road to Total War,* 217–48.

36 Martin van Creveld, *The Transformation of War* (New York, 1991), 37; cf. Robert B. Asprey, *War in the Shadows: The Guerrilla in History,* 2 vols. (Garden City, N.Y., 1975); Walter Laqueur, *Guerrilla: A Historical Study* (London, 1977).

"backward" theater early in the conflict.[37] Nor was the negative correlation between modernization and total war limited to the American Civil War. The brutalization of the eastern front during World War II accompanied – if it was not caused by – the "profound demodernization" of warfare in this theater. The fact that combat here took on the character of a "war of ideologies," writes Omar Bartov, represented the Wehrmacht's attempt "to compensate for the loss of its technological superiority by intensifying the troops' political indoctrination."[38]

All of these criticisms might be described as internal, insofar as they suggest that the narrative of total war results in the neglect or misrepresentation of significant developments within the chronological bounds that mark out the narrative. Another, more fundamental flaw is external, for it raises questions about these chronological bounds and hence about the integrity of the narrative framework itself.

The concept of total war has historically implied agendas beyond the year 1945. Edward Thompson pursued one of these, contriving perhaps the ultimate rhetorical alternative to "total war" when he abandoned his scholarship to do battle against "exterminism."[39] But as a heuristic tool, the concept of total war has offered little help in understanding the varieties of combat that have raged around the globe since the conclusion of World War II. These have included conventional warfare reminiscent of both world wars in their operations, guerrilla campaigns, military raids, civil wars, and several instances of genocide. But all these conflicts have been limited, at least in the essential sense that they have been contained and have not involved the most destructive weapons available. And they cannot be extrapolated into the narrative logic of total war.

Nor can warfare on the other side of the frame. The narrative's greatest disservice has arguably been to promote the systematic misunderstanding of war in the early modern era. The narrative of total war portrays conflict in the eighteenth century, the *terminus a quo*, as a carefully limited and regulated affair, fought out for limited aims, according to accepted rules of engagement by small, professional armies that were recruited from the "nonproductive" sectors of society and kept insulated from civilians, both when the soldiers fought and when they were barracked. This view is a caricature, and it does not comport with the narrative that currently governs the military history of the early modern period. This narrative is called the

37 Fellman, "Nihilist Edge"; cf. McPherson, "From Limited to Total War."
38 Omar Bartov, *Hitler's Army: Soldiers, Nazis, and War in the Third Reich* (New York, 1992), 4, 12–28.
39 E. P. Thompson et al., eds., *Exterminism and the Cold War* (London, 1982).

"military revolution."[40] It is emplotted in what Michael Roberts, the original narrator, has characterized as the "prodigiously increasing" scale of European warfare in the early modern era – the dramatic increase in the size of armies, the expanding scope of their operations, and the heightened impact of warfare on politics and society.

The discursive parallels burnish, if they do not eliminate, the break between the eras that the two narratives purport to frame. "The armies of the Great Elector," Roberts himself has noted, "are linked infrangibly with those of Moltke and Schlieffen."[41] The narrative similarities draw out the omnipresence of armed conflict even in the age of reason, the gravity of the issues at stake, and the enormous impact of warfare on the lives of civilians. Eight of the fifteen conflicts that have merited Professor Wright's designation as "general war" took place between 1700 and 1783.[42] The war aims of Louis XIV were scarcely more limited, and a great deal more tenacious, than those of Napoleon. Before it dissolved in 1762, the coalition arrayed against Prussia in the Seven Years' War aspired to the destruction of that kingdom.[43] To speak of the limited impact of war on civilian life in the eighteenth century is to misconceive the nature and extent of the taxes, levies, and contributions associated with policies of "mercantilism" or "cameralism." The great preponderance of these myriad burdens on the common folk was generated by the need to raise, maintain, and employ armies and navies. Rudimentary forms of conscription – one of the hallmarks of total war – were well in place by the middle of the eighteenth century, not only in Prussia, whose pervasive military culture can hardly be described as "limited," but also in Sweden, Russia, Spain, and parts of the Habsburg empire, while in almost every continental state, military service was the defining characteristic of the ruling estate.[44]

If warfare seems nonetheless limited in the eighteenth century, the per-

---

40 The seminal texts are Michael Roberts, "The Military Revolution," in Michael Roberts, *Essays in Swedish History* (Minneapolis, 1967), 195–225; Michael Roberts, *The Military Revolution, 1560–1660* (Belfast, 1956). See also Geoffrey Parker, *The Military Revolution: Military Innovation and the Rise of the West, 1500–1800* (Cambridge, 1988); Brian M. Downing, *The Military Revolution and Political Change: Origins of Democracy and Autocracy in Early Modern Europe* (Princeton, N.J., 1992); Jeremy Black, *European Warfare, 1660–1815* (New Haven, Conn., 1994); R. A. Stradling, "'A Military Revolution': The Fall-Out from the Fall-In," *European History Quarterly* 24 (1994): 271–8.

41 Roberts, "Military Revolution," 217–18.

42 Wright, *Study of War*, 647–9; cf. Thompson, *Global War*, 87–92; Russell F. Weigley, *The Age of Battles: The Question for Decisive Warfare from Breitenfeld to Waterloo* (Bloomington, Ind., 1991).

43 Weigley, *Age of Battles*, 537.

44 André Corvisier, *Armies and Societies in Europe, 1494–1789* (Bloomington, Ind., 1979); Otto Büsch, *Military System and Social Life in Old Regime Prussia, 1713–1807: The Beginnings of the Social Militarization of Prusso-German Society*, trans. John G. Gagliardo (Atlantic Highlands, N.J., 1996).

tinent comparison is not with the nineteenth century but with the seventeenth. Limitation of war implied above all the discipline and organization of the soldiery into standing armies, which fought exclusively in the service of the state. The absence of these "advances" in the seventeenth century accounted for the appalling vulnerability of civilians to violence at the hands of the *soldateska*. The Thirty Years' War is a chapter out of place in the narrative of total war, not only because of the devastation of civilian populations but also because the "war aims" of all sides in this conflict addressed fundamental questions of the social and moral order, which are thought to be defining features of total war in the twentieth century. The reminiscences of the Thirty Years' War noted by observers in Germany in 1945 were not fortuitous. If the extent of destruction and the motivating force of ideological animosities are to be the indices, this terrible struggle bears comparison with any of the twentieth century's total wars.[45]

The narrative of total war raises as many problems as it resolves. It encourages an undiscriminating view of warfare in the early modern era while it reduces the ambiguities and varieties of military experience in the modern period to schematic patterns of development that are driven somehow by their own logic. Yet it is impossible to abandon the idea of total war, if only because the historiography devoted to it has become so formidable. The concept also speaks to massive and dramatic changes in the conduct and social impact of warfare in the modern era. Despite a host of antecedents and countervailing developments, the analysis of these changes cries out for the sort of structuring principle that the narrative of total war has historically provided. The remarks that conclude this chapter accordingly pose no radical alternative; they represent instead a plea for more critical employment of this evidently indispensable tool.

The effort best begins at the methodological foundations. Although they were indebted in a significant measure to the same intellectual traditions, Max Weber offers historians a more useful approach to total war than does Clausewitz. Clausewitz is not a disinterested authority on this narrative. The project of the Prussian reformers, for whom he served as an ideologist, was based on the proposition that Napoleonic warfare represented a fundamental departure from combat in the eighteenth century.[46] Clausewitz's concept of "absolute war" thus had a direct historical referent, and it reflected a specific agenda for the reform of the Prussian armies in the af-

45 Geoffrey Parker, ed., *The Thirty Years' War* (London, 1984).
46 See Eberhard Kessel, "Die Wandlung der Kriegskunst im Zeitalter der französischen Revolution," *Historische Zeitschrift* 148 (1933): 248–76.

termath of the Battle of Jena. In Clausewitz's reading, "absolute war" represented a reality that was potential in every act of war, but it had found its
fullest historical embodiment in Napoleon's.[47]

Defining total war in Weberian terms is less burdened with philosophical implication in the stuff of the narrative. Total war can be characterized
as an "ideal type." In these terms, the narrative translates into a "developmental model," whose telos represents an unalloyed phenomenon that can
be approximated only empirically. The model must be dynamic, however;
it is to be modified in constant collision with the historical *empirica* through
which it serves as a conceptual guide.

The pivotal question concerns the elements that constitute total war
idealtypisch. The literature has emphasized two orders of factors – those
that pertain to the broadening expanse of warfare and those that have to
do with its heightening intensity. The latter category has produced much
of the confusion. It is not clear what the "intensification" of warfare can
mean, particularly in light of Clausewitz's observations on the nature of
war, which in this context are useful indeed.[48] When, in the opening
chapter of *On War*, he remarked that at "the heart of the matter" war was
nothing but a "duel on a larger scale," Clausewitz alluded to the intensity
of violence inherent in every act of warfare. By the "laws of its own nature," war is "primordial violence, hatred, and enmity." He concluded, "To
introduce the principle of moderation into the theory of war itself would
always lead to logical absurdity."[49] It is irrelevant whether the instruments
of this "primordial violence" were pikes or machine guns; for all the differences in their efficiency or the range of the destruction they wrought,
the one was no less "intense" than the other. Russell F. Weigley has
recently addressed this point in somewhat different terms. "Stable weapons technology," he writes, "did not prevent the slaughter of the typical
eighteenth-century battlefield, where casualties approaching one-fifth of
the troops engaged were not unusual. Such shambles mocked the idea
that the age was one of limited war."[50] At the essential moment of decision by arms (*Entscheidung – im Gefecht*), which Clausewitz likened to

47 The work of Peter Paret is indispensable. For an introduction, see his "Genesis of *On War*" in Carl
von Clausewitz, *On War*, ed. and trans. Michael Howard and Peter Paret (Princeton, N.J., 1976),
3–25; cf. Peter Paret, "Clausewitz as Historian," in *Understanding War: Essays on Clausewitz and the
History of Military Power* (Princeton, N.J., 1992), 130–42; Hans Rothfels, "Clausewitz," in Earle, ed.,
Makers of Modern Strategy, 201. See also Thomas Burger, *Max Weber's Theory of Concept Formation*
(Durham, N.C., 1976); Wolfgang J. Mommsen, "Max Weber und die historiographische Methode
in seiner Zeit," *Storia della Storiografia* 3 (1983): 28–43.
48 See Best, *War and Society*, 63; Bond, *War and Society*, 224.
49 Clausewitz, *On War*, 76–7, 88–9.   50 Weigley, *Age of Battles*, xvii.

"cash payment in commerce," warfare is, by its very nature, an intense business.[51]

The narrative of total war has nevertheless emphasized the progressive heightening of warfare's intensity since the end of the eighteenth century. In a preponderance of cases, the appeal to intensification has been rhetorical, bereft of any definition or measure of this concept. One of the most plausible attempts to bring clarity to it has been to associate intensification with the growing frequency of battle. One historian has thus written that Grant's strategy in the Wilderness Campaign was to "pack several battles of the intensity of Gettysburg and Chickamauga into a compressed time span, each one linked by only a few hours or days of maneuvering."[52] Quincy Wright has argued in similar fashion that the intensity of total war can be gauged in the continuity of battle. World War I hence stands as the classic instance. "The pattern of war," he remarks, "instead of a grouping of dots on a map became a large black spot of ink on a map which spread rapidly until the entire map was blackened."[53] However, Wright's graphic imagery also underlines the problem of defining the intensity of warfare in these terms, which pivot on the definition of a battle, which is itself no less problematic.[54]

Another effort would evade this semantic cloud by measuring the intensity of warfare in the ratio of casualties, or of the volume of fire, to a given geographical area over a given period of time. In this light, "intense" is a valid characterization of the sort of combat that a company of Bavarian infantry experienced in the town of Bazeilles, near Sedan, in September 1870. Here, notes a recent student of the conflict, "the hand-to-hand, house-to-house fighting was of a sort where officers did not always have control over their men."[55] This measure is at least congruent with the narrative of total war, for it reaches its apex in Hiroshima. But it harbors a conundrum (not to say its self-deconstruction). By its own logic, the intensity of warfare must decline with the growing geographical and temporal extension of combat, which is the other conventional measure of total war.

---

51 Clausewitz, *On War*, 97.
52 Earl J. Hess, "Tactics, Trenches, and Men in the Civil War," in Förster and Nagler, eds., *On the Road to Total War*, 485.
53 Wright, *Study of War*, 311.
54 See Thompson, *On Global War*, 90. In my view, Weigley's recent work founders on a similar difficulty, the problematic definition of "decisiveness."
55 Mark R. Stoneman, "The Bavarian Army and French Civilians in the War of 1870–71," M.A. thesis, University of Augsburg, 1994, 63.

Until these difficulties are resolved and the concept of intensity in warfare is better clarified, the narrative of total war is best framed alone in the
second of the conventional measures, the growing expanse of warfare. The
salient developments accordingly are the increasing size of armies, the
broadening scope of operations, the growing comprehensiveness of the effort to support armed forces, and the systematic, calculated incorporation
of civilians into the category of participants. The last of these measures is
pivotal, for in the others the distinctions between the "military revolution"
of the early modern era and developments in the modern period are questions of degree. A state of total war in its "ideal" form – one is tempted to
say "total total war" – is reached in this framing once every man, woman,
and child on the planet is directly involved in the prosecution of war: as
combatants, as providers of material and moral support, or as objects of
military violence. It has not happened, yet. Its closest approximation arguably occurred in 1945 – not in Hiroshima or Nagasaki, but in Los Ala-
mos, where scientists entertained briefly the thought that the heat generated in the first test of the bomb would be intense enough (measured
precisely, in degrees Celsius) to ignite the earth's atmosphere.[56]

It is difficult nonetheless to deny that the broadening embrace of warfare, particularly the calculated erasure of the bounds between combatant
and noncombatant, has been the salient theme in the military history of
the past two centuries. Most of the generalizations conventionally implied
in the narrative of total war are valid. Wars did become larger, longer,
more dependent on complex machinery, and by nearly every index more
costly. The triumph of the idea of popular sovereignty at the end of the
eighteenth century not only fed the growth of armed forces; it also promoted the "lateral" expansion of warfare that accompanied the mobilization of civilians, whose role was to sustain the growing material requirements of these military forces. War became, in Michael Howard's words, "a
conflict not of armies, but of populations."[57] Populations, not just fighting
men in uniform, accordingly became more than incidental targets of military violence, once the machinery of war made the systematic assault on
civilian targets feasible. As Geoffrey Best has remarked, "in as much as 'war
and society' suggests two distinct and separate identities it has been increasingly inappropriate in the twentieth century."[58]

The challenge to historians is to liberate the analysis of these developments from the constraints implied in the conventional narrative of total

56 I owe this piece of information to Aaron Novick, my former colleague at the University of Oregon, who was there.
57 Howard, *War in European History*, 93.   58 Best, *War and Society*, 224.

war. The dramatic broadening of the purview of armed conflict was neither unprecedented nor inexorable, nor was it generated only in the evolving forms and technologies of warfare. The proposition that war and society were ever distinct is but another dubious feature of the conventional narrative; but in the modern era the intersections of the realms have become more massive, transparent, and immediate. The salience of these intersections means the breakdown of the distinctions between military history and the history of society, politics, and culture.[59]

Total war requires total history.[60] If the narrative serves only to set a research agenda around this proposition, it performs a service great enough to justify its retention. The agenda pertains to two dimensions of the problem of total war. On the one hand, the impact of warfare on society and politics has become all-embracing, and historians of warfare must attend to its every phase. On the other hand, the emergence of something approximating total war in the twentieth century was the product of a vast complex of reciprocal changes, which also command the attention of historians of warfare. These changes comprised demographic growth, technological innovation, industrial integration, social conflict, the redefinition of political society, the expansion of public power, and the heightening of diplomatic tension, to say nothing of technological and organizational changes within the narrower realm suggested by the term "military history."[61]

The history of total war also must be cultural history. One need not be a partisan of the linguistic turn to recognize that both dimensions of the problem have had massive cultural consequences, which are no less vital to the study of total war than is the machine gun. To cite but one instance, the extension of the lateral bounds of warfare and the breakdown of residual legal restraints on war accompanied the popularization of new definitions of "the other." These were rigid and sinister enough to sanction the calculated eradication of civilian immunities in war. Of the risks faced by civilians in the twentieth century, Geoffrey Best has noted laconically that "the technical means had been perfected, plausible economic reasons for damaging [civilians] had multiplied, and their own apparently willing participation in the decision to make or to continue war seductively suggested

---

59 See Bond, *War and Society*, 168; cf. Peter Paret, "The History of War and the New Military History," in *Understanding War*, 209–26; John R. Gillis, ed., *The Militarization of the Western World* (New Brunswick, N.J., 1989).

60 Cf. K. Neilson, "Total War: Total History," *Military Affairs* 51 (1987): 17–21.

61 These claims merely underline observations made two decades ago by Jay M. Winter, "The Economic and Social History of War," in Jay M. Winter, ed., *War and Economic Development: Essays in Memory of David Joslin* (Cambridge, 1975), 1–10.

that they deserved to be damaged."[62] The images required to justify this conclusion were also broad enough to threaten the profound conceptual barriers to total war that survived in the gendered distribution of wartime roles. Whatever the public regrets of their advocates, theories of strategic bombing rested on images that implied the inversion of these roles; the central importance of an antagonist's "soft," "vulnerable" side – and the "popular hysteria" that systematic aerial bombardment was to produce – recommended women as legitimate, indeed preferred, targets.

Attending to the pervasive influence of cultural factors is required to rescue the narrative of total war from some of the anomalies that otherwise disfigure it. In 1940 the German army achieved a rapid, overwhelming decision at arms – precisely the kind of spectacular victory that the general staff had scripted in 1914, in hopes of averting the protracted war that eventuated. The feat of the German army in 1940 comported in no way with the narrative logic of total war, insofar as it repudiated the proposition, which was widely held among contemporary military planners, that the dynamics of combat had made long wars inescapable. That the European conflict nonetheless evolved into a "total war" was due less to the dynamics of combat than to the Germans' embrace of an ideology that portrayed the other peoples of the world as *Untermenschen* (subhumans) and prescribed the subjugation, if not the annihilation, of most of them.

Historians evidently cannot dispense with the narrative of total war. But they can employ it more self-consciously, with more caution and discrimination than they have in the past. They can be more sensitive both to its explanatory limitations and to the comprehensive perspective it requires. Its parameters are not impermeable, nor is its logic intractable. The expansion of warfare in the modern era has been a halting process that has contended throughout with countervailing pressures, such as the strategic virtuosity of the German planners in 1940. The historical circumstances that have both promoted and retarded the coming of total war are as many and varied as its social, political, and cultural ramifications. The utility of the narrative ultimately rests on its capacity – and its challenge – to comprehend the full variety of these circumstances and ramifications.

62 Best, *Humanity in Warfare,* 224.

2

Different Path to War

A Comparative Study of Militarism and Imperialism in the United States and Imperial Germany, 1871–1914

IRMGARD STEINISCH

German national unification in 1871 met with the unreserved applause of the government of the United States. As the noted historian George Bancroft, then American envoy in Berlin, commented, "our foreign political interests almost always run parallel with those of Germany."[1] Ulysses S. Grant, U.S. president and Civil War hero, confirmed the United States' friendship to the newly united Germany in his annual messages to Congress when he stressed the mutuality of friendly feelings between the two countries.[2] At this stage, at least, the "German Revolution," as former British Prime Minister Benjamin Disraeli once characterized Germany's national unification and the subsequent dramatic change in the balance of power in Europe,[3] was obviously of little concern to the United States. But during the last decade of German Chancellor Otto von Bismarck's "reign," the friendly feelings that had characterized relations between the United States and the new German Reich increasingly gave way to overt hostility. The skirmishes between German, American, and British consuls on the tiny South Sea island of Samoa in 1884–9, a trifle in itself, marked the beginning of a new era of rivalry and suspicion.[4] By 1897 future president

---

I wish to thank the Social Sciences and Humanities Research Council of Canada for supporting this research with a generous grant.

1 Quoted in Alfred Vagts, "Hopes and Fears of an American-German War, 1870–1915," *Political Science Quarterly* 54 (1939): 515.
2 James D. Richardson, ed., *A Compilation of the Messages and Papers of the Presidents, 1789–1897,* 10 vols. (Washington, D.C., 1901), 7:97, 120–1.
3 See speech in the House of Commons, Feb. 9, 1871, excerpt reprinted in John C. G. Röhl, *From Bismarck to Hitler* (London, 1970), 23.
4 See Clara Eve Schieber, *The Transformation of American Sentiment Toward Germany, 1870–1914* (New York, 1923; reprint, New York, 1973), 39–88; see also Paul M. Kennedy, *The Samoan Tangle: A Study in Anglo-German-American Relations, 1878–1900* (Dublin, 1974).

Theodore Roosevelt expressed the view that war with Germany was not
only likely but also perhaps desirable.[5] Kaiser Wilhelm II was, at times,
equally bellicose; although, paradoxically, he also toyed on occasion with
the idea of a German-American alliance.[6]

But what meaning can be inferred from the changing nature of
German-American relations in regard to the outbreak of World War I? Did
German colonial ambitions and economic rivalry with the United States
foreshadow Germany's readiness to go to war? Or did the rise of American
Germanophobia after 1890 make the entry of the United States into World
War I a foregone conclusion? As the rich literature on German-American
relations demonstrates, no serious studies put forth such far-reaching conclusions. But at the same time, many monographs deal with specific events
and developments in order to explain the various reasons why mutual admiration and goodwill between the United States and Germany turned
into mutual hostility and eventual armed conflict.[7]

High on the list of factors are economic and trade rivalry and the clash
of American democratic ideals with Prussian autocracy and militarism.
Much is also made of the rise of Anglo-American friendship for reasons of
ideological compatibility, political cooperation, and cultural affinity. It has
also been frequently argued that it was in the interests of both American
and British foreign policy to maintain the existing balance of power in Europe.[8] And at the turn of the century only Germany seemed to have the
will and the power to disturb the status quo in Europe and indeed in the
world. That the two anglophone nations differed on the seriousness of the
German threat is evidenced by the fact that in August 1914 Britain went to

5 Richard H. Collin, *Theodore Roosevelt: Culture, Diplomacy, and Expansion: A New View of American Imperialism* (Baton Rouge, La., 1985), 123–4.
6 Reiner Pommerin, *Der Kaiser und Amerika: Die USA in der Politik der Reichsleitung 1890–1917*
(Cologne, 1986), 179ff.
7 See Paul M. Kennedy, "British and German Reactions to the Rise of American Power," in R. J.
Bullen, H. Pogge von Strandmann, and A. B. Polonsky, eds., *Ideas into Politics: Aspects of European
History, 1880–1950* (London, 1984), 15–24; and for brief surveys on the literature, see Reiner Pommerin, *Der Kaiser und Amerika*, 15–22, and Ragnhild Fiebig-von Hase, *Lateinamerika als Konfliktherd
der deutsch-amerikanischen Beziehungen, 1890–1903: Vom Beginn der Panamerikapolitik bis zur Venezuelakrise von 1902–1903* (Göttingen, 1986), pt. 1; Manfred Jonas, *The United States and Germany: A
Diplomatic History* (Ithaca, N.Y., 1984), 311–17; still informative is Otto Graf zu Stolberg-
Wernigerode, *Germany and the United States of America During the Era of Bismarck* (Reading, Pa.,
1937); Alfred Vagts, *Deutschland und die Vereinigten Staaten in der Weltpolitik*, 2 vols. (New York, 1935);
see also Detlef Junker, "The Manichaean Trap: American Perceptions of the German Empire,
1871–1945," German Historical Institute Occasional Paper no. 12 (Washington, D.C., 1995), 9–36.
8 See Jerald A. Combs, *American Diplomatic History: Two Centuries of Changing Interpretation* (Berkeley,
Calif., 1983), pt. 3; Robert E. Osgood, *Ideals and Self-Interest in America's Foreign Relations*, 4th ed.
(Chicago, 1964); see also Henry C. Allen, *Great Britain and the United States: A History of Anglo-
American Relations, 1783–1952* (New York, 1955), and Bradford Perkins, *The Great Rapprochement:
England and the United States, 1895–1914* (New York, 1968).

war. By contrast, the United States entered the conflict in April 1917, belatedly and reluctantly. Yet it was American intervention that assured Germany's defeat, or, to put it another way, "Germany's War Mania"[9] was in the end checked by the American resolve to "defend democracy in the world."[10]

This chapter does not intend to provide a detailed investigation of German-American relations and diplomacy. Instead, it analyzes the dominant ideological concepts in which each nation's route to war is studied. The dichotomy of "German authoritarian militarism" in contrast to "American democracy" is probably the most frequently employed historical model. This is hardly surprising because it captures first and foremost the opposing national images that emerged during World War I and also points to the decisive difference in the political systems of both nations. It also reflects the dominant national paradigm and conceptual framework in which German and American history is usually studied. For example, the concept of the *Sonderweg* (special path of historical development) expresses Germany's past failure to come to grips with the problems of modern industrial society and democracy.[11] However, the concept of American exceptionalism celebrates the United States' achievements in preserving democracy at home and abroad in spite of its massive expansion in territory during the nineteenth century, in addition to its growth in economic and military power, which made it the foremost power in the world by the end of World War I.[12] Not to view American development as "exceptional" is to deny the obvious, commented one historian in a recent debate about American foreign policy.[13] In a negative sense, the same can be said for Germany and its peculiar development.

9 Thus the title of an interesting piece of British war propaganda that also was distributed in the United States: *Germany's War Mania: The Teutonic Point of View as Officially Stated by Her Leaders: A Collection of Speeches and Writings* (London, 1915).

10 See Osgood, *Ideals and Self-Interest*, 260; Ernest R. May, *The World War and American Isolation, 1914–1917* (Cambridge, Mass., 1959); Arthur S. Link, *Wilson*, 5 vols. (Princeton, N.J., 1947-65), vols. 3 and 5.

11 See Hans-Ulrich Wehler, *Das deutsche Kaiserreich 1871–1918* (Göttingen, 1973); and the critique by Thomas Nipperdey, "Wehlers 'Kaiserreich': Eine kritische Auseinandersetzung," in *Gesellschaft, Kultur, Theorie: Gesammelte Aufsätze zur neueren Geschichte* (Göttingen, 1976), 360–89; for a historical account including references to the relevant literature, see Jürgen Kocka, "German History Before Hitler: The Debate About the German Sonderweg," *Journal of Contemporary History* 23 (1988): 3–16, and the various articles in Gordon Martel, ed., *Modern Germany Reconsidered, 1870–1945* (London, 1992).

12 See the controversial accounts by William Appleman Williams, *The Tragedy of American Diplomacy* (Cleveland, 1959); Walter LaFeber, *The New Empire: An Interpretation of American Expansion, 1860–1898* (Ithaca, N.Y., 1963); and Gabriel Kolko, *Main Currents in Modern American History* (New York, 1984); see also Combs, *American Diplomatic History*, 255–7.

13 William E. Weeks, "New Directions in the Study of Early American Foreign Relations," *Diplomatic History* 17 (winter 1993): 96.

Recently, concepts of national exceptionalism as explanatory tools for historical interpretation have come under attack.[14] Although this chapter argues that there are national distinctions that matter a great deai,[15] it needs to be noted that the sheer preponderance of the national historical perspective, both by the number of published works and the volume of archival material, tends to skew historical interpretation in favor of national exceptionalism and uniqueness, even in studies that tackle the task of cross-national comparisons.[16] Most important, however, the critique of national focus touches a central nerve when it points to the frequently self-fulfilling logic in historical investigation.[17] In the historians' quest for meaningful generalizations and their search for historical continuities and national distinctiveness, there is a tendency to rely on evocative concepts such as militarism and autocracy, peace and democracy, national interest and *Weltpolitik* (world policy) to provide the framework for the historical analysis of specific events and national trends. But it could be argued that these concepts infuse too much conformity into the analysis of national developments by constructing too selective an interpretation of events, thus assigning a predetermined pattern to a complex historical process and obscuring similarities in developments between nations. And what are the factors and features that make a nation distinct at a particular point in time? It is this question that is addressed here, as well as whether responses to major developments between 1871 and 1914 in both societies were indeed unique, as is frequently assumed.

14 David Blackbourn and Geoff Eley, *The Peculiarities of German History: Bourgeois Society and Politics in Nineteenth-Century Germany* (Oxford, 1984). This is not the place to further belabor the so-called *Sonderwegsdebatte* of recent years. But for the relevant information, see note 11 to this chapter. For the United States, see the well-referenced and thoughtful article by Ian Tyrell, "American Exceptionalism in an Age of International History," *American Historical Review* 96 (Oct. 1991): 1031–55.

15 Most pertinent for the origins of World War I is Fritz Fischer, *Griff nach der Weltmacht: Die Kriegszielpolitik des kaiserlichen Deutschland 1914/18* (Düsseldorf, 1961). This detailed study started the so-called *Kriegsschuldkontroverse,* or Fischer Controversy, and a steady stream of revisionist writings. For the intricacies of the debate, the various participants, and the relevant publications, see John A. Moses, *The Politics of Illusion: The Fischer Controversy in German Historiography* (London, 1975).

16 Comparative studies are still few and far between. Most recently, see Gabriel Kolko, *Century of War: Politics, Conflict, and Society Since 1914* (New York, 1994); see also Modris Eksteins, *Rites of Spring: The Great War and the Birth of the Modern Age* (Toronto, 1989); for the impact of the industrialization experience in the United States and Germany, see the impressive study by Charles S. Maier, *Recasting Bourgeois Europe: Stabilization in France, Germany, and Italy in the Decade After World War I* (Princeton, N.J., 1975). As my own work suggests, the idea of national uniqueness is less prominent when seen from a socioeconomic rather than a political perspective. See Irmgard Steinisch, *Arbeitszeitverkürzung und sozialer Wandel: Der Kampf um die Achtstundenschicht in der deutschen und amerikanischen Eisen- und Stahlindustrie 1880–1929* (Berlin, 1986).

17 See the critique by Geoff Eley, *From Unification to Nazism: Reinterpreting the German Past* (Boston, 1986), 254–82.

But what is the usefulness of a comparative analysis of such different nations as Imperial Germany and the United States? This chapter argues that it is the obvious incompatibility of the political and social systems that justifies the study of the dominant national paradigms and a closer look at the issues of militarism and naval armament, imperialist expansionism, and lust for world empire. It is important to remember that both nations were latecomers to the imperialist race of expansionism and global power, and it is this fact that provides the *tertium comparationis*. Moreover, the widespread imperialist convictions held in both nations between 1890 and 1914 were intimately tied to their dynamic economic systems, and many contemporaries in Germany and the United States justified an imperialist policy of expansionism on these grounds.[18] At the same time, there were qualitative differences between German and American imperialist expansion and militarism; these issues are discussed in the following sections.

THE EXPERIENCE OF WAR AND THE PROBLEM OF MILITARISM

European diplomats and politicians were notoriously ill informed about the political culture and the political process in the United States. Political and public opinion in Europe during the American Civil War is just one of many examples. As late as 1864 there was widespread skepticism about prospects for a Union victory and therefore for the continued existence of the United States.[19] After April 1865 Europe's diplomats and statesmen became rather apprehensive that the victorious government of the United States, which now commanded the largest army in the world, would first send troops south to expel French troops and the Emperor Maximilian from Mexico and then march armies north to conquer British North America. Or, they thought, perhaps the Americans might dare attack on both fronts simultaneously![20] When no military expeditions materialized – and, on the contrary, the Union army was quickly demobilized – European interest in American expansionism faded as quickly as it had surged. Of course, it was noted in Europe that the government of the United States, working through diplomatic channels, achieved full satisfaction in

---

18 See Woodruff D. Smith, *The Ideological Origins of Nazi Imperialism* (Oxford, 1986), 30–2; Collin, *Theodore Roosevelt*.

19 Worthington C. Ford, ed., *A Cycle of Adams Letters, 1861–1865*, 2 vols. (New York, 1929), 85.

20 Ibid., 254; see also the flurry of diplomatic rumors in Historische Reichskommission / Reichsinstitut für Geschichte des neuen Deutschlands, ed., *Die auswärtige Politik Preussens 1858–1871: Diplomatische Aktenstücke,* 10 vols. (Berlin, 1939), vol. 6.

Mexico, as well as from the British government by the Treaty of Washington.[21]

It was not only Europeans who thought that the United States was different from Europe; Americans had long been of that same opinion. In the public mind, the experience of the bloody and protracted Civil War did not change the idea of the uniqueness of the American republic and its moral superiority to Europe.[22] Indeed, the Civil War, and the subsequent deployment of the U.S. Army in the Southern states during Reconstruction, had a lasting impact on American politics. Not only did the American public, in deference to his military achievements, elect General Ulysses S. Grant president in 1868, but an active military record remained for a time an important asset for high political office, as demonstrated by the careers of succeeding American presidents. At the same time, there was little public enthusiasm for a large standing army, as rapid military demobilization after the Civil War clearly demonstrated. In fact, the regular U.S. Army, fighting against various Native American nations in the western territories and states, was notoriously understaffed and lacking in training.[23] By the early 1880s the U.S. Army, with barely 27,000 men, was so small that Andrew Carnegie, the successful steel industrialist and devoted peace activist, could brag that "the glory of America was that it had no army worth the name."[24] Of course, he did not mention the usefulness of both the regular army and the National Guard in their deployment against striking workers, which, not surprisingly, contributed to the army's lack of popularity, especially within labor circles.[25]

Nevertheless, Carnegie was quite correct in pointing out that it was the absence of institutionalized militarism that gave credence to the well-rooted mystique of the United States as an essentially unmilitaristic society. Not even the refounding of the United States by means of a civil war had dented the cherished political tradition that centered on the undisputed hegemony of civil society and civilian government. For this very reason, the creed of Thomas Jefferson, that the American republic was fundamentally different from Europe and its "nations of eternal war,"[26] remained a constant and well-emphasized theme in American history that even the experiences of two world wars, the Cold War, and the conflict in Vietnam

21 Allen, *Great Britain and the United States.*   22 Combs, *American Diplomatic History,* chap. 21.
23 Warren W. Hassler, *With Shield and Sword: American Military Affairs, Colonial Times to the Present* (Ames, Iowa, 1982), 189–212; Russel F. Weigley, *History of the United States Army* (New York, 1967), 234–94.
24 Quoted in John Mueller, *Retreat from Doomsday: The Obsolescence of Major War* (New York, 1989), 32.
25 Weigley, *History of the United States Army,* 281–2.
26 Quoted in Alfred Vagts, "The United States and the Balance of Power," in Hans J. Morgenthau and Kenneth W. Thompson, eds., *Principles and Problems of International Politics* (New York, 1956), 189.

did not totally dislodge.[27] Hardly any greater contrast to the German historical experience can be conceived.

Germans have been cursed by Bismarck's fateful phrase that German national unification would be achieved by "blood and iron." Ironically, Bismarck's speech was nothing more than sarcastic rhetoric at the time, directed against his liberal adversaries in the Prussian diet; only later was it interpreted as divine providence by nationalist German historians of the *Reichsgründungszeit* (era of the Reich founding). But during the twentieth century it has become the most powerful paradigm to explain what went wrong in German history.[28] Emphasis has been placed on the fateful consequences of Germany's unification by three successive wars, each more impressive in its military terms and political results than its predecessor. The inference is that these wars indicate a peculiar German/Prussian proclivity for war. But was it the prominence of the Prussian military tradition that might have predisposed Bismarck toward the military approach to unification, rather than civil alternatives? And what effect did this have on German society after 1871?[29]

Certainly, the special relationship between civil authority and the military in Prussia was further strengthened during the 1860s and again after 1871.[30] Today, there is little disagreement among historians about the fact that the German chief of staff enjoyed a decisive boost in prestige and political influence during these decades. Moreover, the lack of civil control over the military was perpetuated when the German Reich was founded. The Prussian military leadership retained its constitutionally privileged position and remained directly answerable only to the Prussian king and then the German kaiser. This meant that the military was largely immune from parliamentary scrutiny and civil control, a decisive factor in Germany's push for war during the July crisis of 1914.[31] There also is abundant evidence demonstrating the widespread admiration, even emulation, of the

27 See Combs, *American Diplomatic History,* chap. 21.
28 See Friedhelm Grützner, *Die Politik Bismarcks von 1862 bis 1871 in der deutschen Geschichtsschreibung: Eine kritische historiographische Betrachtung* (Frankfurt am Main, 1986); Hagen Schulze, *The Course of German Nationalism: From Frederick the Great to Bismarck, 1763–1867* (New York, 1985); and, most recently, Hagen Schulze, *Staat und Nation in der europäischen Geschichte* (Munich, 1995), chaps. 2, 3.
29 For a range of divergent views, see Lothar Gall, ed., *Das Bismarck-Problem in der Geschichtsschreibung nach 1945* (Cologne, 1971); see also Wehler, *Kaiserreich;* Lothar Gall, *Bismarck: Der weisse Revolutionär* (Frankfurt am Main, 1983), 340ff., 373ff.; most recently, Ernst Engelberg, *Bismarck: Urpreusse und Reichsgründer* (Berlin, 1986), chaps. 6–11; for a recent narrative account, see William Carr, *The Wars of German Unification* (New York, 1991).
30 See Gordon A. Craig, *The Politics of the Prussian Army, 1640–1945* (Oxford, 1955; reprint, London, 1964), chaps. 6–7.
31 See Fritz Fischer, *War of Illusions: German Politics from 1911 to 1914* (New York, 1975); Konrad H. Jarausch, *The Enigmatic Chancellor: Bethmann Hollweg and the Hubris of Imperial Germany* (Princeton, N.J., 1972); and Volker R. Berghahn, *Germany and the Approach of War in 1914* (London, 1973), 165–210.

military in German society prior to 1914.[32] Moreover, in contrast to the United States, there was an early abolition of the militia in favor of the policy of national conscription, which provided large numbers of male recruits with first-hand military training.

Although there is no doubt about the long military tradition in Prussia, it is still difficult for historians to establish the connections and interactions between the political process and institutionalized militarism in Imperial Germany, on the one hand, and popular and elitist culture, on the other. Nor can one find simple answers to the fundamental question: What made the risk of war such an attractive policy option in the summer of 1914? Was it angst and *Untergangsmentalität* (fear of decline), or the hubris of power in a militarized society?[33] Was there a domestic crisis of such dimension that the ruling military and government elite believed that the time was opportune to wage a war for strategic advantage? Or was the foreign policy menace of "encirclement" by France, Russia, and Britain the major driving force?[34]

German nationalism, as it evolved between 1871 and 1914, was certainly linked to military achievements. The wars of 1864, 1866, and particularly 1870–1, the Franco-German war, quickly became symbols of an emerging German national culture, of which the *Sedantag* (commemoration of the victory over the French at Sedan) is only one manifestation.[35] This should hardly be surprising, given the previous weakness of the various German states, the memory of the military humiliations of the Napoleonic wars, and the sudden great-power status of a united German nation-state. The character of the Wars of German Unification also lent themselves to glorification. They were short, they were limited in their human and material cost, and they resulted in sweeping victories.[36] In contrast, the American Civil War, with its half a million war dead and enor-

---

32 See the classic article by Eckart Kehr, "The Genesis of the Royal Prussian Reserve Officer," in *Economic Interest, Militarism, and Foreign Policy: Essays on German History*, ed. Gordon A. Craig (Berkeley, Calif., 1977), 97–108; very interesting is Dennis E. Showalter's "Army, State, and Society in Germany, 1871–1914: An Interpretation," in Jack R. Dukes and Joachim Remak, eds., *Another Germany: A Reconsideration of the Imperial Era* (Boulder, Colo., 1988), 1–18.

33 See Stig Förster's chapter in this book; see also Berghahn, *Germany and the Approach of War,* 176–9.

34 For an introduction to the extensive literature as well as the range of interpretations, see the interesting articles in Gregor Schöllgen, ed., *Escape into War? The Foreign Policy of Imperial Germany* (Oxford, 1990); see also Isabel V. Hull, *The Entourage of Kaiser Wilhelm II, 1888–1918* (Cambridge, 1982); for the importance of nationalist mass mobilization, see Geoff Eley, *Reshaping the German Right: Radical Nationalism and Political Change After Bismarck* (New Haven, Conn., 1980; reprint, Ann Arbor, Mich., 1991).

35 See Thomas Nipperdey, "Nationalidee und Nationaldenkmal in Deutschland im 19. Jahrhundert," in Thomas Nipperdey, *Gesellschaft, Kultur, Theorie: Gesammelte Aufsätze zur neueren Geschichte* (Göttingen, 1976), 133–72.

36 Dennis E. Showalter, *Railroads and Rifles: Soldiers, Technology, and the Unification of Germany* (Hamden, Conn., 1975); see also Michael Howard, *The Franco-Prussian War: The German Invasion of France* (London, 1961; reprint, London, 1979), 4.

mous devastation to the Southern countryside and economy, clearly exposed the terrors of war, at least to Americans.[37] But few Europeans were interested in this lesson. Moltke's sneering reference to the American Civil War as "a contest in which huge armed rabbles chased each other around a vast wilderness" was shared by many European military experts.[38]

By comparison, the successful Prussian-German wars seemed to be models of military efficiency. Indeed, between 1871 and 1914 the Prussian military organization became the model for planning future war, not only in Europe but also in the United States.[39] Most reform proposals for the reorganization of the U.S. Army used the Prussian military organization as its blueprint, calling for a streamlining of the military bureaucracy and command structure as well as the establishment of the office of general chief of staff. However, support was not forthcoming from the American Congress. Military reforms succeeded only after the Spanish-American War, under the energetic leadership of Secretary of War Elihu Root. But military education had changed earlier. The historicist approach to the study and planning of war, so typical of Prussian military education, was common in the late 1870s, and at West Point, cadets busied themselves with strategic problems for probable and improbable military contingencies. Despite the legacy of the Civil War, but in keeping with the ideas of the influential Prussian military theorist Carl von Clausewitz, war was increasingly viewed as a legitimate instrument of national politics; and it was this theory that came to dominate American military thought and strategy around the turn of the century.[40]

The convergence of military thought between the United States and Germany, despite their very different geopolitical constraints, was largely due to the ascendancy of both nations to great-power status. In fact, between 1871 and 1914 American and German societies shared many characteristics that supported the turn to imperialist policies. Above all, it was their economic and industrial strength, their enormous productivity.[41] In the United States, the managerial revolution and technocratic developments

---

37 See Gerald F. Linderman, *Embattled Courage: The Experience of Combat in the Civil War* (New York, 1987); John Mueller, *Retreat from Doomsday: The Obsolescence of Major War* (New York, 1989).

38 Quoted in Richard A. Preston and Sydney F. Wise, *Men in Arms: A History of Warfare and Its Interrelationships with Western Society,* 4th ed. (New York, 1979), 255.

39 See the survey in Theodore Ropp, *War in the Modern World* (New York, 1962), chaps. 7–8; C. Joseph Bernardo, *American Military Policy: Its Development Since 1775* (Westport, Conn., 1974); on Germany, see Arden Bucholz, *Moltke, Schlieffen, and Prussian War Planning* (New York, 1991), and Michael Geyer, *Deutsche Rüstungspolitik 1860–1980* (Frankfurt am Main, 1984), 24–96.

40 Richard D. Challener, *Admirals, Generals, and American Foreign Policy* (Princeton, N.J., 1973), 12–45; Weigley, *History of the United States Army,* 272–98, 314–41.

41 David S. Landes, *The Unbound Prometheus: Technological Change and Industrial Development in Western Europe from 1750 to the Present* (Cambridge, Mass., 1972), chap. 4.

were particularly pioneering and advanced for the time. Mass production, as well as mass consumption in the age of modern machinery, modern urban living, and the rise of the large corporation were all based on the efficient organization and interaction of large masses of people in a common cause. Furthermore, by the 1890s the belief in the technocratic problem-solving capacity of the expert ushered in a powerful reform movement that set out to improve industry, enhance worker productivity, streamline government, and refurbish the military. Significantly, the scientific management theories of Frederick Winslow Taylor found their most complete expression in the Watertown Arsenal, a federal arms manufacturing plant in Massachusetts.[42]

In Germany the relationship between heavy industry and the military was more direct and notoriously close. The profitable connections between the Friedrich Krupp firm in Essen, Germany's leading arms manufacturer, and the Hohenzollerns, especially Wilhelm II, as well as the Prussian military and government officials, are legendary. So too is the political influence of heavy industry in Imperial Germany.[43] But the interaction between industry, the military, and government went deeper than mere influence peddling. Indeed, during the early stages of mass production some German manufacturers, such as the entrepreneur Alfred Krupp, took their organizational cues from the army in order to ensure the smooth interaction of a large work force in their plants that was necessary for quality production.[44] Also, the extensive state bureaucracies frequently provided examples for the evolving administration of large firms.

The key to success in mass industrial production and modern military operations rested largely on efficient organization. Managerial control was needed, and it is for this reason that the German military model, with its emphasis on organization, communication, and precise planning to ensure the efficient movement of mass armies, must be seen not only in relation to its supposedly proven success and the confines of arms technology but also in its appeal to the new professionalism and managerial practices in industry and mass society at large. Certainly, it was only a small step also to view war as controllable, promising victory to the side that was best informed and best prepared. And it is precisely this idea – that war was subject to a cost-benefit approach – that was most insidious, especially because it had

42 Hugh G. J. Aitken, *Taylorism at Watertown Arsenal: Scientific Management in Action, 1908–1915* (Cambridge, Mass., 1960).
43 Willi A. Boelcke, ed., *Krupp und die Hohenzollern in Dokumenten: Krupp-Korrespondenz mit Kaisern, Kabinettschefs und Ministern 1850–1918* (Frankfurt am Main, 1970).
44 Heinz Reif, "Ein seltener Kreis von Freunden: Arbeitsprozesse und Arbeitserfahrungen bei Krupp 1840–1914," in Klaus Tenfelde, ed., *Arbeit und Arbeitserfahrung in der Geschichte* (Göttingen, 1988), 51–91.

such a decisive impact on international politics and military planning in Europe and the United States. At the same time, as the examples of both the U.S. Army and the Prussian/German army demonstrate, actual military planning and organization fell far behind the ideal of efficient organization and rational analysis. But it was not so much realistic practice as sentiment that guided policies.[45]

The spread of technocratic ideology coincided with an increase in popular enchantment with "war." During the late 1880s and 1890s a trend emerged in Europe and in the United States to view certain types of war as heroic and romantic.[46] For the Germans, it was the wars of national unification. For the British, it was their colonial wars. For the Americans, it was the Civil War, which was now eulogized. This trend reflected the rising tide of imperialist reaffirmation of the nation-state as much as it was a reaction against the confines of urban industrial society. War promised not only national honor but also individual adventure and manly courage. And it is not surprising that the westward expansion of the United States, with its idea of ever-new frontiers and conquests, probably was the main focus of such escapist myth-building for Americans.[47] Not only did the United States join the European nations in imperialist expansion, but war itself also was increasingly seen as inevitable and even desirable. If the "splendid little war" with Spain in 1898 demonstrated anything, it was that a war against a despotic European country could enjoy immense support and popularity among the American public.[48]

This transition from war as horror to war as heroic experience is personified in General William Tecumseh Sherman's change in attitude. During the Civil War, he had branded war as "hell," and he had acted on his insight "the crueller [the war] . . . the sooner it will be over" when he marched his troops through Georgia to break Southern morale. By 1890, however, Sherman was lauding the military "calling" and praising the martial spirit.[49] A similar trend was evident in Germany. General Helmuth von Moltke, who had masterminded the German military victories in the 1860s, put forth similar views in 1880: "Perpetual peace is a dream, and not a pleasant

---

45 Michael Howard, "Men Against Fire: Expectations of War in 1914," *International Security* 9 (1984): 41–57; Stephen van Evera, "The Cult of the Offensive and the Origins of the First World War," ibid., 58–107; see also Paul M. Kennedy, ed., *The War Plans of the Great Powers, 1880–1914* (Boston, 1985); Weigley, *History of the United States Army,* 328–41.

46 See Mueller, *Retreat from Doomsday,* 37–46.

47 A good example is Theodore Roosevelt and his literary work "The Winning of the West" (1894); see David H. Burton, *Theodore Roosevelt: Confident Imperialist* (Philadelphia, 1968), 17–27.

48 See Thomas A. Bailey, *A Diplomatic History of the American People* (Englewood Cliffs, N.J., 1974), 460–1.

49 See Mueller, *Retreat from Doomsday,* 38–9.

one at that; and war is part of God's ordering of the world. In war the most noble human virtues develop courage and self-denial [*Entsagung*], faithfulness to duty and the willingness to sacrifice one's life. Without war, the world would wallow in materialism."[50]

Of course, German and American advocates of militarism had their critics. But it was not until the late 1890s that sober warnings against armed conflict by various pacifist writers and groups gained public support in the two countries. And even then it was difficult for them to maintain a common front. In 1898, for example, some within the fledgling American peace movement regarded the Spanish-American War as a serious setback, whereas others approved of this type of war because it was fought in the name of "liberty and civilization."[51] Only very few of the activists and members of the peace movements in the United States, Germany, or Great Britain rejected war sui generis. What they wanted was a practical deterrent to war.

The Hague conferences on international arbitration in 1899 and again in 1907, which were attended by the United States, Germany, and most other European countries, were important steps in that direction. In 1899, however, support for disarmament was not forthcoming by either the German or the American governments. This would change by 1907, when Germany continued to view the attempts at international arms limitation as an attack on its national security interests, while the United States had by then become an ardent advocate of international disarmament. This reversal in American policy can be largely attributed to concern over the threatening dimensions of the naval arms race, which was undertaken by many European powers and also by Japan.[52] It did not mean, however, that the United States abandoned its own arms buildup, especially when the rivalry among the great powers for colonial empire, economic advantage, and national prestige continued and intensified.

THE ALLURE OF NAVALISM

The idea that a strong navy was paramount to achieving and maintaining great-power status was a key component in Western imperialist ideology and policy during the late nineteenth century.[53] By the 1890s both Germany and the United States had committed themselves to naval expansion.

50 Quoted in Roger Chickering, *Imperial Germany and a World Without War: The Peace Movement and German Society, 1892–1914* (Princeton, N.J., 1975), 392.
51 Roland Marchand, *The American Peace Movement and Social Reform, 1898–1918* (Princeton, N.J., 1972), 24–9.
52 See Ilse Kunz-Lack, *Die deutsch-amerikanischen Beziehungen 1890–1914* (Stuttgart, 1935), chap. 6; Chickering, *Imperial Germany*, chaps. 6, 8; Marchand, *American Peace Movement*, 26–38, 51–7.
53 The concept of imperialism has been vigorously debated. See Wolfgang J. Mommsen, *Theories of Imperialism* (Chicago, 1982), and also Hans-Ulrich Wehler, ed., *Imperialismus* (Düsseldorf, 1979); see

The international consequences of the naval race, which started in earnest in 1898 with German Admiral Alfred von Tirpitz's plan to build a large battle fleet, were considerable. It seriously damaged Anglo-German relations, destabilized the European balance of power, and was a decisive factor in the outbreak of World War I. Furthermore, German naval policy also was largely responsible for the deterioration of German-American relations, while furthering Anglo-American rapprochement.[54]

Not surprisingly, historical research has been most interested in the motives and the rationale behind Germany's disastrous naval policy. Much emphasis has been placed on the theme that naval armament was essential to *Weltpolitik,* the foreign policy of colonial acquisitions and expansion.[55] Whether this German version of imperialism was as popular as it was inept, however, is open to debate. But there is little doubt that naval policy played a central role in the domestic policy of "nationalist integration" in Germany between 1898 and 1914, a strategy designed to further political and social stability in the face of rising socialist influence among the working class.[56] What is most striking in reference to American developments, however, is the fact that German naval theory and planning drew heavily on American models. For example, Tirpitz, the most influential proponent of a German battle fleet, was an ardent disciple of the teachings of the American naval officer and historian Alfred Thayer Mahan. And so was Kaiser Wilhelm II![57]

Mahan's historical analysis, published in *The Influence of Seapower upon History, 1660–1783* (1890), and his subsequent writings were, of course, first and foremost influenced by conditions in the United States and by the British experience of empire building.[58] His analysis emphasized the importance of American naval supremacy in the western hemisphere in order

also Hans-Ulrich Wehler, *Der Aufstieg des amerikanischen Imperialismus: Studien zur Entwicklung des Imperium Americanum 1865–1900* (Göttingen, 1974).

54 Paul M. Kennedy, *The Rise of the Anglo-German Antagonism, 1860–1914* (London, 1980), pts. 3–4; Challener, *Admirals, Generals, and American Foreign Policy,* 25–40.

55 For an informed discussion on the origins and meaning of *Weltpolitik,* see Smith, *Ideological Origins,* 52–82; see also William L. Langer, *The Diplomacy of Imperialism, 1890–1902* (New York, 1956), 415–44; Gregor Schöllgen, *Imperialismus und Gleichgewicht* (Munich, 1984); Holger H. Herwig, *"Luxury" Fleet: The Imperial German Navy, 1888–1918* (London, 1980), 95–110; and Ivo Nikolai Lambi, *The Navy and German Power Politics, 1862–1914* (Boston, 1984), chap. 9.

56 See the groundbreaking essay by Eckart Kehr, "The Social and Financial Foundation of Tirpitz's Naval Propaganda," in Kehr, *Economist Interest, Militarism, and Foreign Policy,* 76–96; and Volker R. Berghahn, *Der Tirpitz-Plan: Genesis und Verfall einer innenpolitischen Krisenstrategie unter Wilhelm II* (Düsseldorf, 1971); Wilhelm Deist, ed., *Marine und Marinepolitik im kaiserlichen Deutschland 1871–1914* (Düsseldorf, 1972); and, more recently, Eley, *Reshaping the German Right,* pt. 2.

57 See Holger H. Herwig, *Politics of Frustration: The United States in German Naval Planning, 1899–1941* (Boston, 1976), 40–1; see also Holger H. Herwig, *The German Naval Officer Corps: A Social and Political History, 1890–1918* (London, 1973), 18.

58 Alfred T. Mahan, *The Influence of Sea Power upon the French Revolution and Empire, 1793–1812* (Boston, 1892), and Alfred T. Mahan, *Sea Power in Its Relations to the War of 1812* (Boston, 1905); see Challener, *Admirals, Generals, and American Foreign Policy,* 12–16, 77.

to protect not colonies but economic spheres of influence. This, however, required the acquisition of naval bases at strategic points in the Caribbean as well as in the Pacific, and a navy strong enough to deal with possible enemies. Although Mahan's "capital ship theory of naval defense" sketched a distinctly American version of empire building, it did not require U.S. naval superiority or even parity with the predominant naval power, Great Britain.[59] This was an important factor in future Anglo-American relations.

Mahan's theories, especially his arguments that nations must expand or die, were steeped in social Darwinist ideology, which was immensely popular among the elite in the United States. It also was widespread in Germany, even if its atheistic and populist implications were despised by the old conservative elites.[60] Nevertheless, the scientific pretension and peculiar thrust of Mahan's imperialist visions helps to explain the ready acceptance of his ideas in both countries. Prominent among Mahan's advocates in the United States were politicians in high offices, including Hilary A. Herbert, secretary of the Navy under President Grover Cleveland; Henry Cabot Lodge, the influential Republican senator; and, above all, President Theodore Roosevelt and his secretaries of state, John Hay and Elihu Root.[61] In Germany, support ranged from navalists such as Tirpitz and Kaiser Wilhelm II to aggressive nationalists such as the historian Heinrich von Treitschke, and even included educated middle-class and social critics such as Max Weber, Gustav Schmoller, and Werner Sombart.[62]

In the United States, social Darwinist convictions frequently helped to unite imperialists and anti-imperialists because neither camp was opposed to the necessity of expanding American influence in the western hemisphere and in Asia. What they argued about was the question of whether economic expansion also mandated territorial acquisition.[63] In Germany, the differences of opinion over imperialism also covered a wide spectrum of political vision. For most advocates, expansion overseas seemed to promise a solution

59 See Harold and Margaret Sprout, *The Rise of American Naval Power, 1776–1918* (Oxford, 1939; reprint, London, 1967), chaps. 13–16.
60 Alfred Kelly, *The Descent of Darwin: The Popularization of Darwinism in Germany, 1860–1914* (Chapel Hill, N.C., 1981), makes it clear that popular Darwinism was associated with liberal and also socialist ideology.
61 See Burton, *Theodore Roosevelt,* 132–41; Osgood, *Ideals and Self-Interest,* 29–41; Richard Hofstadter, *Social Darwinism in American Thought, 1860–1915* (Philadelphia, 1944; reprint, 1959); and Carl N. Degler, *In Search of Human Nature: The Decline and Revival of Darwinism in American Social Thought* (New York, 1991).
62 See Herwig, *Politics of Frustration,* 40–1, 93–109.
63 E. Berkeley Tompkins, *Anti-Imperialism in the United States: The Great Debate, 1890–1920* (Philadelphia, 1970), and Ernest R. May, *American Imperialism: A Speculative Essay* (New York, 1968), chaps. 5, 8.

to Germany's problems of overpopulation and economic crisis; colonies would keep German emigrants within the Reich and yet provide new markets. At the same time, there was a monumental divide between aggressive militarists such as Theodor von Bernhardi, who advocated war as the inevitable route to German survival and world empire, and devoted peace activists such as the widely respected Lutheran church historian Adolf Harnack, who, along with many Germans in the *Bildungsbürgertum* (educated middle classes) and business world, supported German colonial expansion.[64] Furthermore, social Darwinist ideas deeply penetrated the large socialist labor camp, whose leaders in the Reichstag were consistent critics of aggressive imperialism with its navalism and "gun-boat diplomacy."[65]

The impressive rise of industrial capitalism in both the United States and Imperial Germany made Mahan's view of economic expansion, as a new version of empire building, more attractive. It also reinforced social Darwinist justifications for the necessity of empire building. And more important for the United States' experience, it accommodated American political and cultural traditions. For example, Mahan's arguments provided the means for evading the traditional American aversion to colonialism and the maintenance of military institutions.[66] A different set of principles operated in Germany. For the German elites, Mahan's theories justified naval expansion, with or without further colonial acquisitions; the emerging military-industrial complex reflected both German industrial development and its natural expansion overseas.[67] Mahan's theories also provided the justification for challenging British naval superiority for defensive, not offensive, reasons. Indeed, it could be argued that both German and American leaders believed that it was possible to surpass the British Empire as the foremost world power without risking war.[68]

---

64 See Smith, *Ideological Origins of Nazi Imperialism,* chaps. 2, 4; on Harnack, see John A. Moses, "The British and German Churches and the Perception of War, 1908–1914," *War and Society* 5 (May 1987): 23–43.

65 See Kelly, *Descent of Darwin,* 123–41; Heinz Gollwitzer, *Geschichte des weltpolitischen Denkens,* 2 vols. (Göttingen, 1982), 285–306, and Hans-Christoph Schröder, *Sozialismus und Imperialismus: Die Auseinandersetzung der deutschen Sozialdemokratie mit dem Imperialismusproblem und der "Weltpolitik" vor 1914* (Hannover, 1968).

66 See May, *American Imperialism,* chap. 5.

67 See Smith, *Ideological Origins of Nazi Imperialism,* chaps. 4, 6; Gollwitzer, *Geschichte des weltpolitischen Denkens,* 1:23–78, 149–95, 217–52.

68 Of course, many considerations other than Mahan's theories influenced German and American naval policy, but his arguments provided a very useful base for naval propaganda. Certainly, Theodore Roosevelt and Tirpitz recognized this important advantage. See Wilhelm Deist, *Flottenpolitik und Flottenpropaganda: Das Nachrichtenbureau des Reichsmarineamtes 1897–1914* (Stuttgart, 1976), 71ff., 171ff.; see also Howard K. Beale, *Theodore Roosevelt and the Rise of American World Power* (Baltimore, 1956; reprint, Baltimore, 1984), 56–64.

Although Mahan's vision proved viable for the United States, it had disastrous implications for Imperial Germany, for obvious geopolitical reasons. Throughout the late nineteenth century the United States could engage in the rhetoric of war with Great Britain, as President Cleveland did during the border dispute between Venezuela and British Guyana in 1895 and as President Theodore Roosevelt did during the 1901 Alaskan boundary dispute with Canada. In both cases American presidents correctly assumed that the British would back down and sacrifice western hemisphere priorities for the sake of an Anglo-American rapprochement.[69] Imperial Germany had no such option. In fact, its geostrategic location made it impossible for Britain to grant Germany a fleet powerful enough to pose a serious threat to British control of the North Sea, the English Channel, or the North Atlantic. That neither Tirpitz, who had the support of Kaiser Wilhelm II, nor the German Foreign Office comprehended this reality was revealed by the German rejection of British proposals in the period 1912–14 to slow down the naval arms race. It was even more graphically demonstrated in the July 1914 miscalculations about British policy and naval war strategy.[70]

Yet despite its role in destabilizing Anglo-German relations, and despite the fact that the construction of a large battle fleet was extremely costly and a heavy burden on the German taxpayer, there is little doubt that the navy enjoyed great popular support, much more so than the army.[71] The naval buildup in the United States also enjoyed enthusiastic support, especially under the guidance of the assistant secretary of the Navy and later president Theodore Roosevelt.[72] There are, in fact, a number of parallels in the respective naval arms races that should be noted. First, there were heated debates over naval appropriations in the German Reichstag and in the U.S. Congress; but in the end, and against strong opposition, appropriations were granted. In each country heavy industry promoted naval armament and constituted an influential political lobby. This lobby provided significant financial backing to naval circles and political enthusiasts to rally mass support, especially in Imperial Germany.[73]

69 See Ernest R. May, *Imperial Democracy: The Emergence of America as a Great Power* (New York, 1961), 31–55, 225–6.
70 Berghahn, *Der Tirpitz-Plan,* 45–89; Kennedy, *Rise of Anglo-German Antagonism,* 415–24; and the very persuasive analysis by John H. Maurer, "Churchill's Naval Holiday: Arms Control and the Anglo-German Naval Race, 1912–1914," *Journal of Strategic Studies* 15 (Mar. 1992): 102–27.
71 See Wilhelm Deist, *Flottenpolitik und Flottenpropaganda,* 249–96; and Eley, *Reshaping the German Right,* 147ff.
72 Sprout, *Rise of American Naval Power,* 250–85.
73 See Deist, *Flottenpolitik und Flottenpropaganda,* 110ff.; Beale, *Theodore Roosevelt,* 56–64.

It is also noteworthy that the propaganda techniques used by naval lobbying groups in Germany and in the United States were similar. For example, American "boosters" not only modeled their Navy league on the German example but also practiced the art of nationalist propaganda and created *Feindbilder* (conceptions of the enemy) when naval appropriations bills were pending.[74] It was precisely these methods that the German navy and its supporters under the guidance and inspiration of Tirpitz employed; this meant successfully mobilizing anti-British propaganda, and also anti-socialist sentiment, prior to crucial votes in the Reichstag.[75] By the early 1900s in the United States, it was anti-German propaganda that proved most successful in getting naval grants through Congress.

Obviously, Mahan's idea of armed preparedness was easier to sell to the nation if one could identify the enemy, real or imagined. And the success of naval boosterism was impressive. When President Roosevelt's tenure in office ended in 1909, the U.S. Navy ranked third behind the British and German navies but second in regard to first-class battleships.[76] In Germany, the naval policies of Tirpitz did not intend to achieve parity with the Royal Navy but made the German navy strong enough to be a potential threat to British naval superiority.

There can be little doubt that naval propaganda contributed materially to nationalist chauvinism and the development of national antagonisms and also increased international tension. German-American relations are a case in point. Although official relations remained cordial even for some time after the outbreak of World War I, both navies had been busy drafting war plans against each other for more than a decade.[77] In addition, the nationalist press in the United States fanned the flames of Germanophobia, which displaced the traditional rhetoric of Anglophobia; in Germany, anti-Americanism also became more pronounced, especially among ardent nationalists.[78]

Prior to 1914 naval propaganda not only identified the potential enemy, it also provided the vision of national glory. It is this combination that might help to explain why naval propaganda struck a responsive chord in both Germany and the United States. In a sense, the naval armaments race

74 See Herwig, *Politics of Frustration*, 81–3.
75 Wilhelm Deist, *Flottenpolitik und Flottenpropaganda*, 171ff., 194ff., 264–5.
76 Pommerin, *Der Kaiser und Amerika*, 127.
77 See Herwig, *Politics of Frustration*, chaps. 2, 4; see also Pommerin, *Der Kaiser und Amerika*, 179–92.
78 Ibid., 207–20; Roger Chickering, *We Men Who Feel Most German: A Cultural Study of the Pan-German League, 1886–1914* (Boston, 1984), 88–91; Schieber, *Transformation of American Sentiment*, chaps. 5, 6.

can be interpreted as an international competition in national prowess without the immediate threat of war. It was to be the instrument that would translate economic power into political might. Or, to phrase it differently, a large fleet of battleships in a way signified the nation's great advances in industry and technology, as well as the promise of national influence and power throughout the world. It also meant competition but not necessarily conflict with Britain and its empire.

ASSESSING FOREIGN POLICY PERFORMANCE, 1865–1914

By the July crisis of 1914 the foreign policy failures of the government of Kaiser Wilhelm II far exceeded its victories. Neither the "Policy of a Free Hand" nor *Weltpolitik* had advanced Germany's search for empire. Indeed, the territorial expanse of Imperial Germany had changed little since Bismarck's dismissal; it was he, not Wilhelm II, who had laid the foundations of Germany's small colonial empire in Africa and the South Seas. Nor were the territorial gains after 1890 all that impressive: the occupation and lease of Tsingtao in 1898 from China; the purchase of a few more South Sea Islands from Spain in 1899; the division of Samoa between the United States and Germany; and the small territorial addition to Cameroon in 1911, as compensation for French expansion in Morocco.

These minor territorial additions to the German colonial empire stood in disproportionate relation to the aggressive nationalist stance and rhetoric that characterized German foreign policy under the "personal regime" of Wilhelm II and his chancellors, particularly Foreign Minister and later Chancellor Bernhard von Bülow. Even more important, Germany's influence in world politics declined with French diplomatic successes in building alliances, first with Russia (1894) and then with Great Britain (1904). The Algeciras Conference in 1906 demonstrated not only Germany's growing isolation but also the formidable opposition, including that of the United States, arrayed against German imperialist ambitions.[79]

By contrast, American expansion in territory, influence, and power after the Civil War – while it created international tensions, war scares, and, in 1898, even a "little" war – was extraordinarily successful. The acquisi-

---

79 See Imanuel Geiss, *Der lange Weg in die Katastrophe: Die Vorgeschichte des Ersten Weltkriegs 1815–1914* (Munich, 1990), and Imanuel Geiss, "The German Version of Imperialism, 1898–1914: *Weltpolitik*," in Schöllgen, ed., *Escape into War?*, 105–19; see also Kennedy, *Rise of the Anglo-German Antagonism*, 283–5; Burton, *Theodore Roosevelt*, 47–8.

tion of Alaska in 1867, part of Secretary of State William Seward's vision of Manifest Destiny to extend American control over the entire continent, represented a major territorial gain. Contrary to Seward's expectation, and that of many of his contemporaries, Canada rejected political union with the United States, but it became increasingly economically dependent on its neighbor to the south by World War I.[80] The status of the northern dominion also could be used as a valuable pawn in the United States' diplomatic relations with the British. During and after the Civil War, the security of Canada was one of the reasons for British accommodation of American demands; yet, by the 1900s the Canadian government was an active participant in the Anglo-American rapprochement.[81] Among politicians in the United States, Theodore Roosevelt was in the vanguard of those visualizing the compatibility of American and British interests as two fully equal nations who "could dominate the world – to the advantage of civilization."[82] It was a vision many in the American political and military elite shared.[83]

But even more impressive was the success with which the United States used the threat of military intervention to gain hegemony over other regions of the western hemisphere. In 1865 American military potential and Seward's pointed reference to the Monroe Doctrine were sufficient inducement for French Emperor Napoleon III to abandon his ill-fated Mexican adventure.[84] During the 1890s American war rhetoric was equally successful in convincing successive British governments to forgo any additional territorial claims in Latin America. Despite some resistance to American policies in Nicaragua and Venezuela, and against the unilateral abrogation of British treaty rights over a future canal across the Isthmus of Panama, the British government pursued a policy of accommodation. In 1904 it even accepted President Roosevelt's particularly strident interpretation of the Monroe Doctrine that gave the United States sweeping powers to intervene in the internal affairs of countries in Latin America and the Caribbean, in addition to Mexico.[85] As the American revisionist historian Gabriel Kolko writes, "No other imperialist power at this time claimed

---

80 Dexter Perkins, "William H. Seward as Secretary of State," in Glyndon G. Van Deusen and Richard C. Wade, eds., *Foreign Policy and the American Spirit* (Ithaca, N.Y., 1957), 218–26.

81 J. L. Granatstein and Norman Hillmer, *"For Better or For Worse": Canada and the United States to the 1990s* (Toronto, 1991), 1–68.

82 Beale, *Theodore Roosevelt*, 81.

83 Challener, *Admirals, Generals, and American Foreign Policy*, 26–7.

84 Perkins, "William H. Seward as Secretary of State," 223–4.

85 Burton, *Theodore Roosevelt*, 110–29.

such open-ended privileges over so vast an area, and had another done so the result would have produced a European war."[86] This is probably one of the few times when Kolko is in agreement with mainstream historians, especially when he and other historians before him point to the fact that American ascendancy as a world power rested on the twin pillars of tremendous industrial growth and capitalist expansion, on the one hand, and political instability in Europe, on the other.[87]

Economic determinist and structural objectivist interpretations, such as Kolko's assertion "that the United States . . . would not have been any different had chauvinism and social Darwinism been absent in the latter part of the nineteenth century,"[88] have prompted much historical debate. Although it is true, as many critics have pointed out, that such historical determinism belittles the factor of human choice and responsibility in history, it also is true that the great success of industrial capitalism in the United States and Germany made imperialist expansion in both countries a driving force of particular strength and vitality. In this context, it is interesting to note that the view of Great Britain as a declining power, so frequently expressed by leading American and German politicians and intellectuals at the time, rested on the recognition of Britain losing its economic supremacy.[89] Nevertheless, there existed the clear realization in the United States, and in Imperial Germany, that Britain remained the key power broker in the world.

Many historians besides Kolko have long emphasized the fact that American national destiny was not independent from the balance of power in Europe. Certainly, President Roosevelt took full advantage of European rivalry and dissent, as well as British weakness. In simple geopolitical terms the concept of the balance of power remains a convincing tool to explain the imperialist successes of the United States while pointing to the inevitability of failure of Germany's *Weltpolitik*.[90] Because the balance of power in Europe traditionally operated against the hegemony of a single continental power, German imperialist expansion had closely prescribed limits. It was the political genius of Bismarck's foreign policy to have recognized these limits after 1875, when he made it clear that German terri-

---

86 Kolko, *Main Currents in Modern American History*, 42.
87 Vagts, "United States and the Balance of Power," 178–209; Wehler, *Der Aufstieg des amerikanischen Imperialismus*, 24–43.
88 Kolko, *Main Currents in Modern American History*, 40.
89 Kennedy, *Rise of Anglo-German Antagonism*, 312–13; Eckart Kehr, "Anglophobia and *Weltpolitik*," in *Economic Interest, Militarism, and Foreign Policy*, 22–49.
90 Vagts, "United States and the Balance of Power," 178–209; Geiss, "German Version of Imperialism," 105–19.

torial ambitions in Europe were satisfied.[91] At the same time, the much-debated question remains whether even a politician of Bismarck's stature could have withstood the pressures of rising imperialist ambitions after 1890.[92] And it is even more difficult to imagine how Imperial Germany could have realized its imperialist ambitions through partnership with Great Britain, as was the case with the United States.

It is from this traditional balance-of-power perspective that historians have more recently probed the origins of World War I in innovative ways. Comparing the economic performance of the great powers in the prewar years, the British historian Paul M. Kennedy points out that neither Germany nor the United States had much to gain from war because their dynamic economies assured their ascendancy to global-power status.[93] By contrast, he argues, France and Great Britain, which were losing ground both in economic and demographic terms, experienced the good fortune that victory in World War I reversed their decline, if only in the short term. It is this assessment of relative weakness and possible gain that demonstrates the irrationality of Germany's push for war and the economic logic of its defeat. Kennedy's economic perspective makes it easier to understand, however, why Germany's blustering foreign policy was perceived as so very threatening, and not only by its immediate neighbors. It also helps to explain the increasing inflexibility of the alliance system in Europe before the outbreak of World War I. By probing the question of the difficulty of governance in Britain and Germany during times of increasing social strife and political fragmentation, German historian Gustav Schmidt points to the legacy of vast naval expenditures and to the fact that Anglo-German rivalry became the foundation of the domestic and foreign policies of both countries during the 1890s. According to Schmidt, this made not only German but also British foreign policy increasingly nationalistic and uncompromising – so much so that even when British government leaders in 1912 no longer considered Germany a military threat to British security, a policy of political accommodation toward Germany was no longer politically feasible.[94] Reconciliation was unpopular at home and

91 Andreas Hillgruber, "Die 'Krieg-in-Sicht'-Krise 1875: Wegscheide der Politik der europäischen Grossmächte in der späten Bismarck-Zeit," in *Deutsche Grossmacht und Weltpolitik im 19. und 20. Jahrhundert* (Düsseldorf, 1979), 35–52.
92 See Michael Stürmer, "A Nation-State Against History and Geography: The German Dilemma," in Schöllgen, ed., *Escape into War?*, 63–72; and Klaus Hildebrand, "Opportunities and Limits of German Foreign Policy in the Bismarckian Era, 1871–1890: 'A System of Stopgaps'?" ibid., 73–92.
93 Paul M. Kennedy, "The First World War and the International Power System," *International Security* 9, no. 1 (summer 1984): 7–40.
94 Gustav Schmidt, "Great Britain and Germany in the Age of Imperialism," *War and Society* 4 (May 1986): 31–51.

abroad, with Britain's European alliance partners, its dominions, and with the United States, all of which felt that their respective national interests were not served by a British-German rapprochement and colonial concessions aimed at mollifying Germany's imperialist ambitions. Thus, the new balance of power in Europe that emerged after the turn of the century and that centered on the Anglo-German antagonism compounded the foreign policy mistakes and miscalculations of Imperial Germany.[95]

From this global perspective, the emergence and development of the international peace movement before World War I raise some interesting questions. As is well known, American governments of this period were early advocates of the use of international arbitration to resolve international confrontations peacefully. It also should be noted that many of the belligerent imperialists, such as Theodore Roosevelt and Elihu Root, drew close to the peace movement after 1900.[96] By contrast, Imperial Germany's political and military elites continued unabated in their active opposition to the peace movements at home and international arbitration abroad.[97] Could a transnational study help explain these national differences and how they were translated into policymaking? Possibly. For example, it is well known that President Roosevelt received the Nobel Peace Prize in 1906 for his arbitration role in the Russo-Japanese War. But it is perhaps less well known that he was not ready to arbitrate when vital American interests were at stake, as was the case in the 1901 Alaskan boundary dispute with Britain and Canada, where belligerent rhetoric seemed to serve the national interest better.[98] One should also consider in the German case that Wilhelm II and his government sought international agreement in the First Moroccan Crisis, only to be disappointed with the outcome.[99]

As intriguing as these examples might be, they are a reminder that peace activists in both countries also could be intense nationalists imbued with imperialist and social Darwinist values. This was certainly true in Germany and in the United States, where the civilizing mission of the Anglo-Saxon race, at home and abroad, was much emphasized. That this new assertiveness of the United States did not lead to conflict with Great Britain was, as has already been discussed, due not only to geography and the global balance of power but also possibly to common cultural roots. American chau-

95 This is also emphasized by Kennedy, *Rise of the Anglo-German Antagonism,* 441–70, and Geiss, "German Version of Imperialism," 105–19.
96 Beale, *Theodore Roosevelt,* 399–427; Marchand, *American Peace Movement,* 24–9.
97 Chickering, *Imperial Germany and a World Without War,* 218ff.
98 Burton, *Theodore Roosevelt,* 11–12, 42–4.
99 Vagts, *Deutschland und die Vereinigten Staaten,* 2:1948–86.

vinism, Anglophilia, and Germanophobia were certainly essential features of emerging British-American cooperation.[100]

Cultural analyses of imperialism, modernism, and modernity that are transnational in scope might also be a way to see foreign policy in a different power relationship. As the recent work by Richard Collin on the presidency of Theodore Roosevelt demonstrates, the thrust for empire, including the risk of war, went together with a cultural exaltation that stressed national distinctiveness and superiority. By the turn of the century, Collin claims, there was a widespread belief that the American age had arrived.[101] Obviously, the belief in the superiority of one's own culture – a theme only too familiar in German history and historical analysis – was not unique to Imperial Germany, even though it is frequently cited as a major cause of the outbreak of World War I.[102] But it might well be that Germany's sense of mission was more absolute than that of the United States because it lacked Anglo-Saxon restraint. As Modris Eksteins claims, Germany's cultural evolution propelled the nation into the forefront of modernity by the cultural rejection of bourgeois values and its very own capitalist successes. From this perspective, war could be viewed as a form of liberation in 1914.[103]

To date, historians have not embarked on a comparative analysis of President Roosevelt and Kaiser Wilhelm II and their policies, but both men continue to engage the historical imagination, as the volume of literature demonstrates. It is also interesting that contemporary commentators frequently compared the American president and the German kaiser.[104] They were the same age, and both seemed to possess dynamic personalities that, although somewhat erratic, were seen to be in step with the youthful energies of their respective nations. Each man represented a generational change in political leadership, and each seemed to need martial rhetoric and public affirmation of his manly courage. But whereas Theodore Roosevelt is revered for his political success, Wilhelm II is fascinating because of his failures.

100 Burton, *Theodore Roosevelt*, 18, 31.
101 Collin, *Theodore Roosevelt*, pt. 1; and Richard H. Collin, *Theodore Roosevelt's Caribbean: The Panama Canal, the Monroe Doctrine, and the Latin American Context* (Baton Rouge, La., 1991).
102 Modris Eksteins, "When Death Was Young . . . : Germany, Modernism, and the Great War," in R. J. Bullen, Hartmut Pogge von Strandmann, and A. B. Polonsky, eds., *Ideas into Politics: Aspects of European History, 1880–1950* (London, 1984), 25–35.
103 Ibid., 29; see also Modris Eksteins, *Rites of Spring: The Great War and the Birth of the Modern Age* (Toronto, 1990), 90–4.
104 See Beale, *Theodore Roosevelt*, 441ff.

In recent years there have been several attempts to provide a psychohistorical profile of Wilhelm II[105] and to some extent of Bismarck[106] in order to explain Germany's foreign policy, which ended in war. There is no doubt, however, that Bismarck shaped the destiny of Germany, and in a sense that of Europe, between 1862 and 1890; by contrast, it is generally recognized that Wilhelm II was less of a leader and more of a liability to German domestic and foreign policy. And it seems that historical excursions into the psyche of political leaders and their nations only underscore the necessity of clearly identifying divergent interests and power relations in and between nations. As this comparative analysis between American and German imperialist expansionism suggests, determining the relative importance of geostrategic conditions, political structures, and the responsibility of power remains key to explaining the outbreak of World War I. Did the war contain an "irrepressible dynamism" of its own?[107] Perhaps, but that question is beyond the scope of this chapter.

CONCLUSION

In August 1914 the German people might have yearned for empire and maybe also for "true salvation" through war,[108] but it is a historical fact that "the view of not more than a dozen men,"[109] mainly generals, counted most when Germany plunged into war. By contrast, while the ruling elite in the United States was without doubt Anglophile, it took provocative German action, such as the Zimmermann telegram and unrestricted submarine warfare, to turn the United States into a belligerent – and then only after the war had been raging for more than two years.[110] As this comparative study tries to show, decision-making authority and political priorities varied greatly between Imperial Germany and the United States between 1890 and 1914 because of different political structures, social values, power relationships, and the concepts of consensus and loyalty. This dichotomy

105 See Hull, *Entourage of Kaiser Wilhelm II;* most recently, John C. G. Röhl, *Wilhelm II: Die Jugend des Kaisers* (Munich, 1993), and Thomas A. Kohut, *Wilhelm II and the Germans: A Study in Leadership* (New York, 1991), 225–34; see also the earlier and very detailed biography by Michael Balfour, *The Kaiser and His Times* (London, 1964).
106 Otto Pflanze, "Towards a Psychoanalytic Interpretation of Bismarck," *American Historical Review* 77 (Apr. 1972): 419–44; Judith M. Hughes, *Emotion and High Politics: Personal Relations at the Summit in Late Nineteenth-Century Britain and Germany* (Berkeley, Calif., 1983), 210–19.
107 Eksteins, *Rites of Spring,* 315.
108 Eksteins, "When Death Was Young," 28–9.
109 Kolko, *Century of War,* 39. His judgment is based on the many studies of the Fischer school; see also John C. G. Röhl, *The Kaiser and His Court: Wilhelm II and the Government of Germany* (Cambridge, 1994), 162–89.
110 Kennedy, "British and German Reactions," 15–24.

would become most evident during the ultimate crisis situation – whether one's country should go to war.

In recent scholarship, dissatisfaction has been voiced with foreign policy analyses that do not probe beyond the historical affirmation of the nation-state and remain dedicated "to write histories so fully on public life, electoral politics and white men."[111] But as this chapter demonstrates, although cross-national analysis can refocus some of the issues and interpretations, it is extremely difficult to explain the breakdown of the international political system and the outbreak of war in terms other than those of conflicting interests within individual nations and among nation-states.

111 Ian Tyrell, "American Exceptionalism in an Age of International History," 1033ff.; quotation in Michael McGerr, "The Price of the 'New Transnational History,'" *American Historical Review* 96 (Oct. 1991): 1067.

PART TWO

War and Society

3

The Political Economy of Warfare in America, 1865–1914

PAUL A. C. KOISTINEN

INTRODUCTION

This chapter deals with the political economy of warfare in America from approximately 1865 to 1914.[1] By the political economy of warfare I mean the interrelationship of the political, economic, and military structures in devising the means to mobilize the nation's resources for defense and to conduct war. The magnitude and duration of the fighting dictates *what* the nation has to do to harness its economic power, but prewar trends largely determine *how* this mobilization takes place. Four factors determine the method of mobilization. The first is *political:* the size, strength, and scope of the federal government. The second is *economic:* the level of maturity of the economy. The third is *military:* the character and structure of the services as well as their relationship with civilian society and authority. Finally, it is necessary to assess the *state of military technology.*

Patterns of economic mobilization for war have passed through three major stages over the course of American history. The experiences in the War of Independence, the Civil War, and twentieth-century warfare best characterize these stages, which I have labeled preindustrial, transitional, and industrial. In the preindustrial stage, centralized control of economic mobilization was necessary because all institutions were weak. In the transitional phase, control from the center was less necessary for the Union because all institutions were relatively, but not exceptionally, strong. In the Confederacy, however, weak institutions everywhere demanded strength at the center. The failure of adequate centralized authority to emerge in the

---

1 The following analysis is based on Paul A. C. Koistinen, *Mobilizing for Modern War: The Political Economy of American Warfare, 1865–1919* (Lawrence, Kans., 1997), chaps. 1–6. The documentation for these chapters is extensive. In the notes that follow, I can only suggest the range of sources I draw on for my analysis and cite some of the most recent bibliographies.

South opened the door to military subjugation. With the industrial stage, exceptionally strong institutions all around required unbending strength at the center to maintain stability.

The years from 1865 to 1914 mark the beginning of the industrial stage. In this stage, for the first time in American history, all four economic mobilization factors, including the technology of war, changed significantly. Consider the maturity of the economy first: In the period from 1865 to the early years of the twentieth century, the industrial revolution transformed the American economy into a fully mature industrial system. The economy was dominated by large corporations that used various devices to consolidate economic power for the purpose of controlling market forces.

In response to this dramatic change, the size, scope, and strength of the federal government – the second economic mobilization factor – also were transformed. Although the change began in the late nineteenth century, the most significant reforms occurred during the Progressive era. From about 1900 to 1916, the federal government was expanded and restructured to regulate big business and to begin to act as a social welfare agent for the masses.

In terms of the third factor, the character of the armed services and their relationship to civilian society and authority, far-reaching changes again took place. Both the army and the navy completed the process of modernization and professionalization that had begun before the Civil War and included advances in education and training, the growth of professional societies and publications, and structural reforms. All these changes were designed to further the military's corporate identity and improve the armed services' ability to conduct warfare.

The fourth factor, the state of military technology, took on critical significance for the first time. Building a new navy of steel, steam, armor, and modern ordnance required a production team of government officials, naval officers, and industrialists working together, particularly where armor and ordnance were involved. In one way or another, that production team has remained in existence until the present day. Here are located the origins of what today is called the military–industrial complex. New technology would bring similar change to the army in the twentieth century. This reality began to break down the institutional integrity that the army and navy had gradually built up after 1815. Ironically, this process began when the services had reached their most advanced stage of professionalization. In short, changing weaponry altered the nature of military professionalism and the armed services' relationship to the civilian world.

Basic change in all four economic mobilization factors fundamentally

changed the way the economy was harnessed for war. This was only vaguely evident in the very short and limited effort required during the Spanish-
American War of 1898, but the nation experienced the full impact of
modernity when harnessing the economy for World War I, a subject I have
addressed elsewhere and that is beyond the scope of this chapter.[2]

The Spanish-American War, however, had a significant impact on the
third mobilization factor, the nature and character of the military services
and their relationship to civilian society and authority. War mobilization
revealed that the army's system of command and administration was ap-
pallingly flawed. This led to the reforms of Secretary of War Elihu Root
(1899–1904), in which the office of commanding general – created by
Secretary of War John C. Calhoun in 1821 – was scrapped in favor of the
chief-of-staff/general-staff system. A number of years later, the office of
chief of naval operations, and related institutions created earlier, such as the
Naval War College, provided the navy with a comparable structure. Additionally, both services, particularly the navy, made improvements in their
systems of supply.

In developing the foregoing points on the political economy of warfare
from 1865 to 1914, particular attention will be devoted to civil-military relations and the impact of technology. Political and economic developments
are more well known and more easily summarized.

POLITICAL MODERNIZATION

Between 1876 and 1896 the United States entered a period in which the
political and economic systems were more separated from one another than
has ever before or since been the case.[3] This extreme fragmentation came
about as the sectional ideology that had fueled politics before and after the
Civil War became irrelevant. The two major political parties could neither
come to terms with the industrialization taking place nor devise policies
for handling the problems it caused. A drift set in whereby elections be-

---

2 Paul A. C. Koistinen, "The 'Industrial-Military Complex' in Historical Perspective: World War I,"
Business History Review 41 (winter 1967): 378–403. The analysis is expanded in *Mobilizing for Modern
War*, chaps. 6–10.
3 Carl N. Degler, *The Age of the Economic Revolution, 1876–1900*, 2d rev. ed. (Glenview, Ill., 1977),
provides a good introduction to the subject matter and bibliography of the Gilded Age. His work is
extended and updated in the following volumes: Robert H. Wiebe, *The Search for Order, 1877–1920*
(New York, 1967); Morton Keller, *Affairs of State: Public Life in Late Nineteenth-Century America*
(Cambridge, Mass., 1977); Stephen Skowronek, *Building a New American State: The Expansion of National Administrative Capacities, 1877–1920* (Cambridge, 1982); Michael E. McGerr, *The Decline of
Popular Politics: The American North, 1865–1928* (New York, 1986); relevant essays in Mary O. Furner
and Barry Supple, eds., *The State and Economic Knowledge: The American and British Experiences* (New

came more important than issues, leading to elaborate and sophisticated political machines and campaigns for getting out the vote as well as to a high level of political corruption.

In the midst of this drift, some positive developments were taking place. Between approximately 1885 and 1900, party and congressional leaders used party caucuses, committee structures, and new or modified regulations to streamline procedures and transform the two houses of Congress into a reasonably effective national legislature. Meanwhile, beginning with Rutherford B. Hayes and continuing under his successors, the various one-term presidents restored some authority to an executive branch that had been badly weakened by the impeachment of Andrew Johnson and the political incompetence of Ulysses S. Grant. In doing so, they helped pave the way for an effective presidency – the sine qua non of reformed government – and specifically for William McKinley.

The political adjustment to industrialization took place first on the periphery rather than at the center of the social system. This was evident in the operations of the urban political machines and the growing agrarian protest movements. Simultaneously, reform was taking hold within traditional political and governmental circles at the local, state, and national levels. For the most part, these movements were led by mugwumps and new professional elements from the middle to upper classes who were seeking to make the social system more efficient or humane and sometimes both. Their efforts included improved social services, updated public utilities, and more effective forms of governance.

Local and state reforms in time forced Washington to respond to industrialization. Most important, the national government had to address the consolidation of economic power under the modern corporation as the most significant result of the industrial revolution. It did so with the Interstate Commerce Act of 1887 and, at least symbolically, the Sherman Anti-Trust Act of 1890. By setting up an independent regulatory commission with the former statute, Congress created the most basic institution of the twentieth century for dealing with the complexities of a modern industrial economy.

York, 1990); Richard L. McCormick, "Public Life in Industrial America, 1877–1917," in Eric Foner, ed., *The New American History* (Philadelphia, 1990), 93–117; Joel L. Silbey, *The American Political Nation, 1838–1893* (Stanford, Calif., 1991), 141–251; Peter H. Argersinger, *Structure, Process, and Party: Essays in American Political History* (Armonk, N.Y., 1992); Robert C. McMath Jr., *American Populism: A Social History, 1877–1898* (New York, 1993); Mark W. Summers, *The Era of Good Stealings* (New York, 1993); Melvyn Dubofsky, *The State and Labor in Modern America* (Chapel Hill, N.C., 1994); and Charles W. Calhoun, ed., *The Gilded Age: Essays on the Origins of Modern America* (Wilmington, Del., 1996).

Lasting reform at the national level depended on breaking the stalemate that paralyzed the two parties and kept them focused on elections rather than on issues. Beginning in 1884, the party system entered a period of exceptional turbulence that led to the fundamental realignment of 1894–6, in which the Republicans emerged as the nation's majority party based on winning the cities. Industrialization had destroyed the third-party system and ushered in the fourth.

Despite all that it was not, the third-party system was in many ways quite remarkable. In a passive, negative fashion it saw the nation through the most trying period of industrialization. By focusing on local and state issues, the third-party system, along with the various third parties, helped to keep the masses loyal to the existing social system during a twenty-year period of enormous stress. The two parties acted in various ways to ameliorate, rather than to intensify, class antagonisms. Moreover, because a large part of the population, particularly urban inhabitants, consisted of immigrants, both parties had to be sensitive to ethnic, cultural, and religious interests. By focusing on such concerns, the political parties tempered class antagonisms, a strategy that was reasonably effective except during the repeated periods of economic depression. Ethnocultural issues became less consequential in the twentieth century as the economy experienced greater stability, government at all levels became more involved in economic and welfare measures, rates of immigration fell, and labor unions grew in strength.

The fourth-party system, like the third, started with a strong executive.[4] McKinley led with a firm hand, Theodore Roosevelt even more so. Unlike in the third-party system, the dominance achieved by the executive branch in the fourth would be permanent – a necessity in a modern, complex society. During the Progressive years strengthening the executive depended on furthering domestic reform. That effort began with Theodore Roosevelt, both advanced and faltered under William Howard Taft, and was brought to fruition by Woodrow Wilson. By combining the New Freedom with the New Nationalism, President Wilson achieved a new Progressive synthesis: a government–business regulatory alliance as the

---

4 The literature on progressivism is exceptionally rich, with some of the works cited in note 3 relevant to the period. One of the best introductions to the bibliography of the era is Robert H. Wiebe, "The Progressive Years, 1900–1917," in William H. Cartwright and Richard L. Watson Jr., eds., *The Reinterpretation of American History and Culture* (Washington, D.C., 1973), 425–42. More recent publications revise Wiebe's essay and provide additional insight on the subject. See Richard M. Abrams, *The Burdens of Progress, 1900–1929* (Glenview, Ill., 1978); John Whiteclay Chambers II, *The Tyranny of Change: America in the Progressive Era, 1900–1920,* rev. ed. (New York, 1992); McCormick, "Public Life in Industrial America," in Foner, ed., *New American History,* 93–117; and Lewis L. Gould, *Reform and Regulation: American Politics from Roosevelt to Wilson,* 3d rev. ed. (Prospect Heights, Ill., 1996).

principal mode of twentieth-century American political economy. A larger government would begin to act as social welfare agent and regulate business — but under conditions in which the regulated would actually be the
regulator or the regulator would share at least the interests and ideology of
the regulated. The "people in the street" would be included in the bargain
through a modest welfare state that ameliorated the worst features of capitalism and kept the masses loyal to the system.

How all this worked remained elusive during the years of peace because
the activities of government, business, and the masses appeared to proceed
largely on different planes that touched overtly only on occasion. But a
planned wartime economy made the new system clear and palpable. The
functioning of the War Industries Board fully revealed the dynamics of the
government-business regulatory alliance; the operations of the larger wartime economy manifested the main features of a modest welfare state.[5]

Although Progressivism was exceptionally complex and contradictory,
its political economy at the local, state, and national levels had a consistency of sorts. Elite patterns were evident at all levels and centered on limiting
democratic trends. This took place directly through measures restricting
the franchise and indirectly through the creation of independent regulatory agencies staffed by officials who were appointed rather than elected, operated largely outside the public eye, came from the middle- to upper-class
elements, and were designated as professional experts. This trend was of
course most important at the national level because the federal government, the fulcrum of the new regulatory alliance, was growing at the expense of both local and state governments. The importance of appointed
officials in Washington was evident in the growing size and power of the
executive branch and in agencies such as the Interstate Commerce Commission, the Federal Trade Commission, and the Federal Reserve Board.

INDUSTRIALIZATION

The shaping force of the Gilded Age was the transition from an agrarian to
a mature industrial economy in a short period of thirty-five years.[6] The
United States already was a manufacturing nation of importance in 1860,

5 The subject matter and bibliography of the World War I years are covered extensively in my publications cited in note 2.
6 I have written about and cited sources on concentrated corporate power in previous studies. See Paul
A. C. Koistinen, *The Military-Industrial Complex: A Historical Perspective* (New York, 1980), 14–16,
and n. 12; and "Warfare and Power Relations in America: Mobilizing the World War II Economy,"
in James Titus, ed., *The Home Front and War in the Twentieth Century: The American Experience in Comparative Perspective* (Colorado Springs, Colo., 1984), 98–103, and n. 4, 20. A number of studies cited

but by 1900 it had become the world's industrial giant, and by 1910 it was unsurpassed in the output of most industrial products.

In accounting for the growth, most scholars recognize the importance of expanding demand in a population that jumped from 36 million in 1865 to 100 million in 1914. The supply side of growth matched or exceeded demand. Technological innovation, adaptation, and diffusion became exceptionally important in the late nineteenth and early twentieth centuries and multiplied manifold the productive capacity of American industry. Mass-production techniques were especially important in that regard.

Between 1869 and 1899 agriculture reversed positions with industry, dropping from 53 percent to 33 percent of value added in commodity output. That was the case despite the fact that gross farm output nearly tripled between 1860 and 1910, with the enormous push into the Great Plains, greater mechanization, and improved farming techniques.

A national market was basic to the economic growth of both industry and agriculture in the late nineteenth century. Regardless of the numerous academic disputes involving the railroads, most scholars agree that they were essential in transforming the United States from a collection of regional markets to a single national market in which raw materials and semi-finished goods could be moved quickly, reliably, cheaply, and flexibly to centers of production and finished products could be distributed throughout the nation and abroad with similar ease.

Scholars also generally agree that the railroads pioneered in the organization of the modern corporation that was later adapted and refined by industrial firms. Multimillion- and ultimately multibillion-dollar enterprise with a national and even international reach required new and effective management methods. Although corporate structures took many forms, three characteristics stand out: The first involved separating policy-making

in note 2 also are relevant to economic development. Additionally, various statistics introduced in the following sections are taken from U.S. Department of Commerce, Bureau of the Census, *Historical Statistics of the United States: Colonial Times to 1970*, 2 pts. (Washington, D.C., 1975). See also the following sources on the maturation of the economy during the Gilded Age: Glenn Porter, *The Rise of Big Business, 1860–1910* (Arlington Heights, Ill., 1973); Harold G. Vatter, *The Drive to Industrial Maturity: The U.S. Economy, 1860–1914* (Westport, Conn., 1975); Alfred D. Chandler Jr., *The Visible Hand: The Managerial Revolution in American Business* (Cambridge, Mass., 1977); Thomas C. Cochran, *200 Years of American Business* (New York, 1977), 51–170; Susan P. Lee and Peter Passell, *A New Economic View of American History* (New York, 1979), 266–361; Stuart Bruchey, *Enterprise: The Dynamic Economy of a Free People* (Cambridge, Mass., 1990), 308–80; Gerald Berk, *Alternate Tracks: The Constitution of American Industrial Order, 1865–1917* (Baltimore, 1994); Louis Galambos, "The Triumph of Oligopoly," in Thomas Weiss and Donald Schaefer, eds., *American Economic Development in Historical Perspective* (Stanford, Calif., 1994), 241–53, 307–313; Claudia Goldin and Gary D. Libecap, eds., *The Regulated Economy: A Historical Approach to Political Economy* (Chicago, 1994); and Walter Licht, *Industrializing America: The Nineteenth Century* (Baltimore, 1995).

from operations, with the top executives determining strategy, coordinating the various divisions, and planning for the future. Second, control of operations was specialized and then turned over to middle management, which regularly reported to corporate heads to facilitate the latter's decision-making. Finally, elaborate financial controls, including modern accounting systems, were implemented to facilitate sound operations. Here was born business bureaucracy, with separate divisions for production, marketing, finance, and so forth.

The evolution of the corporate structure placed in the hands of managers the means for determining rational prices internally, rather than relying on the pressures of the marketplace. But they could do so only by controlling the external as well as the internal business environment. The external environment turned out to be a harsh one involving brutal and destructive competition. That led corporations to seek security through the consolidation of economic power. The methods used varied according to the nature and needs of the industry involved, with the holding company eventually becoming the favored approach.

By the turn of the century the modern American economy had emerged with a dualistic nature. At the center stood so-called big business – oligopolistic industries consisting of a few large, mass-production firms that did not compete in terms of price, tended to recognize market shares and specialties, and generally conducted their affairs more through corporate decision-making than by market forces. These industries were capital-intensive, benefited from economies of scale, and discouraged entry. Examples include steel, oil, and chemicals. Several hundred corporations comprised this core. On the periphery were the industries subject to competition. What they lacked in size and clout they made up for in numbers, comprising literally thousands of firms. These industries included principally small- to medium-sized firms that were often labor-intensive, were unable to benefit substantially from economies of scale, and regularly faced new competitors because of easy market entry. The textile, lumber, and clothing industries fell into this category.

Mass production brought mass distribution at the expense of the middleman. While the middleman declined in distribution, in finance his function, numbers, and importance grew after the Civil War. The exponentially expanding economy created new wealth and required vast amounts of investment because the large corporations at this stage depended heavily on external financing. The role of the financial intermediaries was that of coordinating savings with investment. Almost all intermediaries, including commercial and savings banks, trusts, building and loan associations, and insurance companies, grew vigorously in size and assets from 1865 to 1910 and served the purposes of encouraging savings, providing investment funds, and increasing the mobility of capital. The outstanding institutions for the rise of big business were the investment banking houses, the most important of which was J. P. Morgan and Co. The economic reach of these firms became so substantial that some scholars and others have concluded that in the late nineteenth and early twentieth centuries the American economy entered a phase of "finance capitalism" – in effect an economy dominated by bankers. If such conditions existed, they were only temporary and had ended before the close of World War I. The twentieth-century American economy was basically one of corporate, not finance, capitalism.

In 1900 as in 1860, therefore, the United States had a vigorous capitalist economy, although one that big business had significantly modified by the turn of the century. Although the shape of the economy did not change substantially between 1901 and 1917, the nation's political economy basically changed with the rise of big government, a subject analyzed here previously.

NAVAL MODERNIZATION

The Gilded Age and the Progressive era were critical periods for the military services. On one level, however, that did not appear to be the case. Drastically reduced in size and importance after the Civil War, the army and navy both returned to their antebellum, peacetime pursuits. For the army, that meant frontier duty; for the navy, it meant showing the flag and protecting commerce. At the same time, however, both services began a process of professionalization that fundamentally altered their outlooks, structures, and roles and prepared them to handle the technological revolution that was transforming weaponry. Although the professionalization process reached maturity only with World War I, it already was well advanced by the early years of the twentieth century. The navy is analyzed first because its progress was faster, its tasks perhaps were simpler, and the pressures of technological change were greater.

According to most naval historians, the years from 1866 to 1881 were the "dark ages."[7] The nation, these historians contend, allowed its navy – top-heavy with officers who faced a bleak future in terms of assignments, promotion, and experience – to rot and rust. Stagnation and neglect, cor-

---

7 The subject matter and bibliography for the navy in the late nineteenth and early twentieth centuries are covered well in three essays in Kenneth J. Hagan, ed., *In Peace and War: Interpretations of American*

ruption and demoralization were the lot of the navy both afloat and on shore.

There is some truth to these charges. But the real complaint of these historians, who are disciples of Alfred Thayer Mahan, is that the nation lost its Civil War dominance and did not keep abreast of the naval revolution so as to maintain a world-class force. A number of dissenting historians have trenchantly pointed out that this approach is ahistorical. During the Gilded Age, the nation faced no major threats to its security and was absorbed in continentalism and commercialism, requiring only a modest fleet.

Moreover, and more important, in the midst of the navy's decline, a professionalizing process that had begun before the Civil War was reactivated, grew in strength and accomplishment, and emphasized preparing the service to fight a modern war. Key to this progress was the founding of the United States Naval Institute in 1873, the Office of Naval Intelligence in 1882, and the Naval War College in 1884. Beginning in 1881 and continuing into the twentieth century, all secretaries of the navy, acting alone or at the direction of Congress, created various boards of naval officers to advise and assist them with the size, nature, and composition of the fleet, ship construction, navy yard expansion and reform, differences between the line and staff, and, in conjunction with the army, the manufacture of ordnance and fortification of the coast. Additionally, as hemispheric and international tensions mounted, existing and ad hoc agencies began to plan for war. These efforts gradually led to modifications in the navy's command struc-

Naval History, 1775–1984, 2d rev. ed. (Westport, Conn., 1984): Lance C. Buhl, "Maintaining 'An American Navy,' 1865–1889," 145–73; Ronald Spector, "The Triumph of Professional Ideology: The U.S. Navy in the 1890s," 174–85; and Richard W. Turk, "Defending the New Empire, 1900–1914," 186–204. Other important studies include Harold and Margaret Sprout, *The Rise of American Naval Power, 1776–1918,* rev. ed. (Princeton, N.J., 1946); Samuel P. Huntington, *The Soldier and the State: The Theory and Politics of Civil-Military Relations* (Cambridge, Mass., 1957), 222–88; Dean C. Allard, "The Influence of the United States Navy upon the American Steel Industry, 1880–1890," M.A. thesis, Georgetown University, 1959; Charles O. Paullin, *Paullin's History of Naval Administration, 1775–1911* (Annapolis, Md., 1968), 309–485; Peter Karsten, *The Naval Aristocracy: The Golden Age of Annapolis and the Emergence of Modern American Navalism* (New York, 1972); Benjamin F. Cooling, *Gray Steel and Blue Water Navy: The Formative Years of America's Military-Industrial Complex, 1881–1917* (Hamden, Conn., 1979); Allan R. Millett and Peter Maslowski, *For the Common Defense: A Military History of the United States of America* (New York, 1984), 233–327; and James C. Bradford, ed., *Admirals of the New Steel Navy: Makers of the American Naval Tradition, 1880–1930* (Annapolis, Md., 1990). A number of useful surveys of the navy have been published in the past decade: Edward L. Beach, *The United States Navy: 200 Years* (New York, 1986); Kenneth J. Hagan, *This People's Navy: The Making of American Sea Power* (New York, 1991); Stephen Howarth, *To Shining Sea: A History of the United States Navy, 1775–1991* (New York, 1991); Robert W. Love Jr., *History of the U.S. Navy, 1775–1941* (Harrisburg, Pa., 1992); Frank Uhlig Jr., *How Navies Fight: The U.S. Navy and Its Allies* (Annapolis, Md., 1993); and George W. Baer, *One Hundred Years of Sea Power: The U.S. Navy, 1890–1990* (Stanford, Calif., 1994).

ture. Secretary of the Navy John D. Long created a Naval War Board to assist him with command functions during the Spanish-American War. After hostilities ended, the secretary made this arrangement more permanent by establishing in 1900 the General Board of the Navy to act as a rudimentary general staff. Although a formal general staff never emerged, the chief of naval operations, a position established by statute in 1915, became the navy's counterpart of the army's chief of staff. Restructuring the shore establishment and command functions usually also involved reforms of the bureau system.

Rear Admiral Stephen B. Luce was the true father of the modern American navy, if any one person can claim that distinction. He set as his principal goal professionalizing the officer corps in its specialty, the science and art of conducting war. The Naval War College (NWC) was his brainchild, a postgraduate school for putting his ideas into action. He served as its first president and received vital support from Captain Henry C. Taylor, who led the college between 1893 and 1897. Both Luce and Taylor were as politically astute as they were strategically talented. To protect the professionalizing process in general and the NWC in particular from the intense animosity of the conservative officers of the line, they reached out to businessmen, politicians, and community leaders, including Theodore Roosevelt, Henry Cabot Lodge, and Nelson W. Aldrich, and, along with various secretaries of the navy, convinced the officer corps of the importance of civilians in modernizing the service. The professionalizing cause received an enormous boost from the publications and popularity of Mahan, who served both as faculty member and as president of the NWC.

The building of a "new navy" became an inextricable part of the modernizing process. In the late nineteenth and early twentieth centuries the nation rapidly ascended from twelfth to second or third place among navies of the world as it built a new fleet of steel, steam, armor, and modern ordnance organized around the battleship. William H. Hunt's appointment as secretary of the navy in 1881 marked the beginning. He was the first of six successive secretaries of good-to-excellent abilities in the last decades of the nineteenth century. Never before had the navy had such capable leadership over a twenty-year period. This was all the more remarkable because control of the White House and Congress alternated between Democrats and Republicans from 1885 to 1897 in a highly charged partisan atmosphere. Bipartisanship was evident, if not fully in force, in relation to the navy. Two critical points stand out about the new navy: First, civilians in the executive and legislative branches made the critical decisions involving the navy, with the officer corps providing the necessary support, expertise, and advice.

Second, naval modernization went through two distinct phases. The first, extending from 1881 to 1889, involved technologically updating the fleet to carry out its defensive mission more effectively. The second, beginning in 1889 and extending into the twentieth century, entailed gradually, and at times deceptively, changing the fleet's mission to an offensive one along the lines set forth by Mahan. Benjamin F. Tracy, secretary of the navy from 1889 to 1893 and generally considered by scholars to have been the most important and talented of those holding the post in the post-Civil War nineteenth century, deftly led the navy and the nation through this crucial transition. He did so to match strategy with diplomacy as the nation began to expand on the world stage and adopt an imperialist role.

Drawing on the efforts of his predecessors, Tracy also instituted reforms for the design and construction of ships, centralized procurement under the Bureau of Supplies and Accounts, and reorganized navy yards, with civil service rules and procedures replacing the spoils system. Most of Tracy's successors continued to revamp the shore establishment. By the time the nation entered World War I, the business side of the navy was reasonably centralized and efficient.

The modernizing process begun in the early 1870s prepared the navy for the Spanish-American War better than for any previous conflict. The officer corps had probably never been of higher quality, and with various reforms the quality of enlisted personnel also was greatly improved. An impressive fleet was easily expanded, and other procurement was carried out efficiently under centralized procedures. More important, planning for war by the NWC and the Office of Naval Intelligence began in 1894 and later was taken over by Secretary Long's Naval War Board, which played a key role in directing the navy during hostilities. Most important, the conduct of the war was always under the centralized control of civilians. Long, his assistant secretary, and his staff closely controlled the naval establishment, all under the supervision of the president. Once war was declared, McKinley directed the war effort from the White House. That included reading, approving, and revising all important orders, consulting with the secretaries of war and navy and their chief advisers or his cabinet on major decisions, coordinating army and navy operations, and generally acting as a strong commander-in-chief. The war revealed weaknesses in the navy yards, naval gunnery, and other areas. Overall, however, the navy performed well.

The Spanish-American War removed many of the prior restraints on naval building and allowed the Progressive administrations to aim for a second- and later a first-place navy. The rapid building began under Long during the Spanish-American War. Among the navies of the world, the

United States moved from sixth to fourth between 1900 and 1902. Theodore Roosevelt – who had a total of six secretaries but actually acted as his own secretary of the navy – made the navy one of his top priorities, achieved a thoroughly remarkable building program, and moved the navy to third, possibly second, place among the nations of the world before leaving office in 1909. Taft continued the building, and Wilson, once he took up preparedness in mid-1915, pushed American naval policy to its logical conclusion: the goal of a navy second to none.

Before leaving the subject of the new navy, we need to address several vital issues. The first is the role of Congress in the naval transformation. Generally, the nation's legislators responded to executive initiatives rather than coming up with their own. Although it rejected, modified, or altered the pace of proposals coming from Republican and Democratic adminis-trations, Congress never set its own naval policy. Between 1881 and 1916, the drive to make an insignificant navy into a peerless force took on nearly inexorable qualities that Congress seemed unable to control. Persistence by the executive branch and international developments acted to break down congressional opposition first to a modern navy, then to an offensive one, and finally to a navy second to none.

The second issue involves the relationship the service developed with pri-vate industry in building a new fleet and the significance of this relationship for modern defense and warfare. In terms of shipbuilding, no extraordinary problems were encountered. By choice, most of the new fleet was built in the nation's ample private yards, not the navy yards. After 1882 the navy be-came the single most important customer for the shipbuilding industry and encouraged new entrants, as was the case with Newport News Shipbuilding Co. Naval building also may have advanced technology in the rolling and casting of steel, but in no extraordinary way. Commercial demand would have produced the same results, although perhaps at a slower pace.

Armor and heavy ordnance, by contrast, presented the Navy Depart-ment with a major challenge. The steel industry was unable to forge these products, making the nation dependent on foreign manufacture, a condi-tion that was unacceptable in terms of national defense. After various in-vestigations, a consensus was reached in 1886 in which it was decided to rely on mixed production for heavy ordnance, with steel firms forging guns while the government finished them, and private firms alone manufactur-ing armor. Shortly thereafter, both the navy and army established gun fac-tories. It was left to Grover Cleveland's secretary of the navy, William C. Whitney (1885–9), to work out the means for developing heavy forging capacity. Accumulating about $4.5 million in past and current congressional appropriations for armor and ordnance, he rigged competitive bidding in 1886 so that the Bethlehem Iron Co. received the entire contract. Prices were pegged to subsidize acquiring the necessary plant and equipment to match the all-steel armor of France's Henri Schneider and the steel forging of Joseph Whitworth of England. Working through active-duty naval officers who simultaneously acted as exclusive agents for the foreign firms and as technical advisers to Bethlehem, Whitney managed to obtain for the steel firm the patent rights, technical assistance, and plant to manufacture armor and ordnance. In short order Bethlehem turned out ordnance forging of the highest order. Armor proved to be more difficult, and Whitney's successor Tracy in 1890 persuaded Carnegie, Phipps Co. to undertake armor production to increase the nation's capacity. Carnegie demanded and received the same inflated prices as Bethlehem, together with government-purchased nickel and technical assistance from the navy. By 1896 the nation had gone from nearly total dependence to total independence in the output of armor and heavy ordnance. But the subsequent twenty years were ones of enormous turmoil as the steel firms and the navy fought endlessly over the price and production of armor. By 1916, Washington had become so disillusioned with the steel firms that it built an armor plant in South Charleston, West Virginia. The facility never went into production.

The construction of a modern navy in time spawned a large collection of industries dependent to varying degrees on continued naval growth. By 1903 three firms made armor for the navy; six, ordnance; nine, projectiles; and seventeen, ships. Subcontractors numbered in the hundreds. Many of these firms combined forces in 1903 under the banner of the Navy League to work for a larger fleet. Although the league was not simply a vulgar collection of merchants of death, motivation was not singularly high-minded. From the outset the Navy League served as the civilian voice of those in the navy pressing for an ever-larger fleet, performed valuable services for its namesake, and did not have an identity separate from that of the service.

Various authors have rightly pinpointed the construction of the new navy as originating the so-called military-industrial complex (MIC). Here for the first time a new weapon system required a production team of government officials, naval officers, and industrialists. This grouping eroded the barriers between private and public along with civilian and military institutions and led to the circulation of personnel among huge, modern, bureaucratic institutions. With a consistently growing offensive fleet, this production team became permanent and deepened and broadened its base. As that took place, increasing numbers of economic, political, and military groups became committed to an expanding navy. Although a complex per se did not exist at this time, the building of a new navy at least suggested that heavy military spending over a prolonged period of time in an industrialized economy could lead to circumstances in which the nation's defense and foreign policies and its economic structure could become dangerously distorted.

The army's decline after the Civil War occurred faster and went further than that of the navy because the former had been much larger and was always a greater source of anxiety within the nation. Moreover, the army also became the object of constant attacks because of its role in Reconstruction, Indian fighting, and labor disputes, and these attacks adversely affected the service.

Decline, however, also included regeneration as the army, like the navy, resumed its pre–Civil War professionalization.[8] In two critical and related ways, army reform differed from that of the navy. First, it took place largely without civilian guidance. Between 1869 and 1899 no secretary of war was genuinely talented, qualified, or interested. Second, army reforms were not influenced significantly by technological advances.

General William T. Sherman served as a bridge between pre- and postwar reform. The Civil War was the primary force motivating Sherman and his allies. That total, relentless war of attrition had seared into them the les-

---

8 Joseph G. Dawson III, *The Late 19th-Century U.S. Army, 1865–1898: A Research Guide* (Westport, Conn., 1990), is an excellent guide to the subject. Also helpful are a series of articles in Kenneth J. Hagan and William R. Roberts, eds., *Against All Enemies: Interpretations of American Military History from Colonial Times to the Present* (Westport, Conn., 1986): Jerry M. Cooper, "The Army's Search for a Mission, 1865–1890," 173–95; William R. Roberts, "Reform and Revitalization, 1890–1903," 197–218; and Timothy K. Nenninger, "The Army Enters the Twentieth Century, 1904–1917," 219–34. Additionally, see Edward M. Coffman, "The Long Shadow of *The Soldier and the State*," *Journal of Military History* 55 (Jan. 1991): 69–82, and William B. Skelton, "Samuel P. Huntington and the Roots of the American Military Tradition," *Journal of Military History* 60 (Apr. 1996): 325–38. Significant studies on the army during this period include Walter Millis, *Arms and Men: A Study in American Military History* (New York, 1956), 131–210; Huntington, *Soldier and the State*, 222–303; Paul Y. Hammond, *Organizing for Defense: The American Military Establishment in the Twentieth Century* (Princeton, N.J., 1961), 10–38; Russell F. Weigley, *History of the United States Army* (New York, 1967), 265–354; Millett and Maslowski, *Common Defense*, 233–327; and Edward M. Coffman, *The Old Army: A Portrait of the American Army in Peacetime, 1784–1898* (New York, 1986), 215–404. The Spanish-American War has received a great deal of attention from scholars, including the following volumes: Graham A. Cosmas, *An Army for Empire: The United States Army in the Spanish-American War* (Columbia, Mo., 1971); John M. Gates, *Schoolbooks and Krags: The United States Army in the Philippines, 1898–1902* (Westport, Conn., 1973); Gerald F. Linderman, *The Mirror of War: American Society and the Spanish-American War* (Ann Arbor, Mich., 1974); Richard E. Welch Jr., *Response to Imperialism: The United States and the Philippine-American War, 1899–1902* (Chapel Hill, N.C., 1979); David F. Trask, *The War with Spain in 1898* (New York, 1981); Stuart C. Miller, *"Benevolent Assimilation": The American Conquest of the Philippines, 1899–1903* (New Haven, Conn., 1982); and John L. Offner, *An Unwanted War: The Diplomacy of the United States and Spain over Cuba, 1895–1898* (Chapel Hill, N.C., 1992).

son that armies existed to fight and that victory depended on marshaling a nation's strength to the fullest and methodically using that might to destroy the enemy. During years of peace, the military's primary goal was to prepare for war. Preparedness required effective command and administrative systems, reliable methods for expeditiously mobilizing and training mass armies, and the selection, evaluation, and training of high-quality officers to lead the troops.

Repeated attempts at reforming the army's system of command and administration at the executive and legislative levels during the 1860s and 1870s were frustrated by divisions among the line, the supply and administrative bureaus, and the secretaries of war. It took the glaring deficiencies revealed during the Spanish-American War and strong civilian leadership to revamp fundamentally the army's structure at the turn of the century. The army also made little headway in the vital but touchy issue of reserves. Commitment among the officer corps to a national reserve created nothing but controversy, leaving the nation with the state militia, now usually designated as the National Guard. After languishing during the 1860s and 1870s, the militia system began to be rebuilt in the 1880s as states provided larger budgets, modified laws, built new armories, and improved training. Overall, the results were marginal.

The army made the most progress with schools, professional associations, and specialized publications that all acted together to further military knowledge, open up debate on key issues, and advance the interests of the army and its specialized branches. Sherman led the way in this regard. In 1868 he reopened the Artillery School at Fortress Monroe and, most important, created the School of Application for Cavalry and Infantry at Fort Leavenworth, Kansas. Beginning without a clear mission as a very basic training school for officers, the school evolved in the late nineteenth and early twentieth centuries into two institutions, the Army School of the Line and the Army Staff College, to prepare outstanding officers for high command and general staff work. During World War I, Leavenworth graduates played a critical role in the success of the American Expeditionary Force. Various branch schools, with a narrower focus than the School of the Line and the Staff College, also were established in the late nineteenth and early twentieth centuries. These included the Engineering School of Application in 1866, the Cavalry and Light Artillery School in 1891, the Signal School in 1904, and numerous others. Army officers also led in establishing professional organizations and publications such as the Military Service Institution of the United States, set up in 1878, and its *Journal of the Military Service Institution of the United States;* the Cavalry Association and in

1885-8 its *Cavalry Journal;* and the Infantry Society in 1893 and what became the *Infantry Journal*. In addition to journals, various monographs were
published, including Arthur L. Wagner's *The Service of Security and Information* (1889), John Bigelow Jr.'s *Principles of Strategy* (1894), and Emory Upton's *Military Policy of the United States* (1904).

The army also advanced in other ways. In 1885 the service established an
intelligence agency eventually called the Military Information Division.
Additionally, various reforms were instituted late in the nineteenth century
to improve the quality of officers. Moreover, with the consolidation of
army posts, officers engaged in field training with whole regiments, and in
the late 1880s a number of regiments came together to exercise as a single
infantry unit for the first time since 1869. Finally, although army reform was
not driven by technology, some progress occurred between 1865 and 1914
with small arms and artillery and the use of motor vehicles and airplanes.

Despite substantial progress in professionalization, the army remained a
collection of parts, not a whole, at the end of the nineteenth century.
With inattentive secretaries of war and largely ceremonial commanding
generals, power within the War Department-army system gravitated toward the supply and service bureaus. Although ably run for the most part,
each bureau was an independent, highly specialized unit proud of its expertise and jealous of its turf. Because the bureau heads acted as the principal advisers to the inexperienced secretaries of war, the department operated without central direction. Moreover, by the last decades of the
nineteenth century the bureaus were becoming hidebound, narrow, and
entangled in red tape. Without centralized control and planning, the army
was unprepared for war, as the conflict with Spain made amply clear.

Although it was not the unmitigated disaster that is often portrayed, mobilization for the undemanding Spanish-American War laid bare a fragmented War Department-army structure badly in need of reform. Commanding General Nelson A. Miles was totally unfit for the office and was
quickly pushed aside. Secretary of War Russell A. Alger performed better
as long as he was under the direction of McKinley, who used the adjutant
general as his de facto chief of staff. But even a strong commander-in-chief
could not bring centralized direction to the army. Recruiting and transporting troops to camps was no problem, and after a slow start all of the
supply bureaus operated with reasonable efficiency. Nonetheless, the supply system faltered badly at critical points because the Quartermaster Department failed to coordinate its mobilization with the railroads, set up and
operate base depots effectively, and use water transportation properly. As a
result, the army campaigns against Cuba often varied between farce and

despair. With time and change, the logistical structure began to function acceptably. But just before and after the armistice, the failures of the Medical Department resulted in epidemics of typhoid, dysentery, malaria, and perhaps yellow fever that swept the camps in Cuba and at home. This created a national furor, leading to a major investigation of the war effort, the resignation of Alger, and the reforms of Elihu Root.

The war had demonstrated that the nation had the economic and political might to quickly and efficiently mobilize human, material, and financial strength. Without an effectively organized army, this might could not readily be converted into military power. That reality was demonstrated on the east coast. But, by contrast, on the west coast mobilization for campaigns in the Philippines was a model of efficiency. The difference was the leadership of the West Point graduate and Civil War veteran Major General Wesley Merritt, who knew how to handle large bodies of troops, plan properly, and use his staff correctly.

Merritt's accomplishments highlighted the fact that the Civil War and the professional growth that followed it had provided the army with all the necessary conditions for modernization. What was needed was new, fresh, outside civilian leadership to guide the army in reaching its potential.

McKinley turned to Theodore Roosevelt's neo-Hamiltonian circles in tapping Elihu Root to bring about the needed change in the War Department-army system. The most important of Root's reforms was creating the chief of staff/general staff to replace the commanding general. As the principal adviser to the secretary of war, the chief of staff commanded both the line and the administrative and supply bureaus and relied on the general staff to carry out his duties and plan for future operations. This system was tailored to meet the nation's peculiar military needs, but it did not work effectively before World War I for a number of reasons. First, officers selected for general staff duties often did not know what they were supposed to do or had conflicting ideas about staff work. Second, and more important, the reforms required strong, aggressive secretaries of war and chiefs of staff in order to be implemented – entities that were lacking most of the time. Third, and most important, the bureaus, fighting to maintain their power, intensely resisted the reforms. For a brief period in 1910–14, when Henry L. Stimson and Major General Leonard Wood were secretary of war and chief of staff respectively, these conditions changed as the bureaus were faced down and the authority of the chief of staff was unquestionably established. However, after Stimson and Wood left office, the momentum was lost as ineffective leaders returned and Congress, at the urging of bureau representatives, statutorily restricted general staff operations. Nonetheless, Stimson and Wood had shifted the locus of power in the War

Department from the bureaus to the chief of staff and prepared the way for Root's system to come into its own during World War I.

Root also rationalized the army's postgraduate education into a tiered system that not only properly trained the officer corps but also acted as an effective means of selecting officers for command duties reaching to the very top of the army structure. It was this system that prepared the officer corps for two world wars in the twentieth century. The final area of Root's efforts involved reforming the National Guard. The changes never worked well. However, they served the purpose of weaning the army from Upton's ideas of a federal militia and pushed it in the direction of mass conscript armies that Winfield Scott had suggested nearly a century earlier and that were used to fight World Wars I and II.

Root, most army reformers, and the bureaus recognized that improvements in the supply area were essential. Consequently, in 1912 the Quartermaster, Subsistence, and Pay departments were consolidated into one bureau. Additionally, to service the nation's small empire in the Caribbean and the Pacific, the Quartermaster Department organized an army transportation service that operated with relative efficiency. In attempts to avoid the railroad confusion of the Spanish-American War, the Quartermaster Corps worked with the American Railway Association to aid its planning for land transportation. Although the corps met all demands for rapid mobilization before World War I, it and the other bureaus were unprepared for the larger conflict because the army-War Department structure was not planning for economic mobilization or even for procurement on a sufficiently broad level.

All of Root's principal reforms tied into and strengthened one another. The general staff and educational reforms gave the army the structure and training essential for full professionalization. Reforms of the National Guard advanced the officer corps' thinking about the use of citizen-soldiers in mass armies. Although Root's reforms appeared incomplete and in some instances failed during the early years of the twentieth century, World War I demonstrated their viability and enormous importance.

CONCLUSION

The far-reaching changes in the economic, political, and military areas from 1865 to 1914 in addition to the rapid technological advances – the four factors shaping the political economy of warfare – make this period one of the most significant for the nation in terms of economic mobilization for war. Indeed, what occurred during these years laid the foundations for most developments involving the economics of warfare in the twentieth century. It is important to recognize, however, that the political economy of warfare can never be more than an extension of a nation's general political economy. Hence, the consolidated corporate structure brought forth a large, regulatory state that in turn created a new American power elite built around a government-business regulatory alliance essential for maintaining balance and stability in the industrially transformed economy. Although both the army and navy were going through a professionalizing process of their own during the Gilded Age, these processes did not significantly affect civil-military relations until building a new navy required extensive intervention by the nation's political and economic leaders on a continual basis beginning around 1881. The army did not require similar attention until the Spanish-American War revealed the glaring deficiencies of its command and administrative systems.

On the eve of World War I, the navy was basically prepared for modern, industrialized warfare. Continuous expansion of the fleet kept the navy in contact with the civilian economy, and further growth during hostilities would be substantial but not overwhelming, allowing the Navy Department to use its peacetime structure to manage wartime conditions. Not so with the army. The Root reforms had streamlined the army to better manage itself but not yet to work within the nation's political economy as the largest, most important wartime procurement agency. That adjustment would take place during World War I, modifying permanently civil-military relations. Technological change in the interwar years and after would keep the army, like the navy, in constant contact with the civilian economy.

A basic aspect of what took place during the late nineteenth and early twentieth centuries was beginning the long and difficult process of preparing the military to work in harmony with the nation's political and economic elites in terms of the economics of defense and warfare. That process was largely completed by 1940. Thereafter, the armed services joined the federal executive and the large corporate structure in constituting the nation's modern, elite power structure, although the military probably still remained a subordinate or secondary power group.[9]

9 I have addressed the elitist nature of American society from the colonial period through the Civil War in *Beating Plowshares into Swords: The Political Economy of American Warfare, 1606–1865* (Lawrence, Kans., 1996). I have also analyzed and cited sources on the modern American "power elite" in *Military-Industrial Complex*, 14–17, and n. 11–17, and "Warfare and Power Relations in America," in Titus, ed., *Home Front and War in the Twentieth Century*, 91–110, 231–43. I cite further sources on power operations in *Mobilizing for Modern War,* chap. 5, n. 1.

4

Hugo Stinnes and the Prospect of War Before 1914

GERALD D. FELDMAN

Very little has been written about preparations in the private economy in Germany for World War I. There is a good reason for this. There were scarcely any preparations in the German private economy for the war, and neither the German government nor the German military called on the private economy to make much preparation for the short war they were anticipating, let alone for the "total war" that was quite beyond their imaginations. Indeed, as I tried to show in a book written some years ago, both the military and civilian authorities and the business community were very slow in and very reluctant about coming to terms with the economic requirements of a long war even after they were in it.[1] Strictly speaking, therefore, the question of the German business community's preparations for World War I is a very thin subject. Current historiographical trends notwithstanding, it is difficult to write about what did not happen or to try to make what is marginal significant out of the conviction that it should be significant. The constraints of mortality being what they are, it is best to concentrate on what matters. I will attempt to do so here by examining the behavior of a major industrialist, Hugo Stinnes (1870–1924), in an effort to understand why there was so little preparation for the war or serious engagement with the dangers of war on the part of German businessmen, to explore how they thought about war, insofar as they thought about it at all, and then to use this case study to make some speculative remarks about the implications of this for the *grande histoire* of prewar German capitalism and international relations, and for the truly significant problem of the political behavior of leading German businessmen during and after the war.

---

1 Gerald D. Feldman, *Army, Industry, and Labor in Germany, 1914–1918* (Princeton, N.J., 1966; reprint, Providence, R.I., 1992).

77

Hugo Stinnes, one of the true giants of prewar German industrial development, was born in 1870 to a Ruhr valley industrial family of coal merchants and coal mine owners. Stinnes used this base to strike out on his own in 1892 and become one of Europe's leading industrialists by his early thirties. Not only did he successfully manage the family mines, build up an international coal marketing operation, and become a leading figure in the Rhenish-Westphalian Coal Syndicate almost from the moment of its founding by Emil Kirdorf in 1893, but he also collaborated with August Thyssen to expand his mining empire and, most important, to create the Rhenish-Westphalian Electric Company, the largest power company in Europe, before the turn of the century. Early in the century, he entered into the iron and steel business by becoming the dominant figure in the Deutsch-Luxemburg Concern, which he expanded to include the Dortmunder Union. This great vertical enterprise had major operations in Lorraine and Luxembourg. In the years before the war, Stinnes moved into commercial shipping by founding the Midgard Lines; his firm had agencies throughout Europe and the Middle East, as well as in the United States and Latin America. Sometimes openly and sometimes employing front men and foreign firms, his firm or the concerns he dominated had major ore holdings in Luxembourg, Normandy, and French Lorraine, docking facilities in St. Petersburg, mines in Wales and in the Ottoman Empire, and important holdings in Belgium. He was, in every sense, an industrial empire builder and quite consciously sought to create a major international enterprise for himself and his family. Much of this was done on the basis of credit, especially from the great banks, with which he had close but sometimes very testy relationships. He also had a very troubled relationship with organized labor, playing a key role in the battle against the great miner strikes of 1905 and 1912 and strongly opposing collective bargaining. Nevertheless, he was pragmatic rather than ideological, and he tended to view all political and social issues from the perspective of economic and market conditions. In general, he exerted considerable political influence on behalf of the social and economic policies favored by heavy industry.[2]

Stinnes's role in World War I and the early Weimar Republic is quite

---

2 A useful biography of Stinnes that concentrates on the postwar period is Peter Wulf, *Hugo Stinnes: Wirtschaft und Politik 1918–1924* (Stuttgart, 1979). I am writing a biography of Stinnes based on his large *Nachlass* (I-220) in the Archiv für Christlich-Demokratische Politik (ACDP) der Konrad-Adenauer-Stiftung, St. Augustin bei Bonn and other papers in private possession (NL Stinnes). Some of this material has been used in Gerald D. Feldman, *The Great Disorder: Politics, Economics, and Society in the German Inflation, 1914–1924* (Oxford, 1993).

well known. He was a strong annexationist from the very beginning of the war and was particularly interested in the German acquisition of Briey-Longwy and control of Belgium, in particular the port of Antwerp. In September 1918, when some of his colleagues were getting nervous, Stinnes still insisted that Germany had to control Antwerp whether the war turned out favorably or not.[3] He was a major supporter of Hindenburg and Ludendorff and firmly believed that "Ludendorff will win," as he said time and again; he organized vast financial contributions to the Fatherland Party; worked closely with such worthies as Alfred Hugenberg, Admiral Alfred von Tirpitz, and Wolfgang Kapp; and ferociously fought against Chancellor Theobald von Bethmann Hollweg.[4] In short, he was a very immoderate imperialist during the war. After the war he emerged as the leading spokesman for German industry, strongly opposed the policy of fulfillment, and conducted what was virtually a private foreign policy with the goal of revising the Versailles Treaty and reconstructing Germany and Europe on the basis of arrangements and deals among the world's business leaders.[5]

The problem posed by this record is that there is scarcely a hint of his wartime behavior or his role in national and international politics prior to the outbreak of the war and, indeed, a remarkable lack of militarism and imperialism in Stinnes's behavior. Because the hundreds of volumes of his papers contain ample evidence of his post-1914 imperialism and political activity, there is no reason to suppose that his massive prewar correspondence would not be equally revealing. What the latter displays, however, is a general lack of engagement with military questions and a very limited interest in foreign policy questions.

The first indication of genuine concern on the part of Stinnes over a major European war is to be found in the summer of 1911 following the Second Moroccan Crisis. His primary anxiety was focused on the consequences that a war might have for his merchant fleet – that is, he was worried about the seizure of his ships at sea. Thus, a group of secret wireless codes was developed to inform his captains in the eventuality of an impending declaration of war between Germany and fourteen other countries. "X zwölf" ("X twelve"), "X dreizehn" ("X thirteen"), for example,

---

3 An excellent study of Stinnes's wartime Belgian policy is Brigitte Hatke, *Hugo Stinnes und die drei deutsch-belgischen Gesellschaften von 1916: Der Versuch der wirtschaftlichen Durchdringung Belgiens im Ersten Weltkrieg durch die Industrie-, Boden- und Verkehrsgesellschaft 1916 m.b.H.* (Stuttgart, 1990).
4 Wulf, *Stinnes*, 29–59.
5 These activities are examined throughout Feldman, *Great Disorder*.

would mean that an impending state of war existed between Germany and the rather odd combination of Greece and China. "X eins," "X zwei," "X vier" ("X one," "X two," "X four") would mean that there was an impending war between Germany and the more likely and fearsome combination of England, France, and Russia. If a "K" were placed before the relevant numbers, then war had been declared. The captains were ordered to head for the nearest possible neutral or German port if they were on the high seas and to clear out of potential or actual enemy ports if it was safe to do so.

The question of impending or actual war with England was particularly touchy because Stinnes had a large and growing investment and operation in England run by a very trusted agent, J. Russell Ferguson. In the event of a crisis, Stinnes's ships were told to contact Ferguson and get instructions from him if they were caught in any potential enemy port in Europe. In the event of war, the captains were instructed to paint over German colors and Stinnes logos so that they would not be easily noticed. Stinnes's two chief concerns, however, were keeping his operations going and saving his ships despite the war. Certain that Switzerland would remain neutral, he decided to use his iron firm of Julius Schoch and Co. and the company's branch Hugo Stinnes G.m.b.H. in Zurich as the contact office for his branches elsewhere. Thus, Ferguson was to have full power to act on behalf of Stinnes coal and shipping interests and was told to get his instructions through Zurich, which would, of course, receive its orders from Mülheim an der Ruhr. In this way, as Stinnes put it, "the connection between France and England, on the one hand, and Germany and Austria could be maintained."[6] It would not quite be "business as usual," but at least the business links would not be severed totally.

Stinnes also worked under the assumption that private property rights would be respected in a war, although he recognized that German merchant ships would be subjected to prize laws. To counter these dangers, he came up with a number of ingenious ideas to protect both his cargoes and his ships. Thus, insofar as cargo was concerned, he instructed Ferguson as follows:

Should Germany happen to be involved in a war, I am firmly determined to avoid under all circumstances that the cargo of my steamers leaving England for Germany should be considered as contraband of war, and that, as a consequence, my steamers should be confiscated. This danger to which my steamers running with coal from England to Germany would be exposed will surely be avoided if I divert

6 Stinnes to Deters, Aug. 28, 1911, ACDP, I-220, no. 262/3.

my steamers to neutral countries instead of allowing them to proceed with their cargoes to Germany. In this connection I am in the first line thinking of Copenhagen, and in the second line of St. Petersburg, provided Denmark and Russia will preserve their neutrality.

Should a war break out I would ask you to direct any steamers loading in British ports to Copenhagen and St. Petersburg instead of Germany, and arrange for clean Bills of Lading being made out in order that the Captain on sea may legitimise himself by means of such Bills of Lading when compelled by the belligerent parties. In this case the cargo could not be considered as contraband of war.

This will remove any danger to my steamers. On the other hand, I am convinced to serve my commercial interest because there is no doubt that in the event of international complications there will be a good chance of disposing of the cargoes of coal in Copenhagen or St. Petersburg with an appreciable profit. I attach special value to this latter point, the more so as the discharging appliances in Copenhagen will soon be finished, and in St. Petersburg available barges in connection with the swimming cranes will facilitate quick discharging.[7]

Exactly why Stinnes would have counted on possible Russian neutrality in 1911 is difficult to say, for although the Russians may not have been terribly interested in Morocco, they did have recent and bitter memories of the role played by Germany in the Annexation Crisis of 1908 as well as treaty arrangements and ties with France and Britain vital to their interests. Nevertheless, Stinnes had invested a great deal in his Russian facilities, had been using the floating docks and barges there to sell coal to the Russian navy through his English outlets, and apparently wished to make as big a sale as possible before the lights went out.[8]

Similarly, when the lights went on again, Stinnes wanted to be sure that he had not lost his ships, or at least the value they represented. Thus, in the fall of 1912 there ensued a new round of correspondence as to how to prevent his merchant ships from being confiscated at the outbreak of war, above all by the English. Stinnes's answer to this problem was to have such ships of his fleet as were endangered sold immediately to his English firm, Hugo Stinnes Ltd. For this purpose, they were to be equipped with the requisite bills of sale and English flags, which they were to hoist when necessary. Furthermore, because there had been a variety of inquiries about the purchase of his ships in England, J. Russell Ferguson was empowered to sell the ships, now English, to other English purchasers for appropriate prices. As Stinnes was informed by the legal experts in the Reich Naval Office and by his English colleagues, however, the sale of ships at sea or in other than their home ports was perfectly allowable in times of peace but

7 Stinnes to Ferguson (in English), Sept. 8, 1911, ibid.
8 On the sales to Russia and the Russian navy, see the correspondence of 1910–11 in ibid., 190/2.

was strictly regulated in the event of war. Sales made for the demonstrable purpose of avoiding confiscation by prize courts would not be recognized, and transfers of interest within the same business organization would certainly not be accepted. That is, Stinnes's "calculated preparations for war" would not wash, and his collection of flags would not do him a bit of good.[9]

In the last analysis, therefore, Stinnes could hope only that his ships loaded with English coal would make it to neutral ports or to German ports. In the case they were home safely, the coal could be sold to the German navy, which of course would be interested in having coal transport ships available in wartime. Stinnes thus developed a growing interest in arrangements whereby the navy would lease or purchase his ships to service the coal needs of the German fleet. Although willing to undertake the necessary technical changes on his old ships and on the new ones he built in conformity with naval coaling specifications, Stinnes was quite insistent that the navy bear the costs, and he was particularly anxious to have the navy take over old ships while he retained ownership of the modern ones for postwar use.[10]

A similarly pragmatic and single-minded concentration on business interests characterized Stinnes's international business activities prior to the war. Because of his far-flung international interests, Stinnes was engaged in many of the "hot spots" of German prewar imperial activity. There is no evidence, however, that his primary concern was anything but finding markets for his goods and making money, which is not to say that he was unwilling to play on government interests or make use of government support when competing with the French in the Near East or in the Balkans, for example. Thus, at the end of 1913, Stinnes, in alliance with the Deutsche Bank, bought out Belgian interests in the Charbonnages Réunis de Bender-Eregli, which held a hundred-year lease on the Turkish coal mines in the Heraclea area. Its major competitor in that area was the French Société d'Heracleé, which was seeking to control the railroad connections and the port facilities in the Heraclea area and levy charges against other companies that would effectively leave only the French mines profitable. Furthermore, the port area was of major importance for ships entering the Black Sea. Although an agreement between the French and German financial groups setting up spheres of interest in Asia Minor was

9 See the documents in ibid., especially Deters to Stinnes, Nov. 5, 1912, and Ferguson to Deters, Nov. 11, 1912.

10 See the correspondence between Deters and Stinnes, Dec. 1911–Feb. 1912, ibid.

supposed to protect German interests in Heraclea, Stinnes and the Deutsche Bank came to the conclusion that the agreement was flawed because it left the French with a potential stranglehold on the coal business through their control of the railroad and harbor facilities. In early 1914, therefore, Stinnes personally expressed his concerns to Chancellor Bethmann Hollweg, urging that the German government refuse to approve the Franco-German financial agreement until German interests in Heraclea were protected. In his appeal to Bethmann, Stinnes placed particular emphasis on the potential German naval interest in the coaling area. At the same time, however, Stinnes also sought to mobilize British interests against the potential French monopoly and supported an attempt, apparently successful, to have the matter ironed out by the financial groups involved in preference to having the governments take up the matter.[11]

Similarly, Stinnes's activities in the Balkans centered on commercial rather than German political or imperial interests. In early 1914 his agents in Serbia argued that the Germans should take advantage of the discrediting of the Austro-Hungarian banks in Serbia in the recent Balkan war and step in with their own financial resources. If the Germans participated in the financing of Serbia, then the Serbs would not be beholden to the French and feel compelled to buy French equipment, which was more expensive and less reliable than that of the Germans. This feeling seems to have been shared by the Serbs, most of whose engineers appear to have been trained in Germany and were very much taken with German products and the German way of doing business. At the same time, however, Stinnes's firms were no less interested in sales to the recently defeated Bulgaria and were reporting confidently that there would be peace in the Balkans for a decade following the Second Balkan War. On a trip to the Balkans and the Near East in April 1914, Stinnes was himself quite impressed with the economic possibilities in Serbia and Bulgaria, noting the "fecundity of the Serbian territory we passed through with its apparently healthy organic constitution composed of many small farms with a populous peasant population and a rich stock of cattle." He was even more impressed with the promise of Bulgaria, "despite the great misfortune which this

---

11 Stinnes to the Deutsche Bank and Stinnes to Bethmann Hollweg, Feb. 26, 1914, NL Stinnes, private papers; undated report by Thomas for Stinnes visit to the chancellor on Mar. 5, 1914, ACDP, I-220, no. 300/5. The naval side was to prove important in October 1914, when Admiral Souchon made arrangements for the *Goeben* and other German naval vessels to get coal from the Stinnes mines in Heraclea, but this appears to have been the first contact with the navy about the coal because Souchon seems not to have known whether the coal was of satisfactory quality. See the correspondence in ibid., no. 272/1.

people has experienced."[12] The fact was that Stinnes was anxious to make money wherever he could, be it in the Balkans or in Brazil. He took a similar view of business with France, and he was busily buying into French enterprises and ore fields in Longwy and Normandy shortly before the war, apparently without much concern about the testy relations between Germany and France.[13]

Indeed, all the evidence available suggests that the remarkable report of the Pan-German leader Heinrich Class concerning a dinner conversation with Stinnes in Mülheim in September 1911, in which Stinnes supported peaceful German expansion and criticized Pan-German attitudes, is an accurate characterization of Stinnes's views. According to Class, Stinnes argued that the Pan-Germans were on the mark in domestic politics but were in error in foreign policy. He praised Bethmann Hollweg for his performance in foreign affairs and made it clear he would oppose the Pan-Germans so long as they fought Bethmann. Stinnes then went on to argue that economic, not military, power was the key to Germany's future in the world and sought to demonstrate this with his own person:

And you see what that means as I slowly but surely get the majority of stock of this or that enterprise, as I gradually gain more and more of the coal supplying of Italy for myself, when I inconspicuously get a foothold in the ore fields of Spain and Sweden, when I secure a position in Normandy. Let things develop quietly for three or four years and Germany will be the uncontested economic ruler of Europe. The French have remained behind us; they are a nation of *petite rentiers.* And the English are too work-shy and without the courage to undertake new enterprises. Otherwise, there is no one in Europe that can compete with us. Therefore, only three or four years of peace, and I can assure you the silent attainment of German predominance in Europe.

To the horror of Class, who was certain that England would never permit such a development, Stinnes treated such attitudes as obsolete and insisted that "the world would now be ruled by economic interests, by the great entrepreneurs and the banks." Stinnes was severely critical of Mannesmann and the noisy efforts to gain control of the ore in Morocco, arguing that more subtle and quiet techniques would have secured not only ore but also valuable farmland in Morocco for German interests. Here again Stinnes insisted that he was showing the way and described his enterprises in England, Denmark, Holland, and Italy; pointed out how he used foreigners to run them and act as fronts for his operations; and controlled the

12 Hugo to Cläre Stinnes, Apr. 14, 1914, ibid., no. 294/5.
13 See the correspondence of 1913–14 with the Deutsch-Luxemburg Mining and Smelting Co. on trade with the Balkans and acquisitions in Longwy and Normandy in ibid., no. 221/2.

majority share of the most important mine in Wales, a mine that supplied the English navy with coal and that Stinnes was using to provide coal to Italy on English ships flying the German flag![14]

It was only natural for Stinnes to describe his empire to Class in nationalist and patriotic terms, and although Stinnes always conflated the public good with his own, it is important not to overemphasize the nationalist aspect. One scarcely finds any such considerations in his extraordinary correspondence with his wife. A letter of July 1913 is far more indicative of the passions that really moved him. Thus, having just closed his books on the business year, he reported the he "emerged with almost one million in taxable income. It is mad to think what one has now to pay for his labor. Nevertheless, it is better this way than if one had earned nothing." His profits drove him to even deeper and more intimate reflections: "Only remain pretty, healthy, and fresh for me so that you can still one day savor the fruits of these work-filled years with understanding and joy-of-life. For what else should I have worked so? The children alone would not have driven me to do it, and the others do not have any understanding for the great international organization and power that shall be built up here."[15]

Stinnes could hardly be unaware of the danger of war, but his business policies, calculations, and hopes were geared toward a long period of peace. As he wrote to his wife in the summer of 1913, "hopefully the people in the Balkans will soon settle down, and to be sure in such a way that a Rumanian-Bulgarian alliance will be the result. Then one can hope for a decade of peace – one would hope even longer because of our boys."[16] This sanguine attitude held when business conditions were good, as in 1912, or when they were bad, as in 1913–14. When assessing business conditions for the Reichsbank in the fall of 1912, he emphasized how much the German coal industry had been strengthened since the last crisis of 1907, made a point of noting the extent to which the prosperity of heavy industry and its increased exports were benefiting the rest of the German economy, expressed satisfaction over the increased size of the German merchant fleet and the fact that Germany was becoming less dependent on British shipping, and confidently stated that Germany would emerge from the existing boom "financially and technically strengthened . . . so that it will no longer lack the means in quiet times to make itself independent at sea and create dependent consumers of all kinds in foreign markets like En-

14 Heinrich Class, *Wider den Strom: Vom Werden und Wachsen der nationalen Opposition im alten Reich* (Leipzig, 1932), 216–19.
15 Hugo to Cläre Stinnes, July 12, 1913, ACDP, I-220, no. 294/5.
16 Hugo to Cläre Stinnes, July 7, 1913, ibid.

gland and France."[17] Although the period from 1913 to 1914 was one of recession, Stinnes does not seem to have altered his plans and intentions, although he certainly responded by reducing prices and demanding increased productivity from his labor force. As demonstrated earlier, Stinnes was expanding his activities and assets both at home and abroad. This was especially the case in England, where he acquired new mining interests in July 1913 in Yorkshire and Nottinghamshire with the obligation to develop the mining interests involved. In 1914 Hugo Stinnes Ltd. signed a contract specifying prices for the sale of this coal to branches of the Stinnes firm throughout Europe and the Near East.[18]

The expansion of Stinnes's trade in iron, steel, and finished products was more problematic, to be sure. It was driven by the advanced technology and high productivity of works whose profitability depended on the fullest possible use of plant facilities. Thus, the report of the Deutsch-Luxemburg Concern for 1912–13 noted with satisfaction that business had been reasonably good despite the Balkan wars and that the sale of railroad material had proven very important in keeping the plants occupied. What worried Stinnes most during this period were the increased interest rates and the burdens of taxation: "The prospects for the future, in view of the advanced technical development of our works, could be characterized as not unfavorable despite the political disturbances and increased cost of money, were it not for the fact that the most serious concern is being created by the way in which those engaged in industry are being one-sidedly burdened with taxes which are gradually becoming unbearable."[19]

Stinnes was less upbeat a year later. In a report written after the Great War had begun, Stinnes admitted that the last year of peace had not been a good one for the Deutsch-Luxemburg Concern:

There can be no doubt that the productive capacity of the iron and steel works has to some extent run ahead of world demand and that even without the beginning of military disturbances a balancing of production and demand would have taken place only slowly with increased financial liquidity and political calm. So one would have had to accept unsatisfactory prices for many products because the technically advanced German works, with their extended energy supply based on gas, find production cutbacks especially disturbing and costly and are often forced

17 Stinnes to the Reichsbankstelle Mülheim/Ruhr, Oct. 3, 1912, NL Stinnes, Privatbesitz.
18 On July 14, 1913, he acquired the mines from Arnold Lupton for £20,000 with the promise to raise no less than £1.1 million in shares. I am grateful to Antje Hagen for this information based on her research in the Public Record Office, Document BT 31/21598/130099. On the coal contract of 1914, see ACDP, I-220, no. 224/7.
19 Deutsch-Luxemburg Geschäftsbericht, Oct. 1913, ACDP, I-220, no. 080/7. The Stinnes papers provide strong evidence that he composed the general introductions to these reports.

to produce at loss-bringing prices. The war hit us when we were confronted with a business situation which was in no way very promising for the coming years.[20]

This did not mean that Stinnes welcomed the coming of war any more than he had under the deteriorating business conditions of 1913–14. His business activities in England and elsewhere would have been unintelligible if this had been the case. Indeed, there is no record of Stinnes's showing much interest in producing for the army and navy at all. In 1909, for example, when Reichstag Deputy Baron von Oppersdorff was trying to reduce prices charged to the navy by creating some competition for Krupp and the Dillinger Hütte in the production of armored plate and turned thus to Deutsch-Luxemburg, Director Knupe advised Stinnes that the costs of building the necessary plant would be too high and that it would be hard to compete with the existing plants. Stinnes apparently told this to Oppersdorff in a personal meeting, and he stayed out of the business.[21]

More generally, Stinnes seems to have had a skeptical view of the military but more positive feelings about Admiral Tirpitz, with whom he cooperated in supplying coal for secret coaling stations used by the German navy in the Far East.[22] This enthusiasm for selling coal to the navy did not extend to paying taxes for the naval race and heavy armaments expenditures, however, which Stinnes thought too high. Although he felt that French military policy made an increase in the army unavoidable, he was hopeful in February 1912 that the fleet increases could be kept in moderate bounds through an agreement with England. He warned that "the burdens of the state and municipal taxes in Germany have begun to be unbearable and that the further development of our industry will cease if there is no limitation of expenditures."[23] He did not think Germany could sustain 20 percent income taxes when its cost of living was already higher than those of England, Belgium, and France.

Although Stinnes's relationship with the Conservatives had been quite testy in 1909–10, and he had even threatened to make common cause with the Socialists if the Conservatives were not more supportive of industrialist interests, he came down on their side with respect to a Reich Inheritance Tax in 1912, arguing that direct taxation should be left to the states, that the states should be required to supplement their matricular payments to the Reich, and that an increased tax on assets in Prussia for such purposes

20 Business Report of Oct. 28, 1914, ibid.
21 Oppersdorff to Deutsch-Luxemburg, Feb. 28, 1909, and subsequent correspondence, ibid., no. 214/3.
22 Class, *Gegen den Strom*, 218–19.
23 Stinnes to the *Rheinisch-Westfälische Zeitung*, Feb. 12, 1912, NL Stinnes, family papers.

was preferable to introducing direct Reich taxation.[24] Although his argument that there would be substantial costs involved in changing the tax system had some cogency, he was, like his Conservative allies, manifestly resistant to accepting the political and social implications of Germany's increased military requirements for the German fiscal system.

Stinnes was not alone in this anxiety that the money needed for industrial development would be eaten up by military expenditure and war preparation. The great German banks were especially sensitive to the consequences of international complications and war scares for their capacity to satisfy the liquidity requirements of their national and international customers. The entire German credit system for big industry was based on the generous supplying of credit by the big banks, which counted on their ability to discount their bills at the Reichsbank while maintaining relatively low reserves themselves. The interrelationship between the credit system and the international situation is well illustrated by a letter from Arthur Salomonsohn and Ernst Russell of the Disconto-Gesellschaft to Max von Schinckel of the allied Norddeutsche Bank in December 1912. They complained bitterly about negative consequences of the recent fighting in the Balkans for the money market:

The most unbelievable demands are made upon us from all sides, and although our status is significantly more liquid than it was last year, to our regret we must still turn very heavily to the Reichsbank, and the closer the end of the month comes, the worse it is, for our affiliated banks and other friends seek to make good their balances by keeping their bills in their portfolios and pumping more out of us, which naturally leads to the weakening of our portfolio. We try to defend ourselves as hard as possible, but finally there is nothing less to do but for us to jump into the breach.

Under such circumstances, the bankers greeted with great enthusiasm the good news about the international situation and promises of peace:

If the horrible money shortage, which even exceeds that of 1907, naturally is to be blamed on the political conditions and the foolish fear of a large portion of the public, which withdraws its deposits and tries to hoard them, one still in general believes here that the fear of war is no longer justified. The day before yesterday, Dr. Salomonsohn had a lengthy discussion in the Foreign Office, and we can tell you in strictest confidence that there too the officials have a completely calm view of the situation and definitely believe that we will move forward without war since, according to the latest news, the Russians have now very energetically pressed the Serbs to come to an understanding. All the sensational rumors that

---

24 Ibid. and Cläre Stinnes diary for 1909–10 (private papers) for his political conflicts with the Conservatives. Stinnes's politics were right-wing National Liberal.

have been spreading about the stock markets are completely without foundation. Today the Berliner Handelsgesellschaft showed us a telegram from Fürstenberg in which he reports that he has learned from a very highly placed source that an understanding between Austria and Russia is being achieved.

If you are very correct, therefore, in holding very tightly on to your purse strings, we still believe that you do not have to take the eventuality of involvement in a war by Germany into your calculations.[25]

The Reichsbank, which always had to consider the danger of war, was not much taken with such an attitude and, since the economic crisis of 1907, had expressed growing concern about the low reserves of the banks and the excessive use of the Reichsbank as a lender of last resort. The great German banks constantly resisted Reichsbank pressures to increase their reserves and thereby reduce the danger that the Reichsbank would have insufficient reserves of its own in the event of war. By the spring of 1914 the Reichsbank was so fed up with the unwillingness of the private banks to respond to its pleas that it held a meeting with the leading Berlin bankers on June 15 at which Reichsbank president Rudolf von Havenstein insisted that legal action would be taken to force them to take the required measures if they did not do so voluntarily. Needless to say, industry was an interested party with respect to such demands because the proposed increase in the size of bank reserves would inevitably decrease the availability of credit, and some bankers in the Rhineland hoped to mobilize industrialists against the Reichsbank policy. Further discussions were scheduled for the fall, by which time, however, war had begun. There can be little doubt that the Reichsbank intended to force the question, but the delay is yet another indication of the business community's resistance to any preparedness measures that might slow down the economy.[26]

There can be no question that the Second Moroccan Crisis of 1911 and the tensions in and over the Balkans among the great powers had increased awareness of the danger of war and produced a growing recognition of the advisability of some economic preparations for war. There was an extraordinary reluctance, however, to translate such worries into effective action or to think beyond immediate self-interest. Here again, Stinnes is a good example. On July 18, 1914, he reported to a military officer with whom

25 Salomonsohn and Russell to Max von Schinckel, Dec. 11, 1912, Historisches Archiv der Deutschen Bank, K1/782.
26 See Reinhold Zilch, "Zum Plan einer Zwangsregulierung im deutschen Bankwesen vor dem ersten Weltkrieg und zu seinen Ursachen: Dokumentation," in B. A. Aisin and W. Gutsche, eds., *Forschungsergebnisse zur Geschichte des deutschen Imperialismus vor 1917* (Berlin, 1980), 229–56. For banker efforts to mobilize industrialists against the new policy, see Gwinner to Walter Bürhaus, July 22, 1914, Historisches Archiv der Deutschen Bank, S 83.

he was acquainted that he had discussed the problem of economic preparations for war with Alfred Hugenberg of the Krupp concern and that the larger firms in the Ruhr would probably meet with the military authorities in September or October to discuss these problems. What is most revealing, however, is the way in which the issues were conceived. Stinnes went on to point out that it was foolish for the great banks to be forced by the Reichsbank to have substantial cash reserves lying fallow and collecting no interest, and he suggested that they be used instead as credits for the purchase of food supplies and consumer articles by the large enterprises of the industrial districts. Stinnes went on: "I believe that the great Rhenish-Westphalian works would even be willing to pay a moderate interest rate for the capital that would be lent to them if they could secure the means necessary for the workers and for the consumers. . . . The leading people in industry and in public life must make sure that the many millions of persons living behind the front can survive and have work; otherwise there will be revolution and murder and bloodshed, and the campaign will be lost."[27] In short, the outbreak of war was seen by Stinnes as an immense financial and economic catastrophe with dangerous social possibilities, and the economic preparations necessary were conceived in terms of keeping the population fed and busy so that the soldiers could do their work. Indeed, there are parallels between this catastrophic conception of the mobilization and of the demobilization four years later.[28]

In any case, the economic preparations for war that concerned Stinnes most in mid-July 1914 were not for the war with the Entente but for the war with labor. As he informed the directors of the Deutsche-Luxemburg company on July 17, 1914, the labor difficulties he anticipated in Scotland at the end of the month and in Cardiff at the end of the year suggested that the next economic recovery would lead to grave labor difficulties and coal shortages because the miners would take advantage of the situation to strike. It was important that the German works be ready for this eventuality by having sufficient coal and coke stored up to withstand a six-week strike. As he concluded, "In my view, it is not at all to be ruled out that the next great strike movement will be an international one and will create conditions in combustible materials that we have never experienced before. I am firmly of the view that we will face such conditions one day, and I want us to be well armed to meet them."[29] He wrote in no less alarming terms to Director Goldenberg of the Rhenish-Westphalian Electric Power

27 Stinnes to Henke, July 18, 1914, ACDP, I-220, no. 294/2.
28 See Richard Bessel, *Germany After the First World War* (Oxford, 1993), chaps. 2, 4–5.
29 Stinnes to Deutsch-Luxemburg, July 17, 1914, no. 088/2.

Company (RWE): "I am not at all very much taken with the entire international situation on the coal market from the perspective of the consumers. I fear, as do my British officials, that the setting in of an upturn in the business conditions will lead to a great shortage of coal and international labor unrest, eventually a strike, and I am therefore very much for the RWE laying in much larger reserves of coal than has usually been the case."[30] In fairness to Stinnes it must be said that it would have been difficult for him to realize the full seriousness of the international situation in mid-July or even in late July given the kind of information he was receiving. Thus, on July 22, his son Hugo Jr. wrote from London that Ferguson thought the Irish Home Rule issue very serious but that, on the bright side, "the relationship between Germany and England gets *better* from day to day. The Conservatives as well as the Liberals are in a very friendly mood to Germany. One no longer talks about a German attack."[31] Indeed, as late as July 28, Stinnes and his colleagues in Mülheim, while certainly terribly worried, were hopeful that the war between Austria-Hungary and Serbia would be localized.[32]

In a few days they would know better, and the process of adapting to war and to doing business in war would begin, albeit very slowly. By the middle of August, Stinnes and the provincial presidents of Rhineland-Westphalia were worried that excessive support payments to laid-off workers and officials and to the families of drafted men might lead "to the war having to be ended prematurely as a result of the wasting of money."[33]

Apparently, Stinnes understood a great deal more about private than public credit, and he obviously had some way to go before becoming, as he was later called, a "king of the inflation." Thus, in August 1914 he urged the Westfälische-Anhaltische Sprengstoff AG (WASAG), of whose supervisory board he was chairman, not to put its money into time accounts at the bank because it was quite possible that the Reich would need to put off payments to the firm and pay later with interest calculated at the Reichsbank discount rate. He had little patience, however, for the "groundless and foolish" behavior of workers at these dynamite plants who were refusing to accept paper money or changing their paper money into silver, and he instructed that the firm "enlighten" the workers to accept paper money and to increase its supply of five and ten mark notes.[34] Within a few months

30 Stinnes to Goldenberg, July 17, 1922, ibid., no. 159/3.
31 Hugo Stinnes Jr. to Hugo Stinnes Sr., July 22, 1914, ibid., no. 299/1.
32 Amtsrichter Thomas (Hugo Sr.'s personal secretary) to Hugo Stinnes Jr., July 28, 1914, ibid., no. 302/4.
33 Stinnes to Mayor Plassmann of Paderborn, Aug. 15, 1914, ibid., no. 177/1.
34 Stinnes to WASAG, Aug. 2 and 12, 1914, ibid., no. 249/1.

the Reich would be subsidizing the building of plants at the WASAG rather than borrowing from the company, and there would be no choice about accepting paper money or problems with its supply. By then Stinnes had emerged as one of Germany's leading annexationists and was soon to become one of its great producers for the war effort.

What conclusions can be drawn or hypotheses presented in the face of this record? Certainly Stinnes is an important case, but it should be emphasized that, however colorful and unique a personage he was, his behavior and attitudes with respect to the problem of preparing for war in Imperial Germany appear to be typical. The first conclusion that must be drawn, therefore, is that the great industrialists and the great bankers showed very little interest in preparing for war and did not want to think about it. Excessive military expenditure, high taxes, and reduced credit were all viewed as threats to economic development and prosperity. Second, when they did think about war, it was as a potential social and economic catastrophe that might be bearable if it were of short duration. The great chemical industrialist Carl Duisberg, who, like Stinnes, was to end up heavily engaged in war production and an annexationist, hoped for peace to the last minute and believed that the war would set back German economic development for a decade.[35]

Third, the industrial and economic expansion of German businessmen abroad may have been partially legitimized as an expansion of Germany's power, but this was in no way a primary motive. Businessmen may have been willing to use the resources of their government where it proved useful or necessary, but there was a strong disinclination to allow government involvement in their affairs. In the case of Stinnes, there does not seem to be any continuity whatsoever between the international expansion of his business operations and his subsequent rabid annexationism. Certainly he supported annexations in some of the areas in which he had been economically active, but this hardly could have been the case with respect to what appears to have been his most important international preoccupation

---

35 See Carl Duisberg to Emil Fischer, letters of Aug.–Sept. 1914, Emil Fischer papers, Bancroft Library, University of California, Berkeley. The few firms that did produce for the war effort, such as Krupp, were subjected to a great deal of criticism in the Reichstag and the press especially, but not exclusively, from the left, and there was much talk of breaking their "monopoly." At an investigatory committee meeting in June 1914, Duisburg at once defended Krupp and the other German munitions producers as more efficient than the state factories and, as a nonmilitary producer, pointed out that if he were subjected to the kind of attacks to which Krupp had been subjected, he would long ago have told the government that "you should go and make your cannon yourself or buy them where you want; I don't give a hoot about these contracts." He also praised Krupp and the other munitions manufacturers for being great exporters. See Carl Duisburg, *Abhandlungen, Vorträge und Reden aus den Jahren 1882–1921* (Berlin, 1923), 788–804.

prior to the war, namely, his mining interests in England. There is no evidence that he contemplated the possible annexation of Briey-Longwy or Belgian territory prior to the outbreak of the war, and he never contemplated annexing Wales at any time!

Joseph Schumpeter's theses on the incompatibility of imperialism and capitalism are supported rather than undermined by Stinnes's performance, especially if one thinks of capitalism in terms of an international system.[36] While the chief opposition to the modernization of the German taxation system may have come from "atavistic" conservatives who were nonetheless highly militaristic, Stinnes's position reflected a very modern businessman's hostility toward high taxes and big government. Whatever the motives, however, it proved extraordinarily difficult for the German military to raise the money it needed, and, as has recently been argued, this may have increased the military's willingness to take advantage of such superiority as it possessed in 1914.[37]

Finally, is there any relationship at all between prewar industrial expansionism and wartime industrialist annexationism? The case study undertaken here suggests that the relationship lies not in a continuity of goals and ambitions but rather in the discontinuity of development produced by the war. Where continuity could be found was in German political culture, which had nurtured a business community habituated to the pursuit of interest politics and unused to taking political responsibility for its demands. Germany's extraordinary economic growth in the prewar period depended on increasing international trade and interdependence and on international stability. Businessmen expected the growth to continue and paid scant attention to the vulnerabilities of the system. In the end, politics ruined economics, and German businessmen blamed British jealousy, as in the case of Carl Duisberg, or Russian Pan-Slavism, as in the case of Stinnes, for the collapse. They drew the unpleasant conclusion that one could not operate in the old way and that one had to secure by force that which had been undermined by Germany's enemies. As the business report of the Deutsch-Luxemburg Concern argued in November 1914, the war had to be used to secure the economic well-being of Germany

because unfortunately the war had increased the tendency in all the affected countries to lock one another out after the coming of peace and to limit the international exchange of goods, in other words, to carry on the political war economically. It will be one of the greatest tasks we have, to work against these strong

---

36 Joseph Schumpeter, *Imperialism and the Social Classes* (New York, 1951).
37 See Niall Ferguson, "Public Finance and National Security: The Domestic Origins of the First World War Revisited," *Past and Present*, no. 142 (Feb. 1994): 141–68.

tendencies both at home and abroad, for the greatest possible international exchange of goods and competition is necessary for the maintenance of economic health, and it is at the same time the best means to bring the hostile peoples closer together again. In the transition, however, German industry and labor must unconditionally have the opportunity to have profitable activity in a secure and expanded national territory and thereby find compensation for the fearful losses in the war.[38]

The goal of self-protection, which rapidly became indistinguishable from self-aggrandizement, rather quickly triumphed over the goal of economic reconciliation. The extraordinary obtuseness of Stinnes and his industrialist colleagues about the political and international implications of their annexationism was matched only by their unwavering postwar demand that the victors of World War I supply Germany with loans for the reconstruction of Germany's finances and economy, so that Germany might pay a very limited amount of reparations and return to its proper place in a reconstructed international capitalist system.[39] Certainly there was some disingenuousness in this behavior, but it would be a mistake to downplay the genuine conviction that made it possible, a conviction rooted in the experience of the pre-1914 period and the quest for a restoration of the lost paradise it came to represent. The great German businessmen dealt with this loss as children of the political culture in which they had been nurtured. This explains why German businessmen could be so convinced about the justifiability of their annexationism and no less convinced in their demands for a restoration of German equality in international trade and commerce after the war. It was the state and politics that ruined things, something the Germans felt the French never seemed to understand, to their great frustration, but that they thought the British and the Americans ultimately did understand, even if the Anglo-Americans were not always convinced by German economic behavior. There was much truth to this perception. In 1922, in trying to explain why the German industrialists seemed to prefer ruining their finances and economy to swallowing the bitter but necessary Anglo-American medicine of stabilization and deflation, the American ambassador Alanson Houghton argued that "[T]he truth, I believe, is that the German bankers and industrialists are mighty poor economists. They have had plenty of experience in a constantly growing and expanding volume of industry and trade, they have had no experience whatever, until the present, in a decreasing volume of industry and trade, such as, for instance, both the United States and England have experienced

38 Business Report, Nov. 1914, ACDP, I-220, no. 080/7.
39 This is discussed in some detail in Feldman, *Great Disorder*, 321ff.

several times. The net result is that they do not understand the present situation. They are, I believe, not competent to meet it. They need English and American help in particular to work themselves out of the hole into which they have fallen."[40] They may have been poor economists, but they did believe in the primacy of economics, and this doctrine seems to have served the German business community well, whereas war and conquest have not. Perhaps there is a longer history here that deserves further consideration and attention.

40 Houghton Report to the secretary of state, Dec. 27, 1922, U.S. National Archives, Decimal file, no. 862.00/1199.

5

War Preparations and Ethnic and Racial Relations in the United States

BRUCE WHITE

Ethnic and racial issues in the United States were most closely related to the theme of total war during the period from American entry into World War I in 1917 through the mid-1920s, when the mobilization of the population for war produced a demand for 100 percent Americanism and the Espionage and Sedition acts, followed by the Red Scare, race riots, the revival of the Ku Klux Klan, immigration restriction, and the executions of Nicola Sacco and Bartolomeo Vanzetti. North Americans are still periodically reminded of this era – whether by living through the McCarthy era of the early 1950s, experiencing the Trudeau government's invocation of the War Measures Act in Canada in 1970, or simply by driving through Kitchener, Ontario, and remembering that it was formerly named Berlin.

A great deal has been written about the Americanization crusade, darkening attitudes toward German Americans and Irish Americans, and the preparedness movement in the years leading up to American entry into the war, but little has been written on how the military's relationships with ethnic and racial minorities and American expansion overseas relate to increasingly negative attitudes toward minorities within the United States. In addition, the attitudes of ethnic and racial minorities themselves toward the wars and war scares of the pre-World War I period have not been adequately explored, and almost nothing has been written comparing the Canadian and American experiences. It is my purpose in this chapter to assess the role that these factors played in the gradual triumph of a more restrictive and ultimately ominous side of *e pluribus unum,* when most Americans became convinced that group loyalties were incompatible with loyalty to the nation. By 1917, Merle Curti has argued, this narrowed concept of loyalty was closely identified with preparedness and military might, as

97

Americans sought "the unifying principle, the patriotic discipline" that would redeem the nation.[1]

Most historians focus on the years immediately preceding American entry into World War I, but a broader canvas is needed. It was during the period between 1860 and 1924, Philip Gleason has argued, when "ethnicity assumed greater salience as an element in the national identity than it has had at any other time before or since. Especially during the first quarter of the twentieth century, the ethnic factors of 'race,' nationality, language, and so on were the issues that sprang immediately to mind when Americans asked themselves, 'What does it mean to be an American? What kind of Americanism do we want?'"[2] Americans were preoccupied with such unsettling changes as the new stream of immigration from southern and eastern Europe and the dislocations created by rapid industrialization and urbanization in a society characterized by localism, individualism, and privatism; but also important were questions raised by the role of the military, war scares, and participation in warfare itself.

Military involvement with ethnic and racial minorities had been continual from the earliest colonial militias, but the relationship began to change in the late nineteenth century. Heretofore, military service and participation in America's wars had meant opportunity for immigrants and African Americans. Foreign-born soldiers had at times constituted a majority of the enlisted ranks in both the antebellum and postbellum frontier army, and half the enlisted men in the late-nineteenth-century Navy were immigrants. Black regiments, despite the discrimination they experienced, were a valued, regular part of the army following the Civil War, offering opportunities and status unavailable elsewhere, and the navy accepted black applicants without discrimination.[3]

Like most civilians, however, military men did believe in a hierarchy of ethnic groups. Naval officers spoke most highly of English, Scottish, and

1 Merle Curti, *The Roots of American Loyalty* (New York, 1968), 223–4.
2 Philip Gleason, "American Identity and Americanization," in Stephan Thernstrom, ed., *Harvard Encyclopedia of American Ethnic Groups* (Cambridge, Mass., 1980), 46.
3 On immigrants in the army, see Bruce White, "Ethnicity, Race, and the American Military: From Bunker Hill to San Juan Hill," in Major David MacIsaac, ed., *The Military and Society* (Washington, D.C., 1976), 113–30, and Jack D. Foner, *The United States Soldier Between Two Wars: Army Life and Reforms, 1865–1898* (New York, 1970). On African Americans, see Jack D. Foner, *Blacks and the Military in American History* (New York, 1974), 52–108; Marvin E. Fletcher, *The Black Soldier and Officer in the United States Army, 1891–1917* (Columbia, Mo., 1974); Gerald W. Patton, *War and Race: The Black Officer in the American Military, 1915–1941* (Westport, Conn., 1981), 3–31; and Warren L. Young, *Minorities and the Militia: A Cross-National Study in World Perspective* (Westport, Conn., 1982), 191–202. For the Navy, see Peter Karsten, *The Naval Aristocracy: The Golden Age of Annapolis and the Emergence of Modern American Navalism* (New York, 1972), 207–18, and Frederick S. Harrod, *Manning the New Navy: The Development of a Modern Naval Enlisted Force, 1899–1940* (Westport, Conn., 1978).

Scandinavian immigrants, although army officers in the late nineteenth century were often hostile toward English soldiers; many of them, it was believed, had deserted from the British Army in Canada and, if they did not desert again, were continually complaining, drunk, or shirking their duties. Naval officers were most hostile to the Irish, often calling them "stupid turf-lumps." Impressions of the German soldier and sailor were somewhat mixed but rose significantly following the German successes in the Franco-Prussian War. Both services admired and copied the German General Staff system, and in October 1898, one naval officer expressed the opinion that America's next foe would be Germany, a population much more "worthy of our steel" than the Spanish.[4] In the Pacific, naval officers spoke highly only of the Japanese, who, although "yellow" and not socially acceptable, were also "aggressive, ambitious, and imbued with a deference and a fine sense of honor," not unlike the English or the naval aristocracy itself.[5]

The situation of the Native American soldier followed a different course from that of European immigrants or African Americans. Most picked the wrong side during the American Revolution, the War of 1812, and the Civil War, and many were on the wrong end of an army rifle during the frontier wars. Their service as scouts was highly valued, although an experiment with Indian troops and companies as an integral part of the army after the Indian wars were over was an abject failure; the army was led to adopt a continuing policy of thorough integration into white units at the same time segregation was becoming more rigidly established for black soldiers.[6]

By the 1880s the army, navy, and veterans' organizations began to react negatively to the "new immigration" from southern and eastern Europe, as did civilians. In 1894 federal legislation banned the foreign-born from first enlistments in the army, and by 1903 the *Army and Navy Journal* found it amusing that Europeans believed that the army contained many immigrants, calling it "the most inexplicable of European fallacies."[7] The army

---

4 Quoted in Karsten, *Naval Aristocracy,* 214.   5 Ibid., 215.

6 On the failure of Native American troops and companies, see Eric Feaver, "Indian Soldiers, 1891–95: An Experiment on the Closing Frontier," *Prologue* 7 (summer 1975): 109–18; Bruce White, "The American Indian as Soldier, 1890–1919," *Canadian Review of American Studies* 7 (spring 1976): 15–25; and Michael L. Tate, "From Scout to Doughboy: The National Debate over Integrating American Indians into the Military, 1891–1918," *Western Historical Quarterly* 17 (Oct. 1986): 417–37. For an overview of relationships from the earliest colonial settlements through the Vietnam War, see Bruce White, "The American Army and the Indian," in N. F. Dreisziger, ed., *Ethnic Armies: Polyethnic Armed Forces from the Time of the Habsburgs to the Age of the Superpowers* (Waterloo, Ont., 1990), 68–88.

7 *Army and Navy Journal* 41 (Dec. 3, 1903): 344. On veterans' organizations, see Stuart McConnell, *Glorious Contentment: The Grand Army of the Republic, 1865–1901* (Chapel Hill, N.C., 1992), 208–10; Wallace Even Davies, *Patriotism on Parade: The Story of Veterans' and Hereditary Organizations in America, 1783–1900* (Cambridge, Mass., 1955), 293–9; and Rodney G. Minott, *Peerless Patriots: Organized Veterans and the Spirit of Americanism* (Washington, D.C., 1962), 24.

continued to enlist immigrants despite the 1894 legislation, but the comments of military men about immigrants became increasingly vitriolic. True patriotism, wrote Colonel James S. Pettit in a prize-winning essay in 1906, "is constantly being diluted by the accession of foreigners who are pleased to style themselves German-Americans or Irish-Americans, as though they desired to serve two masters."[8] The new influx of immigrants, Lieutenant Roy W. Winton warned, had upset the homogeneous nature of American society. The United States had taken the "hide, hoof, and horn of European offerings balking only at Asia . . . ," and America was in danger of "losing its soul" and undergoing national disintegration.[9]

After 1910, retired officers became active in the nativist and patriotic organizations that proliferated after the turn of the century. Nelson A. Miles, a former commanding general of the army, was prominent in the organization in 1911 of the Guardians of Liberty, a virulently anti-Catholic and anti-immigrant organization.[10] General Samuel B. M. Young became president of the Association for National Service and commander in chief of the Military Order of the Loyal Legion of the United States. He was active in the planning for a National Committee of Patriotic and Defense Societies to coordinate the work of the various organizations.[11]

Military men were reacting not only to events at home but to those abroad as well. Service in the Spanish-American and Philippine-American wars and subsequent occupation duty deepened racist sentiments, which were already intensifying in the United States during the 1890s. "All the Cubans we have met here," Major General William Rufus Shafter wrote to his mother, "are dirty, nasty niggers who eat our rations, will not work and will not fight."[12] Writing in 1905, Major Charles E. Woodruff, an army surgeon, concluded that it would be a fatal step for the blond, blue-eyed Teuton to expand into tropical climates, because, according to him, only the dark-haired races could withstand intense sunlight. Woodruff was even concerned about the fate of Aryans in the American South. Four years later, however, he was more confident, stating that the "higher races" were

8 Colonel James S. Pettit, "How Far Does Democracy Affect the Organization and Discipline of our Armies and How Can Its Influence be Most Effectively Utilized?" *Journal of the Military Service Institution of the United States* 38 (Jan.–Feb. 1906), 71.

9 Roy W. Winton, "The Patriotic Ideal," *Infantry Journal* 8 (1912): 637–47, and "The Problem of Patriotism," *Infantry Journal* 9(1913): 773–7.

10 On the Guardians of Liberty, see "Guardians of Liberty," *Literary Digest* 45 (July 27, 1912): 152–3; Robert Wooster, *Nelson A. Miles and the Twilight of the Frontier Army* (Lincoln, Neb., 1993), 255–6; and Thomas J. Curran, *Xenophobia and Immigration, 1820–1930* (Boston, 1975), 130.

11 General Young's involvement in these organizations is detailed in the Samuel B. Young papers, United States Army Military History Institute, Carlisle Barracks, Pennsylvania.

12 Shafter to his mother, Aug. 2, 1898, William Rufus Shafter papers, Stanford University.

destined to control the tropics, even if acclimatization and colonization were not possible.[13]

In both the Caribbean and the Pacific, occupation duties brought black soldiers into contact with the civilian population, intensifying the prejudices of white officers and raising fears of sexual liaisons.[14] In the United States successive classes at the Army Service Schools at Fort Leavenworth, Kansas, were instructed on racial matters by Le Roy Eltinge. "So great is the mental difference between peoples," Eltinge concluded in a lecture published in 1915 as *Causes of War,* "that they can never fully understand one another. You think with not only a different brain but a different kind of brain than does your Filipino or negro servant. . . . To make it a little more personal, how would you feel about having your daughter or your sister marry a black, yellow or red man?"[15] American expansion overseas not only stimulated thought about ethnicity and race but also led to the development of war plans in response to conflict situations and concerns about the rising power and expansionist tendencies of Germany and Japan, as well as the continuing revolutionary situation in Mexico. Ultimately, such concerns would raise questions about the loyalties of internal minorities as well. The navy was particularly alarmed about German designs on the Far East and the Caribbean and had absorbed Mahanian doctrines about the inevitability of conflict arising from trade ambitions, with a resulting climactic battle of fleets. These concerns were more than academic; as early as the late nineteenth century, Germany had been producing war plans against the United States. These included the destruction of the American fleet, invasion of the West Indies, and attacks on American port cities.[16]

The U.S. navy established an Office of Naval Intelligence in 1882; it came under the supervision of the General Board of the Navy and gradu-

---

13 Charles E. Woodruff, *The Effects of Tropical Light on White Men* (New York, 1905), and Charles E. Woodruff, *The Expansion of Races* (New York, 1909).

14 Fletcher, *The Black Soldier and Officer,* 153, and Charles L. Moskos Jr., "Racial Integration in the Armed Forces," *American Journal of Sociology* 72 (Sept. 1966): 133–4.

15 Le Roy Eltinge, "Causes of War," appended to Eltinge, *Psychology of War* (Fort Leavenworth, Kans., 1915), 14–15.

16 For the development of war planning, see Jeffrey M. Dorwart, *The Office of Naval Intelligence: The Birth of America's First Intelligence Agency, 1865–1914* (Annapolis, Md., 1979); Holger H. Herwig, *Politics of Frustration: The United States in German Naval Planning, 1899–1941* (Boston, 1976), 93–109; Holger H. Herwig and David F. Trask, "Naval Operations Plans Between Germany and the United States of America, 1898–1913: A Study of Strategic Planning in the Age of Imperialism," *Militärgeschichtliche Mitteilungen* 2 (1970): 532; J. A. S. Grenville, "Diplomacy and War Plans in the United States, 1890–1917," *Transactions of the Royal Historical Society,* 5th series, 11 (1961): 1–21; and G. J. A. O'Toole, *Honorable Treachery: A History of U.S. Intelligence, Espionage, and Covert Action from the American Revolution to the CIA* (New York, 1991), 200–11.

ally moved toward war planning, espionage, and, ultimately, domestic intelligence. To coordinate planning between the services, a Joint Army and Navy Board was created in 1903; it developed color-coded symbols for war plans with various countries, including black for Germany, orange for Japan, green for Mexico, and red for Great Britain. The War Department created a Military Information Division, but after this division was placed within and almost swallowed up by the Army War College, intelligence planning was limited to concerns about Mexico and Japan. The army sent intelligence agents into Mexico and American border communities as early as the 1890s, prepared a war plan against Mexico in 1911, and periodically mobilized troops along the border, culminating in the Punitive Expedition of 1916 into Mexico.[17] Military men took note of Japan's military successes against Russia in 1904 and 1905, but it was a domestic crisis that led to the development of War Plan Orange. Japan's anger after the San Francisco Board of Education in 1906 required children of Asian parentage to attend segregated schools led President Theodore Roosevelt to have the army prepare a war plan, which included defense of the Pacific coast and the relocation of Japanese aliens to camps in Utah.[18] In 1912 the Army War College developed a plan for widespread surveillance of Japanese aliens after receiving reports of contingency plans being made to destroy railroads, bridges, and tunnels in the west.[19] A war scare also arose the following year because of Japanese reactions to the Alien Land Act in California, although a war plan by the Joint Board seemed too militaristic to President Woodrow Wilson, and he ordered the Board to cease operations. The navy was more concerned about the potential disloyalty of German Americans, primarily because of the fears of Captain C. D. Sigsbee, who became head of the Naval Intelligence Office in 1900. The former captain of the U.S.S. *Maine* might have been expected to be somewhat nervous, but Sigsbee's fears approached paranoia. In 1903, in the belief that Germany was planning to invade the United States, he recommended an investigation of sailors with Germanic names, including examinations for tattoos that might show loyalties to the Fatherland.[20] In 1913 the navy developed War Plan Black, which envisioned a German invasion of the Caribbean, and in 1915 a plan was drawn up for an "Information Service

---

17 W. Dirk Raat, *Revoltosos: Mexico's Rebels in the United States, 1903–1923* (College Station, Tex., 1981), 194–8, 265–6.
18 Harry P. Ball, *Of Responsible Command: A History of the U.S. Army War College* (Carlisle Barracks, Pa., 1983), 109–10, and Edward S. Miller, *War Plan Orange: The U.S. Strategy to Defeat Japan, 1897–1945* (Annapolis, Md., 1991), 21.
19 Joan M. Jensen, *Army Surveillance in America, 1775–1980* (New Haven, Conn., 1991), 120.
20 Herwig and Trask, "Naval Operations Plans," 23; Herwig, *Politics of Frustration,* 84.

in the Naval Defense Districts," which would appoint district information officers to organize intelligence services within their districts, including a network of local informants to ferret out internal subversion.[21] The following year the War College Division of the War Department General Staff developed a plan, including a "national secret service" under military control, that would institute censorship, surveillance, registration, and plans for internment of aliens from Germany, Austria, and Bulgaria.[22] By this time, however, civilian concerns about the loyalty of minority groups had eclipsed military ones. In March 1917 the War Department was severely criticized by the Department of State for its lack of concern about possible subversive activities by enemy aliens. Secretary of War Newton D. Baker, however, continued to recommend that enemy aliens not be interned or arrested unless they had committed actual crimes.[23]

It was not until the United States entered World War I that fear of subversion mounted to hysteria; before American entry, overt actions were mainly directed against real or suspected German espionage activities. Germany actually made relatively few efforts to enlist the active aid of German Americans, except to call for the return of reservists, to encourage engineers and skilled workers in the munitions industry to quit their jobs, and to urge immigrants to work for continued American neutrality. Some efforts were made to have Hungarian Americans foment unrest in industrial and mining centers, Irish Americans were enlisted to plant explosive devices in the holds of ships carrying ammunition, and Irish-American nationalists engaged in some anti-British planning in coordination with Indian nationalists living in the United States. Franz von Papen, the German military attaché in Mexico and the United States, was in contact with the Gadar organization, which advocated the violent overthrow of British rule in India; most of its support came from Sikh laborers from Punjab living in California.[24]

In 1915 a plot was formulated by Mexican *revoltosos* and Mexican Americans living in Texas for an armed uprising of Mexican Americans and blacks in seven western states. Anglo males were to be killed, and the former states would become a separate socialist country. There also were plans for a black republic in several states. The only overt violence was a series of raids in southern Texas, resulting in bloody reprisals that scattered

21 Dorwart, *Office of Naval Intelligence,* 103.
22 "Possible Rupture with Germany," memorandum for the Chief of Staff, Feb. 29, 1916, File 9433, General Correspondence, record group 165, Records of the War Department General and Special Staffs, War College Division, National Archives, Washington, D.C.
23 Joan M. Jensen, *The Price of Vigilance* (Chicago, 1969), 29.
24 O'Toole, *Honorable Treachery,* 221–35.

the insurgents. This "Plan of San Diego" was encouraged or instigated by factions in Mexico attempting to influence the course of the revolution, but German involvement is problematic. Friedrich Katz has concluded that had this been the case, the United States would have pursued the issue following the war, when a German-American claims commission made intensive investigations of subversion by German agents.[25]

If incidents such as the Plan of San Diego did not create undue alarm before American entry into World War I, the growing campaign for Americanization of immigrants was already becoming something of a crusade. In addition, the campaign for preparedness attracted a growing number of supporters, even if this was a divisive issue in a nation that had always been suspicious of a large military establishment in peacetime. Following the outbreak of war in Europe in 1914, proposals for Universal Military Training (UMT), an even more contentious issue, were being made and receiving considerable publicity.

Military men participated in all three of these movements, although Americanization and Universal Military Training were as divisive within the military as outside it. Both movements were spearheaded within the army by Leonard Wood, a physician who had entered the army as a contract surgeon with the aid of his friend Theodore Roosevelt. Wood, however, was disliked and distrusted by a good many army officers, for he was never considered a real professional by many career men. His arguments for a mass citizen army that could be trained in a relatively short period were not popular among career officers brought up on the teachings of Emory Upton; the army, they believed, should be a thoroughly professional organization of career officers and long-term soldiers. In addition, most officers accepted the proscription against political activity, particularly after President Wilson forbade public statements by the military, and Wood was a partisan and vocal Republican with political ambitions, a man who regarded free speech less as a right than a continuous obligation. For political reasons Wilson did nothing to stop Wood's public pronouncements, thus endearing neither man to the military.

Wood's call for Americanization resonated among social conservatives who feared the fragmentation of American society, and he shared some of their fears of ethnic and racial minorities. Arguing against the admission of Asian laborers in a letter to Theodore Roosevelt in 1905, he concluded

---

25 Raat, *Revoltosos*, 262–4, and Friedrich Katz, *The Secret War with Mexico: Europe, the United States, and the Mexican Revolution* (Chicago, 1981), 339–44.

that America had "enough national weakness and humiliation from the negro to avoid further trouble by the introduction of races with which we
can never mingle. . . . The introduction of any race with which we cannot
intermarry is in my opinion a most horrible mistake."[26] In 1915 he wrote
to Roosevelt expressing the hope that the west coast "will always maintain
its policy of being a 'white man's country.' God knows we have problems
enough with the development of the negro – we don't want the yellow
man. As a matter of fact, in my opinion, we don't want anyone with
whom our descendants can not intermarry without producing a breed of
mongrels; they must at least be white."[27] The more democratic implications of the concept of a citizen army would be developed only later, by
Wood's disciple John McAuley Palmer.

Wood's call for Universal Military Training was supported by another
former army chief of staff, Hugh Scott, and by some of the younger officers assigned to the War College Division of the General Staff. UMT,
Scott argued, would accomplish the physical and moral uplift of Americans as well as the Americanization of the foreign-born. It was an idea beginning to attract not only social conservatives but Progressive reformers as
well. In 1916, for example, Frances A. Kellor, a social worker with strong
Progressive commitments, published *Straight America: A Call to National Service,* in which she argued for Americanization through military preparedness, universal service, and industrial mobilization.[28]

Concerns about cohesiveness began to be seen as more pressing than up-
lifting the foreign-born. The latter motive, although often expressed, was
sometimes less than convincing. Publicity generated by the Plattsburg officers' training camp, for example, stressed the extent to which the movement brought all classes and ethnic groups together. "We at Plattsburg," asserted *The Plattsburger,* "are of all kinds and all creeds. We are rich and we
are poor. We came from the fashionable avenues of the great cities. We
have come even from overseas. The four winds of the earth sent us together," and "into the melting-pot we went." The publication continued, "The
foreign-born among us gathered much from the native born, the latter
learned that there were foreign born so willing at heart that they could become thorough Americans by the simple process of rubbing elbows."[29]

---

26 Wood to Roosevelt, Dec. 13, 1905, reel 61, Theodore Roosevelt papers, Library of Congress,
   Washington, D.C.
27 Wood to Roosevelt, Mar. 5, 1915, reel 199, ibid.
28 See the discussion of Kellor in John Higham, *Strangers in the Land: Patterns of American Nativism,
   1810–1925* (New Brunswick, N.J., 1988), 242–4.
29 "Plattsburg – Ideals and Achievements," *The Plattsburger* (New York, 1917): 16.

The reality was that the camp was composed largely of a white, Northeastern elite; more than 90 percent of the Plattsburgers were college graduates.[30]

By 1916 the campaign for preparedness and Americanization through universal military training was receiving wide publicity. On May 14 a massive Citizens' Preparedness Parade took place in New York City, the size of which was calculated by the *New York Times* at 135,683 marchers. The procession, organized into 63 divisions with more than 200 marching bands participating, took eleven hours to pass the reviewing stand. Practically every trade and profession was represented, and the military was much in evidence. Thousands of National Guardsmen marched, Spanish-American War veterans were represented, and two of the three reviewing officers were military men – General Leonard Wood of the army and Rear Admiral Nathaniel R. Usher, Commandant of the Brooklyn Navy Yard. The third, John Purroy Mitchel, reform mayor of New York City, had been an enthusiastic volunteer at the Plattsburg officers' training camp the previous year.[31]

On the same day that his friend Leonard Wood was standing for eleven hours, saluting the flag each time it passed, Theodore Roosevelt was hosting a preparedness parade of his own at Sagamore Hill, attended predominantly by detachments of Boy Scouts from Irvington-on-Hudson and Glen Cove and by 150 members of the men's Bible class from the Oyster Bay Methodist Church. The latter group arrived in a cavalcade of fifty automobiles, with flags flying. Late in the afternoon Roosevelt went outside to watch the precision drilling of the Scouts. "How did you get here from Irvington?" he shouted to one scoutmaster. "We marched," the leader replied. "Started at 10

30 John Garry Clifford, *The Citizen Soldiers: The Plattsburg Training Camp Movement, 1913–1920* (Lexington, Ky., 1972), 65–6. More genuine concerns for the advancement of the foreign-born would be expressed and implemented when civilian reformers cooperated with army officers in training foreign-born soldiers after the establishment of the Foreign- Speaking Sub-Section in January 1918. Considerable attention was paid to the social and cultural needs and desires of immigrant soldiers, although for the military special treatment was a necessity; almost 25 percent of draftees, according to official statistics, were unable to read and understand an English-language newspaper or write letters home. Intelligence tests conducted during the war were later used for racist purposes, although this was a civilian initiative; the army simply found the tests useful for purposes of classification and assignment. See Nancy Gentile Ford, "War and Ethnicity: Foreign-born Soldiers and United States Military Policy During World War I," Ph.D. diss., Temple University, 1994; Bruce White, "The American Military and the Melting Pot in World War I," in J. L. Granatstein and R. D. Cuff, eds., *War and Society in North America* (Toronto, 1971), 37–51; and Daniel J. Kevles, "Testing the Army's Intelligence: Psychologists and the Military in World War I," *Journal of American History* 55 (Dec. 1968): 565–81.
31 *New York Times*, May 14, 1916. Mitchel's flamboyant enthusiasm, however, would later cost him his life. Disdaining to fasten his safety belt while training as a pilot, he fell out of his airplane. Edwin R. Lewinson, *John Purroy Mitchel: The Boy Mayor of New York* (New York, 1965), 254.

o'clock this morning. Fifty minutes' hike, ten minutes' rest. Just like the army.'"By George, I'm proud of you," Roosevelt replied. "The real democracy comes from the democracy of the dog tent."[32]

Four days later, the Academy of Political Science held an all-day debate at Earl Hall, Columbia University, on the desirability of universal military training. A few participants spoke in opposition, including Oswald Garrison Villard, who warned against fostering the spirit of militarism. The large majority, however, from a variety of backgrounds, enthusiastically supported the idea. None received such tumultuous applause as Henry Breckinridge, a former assistant secretary of war. "Universal Military Training," he concluded in ringing tones, "is the only way to yank the hyphen out of America. With German and English, Russian and Austrian, Italian and Turk, all rubbing elbows in common service to one country out comes the hyphen, up goes the Stars and Stripes and in a generation the melting pot will have melted." The following morning the *New York Times* summarized the debate under the headline "Sees end of Hyphen in Universal Drill."[33]

Ethnic and racial minorities, however, were not simply the objects of discussion and growing concern; they also were affected by, they reacted to, and sometimes they influenced the course of war preparations, war scares, and warfare itself during this period. There were varying reactions among the large number of groups in the United States by the late nineteenth century, but certain patterns are evident. Before the outbreak of war in Europe in 1914, minorities were, on the one hand, influenced by how events would affect their own situation, and the need for acceptability by conforming during wartime was great. On the other hand, there was a tendency to be more reluctant than the general population to support American entry into the Spanish-American War and to be more critical of American imperialism, especially during the Philippine-American War. Ties to the homeland also played a part in determining the attitudes of some ethnic groups.

The war scares of the 1890s all involved ethnic minorities. Carl Schurz exchanged letters with Bismarck during the Samoan crisis of 1889, and the war scare with Italy in 1891 was precipitated by the lynching of eleven Italian Americans in New Orleans. A causative factor of tensions with Chile in 1891 was the appointment and actions of Patrick Egan, a refugee from Ireland, as U.S. minister to that country. Some Irish-American nationalists also did their best to worsen relations with Britain during the Venezuelan

---

32 *New York Times*, May 14, 1916.
33 Ibid., May 19, 1916. Breckinridge developed his arguments further in "The Solving of the Hyphen," *Forum* 56 (Nov. 1916): 583–8.

boundary dispute of 1895, while English, Scottish, and Canadian immigrants sided with Britain.

Ethnic and racial groups also reacted to growing tensions with Spain over the revolt in Cuba, particularly because anti-Catholic sentiment in the United States was heightened. Although the wave of nativism of the early 1890s had largely subsided by 1898, suspicions of "Pope-ridden Spain" remained. It was reported in the press that "the Pope had ordered Catholics in the United States not to fight Spain, that 700,000 armed American Catholics were preparing for an uprising, [and] that an explosion of a powder mill in California was caused by the inmates of a nearby Jesuit monastery."[34] Irish Americans were particularly singled out by several American newspapers, probably because of their strong defense of "everything Catholic and everything Irish."[35]

Before the declaration of war against Spain, some ethnic religious leaders argued for a peaceful settlement. In Chicago, for example, Rabbi Joseph Stolz denounced "savages" who were agitating for war, and a survey of the German-language press found that all but one newspaper or journal was for a peaceful settlement.[36] Some German Americans were influenced by Carl Schurz's opposition to American intervention, and some who had fled militarism feared the same trend in the United States. There was some pacifist dissent; the *Nye Normanden,* for example, a Norwegian-American pacifist journal, condemned "war insanity" and feared what American expansion would bring.[37] The war, however, was too short for pacifist opposition to crystallize, and pacifist groups such as the Mennonites did not have to face the issue of conscription. Mennonites made clothing for soldiers, and some bought war bonds and engaged in Red Cross work[38]; other ethnic groups generally declared their support once the nation was actually at war.

Roman Catholics felt that a public display of loyalty to the United States was a necessity; the largely Irish clerical hierarchy also realized that an appeal for unity would help to defuse the "Cahenslyite" controversy, in which non-English-language groups were seeking more autonomy. Irish-American nationalists interpreted the crisis, like all international events, in terms of their hostility toward Britain. The *Boston Pilot,* for example, argued that Spanish treatment of Cubans was comparable to England's treat-

---

34 Frank T. Reuter, *Catholic Influence on American Colonial Policies, 1898–1904* (Austin, Tex., 1967), 10.
35 Ibid., 13.
36 Ernest R. May, *Imperial Democracy: The Emergence of America as a Great Power* (New York, 1961), 140.
37 Arlow W. Andersen, *Rough Road to Glory: The Norwegian-American Press Speaks Out on Public Affairs, 1875 to 1925* (Philadelphia, 1990), 76.
38 Peter Brock, *Pacifism in the United States from the Colonial Era to the First World War* (Princeton, N.J., 1968), 902–3.

ment of Ireland.[39] Bohemian-American and German-American pro-Cuban committees were organized, and the Polish-American leader Francis Fronczak organized rallies and made speeches urging support for the war and volunteering for military service. At one rally, when an appeal for enlistment was made, the rush forward by would-be recruits was so great that the stage collapsed.[40] Most Cuban immigrants were poor and apolitical, but some members of the Cigar Makers' Union demonstrated for the Cuban cause. Ethnic groups that traditionally voted Republican were inclined to support President William McKinley.

African Americans tended to view the war in terms of how it would affect their status at home, although many sympathized with the Cubans in revolt. Unlike most Americans, who applauded the Creole revolutionary *junta* members in the United States whom they viewed as light-skinned compared with the "dark Spaniards," African Americans saw Cubans as an oppressed black people; they praised the exploits of the black general Antonio Maceo. They took great pride in the participation of the black regiments in the war and realized that their public patriotism would reflect to their credit, but they also feared the stifling of subsequent Cuban independence and the importation of white racial prejudice to the island. The Philippine-American War resulted in an outcry among many African Americans against American imperialism and suppression of Filipino aspirations, particularly as reports of atrocities mounted. The performance of black soldiers was again a source of pride, and black soldiers were inclined to support the American presence, but the African American press was mainly anti-imperialist, as were the majority of black ministers. Some clergymen, though, saw opportunities for missionary endeavors, and the African Methodist Episcopal Church was split on the issue. There was a growing feeling that American imperialism would threaten the position of blacks in the United States and lead to an intensification of racism. An attempt was made by blacks to organize a "Colored Auxiliary of the Anti-Imperialist League," but blacks found anti-imperialists to be as racist as proponents of the "white man's burden."[41] Some African Americans were interested in colonization and in business opportunities in the Caribbean and Asia, but this interest was short-lived.

---

39 Reuter, *Catholic Influence on American Colonial Policies*, 6.
40 Victor R. Greene, *American Immigrant Leaders, 1800–1910: Marginality and Identity* (Baltimore, 1987), 120–1.
41 Willard B. Gatewood Jr., "Black Americans and the Quest for Empire, 1898–1903," *Journal of American History* 38 (Nov. 1972): 545–66, and Willard B. Gatewood Jr., *Black Americans and the White Man's Burden, 1898–1903* (Urbana, Ill., 1975); Richard E. Welch Jr., *Response to Imperialism: The United States and the Philippine-American War, 1899–1902* (Chapel Hill, N.C., 1979), 101–16.

Other ethnic groups also expressed anti-imperialist attitudes. Catholics were fearful of mistreatment of Philippine Catholics and expected Protestant evangelization, but their suspicions were lessened by the astute handling of the issue by Theodore Roosevelt, especially the successful mission of William Howard Taft to Rome in 1902. Frank T. Reuter has argued that the successful resolution of this issue aided in lessening anti-Catholic prejudice in the United States and created a heightened respect for Catholic sensibilities.[42] According to Stuart Creighton Miller, German Americans were the group most opposed to annexation of the Philippines, in part because of fears that American expansion would lead to war with Germany. The tensions with Germany in Samoa and Manila Bay did, in fact, lead some military men to predict war in the near future.[43]

The outbreak of the Boer War – at "about tea time" on October 1, 1899, as the *London Times* put it – caused an intense reaction among some American ethnic groups. Not surprisingly, Dutch Americans strongly supported the Boers, not only because of ethnic loyalty but also because of long-standing rivalries with the English.[44] German Americans were also sympathetic to the Boers because of ethnicity and because of their anti-imperialistic views. Norwegian Americans saw parallels with Norway's aspirations for independence from Sweden and thought positively of the Boers as a Bible-reading, family-centered people.[45] Irish Americans did more than sympathize. Fenian raids into Canada were again considered, and when plans for military service in South Africa were thwarted, the Ancient Order of Hibernians organized under the guise of a Red Cross unit a corps that managed to join and fight with Boer forces.[46]

By the summer of 1900 public opinion in the United States was solidly on the side of the Boers, and both political parties, especially the Democrats, expressed sympathy for the Boer cause. Had the South African War started a few years earlier, the McKinley administration might have supported the Boers or at least expressed neutrality. By 1899, however, the rapprochement with Britain and the passionate Anglophilic sentiments of Secretary of State John Hay led the government to side with Britain.[47]

42 Reuter, *Catholic Influence on American Colonial Policies,* xi, 136–59.
43 Stuart Creighton Miller, *"Benevolent Assimilation": The American Conquest of the Philippines, 1899–1903* (New Haven, Conn., 1982), 19–20.
44 Linda Pegman Doezema, "The Dutch Press," in Sally M. Miller, ed., *The Ethnic Press in the United States: A Historical Analysis and Handbook* (Westport, Conn., 1987), 75.
45 Andersen, *Rough Road to Glory,* 83.
46 John H. Ferguson, *American Diplomacy and the Boer War* (Philadelphia, 1939), 65–7.
47 For the view that there was no need for a rapprochement because there was no real estrangement, see Alexander DeConde, *Ethnicity, Race, and American Foreign Policy: A History* (Boston, 1992), 55–9.

Also, by 1899 the United States faced an insurrection in the Philippines in which some officials saw parallels with British efforts against the Boers.

African Americans faced the unpleasant task of choosing imperialism or racism, or so it seemed at the outset. Anti-imperialist sentiments about the Philippines initially elicited more criticism of the British than of the Boers. Also, black attitudes were influenced by the campaign to discredit the back-to-Africa movement of Bishop Henry McNeal Turner of the African Methodist Episcopal Church, although warning flags should have gone up when Bishop Turner and his party were issued passports identifying them as "honorary whites" while traveling in the Transvaal. Gradually, as the racial attitudes of the Boers became better known, Boer racism seemed the greater evil. Following the war, however, African Americans began to see similarities between the racial settlement in British South Africa and that of the American South. Ultimately, African Americans "found little to justify the faith which they had placed in the racial liberality of the British during the Boer War."[48]

If the wars at the turn of the century were troubling to some, however, this was an era of renewed confidence for most Americans. The upturn in the business cycle in the mid-1890s, the "splendid little war" against Spain, the bracing leadership of Theodore Roosevelt, and the confidence of Progressives in effecting environmental change – all stimulated renewed hope. Even the outbreak of war in Europe in 1914 seemed, initially, to be of limited concern to the United States; a policy of strict neutrality seemed the logical course. Whatever choices the United States might make, however, would raise strong ethnic and racial feelings and loyalties. For immigrants whose homelands were within the Habsburg, German, Russian, or Ottoman empires, the war was of immediate relevance. The heightened aspirations of subject peoples in Europe found among their counterparts in America support that was cultivated by appeals from Europe and the activities of exiles and emissaries to the United States.

The Habsburg Empire had come into being resisting the Muslim Turks; increasingly, it had become dominated by the Austrian Germans and the Magyars of Hungary. By 1914 the empire was a cauldron of restive ethnic groups seeking cultural and political autonomy. Some Magyars, themselves the oppressors of other ethnic groups, sought an independent state, a movement supported by the American Hungarian Federation, which had been established in 1906. Pressure to remain loyal was applied by the Hun-

---

48 Willard B. Gatewood Jr., "Black Americans and the Boer War, 1899–1902," *South Atlantic Quarterly* 75 (spring 1976): 244.

garian government to churches, ethnic organizations, and the press through the American Action program; it had some success, particularly among Calvinists. Emotional and ideological ties resulted in considerable Empire loyalism among Magyar immigrants, even if filtered through American experiences and arrived at with some agonizing. "The fact that fate had endowed . . . [us] with two homelands," wrote one immigrant, "now fell upon us like a lash that tore into our very souls."[49]

Czech Americans were more united than Magyars in seeking independence, through the Slav Press Bureau and the Committee for the Liberation of the Czech People (which became the Bohemian National Alliance after June 1914) and through the exhortations of Thomáš Masaryk, who became "the intellectual spokesman and mentor of all the American Slavs."[50] Slovaks, although differing from Czechs in language, level of socioeconomic development, and attachment to the Catholic Church, initially handicapped by rivalries among Slovak-American leaders and suspicious of Czech domination, put aside their differences to merge the Slovak League into a movement for an independent Czecho-Slovakia.[51]

Southern Slavs were deeply divided by history, language, and culture, particularly between the Orthodox Serbs, with Byzantine and Ottoman influences, and the Catholic Croats and Slovenes, with Latin and Western influences. A number of Croats and Slovenes in the United States preferred to remain within the Empire, although many supported autonomy if Serbs were not to be in the new state. Serbs tended to favor the creation of a Yugoslavia that would be, in essence, a greater Serbia. Some favored a republic and some a monarchy, although all three ethnic groups were angered by the Treaty of London in 1915, in which the Allies promised Slavic territory to Italy. Divisions persisted until the United States declared war on Germany in 1917, which united these and other ethnic groups in support of the American war effort.[52]

The majority of Ukrainians were recent arrivals in the United States and lacked spokespersons and organization. The Federation of Ukrainians in

49 Quoted in Steven Bela Vardy, *The Hungarian-Americans* (Boston, 1985), 91.
50 Victor S. Mamatey, *The United States and East Central Europe, 1914–1918: A Study in Wilsonian Diplomacy and Propaganda* (Princeton, N.J., 1957), 31.
51 Thomas Capek, *The Czechs in America* (New York, 1969), 265–78; Otakar Odlozlik, "The Czechs," in Joseph P. O'Grady, ed., *The Immigrant's Influence on Wilson's Peace Policies* (Lexington, Ky., 1967), 204–23; Victor S. Mamatey, "The Slovaks and Carpatho-Ruthenians," in ibid., 224–49; and Marian Mark Stolarik, *Immigration and Urbanization: The Slovak Experience, 1870–1918* (New York, 1989), 212–35.
52 George J. Prpic, *South Slavic Immigration in America* (Boston, 1978), 93–7, and Prpic, *The Croatian Immigrants in America* (New York, 1971), 233–50.

the United States, created in 1915, declared for the creation of a sovereign state, although outspoken supporters of Austria then founded the Ukrainian National Committee. By the time the United States entered the war, anti-Austrian sentiment prevailed among Ukrainian Americans.[53] Armenian Americans were naturally bitter about successive massacres by the Turks but were not numerous or politically organized until 1918, when they pressed President Woodrow Wilson to aid the newly declared Armenian republic. Among southern European immigrants, Greek Americans were more attuned to European events than were Italian Americans. Many Greek Americans had returned to fight in the Balkan wars of 1912–13, creating a wave of Greek patriotism in the United States. Italians were influenced more by local and regional loyalties and rivalries, and faced discrimination and violence, including lynchings, at home. Encouraged by the territorial promises of the Treaty of London and the entrance of Italy on the side of the Allies in 1915, Italian Americans became more engaged with war issues, although not many reservists returned to fight.

Italian Americans constituted a much larger minority than their political influence might indicate; the same was not true, however, of Polish Americans, the largest eastern European minority in the United States in 1914. This was an ethnic group with a proud national past, although Poland was currently partitioned among Germany, Russia, and Austria-Hungary. The Polish-American press consisted of fifteen daily newspapers with a circulation of 220,000 and sixty periodicals with a readership of more than 100,000. Polish Americans agreed on the reassertion of an independent Poland but were divided over the strategies to be pursued and the alliances to be sought. The Polish National Alliance stood for an independent, pro-Russian Poland and argued that American Poles constituted the "fourth province of Poland," in addition to the Austrian, German, and Russian segments. The Polish Roman Catholic Union also favored an independent Poland, but under clerical dominance. The Committee of National Defense leaned toward the Central Powers, supporting Joseph Pilsudski's arguments for an Austrian-oriented state and the creation of a Polish Legion in the Austrian Army. The arrival in the United States of the renowned pianist and patriot Ignacy Jan Paderewski as the unofficial representative of the Polish National Committee had a significant impact on American opinion, and both the Wilson administration (which was seeking the Pol-

53 Myron B. Kuropas, *The Ukrainian Americans: Roots and Aspirations, 1884–1984* (Toronto, 1991), 135–43, and Clarence A. Manning, "The Ukrainians and the United States in World War I," *Ukrainian Quarterly* 13 (Dec. 1957): 346–54.

ish vote) and Americans in general strongly supported the cause of Polish independence.[54]

The reactions of southern and eastern European immigrants to the outbreak of the war thus revealed differing strategies and emotional and ideological attachments, although leading in the direction of greater autonomy for their ethnic group. At the same time, they were coming under increasing pressure in the United States as a result of the growing Americanization crusade and American fears of involvement in the European struggle. For the first time since the 1790s, and transcending this era in important ways, a wave of ethnocentrism coincided with a foreign policy crisis. In addition, a preparedness debate was emerging that focused on the defense of the United States against an invasion, directing attention to internal loyalties.

Polish Americans benefited from broad American support for their cause; the same was true of Jewish Americans. Without as yet a homeland, and with an understandably low rate of repatriation, American Jews were more oriented toward aid to European Jews in general. Antipathy toward Russia for its brutal pogroms was a stumbling block in the way of support for the Allies until the overthrow of the czar in March 1917, and some Jewish Americans, such as the banker and philanthropist Jacob H. Schiff, openly supported Germany. The situation was changing, however, and Jewish Americans were shifting over to the Allied side. The entrance of Turkey into the war and the treatment of Jews in Palestine focused attention on this region, and the growing influence of Zionists in America, with international connections and pro-Allies sentiments, was beginning to be felt. Of considerable importance was the assumption of leadership of the movement in the United States by Louis D. Brandeis, a man of considerable organizational ability and prestige who used his friendship with President Wilson to full advantage. "Zionism under Brandeis," Morton Tenzer has commented, "combined both American patriotism and Jewish nationalism in a form acceptable to the broader American society," and the center of Zionism began to swing toward the United States.[55]

---

54 Zofia Libiszowska, "Polish-Americans and Wilson's Polish Policy on the Eve of World War I," in Hélene Christol and Serge Ricard, eds., *Hyphenated Diplomacy: European Immigration and U.S. Foreign Policy, 1914–1984* (Aix-en-Provence, 1985), 31–40; and Louis L. Gerson, *The Hyphenate in Recent American Politics and Diplomacy* (Lawrence, Kans., 1964), 70–2.

55 Morton Tenzer, "The Jews," in O'Grady, ed., *Immigrants' Influence on Wilson's Peace Policies,* 297. See also Henry L. Feingold, *Zion in America: The Jewish Experience from Colonial Times to the Present* (New York, 1974), 83–95. For the role of the Yiddish press, see Joseph Rappaport, "Jewish Immigrants and World War I: A Study of American Yiddish Press Reactions," Ph.D. diss., Columbia University, 1951.

Northern Europeans were relatively insulated from pressures for conformity before 1917 because of their greater assimilation and acceptability, which explains why the lack of enthusiasm for the Allied cause by Norwegians and Swedes in the United States did not create more of a backlash. In part their advocacy of neutrality stemmed from their traditional Republicanism, the isolationism of rural and small-town midwesterners, and sympathy for the plight of German Americans in this region. Many were members of the Nonpartisan League and suspected that eastern financiers and industrialists were conspiring with British capitalists for American entry into the war. The Swedish-American press was more openly pro-German, at least initially, and was outspoken in its condemnation of Russia. Swedish Lutheran ministers felt an affinity with their German counterparts who lived in the homeland of Martin Luther, and Swedish Americans resented increasing anti-hyphenism. In Iowa, for example, they reacted bitterly to the unilateral proclamation of the governor forbidding public worship in a foreign tongue. Half of the Norwegian Americans in Congress voted against the declaration of war, and in a 1939 survey by the Works Progress Administration in North Dakota, 105 first-generation Norwegians out of 121 responded that they had opposed American entry into the war.[56] The Dutch-American press also initially printed anti-British and pro-German statements, although it shifted to the Allied side by 1917.

If Swedish and Norwegian Americans could advocate neutrality without triggering recrimination, the same could not be said of German Americans. Although German immigrants had heretofore enjoyed considerable prestige in the United States, the image of Germany as autocratic, militaristic, and expansionist grew after the turn of the century. After 1914 German Americans were increasingly viewed with suspicion, an image strengthened by the chauvinistic support of the fatherland and denunciation of England by the National German-American Alliance and the German-American press. By 1915 the submarine issue was creating fear and revulsion among Americans. Following the sinking of the *Lusitania*,

56 For Norwegian Americans, see Jon Wefald, *A Voice of Protest: Norwegians in American Politics, 1890–1917* (Northfeld, Minn., 1971), 73–8; Andersen, *Rough Road to Glory*, 127–46; Lowell J. Soike, *Norwegian Americans and the Politics of Dissent, 1880–1924* (Northfeld, Minn., 1991), 155–97; and Odd S. Lovoll, "North Dakota's Norwegian-Language Press Views World War I, 1914–1917," *North Dakota Quarterly* 39 (winter 1971): 73–84. For Swedish Americans, see Sture Lindmark, *Swedish America, 1914–1932: Studies in Ethnicity with Emphasis on Illinois and Minnesota* (Uppsala, 1971), 64–78; and George M. Stephenson, "The Attitude of Swedish Americans Toward the World War," *Proceedings of the Mississippi Valley Historical Association* 10 (1918–19): 79–94.

for example, one journal compared the event with the crucifixion of Christ as one of the most perfidious in history.[57]

The German-American population by this time exceeded eight million, with the two-million-member Alliance the largest ethnic organization in the United States. Despite this seeming strength, however, the reactions of German Americans before the war stemmed less from chauvinism than from a perceived weakness and defensiveness. The migration from Germany was an exceedingly diverse one, diminishing markedly after the turn of the century, and the second generation was assimilating rapidly. Several historians have argued that German-American assertiveness was a means of unifying the ethnic group, even to the point of arguing German supremacy and cultural superiority.[58] German Americans considered the Prohibition movement a social and cultural attack on them. They also felt that the defense of German Americans as an ethnic group was a necessary counterweight to Anglo-American cultural and political influences, especially after Anglophile sentiments mounted after 1914.

There also was a considerable difference in the tone of the German-American press and what was being advocated. Calls for American neutrality in 1915 and 1916 were not dissimilar to mainstream public opinion a year earlier, and advocacy of a ban on passenger travel by Americans on armed merchant ships, an embargo on shipments of arms to the belligerents, and a ban on loans to the warring countries also had considerably broader support. The Hitchcock bill before Congress in 1914 to place an embargo on munitions had a chance of passing, as did the Gore-McLemore resolutions the following year calling for a passenger ban. The United States had, in fact, embargoed the shipment of munitions to Mexico in 1913, and Norway, Sweden, Denmark, the Netherlands, Italy, and Spain all imposed an embargo on such shipments. Opposition by the Wilson administration, however, doomed these proposals for disengagement from the European conflict.

It is arguable that these actions, more than anything else, would have benefited ethnic minorities and even resulted in preserving American neutrality, although this assertion must be balanced against the probable consequences to the United States of a negotiated peace or a German victory.

---

57 Andrew P. Yox, "The Fall of the German-American Community: Buffalo, 1914–1919," in William Pencak, Selma Berrol, and Randall M. Miller, eds., *Immigration to New York* (Philadelphia, 1991), 135. Frederick C. Luebke, *Bonds of Loyalty: German-Americans and World War I* (DeKalb, Ill., 1974), remains the best overall study.

58 See, esp., Andrew P. Yox, "Bonds of Community: Buffalo's German Element, 1853–1871," *New York History* 66 (Apr. 1985), 142, 149–50; and David W. Detjen, *The Germans in Missouri, 1900–1918: Prohibition, Neutrality, and Assimilation* (Columbia, Mo., 1985), 180.

Following the resumption of unlimited submarine warfare by Germany, however, the issue was joined. A Philadelphia woman later recalled how, before the war, the beer wagons of German-American brewers in her city had an American flag on one side and a German one on the other. "My mother took me to the window," she recalled, "when the U.S. declared war on Germany and told me to look well at those flags on that big wagon; that I would never see them together again. It truly was the end of an era."[59]

As was the case with German Americans, Irish Americans were mobilized by increasing anti-hyphenism and found their influence and reputation diminished by an increasingly narrow definition of patriotism and loyalty. President Wilson was angered during the 1916 election campaign because of increasingly sharp attacks by Irish-American nationalists. After Jeremiah O'Leary, an Irish-American leader who opposed Wilson's reelection, sent him an intemperate telegram predicting his defeat, Wilson replied that he "would feel deeply mortified to have you or anyone like you vote for me. Since you have access to many disloyal Americans and I have not, I will ask you to convey this message to them."[60] Irish Americans were politically important in eastern cities, but the strident anti-British and pro-German statements of the Clan-na-Gael, a radical Irish-American organization, and other nationalists alienated most Americans. The Clan-na-Gael was supported by only a minority of Irish Americans, but many were antagonized by Wilson's support of the anti-clerical Carranza regime in Mexico, and the entire ethnic community was outraged by the ruthless suppression of the Easter Rebellion in Ireland in 1916 by the British and by the subsequent execution of nationalist leaders, including Roger Casement. Wilson's refusal to protest Casement's death sentence was particularly galling to these groups.[61]

The loyalties of socialists also were increasingly scrutinized by Congress and by preparedness advocates, and, although the dominance of the Nonpartisan League in its area of influence in the Midwest protected it somewhat from attacks on its socialist platform, southern and eastern European immigrants were increasingly depicted as being malleable and particularly receptive to radical ideas. Aliens, it was charged, were primarily responsible for the dissemination of such ideas in America. Opposition to the In-

59 Quoted in Alfred Bergdoll, "The Curse of the Bergdoll Gold: A Biography of Grover C. Bergdoll," MS, box 4, Bergdoll family papers, Balch Institute, Philadelphia.
60 Quoted in Dean R. Esslinger, "American German and Irish Attitudes Toward Neutrality, 1914–1917: A Study of Catholic Minorities," *Catholic Historical Review* 53 (July 1967): 211.
61 The continuing Irish-American connection with Ireland is well outlined in Thomas E. Hachey, "Irish Republicanism Yesterday and Today: The Dilemma of Irish Americans," in Winston A. Van Horne and Thomas V. Tonnesen, eds., *Ethnicity and War* (Madison, Wis., 1984), 150–73.

dustrial Workers of the World stimulated the growth of Americanization programs, and advocates of a literacy test incorporated further restrictions on immigrants into proposed legislation.[62]

The visibility of immigrants in strikes and the collective organization of workers in immigrant communities heightened apprehensions. A majority of American socialists, however, and almost all of the Socialist Party leadership continued to oppose the preparedness program and American entry into the war. Some immigrant socialists supported the Allies out of hopes for independence of their homelands or supported the Central Powers out of emotional or religious commitments, but the majority of ethnic socialists, unlike their counterparts in Europe (except Italy), continued to oppose American entry.[63] As Glenn Altschuler has pointed out, ethnicity posed a dilemma for socialists in a capitalist society. Ethnic and racial loyalties could erode class solidarity, but, on the other hand, they viewed Americanization in a capitalist system as simply a means of ensuring the docility of the workers.[64]

Minority-group pacifists, as might be expected, also generally opposed the war. Moravians and Schwenkfelders had abandoned pacifism by this time, but Mennonite pacifism had been reinvigorated by migration from Russia in the 1870s, as well as by a more organized dissemination of pacifist ideas by the church press, Sunday schools, and Bible conferences. Membership in the peace movement, however, did not necessarily mean sympathy for ethnic and racial minorities. David Starr Jordan, for example, opposed both imperialism and American entry into World War I but was a firm believer in the inferiority of non-Anglo-Saxons.[65]

African Americans and Native Americans had differing views of the meaning of the war in Europe. Initially, most black Americans saw little relevance in the events overseas, although some favored France as a nation more favorable toward racial minorities. By 1917, however, many African Americans had internalized President Wilson's call for a world made safe

62 William Preston Jr., *Aliens and Dissenters: Federal Suppression of Radicals, 1903–1933* (New York, 1966), 45, 74–6, 80–7.

63 David A. Shannon, *The Socialist Party of America: A History* (Chicago, 1967), 82–9; Paul L. Murphy, *World War I and the Origin of Civil Liberties in the United States* (New York, 1979), 53–7; and David Montgomery, "Nationalism, American Patriotism, and Class Consciousness Among Immigrant Workers in the United States in the Epoch of World War I," in Dirk Hoerder, ed., *"Struggle a Hard Battle": Essays on Working-Class Immigrants* (DeKalb, Ill., 1986), 327–51.

64 Glenn C. Altschuler, *Race, Ethnicity, and Class in American Social Thought, 1865–1919* (Arlington Heights, Ill., 1982), 59–60.

65 Ralph Henry Gabriel, *The Course of American Democratic Thought,* 2d ed. (New York, 1956), 384–5. See also Paul Crook, "War as Genetic Disaster? The First World War Debate over the Eugenics of Warfare," *War & Society* 8 (May 1990): 47–70.

for democracy and could see the relevance to their own situation and for black peoples everywhere. "This war," declared W. E. B. DuBois, "is an End, and, a Beginning. Never again will darker people of the world occupy just the place they have before."[66] Most African Americans heeded his call to "close ranks" behind the war effort. Native American attitudes were complicated by the insistence of some on the independent status of Indian nations, particularly among the Iroquois, and by confusion over the questions of citizenship and susceptibility to the draft and of the desirability of participating in a "white man's war." In most cases, however, there was support once the United States entered the war, with resistance confined to bands most isolated from tribal and white influences or reacting to ongoing factional disputes.[67]

With the exception of Native Americans, the loyalties of ethnic and racial minorities were being increasingly monitored by the Wilson administration, with the president moving considerably closer to an anti-hyphenate, pro-preparedness position. As a younger man, Woodrow Wilson had made derogatory comments about southern and eastern Europeans out of fears that ethnic and racial tensions would fragment the nation and eclipse the broader national interest. Subsequently, his attitudes toward these ethnic groups moderated, and by 1914 his deepest antipathies were toward African Americans and Asians. Initially, Wilson advocated neutrality in part out of fear of ethnic and racial conflict if the United States entered the war, as well as concern over the repression a wartime situation would bring. He continued to defend the idea of asylum and to oppose a literacy test, although his criticism of hyphenated Americans deepened by 1915; his growing belief that group loyalties were not compatible with loyalty to the nation both mirrored and influenced the national mood.[68]

This most unmilitary of presidents now embraced military preparedness, and during his years in the White House he was to preside over a number of armed interventions. Although the thrust of the preparedness movement was undeniably defensive, Wilson and some other preparedness advocates had a broader purpose in mind. For some, as John Chambers has ob-

---

66 Quoted in Arthur E. Barbeau and Florette Henri, *The Unknown Soldiers: Black American Troops in World War I* (Philadelphia, 1974), 7. See also Francis L. Broderick, *W. E. B. DuBois: Negro Leader in a Time of Crisis* (Stanford, Calif., 1959), 106–12, and David Levering Lewis, *W. E. B. DuBois: Biography of a Race, 1868–1919* (New York, 1993), 503–30.
67 White, "The American Army and the Indian," 81–2. See also Russel Lawrence Barsh, "American Indians and the Great War," *Ethnohistory* 38 (summer 1991): 276–303.
68 The best discussion of Wilson's attitudes toward immigrants is in Hans Vought, "Division and Reunion: Woodrow Wilson, Immigration, and the Myth of American Unity," *Journal of American Ethnic History* 13 (spring 1994): 24–50.

served, "the largely unspoken rationale for a larger army was to support a more active U.S. role in the world."[69] The goals would be a democratized world and American economic expansion.

These ambitions had singular roots in the American past; a comparison of the Canadian experience during this period, however, helps sharpen the focus on American developments. An obvious difficulty in comparing the two is the earlier entrance of Canada into World War I, but several broad and continuing differences are illuminating – the presence in Canada of two founding ethnic groups, the British connection, and the nature and timing of the migration from southern and eastern Europe.

Tensions between English and French Canadians were continuing, especially because of Anglophone domination of Quebec, but the crisis that developed over the Military Service Act of 1917, which imposed conscription, was more the result of mounting discriminatory attitudes and policies than an endemic dilemma. French Canadians did not internalize the obligation for imperial defense or glory in the accomplishments and conquests of the British Empire, as did most English Canadians, but were initially supportive in successive crises if the crises were couched in terms of nationalism. Quebecois joined the military effort to put down the Northwest Rebellions and the Indian uprising of 1885 but were alienated by the trial and execution of the métis leader Louis Riel, which heightened increasing tensions over the linguistic and educational rights of Francophones in the western territories. French Canadians were in the Canadian contingent to South Africa, although as the war dragged on ill feelings mounted, street riots broke out in Montreal, and a nationalist movement led by Henri Bourassa developed.[70]

The militia structure in Canada, modeled on Britain's, was increasingly Anglophone in composition, especially in the upper ranks, with English as the sole language of command. This situation was exacerbated by the appointment in 1911 of Colonel Sam Hughes as minister of militia, a man of pronounced anti-French Canadian and anti-Catholic prejudices. Initially, French Canadians were almost as unanimous in supporting the Allies as

69 John W. Chambers II, *To Raise an Army: The Draft Comes to Modern America* (New York, 1987), 112.
70 Most English Canadians supported the British, although Carman Miller has shown that many Canadian farmers sympathized with the Boers as pious farmers, and some Protestant clergymen, the left wing of the labor movement, most German Canadians, and some Irish Canadians opposed the war. See Carman Miller, "English-Canadian Opposition to the South African War as Seen Through the Press," *Canadian Historical Review* 55 (Dec. 1974): 422–38. The broader issues of the period are best discussed in Robert Craig Brown and Ramsay Cook, *Canada, 1896–1921: A Nation Transformed* (Toronto, 1974).

were English Canadians, but discriminatory policies and anger over restrictions on the French language in the Ontario educational system resulted in an extremely negative reaction in Quebec when conscription was imposed in 1917. Anti-conscription rallies and riots ensued, leading to a lasting heritage of bitterness in the province over this issue.[71] The fact of two founding groups did not inevitably divide Canada, but the developing heritage of conflict over hegemony produced a significantly different situation from that in the United States. Discrimination against French-Canadian military units contrasted sharply in Canada with enthusiasm for and encouragement of military units by other ethnic groups, reflecting the British heritage in this regard. Canadians were especially enthusiastic about Orange and Scottish Highlander units, with a number of the latter formed in the late nineteenth and early twentieth centuries. In 1914 several battalions of the Canadian Expeditionary Force were given Scottish designations.[72] Irish-Canadian units also were popular. In Montreal in 1916, for example, the Department of Militia readily gave permission for the formation of the Irish Canadian Rangers, who wore shamrocks on their caps and a harp on their collars; "Irish descent" was a prerequisite for joining.[73]

In sharp contrast to the situation in the United States, Irish Canadians were almost unanimously supportive of Canadian entrance into the war on the side of the Allies. The roots of this difference are historical. In upper Canada, the nineteenth-century migration from Ireland was more Protestant than Catholic and primarily rural, with discrimination relatively mild and upward mobility significant. Donald Akenson has suggested that the urban, ghettoized nature of the Irish-American migration helps to explain why Irish nationalism flourished in the United States but not in Canada.[74] By the early twentieth century, most Irish Canadians were integrated into

---

71 Desmond Morton, "French Canada and War, 1868–1917: The Military Background to the Conscription Crisis of 1917," in Granatstein and Cuff, eds., *War and Society in North America,* 84–103; R. H. Roy, "Conscription and Voluntarism: The Canadian Experience," in Russell F. Weigley, ed., *New Dimensions in Military History: An Anthology* (San Rafael, Calif., 1975), 203–23; and Young, *Minorities and the Military,* 96–108.
72 George F. G. Stanley, "The Scottish Military Tradition," in W. Stanford Reid, ed., *The Scottish Tradition in Canada* (Toronto, 1976), 150–1.
73 Robin B. Burns, "Who Shall Separate Us? The Montreal Irish and the Great War," in Robert O'Driscoll and Lorna Reynolds, eds., *The Untold Story: The Irish in Canada,* 2 vols. (Toronto, 1988), 2:571–2.
74 Donald H. Akenson, "Ontario: Whatever Happened to the Irish?" in Donald H. Akenson, ed., *Canadian Papers in Rural History,* 10 vols. (Gananoque, Ont., 1982), 3:204–56. Akenson's conclusions are supported by Gordon Darroch and Michael Ornstein, "Ethnicity and Class, Transitions over a Decade: Ontario, 1861–1871," *Historical Papers* (continued by the *Journal of the Canadian Historical Association*) (1984): 111–37.

the social and political structure; they were also emphasizing the British connection to distinguish themselves from southern and eastern European Catholics and from French Canadians.

In Montreal, there was almost unanimous Irish enthusiasm for the war; only one Irish Canadian publicly expressed disaffection, and that was in the wake of the Easter Rebellion of 1916. The heavily Irish constituency of St. Ann's supported the Union government and its decision for conscription in 1917, although there was less enthusiasm in the working-class districts of the city and support for home rule for Ireland.[75] Participation by Catholics in the war effort was even more striking in Toronto, both in terms of enlistment for service and of organizational activities on the home front. To some extent, this may have been for increased acceptability, but, as Mark McGowan has shown, the respectability of Toronto's Catholic population, at least English-speaking Catholics, was long-standing, and Toronto Catholics' enthusiasm showed obvious signs of dedication to the nation and to the empire. The *Catholic Register* urged its readers to defend the empire above all, "so effectually that 'Pax Britannica' may rejoice the world for another half century." When Father Michael Moyna removed the British Ensign from the coffin of a soldier, he was immediately censured by the Church hierarchy.[76]

Although most German Canadians came from areas outside Germany and there was little loyalty among them to Imperial Germany, the reputation of Germans, as in the United States, went from one of considerable respectability to one of suspicion and hostility. In Canada there was the added initial fear of an invasion from the United States that would be led by German Americans and aided by Canada's Germans and immigrants from the Austro-Hungarian Empire.[77] Surprisingly, however, only 1,192 Germans were interned during the war, compared with 5,954 classified as Austro-Hungarians, most of whom were Ukrainians in the Canadian west. To some extent internment in western Canada was of the destitute and unemployed, but there also was considerable hostility toward Ukrainian immigrants, much more so than there was south of the border.

A policy of peopling the Canadian prairies had led to a substantial population of southern and eastern Europeans in the west, although these groups were less important politically than in the United States. The war

75 Burns, "Who Shall Separate Us?" 571–83.
76 Mark G. McGowan, "'To Share in the Burdens of Empire: Toronto's Catholics and the Great War, 1914–1918," in Mark G. McGowan and Brian P. Clarke, eds., *Catholics at the "Gathering Place": Historical Essays on the Archdiocese of Toronto, 1841–1991* (Toronto, 1993), 177–207.
77 John Herd Thompson, *Ethnic Minorities During Two World Wars* (Ottawa, 1991), 5.

brought hostility toward all "enemy aliens," although the focus in the west was particularly against Ukrainians, a substantial population that had migrated recently and was communal in organization. Many Ukrainians were reservists in their homeland, and in 1914 Bishop Nicolas Budka issued a pastoral letter urging support of Franz Joseph and the return of reservists to fight for the empire. Although Budka retracted this request shortly afterward, the impression of disloyalty remained. Also, many Ukrainians had been vocal in resisting the abolition of bilingual schools in Manitoba (later also in Saskatchewan), a protest that was not well received in western Canada.[78]

Suspicions were heightened by the fact that Ukrainians were a leading foreign-language group in the Canadian socialist movement. Conflict with the Anglo-Saxon leadership of the Socialist Party led to the establishment of a separate Ukrainian Social Democratic Federation and the formation of the Canadian Social Democratic Party, in which Ukrainian socialists played a major role.[79] These activities invited repression of all socialist or nationalist activities in the west, sometimes with British involvement or direction, as when British officials, in conjunction with the Canadian government, suppressed the Gadar Party of Indian nationalists.[80] Although Canada, in its desire to people the west, had given exemption from military service to groups such as the Doukhobors, Hutterites, and Mennonites, wartime hysteria led to considerable repression against them, including loss of the right to vote.[81]

In Canada the war would bring the repressive War Measures Act, the Wartime Elections Act, and, in their wake, the Winnipeg General Strike of 1919. In both countries, even fervently expressed loyalty by immigrants not from Central Power countries, which brought increased acceptability in 1917 and 1918, would not protect them after the war was over. In the United States, however, in the midst of the 100 percent Americanism and

78 Joseph A. Boudreau, "Western Canada's 'Enemy Aliens' in World War One," *Alberta Historical Review* 12 (winter 1964): 6.
79 Donald Avery, "Divided Loyalties: The Ukrainian Left and the Canadian State," in Lubomyr Luciuk and Stella Hryniuk, eds., *Canada's Ukrainians: Negotiating an Identity* (Toronto, 1991), 273.
80 Howard Palmer, "Ethnicity and Politics in Canada: 1867–Present," in Valeria Gennaro Lerda, ed., *From "Melting Pot" to Multiculturalism: The Evolution of Ethnic Relations in the United States and Canada* (Rome, 1990), 182.
81 Thomas P. Socknat, *Witness Against War: Pacifism in Canada, 1900–1945* (Toronto, 1987), 74–9. For the military experiences of African Canadians and Native Canadians, see James W. St. G. Walker, "Race and Recruitment in World War I: Enlistment of Visible Minorities in the Canadian Expeditionary Force," *Canadian Historical Review* 70 (Mar. 1989): 1–26; Robin W. Winks, *The Blacks in Canada: A History* (New Haven, Conn., 1971), 312–20; James Dempsey, "The Indians and World War One," *Alberta History* 31 (summer 1983): 1–8; and Janice Summerby, *Native Soldiers: Foreign Battlefields* (Ottawa, 1993), 5–19.

growing war hysteria following American entry into the war, Roger Baldwin, a young social worker and conscientious objector, founded the National Civil Liberties Union, subsequently renamed the American Civil
Liberties Union, in defense of free speech and opinion against all public
and private attempts to abridge it. If enforced conformity during wartime
has been an American trait, an irreverent attitude toward authority, from
Thomas Paine's to Henry David Thoreau's to Daniel Ellsberg's, has also
been an enduring American characteristic.

6

Religion and War in Imperial Germany

GANGOLF HÜBINGER

In the early evening hours of August 1, 1914, when news of German mobilization was spreading, Kaiser Wilhelm II surprised the jubilant crowd
that had gathered outside his Berlin residence, the *Stadtschloss,* by delivering
an unusual speech:

From the bottom of my heart, I thank you for the love and loyalty you are showing. In the struggle that is now impending, I will recognize no parties any more
among my people. There will only be Germans among us now. And whichever of
the parties actually opposed me in the course of the past battle of opinion, I for-
give them all. The only thing that is important now is that we keep together like
brothers, then God will help the German people to triumph.

Accompanied by the chimes of the bells of the Berlin cathedral, the
crowd sang the hymn "Now Thank We All Our God."[1] Making reference
to God in case of war had been a normal habit among German princes,
especially among the Protestant ones. When the Battle of Sedan was over
and Napoleon III had been taken prisoner, Wilhelm II's grandfather, the
Prussian king and later German emperor Wilhelm I, hailed the German
victory over France with the following words: "What a turn [of events] by
divine providence." Both of the foregoing quotations illustrate the traditional Prussian notion of the state as a unity of throne and altar; however,
there is a big difference as regards the intent and impact of these religious
phrases. In 1871 most Protestants claimed the unification of the German
Reich exclusively for themselves. Historians constructed a direct line of
development from the Reformation to the foundation of the Reich, from
Luther to Bismarck. In place of "divine providence" (*Gottes Fügung*), the
national Protestants preferred the phrase "divine guidance" (*Gottes
Führung*). On Sedan Commemoration Day, which had become the na-

1 Quoted in Gunther Mai, *Das Ende des Kaiserreichs* (Munich 1987), 13–14.

125

tional holiday of the German Reich, this modified slogan – "What a turn [of events] by divine guidance!" – was used as a decoration for the Brandenburg Gate. The political symbols, the festivities, and the monuments were manifestations of a mentality that denied full citizenship to Catholics as well as to the nonreligious Social Democrats. In the course of the Kulturkampf, and with the help of Bismarck's antisocialist laws, these two groups were declared "enemies of the Reich" and thus were excluded from a nation defined in mainly Protestant terms. A civil religion of the kind that after the Civil War united and integrated American society could not develop in Imperial Germany. To this extent, the German tradition differs radically from American tradition. Germany remained, in spite of the secularization and industrialization that took place, a religiously deeply divided country.[2] So when Wilhelm II, on August 1, 1914, demanded "total" mobilization from his "subjects," he meant to address not only the Social Democrats, who for a long time had been vigorously persecuted by the political establishment, but also all those portions of the Reich's population that had so far been given the cold shoulder for religious reasons. The question that arises here is: How great was – as seen from a religious point of view – the readiness in a fragmented German society to wage a war that from the outset was not a cabinet war but, as a national war that mobilized the masses, a total war?

"Anticipating war?" This question was asked in the historical literature on Wilhelmine Germany as early as 1986, with special regard also to the concept of "religion" as a determining cultural factor.[3] The question dealt with in this book has a somewhat different tenor in that it is rendered much more sharply: "Anticipating total war?" The historian Roger Chickering is right in maintaining that the ideal concept of "total war" needs to be specified if we want to differentiate nineteenth- and twentieth-century wars from the type of war represented, for example, by the Thirty Years' War. He defines modern total war as "the product of a vast complex of reciprocal changes, which comprised, among others, demographic growth, technological innovation, industrial integration, social conflict, the redefinition of political society, the expansion of public power."[4] Accordingly, the wars of industrial mass societies in modern times acquired a new quality. And

2 Gangolf Hübinger, "Confessionalism," in Roger Chickering, ed., *Imperial Germany: A Historiographical Companion* (Westport, Conn., 1996).
3 Martin Greschat, "Krieg und Kriegsbereitschaft im deutschen Protestantismus," in Jost Dülffer und Karl Holl, eds., *Bereit zum Krieg: Kriegsmentalität im wilhelminischen Deutschland 1890–1914* (Göttingen, 1986), 33–55; August-Hermann Leugers, "Einstellung zu Krieg und Frieden im deutschen Katholizismus vor 1914," ibid., 54–73.
4 See Roger Chickering's essay (Chapter 1) in this book.

along with this, there was a change also in the cultural patterns of inter-preting war.

Religion often claims to be a final arbiter with respect to the ethical im-plications and legitimation of power struggles. Consequently, two precon-ditions must be satisfied before one can really speak – beyond the tradition-al sacralization of war[5] – of a social mobilization for "total war."

1. The distinction between ethics and politics is erased. Religion then aims at rendering ethical the power struggle between modern nation-states. As a con-sequence, nationalism is assigned religious functions.
2. The distinction between the individual and society is erased. As a conse-quence, religion furthers the *Volksgemeinschaft* (organic national community) and works toward a militarization of man's conscience and of social life, put-ting both into the service of such a community.

From a statistical perspective, religious affiliations remained extremely stable in both the Reich and in the individual German states. In 1910 the German Reich encompassed 40 million Protestants (61.6 percent of the total population), 23.8 million Catholics (36.7 percent), 615,000 Jews (0.5 percent), and half a million people who belonged to other religious groups. The same proportions apply to Prussia, which accounted for 60 percent of the entire population of the Reich. In Baden and Bavaria, the two states that represented the greatest political and cultural counterweight to Prussian hegemony, there were twice as many Catholics as Protestants. But Protestants were nonetheless significantly overrepresented among the economic and political elites of these states, a fact that led to bitter contro-versies among the members of the two largest churches. Groups not affili-ated with a recognized church played a statistically insignificant role in the religious context of Wilhelmine Germany. Nonetheless, the rise of free-thinking and sectarian movements among the middle classes, such as the readers of Paul de Lagarde, provided the basis for a more aggressive type of nationalism.

In terms of content and method we may differentiate among three lev-els on which religion was involved in the transmission of ideas of war through agents such as the established churches, independent theological writers and journalists, and either large politicized associations of a confes-sional type or small sectarian societies.

---

5 See the exemplary regional study by Werner Blessing, "Gottesdienst als Säkularisierung? Zu Krieg, Nation und Politik im bayerischen Protestantismus des 19. Jahrhunderts," in Wolfgang Schieder, ed., *Religion und Gesellschaft im 19. Jahrhundert* (Stuttgart, 1993), 216–53.

1. *The first level might be termed the religious interpretation.* This rubric refers to the activities of theologians, whether bishops, professors, or pastors. Sources of primary importance include pastoral letters, scholarly treatises, and sermons.[6]
2. *The second level concerns the cultural preservation of belligerent feelings and war experiences in the context of the controversies among the various religious circles.* This refers to the activities of the religious parties and their presses, as well as to the way in which these parties exercised control on a symbolic level through festivities, memorial days, rites, symbols and icons, and monuments. The two leading mass organizations opposing each other in this context were the Protestant League (Evangelische Bund) and the People's Association for Catholic Germany (Volksverein für das katholische Deutschland).
3. *The third level refers to the way religion helps to spread a war-oriented, belligerent mentality and attitude in everyday life.* This includes activities ranging from war games among high school bible circle members to the unopposed incorporation of denominational youth groups into the military-oriented governmental "youth welfare" program.[7]

There were some Protestant clergymen who went as far as setting up so-called boys' battalions, and the Prussian War Ministry felt called on to stop them in their eagerness.[8] And there were some professors of theology who stood up to legitimize the right of war.[9] However, neither in the everyday religious life of the man in the street nor in the sphere of university teaching did all this have an effect that could in any way be termed "total" in the sense of erasing the distinction between ethics and politics. Rather, the social driving forces of a militarization of public thinking to such an extent that one can speak of "anticipating total war" developed in the "intermediate" public sphere between popular mentality and theological reflection – in other words, by the control exercised over the political public by denominational associations and their press media, inasmuch as these associations helped to broaden the stream, or intensify the impact, of the nationalist agitation-minded leagues. There are good reasons indeed why research

---

6 For some examples in this context, see Karl Hammer, *Deutsche Kriegstheologie 1870–1918* (Munich, 1971). The leading denominational encyclopedias – fully in line with the classical practice among European nation-states – adopted the argument that war must be seen as an unrenounceable instrument in the service of state policy, which means that war can be interpreted theologically as representing anything between a punishment by God and an act of political ultima ratio. Cf. "Krieg" and "Kriegsrecht," in *Staatslexikon,* 5 vols. (Freiburg im Breisgau, 1894), 3:863–93 (Catholic), and "Krieg," in *Die Religion in Geschichte und Gegenwart* (Tübingen, 1912), 3:1770–80.

7 The militarization of education is stressed – certainly in a quite one-sided manner at times – by Christa Berg, ed., *Handbuch der deutschen Bildungsgeschichte,* vol. 4: *1870–1918: Von der Reichsgründung bis zum Ende des Ersten Weltkrieges* (Munich, 1991), 501ff.

8 See Klaus Saul, "Der Kampf um die Jugend zwischen Volksschule und Kaserne: Ein Beitrag zur 'Jugendpflege' im Wilhelminischen Reich 1890–1914," *Militärgeschichtliche Mitteilungen* 9 (1971): 126.

9 Ferdinand Kattenbusch, *Das sittliche Recht des Krieges* (Giessen, 1906); see also Greschat, "Krieg und Kriegsbereitschaft," 43–4.

addressing the relationship between nationalism, imperialism, world politics, and war mentality has come to place new weight now on the rising middle classes and the intelligentsia, rather than on a more narrowly conceived economic interpretation.[10] The historian Hans-Ulrich Wehler calls the nationalism of this epoch a political religion that worked as a diversion from, or counterbalance to, the crises generated by modernization.[11] For Eric J. Hobsbawm, "the alliance of nationalism and religion is obvious enough."[12] Dieter Langewiesche provides an analysis of the dialectics of participation and aggression that pervade and characterize all types of nationalism even before World War I. This dialectic works in two ways: toward homogeneity and toward exclusion, thus defining the prevailing images of "self" and "other." The civil values of the nineteenth century, whether liberal or conservative in nature, got discarded and lost as nationalism became more radical. The result was a populism that, in the years after World War I, became the source from which the fascist movements in particular could draw their support.[13]

In this chapter I focus on the extent to which the radical nationalism of the Wilhelmine era – from which a total war mentality later developed – was actively supported by religious communities.

To answer this question, one finds ample material in connection with the Protestant League for Preserving German-Protestant Interests (Evangelischer Bund zur Wahrung der deutsch-protestantischen Interessen). The league was founded in 1886 as a parallel organization to the Pan-German League (Alldeutscher Verband). Anchored in the same liberal-conservative constituency as the latter, the Protestant League pursued a radicalization of nationalist middle-class ideology and grew to a membership of half a million. And yet the Pan-German League – also a "distinctly Protestant phenomenon"[14] – proved unable to attract more than approximately 20,000 members.[15] At the turn of the century the Protestant League issued an extensively illustrated two-volume review of Protestant achievements in the political, economic, and cultural fields. The editor of this review was Carl Werckshagen, who tried, in this context, to extend the prevailing historical

---

10 Wolfgang J. Mommsen, *Der autoritäre Nationalstaat* (Frankfurt am Main, 1990), 184.
11 Hans-Ulrich Wehler, *Deutsche Gesellschaftsgeschichte* (Munich, 1995), vol. 3.
12 Eric J. Hobsbawm, *Nations and Nationalism Since 1780: Programme, Myth, Reality,* 2d ed. (Cambridge, 1992), 124, 150.
13 Dieter Langewiesche, *Nationalismus im 19. und 20. Jahrhundert: Zwischen Partizipation und Aggression* (Bonn, 1994).
14 Roger Chickering, *We Men Who Feel Most German: A Cultural Study of the Pan-German League, 1886–1914* (Boston, 1984), 138.
15 See Gangolf Hübinger, *Kulturprotestantismus und Politik: Zum Verhältnis von Liberalismus und Protestantismus im wilhelminischen Deutschland* (Tübingen, 1994), 52ff.

concept of a patriotic German nation, developed from the spirit of the Reformation, in such a way as to connect it directly to imperialist world politics. In the introduction to the first volume he wrote: "But our review will have to reach far beyond the limits given by our mother tongue and by the boundaries of the peoples that belong to our race, in order to show how Protestantism has become the main supporter of spiritual culture in the world, and how it carries as a colonizing power the gospel of the beatifying evangelical truths into even the most remote regions of the world."[16] In this way a religious nationalism systematically gained ground in Imperial Germany. It was promoted, from the outset, by liberal Protestants and became increasingly accepted by conservative Protestants, who had their roots in a quite different tradition. In his *Deutsche Geschichte* (German history), Thomas Nipperdey characterizes this increasingly belligerent religious nationalism, which he calls *Kirchennationalismus,* and its impact on German political culture as follows:

The notion of throne and altar was expanded to form a trinity of throne, nation and altar; the pathos of obedience to the king and the state now also included the nation, affirmation of the state developed into a glorification of the nation. In other words: Since nationalism had now become established and right-wing, it could and had to be adopted also by the conservative-minded Established Church. And more than any other institution the Church was in a position to lend meaning to the newly created Reich. State Protestantism thus became imperial Protestantism (*Reichsprotestantismus*).[17]

A nationalism that in this way assumed the functions of a political religion remained alien to Catholics and Jews. Only on the periphery did a comparable nationalist Catholic movement develop in the form of the German Association (DeutscheVereinigung). For the German Association, it certainly meant more than just performing an obligatory Byzantine act when it greeted the emperor on his birthday with the following homage: "Our Emperor's dictum, 'Germany to lead the world,' . . . will never become true unless each individual will show the same sense of duty and will work with the same selfless devotion for our nation as our beloved Emperor, who now enters his fifty-second year, has always done."[18] Such utterances notwithstanding, the relationship of the churches to nationalistic creeds remained nonetheless asymmetric.

16 Carl Werckshagen, ed., *Der Protestantismus am Ende des 19. Jahrhunderts in Wort und Bild* (Berlin, 1900), 1:1–2.
17 Thomas Nipperdey, *Deutsche Geschichte 1866–1918*, vol. 1: *Arbeitswelt und Bürgergeist* (Munich, 1990), 488.
18 Emperor's birthday, in *Deutsche Wacht: Wochenschrift der Deutschen Vereinigung,* no. 3 (1910): 70.

Generally, a topic such as religion and war cannot be restricted to a comparison of two large denominational groups, for both these churches no doubt incorporated a modernistic as well as a modern-fundamentalist camp, with the latter, in turn, split up into a small pacifist and a certainly dominant militant wing. More important, Wilhelmine Germany was not so much the epoch of de-Christianization as one of a withdrawal of the established churches from public life.[19] It was the time of "vagabond religiosity," which included pacifist groups (as in the case of the Tolstoians[20]) but was characterized on the whole by a much stronger and growing bellicosity cast within the categories of national or racial (*religiös-völkische*) religion. These found expression, for example, in the cult of Paul de Lagarde, as Fritz Stern has pointed out in his important book on the politics of cultural despair.[21]

PROTESTANTISM AND CATHOLICISM: A COMPARISON

During the war against France in 1870–1, German Catholics and Protestants supported Prussian politics in patriotic solidarity. Moreover, both groups experienced the war fever of 1914. In the hectic phase of German foreign and colonial politics between 1905 and 1909, the Catholic Center Party (Zentrumspartei) gave up all reservations it had entertained in previous decades and began, under the leadership of Matthias Erzberger, to support the politics of unreserved armament pursued by the government. As regards the missionary activities of both churches, the predominant attitude was one that was well in conformity with official colonial politics. However, it is to be noted that on the Catholic side nothing existed like the ethical imperialism of Paul Rohrbach, a liberal ex-theologian who did not hesitate to interpret overseas colonization as an instrument of the world supremacy of Christ.[22] So here we have evidence that hints at asymmetries that existed between the two rivaling denominational camps – asymmetries, moreover, that seem to be significant. They may be summed up by the following thesis: For Catholicism, national and international politics were absolutely compatible, whereas in the Protestant main-

---

19 For an overview, see Kurt Nowak, "Kirche im Kaiserreich – Kampf um die Leitkultur," in *Geschichte des Christentums in Deutschland: Religion, Politik und Gesellschaft vom Ende der Aufklärung bis zur Mitte des 20. Jahrhunderts* (Munich, 1995), 149–204.

20 For more details, cf. Edith Hanke, *Prophet des Unmodernen: Leo N. Tolstoi als Kulturkritiker in der deutschen Diskussion der Jahrhundertwende* (Tübingen, 1993).

21 Fritz Stern, *The Politics of Cultural Despair: A Study in the Rise of the Germanic Ideology* (Berkeley, Calif., 1961).

22 For an overview of the differences between Protestantism and Catholicism, see Helmut W. Smith, *German Nationalism and Religious Conflict: Culture, Ideology, Politics, 1870–1914* (Princeton, N.J., 1995).

stream there was a tendency to dramatize the difference between national-ism and internationalism, with a view to stigmatizing Catholics as nonpa-triotic.

After 1908 at the latest, when the struggle between church and state had abated and one generally felt, furthermore, that the German Reich was be-coming increasingly isolated, the German Catholics decisively supported, on the occasion of their yearly assemblies (*Katholikentage*), the notion of a common readiness to defend the nation while dissociating themselves from Pan-German and German-racial agitation.[23] The People's Association for Catholic Germany also began to deal with colonial and naval politics in its civic educational work. Like the Catholic Center Party, the Volksverein also found it necessary to acquire colonies and secure them by military action for reasons that were based in the economic dynamics of modern industri-al nations. At the same time, however, the Volksverein also criticized in its pamphlets the "presumptuousness of militarism" that it believed to stand in the way of international understanding.[24] Such "delayed" nationalism and reserved militarism found no acceptance among the nationalistic Protestant associations. Quite often, Catholics were barred from membership in the veterans' associations (*Kriegervereine*).[25]

The Protestant League cheered the "Bülow bloc." This bloc consisted of conservatives as well as right-wing and left-wing liberals, as the realization of a Protestant coalition had been finally achieved – and by which they hoped to keep the Catholics and Social Democrats out of political power. As "a picture for every German" – for 20 pfennigs in miniature and for two (German) marks as a wall poster – the Protestant League sold a political-allegorical image imparting a fusion of religion and politics:

On this . . . print, Luther and Bismarck are shown below a gnarled oak tree as de-fenders of German honor, German faith, German power. The idea of a joint ren-dering of the two greatest Germans has been carried out so uniquely and beauti-

---

23 See Horst Gründer, *Christliche Mission und deutscher Imperialismus 1884–1914* (Paderborn, 1982); Walter Mogk, *Paul Rohrbach und das "Grössere Deutschland"* (Munich, 1972).

24 "For however heterogeneous we Germans may be in our thinking and beliefs, there is one thing in which we feel united: in our patriotism. [Stormy applause.] And if the necessity should ever arise – God forbid that this will happen! – , the "Wacht am Rhein" [guarding the Rhine] [vigorous ap-plause] will stand there united and as firmly and loyally as in the past, and not only [guarding] on the Rhine but also [guarding] along the Memel River as well and [guarding] on any shoreline on our German seas." The message of greeting from Switzerland also earned applause: "When Catholics as-semble, the meeting is international. [Applause.] But this speaks in no way against our patriotism. [Applause.]" Quotations taken from the welcoming speeches in *Verhandlungen der 55. Generalver-sammlung der Katholiken Deutschlands* (1908), 180, 182.

25 For more details, see Horstwalter Heitzer, *Der Volksverein für das katholische Deutschland im Kaiserreich 1890–1918* (Mainz, 1979), 224–7.

fully in this art print that it may well be considered to be a true gift to the German people.[26]

The Protestant League, with its nearly three thousand local groups, probably was the most effective disseminator of a radicalized middle-class nationalism, given the power it exercised in defining "Germanness." It was an organization that was as militant in its external relations as it was restrictive and exclusive in its internal approach.

To underpin and enhance this comparison of the two Christian denominations and their attitudes toward the war, let us take a look at the German Jews. In terms of number, their proportion of the population was small, amounting to only 1 percent. However, they were overrepresented in the propertied middle classes (*Besitzbürgertum*) and among the educated middle classes (*Bildungsbürgertum*), especially the free professions. In political terms, the Jews were finally granted their civil rights in Imperial Germany. In social terms, however, they were still denied promotion to higher-rank public offices, including military careers and the prestigious rank of reserve officer. Both wings – the liberal and the orthodox Jews – nonetheless showed a marked loyalty toward the Kaiser and the Reich. Considering their struggle for full assimilation, this loyalty of the Jews might have developed into national chauvinism had there not been widespread anti-Semitism, which was particularly dominant in the 1890s. This modern, new type of anti-Semitism, which differed from traditional anti-Judaism by its use of militant racist stereotypes, saw in the Jews a threat to national homogeneity. The Protestant-affiliated Associations of German Students also joined in the common Jew-baiting, even using slogans that advocated physical annihilation: "Wherever we look: Jewish or French influence. It is the task of the Christian-Germanic youth to eradicate all this because the future belongs to us."[27] In the modernization crisis of the late nineteenth century a cult of "Germandom," of Germanic ideals and the Nordic man, arose that assumed a religious quality and in fact became quite widespread among the educated. And part of the activism inherent in this new racial discourse was a new, pagan, quasi-religious self-definition of the belligerent German *Herrenmensch* (member of the master race).[28]

26 Margaret L. Anderson, "Windhorsts Erben: Konfessionalität und Interkonfessionalismus im politischen Katholizismus 1890–1918," in Winfried Becker and Rudolf Morsey, eds., *Christliche Demokratie in Europa* (Cologne, 1988), 87. As regards the instrumentalization of religion, see also Thomas Rohrkrämer, *Der Militarismus der "kleinen Leute": Die Kriegervereine im Deutschen Kaiserreich 1871–1914* (Munich, 1990), 203–14.

27 Several reprints in *Monatskorrespondenz des Evangelischen Bundes* 23 (1909): 167.

28 Diederich Hahn in his opening speech on the occasion of the 1881 Kyffhäuserfest (Kyffhäuser festival) held by the Associations of German Students, quoted from Norbert Kampe, *Studenten und*

RACIAL, NONDENOMINATIONAL RELIGIOUSNESS

A considerable potential for the development of aggressive racial attitudes accumulated outside the established churches in free, sectlike religious groups. What these groups tried to do was to set against the decadence of a bourgeois-capitalist culture the religious dedication with which the individual should sacrifice himself to his ethnic community as a whole. Max Maurenbrecher, the influential free-thinking preacher at the beginning of the twentieth century who in his writings tried to reconcile Marx and Nietzsche, socialism and nationalism, Germanness and Christianity, quit the Social Democratic Party in 1913 because he no longer could tolerate the party's stance on issues of military and foreign policy.[29] A religious cult was being made of Paul de Lagarde, whose *Deutsche Schriften* (German writings) helped to spread not only the idea of a Protestant national church but also the racial anti-Semitism of the educated middle classes. The influential Eugen Diederichs, a Jena publisher who remained an opponent of the Pan-German "new right" throughout World War I, made Lagarde the torch bearer of a mystically oriented religious literature that was expected to generate "a common emotion that will run through the entire body of the people."[30] Diederichs also published the writings of Arthur Bonus, an ex-clergyman of a Niederlausitz working-class parish who advocated a Germanic Christianity characterized by a national will to power.[31] Even in wide circles of liberal cultural Protestantism[32] there was a readiness to support the so-called "ideas of 1914"[33] in a manner that gave priority to a romantic-idealistic and totalizing view over and against the critical rationality of the Enlightenment.

"Judenfrage" im Deutschen Kaiserreich (Göttingen, 1988), 48. See also the various studies by Shulamit Volkov, *Jüdisches Leben und Antisemitismus im 19. und 20. Jahrhundert* (Munich, 1990), who interprets anti-Semitism as a "cultural code" of Wilhelmine society.

29 See Klaus von See, *Barbar, Germane, Arier: Die Suche nach der Identität der Deutschen* (Heidelberg, 1994).

30 "Confidential circular to our friends," Mannheim, July 1913; copy in the state library of Schleswig-Holstein, Kiel.

31 Quotation from *Die Kulturbewegung Deutschlands im Jahre 1913: Ein Verzeichnis der Neuerscheinungen des Verlages Eugen Diederichs* (Jena, 1913), 2. Cf. ibid.: "A *Volkstumsbewegung* must give us a conscious sense of race. England, because of the fact that it developed such a *Volkstumsbewegung*, must give us a conscious sense of race: racial sense, has acquired a big advantage, and we will not be able to compete with England for world dominance if we continue to bring to bear, one-sidedly, industrial power but lack inner concentration." The volume containing Paul de Lagarde's writings was published as *Deutscher Glaube, deutsches Vaterland, deutsche Bildung* (Jena, 1913).

32 Arthur Bonus, *Zur religiösen Krisis*, vol. 1: *Zur Germanisierung des Christentums* (Jena, 1911).

33 The pacifist attitude of the Marburg theologian Martin Rade represents a clear exception. At the 5th World Congress for Free Christianity and Religious Progress held in Berlin in 1910, Rade chaired the section "Religion and Peace," which was designed to help in the reduction of international tensions. Participants came from Britain, France, the United States, and elsewhere.

There are – in summation – two types of radical nationalism that initiated a belligerent mentality in Germany and mutually reinforced themselves in the course of the war. We have, first, an older type of chauvinism, its typical representatives being the Pan-German League and the Protestant League. Politically minded pastors such as Reinhard Mumm, a conservative member of the German Reichstag and chairman of a number of Protestant associations, Gottfried Traub, a liberal member of the Reichstag and chairman of the Protestant Association (Protestantenverein), and the free-thinking preacher Max Maurenbrecher were among the leading figures who supported, in their respective religious circles, an instrumentalization of religion for aggressive power politics. Later, in 1917, Traub and Maurenbrecher were among the founders of the chauvinist Deutsche Vaterlandspartei (German Fatherland Party). Second, we have a newer type of extreme nationalism that transformed religion into a racial myth. This concept found acceptance especially in educated circles on the periphery of or outside the churches, with recourse taken to Lagarde, to the superman cult of the Nietzscheans, or to Bonus's concept of a Germanic Christ. This new type of extreme nationalism became in itself "a political religion under the conditions of secularization."[34] Its basic elements – such as the charismatic relation between leaders and groups of followers, with these groups combining to form an organic national community in order to counteract and overcome the particularization that characterized bourgeois society – were readily accepted by the youth movement in particular.

The latter, militant type of nationalism has its roots in the period before World War I. "Siegfried oder Christus" is the battle cry that highlights the contrast between Germanic heroism and the values of a Christian civic society. In the case of "Fidus" (Hugo Höppener), whose mystical and erotic paintings were fully in line with the taste of the time, "Siegfried" becomes "Michael" in 1933.[35] But this makes no difference in the context of the new pagan and racial religion that gained influence during the war and was used during the Weimar Republic by the National Socialists for their own purposes.

34 See Friedrich Wilhelm Graf, "Protestantische Theologie in der Gesellschaft des Kaiserreichs," in Friedrich Wilhelm Graf, ed., *Profile des neuzeitlichen Protestantismus* (Gütersloh, 1992), 2, pt. 1:94.
35 See Stefan Breuer, *Anatomie der konservativen Revolution* (Darmstadt, 1993), 194.

7

Socializing American Youth to Be
Citizen-Soldiers

DAVID I. MACLEOD

Despite "interesting" changes in battlefield technology, the U.S. War Department assured American draftees in 1917 that victory still depended
"more on nerve and fighting spirit" than on "weapons and armor." The
"spirit" animating the new national army would combine "democratic feeling, . . . love for the Nation, and . . . Americanism." The prospective "citizen-soldier" – a term repeated incessantly throughout the *Home Reading
Course for Citizen-Soldiers* sent to every conscript – was to learn perfect respect for the American flag, practice saluting, and expect many hours of
close-order drill to learn "precision, teamwork, and . . . prompt and un-
hesitating obedience." He was to realize that "the soldier is not an individual player in the great game of war; he is valuable chiefly as a member of a
team."[1] In the pamphlet's most insistent metaphor, squads, companies, regiments, and divisions all were teams. Indeed, the whole army, the draftee
learned, "is handled just like a football team. . . . When the signal is given,
all work together – all play the game – teamwork." Yet just as in sports, the
soldier also would need individual "spirit, tenacity, and self-reliance," the
last a virtue particularly "characteristic of the American." Simple skills
would suffice: "Many men . . . become expert in picking up enemy bombs
before they explode and throwing them back."[2]

However disingenuous these reassurances, they appealed to long-standing beliefs about American military prowess and the proper socialization of

The author would like to thank William McDaid and members of the Central Michigan University
history department faculty seminar for comments, but I absolve them of responsibility for any remaining errors.

1 U.S. War Department, *Home Reading Course for Citizen-Soldiers* (Washington, D.C., 1917), 49-51,
   quotations on 58, 61, 54, 41, 25; Ronald Schaffer, *America in the Great War: The Rise of the War Welfare
   State* (New York, 1991), 177.
2 War Department, *Home Reading Course*, 27-9, quotations on 44, 61, 10, 59.

male youth. The established American practice was to fight large-scale wars with masses of civilian volunteers who needed only to be real men and good citizens in order to be promising soldiers. Given this tradition of reliance on relatively untrained "citizen-soldiers," many pre-World War I Americans found it hard to distinguish between building manly character and preparing young males for military service. The same "essentials of virile and successful manhood" seemed vital "in the Army or out of it."[3] This confusion was especially prevalent among the long-settled northeastern middle and upper classes, who equated national interests with their own.

Direct military training for schoolboys and college students before 1914 was limited and mostly ineffective. But indirect preparation was common, as many American boys – especially those of the white upper and middle classes – underwent a socialization designed to combine individual aggressiveness, vigorous outdoor life, team play, and militant patriotism. While learning to emulate approved models of manly character, they also were being socialized as future citizen-soldiers.

Organized adult endeavors along these lines intensified amid the jingoism of the 1890s, again after 1910 with the advent of Boy Scouting, and especially after 1915. Such preparation bolstered the faith that young Americans, as self-reliant, manly, patriotic team players, needed only a little technical training to be ready for war.

The American idealization of team sports and trust in such indirect military preparation reflected a relative optimism absent from the rhetoric of prewar German youth work. Because Americans lacked the German fear of foreign encirclement, and the sense of domestic crisis among the American upper and middle classes was less acute than their German counterparts' fear of socialist youth, the tenor of youth work was generally less alarmist in the United States than in Germany after 1911. But more than tone distinguished American from German efforts to indoctrinate youth. While adult-sponsored youth groups in both countries divided along class lines, different configurations resulted. Frightened by the growth of socialist youth groups, German elites focused their efforts on inculcating conservative patriotism and pro-military attitudes among working-class youth. Although membership statistics are imprecise, by 1914 the resulting organizations almost certainly enrolled a larger proportion of their country's young males than did any American youth group. Germany's middle-class Wandervögel, on the other hand, furnished idealistic volunteers when war came but tried before 1914 to distance themselves from the excesses of

3 Ibid., 10.

German militarism. Although the Wandervögel loom large in the historiography of German youth, their membership was smaller than that of adult-sponsored American groups for middle-class youth or even the German Boy Scouts (Pfadfinderbund), let alone the Jungdeutschlandbund.[4]

By contrast, white middle-class youth workers in the United States were much more concerned with training boys of their own class for social leadership. Many such American men feared that their own and their sons' masculinity was being eroded by the growing influence and activism of women and by the conditions of white-collar life, while burgeoning numbers of immigrants threatened the predominance of old-stock elites whom Theodore Roosevelt accused of "race suicide."[5] Gender tensions and concern for Anglo-Saxon superiority ran just beneath the surface of middle-class American youth work. The leaders could not seek harmony by invoking a foreign threat because no credible menace existed before 1915. One major agency for middle-class youth, the Young Men's Christian Association (YMCA), was committed to internationalism, and the Boy Scouts of America initially muted scouting's military elements more than the German Boy Scouts. American youth work for lower-class boys took the form of boys' clubs, whose recreational and educational programs would harmlessly preoccupy street boys but whose directors made few claims to building character or training boys for social leadership. Boys' club programs lacked the patriotic and military overtones of Boy Scouting or even of American football.[6] American Boy Scout troops were affiliated primarily with Protestant churches of the white middle class, whereas football was preeminently the sport of upper- and middle-class preparatory schools, high schools, colleges, and universities.

Geographic isolation shaped American attitudes. By 1911 the United States had built a powerful navy but had, like Britain, eschewed the Prussian model of mass-conscript armies. By European standards, American land forces were tiny. Although the state militias (called the National Guard) offered further reserves, regular army officers thought them to be of poor quality. The absence of serious external threats made preparation of the young for military service a less pressing issue than it was on the continent of Europe. Indeed, as European tensions mounted, a cautious, socially respectable American peace movement reached the height of its

---

4 See Derek S. Linton's essay in this book (Chapter 8); Derek S. Linton, *"Who Has the Youth, Has the Future": The Campaign to Save Young Workers in Imperial Germany* (Cambridge, 1991); Peter D. Stachura, *The German Youth Movement, 1900–1945* (London, 1981), 20–36.

5 Theodore Roosevelt, "Twisted Eugenics," *Outlook* 106 (Jan. 3, 1904): 32.

6 David I. Macleod, *Building Character in the American Boy: The Boy Scouts, YMCA, and Their Forerunners, 1870–1920* (Madison, Wis., 1983), 63–71.

influence between 1907 and 1914. After 1914 "preparedness" advocates such as General Leonard Wood trumpeted implausible warnings of invasion in their crusade for the rapid expansion of the U.S. Army.[7] In 1916 one publisher even issued a series of boys' adventure stories set during a German conquest of the eastern United States brought on by American "folly in not having prepared for real war." Such alarmism was rare before 1914, however, and invasion fantasies cannot have loomed large in the imaginations of the young.[8]

For internal use, American governments did not need large or well-trained armies. The Civil War appeared unique. Subjugation of Native Americans had the effect of total war on them but required only a tiny force of U.S. troops. To most American elites, domestic order, control of labor, and the assimilation of immigrants seemed much more pressing issues than security against military attack. For suppressing civil disturbances, militia cost much less than professional troops. By one count – probably low – National Guard units did riot duty 328 times between 1886 and 1895, most often to quell strikes or other manifestations of labor strife. Local Guard units, which required almost no effortful training and offered a convivial social life, recruited readily, enlisting some working-class youths but keeping command in middle-class hands. There was no need to prepare boys for future Guard duty; adventuresome youths could join immediately. Boyishly, Marquis James recorded his delight on being accepted at age fifteen in 1906: "Hoop-ee. I am a Real Real Soldier in a Real Real army. Yes, sir. I have enlisted as a private in Oklahoma National Guards 1st Regiment Co. K. I have the honor of being the youngest soldier in Oklahoma."[9] Accordingly, when American socialists – who had no significant youth movement of their own – attacked high school cadet corps or the Boy Scouts for fostering militarism, they worried not that boys would be

---

7 John Whiteclay Chambers II, *To Raise an Army: The Draft Comes to Modern America* (New York, 1987), 68, 75, 85–6; and John Whiteclay Chambers II, ed., *The Eagle and the Dove: The American Peace Movement and United States Foreign Policy, 1900–1922,* 2d ed. (Syracuse, N.Y., 1991), xxiii.

8 H. Irving Hancock, *At the Defense of Pittsburgh, or the Struggle to Save America's "Fighting Steel" Supply* (Philadelphia, 1916), 255. The other titles (same author and date) were *The Invasion of the United States, or Uncle Sam's Boys at the Capture of Boston; In the Battle for New York, or Uncle Sam's Boys in the Desperate Struggle for the Metropolis;* and *Making the Last Stand for Old Glory, or Uncle Sam's Boys in the Last Frantic Drive.* See also Barbara A. Bishop, comp., *American Boys' Series Books, 1900 to 1980* (Tampa, Fla., 1987). My thanks to Francis Molson for this material.

9 Marquis James, *The Cherokee Strip: A Tale of an Oklahoma Boyhood* (New York, 1965), 144; Chambers, *To Raise an Army,* 65–6; Robert Reinders, "Militia and Public Order in Nineteenth-Century America," *Journal of American Studies* 11 (1977): 93–8; Gerald F. Linderman, *The Mirror of War: American Society and the Spanish-American War* (Ann Arbor, Mich., 1974), 66; Martha Derthick, *The National Guard in Politics* (Cambridge, Mass., 1965), 19.

led off to foreign wars but that they would learn to aid the militia as "suppressors of the working class."[10]

Americans assumed that in the case of serious warfare, volunteers would flock to the colors. Besides George Washington, the archetypes of the American ideal of the "temporary citizen-soldier" were the Minute Men, who had left their farms to humble Britain's red-coated regulars in 1775. Patriotic history taught Americans to view themselves as peace-loving civilians who went to war reluctantly – though surprisingly often.[11]

Thus Americans could combine considerable truculence with assurance that militarism was an alien phenomenon, primarily Prussian and secondarily French, that they identified with the European powers' universal training of conscripts. Two American Boy Scout officials decried militarism as a belief in "cold, deadly competition between men, in which the clever adversary outwits or outmaneuvers his less unscrupulous or less aggressive opponent."[12] Who would train boys for that?

The Spanish-American War did little to change popular views. So many men eager to fight rushed to volunteer that failure to see combat became the major morale problem. Impatient with discipline, volunteers saw war not as "concerted group action" but as a "personal encounter" in which superior American character would prevail. Although American forces performed poorly, spurring major military reforms after 1900, rapid victory sustained popular faith in the volunteer principle. As late as 1914, a preparedness advocate complained that "public sentiment . . . boasts and believes in the superiority of untrained American arms over the best trained troops in the world."[13]

Paradoxically, American avoidance of universal military training for young men made it seem all the more vital to foster in growing boys the patriotic enthusiasm that would lead them to volunteer and the qualities of character that would enable them to prevail in battle. Enthusiasts for cadet

10 *The Masses* 3 (May 1912): 3, quoted in W. Bruce Leslie, "Coming of Age in Urban America: The Socialist Alternative, 1901–1920," *Teachers College Record* 85 (1984): 468; Kenneth Teitelbaum, *Schooling for "Good Rebels": Socialist Education for Children in the United States, 1900–1920* (Philadelphia, 1993), 29–31.

11 Chambers, *To Raise an Army*, 265, facing 148; Ruth Miller Elson, *Guardians of Tradition: American Schoolbooks of the Nineteenth Century* (Lincoln, Neb., 1964), 325; Boy Scouts of America, *The Official Handbook for Boys* (Garden City, N.Y., 1911), 239–40, 338–9 (hereafter BSA, *Handbook*).

12 Norman E. Richardson and Ormond E. Loomis, *The Boy Scout Movement Applied by the Church* (New York, 1915), 23; Chambers, *To Raise an Army*, 2, 70; Benjamin F. Trueblood, "Military Drill in the Schools," *Century Magazine* 48 (1894): 318; Ernest Howard Crosby, "The Military Idea of Manliness," *Independent* 53 (1901): 874.

13 Linderman, *Mirror of War*, 99–103, quotations on 77, 95; Ira L. Reeves, *Military Education in the United States* (Burlington, Vt., 1914), 29; Chambers, *To Raise an Army*, 67.

corps in secondary schools believed that these institutions were "training our Minute Men of the future."[14] Because the boys were too young for immediate military service, however, many American educators and youth workers condemned specifically military training. Especially after 1900, efforts to raise manly citizens shifted away from military drill toward a wider range of preparatory activities. American youth work was heavily influenced by British precedents. In both countries, adults used team sports and outdoor recreation to foster individual aggressiveness, group loyalty, and militant patriotism – all without believing themselves militaristic.

Uniforms, drill, and parades figured prominently in nineteenth-century American popular culture. At election time, partisan companies of men and boys paraded in uniform, although this style of campaigning was fading by the early 1890s. Antebellum boys got up their own cadet companies to imitate the militia.[15] This enthusiasm waned, however, as the militia faded after the Civil War. By the time the National Guard revived around 1880, team sports were taking hold, and boys were much more likely to organize themselves for baseball.

By the 1890s most boys' drill companies were adult-sponsored, as men tried to impose an old-fashioned boyhood under adult control. In part, drill was merely an expedient, much as youth workers later used basketball; when men of the 1890s ran out of ideas they marched the boys around the hall. Yet they also hoped to inspire enthusiasm while teaching persistence and precision. In an era when Protestants worried that boys were finding faith effeminate and quitting Sunday school in droves, advocates of muscular Christianity repackaged religion in athletic and military metaphors. Taking Christian militancy literally, a surprising number of churches sponsored cadet companies by the early 1890s.[16]

The best known of these were affiliated with the Boys' Brigade. William Smith, a Glasgow businessman and officer in Britain's Territorial Forces (analogous to the American National Guard), formed the first company in 1883, hoping to interest rowdy boys in his mission Sunday school. The idea found a lively publicist in Henry Drummond, a propagandist for athletic Christianity who commanded a transatlantic audience. Drummond promised easy control: Just "put a fivepenny cap on [boys] and call them

14 Day Allen Willey, "Training Our Minute Men of the Future," *Outing* 51 (1908): 603–7.
15 Michael E. McGerr, *The Decline of Popular Politics: The American North, 1865–1928* (New York, 1986), 23–9, 142–7; Josephus Daniels, *Tar Heel Editor* (Chapel Hill, N.C., 1939), 174–5; Charles Dudley Warner, *Being a Boy* (Boston, 1878), 207–10; William Dean Howells, *A Boy's Town* (New York, 1890), 121–5, 187.
16 Joseph F. Kett, *Rites of Passage: Adolescence in America, 1790 to the Present* (New York, 1977), 196–8; B. O. Flower, "Fostering the Savage in the Young," *Arena* 10 (1894): 423–5.

soldiers, which they are not, and you can order them about till midnight." Although reality never matched Drummond's hyperbole, Brigade companies spread erratically among high-status American congregations and reached a peak enrollment of about 16,000 around 1894.[17]

But military drill had other common uses that were more overtly repressive and unappealing to the young. Authorities commonly imposed long drills on students whom they deemed obstreperous or racially inferior. Students at the Hampton Institute, a model teacher training school for African Americans, and at most schools for Native Americans lived under rigid military discipline intended to deaden independence. Boys and often girls marched long hours in drill formation. Although older students volunteered in large numbers to fight in World War I, many found the schools' regimen hateful. Juvenile reformatories also imposed military drill. Prosperous parents whose sons proved recalcitrant or failed in school often packed them off for equivalent discipline to one of the private military academies that proliferated in the late nineteenth century.[18]

While full-blown military drill in these cases was a device for controlling youths who had been stigmatized as racially inferior or grossly undisciplined, a milder version pervaded the overcrowded public schools in American cities. William T. Harris expressed a consensus in 1872 that "military precision is required in the maneuvering of classes." In the St. Louis system, where discipline was unusually severe, children of the early 1890s had to spend several daily recitation periods standing "perfectly motionless, their bodies erect, their knees and feet together, the tips of their shoes touching the edge of a board in the floor." Any movement brought reproof.[19] Thus military drill may have reminded many American youngsters not of recreation but of constraint and boredom.

This was true in cadet corps once the novelty wore off. The boys grew so restless that one Brigade captain considered it cause for congratulation when his company got through an evening's display drill without throwing

---

17 Henry Drummond, "Manliness in Boys – By a New Process," *McClure's* 2 (Dec. 1893): 70; Macleod, *Building Character*, 42–4, 87–92; John Springhall, Brian Fraser, and Michael Hoare, *Sure and Steadfast: A History of The Boys' Brigade, 1883–1983* (London, 1983), 76–8.

18 James D. Anderson, *The Education of Blacks in the South, 1860–1935* (Chapel Hill, N.C., 1988), 58; Michael C. Coleman, *American Indian Children at School, 1850–1930* (Jackson, Miss., 1993), 86–8; Wilma A. Daddario, "'They Get Milk Practically Every Day': The Genoa Indian Industrial School, 1884–1934," *Nebraska History* 73 (spring 1992): 9; Robert M. Mennel, *Thorns and Thistles: Juvenile Delinquents in the United States, 1825–1940* (Hanover, N.H., 1973), 103–9, 116; Richard Gwyn Davies, "Of Arms and the Boy: A History of Culver Military Academy, 1894–1945," Ph.D. diss., Indiana University, 1983, 2–17, 56.

19 Harris quoted in David B. Tyack, *The One Best System: A History of American Urban Education* (Cambridge, Mass., 1974), 50; Joseph M. Rice, *The Public-School System of the United States* (New York, 1893), 98. Harris was superintendent in St. Louis until 1880.

chairs or destroying property. Yet the best the editor of *Brigade Boy* could suggest was more of the same: "Mix up commands. Rip out four or five movements all to be done at one command and in succession, and your boys will begin to show signs of interest in you."[20] Brigade spokesmen asserted that marching drill was merely a device to inculcate virtues needed in civilian life, such as alertness and obedience; yet they hinted that Brigade work would also prepare cadets for future military service. The temptation was to add more overtly military features to try to revive flagging interest. Some officers staged sham battles that pleased neither pacific churchmen nor military officers seeking professional competence. Tactics favored massed charges and glorious sacrifice; in one engagement the colonel was killed three times over. Unlike the Boy Scouts of America, the United Boys' Brigades of America never acquired an effective central organization. Membership declined to 12,000 by 1909 and then fell sharply as scouting eclipsed the Brigades.[21]

Direct military training in public schools and colleges was for the most part equally small-scale and ineffective, inoculating more youths against military enthusiasm than it inspired. The one exception in terms of scale was cadet training at land-grant colleges. In 1862, when the Morrill Act granted land to support colleges teaching "agriculture and the mechanic arts," the Civil War was raging and Congress added a requirement that instruction include "military tactics." When the emergency passed and the requirement remained, land-grant colleges complied, but with limited enthusiasm. Aggregate enrollments for military drill were impressive: 29,036 students in the 1913–14 school year. In theory these students graduated ready to serve as junior officers in the National Guard or volunteer units raised in a national emergency. In practice, however, many of the army officers who were serving terms of exile as professors of military science merely put the students through basic marching drills – inadequate training for privates, let alone officers. Many students found the experience "uninteresting and even distasteful," conceded one such officer. At the University of Wisconsin in 1886, students who had completed their military requirement returned to throw dumbbells and yell at those drilling; disruptions continued in the 1890s, with recalcitrant students receiving only token punishment.[22]

20 *Brigade Boy* 2 (1903): 185; *American Brigadier* 1 (Feb. 1907): 33.
21 United Boys' Brigades of America, Massachusetts Division, *The Boys' Brigade* (n.p., [late 1890s]), 1; *Brigade Boy* 2 (1903): 156–7; *American Brigadier* 1 (July 1907): 7; Macleod, *Building Character*, 88–92.
22 Reeves, *Military Education*, 25, 68–9, 86–93, 101, quotation on 85; *Report of the Commissioner of Education for the Year Ended June 30, 1914*, 2 vols. (Washington, D.C., 1915), 2:281 (hereafter *RCE* plus ending date); Merle Curti and Vernon Carstensen, *The University of Wisconsin: A History, 1848–1925*, 2 vols. (Madison, Wis., 1949), 1:415–17, 676. Military training seldom caught

Elsewhere the program droned on with less controversy but few results. Although graduates poured forth, the federal government could not trace them in an emergency. Very few joined even the National Guard, and almost none the regular army. Far from socializing American youths for war, armory drill bored them. When General Leonard Wood and his associates organized volunteer military training camps for current or prospective college students (160 students in the summer of 1913 and 667 in 1914), the purpose was to find a better way to form an enthusiastic reserve of future officers. Sons of the elite flocked to training that went well beyond drill, mimicking army camp life and taking the would-be leaders out on maneuvers.[23]

More controversial than drill at land-grant colleges but equally ineffective were schemes for drilling high school boys. Dr. D. A. Sargent, a prominent physical educator and opponent of such drill, commented sarcastically: "As parents . . . do not take kindly to warlike preparations, especially if they presage the sacrifice of their own children, the argument most generally advanced in favor of the introduction of military drill into our school system is that it furnishes an admirable means of physical training."[24] Boston and a few other cities had had high school cadet corps since the Civil War. Then in 1893 the Grand Army of the Republic (GAR), the main organization of Union veterans, resolved to support schoolboy drill. Former President Benjamin Harrison touted the benefits: "A military drill develops the whole man, head, chest, arms, and legs proportionately. . . . It teaches quickness of eye and ear, hand and foot; qualifies men to step and act in unison; teaches subordination; and, best of all, qualifies a man to serve his country."[25]

Despite the jingoism of the time, the movement failed to win support from New York state or the federal government. Reputedly 30,000 boys drilled as American Guards in New York City, but with parents paying for the uniforms, the companies were ephemeral. Drill in public high schools won some limited popularity in the Northeast and Far West, where the sense of foreign threat was strongest, but almost none in the Midwest. Nationwide, reported enrollment of high school cadets rose only slowly to peaks of

on where it was voluntary. See, for example, Orrin Leslie Elliott, *Stanford University: The First Twenty-Five Years* (Stanford, Calif., 1937), 111.

23 Reeves, *Military Education*, 95–6; John Garry Clifford, *The Citizen Soldiers: The Plattsburg Training Camp Movement, 1913–1920* (Lexington, Ky., 1972), 1–24.

24 D. A. Sargent, "Should We Have Military Training in the Schools," *Journal of Proceedings and Addresses* (National Education Association) 35 (1896): 920 (hereafter *NEAP*).

25 "Military Instruction in Schools and Colleges," *Century* 47 (1894): 469; Henry M. MacCracken, "Military Drill in the Schools of the United States," *RCE* 1898–9, 479–80.

9,771 for public high schools in 1903 and 9,743 for private high schools the following year. These cadets constituted just 4 percent of all public high school boys and 19 percent of private secondary school boys – and this at a time when the majority of American teenagers were not in school. Aggregate drill enrollment declined only slightly by 1914 but represented a much smaller fraction of the growing male high school population.[26]

Why had school cadet corps failed to catch on? While some school principals praised drill for improving boys' posture and obedience, more feared militarism and worried that compulsory drill was a disincentive for boys to stay in school. Sargent convinced many educators that the strain of military drill in fact harmed growing boys, who needed free exercise. In practical terms, moreover, uniforms were expensive, instructors scarce, and camps and excursions – without which interest plummeted – hard to supervise.[27]

Cadet corps further lacked a large base of unequivocal support. Much as in Germany, American officers of the regular army strongly favored physical conditioning and premilitary training in high school but did not want boys to graduate with an exaggerated sense of their own military competence. National Guardsmen did not unanimously support high school drill either. Critics delighted in reporting complaints by Guard officers that cadet corps hurt enlistments by making boys dislike soldiering. Always there loomed the threat of boredom, which intensified as livelier alternative forms of recreation, such as team sports, proliferated. Starting in 1911, Lieutenant Edgar Steever achieved highly publicized success with a cadet program in Wyoming high schools that centered on competitive wall scaling, but the acclaim for his methods merely highlighted the failure of ordinary drill.[28] The core problem, in short, may have been that too few boys really liked marching drills.

Alone among proponents of cadet training, Steever noted that it offered girls no role. Reinforcing traditional gender roles, he added "a note of

26 Mary Dearing, *Veterans in Politics: The Story of the G.A.R.* (Baton Rouge, La., 1952), 480–1; Stuart McConnell, *Glorious Contentment: The Grand Army of the Republic, 1865–1900* (Chapel Hill, N.C., 1992), 231; MacCracken, "Military Drill," 481; *RCE* 1903, 2:1824–5; *RCE* June 30, 1904, 2:1752–3; *RCE* June 30, 1914, 2:411–29.
27 MacCracken, "Military Drill," 482–5; William D. Parkinson, "The Public School and Military Drill," *Journal of Education* 82 (1915): 452–3; Sargent, "Should We Have," 920–9; William C. Allen, "Militarizing Our Schools," *Journal of Education* 74 (1911): 566; George W. Ehler, "Military Drill and Physical Education," *American Physical Education Review* 20 (1915): 539–41; Willard S. Small, "Educational Hygiene," *RCE* June 30, 1916, 1:317–23; Wilmot E. Ellis, "Honorable Mention Essay," *Journal of the Military Service Institution of the United States* 46 (1910): 219–26 (hereafter *JMSI*).
28 "Comment and Criticism," *JMSI* 11 (1890): 338; James J. Mayes, "Gold Prize Essay," *JMSI* 46 (1910): 171–92; D. C. Bliss, "Military Training in the High School," *School Review* 25 (1917): 163–6; "Massachusetts Commission on Military Education," *School Review* 25 (1917): 168; George Creel, "Wyoming's Answer to Militarism," *Everybody's* 34 (1916): 150–9.

chivalry" by recruiting girls as sponsors for each squad. By 1917 he recognized the totality of modern war and advocated that girls be trained to work in civil defense and manage refugees.[29] In gender as in much else, pre-1914 American advocates of cadet training were not preparing for total war.

While direct military training for boys accomplished little, indirect forms of socialization intensified from the 1890s onward and flourished with little opposition. They drew on two main sources of strength: assertive patriotism and fears for the masculinity of boys from prosperous urban families. While winning support from many Americans who considered themselves peace advocates, patriots and character builders inculcated attitudes that were, in the American context, effectively premilitary.

Much of the native-born white middle class confronted the turmoil of the 1890s with an upsurge of militant patriotism. This often took the form of campaigns to Americanize immigrants and prepare all young people for service to the nation. Because the United States lacked the personalized focus of loyalty furnished by a monarch and was in theory a society of free individuals without a fixed social hierarchy, patriots felt all the more strongly that children must learn unquestioning loyalty to the nation as an abstract entity.

Much of the new socialization centered on veneration of the flag as the symbol of American nationhood. As late as 1888, few schoolhouses flew the American flag. That year, two GAR posts in New York City began competing to bestow flags on schools. The practice spread, other patriotic societies joined in, and by 1905 eighteen northern and western states required that schoolhouses fly the American flag. New Jersey law even mandated that pupils "take an active interest in the raising and lowering of the flag."[30]

Increasingly, pupils did so by reciting a formal pledge of allegiance, first published by *The Youth's Companion* in 1892. Facing the flag, every pupil was to give "the military salute" and repeat slowly: "I pledge allegiance to my Flag and the Republic for which it stands: one Nation indivisible, with Liberty and Justice for All." As they said the words "to my Flag," pupils were to extend their right hands "gracefully, palm upwards, towards the Flag," and hold that stance until the end. One celebration would have had little impact; what made reverence for the flag so characteristically Ameri-

---

29 Creel, "Wyoming's Answer," 154; Captain E. Z. Steever, "The Wyoming Plan of Military Training for the Schools," *School Review* 25 (1917): 149.

30 Charles F. Speierl, "Civil War Veterans and Patriotism in New Jersey Schools," *New Jersey History* 110 (fall-winter 1992): 51; McConnell, *Glorious Contentment*, 228, 230; Scot M. Guenter, *The American Flag, 1777–1924: Cultural Shifts from Creation to Codification* (Rutherford, N.J., 1990), 105, 109, 124.

can was the practice of reciting the pledge to start each day at school. The pace at which this ritual spread before World War I is uncertain, but it was probably fairly rapid in northern states.[31]

The intensity of classroom nationalism may have subsided somewhat after 1900, as progressive-oriented education for citizenship focused less on masculine concerns of war and national rivalry than on state and local issues emphasized by women reformers. Still, the new civics spread slowly, and teachers continued to administer strong doses of patriotic indoctrination. Jewish immigrants who attended school in New York City before World War I recall learning a highly idealized American history.[32]

As the historian Ruth Miller Elson has shrewdly noted, the textbooks whose contents nineteenth-century American students memorized preached boring sermons against war and then filled pages with dramatic battle narratives. They duly condemned aggressive warfare and pronounced all American wars defensive. Students learned that a citizen's highest duty was to fight for his country, his greatest glory to die for it.[33]

At least on a superficial level, such instruction generated strong identification with American heroes. Several turn-of-the-century studies asked American schoolchildren whom they would most like to resemble.[34] The youngest often named personal acquaintances, but the numbers selecting figures from American history rose rapidly with age. In one study, more than 70 percent of children ages eleven through sixteen named historical personages, mainly American; in another, more than 70 percent of white boys in Nashville, Tennessee, picked historic Americans as their ideals.[35] A major influence was the cult of admiration for George Washington fostered by the schools; on average, at least one-quarter of the children obligingly named Washington as their exemplar. Besides his legendary honesty, he

31 Francis Bellamy, "The Official Programme of the National School Celebration of Columbus Day," *Youth's Companion* 65 (1892): 446, quoted in Guenter, *American Flag,* 130–2; McConnell, *Glorious Contentment,* 229. By contrast, a woman born in 1896 who attended the underfunded schools for African Americans in rural Virginia recalls no recitation of the Pledge of Allegiance or instruction in American history. Margaret S. Carter and Charles M. Carter, "The Value of an Education," *Phylon* 49 (1992): 97.

32 "Education for Citizenship," *RCE* June 30, 1913, 1:9–10; Arthur William Dunn, "The Trend of Civic Education," *RCE* June 30, 1914, 1:408–10; James Mahoney, "American Citizenship in the Educational Surveys," *RCE* June 30, 1914, 1:564, 580; Stephan F. Brumberg, *Going to America, Going to School: The Jewish Immigrant Public School Encounter in Turn-of-the-Century New York City* (New York, 1986), 126–7.

33 Elson, *Guardians of Tradition,* 283–4, 322–34.

34 Estelle M. Darrah, "A Study of Children's Ideals," *Popular Science Monthly* 53 (1898): 88–99 (1,440 elementary school children, ages 7–16, in St. Paul, Minn., and San Mateo County, Cal.); Will Grant Chambers, "The Evolution of Ideals," *Pedagogical Seminary* 10 (1903): 101–43 (2,333 elementary school children, ages 6–16, in New Castle, Pa.); David Spence Hill, "Comparative Study of Children's Ideals," *Pedagogical Seminary* 18 (1911): 219–31 (1,431 white elementary school children, ages 7–15, in Nashville, Tenn.).

35 Darrah, "Children's Ideals," 89–90; Hill, "Comparative Study," 220.

personified the citizen-soldier ideals of service to his country and military valor. The power of school training to teach admiration for political and military leadership was such that in two of three studies, a majority of girls named male ideals. Estelle Darrah, the pioneer investigator, blamed the fact that "historical instruction in our public schools presents only male characters and that it deals almost entirely with conquest and war." Compared with boys, however, girls did choose more acquaintances and more individuals – often women – who were noted for service without military overtones. Boys commonly chose men with records of military accomplishment. One study concluded that "boys have a constantly increasing admiration for military powers up to the age of fifteen, when fully one-third of them prefer it to other forms of renown."[36]

These findings may be overstated, as schoolchildren may have written what they thought their elders wanted. Yet comparative studies, which would have suffered from the same flaw, suggest that turn-of-the-century American children identified more strongly with national heroes than did their English and German contemporaries or American children of later decades. American children of the 1920s, 1940s, and 1950s were much less likely to choose historical figures as exemplars. The cult of Washington faded, and commercial entertainment supplied rival ideals. Turn-of-the-century investigators replicated the American studies with children in English and German state schools. The responses were somewhat unrepresentative because these schools drew from lower-middle- and lower-class children who may have been less socialized than wealthier children to identify national interests with their own. Still, the results diverged substantially from American patterns. At every age from nine upward, at least 20 percent fewer English children chose "historical or public characters" as ideals. Approximately 40 percent of German children chose public figures (historic or contemporary) at age fourteen, compared with 80 percent of American children.[37] At least at the level of verbal response, unusually large numbers of American boys in the pre World War I decades had learned to profess identification with national heroes and ideals of military glory.

Other evidence suggests, however, that American boys were not preoccupied with dreams of war. The veterans who visited schools before Memorial Day to tell students "'how grandly' the soldiers of the Civil War

---

36 Darrah, "Children's Ideals," 96; Chambers, "Evolution," 132.
37 Fred I. Greenstein, *Children and Politics,* rev. ed. (New Haven, Conn., 1969), 137–43; Earl Barnes, "Children's Ideals," *Pedagogical Seminary* 7 (1900): 3–12 (2,100 Board School children, ages 8–13, in London); Henry H. Goddard, "Ideals of a Group of German Children," *Pedagogical Seminary* 13 (1906): 208–20 (1,590 *Mittelschulen* and *Volkschulen* pupils, ages 7–16, in Göttingen). The emperor, named by 12 percent of boys, did not rival Washington.

had died" were old and no longer glamorous. Growing up in Michigan around 1910, the future Civil War historian Bruce Catton "now and then" refought the Civil War with friends, but "the game that got most of our attention was baseball." This was typical. Although war toys sold widely from the 1880s onward, boys seldom listed them among the items they played with most. Cap pistols came on the market in the 1870s and the Daisy Air Rifle in 1900, but boys often used these in nonmilitary play as hunters, cowboys, and cops and robbers.[38] Baseball and other new team sports had evidently displaced war play. When asked about their amusements, only 55 of 1,000 Massachusetts schoolboys of the late 1890s mentioned playing war and just 3 considered it a favorite activity, compared with 679 who mentioned baseball and 241 who declared it a favorite. In 1914, 1,108 fifth- through eighth-grade boys in Springfield, Illinois, described what they had done over Easter vacation: Only 0.5 percent had played soldiers, whereas 3.7 percent had played cops and robbers, 27.6 percent had seen movies, and 71.0 percent had played baseball.[39] Assertions that every boy wanted to play soldier were outdated.

The range of popular books published for American boys indicates that publishers expected them to be moderately but not overwhelmingly interested in warfare – at least before 1915. Although sometimes set during the American Revolution and filled with patriotic enthusiasm, dime novels between the 1860s and 1900 mostly featured Wild West adventures, stories of criminals, and hordes of detectives. In the early twentieth century, series books about boys poured onto the market; one bibliography lists 1,200 from the late 1890s through 1914. Of these, 31 percent were simple adventure stories, often involving detection and catering to boys' fascination with radio, airplanes, motor cars, and motorcycles. Stories of Boy Scouting (9 percent) and outdoor life (8 percent) also centered on adventure. More than 17 percent featured school life and sports. By contrast, stories set in some American war totaled only 9 percent of the titles. The American Revolution led at 3 percent, followed by warfare with Native Americans and the Civil War; other conflicts, including even the recent Spanish-American War, made little showing. A further 2 percent of the stories took

38 Gerald F. Linderman, _Embattled Courage: The Experience of Combat in the American Civil War_ (New York, 1987), 297; Bruce Catton, _Waiting for the Morning Train: An American Boyhood_ (Garden City, N.Y., 1972), 43–4; T. R. Croswell, "Amusements of Worcester School Children," _Pedagogical Seminary_ 6 (1899): 318, 342, 354; G. L. Freeman and R. S. Freeman, _Yesterday's Toys_ (Watkins Glen, N.Y., 1962), 56.
39 Croswell, "Amusements," 317, 321; Lee F. Hanmer and Clarence Arthur Perry, _Recreation in Springfield, Illinois_ (Springfield, Ill., 1914), 24. Zach McGhee, "A Study in the Play Life of Some South Carolina Children," _Pedagogical Seminary_ 7 (1900): 459–78, does not mention soldier play.

place at West Point or elsewhere in the army. Annapolis and the navy, whose new fleet lent the service glamor, fared better with 4 percent of titles.[40] Whether series publishers shaped or catered to boys' tastes in fantasy, it appears that their readers dreamed only intermittently of military combat and often preferred other adventures.

Boys apparently liked to imagine winning easily and individually or with a small gang of chums. The Boy Scouts of America's chief scout librarian charged that series books were "blowing out the boys' brains" with idle dreams of effortless triumph, teaching disdain for disciplined training and respectful obedience. The relative infrequency of military themes in pre-war books did not result from squeamishness about war stories; more than one-third of series books published from 1915 through 1917 and more than half in 1918 and 1919 sent their heroes off to World War I. But even the wartime books did not teach the submission of the individual demanded by modern armies. Instead, boys dreamed of exploits alone or with a small group of friends. Perhaps to meet such expectations, the War Department's *Home Reading Course* opened with tales of individual heroism and balanced sermons about obedient teamwork with assertions that personal initiative remained important.[41]

The adventurous hero answered contemporary American anxieties about loss of manliness. These fears, which crested in the 1890s and remained at flood stage through the 1910s, particularly troubled the urban upper and middle classes. Men of the new middle class worried that they were sitting all day in offices and doing other men's bidding. Their sons, they feared, also were leading sedentary lives, raised by mothers and taught mostly by women teachers. In their fear of women's advancement, nervous males came to regard manliness as "less the opposite of childishness than the opposite of femininity." For boys the word "sissy" (originally meaning sister) turned into a fighting insult between 1880 and 1900.[42] The prominent psychologist G. Stanley Hall charged coeducational public schools with rewarding prissy feminine virtues. Women teachers, ranted Admiral F. E. Chadwick in 1914, were nurturing "a feminized manhood, emotional, illogical, noncombative." Though neither militarist nor misogynist, the

---

40 Merle Curti, "Dime Novels and the American Tradition," *Yale Review* 26 (1937): 761–78; E. F. Bleiler, ed., *Eight Dime Novels* (New York, 1974), viii; Bishop, *American Boys' Series Books*.
41 Franklin K. Mathiews, "Blowing Out the Boy's Brains," *Outlook* 108 (1914): 652–4; Peter A. Soderbergh, "The Great Book War: Edward Stratemeyer and the Boy Scouts of America, 1910–1930," *New Jersey History* 91 (1973): 244; War Department, *Home Reading Course*, 3–5.
42 Kett, *Rites*, 173; Peter N. Stearns, "Girls, Boys, and Emotions: Redefinitions and Historical Change," *Journal of American History* 80 (1993): 48; Peter G. Filene, *Him/Her/Self: Sex Roles in Modern America*, 2d ed. (Baltimore, 1986), 98.

Boy Scouts of America's chief scout, Ernest Thompson Seton, fulminated in 1910 that urban culture was turning "our robust, manly, self-reliant boyhood into a lot of flat-chested cigarette-smokers, with shaky nerves and doubtful vitality."[43]

Adults nervous about loss of vitality among boys of the native-born middle class were eager to nourish what Theodore Roosevelt called "the great fighting, masterful virtues." A Methodist pastor praised the Boys' Brigade because it suited "the military Berserker instinct in every Anglo-Saxon boy."[44] Turn-of-the-century American child-rearing advice accepted anger directed at peers more readily than before or since. When Roosevelt brought boxing into the White House, parents began to give their sons boxing gloves. Contact sports won praise for teaching temper control, yet boys were not to duck a worthy fight. "To be angry aright is a good part of moral education," preached G. Stanley Hall. "An able-bodied young man, who can not fight physically, can hardly have a high and true sense of honor, and is generally a milk-sop, a lady-boy, or a sneak."[45]

Whereas women reformers such as Jane Addams espoused a positive vision of peace based on social and political justice, American men so strongly equated the fighting virtues with masculinity that they had trouble imagining peace as more than mere avoidance of war and thus as temporary.[46] The most celebrated attempt at this was the philosopher William James's 1910 essay "The Moral Equivalent of War." James accepted the premise that the fighting virtues must be preserved, describing the militarists' faith with a rhetorical gusto that suggested his divided emotions. "Apologists for war" believed, he wrote, that war's "'horrors' are a cheap price to pay for rescue from . . . a world of clerks and teachers, of coeducation and zoophily, of 'consumers' leagues' and 'associated charities,' of industrialism unlimited and feminism unabashed. No scorn, no hardness, no valor any more! Fie upon such a cattle-yard of a planet!" James insisted, however, that modern total war, "when whole nations are the armies," ren-

---

43 Chadwick, "The Woman Peril in American Education," *Educational Review* 47 (1914): 116, quoted in David Tyack and Elisabeth Hansot, *Learning Together: A History of Coeducation in American Schools* (New Haven, Conn., 1990), 146–200; Seton, "The Boy Scouts in America," *Outlook* 95 (1910): 630; Macleod, *Building Character*, 44–9.

44 Theodore Roosevelt, *The Strenuous Life* (New York, 1901), 1–7; E. R. Dille, "The Boy: The Raw Material," *Boys' Brigade Bulletin* 1 (Nov. 15, 1892): 9.

45 G. Stanley Hall, *Youth: Its Education, Regimen, and Hygiene* (New York, 1907), 94; Stearns, "Girls, Boys, and Emotions," 44–6. Somewhat later studies found that American parents prompted boys to fight when provoked, whereas French and German children were to ask adults to intervene. Carol Zisowitz Stearns and Peter N. Stearns, *Anger: The Struggle for Emotional Control in America's History* (Chicago, 1986), 99–100.

46 Chambers, *Eagle and the Dove*, xvii.

dered war "absurd and impossible from its own monstrosity." While decry-
ing the narrowly commercial selfishness of his era and accepting the military claim of service, he proposed an alternative program of universal,
strenuous, but peaceful service: "To coal and iron mines, to freight trains,
to fishing fleets in December, to dish-washing, clothes-washing, and win-
dow-washing . . . would our gilded youth be drafted off, according to their
choice, to get the childishness knocked out of them, and to come back
into society with healthier sympathies and soberer ideas."[47]

James did *not* propose sport as a substitute for war. He was advocating
humble work as a schooling in democracy and scorned "'mere vital excitement' as an end in itself."[48] But the "moral equivalent of war" became a
handy catch phrase for his era, divorced from James's specific proposal. In
others' writings (James died in 1910), his idea – brutally simplified – blended into a turbid stream of metaphor that depicted both sports and scouting
variously as substitutes or preparation for war. The two functions proved
hard to separate. Much as many male peace advocates also supported
American naval rearmament, so youth workers could portray their programs as entirely nonmilitaristic while stating with equal pride that their
training would prepare boys to be good citizen-soldiers in any emergency.
When George E. Johnson, a leading playground organizer, wrote "Play as a
Moral Equivalent of War" in 1912, he praised sport as both a substitute and
a preventive for war: "Play preserves, purifies, perpetuates the martial capacities, while it diminishes the belligerent spirit." Yet he added that team
sports, although less "sacrificial" than warfare, taught "hardy endurance,
sometimes [of] painful injuries." Above all, "in the development of the ideal of team work, of self-subordination, of co-operation, lies the very
essence of the spirit of voluntary enlistment and sacrifice in war. So long as
our youth are trained in the school of our great co-operative games, there
can be no degeneracy in the spirit of the volunteer soldier, which has always characterized the American people."[49]

Johnson's article followed decades of assertions that team sports taught
military virtues. In 1887 Alexander Johnston epitomized the genteel view
of war in his "satisfaction" that football was "doing for our college-bred
men, in a more peaceful way, what the experience of war did for so many of
their predecessors in 1861–65, in its inculcation of the lesson that bad tem-

47 William James, "The Moral Equivalent of War," *McClure's* 35 (1910): 464–5, 467.
48 Quoted in George M. Fredrickson, *The Inner Civil War: Northern Intellectuals and the Crisis of the
   Union* (New York, 1965), 229–38.
49 Michael A. Lutzker, "The Pacifist as Militarist: A Critique of the American Peace Movement,
   1898–1914," *Societas* 5 (1975): 87–104; George E. Johnson, "Play as a Moral Equivalent of War,"
   Playground 6 (1912): 120–2.

per is an element quite foreign to open, manly contest." With equal complacency, a high school principal observed in 1902 that love of team sports

is a more marked characteristic of the Anglo-Saxon than of any other race. Games like football, baseball, and cricket are not popular in France, Germany, Italy, or Spain. The English, and, in a greater degree, the Americans, are fond of such games. It is probable that such a liking will always be characteristic of the dominant races, for the world can never be both won and permanently retained except on a social, co-operating, altruistic plan.[50]

By then the group emphasis mattered. Fearing loss of social cohesion and recognizing that middle-class youths must learn to thrive in large organizations, Progressive-era youth workers sought to inculcate conformity with group needs. Team games promised to teach the group orientation demanded by modern business and military life, yet without endangering boys' masculinity. According to Luther Gulick, the organizer of New York City's Public Schools Athletic League, players learned "heroic subordination of self to the group." On another occasion, Gulick declared that interschool athletics taught "high corporate morality."[51]

Football in particular became a metaphor for manliness and military prowess. Although more widely played, baseball lacked the prestige of football, which spread downward from elite colleges. Baseball seemed too individualistic, hinging as it did on the solitary contest of pitcher and batter and lacking the close physical contact of "fighting plays." American football, with its mass charges against the opposing line of players, resembled a miniature battlefield, complete with casualties.[52] As these mounted, defenders and critics debated the game in military terms. Athletic injuries, Henry Cabot Lodge told Harvard alumni in 1896, were "part of the price which the English-speaking race has paid for being world conquerors." Conceding the point of racial pride – "No Saxon community will ever abandon a game simply because it is rough" – a critic questioned the value of fifteen football deaths in 1904: "Is not the atmosphere of *Dulce et decorum est pro patria mori* a little too intense on the modern football field?"[53] Al-

50 Alexander Johnston, "The American Game of Foot-Ball," *Century* 34 (1887): 898; Reuben Post Halleck, "The Social Side of High-School Life," *NEAP* 40 (1902): 460.
51 Gulick quoted in Kett, *Rites,* 203; Gulick, "The New Athletics," *Outlook* 98 (1911): 599–600, quoted in Timothy P. O'Hanlon, "School Sports as Social Training: The Case of Athletics and the Crisis of World War I," *Journal of Sport History* 9 (1982): 10; Daniel T. Rodgers, "Socializing Middle-Class Children: Institutions, Fables, and Work Values in Nineteenth-Century America," *Journal of Social History* 13 (1980): 363.
52 Johnson, "Play," 116; Johnston, "American Game," 892; Joe L. Dubbert, *A Man's Place: Masculinity in Transition* (Englewood Cliffs, N.J., 1979), 179–81.
53 Lodge quoted in John Rickards Betts, *America's Sporting Heritage, 1850–1950* (Reading, Mass., 1974), 195; Paul van Dyke, "Athletics and Education," *Outlook* 79 (1905): 392.

though rules reform reduced casualties, the 1909 death of a West Point cadet of injuries suffered in a twelve-man pileup prompted an editor of *The Army and Navy Journal* to inveigh against the danger and "military worthlessness of football," arguing that modern firepower had made massed attacks obsolete and reduced football to "a relic of the past rather than a preparation for the exigencies of modern battle." Yet many officers still agreed with Colonel James Parker of the Eleventh Cavalry, who advised his regiment that "football is calculated to bring out and develop the most valuable soldierly qualities – courage, ready obedience and unflinching fortitude under pain and stress."[54] To its military supporters, football furnished broad socialization rather than specific training for battle.

Despite its risks, around 1900 football spread rapidly from colleges into high schools, typically becoming the first school-sponsored sport. By 1914 some 450 colleges and 6,000 secondary schools had football teams. Meanwhile, secondary school enrollment more than tripled, from 407,919 in 1893–4 to 1,373,661 in 1913–14, bringing more youths – still primarily middle class – under school influence.[55]

With girls outnumbering boys in high school, enthusiasts touted football as an all-male preserve. It was all-male not only literally – all teams were sex-segregated anyway – but also symbolically. While many girls played baseball and basketball, almost none played football. Overall, boys' sports received much more support than girls'.[56]

Despite educators' subsequent rationalizations, however, the schools' initial takeover of student athletics did not follow from any carefully planned scheme to socialize boys. In most high schools of the late nineteenth century, students organized the first teams but could not prevent the use of hired ringers. With mismatched players and weak refereeing, play was brutal. School principals intervened defensively to protect their schools' reputations and only later started expatiating on the necessity of athletics to build character and loyalty.[57]

Neither should we overestimate football's influence on boys. Except at small high schools, interschool athletics reduced the majority of students to

54 William Everett Hicks, "The Military Worthlessness of Football," *Independent* 67 (1909): 1201, 1203.
55 Betts, *America's Sporting Heritage*, 129; Galen Jones, *Extra-Curricular Activities in Relation to the Curriculum* (New York, 1935), 20; *RCE* 1893–4, 1:33; *RCE* June 30, 1914, 2:411, 425.
56 Dubbert, *A Man's Place*, 178–9; F. D. Boynton, "Athletics and Collateral Activities in Secondary Schools," *NEAP* 42 (1904): 206–14; Croswell, "Amusements," 321; George E. Johnson, *Education Through Recreation* (Cleveland, 1916), 28–9, 54–5.
57 Jeffrey Mirel, "From Student Control to Institutional Control of High School Athletics: Three Michigan Cities, 1883–1905," *Journal of Social History* 16 (1982): 83–100; Thomas W. Gutowski, "Student Initiative and the Origins of the High School Extracurriculum: Chicago, 1880–1915," *History of Education Quarterly* 28 (1988): 61–72.

spectators, although a principal claimed that onlookers were developing "loyalty" and "social morality." Few schools had extensive intramural programs. Furthermore, a majority of teenagers were not in high school. As late as 1918, only about one-third of American pupils reached that level.[58]

Despite much more school support, football never quite displaced the less military game of baseball in the affections of American boys. More turn-of-the-century boys picked baseball than football as their favorite recreation. Only a fraction, moreover, played either sport with a formally organized team – a fact that troubled recreation workers, who believed that only teams with adult coaching developed intensity and discipline. Worse yet, a 1913 play census of Cleveland reported that the majority of children found outdoors were "just fooling" or "not playing anything in particular."[59] Organized sports had not fully reshaped American childhood.

Some limits to socialization through sport reflected cultural conflicts. Practical-minded immigrants missed the sacrificial idealism and militant Anglo-Saxonism that linked romantic notions of sport and war. When Leonard Covello, who was attending high school in New York City just after 1900, reported an athletic triumph, his father was incredulous: "We kill ourselves. We work so that he can have some future – and he spends his time at school playing!" Nor did boys necessarily value purely symbolic honors. A coach at the Boys' Club of New York City reported that his boys had no interest in maintaining "the strict amateur standing of the amateur sportsman. They desired always to play for some stake . . . [but] were easily dissuaded from playing for money and perfectly satisfied to play for a prize instead." To idealizers of war and sport, such commercial practicality was anathema.[60]

Yet these limitations to the influence of sports may not have mattered hugely. Even spectators could absorb cultural values from sports. By balancing individual stardom and group cohesion, team sports were on their way to becoming the master metaphor for twentieth-century American masculinity. And among the influential American upper-middle and upper classes, faith in sport as a nursery of character and martial virtues may well have trivialized war and made it seem less forbidding. If football resembled war, then in some sense war itself was a game. The search for equivalents obscured James's warning that modern warfare is unthinkably destructive.

58 Franklin Winslow Johnson, "The Social Organization of the High School," *School Review* 17 (1909): 672; Commission on the Reorganization of Secondary Education, *Cardinal Principles of Secondary Education* (Washington, D.C., 1918), 8.
59 McGhee, "Play Life," 464–5; Croswell, "Amusements," 321; Johnson, *Education*, 49–59.
60 Leonard Covello, *The Heart Is the Teacher* (New York, 1958), 50; Boys' Club of the City of New York, *Annual Report* (New York, 1904), 22–3.

Boy Scouting – another great enthusiasm of the pre-World War I American middle class – was somewhat closer to James's spirit but also tried to be both *non*military and *pre*military. These tensions were especially evident in the parent British movement.

An English general, Robert S. S. Baden-Powell, founded Boy Scouting in 1908. His scheme for teaching boys helpfulness and discipline won support from elites fearful of imperial decline, troubled by the growing power of Germany (which Baden-Powell indiscreetly declared Britain's "natural enemy"), and disturbed by the army's poor performance in the Boer War.[61] Scouting began as an effort to enliven the Boys' Brigade and drew on Baden-Powell's experience with military scouting. Baden-Powell rejected prolonged drill for boys as stultifying and turned instead toward freer outdoor life. Believing that British boys lacked initiative, Baden-Powell advocated that they pursue most scout activities in small patrols with boy leaders, though he grouped the patrols into troops under adult scoutmasters. He emphasized camping and civilian service, insisting that his were "peace scouts."[62]

Maintaining this distinction proved difficult in an era of militarism. Baden-Powell himself urged boys to practice leading a running target by sighting along their scout staves. Having constantly to fend off proposals to make scouting a cadet scheme, he made clear that scouting could be premilitary. And whatever Baden-Powell's intentions, many of his supporters were military enthusiasts. According to an American scout official who observed British scout troops early in 1914, the movement was "semimilitary" and the boys were "drilled as proficiently as any body of army men."[63]

Although many Americans first learned of scouting through descriptions of it as a military movement (*Harper's Weekly* featured "England's Boy Army" in March 1910), it took shape in the United States under mostly nonmilitary auspices. Edgar M. Robinson, a Canadian who headed YMCA's boys programs in the United States, learned in May 1910 that William D. Boyce, a Chicago newspaper publisher, had incorporated the Boy Scouts of America, that the Hearst newspapers hoped to exploit

---

61 Baden-Powell quoted in John Springhall, *Youth, Empire and Society: British Youth Movements, 1883–1940* (London, 1977), 128n.
62 R. S. S. Baden-Powell, *Scouting for Boys: A Handbook for Instruction in Good Citizenship*, rev. ed. (London, 1909), 11; Macleod, *Building Character*, 134–41; Tim Jeal, *The Boy-Man: The Life of Lord Baden-Powell* (New York, 1990), 357–97.
63 Samuel A. Moffatt, "Observations of the Boy Scout Movement in England," *American Youth* 3 (1914): 157–8; Baden-Powell, *Scouting for Boys*, 275; Macleod, *Building Character*, 139; Jeal, *Boy-Man*, 448–9.

scouting as a circulation gimmick, and that several groups including the
Hearst affiliate were organizing Boy Scout groups on lines avowedly more
military than Baden-Powell's. Robinson persuaded Boyce to let the
YMCA take over, then organized the Boy Scouts of America as an independent, inclusive organization that co-opted all but the Hearst group of
scouts. Baden-Powell gave the BSA's organizers a very free hand. Although
they had to placate military enthusiasts, Robinson's group was unburdened
by the imperial anxieties that plagued contemporary Britain and Germany,
and instead emphasized civic and moral concerns attuned to Progressive-
era America. Ernest Thompson Seton, the British-born nature writer who
became chief scout, disliked military discipline and privately delighted in
puncturing Americans' "noxious self-satisfaction" about their past. Administration was chaotic, however, until James E. West, a lawyer and child welfare worker, took over as executive secretary in 1911.[64]

In their quest for inclusiveness as the only legitimate American Boy
Scout movement, the early organizers papered over a wide range of opin-
ions. Inclining toward pacifism or at least internationalism were Seton and
a number of YMCA men. Protestant churches sponsored half the early
troops, and about one-quarter of the scoutmasters were clergymen. As the
Boys' Brigade had found, cadet schemes increasingly troubled Progressive-
era churchmen. One of the country's foremost peace advocates, David
Starr Jordan, joined the BSA's National Council, while another, Andrew
Carnegie, became the largest outside donor to the headquarters' budget.[65]
At the same time, leading proponents of military preparedness backed the
BSA. General Leonard Wood joined the National Council. Theodore
Roosevelt lent his name as vice president of the Boy Scouts of America
and issued a statement of support saying that scouting aimed "to make boys
good citizens in time of peace, and incidentally to fit them to become
good soldiers in time of war."[66]

Was Boy Scouting indeed *premilitary*? By ducking the question, the
movement could please nearly everyone. Educators eager to forestall cadet
training in the schools praised scouting as a nonmilitary alternative. Yet
military officers also saw scout training in first aid and camp life as valuable.[67] Because Boy Scouts were still young, the question of their future

---

64 Sydney Brooks, "England's Boy Army," *Harper's Weekly* 54 (Mar. 26, 1910): 9–10; Seton quoted in
Macleod, *Building Character,* 146–67, 181.
65 Macleod, *Building Character,* 191, 194, 207; John L. Alexander, ed., *The Sunday School and the Teens*
(New York, 1913), 319; BSA, *Annual Report* 3 (Feb. 1913): 5.
66 "Boy Scout Leaders Dine Baden-Powell," *New York Times,* Sept. 24, 1910, 8.
67 "Report of the Committee on Military Training," 789; Capt. Howard J. Hickok, "Honorable Mention Essay," *JMSI* 51 (1912): 192–4.

military service could be left in abeyance or blurred by the language of moral equivalence. Boy Scout spokesmen sometimes echoed James's words. Less elegantly, the BSA enunciated its own formula: "As an organization the Scout Movement is neither military in thought, form or spirit, although it does instill in boys the military virtues such as honor, loyalty, obedience and patriotism."[68]

Most of the BSA's national leaders did not see themselves as preparing boys for war and, as believers in progress, were shocked by Europe's resort to "ancient methods" in 1914. James West issued an odd, troubled statement absolving scouting of blame.[69] *Boys' Life,* the BSA's magazine for boys, followed in November with a vehemently antiwar "War Issue" that the president of the BSA urged parents to read. It began with pacifist messages from Andrew Carnegie and David Starr Jordan. Cyrus Townsend Brady warned boys that a soldier's job was "to kill and destroy . . . just that and nothing else." In grisly detail he described men dying, cursing and screaming, alone in no man's land, while others were "shot into unrecognizable lumps of flesh."[70] British and German troops butchered each other in one illustration, while in another a Boy Scout led a female figure labeled "Civilization" toward "peace." Surely here was evidence that scouting was not premilitary. Leonard Wood quit the National Council. Roosevelt stayed on but fumed in 1915 that the BSA had been "part of the wicked and degrading pacifist agitation of the past few years."[71]

Yet Boy Scouting also taught boys uncritical patriotism and performance of duty – which are all that government needs once one's own country goes to war. With no hint of irony, the "War Issue" praised cheery German and British Boy Scouts who harvested crops or reported spies; it also included a story of American frontier warfare in which Daniel Boone's forces killed thirty-seven Native Americans. After recounting the numerous wars in American history, the *Official Handbook for Boys* pronounced: "There is no country in the world less warlike than ours."[72] Under West the Boy Scouts of America had wrapped itself in symbols of American na-

---

68 BSA, *Annual Report* 3 (Feb. 1913): 5; BSA, *The Official Handbook for Boys,* rev. ed. (New York, 1914), 12; *Scouting* 2 (July 1, 1914): 8; Richardson and Loomis, *Boy Scout Movement,* 19–24.

69 "Scouts in the Warring Nations," *Scouting* 2 (Aug. 15, 1914): 1.

70 Cyrus Townsend Brady, "What War Is – Just One Battle," *Boys' Life* 4 (Nov. 1914): 7–9; "President Livingstone's Statement," *Scouting* 2 (Nov. 1, 1914): 1.

71 Leonard Wood to James West, Nov. 9, 1914, box 276, ser. 1; Theodore Roosevelt to James West, Nov. 30, 1915, vol. 94, ser. 2, both in Theodore Roosevelt papers, Library of Congress, Washington, D.C.

72 BSA, *Handbook* (1911), 339; Alfred H. Loeb, "What I Saw Scouts Doing in Europe," *Boys' Life* 4 (Nov. 1914): 9–10; and Everett T. Tomlinson, "Scouting with Daniel Boone," *Boy's Life* 4 (Nov. 1914): 11–13.

tionhood. Somewhat to Baden-Powell's displeasure, the BSA had superim-posed the American eagle on the Boy Scout fleur-de-lis. The top rank was Eagle Scout. And BSA members wore a uniform so similar to the U.S. Army's that Congress exempted them from legislation against civilian use of uniforms resembling the armed forces'.[73]

At the local level, some early troops were openly military. In one Indiana town, two hundred Boy Scouts drilled under a Spanish-American War veteran, with boy sergeants instead of patrol leaders. The rival American Boy Scouts (the remnant Hearst group) marched with rifles, and the BSA had to warn its own troops against using staves as dummy muskets.[74] Until 1915, however, troop activities grew steadily less military.

The effect on American boys is uncertain. Publishers saw a wave of enthusiasm and flooded the market with Boy Scout books. But these shared only a name with the movement and promised excitement no troop could deliver. Although the authors often sported military pseudonyms, the heroes were mostly boy detectives in scout uniforms.[75]

Reality was more prosaic. Scout promotion requirements were relatively formalized, like schoolwork. As an extreme example, the Civics badge required only that a boy draw a map of his city and memorize disconnected information about the structure of government. Compared with later years, few early scouts won promotion.[76]

Boy Scouts loved hiking and camping. The future behaviorist B. F. Skinner wrote home in delight in 1915: "Everything runs like clockwork. This afternoon we had water races and tomorrow a quoit tournament. Thursday we have a game of 'lost battalion' and Friday we are going to give a show and invite the people around the lake. Not an idle moment. We have sentry duty and Ebbe [his brother] is on to-night. . . . It's great and nobody kicks." Such experiences were hard for individual scoutmasters to provide, however, and dangerous in untried hands. As a result, only a fraction of Boy Scouts camped for any length of time until the BSA organized large camps with paid staff, mostly after 1914.[77]

73 Macleod, *Building Character*, 148–9, 157, 178.
74 Robert W. Peterson, *The Boy Scouts: An American Adventure* (New York, 1984), 57; *Scouting* 1 (Sept. 15, 1913): 5. Never numerous outside New York City but an embarrassment there, the American Boy Scouts became the United States Boy Scouts in 1913 and (under BSA pressure) American Cadets in 1918. Macleod, *Building Character*, 157. For pictures see Kett, *Rites*, 213ff.
75 E.g., Major Archibald Lee Fletcher, *Boy Scouts in Alaska, or The Camp on the Glacier* (Chicago, 1913). Bishop, *American Boys' Series Books*, lists 111 Boy Scout titles through 1914. Then the fictional Boy Scouts went to war in 60 of 100 titles from 1915 through 1919.
76 BSA, *Handbook* (1911), 29–30; Macleod, *Building Character*, 249.
77 B. F. Skinner, *Particulars of My Life* (New York, 1976), 89; *Scouting* 2 (Aug. 1, 1914): 4; Macleod, *Building Character*, 241–2.

As a source of group cohesion, the patrol system remained weak. Whereas Baden-Powell thought that British boys lacked initiative, Americans feared more that theirs lacked discipline; most scoutmasters ran virtually all activities themselves on a troop basis. American scouting attempted to socialize boys to control in large groups by adult officers.[78]

Mustered in groups, Boy Scouts sometimes won nationwide attention, notably in 1913 when they battled Ohio Valley floods. Like many Progressive-era adults, Boy Scouts more typically learned to equate public service with brief crusades in which everyone pledged good intentions. In one such campaign, for instance, Boy Scouts signaled the date of fire-prevention day from Pittsburgh's tallest building and then distributed 100,000 "safety first" cards.[79]

Despite such public achievements, the BSA was still just beginning to recruit a mass membership when war struck. In 1914, 103,395 boys enrolled but 86 percent were new that year. These were disproportionately sons of white-collar fathers or skilled workers, as many immigrant, working-class parents could not afford the cost of scout uniforms and mistrusted scouting as a school of militarism. Membership grew rapidly to 185,251 in 1916 and to 377,577 by 1918; but the BSA lived on its public image, recruiting streams of new boys to replace those who dropped out. Through 1920 fewer than half of each year's scouts returned the following year. Such rapid turnover suggests that scouting did not teach many boys persistence and implicit submission to military discipline; only a fraction stayed long enough to be seriously affected. Furthermore, a good many early Boy Scouts were below the official minimum age of twelve. Once the age requirement was better enforced, a majority still quit before their fifteenth birthday and eight of nine before they turned seventeen. Studies of American teenagers in more recent decades have found that they tend to pass from naïvely authoritarian toward more differentiated views with increasing age. Although critics later alleged that Boy Scouts too readily accepted authoritarian leadership, many early scouts were too young to take permanent shape politically.[80] Clearly, school instruction and sports reached more boys. Yet Boy Scouting offers the clearest indication of middle-class adults' interest in preparing boys to be citizen-soldiers and of their lingering ambivalence about doing so directly.

78 Macleod, *Building Character,* 270–4.
79 Harold P. Levy, *Building a Popular Movement: A Case Study of the Public Relations of the Boy Scouts of America* (New York, 1944), 26; *Scouting* 2 (Dec. 1, 1914): 2.
80 Chambers, *To Build an Army,* 109; Macleod, *Building Character,* 154, 215–20, 280–1; Joseph Adelson, "The Political Imagination of the Young Adolescent," *Daedalus* 100 (1971): 1022–7; Levy, *Building,* 83–92.

The slow growth of equivalent programs for girls furnished further evidence that Americans were not anticipating total war. Combat was still idealized as a form of masculine character building with little attention to the civilian mobilization of both sexes that total war would entail.[81]

Camp Fire Girls, the largest new organization, took a conservative approach to gender roles. With help from James West and Seton, in 1911 Luther Gulick and Charlotte Vetter Gulick designed a program intended to put romance into domestic work. Luther Gulick declared it would be "fundamentally evil" to copy Boy Scouting; because girls must learn "to be womanly," the "domestic fire" became the group's symbol. Girls wore a "ceremonial gown" for the "Indian maiden" look. Their citizenship training was mildly reformist, including conservation and "United States history as it affects women's welfare" – not, as in boys' groups, history centered on wars. If Camp Fire Girls were socialized for war, it was for self-abnegating service on the home front. Whereas Boy Scout promotion requirements obliged boys to earn and save money, Camp Fire Girls could win honors by earning money and giving it away. The organization grew rapidly, claiming 60,000 girls in 1914 (probably an overestimate) and 94,445 in 1917.[82]

The Girl Scouts, founded in 1912 by Juliette Low on the model of Baden-Powell's Girl Guides, blended domestic skills with an assertive public style that resembled Boy Scouting's. The early Girl Scouts stressed outdoor exercise and practiced marching drills. But the organization was much smaller than Camp Fire – perhaps 2,000 scouts when war came in 1914.[83]

In the end, war confounded many expectations. Pressure from preparedness advocates drove the Boy Scouts down a path toward greater militancy. In October 1915 the BSA shifted emphasis, declaring that "the Boy Scout movement is not anti-military. The Boy Scout Movement neither promotes nor discourages military training. . . . It is in reality as strong a factor as any other one agency which the country now has for preparedness, since it develops the character of boys and assists them in securing a proper con-

---

81 Girls also impressed adults as being already more compliant to their wishes. Perhaps twenty times as many groups were doing youth work with boys in 1910 as with girls. Hartley Davis with Mrs. Luther Halsey Gulick, "The Camp-Fire Girls," *Outlook* 101 (1912): 189.

82 Gulick quoted in Helen Buckler et al., *WO-HE-LO: The Story of Camp Fire Girls, 1910–1960* (New York, 1960), 11, 22, 27–33, 83, 147, quotations on 55, 139; BSA, *Handbook* (1911), 17.

83 Mary Aickin Rothschild, "To Scout or to Guide? The Girl Scout-Boy Scout Controversy, 1912–1941," *Frontiers* 6 (1981): 117; Charles E. Strickland, "Juliette Low, the Girl Scouts, and the Role of American Women," in Mary Kelley, ed., *Woman's Being, Woman's Place: Female Identity and Vocation in American History* (Boston, 1979), 259.

ception of a citizen's responsibility." Trained scouts "will . . . prove themselves more virile and efficient in any emergency which calls for their services as citizens of the country." More and more scoutmasters drilled their troops.[84] Seton left the BSA in late 1915 amid charges that he "was in harmony with the views of anarchists and radical socialists on the question as to whether the Boy Scouts of America should stand for patriotism and good citizenship." As public opinion shifted, Boy Scout leaders counterbalanced their continuing opposition to full-scale cadet training with strident emphasis on patriotism and "the proper attitude of mind towards duly constituted authority." After 1917 scoutmasters had to be citizens, and non-American boys had to swear allegiance before joining.[85]

Once the United States declared war, troops celebrated with massive parades. The Boy Scouts scored a public relations triumph by selling $354,859,262 worth of war bonds. The boys were still unready for sustained effort, however. Liberty Loan drives that required them to push hard for a week or so succeeded fairly well (though only 7 to 9 percent of Boy Scouts sold ten or more bonds), whereas a scheme to have them raise gardens – which demanded that they toil a whole season – failed as they got bored.[86]

War caused a boom in Girl Scout membership. Well before 1917 they turned to militant preparedness, adopting an army-style uniform like the boys'. During the war, Girl Scouts sold bonds and marched in parades, just as the boys did. When several thousand marched through Boston in 1919, a reporter wrote approvingly that "the young girl soldiers manifested every evidence that they are just as militaristic as their brother scouts." Girl Scout ranks swelled to 50,000 by 1920.[87]

The approach of war brought reflexive calls for cadet training in schools. The proportion of high school boys enrolled for drill rose from just under 3 percent in 1913–14 to nearly 5 percent in 1915–16, then shot up to 15 percent for 1917–18. As usual, drill taught neither perseverance nor militarily useful skills. Boys did endless close-order drill, got bored, and

84 BSA, *Annual Report* 6 (Feb. 1916): 19; Macleod, *Building Character,* 180.
85 *New York Times,* Dec. 7, 1915, 4; BSA, *Annual Report* 7 (Mar. 1917): 12, quotation on 24. Seton's departure also resulted from complex personal rivalries.
86 William D. Murray, *The History of the Boy Scouts of America* (New York, 1937), 101–36; statistical table, *Scouting* 6 (Mar. 15, 1918): 15; "To Every Scout," *Scouting* 6 (May 1, 1918): 1–2; "Are We 100% Loyal?" *Scouting* 6 (July 1, 1918): 8; BSA, *Annual Report* 9 (May 1919): 34.
87 "Thousands Applaud Girl Scouts as They March Through the Back Bay," unidentified clipping in historical scrapbook, vol. 5, Boy Scouts of Canada, National Council Library, Ottawa; Strickland, "Juliette Low," 259.

stopped attending. "Possibly Chicago officials have been led to form battalions of death," gibed an editorial on the dwindling turnout.[88]

Yet idealism remained high, especially among home-front opinion leaders who were convinced that sport and character had equipped young Americans for victory. Praising the eagerness with which athletes volunteered for officers' training programs, a Harvard dean asserted in 1918: "This war has come nearer justifying our methods in intercollegiate athletics than we had thought possible." In a "Dad" to "Tom" letter published as an editorial by the *Ladies' Home Journal,* father assured son that "you and the other chaps have gone over . . . to demonstrate the right kind of manhood, for it is that which weighs in a fight and wins it." Socialized to expect leadership positions and to believe in national service, graduates of elite preparatory schools and colleges volunteered in such numbers that Princeton University called a mass meeting in March 1917 to dissuade students from rushing off to enlist.[89]

Ironically, Woodrow Wilson's administration, fearful of uncontrollable volunteer units such as the one that Theodore Roosevelt proposed to lead and aware that Britain's pell-mell volunteering had wasted skilled workers as infantrymen, turned to conscription to secure the masses of troops it needed. Still, 23 percent of the U.S. forces were volunteers, especially the officers, who included many products of Leonard Wood's summer training camps. Fragmentary evidence suggests that the educated middle class, both volunteers and draftees, went to war somewhat more enthusiastically than did farmers or laborers.[90]

The Wilson administration's reluctance and inability to apply broadly effective coercion made draft registration almost voluntary, dependent on government propaganda and popular patriotism. In this situation, a generation of socializing boys to loyalty and obedience may have helped at least marginally to spur compliance. However, nearly one-fifth of the draftees were foreign-born and more than one-eighth African American. These groups and the working class had generally been bypassed by much of the prewar effort to inculcate manly patriotism. Although schooling and sports

88 "Lax Military Training for Boys," *School Review* 26 (1918): 289; "Military Training," *School Review* 26 (1918): 366–7; *RCE* June 30, 1914, 2:411, 415, 425, 429; *RCE* June 30, 1917, 1:513, 523, 527; *Statistical Abstract of the United States, 1921* (Washington, D.C., 1922), 124–5.
89 L. B. R. Briggs, "Intercollegiate Athletics and the War," *Atlantic Monthly* 122 (1918): 303; "Tom," *Ladies' Home Journal* 34 (Oct. 1907): 4, quoted in Filene, *Him/Her/Self,* 96; David M. Kennedy, *Over Here: The First World War and American Society* (New York, 1980), 146–7; Schaffer, *America in the Great War,* 186.
90 Chambers, *To Raise an Army,* 125–44, 174–85, 200, 233; Kennedy, *Over Here,* 147–50; Mark David Meigs, "Uplift and Optimism: Voices of American Participants in World War One," Ph.D. diss., University of California, Berkeley, 1990, 85.

may have furnished some socialization along these lines, the typical conscript had had limited education: 6.9 years for native-born whites, 4.6 for foreign-born whites, and 2.6 for African Americans from the underschooled South.[91] Even among the middle class, only modest numbers of youths had as yet passed through scouting, which had achieved large enrollments only recently. Nor could the majority have played football on the select squads chosen for interschool competition, although popular culture and casual play spread the ethos of team sports much more widely and small high schools did place most male students on teams. What sports and patriotic indoctrination provided was inspiration to the sorts of young men most likely to become officers and a metaphorical language for representing war to conscripts that was consistent with middle- and upper-class efforts at hegemony and at least familiar to some of the draftees. By securing middle-class approval – and sometimes personal involvement as scoutmasters or team supporters – organized socialization also reinforced the expectations of men in power in many communities that youths should be loyal team players.

Additionally, in pressuring civilians to participate in ostensibly voluntary programs on the home front, the government drew heavily on juvenile patriotism. Boy Scouts and Girl Scouts beat the drum for Liberty Loan drives and extracted hundreds of millions of dollars in sales.[92] As long as the government of the United States clung to coercive voluntarism, propagandizing of and by youth would be essential to anything approaching total war.

Despite the military professionals' belief that new troops needed thorough training – the American General Staff wanted two years' – Allied losses by early 1918 forced the United States to send forces in haste, relying once more on the spirit of relatively untrained citizen-soldiers. Many doughboys shipped out to France with training that, except for physical conditioning, scarcely surpassed that of some cadet companies. Some men sailed having never fired a rifle. Time in training camp passed in maintenance, calisthenics, marches, and endless drills.[93]

Published narratives by combatants and even some early letters home exude the exalted air of prewar middle- and upper-class male socialization. "I think soldiering makes real men," a young lieutenant wrote his family. Although the dream of war as dangerous sport seemed most apposite in

91 Kennedy, *Over Here*, 150–7, 162, 165, 188.
92 Macleod, *Building Character*, 181; Florence Woolston, "Billy and the World War," *New Republic* 17 (Jan. 25, 1919): 369.
93 Kennedy, *Over Here*, 169–70; Edward M. Coffman, *The War to End All Wars: The American Military Experience in World War I* (New York, 1968), 55–6, 65–8.

aerial combat, the Americans and British shared a tradition of trying to see even ground war in similar terms. The poet Alan Seeger described the "frequent encounters and ambuscades" as "very good sport."[94] Such thinking merged easily with popular Anglo-Saxonism. The bestselling *Private Peat* told readers that "if the German hordes, with their iron power behind them, had had five per cent of the Anglo-Saxon sporting blood in their veins, they would have licked us long ago." Writers once again idealized mass charges of the Civil War variety and echoed the pieties of glorious sacrifice. Clearly, romantic views of sport and war had led some articulate young Americans to the verge of battle. But these effusions were unrepresentative, written mostly by men composing self-consciously for publication, by romantics like Seeger who had volunteered 25,000 or more strong to serve with British or French forces before the United States joined the war, or by young officers who had not yet seen combat. These were the middle- and upper-class young men influenced most by prewar socialization to the ideal of the citizen-soldier and most likely to be volunteers and officers. Many draftees had simply complied a step at a time, registering, accepting induction, and finding obedience easier than resistance.[95]

The socialization of pre–World War I American youths for war had been vague, romantic, euphemistic in its conflation of sport and war, and often focused narrowly on the sons of the middle and upper classes. Formal military instruction through drill had won little popularity and probably had little effect. But indirect socialization for patriotic masculinity may have mattered more. Through extended schooling, sports, and sometimes youth programs such as scouting, middle- and upper-class boys had learned to revere the flag, obey orders, and work for the team. Once they were at the front, patriotism, obedience, loyalty to their team of buddies, and, if necessary, compulsion would carry most forward.[96]

94 Albert Angier, quoted in Filene, *Him/Her/Self,* 100; Alan Seeger, *Letters and Diary* (New York, 1917), 205, quoted in Charles V. Genthe, *American War Narratives, 1917–1918: A Study and Bibliography* (New York, 1969), 49; Frank Freidel, *Over There: The Story of America's First Great Overseas Crusade,* rev. ed. (Philadelphia, 1990), 78, 135.

95 Harold Peat, *Private Peat* (Indianapolis, 1917), 85, quoted in Genthe, *American War Narratives,* 36; Meigs, "Uplift and Optimism," 98, 128–30; Schaffer, *America in the Great War,* 182–97. Belief that Germans did not "play the game" may, in the minds of some Anglo-American combatants, have excused some Allied atrocities. Genthe, *American War Narratives,* 91; Freidel, *Over There,* 115.

96 Estimates of subsequent disillusionment vary, but the war ended victoriously so soon after most saw combat that many American veterans apparently continued to envision war in the romantic terms they learned before they saw combat. Kennedy, *Over Here,* 212–29; Schaffer, *America in the Great War,* 194–7.

8

Preparing German Youth for War

DEREK S. LINTON

It is tempting to construct a genealogy that leads inexorably from the numerous calls for premilitary training of young males in Bismarckian and early Wilhelmine Germany to the rapid proliferation of militarized organizations for male adolescents in the years immediately preceding the outbreak of World War I.[1] Such a temptation, however, should be stoutly resisted. After all, Field Marshall Freiherr Colmar von der Goltz, who in 1911 founded the largest of such organizations, the Young Germany League (Jungdeutschlandbund), had advocated the systematic premilitary training of primary school students since 1876.[2] Yet his proposals had invariably been dismissed as well meant but potentially dangerous. Conservatives associated these proposals with French conceptions of "the nation in arms," and the Prussian War Ministry worried that the implementation of such training would embolden and lend credibility to left-leaning and socialist proponents of short-term militia-type armies.[3] Thus, premilitary training threatened to undermine military professionalism. Indeed, up until 1914 such apprehensions about professionalism impelled the military to enforce an inviolable taboo against teaching young males to handle weapons before enlistment.

Moreover, until the prewar years, voluntary youth associations that heavily emphasized a component of premilitary training generally

---

1 Such a perspective characterizes the work of Klaus Saul's "Der Kampf um die Jugend zwischen Volksschule und Kaserne: Ein Beitrag zur Jugendpflege im wilhelminischen Reich 1890–1914," *Militärgeschichtliche Mitteilungen* 1 (1971): 97–142, and the article by Christoph Schubert-Weller, "Vormilitärische Jugenderziehung," in Christa Berg, ed., *Handbuch der deutschen Bildungsgeschichte*, vol. 4: *1870–1918: Von der Reichsgründung bis zum Ende des Ersten Weltkrieges* (Munich, 1991), 503–15. Schubert-Weller in particular largely draws on programmatic statements before 1909 without much attention to their consequences, and he completely neglects the central importance of the growth of Social Democratic youth work for the actual implementation of premilitary training.
2 Colmar Freiherr von der Goltz, *Jung-Deutschland: Ein Beitrag zur Frage der Jugendpflege* (Berlin, 1911), 5–17.
3 "Auszüge aus dem gemeinsamen Immediatbericht des preussischen Kultus-und Kriegsministerium, 28.9.1906," reprinted in Saul, "Der Kampf um die Jugend," 126–9.

foundered. Thus, in the 1890s the Central Committee to Promote Youth and Popular Sports in Germany (Zentralausschuss zur Förderung der Jugend und Volksspiele in Deutschland), organized by Emil von Schenkendorff, a National Liberal Party member of the lower house of the Prussian parliament, undertook a sustained campaign to encourage German youth to engage in sports and gymnastics in order to improve their health, counter precocious maturity, and enhance Germany's defensive capabilities.[4] Yet despite financial support, approval from the Kaiser and the Prussian bureaucracy, and endorsements from numerous notables and urban administrators, this campaign ultimately withered in the face of concerted opposition from the German Gymnasts. The German Gymnasts, the largest, oldest, and most "establishment" middle-class gymnastics association, objected vociferously to the Central Committee's aspiration to monopolize sports activities for youth. Even less successful was a uniformed youth militia (*Jugendwehr*) in Berlin started by a captain of the reserves in 1896.[5] This organization was launched to save post-school-age males from the moral dangers of the large city through a program combining such premilitary preparation as marching and drilling with edifying recreational activities, such as visiting museums. It soon attained a maximum membership of 1,000 and then stagnated. It also was unable to secure funding from the government. Certainly some of the same anxieties that prompted these early organizing attempts – anxieties over the supposed dangers of urban life, the ostensibly declining fitness of young males, and deficiencies in national military preparedness – figured prominently as justifications for the organization of militarized youth groups in the prewar years. Moreover, some of the same persons who had long promoted premilitary training, including Freiherr von der Goltz, also were instigators of the prewar foundation fever. But despite continuities in anxieties, ideology, and personnel, explaining the extraordinary burst of organizational activity after 1908 and the sharp contrast between the modest success of earlier endeavors and the effectiveness of prewar efforts requires a concentration on the specific political and institutional constellation of late Wilhelmine Germany, especially the years between the passage of the new Imperial Association Law in 1908 and the outbreak of the war.

Hence this chapter will first explore the ideological climate that made the prewar militarization of youth work possible, then turn to the institu-

4 Saul, "Der Kampf um die Jugend," 98–9; Schubert-Weller, "Vormilitärische Jugenderziehung," 505–6.
5 Major Menzel, "Die Jugendwehr," in Deutsche Zentrale für Jugendfürsorge, ed., *Handbuch für Jugendpflege* (Langensalza, 1913), 410–16.

tional nexus that facilitated the rapid expansion of militarized associations. It will then take up the rapid growth of the Social Democratic Party (Sozialdemokratische Partei Deutschlands or SPD) youth organization following the passage of the Imperial Association Law in 1908 and relate this growth to the formation of officially sponsored militarized youth groups by discussing the forms, goals, and activities that defined these associations. Finally, it will speculate about the effects produced by this militarized youth work in terms of preparing German youth for war. In addressing these issues, this chapter attempts to make the prewar militarization of youth work operate as a lens that can focus light on broader historiographical questions about the relation between Imperial Germany's domestic situation and its aggressive foreign policy in the summer of 1914.

Starting in the 1890s large sectors of the educated middle class abhorred what they believed to be the physically debilitating and morally deleterious consequences of industrial society and the urban environment for adolescents, especially adolescent workers. Representative of this trend was the study on dangers to the health of young laborers written by the social and racial hygienist Dr. Ignaz Kaup in 1911 for the influential Society for Social Reform (Gesellschaft für Soziale Reform).[6] Kaup held labor in factories and workshops responsible for the imperiled health of post-school-age workers. Their health was further worsened by urban pleasure seeking, as exemplified by smoking, immoderate drinking, and early sexual relations that accompanied the premature independence of young employees. According to Kaup, deteriorating health manifested itself in a precipitous decline in the fitness of urban males for military service. Thus, the military acceptance rate for urban-born males employed in industrial or commercial firms dropped from 53.8 percent in 1902–3 to 49.7 percent by 1907–8. Dr. Max von Gruber, the *völkisch* hygienist at the University of Munich, skeptically challenged Kaup's citation of the military fitness rates as evidence because the rapidity of the decline indicated that it was more likely attributable to greater selectivity by military doctors faced with larger birth cohorts than to biological degeneration.[7] Nonetheless, at the general assembly of the Society for Social Reform, he concurred that the unsatisfactory health and weak physiques of urban youth were the result of occupational dangers compounded by social poisons such as tuberculosis, venereal dis-

---

6 Dr. med. Ignaz Kaup, "Schädigungen von Leben und Gesundheit der Jugendlichen," in *Die Jugendlichen Arbeiter in Deutschland*, 6 vols., Schriften der Gesellschaft für Soziale Reform, no. 3 (Jena, 1911), 4:8–55.

7 Prof. Dr. v. Gruber, "Referat: Berufschutz der Jugendlichen," in *Verhandlungen der 5. Generalversammlung der Gesellschaft für Soziale Reform am 12. und 13 Mai 1911 in Berlin* (vol. 4 of *Die Jugendlichen Arbeiter in Deutschland*), Schriften der Gesellschaft für Soziale Reform, nos. 5–6 (Jena, 1911), 12–51.

ease, and alcoholism. Rather than simply express antipathy to the metropolis, however, hygienists and social reformers proposed a combination of
expanded protective legislation and programs for physical exercise to improve the health of young laborers and thereby safeguard Germany's future
soldiers.

Further cited as evidence of the negative effects of urbanism on the
physical capacities of youth was the diminished responsiveness and atrophy
of their sensory organs.[8] Imperial encounters had demonstrated the extraordinary sensitivity of "natural peoples," such as the Hereroes in Southwest
Africa, to barely discernible changes in the environment. The sensory
acuteness of native populations was admired, even as they were being
slaughtered. By contrast, German officers lamented the inability of their
men to decode the signs of nature, to find their bearings in strange terrain,
to detect danger with their eyes and ears. However, officers believed that
this loss of sensory acuity could be halted and reversed through systematic
training and exercising of the senses.

In addition to the physical dangers arising from industry and the large
city, officials and middle-class social reformers listed with alarm a host of
moral dangers that confronted urban youth.[9] Young workers were considered less dependent on their families than in the past, and most broke with
the churches soon after confirmation. Unskilled youth utterly lacked commitment to their jobs and instead simply regarded their work purely as a
means to earn money for amusement. With their earnings in hand, they
gravitated to the new forms of mass entertainment, to the cheap thrills offered by the dance hall, bars, and cinema. Young workers were mesmerized
by the exciting *demimonde* portrayed in films and the siren song of adventure bruited by the lurid "penny dreadfuls." Not only did urban shop win-
dows bombard their senses with beguiling images and sanction materialism,
but by doing so they contributed to the discontent that accelerated the upward spiral of juvenile delinquency.[10] Youths who succumbed to the mere-
tricious temptations of the streets were unlikely to submit to military discipline or harness their strength to improving Germany's industrial efficiency.
Already in 1900 the Munich educational reformer and school superintendent Georg Kerschensteiner had advocated forming military-style youth
organizations modeled along the lines of the British Boys' Brigades in or-

8 See, e.g., Von der Goltz, *Jung-Deutschland*, 26–36.
9 For a full treatment of this moral discourse and the resulting reform proposals, see Derek S. Linton,
   "Who Has the Youth, Has the Future": The Campaign to Save Young Workers in Imperial Germany (Cambridge, 1991), 48–72.
10 Paul Köhne, "Kriminalität und sittliches Verhalten der Jugendlichen," in "Die Jugendlichen Arbeiter
   in Deutschland," *Schriften der Gesellschaft für Sozialreform*, no. 2 (Jena, 1910), 4:10–11, 15.

der to avert decline by instilling discipline in young, unskilled workers and teaching them to rely on their middle-class superiors for moral guidance.[11]

The writings of educators such as Kerschensteiner and conferences convened by such middle-class reform associations as the Evangelical Social Congress (Evangelisch-sozialer Kongress) and the Center for Workers' Welfare Institutions (Centralstelle für Arbeiter-Wohlfahrtseinrichtungen) first called attention to the endangering environment and supposed behavioral problems of lower-class urban youth at the turn of the century.[12] Such writings and conferences stimulated a wave of interest in youth within the *Bildungsbürgertum* (educated middle classes), interest that the German states soon fostered and reinforced. Clergymen rapidly translated this interest into new forms of youth work. Younger and more energetic urban Protestant ministers, such as Walther Classen and Clemens Schulz in Hamburg and Günther Dehn in Berlin, criticized the exclusive focus on religious devotion that had previously hampered the youth work of the Inner Mission of the Evangelical Church (Innere Mission der evangelischen Kirche).[13] Instead, these urban ministers built large youth organizations, many in rough proletarian districts, such as Hamburg's St. Pauli waterfront district or Berlin-Wedding, that stressed sports, recreation, and sociability. Such breaks with traditional Protestant approaches to youth depended more on the individual initiative of charismatic pastors, however, than on a new consensus about the institutional reorientation of the Evangelical Church. By contrast, the Catholic Church made a wholehearted effort to organize young Catholics.[14] In 1895 Joseph Drammer, a founder of the populist People's Association for Catholic Germany (Volksverein für das katholische Deutschland) and chairman of the Cologne Association of Young Workers (Kölner Jungarbeiterverein), initiated a campaign to set up a committee for youth affairs in every diocese. In response to the awakened interest in the affairs of young workers and the organizational drive of the SPD, the church centralized and coordinated these committees in 1908 when it established a national Catholic youth secretariat in Düsseldorf. By 1911 the

---

11 Georg Kerschensteiner, "Staatsbürgerliche Erziehung der deutschen Jugend," in *Berufsbildung und Berufsschule: Ausgewählte Pädagogische Schriften* (Paderborn, 1966), 1:26, 80–1.

12 See *Die Verhandlungen des elften Evangelisch-sozialen Kongresses abgehalten zu Karlsruhe 7–8 Juni 1900* (Göttingen, 1900), and *Fürsorge für die schulentlassene Jugend: Vorberichte und Verhandlungen der IX. Konferenz: Schriften der Centralstelle für Arbeiter Wohlfahrtseinrichtungen*, no. 16 (Berlin, 1900).

13 Jürgen Reulecke, "Bürgerliche Sozialreformer und Arbeiterjugend im Kaiserreich," *Archiv für Sozialgeschichte* 22 (1982): 321–3. For an expanded discussion of Protestant youth work, see Linton, *Who Has the Youth, Has the Future*, 98–107.

14 Karl Mosterts, "Verband der katholischen Jünglingsvereinigungen Deutschlands," in Herta Siemering, ed., *Die deutschen Jugendpflegeverbände* (Berlin, 1918), 134–46; see also Linton, *Who Has the Youth, Has the Future*, 107–15.

more than 3,800 Catholic youth groups, mostly parish sodalities that offered a mixture of religious instruction, recreation, and social events, could boast a membership of 365,000. The youth secretariat published a national newspaper, *Die Wacht,* which was distributed to members of all Catholic youth associations. With its well-written articles and stories, often secular and informational, this paper could compete on even terms with the socialist youth paper, the *Arbeiter-Jugend.* Moreover, the burgeoning industrial cities of the Rhineland and Ruhr proved to be the bastions of Catholic youth organization.

Even more important for the organization of young laborers under state and middle-class auspices was the transformation of industrial continuation schools (*gewerbliche Fortbildungsschulen*) from voluntary evening schools that taught mechanical drawing to young craft apprentices into obligatory part-time schools with a wide array of vocational courses for all young male laborers.[15] Such a transformation was proposed by Kerschensteiner in his highly influential essay on civic education, *Staatsbürgerliche Erziehung der deutschen Jugend,* published in Erfurt in 1901. Here, Kerschensteiner elaborated on what should be done to close the dangerous gap in official socialization institutions for youth between the completion of primary school and their entry into the army. He argued that by building on young workers' interest in vocational advancement, continuation schools not only could improve industrial efficiency, but they also could spell out linkages between the indispensability of cooperation in the world of work and the need for harmony in civil life, thus subtly undercutting the class-struggle message of the socialists. These schools also were to sponsor extensive recreational programs that would improve the health of young workers, instill self-discipline, and guide youths to wholesome pursuits in their free time – all of which would counteract the moral perils of urban life. As mentioned previously, in the case of the unskilled who lacked an immediate attachment to their work, he hoped that militarized organizations analogous to the British Boys' Brigades might substitute for the discipline of craft or skill. By 1910 every Prussian city with a population of more than 100,000 had made such schools mandatory for all young male laborers after their completion of primary school at age fourteen. That year there were more than 2,000 such schools in Prussia, and enrollment totaled over 350,000. On a somewhat smaller scale, continuation schools in other German states, most notably Saxony and Bavaria, followed a similar trajectory.

15 For an overview of these schools, see Klaus Harney, "Fortbildungsschulen," in Christa Berg, ed., *Handbuch der deutschen Bildungsgeschichte,* vol. 4: *1870–1918* (Munich, 1991), 380–9; and for their development at the local level, see Linton, *Who Has the Youth, Has the Future,* 73–97.

Many municipalities instituted continuation schools for commercial as well as industrial employees. In general, these schools required three years of compulsory attendance. Students attended classes several evenings during the workweek for a total of six or eight hours weekly. Course work was divided among vocationally related instruction, German, and civic education. Moreover, many of these schools sponsored extensive extracurricular recreational programs along the lines suggested by Kerschensteiner. Instructors from the German Gymnasts oversaw athletic programs, while school choirs and brass bands appealed to the musically inclined and a host of clubs catered to the more sedentary. Well-appointed reading rooms stocked with numerous illustrated journals and a lending library also were standard features of the urban continuation schools. Apart from providing recreation away from the socialist and labor milieu, continuation schools strove to reinforce the patriotism and monarchical spirit propagated by the primary schools. They staged carefully orchestrated celebrations of national holidays such as the Kaiser's birthday and the 1913 centenary of the Wars of Liberation against Napoleon. Thus, before the war, mandatory municipally controlled continuation schools with educational programs stressing vocational skills, civics, and recreation enrolled the majority of young male urban laborers. In addition, a substantial number of teachers, clergymen, and members of the German Gymnasts had accumulated considerable experience in working with adolescent male workers. This state of affairs meant that both the institutional preconditions and personnel were present that aided the subsequent formation of militarized youth groups.

Serious middle-class concern about the physical and moral degeneration of young workers as a result of rapid urbanization and the consequent belief that this decay would sap Germany's potential military strength and diminish its industrial efficiency were the necessary ideological prerequisites for the militarization of youth work. The mandatory continuation school provided an institutional focus that would facilitate the organization of such groups. But the immediate stimulus to nationwide formation of militarized youth groups was the rapid growth of the socialist youth movement following passage in 1908 of the Imperial Association Law. Interior Minister Bethmann Hollweg had omitted any restrictions on the political organization of youth in his original legislative draft because he considered them unenforceable.[16] But in the face of pressure from both conservative and liberal Reichstag deputies who believed that the absence of such pro-

---

16 Karl Erich Born, *Staat und Sozialpolitik seit Bismarcks Sturz: Ein Beitrag zur Geschichte der innenpolitischen Entwicklung des Deutschen Reichs 1890–1914* (Wiesbaden, 1957), 217–22.

hibitions would accelerate the SPD's politicization of youth, he added a section in the final version prohibiting political activity by youths under the age of eighteen. Ironically, it was the SPD's reaction to this prohibition that would set in motion the sort of stunningly rapid growth of socialist youth work that the law had been intended to forestall and that would usher in a new phase in the battle for hegemony over young workers.

Two socialist youth movements already existed prior to 1908: one in southern Germany, the other in the north.[17] The south-German organization, founded by the revisionist lawyer Ludwig Frank in 1904, centered its agitation on opposition to the military. It was at the conference of the south-German group in 1906 that the radical socialist Reichstag deputy Karl Liebknecht delivered the address subsequently expanded into his well-known pamphlet *Militarismus und Antimilitarismus, unter besonderer Berücksichtigung der Internationalen Jugendbewegung* (Leipzig, 1907). In northern Germany, by contrast, more stringent state laws forbade political activity by youth. There the Federation of Free Youth Organizations avoided overt politics and instead limited itself to defending the economic interests and fostering the sociability of apprentices, journeymen, and young factory workers. Both organizations were decentralized, and both enjoyed considerable independence in relation to the SPD.

The new Imperial Association Law had several contradictory effects on the relation of the SPD to youth work. On the one hand, the south-German movement was deradicalized. Moderate spokespeople of the Free Trade Unions (Freie Gewerkschaftsbund), increasingly decisive in determining party policy, denounced the antimilitarism of the south-German youth because they concluded that opposition to the military would provoke an unequal confrontation with the state and hence was doomed to inevitable failure.[18] They also argued that the law compelled the SPD to bring youth activities under centralized control of party elders. On the other hand, both the SPD and the Free Trade Unions agreed to budget greater resources and energy than before to their youth work in order to imbue young workers with a "proletarian world view." They backed this decision by setting up a national commission on youth affairs, staffed by such prominent party and trade-union leaders as Friedrich Ebert, Carl

17 Karl Korn, *Die Arbeiterjugendbewegung* (Berlin, 1922), 36–75, is still the best work on the early years of the movement; see also Hermann Giesecke, *Vom Wandervogel bis zur Hitlerjugend* (Munich, 1981), 38–59.
18 *Protokoll der Verhandlungen der 6. Kongresses der Gewerkschaften Deutschlands, Hamburg, 22–27. Juni 1908*, 320–35; Carl E. Schorske, *German Social Democracy, 1905–1917* (New York, 1972), 106–8; Dieter Fricke, *Die deutsche Arbeiterjugendbewegung 1869–1914* ([East] Berlin, 1976), 347–9.

Legien, and Luise Zietz. The SPD also began publishing a national news-paper for young workers, *Arbeiter-Jugend,* that even fierce opponents of the SPD admired for its high quality. Local SPD groups throughout Germany began holding educational events that introduced such themes as the materialist conception of history and the history of labor movements, sponsoring recreational activities such as summer hikes, and staging cultural events with readings from radical poets such as Heinrich Heine. In order to keep from being dissolved for holding political events with youth in attendance, presiding SPD members assiduously prevented any overt discussion of political issues. Despite this restraint, local police often suspected that adult SPD members were covertly disseminating antimilitarist propaganda, and police officials often broke up youth movement meetings on the flimsiest of pretexts.[19] Nonetheless, by 1910 subscriptions to *Arbeiter-Jugend* reached approximately 65,000, and local youth commissions held more than 1,800 lectures and more than 300 artistic events that year.[20] Thus, the paradoxical effect of the tough new Association Law was to unleash the exponential growth of SPD youth work.

Government officials responded to this growth in part by heightening police surveillance and sharpening repressive measures against the socialist youth movement. But in addition to repression, they, along with clergymen, teachers, and a host of youth reformers, resolved to redouble their efforts to win the hearts and minds of young workers. They were committed to loosening the grip of the SPD by intensifying their efforts to bind these young workers to the Wilhelmine state and to middle-class society. The preexisting middle-class discourse on working-class youth and its embodiment in continuation schools as an institutional locus made such efforts feasible. The militarized youth group proved to be the most effective vehicle.

Although the Jungdeutschlandbund was by far the largest of these militarized youth groups and the one that depended most clearly on the continuation schools for its success, two precursor organizations blazed its trail: the German Boy Scouts (Deutsche Pfadfinder) and the Bavarian Defense Force Association (Bayerischer Wehrkraftverein). The founders of the German Boy Scouts sometimes purported to trace the organization's ancestry back to the father of German gymnastics, the ascetic and irrationalist

19 For illustrations of SPD youth activity and repression on the regional level, see Derek S. Linton, "Zur sozialdemokratischen Jugendbewegung im rechtsrheinischen Industriegebiet während des Kaiserreiches," in Burkhard Dietz, Ute Lange-Appel, and Manfred Wahle, eds., *Lebens- und Arbeitswelten von Jugendlichen im rechtsrheinischen Industriegebiet* (Bochum, 1996), 63–84.

20 *Jahresberichte: Zentralstelle für die arbeitende Jugend Deutschlands Juli 1910–Juni 1911* (Berlin, 1911), 3–11.

romantic nationalist Friedrich Jahn, during the Napoleonic occupation.[21] This falsified genealogy both played down the scouts' English origins and elevated their nationalist appeal by aligning them with a heavily mythologized foundational event of German nationalism, the Wars of Liberation against Napoleon. This supposed bond was especially trumpeted during 1913 when the centenary was commemorated with a host of officially sponsored patriotic festivities. But in Germany as in England, the real and more proximate roots of the Boy Scouts lay in colonial wars in Africa. Both authors of the *Pfadfinderbuch,* Staff Doctor Alexander Lion and Major Maximillian Bayer, had served in the genocidal war against the Herero in Southwest Africa. According to these two officers, the heroic deeds of the German forces there would "form an eternal page of glory in German history."[22] It was their experience in this brutal colonial war that forged their immediate identification with Robert Baden-Powell, the hero of the siege of Mafeking during the Boer War and the innovator of the scouting movement. Although the two officers adopted much of the program from Baden-Powell's *Scouting for Boys,* on which they largely based the *Pfadfinderbuch* of 1909, they modified Baden-Powell's message substantially to infuse it "with a thoroughly German spirit."[23] They underlined this "German spirit" much more in later editions and placed greater emphasis on premilitary training of members.

As organized by Lion and Bayer, the *Pfadfinder* (scout) movement was steeped in the anti-industrial, anti-urban, "back to nature" and medieval sentiments that pervaded the turn-of-the-century life-reform movements. The scout was to imitate the character traits of the virtuous medieval knight: his honor, his faith in God, and his loyalty to his lord and people.[24] Like the huntsman, he was to cultivate the art of closely observing nature and learn to camp in the open in order to accustom himself to surviving in the wild, because those who failed to acquire these skills soon became disoriented when they arrived in the colonies. Through sports and exercises, the *Pfadfinder* would test and increase his strength and endurance. At the same time he was to avoid squandering his health by smoking and drinking. The *Pfadfinder* also was to practice personal cleanliness and hygiene. Thus, the scout was being introduced to hygienic, urban ways of life promoted by physicians and hygienists even as he supposedly reverted to a

21 Oberstabarzt Dr. A. Lion and Major Maximillian Bayer, *Jungdeutschlands Pfadfinderbuch,* 5th ed. (Leipzig, 1914), 1–2.
22 Ibid., 7.
23 Karl Seidelmann, *Der Pfadfinder in der deutschen Jugendgeschichte,* 2 vols. in 3 pts. (Hannover, 1980), pt. 1:27–32.
24 Lion and Bayer, *Jungdeutschlands Pfadfinderbuch,* 11–17, 204–7.

pristine natural existence. Fear of God was also mandated, although within a framework of religious tolerance. In the military metaphors favored by the two officers, "Protestants, Catholics, Jews, Mohammedans are united in the main points; they all honor one God, they are all soldiers of one army, although they belong to different branches and therefore wear different uniforms."[25] But the militarism of the *Pfadfinder* certainly was not entirely metaphorical. Each *Pfadfinder* was expected to be loyal to the Kaiser and to the military, which "was always armed and ready for combat in order to protect the peace and honor of the Reich."[26] Although the patriotism of modern youth had been questioned, Lion and Bayer avowed that it had recently been displayed in Southwest Africa. Patriotism was all the more necessary because the wealth and commercial success of the Reich, as well as its military and naval power, had aroused the envy and hostility of its neighbors. If the peacekeeping art of the diplomat failed, "then the sword decides. And then we must fight for our place in the world, the freedom of our German people, for our honor."[27] The *Pfadfinder* was supposed to be conscious of the formidable power of the Reich and be ready to defend it. Thus, in a context in which the founders envisaged Germany encircled by jealous enemies, the scouting slogan "always prepared" assumed a connotation of watchful and warlike armed vigilance.

Initially, the *Pfadfinderbuch* with its accents on character building, conformist patriotism, religion, sports, and camping and its incongruous but widespread juxtaposition of pseudoprimitivism and medievalism with modern colonialism and healthy modes of urban life captured the interest of gymnasia teachers throughout Germany, who founded small autonomous groups along the lines recommended by Lion and Bayer.[28] These local *Pfadfinder* groups probably recruited much the same type of gymnasia student who joined the Wandervögel in the middle-class Berlin suburbs. But on January 18, 1911, Lion and Bayer inaugurated the nationwide German Scouting League (Deutsche Pfadfinderbund) in Berlin. The choice of date was hardly fortuitous because it was heavily freighted with symbolic significance. Not only was it the anniversary of the birth of the Prussian monarchy and the proclamation of the empire at Versailles, but it also coincided with Kaiser Wilhelm's long-awaited proclamation of a decree on youth (*Jugendpflege-Erlass*), which coordinated and gave a further fillip to state and middle-class youth work. The Pfadfinderbund, which was headed by an executive committee and advisory council composed of military officers,

---

25 Ibid., 15.
27 Ibid., 205–6.

26 Ibid., 13.
28 Seidelmann, *Der Pfadfinder*, 35–6.

teachers, mayors, and businessmen, quickly erected a centralized national organization that directed the large number of local and regional branches. These branches were organized as small, disciplined groups in a military-style hierarchy under the leadership of field masters, usually junior officers or teachers by profession. Members wore a common uniform, in part to eliminate the external signs of social distinction. Bayer brusquely dismissed as a fairy tale the notion that the Pfadfinderbund gathered its recruits exclusively from the upper-middle-class gymnasia because by 1913 more than half the members had attended only primary school.[29] Some scattered evidence from memoirs tends to confirm that the camping and sporting programs of the *Pfadfinder* also appealed to young workers.[30] By the start of the war the scouts claimed approximately 90,000 members belonging to 375 local groups serving under the command of about 2,000 field masters. But by that time the Pfadfinderbund had affiliated with the Jungdeutschlandbund, and its activities and goals had become virtually indistinguishable from those of the broader group. This merger was sealed with Freiherr von der Goltz's preface to the fifth edition of Bayer's and Lion's book, which appeared in 1914 under the title *Jungdeutschlands Pfadfinderbuch.*

The second organization that clearly served as a precursor of the Jungdeutschlandbund was the Bayerischer Wehrkraftverein. Originally called into life in 1909 by forty Bavarian officers as a local Munich association, it was a response to a Bavarian adaptation of a Prussian War Ministry decree urging officers to make greater efforts to elicit more interest and involvement from youth in military affairs.[31] The following year these officers were working with 250 continuation-school students. They soon approached gymnasia students as well, although units from the gymnasia and continuation schools were kept separate. Munich school superintendent Kerschensteiner became an honorary member, and the school authorities assisted the officers by allowing them privileged access to the schools. The Wehrkraftverein was also supported by the Bavarian War and Education ministries. Moreover, Prince Regent Luitpold became the organization's patron and endowed it with 30,000 marks. With such substantial establish-

---

29 Hauptmann M. Bayer, "Der deutsche Pfadfinderbund," in Deutsche Zentrale für Jugendfürsorge, ed., *Handbuch für Jugendpflege,* 408.

30 See, e.g., Karl Öttinger, "In der Arbeiterjugend," in Detlef Hoffmann, Doris Pokorny, and Albrecht Werner, eds., *Arbeiterjugendbewegung in Frankfurt 1904–1945* (Frankfurt am Main, 1978), 123.

31 For the Bayerischer Wehrkraftverein, see Seidelmann, *Der Pfadfinder,* 37–9; Siemering, ed., *Die deutschen Jugendpflegeverbände,* 50–1; and Saul, "Der Kampf um die Jugend," 116–17, from which the following quotations are taken.

ment backing the group flourished, attaining a membership of 10,000 by 1914, although apparently more were recruited from the gymnasia than from continuation schools.

In terms of activities, members participated in Sunday war games or hikes that were supplemented by exercises in reading maps, judging distances, and acquiring the sort of observational skills that would be useful for soldiers in the field. Members also engaged in such sporting activities as swimming and gymnastics. In contrast to other militarized youth groups, the Wehrkraftverein prided itself on conducting hikes even in inclement weather and on its single-minded emphasis on physical fitness, war games, and hikes rather than on social or cultural events. Thus, its raw physicality was even more crude than that of the *Pfadfinder*. Even its limited educational endeavors were strictly functional because they were supposed to buttress and deepen the national and monarchical sentiment of members and inspire them to heroism and self-sacrifice by teaching them about great men and exemplary deeds from Germany's past. One of the high points of the Wehrkraftverein's existence was the participation of 4,000 members in the celebration of the centenary of the War of Liberation at the Befreiungshalle near Kehlheim.

Obviously such nationalist programs were also in part directed against the socialist youth movement. But this antisocialism was made manifest in several public pronouncements by the Verein. Organizational guidelines asserted that the Wehrkraftverein conceived of itself as a counterweight to "the predominance of the fantasts of eternal peace"; and when it united with the South-German Association of Young Catholic Men in 1914, the aim of this alliance was to construct a bulwark against "the serious threat to youth released from the primary schools by propaganda on behalf of unbelief, immorality, and rebellion against every authority," thinly veiled code words for socialist views.

This Bavarian venture sparked interest among staff officers in Berlin, an interest given further impetus by the imperial youth decree of January 18, 1911. This decree called for a national effort to save youth from the consequences of Germany's recent economic transformation, an effort that would be crowned with success only if it engaged all "who have a heart for youth and who are prepared to further their patriotic education."[32] To meet the Kaiser's goal, General von Jacobi soon prevailed on his friend Field Marshall Freiherr Colmar von der Goltz, the longstanding advocate

---

32 For the text of the Kaiser's decree, see *Handbuch für Jugendpflege,* 853–61.

of premilitary training for young males, to launch a nationwide youth organization similar to the one in Bavaria.[33] This idea fit in well with von der Goltz's perspective because the field marshal, an archconservative and favorite of the Kaiser, was increasingly convinced that Germany would soon be compelled to fight a large-scale preemptive war against Russia and France. Moreover, he had long decried the softness and pleasure seeking that had accompanied Germany's transformation from an agrarian to an industrial state. Hence he was immediately enthusiastic about launching such a project. By June he had drawn up plans that he discussed with the Kaiser, who approved them.

The Jungdeutschlandbund was to aspire "to make our youth able bodied and truthful, strengthen them physically and mentally, train them in orderliness and obedience, inspire them with dedication and esprit de corps, so that they will recognize that service to the Fatherland is the highest honor of the German man."[34] These largely military virtues were to be implanted in the young through hikes, marches, war games, camping, and sports. One added advantage of this organization was that those officers involved in its work would have to teach by example, without the coercive sanctions available within the army. Moreover, von der Golz hoped that working-class youths would come to trust their upper-class officers, thus reducing social antagonism. Officers would inspire their charges with stories of Prussian history and heroes while also acquainting them with practical skills, such as first aid.

Despite royal approval, plans for the Jungdeutschlandbund did not meet with universal assent. The mass middle-class Imperial League Against Social Democracy and a number of generals pressed for the Jungdeutschlandbund to confront the socialist youth movement openly. Freiherr von der Golz demurred, however, arguing that injecting blatantly antisocialist propaganda into youth work would preclude having any impact precisely on those young people whom he most hoped to reach. Adult organizers of religious youth groups were chary of the league's secularism and its one-sided emphasis on physical fitness. The German Gymnasts feared competition from a well-funded, government-supported youth group. Even the Prussian minister of education, aware of such concerns, expressed reservations about "new general experiments," worrying that the league would

---

33 For the Jungdeutschlandbund and documentation of the following, see Saul, "Die Kampf um die Jugend," 118–23; Schubert-Weller, "Vormilitärische Jugenderziehung," 511–12; and Linton, *Who Has the Youth, Has the Future,* 154–61.
34 Reinhard Höhn, *Sozialismus und Heer,* 3 vols. (Bad Harzburg, 1969), 3:523–4.

undercut existing programs. Hence he obtained a promise that the League would confine itself to improving the physical fitness of youth.

The foundations of the Jungdeutschlandbund were laid with great care. Funding was secured from some of Berlin's wealthiest bankers, merchants, and industrialists. The league solicited directors of continuation schools for their evaluations of the likelihood of success in their institutions, inquiries that generally received optimistic replies. Notables including military men, administrative officials, clergymen, educators, and businessmen were induced to serve on executive committees in targeted municipalities. These committees also sponsored fund-raising events, such as elite charity balls, to ensure that the league would be adequately financed. Public announcements of the league's existence first appeared in middle-class newspapers on May 1, 1912, announcements that underscored the league's antisocialism because they coincided with the major annual socialist holiday. The antisocialist animus emerged clearly in the text of its ads as well. Although the announcements testified to the league's nondiscriminatory inclusiveness, they noted that the league recognized "no distinction on the basis of religion or political party [only] as long as they [i.e., youth] stand on the basis of love of the Fatherland and faithfulness to the Kaiser and Reich."[35]

Within months of this initial announcement, the Jungdeutschlandbund had become established in the Prussian continuation schools in major urban centers. The account included in the annual report of Düsseldorf's industrial continuation school exemplifies the league's mode of operation.

The continuation school also adhered to the Young Germany League movement and immediately after the formation of the Düsseldorf area troop provided the overwhelming majority of participants in its war games. Altogether about 1,250 students took part in the five war games, which were led by local officers, both active and reserve. The leaders rapidly concluded that it wasn't sufficient to be active intermittently in war games at which a different group of students appeared every time depending on chance and inclination, but rather that steady and systematic work with the same group of students was necessary. Consequently, in October 1912 the so-called quadruple alliance was formed, consisting of four reserve officers who wished to dedicate themselves to youth work in the continuation school. These were joined by an additional fifteen reserve officers and about forty-four members of veterans' associations (officials, teachers, businessmen, etc.) who had already declared their intention of being active in youth work at least once a week. After thorough deliberation, they decided that basic training would be imparted in gym halls; and then, during the summer, war games, hikes, and similar activities

35 *Düsseldorfer Tageblatt,* May 1, 1912.

would be held. These gentlemen took over sections formed by the continuation school classes, each with thirty students.[36]

Thus, by the winter of 1913 a network of reserve officers and veterans had created a comprehensive program of drill and gymnastics geared toward preparing for summer war games, although they had learned through previous experience that student interest could be retained only if the drills and exercises were short and changed frequently. The war games, usually held on Sunday mornings, were especially popular. These games had been pioneered by the Boy Scout movement in Britain and then adapted by the *Pfadfinder,* although their British origins were often concealed.[37] For the games, uniformed members of the league were divided into two opposing armies. These war games relied on collective cooperation within one group and hostility toward another, rather than on individual competition – a rule within these militarized youth groups because Freiherr von der Goltz, like many other youth savers, believed that individual achievement would give rise to youthful conceit and hence destroy modesty and obedience. While a fife-and-drum corps roused the future combatants with military marches, the two armies maneuvered for several hours before lining up for battle. Victory was decided by a short clash fought with padded bamboo poles. Presiding officers then conducted a postmortem analysis. The afternoon was spent learning first aid and singing patriotic songs.

Such activities and the careful organization contributed to the growth of the Jungdeutschlandbund. The combination of war games, gymnastics, and marching practiced by the league clearly appealed to many young laborers. Nor is there any evidence that the patriotic propaganda repelled them, because it was essentially familiar from nationalist indoctrination in the schools. By 1914 the league claimed an official membership of 750,000. This figure was egregiously inflated because it included numerous Catholic and Protestant youth groups and regional associations such as the Bayerische Wehrkraftverein, which were nominally affiliated with the Jungdeutschlandbund but which otherwise retained their autonomy. A more realistic estimate would place membership in the 70,000 range, approximately the number registered in the 761 companies like the one at the Düsseldorf industrial continuation school. Even this lower figure indicates the impressive growth during the league's first two years. By 1913 its membership probably already surpassed that of the socialist youth movement.

---

36 Stadtarchiv Düsseldorf III 3629: Die Gewerbliche Fortbildungsschule, *Jahresbericht* (1912–13), 46–8.
37 Ibid., 47–8, and Dr. jur. Reimers, "Das Kriegspiel im Dienst der Jugendpflege," in *Ratgeber für Jugendvereinigungnen* (Zentralstelle für Volkswohlfahrt, 5, no. 2–3 [1911]): 31–3.

In evaluating this success, however, one should bear in mind that the Jungdeutschlandbund relied on such enormous advantages as sponsorship by the Kaiser and the army, funding from wealthy patrons, and privileged access to the continuation schools, advantages that were denied its rivals. Moreover, both Catholic and Social Democratic critics of the league marshaled evidence that teachers and administrators often pressured continuation-school students into joining.[38] Such heavy-handed tactics as well as the league's rather blatant desire to monopolize youth work generated antagonism. The German Gymnasts protested against their displacement from continuation-school gymnastics instruction. Clergymen denounced Sunday war games, the denominational mixing of members, and the celebration of raw physicality to the detriment of spirituality within the league. Relations between the league and the Catholic Youth Associations were perennially strained. Although the secretariat decided that Catholic youth associations should affiliate with the league, they should do so only if the league agreed to respect the autonomy of Catholic youth organizations and postpone war games until Sunday afternoons rather than hold them in the mornings – stipulations that the league initially accepted and then violated. Moreover, the Catholic youth paper, *Die Wacht*, expressed concern over the Jungdeutschlandbund's contribution to the bellicose atmosphere that was increasingly engulfing Germany. In an article published in October 1913 titled "Youth Care and War," it questioned the league's apparent goal of converting "all of Germany into a giant barrack."[39] The article pointed out that Catholics certainly recognized the vital importance of military preparedness and thought that the premilitary training of youth through hikes and gymnastics was a suitable way of achieving this aim when it was kept within reasonable bounds; but devoting every spare minute to military drilling, wearing uniforms on hikes, and promoting bombastic patriotism were excessive. Moreover, such behavior seemed counterproductive when opportunities for easing tensions with France and Britain appeared to be improving. But such criticisms had no impact on Freiherr von der Goltz and his associates.

38 For socialist claims, see "Nationale Jugendpflege," *Düsseldorfer Volkszeitung,* Dec. 11, 1912; for the German Gymnasts, Stadtarchiv Düsseldorf III 2178: Jugendpflege, no. 254, the reply of the industrial continuation school director Gotter to the German Gymnasts of June 19, 1913. Catholic youth association discussions of recruitment by and conflicts with the league are to be found in Historisches Archiv des Erzbistums Köln Tit XXIII, Bd. 1: Generalsekretariat der Jugendvereine, 1908–19, a sheet dated Mar. 1913 for the accusation of coercion by the league; and especially the "Bericht über die Stellung der kath. Jugendvereinigungen gegenüber dem Jungdeutschlandbund," Mar. 1913, 1–4; see also Heinrich Muth, "Jugendpflege und Politik," *Geschichte in Wissenschaft und Unterricht* 12, no. 10 (Oct. 1961): 610–12.
39 "Jugendpflege und Krieg," *Die Wacht* (Oct. 1913): 123.

Indeed, League leaders could and did justify their aggressive recruitment and untrammeled physicalism on the grounds that the league was the most effective youth movement in terms of countering and neutralizing the socialists. Despite Freiherr von der Goltz's assurances about its political non-alignment, the league made little secret of its deep hostility toward the *Arbeiterjugendbewegung* (working-class youth movement) Thus, the league's 1913 annual report asserted that "the more important Social Democrats find it to sow divisiveness and class hatred even in the hearts of the young, the more we must strive to implant a sense of unity of our people, bound by love for their common Fatherland in the hearts of the young."[40]

Despite the transparently antisocialist rhetoric and animus of the league, the socialist press initially reacted with irony and derision to its formation. It seems to have believed that the league would recruit only upper-class boys who fancied dressing in uniforms and playing soldier.[41] But as the Jungdeutschlandbund proved capable of attracting large numbers of young laborers, anxiety-ridden and even panic-stricken warnings to young workers and their parents replaced this initial complacency. This new tone was struck in the 1912–13 annual report of the SPD youth committee of Elberfeld-Barmen.

Playing at soldiering has assumed extremely dangerous dimensions in Wuppertal. Not fewer than eight different youth organizations exist here. Six of them recruit in large part, several of them exclusively, from the ranks of proletarian youth. Whoever is familiar with the spirit that is bred in these military youth groups will be able to measure the extraordinary danger that threatens the proletariat from this direction. . . . When young workers are involved in this hurly-burly for long, then the nationalist brain-washing is so effective that at least an intellectual emancipation becomes very difficult, even if perhaps later they can be won organizationally.[42]

Even more dramatic was the *Düsseldorfer Volkszeitung*'s admonishing and importuning of socialist parents: "Worker parents, keep your children away from Young Germany. Don't hand them over to Prussian 'youth care.' As an animal defends its child against enemy attacks, so should every worker-mother, every worker-father defend his or her children from the attack of Prusso-German 'youth care.'"[43]

Prussian officials in the Düsseldorf administrative district reported with considerable satisfaction in 1913 that state-sponsored "youth care" in gen-

40 Höhn, *Sozialismus und Heer,* 548.
41 "Wie Jungdeutschland gegründet wird," *Arbeiter-Jugend* (May 11, 1912).
42 Hauptstaatsarchiv Düsseldorf 16005: Sozialdemokratischer Verein Elberfeld-Barmen, "Bericht des Jugendausschusses Elberfeld-Barmen über seine Tätigkeit in der Zeit vom 1. Januar 1912 bis 31. März 1913," 41.
43 *Düsseldorfer Volkszeitung,* Oct. 26, 1912.

eral and the activities of the Jungdeutschlandbund in particular had con-
strained the growth of the SPD's youth movement and had spread dismay
within the party.[44] By July every party branch in Düsseldorf had held a lecture on "the bourgeois and proletarian youth movements" and debated
whether or not to impose punitive sanctions against party members who
permitted their sons to participate in the activities of the Jungdeutschlandbund. Thus, by 1913 the increasingly militarized government-sponsored
youth-work program had been effective in containing the growth of the
socialist youth movement and had exacerbated the deepening demoralization that had gripped the SPD as its resounding electoral victory in 1912
proved hollow and the party's growth approached a limit. Thus, the following summer, when war was declared, government officials could be
fairly certain that the SPD's influence among post-school-age youth was
quite limited and that many young workers would rally to the nationalist
cause without hesitation or reservation. Far from opting for war at a moment of intensifying domestic crisis, the decision for war came at a time
when the SPD and its youth movement had been forced on the defensive
and had lost confidence and momentum.[45]

There can be little doubt that the militarization of youth work that
came to the fore after 1908 and reached its prewar culmination in the
Jungdeutschlandbund was successful in containing and constraining the socialist youth movement, the major goals of these militarized formations.
They had been founded less because of fears about Germany's international position than to overcome the ostensibly degenerative effects of urbanism and industrialism and to counter the growth of the SPD's youth-work
program. Thus, one could certainly characterize such youth organizations
as a response by the state and sectors of the *Bildungsbürgertum* to the perceived effects of "classical modernity."[46] Neither the perception of these effects nor the response of upper- and middle-class youth savers was unique
to Germany. After all, such British youth associations as the Boys' Brigades
and Boy Scouts clearly offered models to Kerschensteiner, Bayer, Lion, and
von der Goltz. Anxieties about a generation of weakened, pleasure-

---

44 Hauptstaatsarchiv Düsseldorf 42809: Der Regierungspräsident an den Herrn Minister des Innern in
   Berlin, Dec. 18, 1913.
45 An extensive literature exists both on the internal situation within the SPD and the domestic political conjuncture in Germany on the eve of the war. Still best on the situation within the SPD is
   Dieter Groh, *Negative Integration und revolutionärer Attentismus* (Frankfurt am Main, 1973), 461–575.
   Hans-Ulrich Wehler's claim that the war represented a "flight forward" by antidemocratic German
   elites still spawns controversy. For the various positions, see Hans-Ulrich Wehler, *The German Empire, 1871–1918* (Leamington Spa, 1985), 192–201, and David Kaiser, "Germany and the Origins
   of the First World War," *Journal of Modern History* 55, no. 3 (Sept. 1983): 442–74.
46 For this concept, see Detlev J. K. Peukert, *The Weimar Republic* (New York, 1989), 81–5.

seeking, neurasthenic working-class male youth and the negative effects
these enfeebled and etiolated youth would have on domestic order, national efficiency, and military preparedness were as ubiquitous in Great Britain
after the Boer War as they were in Germany after 1900.[47] Youth movements in both nations sought to establish a rigidly fixed normative image of
working-class youth: chivalrous, strong, upright, loyal, obedient, and conformist nationalist males, in contrast to the amusement-loving, loafing
street youths notably labeled *Halbstarken* in Germany.[48] However, sharper
class tensions and the rapid growth of the SPD's youth movement clearly
made these anxieties somewhat more charged in Germany, and hence
much of the middle class regarded the militarization of youth work with
greater urgency and favor than was the case in Britain.

Despite the essentially domestic genesis of the militarization of youth
work, fears about industrial competitiveness, military preparedness, and
Germany's international standing in relation to its European rivals further
legitimated the youth-care venture. Hence, the international circumstances
and repercussions of these militarized youth formations should not be excluded from consideration. First, these organizations were very much
products of the age of imperialism. Just as the Boer War sparked the formation of the Boy Scouts in Britain, the protracted suppression of the
Herero revolt served as a reference point for the activities of militarized
youth groups in Germany. The emphasis on building strength and stamina,
educating the senses, and teaching survival skills in the wild arose from deficiencies of young German troops in Southwest Africa. Indeed, many aspects of premilitary training were far more appropriate for fighting colonial
wars than they were for the sort of mechanized warfare that defined World
War I. It is an open question whether this sort of premilitary training had
any significant military consequences, although presumably youths who
belonged to such organizations became accustomed to following orders
and maneuvering in small groups and therefore may have been easier to
train and may have acculturated more readily to military life.

Second, whatever the contribution of these groups to military effectiveness, as the Catholic youth paper *Die Wacht* indicated, these youth groups
helped poison the already bellicose atmosphere in Germany in the years
following the Second Moroccan Crisis. They propagandized their youthful
members with a vision of a wealthy and powerful Germany surrounded by

---

47 See, e.g., John Springhall, *Youth, Empire, and Society* (London, 1977), and Harry Hendrick, *Images of Youth* (Oxford, 1990).
48 Clemens Schulz, "Die Halbstarken," *Die Entwicklungsjahre*, 2d ed. (Leipzig, 1912), 7, 12, 28–33. Günther Dehn, *Grossstadtjugend*, 2d ed. (Berlin, 1922), 82–92.

hostile and envious neighbors with whom war had become virtually inevitable. The crescendo of patriotic zeal that marked the centenary of the War of Liberation deliberately conjured up images of an expansionist and tyrannical France. Every youth group from the Wandervögel on the Hoher Meissner to the Bayerischer Wehrkraftverein, in addition to unorganized continuation-school students, celebrated this major festivity of the prewar conjuncture with perfervid patriotic outpourings and calls for generational sacrifice and renewal in the spirit of the father of German gymnastics, Turnvater Jahn, and the volunteers of 1813.[49] Such events, along with the everyday propaganda and war games of the militarized youth groups, made war seem a heroic and glorious game, a test of a generation and an escape from the treadmill drudgery of work and the daily routines of urban life. Escapism was evidently in demand, as demonstrated by young workers' receptivity to the early cinema or their consumption of penny dreadfuls. Whereas the cinema and penny dreadfuls offered escapist fantasies about distant lands, exotic milieux, and the promise of sensual pleasure, the militarized youth organizations presented an alternative escape through the adventure of war and ascetic self-denial and sacrifice in the spirit of Turnvater Jahn. Through such appeals, these organizations clearly shaped the attitudes of thousands of youths who did not merely accept war but who even viewed war with enthusiasm, as an opportunity for heroism and glory. However, the concrete image of war remained unfocused and blurred, a curiously indistinct image that oscillated between medieval chivalry and colonial warfare. Moreover, the focus on glory and chivalry, although conducive to acceptance of war in the abstract, may well have paved the way for the disillusion that would set in as the grim and deadly realities of modern mechanized warfare proved to have little in common with the experiences of the volunteers of 1813 or with summer war games fought with padded bamboo poles.

---

49 For documentation of the Wandervögel's celebration, see Winifried Mogge and Jürgen Reulecke, *Hoher Meissner 1913* (Cologne, 1988).

9

Heroes and Would-Be Heroes

Veterans' and Reservists' Associations in Imperial Germany

THOMAS ROHKRÄMER

The term *total war* came into existence in connection with World War I as a slogan used by leading participants such as Georges Clemenceau and Erich Ludendorff to propagate or justify an unlimited war effort.[1] It subsequently gained wider usage in politics and in more theoretical discourses because it seemed to grasp the peculiarities of twentieth-century warfare in contrast to previous wars: that is, an increasing size of armies, a broadening scope tending toward a global scale, and the systematic mobilization of the "home front" for the war effort (mass production of weapons, scientific development of war technology, mobilization of all members of society), which simultaneously meant that combatants and noncombatants alike gained military significance and were thus targeted by blockades or wide-ranging weapons of mass destruction. Because the population did not consist of powerless chess pieces, this "total" mobilization also demanded an ideological mobilization to justify the immense effort. A rigid friend-enemy thinking that demonized the enemy (leaders and common people alike) and raised apocalyptic as well as euphoric expectations seemed necessary to justify the high price of war and the inhumane measures taken.

The concept is very suggestive at first because it seems to grasp essential features of modern warfare, but the scrutiny devoted to it over the last years has revealed serious weaknesses.[2] One can distinguish three problematic areas:

1. The characteristics of total war mentioned in the foregoing paragraphs have occurred independent of one another at very different points in history. Wars between simply structured, small communities have involved all members of

1 See Roger Chickering's essay (Chapter 1) in this book.
2 Many concrete examples are provided in ibid.

189

society as participants in the war effort and as potential victims; every war seems to have a tendency, as Clausewitz rightly stressed, to become unlimited and "absolute"; the complete destruction or expulsion of the enemy has occurred in many wars but not in a modern war; and the intensity of war and its impact on society have been at least as "total" in premodern as in modern times.

2. Modern wars are not necessarily total. After 1945 none of the many wars have escalated into a global nuclear conflict; the potential of modern science and technology has been used particularly to conduct wars on every level of intensity; today the main military effort of the armies of industrialized countries appears to be aimed at using technological advantage for quick and inexpensive interventions at different points of an international crisis, whereas a global war between major powers has become increasingly unlikely.

3. Total war is an absolute term that can never quite match reality. Although there clearly is a tendency in major modern military conflicts toward a total war effort, a total war in its pure form has never occurred and cannot occur because there are always forces limiting the war effort and because the different features rule one another out when taken to the extreme.[3]

At the conference that resulted in this book, most participants tended toward overcoming these problems by taking the concept of total war as an ideal type that can be approximated only empirically. This attempt to turn the concept into an analytical tool to measure the degree of totality in every war overcomes most of the problems mentioned previously but creates its own difficulty. The features associated with the concept of total war clearly are connected with the modern age. An efficient state bureaucracy, a high level of industry, and powerful means of transportation and communication clearly are necessary prerequisites for the increased size of armies, the growing involvement of noncombatants, the expanded scope of operations, and the technological-scientific character of warfare.

To purify the concept from all these historical characteristics would not only violate the common usage, it would also tend to make it lose most of its value as a tool for analyzing the particularities of modern wars.[4] To overcome all these problems, I would like to discuss the usage of both Clausewitz's term *absolute war* and the term *total war*. The former could be used as an ideal-type to characterize the tendency in all wars toward unlimited violence, whereas the latter could be reserved for industrialized warfare between highly organized societies. According to this definition,

---

3 The totality of destruction possible in nuclear warfare annihilates the anthropological factors.

4 See, e.g., von Trotha's contribution to this book (Chapter 19); he understands "total war" as a mobilization of all members of the societies involved and a dehumanization of the enemy that results in the war aim of complete annihilation or expulsion.

absolute war would be the more general term, whereas total war would specifically mean absolute war in its modern form. As premodern wars knew limitations because of nonmilitary considerations and frictions, so modern wars are not necessarily total in character. But if a modern war threatens the existential interests of the participants, there is a clear tendency toward absolute warfare in the form of total war.

This definition suggests that there is a tendency toward a totalization of the war effort in all major modern military conflicts independent of the participants' intentions. But this does not mean that ideological factors or developments in times of peace can be neglected. On the contrary, in my analysis of the veterans' and reservists' associations I try to show that cultural changes in the prewar period in Imperial Germany caused a militarization of attitudes that prepared the population for a major war, for extreme sacrifices, and for military measures not limited by humanitarian considerations. This mentality at least made the proclamation of war in 1914 and the gradual totalization of war more readily acceptable.[5]

Militarism was one of the most influential ideologies in Imperial Germany. It was promoted by the government primarily for its domestic function of integrating the people and diverting social tensions toward an outside enemy.[6] But in the 1890s the ideology started to develop its own dynamics. The Wilhelmine era was characterized by an increasingly radical militarization of the people that demanded an aggressive foreign policy. Although most civilian promoters of German expansionism did not anticipate a total war, they did contribute to the movement toward one. They all spread an ideology necessary to legitimate the human sacrifices involved in modern warfare, and some even went so far as to put pressure on the government to move toward more and more daring gambles in trying to achieve the status of a world power.[7]

As a popular mass movement of common people, the ex-servicemen's association is an ideal lens through which to look at the militarism of large parts of the German population and its radicalization after 1890.[8] Veterans'

---

5 On the preparedness for war in Germany in 1914, see Thomas Rohkrämer, "August 1914 – Kriegsmentalität und ihre Voraussetzungen," in Wolfgang Michalka, ed., *Der Erste Weltkrieg: Wirkung, Wahrnehmung, Analyse* (Munich, 1994), 759–77.

6 Hans-Ulrich Wehler, *Das Deutsche Kaiserreich 1871–1918* (Göttingen, 1973).

7 Roger Chickering, "Der 'Deutsche Wehrverein' und die Reform der deutschen Armee 1912–1914," *Militärgeschichtliche Mitteilungen*, no. 1 (1979): 7ff.

8 For a more detailed account, see Thomas Rohkrämer, *Der Militarismus der "kleinen Leute": Die Kriegervereine im Deutschen Kaiserreich* (Munich, 1990); for further references to relevant literature, see also Harm-Peer Zimmermann, *"Der feste Wall gegen die rote Flut": Kriegervereine in Schleswig-Holstein 1864–1914* (Neumünster, 1989).

associations already existed before the German Empire[9] but it was only in the wake of the Franco-Prussian War that they gained "the character of a general mass movement."[10] The veterans were proud of their contribution to a victorious war, which was followed by what they regarded to be the glorious culmination of history: the unification of Germany. Now they wanted to celebrate the memory of this "heroic" time in their life, in which they believed themselves to have made history.[11] Apart from this primary function, the veterans' associations wanted to promote nationalistic and monarchical thinking, preserve the comradeship the soldiers had experienced during their military service, and support one another in times of need. Thus, the main activities were the running of a private insurance system for its members, the burial of deceased members with military honors, and celebrations at the birthday of the emperor and the sovereign of the state, as well as on *Sedantag* or on the dates of other important battles of the Franco-Prussian War. In many cases the activities were not much different from those of a social club. Many clubs seemed to have taken the official goals rather lightly and were happy to turn to eating, drinking, and dancing after a short speech and the singing of the national anthem.[12] Nevertheless it was not by accident that the men organized in veterans' associations. It was their time as soldiers of which they were proud, and they wanted to present themselves in that role to the wider community in order to gain respect and prestige.

At the turn of the century the associations, which had started independently on a local level, united in centralized bodies - first within the different states (the *Landesverbände*), then in 1899 on the national level in the Kyffhäuserbund – a process strongly promoted by government officials who wanted to have more control over the associations. Another important change was that, from the 1890s onward, most local associations began to accept reservists in addition to war veterans. This was a crucial step: First of all, it meant that the associations would not gradually wither away with the deaths of the veterans but that the general conscription in Germany would

---

9 Zimmermann, *Kriegervereine in Schleswig-Holstein*, 95ff., 114–17; Eckhard Trox, *Militärischer Konservatismus: Kriegervereine und "Militärpartei" in Preussen zwischen 1815 und 1848–49* (Stuttgart, 1990).
10 Alfred Westphal, *Das deutsche Kriegervereinswesen: Seine Ziele und seine Bedeutung für den Staat* (Berlin, 1903), 4.
11 Jakob Burckhardt sarcastically described this nationalistic view of history as a reinterpretation "in which the whole world history from Adam onward is covered with a victorious-Germany paint" (Jakob Burckhardt, *Briefe*, 10 vols. [Basel, 1949–86], 5:182–3); see also Martin Doerry, *Übergangsmenschen: Die Mentalität der Wilhelminer und die Krise des Kaiserreichs*, 2 vols. (Weinheim, 1986), 1:31ff.
12 César, quoted in *Sozialdemokratische Partei-Correspondenz*, no. 21, Aug. 12, 1906, 313–14; see also Zimmermann, *Kriegervereine in Schleswig-Holstein*, 422–9.

produce plenty of potential members. Second, it meant a clear change in ideological content. The associations no longer celebrated a particular historical event and the memories connected with it, but rather the general principle of being associated with the German army. The glorification of a specific war was replaced by a general glorification of Germany's military forces. This meant an important step away from personal pride about a particular achievement and toward a general militaristic attitude.

The Kyffhäuserbund grew into a huge organization. With nearly 3 million members in 1913 – about 15 percent of the adult male population – it became the largest association in the German Empire. There still are quite a few uncertainties about the social structure of its membership, but assessments of the time agree with the remaining statistical evidence that the associations consisted mainly of workers, farmhands, and the lower-middle class. According to a statistic of the Prussian association "Deutscher Kriegerbund" from 1911, 28.8 percent of its members were farmhands and small farmers, 27.8 percent workers, 24.9 percent tradesmen (*Gewerbetreibende*) and craftsmen, and 18.5 percent civil servants and white-collar workers.[13] Regional studies also support the view that it was mainly the common people who were members of the veterans' and reservists' associations.[14]

In the following sections I want to concentrate on two aspects through which the associations promoted a mentality necessary for leading a total war: first, a belief in the state and its official representatives connected with growing enmity against the Social Democratic Party and, second, an extreme militarism oriented toward a future war. Finally, I will look beyond the veterans' and reservists' associations to find further support for my thesis that the radicalization of militarism was partly due to a conflict between the veterans of the Wars of Unification and the following generation.

I

In the founding period the governments tended to be distrustful of veterans' associations of common people and spied on them in order to stop any potential politicization.[15] But soon it became clear that there was no real danger. The associations were characterized by a general acceptance of the army and the monarchical state. In a sense, this was only logical. If the as-

---

13 *Parole: Deutsche Kriegerzeitung* 37 (May 7, 1913), 993.
14 Rohrkrämer, *Der Militarismus*, 34–6; Zimmermann, *Kriegervereine in Schleswig-Holstein*, 328–38.
15 If not otherwise indicated, this section is based on Rohrkrämer, *Der Militarismus*, 36–54.

sociations' members wanted to be proud of the part they had played in the Wars of Unification, it was easiest simply to accept fully the war's results.

But this respect for authority did not translate into corresponding political decisions. Many members did not see a contradiction between their nationalist convictions and their support for anti-monarchical parties and interest groups, in particular the Social Democrats and the socialist trade unions. These members had a "good-boy orientation" (Lawrence Kohlberg): They accepted all authorities they encountered in different spheres of their lives without being concerned about contradictions between them.

At first the state authorities were satisfied as long as the veterans' and reservists' associations did not become involved in politics. But with the growing fear of the Social Democratic Party, which gained votes with every election, this attitude changed. Now state authorities saw the associations as an ideal political tool. On the one hand, they wanted to "protect" the common people who still held respect for army and monarchy from "bad" influences by banning from membership supporters of the Social Democrats and, at least in theory, of the socialist trade unions; on the other hand, they hoped that the associations could be used as a forum to propagate the "right" convictions. This policy was justified with the argument that (voluntary) membership in a veterans' and reservists' association meant the continuation of a soldier's obligations, in particular the oath to serve his king and fatherland. Thus, the support of an anti-monarchical party or interest group did not agree with the obligations of membership.

To realize this strategy of controlling the veterans' and reservists' associations it was first of all necessary to convince the free associations to gain official status by joining the *Landesverbände* because only official associations could be forced to adopt statutes banning supporters of the Social Democrats from membership. The emperor himself promoted the centralization of the veterans' and reservists' associations, which offered the privileges of an official flag and badges as well as participation in official parades and celebrations. The gradual decline of the percentage of free associations[16] shows that these privileges were more important to most veterans and reservists than their political freedom.

The other part of the strategy was that conservative elites – army officers, owners of estates, higher civil servants, and the educated middle class – were encouraged to join the veterans' and reservists' associations, control the ex-

---

16 In Prussia, 38 percent were still independent in 1892; in 1899, it was only 11 percent. Rohkrämer, *Der Militarismus*, 28, 273.

clusion of Social Democrats, and pass conservative convictions on to the other members. As the previous discussion of the associations' social composition has shown, the government's appeals to the higher social strata to join the association were not very successful – mainly because the elitist attitudes of these people stopped them from mixing with the common people. But a look at the social composition of the associations' leadership shows that the few who did join tended to occupy the positions of power. Although the common member could still become head of a local branch (although the lower class was already clearly underrepresented on this level), the leadership of the *Landesverbände* and the Kyffhäuserbund came completely into the hands of the middle and upper classes.[17] With differences in emphasis – some were skeptical about the effects of aggressive propaganda and perpetual interference in local affairs – they all accepted and followed the political agenda outlined previously. Thus, a spontaneous feeling of comradeship was instrumentalized for political reasons. The familiar atmosphere in the associations and the general trust among comrades was to be used to influence the common people.

The strategy of manipulation did not succeed altogether. The attempt to break the power of the trade unions failed completely: The members were not prepared to leave an organization that was so important to their material well-being, and the veterans' and reservists' associations could never enforce the ban on trade unionists because it would have hurt mainly their own organizations. The attempt to control the votes of their members also was not wholly successful, as can be seen from the reports throughout the period of members who were banned for voting for the Social Democrats. But all in all, the policy must have had a substantial effect because members whose political convictions were not strong would not risk being expelled from an association that offered social contacts and a modicum of financial support in times of need.

It is surprising to see that there never was an open protest against this policy. Some members secretly tried to circumvent the rule and voted for the Social Democratic Party, but none ever demanded freedom from political control, although the associations' democratic structure did not exist only on paper: If a majority of the local branches strongly opposed a poli-

---

17 Zimmermann, *Kriegervereine in Schleswig-Holstein,* 338, found out that in 900 local associations 30 percent of the leadership was from the lower classes, 53 percent from the middle classes, and 15 percent from the upper classes in comparison to a social composition of the general membership of 51 percent, 42 percent, and 3 percent respectively. In Bielefeld even the heads of the local associations were of a higher social background (Michael Siedenhans, "Nationales Vereinswesen und soziale Militarisierung: Die Kriegervereine im wilhelminischen Bielefeld," in Joachim Meynert et al., eds., *Unter Pickelhaube und Zylinder* [Bielefeld, 1991], 381–2).

cy (for example, reforms concerning the association's structure or member-ship fees), the leadership did not get its way. But in regard to the politiciza-tion of the organization, they shied away from discussion not only because they felt intellectually inferior but also because they sensed – not on an emotional, but on an intellectual level – the contradiction between being a member in an association that glorified and celebrated the monarchical state and supporting a socialist party that at least claimed to support a revo-lution. The associations' leadership was able to exploit this contradiction in its actions.

Probably more influential than direct manipulation were the activities at the local level, which held much more importance for the majority of the members than the political stance of the *Landesverbände* and the Kyffhäuserbund. Nationalistic and militaristic thinking found their strongest voices in the local branches and were publicly expressed and even staged with the performance of public rituals.[18]

The motivation for founding or joining a veterans' and reservists' associ-ation was the attempt to keep alive the feeling of comradeship that had its origin in the war experience or common military service, to realize some security through an insurance system, to obtain an honorable burial cere-mony, and, last but not least, to identify with the army and the new state. The associations' activities – weekly meetings, attendance at burial cere-monies, social frolics, celebration of national memorial days, and atten-dance of official parades – reflected these interests. Although social activi-ties were no different from those of other clubs, public ceremonies were celebrated with great clamor: They included several marches through the village with flag and music, public speeches that ended with a "hurrah" for the emperor and fatherland, and a festivity at the end – all of which amounted to an exceptional social event, at least in smaller places. These occasions, which could dominate the life of a village or small town for two days, fulfilled several functions for the members.

The celebrations were usually described as collective experiences. In the celebration of the emperor, the sovereign of the state, or the German fa-therland, the individual member got the feeling of being part of a strong and important group, homogeneous in its determined effort to support king and country. An official flag, badges, and other little privileges dem-onstrated to the public the special connection of the association with the state.

---

18 The following is based on Rohkrämer, *Der Militarismus,* 55–77.

All public appearances of the "army in civilian clothes," as the veterans' and reservists' associations liked to call themselves, had to follow a strict military procedure. The flag had to be collected according to military fashion, the participants were dressed uniformly and decorated with badges and medals, and all the actions (marching, greeting, etc.) were handled in a military manner. Particulars about the ceremony – for example, whether to salute or to doff hats in front of the emperor – could give rise to long and heated discussions.

The disciplined and uniform public appearances symbolized not only the members' proud identification with the army but also the priority of the collective over the individual member. By following the procedures in every particular detail the participants showed their willingness to suppress individual wishes and desires in the interest of the whole group.

Discipline was based on command and obedience. In the ceremonies, the president of the association gave military commands and the rest of the membership had to act accordingly. Everyone had a clearly determined place in a precisely structured hierarchy, which stretched from God and the emperor to the humblest member of society. On the one hand, the hierarchical thinking could lend security because the individual knew where he belonged and drew his importance, no matter how small, from his contribution to the whole. On the other hand, it also could support the feeling of comradeship because all appeared equal in their loyalty to the highest authorities.

Although the ceremonies copied military fashions as authentically as possible, everything was of course more relaxed. While the veterans and reservists could show themselves as "true" soldiers, hardship was a thing of the past. They thus profited from the prestige of the role without suffering the disadvantages the role entailed in reality.

The leaders of the *Landesverbände* were often embarrassed when the common members gave one another military ranks according to the hierarchy in the local associations, addressed one another as "lieutenant" or "captain," or decorated their civilian clothes "with shoulder straps, big, wide, colorful sashes and sabers," but they could not stop them.[19] These pompous self-presentations pointed out the most important individual reason for participating in these ceremonies. Although the member had to adapt to a strict order, he was rewarded with an increase in social prestige. The veterans and reservists were proud to identify with the highly respect-

19 *Parole* 79 (Oct. 6, 1909): 215.

ed army and nation and display their special status to the public. In the following quotation an author described the strong impression such a presentation of fellow citizens in military fashion made on him in his early youth:

> There was one period of exceptional military importance for me each year. During the three days of Whitsuntide the marching of the uniformed shooting association consisting of 30 to 40 honorable citizens turned the town and its surroundings upside down. Already in the morning of the first Whitsun day . . . the town musicians, today in the uniforms of the grenadiers, marched through the streets of the town to blow the reveille. At noon the civilian riflemen assembled on the market. We stared at them with admiration, especially when the good-natured soupboiler L. and the harmless tanner S. suddenly appeared in unexpected clamor and displayed a roughness and a pride, which we had never expected in them. . . . The neat uniforms, the shining leather, the sparkling rifles with their long bayonets gave their bearers a completely different appearance. . . . But the main joy was to see the leader Mr. U., owner of the mill, gallop toward us on a proud brown horse, a wide, well-fed animal that usually had to work in the business. But today it was as well presented as its rider. This is how I imagined Napoleon in the fantasies of my youth. With the dignity and self-confidence of a general the "major," as he was called today, led his troops under the sound of brass and drums to a green, on which they had their shooting competition. Late in the evening the corps alarmed the town once again on its return. Accompanied by music the officers were brought home to their housewives in order of their rank, and after the sergeant had been delivered home as well, the last few would disperse. . . . Events of this kind and impressions gained from books filled my fantasy as a child, and I was determined to become a soldier.[20]

Thus, the veterans and reservists learned that the often painful process of fitting into a hierarchical institution had its own rewards. The total acceptance of authority not only was the easiest way to get by; it also led to an increase in social respectability.

One can thus conclude that the veterans' and reservists' associations contributed to the spread of authoritarian attitudes that uncritically accepted the state and its representatives. The glorification of the army and its hierarchical, often brutal structure meant a general acceptance of hierarchical organizations based on command and obedience. Instead of limiting authoritarian structures to areas where they were unavoidable, the members of the associations tended to see them as models for all kinds of institutional and personal interactions.

The fight against the Social Democrats, although carried into the veterans' and reservists' associations from the outside, fits into that pattern.

---

20 Gustav von Schubert, *Lebenserinnerungen* (Stuttgart, 1909), 7–8.

Again, the members grudgingly accepted authority instead of making use of democratic structures or leaving the associations. Their social prestige, drawn from membership in the association, obviously was more important to them than freedom from control. The direct effect of this policy against the Social Democrats was the weakening of the party most strongly opposed to an aggressive foreign policy; it indirectly perpetuated an attitude that accepted political control by superiors.

The rejection of all working-class organizations meant that the whole idea of representing class interests was rejected in favor of patriarchal structures. Instead of fighting for their own cause, the common people were supposed to put their trust in the benevolence of the monarchical state. They were trained to be obedient citizens, trusting the state and its representatives. This authoritarian attitude was an important prerequisite for a total-war effort, which is dependent on a cooperative population.

II

The German Empire was by and large satisfied with the international status quo until the 1890s, when the dream of Germany as a colonial world power came into play. The same trend can be witnessed in the veterans' and reservists' associations. In this section I highlight one explanation for this: Because the members of the older generation presented themselves as heroes after their participation in the wars of unification, the members of the younger generation, who had never participated in a war, felt inferior. They dreamed of proving their military qualities in order to step out of their fathers' shadows. Thus, they turned the backward-looking glorification of the Franco-Prussian War into a forward-looking militarism that touted German expansion and future war in which these "would-be heroes" could prove themselves to be "true heroes" like their fathers.

Among high-ranking officers in the imperial army it was generally accepted that wars were a necessary part of human existence. Colmar von der Goltz summarized this opinion with the words: "Wars are human fate, are the unavoidable destiny of nations. Eternal peace is not given to the mortals in this world."[21] Attempts to abolish wars appeared as illusory as attempts to limit their destructiveness. Because there was no power to enforce international treaties, the escalation of every important military conflict seemed unavoidable since a nation would never refrain from using

21 Colmar Freiherr von der Goltz, *Das Volk in Waffen* (Berlin, 1899), 430.

all available means to win.[22] The history of the nineteenth century, in which wars had become increasingly destructive, seemed to prove beyond a doubt that the reality of warfare was determined by nothing but military logic. Even a so-called preventive war, "not as a defense against an immediate, unavoidable danger, but as a precaution [*Vorbeugung*] against future dangers in the interest of Germany," was seen as legitimate and was frequently considered.[23]

By contrast, the common soldiers' memories of the wars of unification were more ambivalent, even if the authors were strong nationalists. Although proud of the part they had played in the war, the vast majority stressed the horrors of warfare. Their elaborate attempts to justify the war against France as a necessary defense shows that they needed a moral legitimation for their actions. Some even criticized as cynical the acceptance of war as part of the natural order by pointing out the suffering involved:

A wise and famous man has called the war "an element of the godly order," and a learned German professor, equipped with all the scientific tools, characterized the war as a healthy and good institution, as "absolutely indispensable for cultural development, for the spread of civilization." Either these kinds of human beings have never seen the horrors of a battlefield or they are calculating, cold, egotistical natures who are only concerned about their own fate, and have no heart which can be moved by thousands of blood-witnesses, who have watered the ground with their hearts' blood.[24]

Most veterans agreed that nothing was more important than that fate would "save us from war," and hardly anyone dreamed of service in a future war.[25] They accepted the necessity to defend their country but hoped for a long period of peace.

Despite this critical attitude toward war, the veterans did not regret their service. They were proud of the memory and saw it as the ultimate test, which had turned them into better human beings and "real men."

Whoever has gone to war with full enthusiasm and with the youthful ideal of self-sacrifice, whoever has stood in enemy fire and realized that he could overcome his fear of death with manly courage comes back (if he is fortunate to survive) as a different person, as a stronger character. . . . He is a man.[26]

22 Cf., e.g., Helmuth Graf von Moltke, *Gesammelte Schriften und Denkwürdigkeiten des General-Feldmarschalls Grafen Helmuth von Moltke,* 8 vols. (Berlin, 1891-3), 5:195.
23 Helmuth Graf von Moltke, *Ausgewählte Werke,* 4 vols. (Berlin, 1925), 3:13.
24 Friedrich Freudenthal, *Von Stade bis Gravelotte: Erinnerungen eines Artilleristen* (Bremen, 1898), 148.
25 *Kriegs-Erinnerungen eines bayrischen Jägers aus den Jahren 1870/71* (Nuremberg, 1894), 101.
26 Ludwig Hütz and Otto Schmalz, ed., *Kriegserlebnisse bayrischer Artilleristen aus den Jahren 1870–71* (Munich, 1902), 283.

Especially young soldiers had experienced the war as a rite of passage that had turned them into respected members of society. Because no achievement in the nonmilitary sphere could, in their eyes, compete with defending one's country, they felt equal to anyone, even the most distinguished members of society. The soldierly image of manliness and heroism mixed with the pride in the role they had played in bringing about German unification.

What I gained from the war and what I could only gain there . . . is . . . the exhilarating feeling that I was among those who were Germany's force in 1870/71 and who fulfilled a glorious task. I am aware that it is nothing special to have done what thousands of others have done. . . . But I thank God that I served in the war. The self-confidence I have, whether it is great or small, the belief in God, all this I could not have if I had not enthusiastically taken my place in times of danger, if I had not done my part that a great time had not found a weak people [*Volk*].[27]

The veterans were convinced that their military deeds entitled them to privileged status for the rest of their lives. The rest of society, especially the younger generation, was supposed to look up to them with respect, listen to their advice, and follow their example. The following quotation from a short story expresses the position they sought:

Father, tell us how you conquered the French flag. . . . Father Wedekind leant back against the big lime tree, under which the bench stood, looked into the evening sun, while the children gathered around him and the neighbors moved closer. . . . The listeners were absolutely silent. The hearts of some boys, who had to go to the army soon, were beating in anticipation and the children hung on his every word.[28]

The veterans stylized storytelling about the war into a patriotic deed that was supposed to educate the younger generation by passing on respect for military virtues. But a closer look at the veterans' and reservists' associations shows that the reservists saw the veterans' behavior in a very different light: They experienced it as a continuous self-glorification, designed to turn the younger generation into second-class beings. If the associations accepted reservists, which did not happen in all cases, the veterans put on their medals to show their status, demanded seats of honor at ceremonies and social events, and expected to be greeted by the young with special honors.[29]

27 Heinrich Schmitthenner, *Erlebnisse eines freiwilligen badischen Grenadiers im Feldzuge 1870/71* (Karlsruhe, 1891), 139.
28 *Parole* 1 (Jan. 3, 1896): 3–4.
29 *Parole* 63 (Aug. 10, 1910): 203 (Parole-Buch); *Parole* 22 (May 31, 1895): 371.

The same arrogance was apparent in the supraregional bodies: When the president of the Prussian veterans' and reservists' associations died, no reservist was invited to the burial ceremony.[30] In the associations' magazine, the journalists demanded admiration of veterans by the younger generation;[31] they glorified the wars of unification while describing the present as a period of decline;[32] and they kept reminding the younger members of a constant duty to be thankful.

But what about you, you men who did not fight four decades ago, who did not contribute when our fatherland was built, who only experienced the warmth of peace! What about you, who only became adults after Germany's resurrection! . . . Are you conscious of the blessings that grew out of German blood? Be honest. . . . Many will have to admit to themselves that they have never thought about it but have lived a comfortable life without realizing the heavy and serious duty of thankfulness they owe to those who have created an orderly and blooming state for them.[33]

In another short story printed in the magazine of the veterans' and reservists' associations, two veterans agree that all members of the younger generation were wimps, and in their eyes no maneuver could compare with the hardship of war.

What is the physical hardship of the hottest day in an autumn maneuver, what the suffering of sleeping in the rain for a night in comparison to the demands of a real war. . . . We know what a real war is like, and we can tell it to our youth.

Many reports about conflicts between veterans and reservists show that the latter rejected this insatiable narcissism. Occasionally they rebelled against the veterans' self-glorification, but they never altogether succeeded in gaining equal status. Reservists remained in associations where they were often treated as second-class members, and they did not break with their fathers' value system in which the warrior was the ideal role model and only true man. Thus, they were forced to hope for a more aggressive foreign policy and a future war in which they could prove their own "manliness" and soldierly qualities. Their attempts to step out of the shadows of their fathers led the reservists to become increasingly militant. As they could gain nothing from a backward-looking glorification of the Wars of Unification, they had to promote the rise of a forward-looking militarism that tried to establish Germany as a world power, possibly by means of war.[34]

---

30 *Parole* 42 (Oct. 16, 1896).
32 Rohkrämer, *Der Militarismus*, 182–3.
34 See, e.g., *Parole* 27 (July 5, 1895): 455.

31 *Parole* 37 (Sept. 10, 1897): 604.
33 *Badisches Militärvereinsblatt* (Aug. 1, 1902): 257.

The veterans had always stressed both peacefulness and soldierly qualities as national characteristics. The true German, they said, would dream
of peace but always be prepared to defend himself. And in case of war he
was not only supposed to be superior to all other nations but also would
discover that he was an adventurer at heart, happy to give up the existence
of a civilian for the exciting life of a soldier. "People in arms" (von der
Goltz), they thought, was the natural and necessary state for the German
people – always prepared to defend themselves in a world governed by the
power of weapons. The reservists accepted the moral obligation not to be
aggressive. Although they dreamed of proving their soldierly qualities,
they still believed in a just war tradition that ruled out offensive wars. For
the veterans there was no difficulty in combining the two qualities: Because they had already fought in a war, they could now present themselves
as peaceful without risking the loss of their soldierly image. But the young
generation in the German Empire was caught in a quandary: On the one
hand, they could prove their manliness only in a war because all civil activities could not compete with military combat. But on the other hand,
they were not permitted to look for a situation in which to prove themselves because a true hero was not supposed to be aggressive. Just as a western hero needs a "bad guy" to prove himself as good and strong, a soldierly
hero needs a foreign aggressor. Thus, the reservists had to hope for a future war without being permitted to admit it. They had to interpret the
actions of others as aggressive to see themselves in a defense position in
which they could prove themselves. As long as the image of a peaceful
warrior was not fundamentally challenged, the problem involved could be
solved only by interpreting other nations' actions as aggressive. This argument is not to deny that there were objective reasons for concern. Since
the annexation of Alsace-Lorraine the enmity between France and Germany remained deep and bitter, and the other European powers also were
suspicious of the new hegemonic power. In addition, Germany's geographic position in the center of Europe gave reason for concern, although its importance should not be overestimated.[35] But independent of
concrete events, the veterans' and reservists' associations always felt threatened. The consistency of the attitude suggests that it was a subjective feeling rather than the result of an objective analysis that made them expect
an attack on Germany.

The vague feeling of danger led to the often-expressed belief in the

---

35 Hans-Ulrich Wehler, *Entsorgung der deutschen Vergangenheit? Ein polemischer Essay zum "Historiker-
streit"* (Munich, 1988), 174ff.

unavoidability of a future war.[36] Only a strongly armed Germany could
deter its enemies from starting a war. "If you want peace, prepare for
war."[37] But the alleged dangers and the resulting policy of distrust and
strength were not primarily seen as necessary evils but rather as an important means to maintain the soldierly spirit in Germany. Although it was
supposed to be a national characteristic, the fading of the fighting spirit
was always seen as a danger that could be counteracted only by the permanent expectation of war. "Nothing is as demotivating as permanent
freedom from dangers, and nothing strengthens as much as permanent
danger. . . . May we be saved from a war! But may the ghost of war be
permanently at our borders."[38] The alleged danger of war was instrumentalized for creating a militaristic mentality and "obedient citizens" who
would sacrifice their own interests for their country. Even colonial wars
were thus seen in a positive light.[39]

Whereas foreign policy under Bismarck still had been limited and realistic in its goals, this modesty could not be maintained in the age of imperialism. The idea of a colonial empire became increasingly popular, and
Germany decided to challenge the other major powers and gain "a place in
the sun." As the established colonial powers strongly resisted the revisionist
newcomer, a "cold war" developed in which the German government
consciously accepted the risk of war in order to achieve its goals.[40]

This political development corresponded with the psychological needs
of the reservists. Only an offensive foreign policy could give them the
hope of fighting in a future war. But as they still felt committed to the
principles of the just-war tradition, which condemned provoking a war,
they had to deny the aggressive character of Germany's attempt to establish
itself as a world power. Its foreign policy was seen as a legitimate attempt to
gain a position it deserved because of its size and might. Economic growth,
which depended on raw materials and markets; population growth, which
demanded new areas for settlement; Germany's cultural achievements,
which should be used to advance the "uncivilized" world – all these reasons
were given as the justification of the necessity for expansion.[41]

---

36 The spread of this topos through the whole of society is shown in Wolfgang J. Mommsen, "Der
Topos vom unvermeidlichen Krieg: Aussenpolitik und öffentliche Meinung im Deutschen Reich
im letzten Jahrzehnt vor 1914," in Jost Dülffer and Karl Holl, eds., *Bereit zum Krieg: Kriegsmentalität
im wilhelminischen Deutschland 1890–1914* (Göttingen, 1986), 194ff.
37 "Der Gesetzentwurf über die Änderung der Wehrpflicht," *Parole* 50 (Dec. 15, 1887).
38 *Parole* 55 (July 9, 1905): 261.   39 *Parole* 1 (Jan. 5, 1910): 2–3.
40 Volker R. Berghahn, *Rüstung und Machtpolitik: Zur Anatomie des "Kalten Krieges" vor 1914* (Düsseldorf, 1973), 24.
41 *Parole* 18 (Mar. 5, 1911): 173.

After the turn of the century international tensions led to an arms race among the major powers. The Prussian veterans' and reservists' associations vaguely realized the futility of a policy that became increasingly expensive without leading to positive results, but they interpreted Germany's policy as a strenuous but necessary determination to keep up with the other powers. Even if military spending became an "unbearable weight," its necessity was beyond question because the other countries were seen as initiators, whereas Germany only pursued its legitimate goals. Attempts to break out of the cycle were pushed aside as naïve.[42]

The most important political attempts to gain control over growing international tensions were the peace conferences of 1899 and 1907 in The Hague. At the same time national peace movements came into existence that attempted to establish a stable and peaceful international order. The German peace movement, which was founded in 1892, appealed to the government to promote understanding among nations, an international body of law, and a world court that could resolve international conflicts peacefully.[43] But the veterans' and reservists' associations fiercely attacked all these attempts to control military dynamics by calling them "sentimentally humanitarian":[44] "The call 'Lay down your weapons!' is drowned out by the trumpet of war and the far-reaching thunder of cannon; eternal peace is a lovely fairy tale from a strange and remote world; among the peoples of this earth, war is reality."[45] The aggressive polemics against international peace initiatives and a peace movement without any real influence betrayed the fact that veterans' and reservists' associations and the nationalistic public interpreted those attempts to limit the danger of war not only as naïve but also as a personal threat.[46] The representatives of the peace movement were not seen as harmless idealists but as positively dangerous. They were associated with the enemy, fulfilling its intention of weakening Germany by spreading the belief in international conventions and stopping necessary armament programs.[47] On top of this, they were charged with undermining the "soldierly spirit" of the Germans. By blaming militaristic attitudes for the dangers of war, the peace movement attacked the core of the nationalistic worldview, and the veterans' and reservists' associations reacted with the accusation that the pacifists were destroying the basis of Germany's power. "We must fight with all our strength against the spread of the idea

---

42 *Parole* 3 (Jan. 15, 1897): 37–8.
43 Karl Holl, *Pazifismus in Deutschland* (Frankfurt am Main, 1988), 41 102.
44 *Parole* 69 (Aug. 26, 1903): 681.   45 *Parole* 91 (Nov. 12, 1905): 902.
46 Roger Chickering, *Germany and a World Without War: The Peace Movement and German Society, 1892–1914* (Princeton, N.J., 1975), 418.
47 *Parole* 31 (Apr. 17, 1907): 301.

of eternal peace. It is absolutely suicidal to kill the soldierly spirit in our people."[48]

Pacifism was regarded as moral decadence, a symptom of the "wimpish, feminine character" of the present,[49] when soldierly virtues like courage were on the decline.

> The lesson of wars is: Only nations who maintain their ability to defend their existence at any time with weapons and to achieve and secure a place in the sun progress and have a future. A weak nation is not feared, it is despised, attacked, defeated, and vanishes. The strong and courageous own the world. . . . Whoever disarms discourages the opponent from disarming as well. On the contrary, it encourages him to attack as soon as the other is sufficiently weakened. Every war is a reminder for Germany to reject any thought of disarmament. Instead, it has to rely on its own strength so that the enemies will be deterred by fear.[50]

War was seen as a positive element of reality that should not be limited by international conventions. In accordance with leading theoreticians of warfare, the veterans' and reservists' associations were convinced that Germany had to prepare for an absolute war.[51]

But the attempt to interpret world politics purely as a defense of Germany's legitimate rights had to fail eventually because the argument of "existential interests" was clearly extended beyond any plausibility. In this situation the concept of social Darwinism offered a more flexible and coherent theory to justify the striving for world power. Its modern, scientific appearance made it look as if it were objectively proven beyond political doubt.

In Wilhelmine Germany, nationalists began to use the theory of evolution, which had originally fascinated progressive forces, as a model to explain international relations. Under neglect of the wider theory, the principle of selection was interpreted literally as a "fight for existence,"[52] a permanent battle for power not among individuals but among nations or races. Social Darwinism justified the permanent preparation for physical conflicts because military power was assigned prime importance for the survival of the collective. In reality, this ideology justified the egotism of nations and undermined the belief in any attempt to limit modern warfare.[53]

---

48 *Parole* 45 (June 9, 1909): 441.   49 *Parole* 10 (Feb. 6, 1910): 89.

50 *Badisches Militärvereinsblatt* 47 (Nov. 17, 1911): 413.

51 See, e.g., von Moltke, *Gesammelte Schriften,* 7:139–40; and von der Goltz, *Das Volk in Waffen,* 9, 128.

52 This is the literal meaning of the common translation of Darwin's "survival of the fittest" or "Kampf ums Dasein."

53 Hans-Günter Zmarzlik, "Der Sozialdarwinismus in Deutschland als geschichtliches Problem," *Vierteljahreshefte für Zeitgeschichte* 11 (1963): 250–1; and Paul Weindling, *Health, Race, and German Politics Between National Unification and Nazism, 1870–1945* (Cambridge, 1989), 25; see also Hans-

With this theory, militaristic thinking interpreted war as the human version of natural selection. As an animal could not escape from Darwin's laws, human beings could not avoid the law of the battle for dominance – that is, war. From a personal challenge, war turned into an objective touchstone of natural selection. "In the lives of individuals and nations the fight for existence is the moving force, and the conflict and competition of interests will – in extreme cases – always . . . be solved by a war."[54]

War was taken out of the normative sphere because it was seen as the natural basis of human existence. Moral arguments now appeared to be merely a cheap excuse to avoid conflict. While the weak tried to maneuver through life without disturbing others, the strong were courageous enough to risk their lives in trying to reach their goals. "Unworthy is the nation that is not prepared to risk everything for her honor. Like the individual without honor, a people without nationalist feelings, without the joyful preparedness to defend a good right with the sword is despicable."[55] The evolutionary "survival of the fittest" did not appear to be a regrettable part of human existence but rather a necessary prerequisite for progress because it eliminated the inferior. A victory in war was thus taken as proof of moral superiority.[56]

Whereas the vast majority of veterans had rejected the view that the war had improved the participants, the social Darwinists were convinced of a war's positive influences:

In a war a *Volk* has to pass the test whether it still has enough strength, unity and willpower to influence world history. In a war the highest virtues of human beings find their expression: entire peoples rise to risk everything – possessions and blood, physical health and life – to defeat the enemy. The addiction to worldly success and possessions, to luxury and sensual joys stops being the prime motivation for human actions, and the most honorable thought, the sacrifice of one's life for the fatherland, overcomes human egotism.[57]

Whereas the traditional conservative militarism had postulated that the fear of international danger was enough to keep up the "soldierly virtues," the new militarism based on social Darwinism was convinced that only the occasional war could prevent the decadence and decline of the people. Male virtues, which could be evoked only by war, were said to be indispensable to civil society as well. Wars should bring forth citizens prepared to sacrifice their own interests for the common good.

Ulrich Wehler, "Sozialdarwinismus im expandierenden Industriestaat," in Imanuel Geiss et al., eds., *Deutschland in der Weltpolitik des 19. und 20. Jahrhunderts: Fritz Fischer zum 65. Geburtstag* (Düsseldorf, 1973), 132ff.

54 *Badisches Militärvereinsblatt* 15 (Apr. 7, 1911): 140–1.   55 *Parole* 88 (Nov. 2, 1904): 873.

56 See, e.g., *Badisches Militärvereinsblatt* 17 (Apr. 28, 1899): 155; *Parole* 88 (Nov. 2, 1904): 873.

57 Ibid.

With these social-Darwinist arguments, war appeared in a completely new perspective. Before, it had been one of many elements of human existence; now it became the central one. Any hope for peace appeared illusory because life was seen as a permanent struggle for existence. Peaceful periods were nothing but a short rest, while war became the essence of life.

By basing their arguments on social-Darwinist thought, the veterans' and reservists' associations clearly broke with the concept of a just war, which the veterans had still maintained. This ideological change overcame the tension between the dream of world power and moral inhibitions to admit to an offensive foreign policy. If history was an eternal fight for existence in which only the strongest survived, then the only alternatives were expansion or decline. In this perspective, a permanent increase in military strength and the striving for world power lost their aggressive elements because expansion appeared as the only chance to secure one's own existence.

Many historians have noticed a clear political change in the 1890s. The period between 1887 and 1893, particularly from 1890 to 1893, was a period of exceptionally high military spending; in the 1890s imperialist propaganda reached new heights, "national" leagues started to play a big part in politics, Germany turned into a revisionist country trying to alter the map of the world, and an expansionist "bourgeois" militarism began to challenge a traditional militarism that was primarily interested in maintaining the status quo at home. In domestic politics the conservative dream of preserving the social order was challenged by new concepts of a *völkisch* nationalism that wanted to create a "true" homogeneous community based on race. There clearly was a common element to all these changes: Whereas the Bismarckian empire was interested primarily in maintaining the status quo (which did not exclude making use of opportunities in foreign policy as long as it was fairly safe), the 1890s witnessed the rise of a new policy – restless, aggressive, and oriented toward new goals.

Gerhard Ritter explained these developments as a new dominance of military thinking over a political reason of state. Instead of trying to achieve stable conditions with a limited war, the Wilhelmine period was interested only in unlimited, destabilizing expansion.[58] This distinction is problematic because we cannot know whether a more successful policy would have satisfied Germany's ambitions. But if we look at the history of

---

58 Gerhard Ritter, *Staatskunst und Kriegshandwerk: Das Problem des "Militarismus" in Deutschland* (Munich, 1965), 1:19–23.

mentalities and ideas, we can explain the radicalization of military thinking more easily. In the 1860s and 1870s war was still an exceptional event – that is, a unique challenge for the individual soldier and the last resort in a question of essential importance for the state. By contrast, social Darwinism turned war into the essence of national existence. The new militarism regarded war as the natural form of existence, while peace was degraded to nothing but a period of preparation for the next war. As social Darwinists interpreted all aspects of life as a kind of war, peace gained the appearance of a "cold war."

According to this rationale, the veterans' and reservists' associations argued in accordance with military officers such as Friedrich von Bernhardi that Germany could not avoid a war for world dominance in the near future. The Germans had to erase the inhibitions in their hearts, put all efforts into an arms buildup, and pick an advantageous moment to attack their competitors. Because a future war seemed unavoidable, such an attack did not appear as aggression but rather as a preventive strike.

First of all it is necessary to realize . . . that a period of peace and quiet has not arrived yet, that the prophecy of a last battle for Germany's existence and importance is not the fantasy of ambitious fools, but that this battle will come one day, unavoidably, with full force and the seriousness that characterizes every decisive battle between nations when they have to accept a new international order.[59]

The veterans' and reservists' associations expected the future war to exceed all previous ones in intensity: bigger armies and more efficient weapons on the one hand, higher demands on the soldiers on the other. This is why they demanded that the remaining "peace"-time be used to prepare for the big showdown. Already at the beginning of our century this mass organization of the common people demanded a mobilization of all parts of society to prepare for a war on an unprecedented scale.

The bitterness of World War I was already apparent in the period of preparation. The "complete effort of the nation" was demanded to evoke and cultivate soldierly virtues in all citizens.[60] As weapons became more efficient and destructive, so the human "material" had to improve its physical and psychological fitness. The veterans' and reservists' associations not only raised this demand in their magazines but also tried to implement it in the associations' activities. Thus, they started with different forms of paramili-

---

59 *Parole* 17 (Apr. 21, 1908): 313–14. (It is an unmarked quotation from Goltz, *Das Volk in Waffen*, 426).
60 *Parole* 47 (June 14, 1914): 466.

tary training in their local associations. In the 1890s, 193 medical companies were founded in Prussia and 44 in Baden; by the twentieth century they had increased to 700 and 100, respectively. Members were trained by doctors and themselves organized little maneuvers to practice. They helped in cases of civil emergencies, but their main purpose was service under the Red Cross in case of a future war.[61] Also, target practice spread shortly before World War I. After 1907 the Kyffhäuserbund had tried to get old weapons from the army, and in 1909 they received 75,000 rifles, which were used diligently to improve the members' military capabilities.[62] The veterans' and reservists' associations even organized "war games" for their members to practice all skills necessary for a future war.

A fresh, lively activity is spreading through our associations. The members not only want to meet for celebrations and other social events but also want to prove that the old soldierly spirit is still alive in the "army in suits" [veterans' and reservists' associations]. All over the German fatherland, usually on Sundays, the young and quite a few old soldiers move into the fields to see whether the hand that was once so calm and secure in using a rifle can still handle the weapon and whether the command "Jump up – march, march!" which is so well-known to all infantrymen, still has its mobilizing force. Shots of the different patrols can be heard through forests and valleys, their sound rolls continuously over the field until a "Hurrah" of many voices marks the high- and endpoint of the battle.[63]

The military activities, which were intended mainly for the young members, probably had only a small training effect. But they showed that the common people in the veterans' and reservists' associations wanted to present themselves as potential soldiers in combat. They expected a war in the near future and wanted to be prepared.

After this it is not surprising that the veterans' and reservists' associations greeted World War I with enthusiasm. They were thrilled by the chance of going to war and were triumphant about the first German victories: "It is a joy to be a German: One attack after the other! One victory after the other!"[64] At last the people seemed to be united and prepared to sacrifice everything in the fight against the enemy. And the war was immediately perceived as a chance to establish Germany as a leading world power. Thus, the veterans' and reservists' associations demanded

---

61 *Geschäftsbericht des Deutschen Kriegerbundes and Badisches Militärvereinsblatt* 44 (Nov. 4, 1898): 373–5 and 28 (July 7, 1911): 259–61.
62 *Geschäftsbericht des Kyffhäuser-Bundes,* 1908, 27ff., and 1909, 15.
63 *Parole* 15 (Feb. 19, 1913), 42–4.
64 *Parole* 67 (Aug. 25, 1914): 678.

that we not only want to be freed from the heavy pressure, but also must gain securities for the undisturbed establishment of a future Germany. Peace shall make us "bigger and stronger." . . . After our patience and peacefulness have been enormously provoked [*in unerhörter Weise schnöde herausgefordert*] for long years, now is the time of reckoning. We want to, and shall, settle all accounts with our enemies.[65]

War thus seemed to offer the opportunity to realize all national and personal ambitions. The new militarism made war appear a blessing. In this sense we can say that a "war with words" was one of the factors that prepared the ground for a real war of unprecedented intensity. As an author of the time said:

The battle with words has prepared the battle with cannons, has intensified the unleashed war, and has created more enmity than the battle with weapons could ever have done. Words have created the atmosphere in which the tension burst. Words are still covering the facts like clouds, and with their fantastic shapes they stop our eyes from perceiving the reality. The power of suggestion has never triumphed as much as in our days.[66]

III

Previous studies of generational conflicts at the turn of the century have naturally concentrated on the youth movements, life-reform movements, and avant-garde art movements.[67] The study of the veterans' and reservists' associations has suggested that wider parts of society were affected by tensions between old and young and that these tensions were caused by the way in which the Wars of Unification were remembered. The veterans' glorification of their deeds and their demands for a privileged position in society were a permanent insult to the next generation, which did not have a chance to compete with its fathers' soldierly image in a quiet time of peace and stability. To step out of their fathers' shadows, the members of this generation either had to question and break with militaristic values or were forced to hope for military conflicts in the future. Thus, the nationalistically minded younger generation turned a backward-looking glorification of the army's role in German unification into a forward-looking mili-

---

65 *Parole* 75 (Sept. 20, 1914): 748.
66 Cincinnatus [Josef Lettenbauer], *Der Krieg der Worte* (Stuttgart, 1916), 8–9.
67 A connection between these movements is suggested in Corona Hepp, *Avantgarde, Moderne Kunst, Kulturkritik und Reformbewegungen nach der Jahrhundertwende* (Munich, 1987). For a brief discussion of the connection between politics and age, see Thomas Nipperdey, "Jugend und Politik um 1900," in Walter Rüegg, ed., *Kulturkritik und Jugendkult* (Frankfurt am Main, 1974), 87–114.

tarism that aimed to establish Germany as a world power, possibly by means of a war.[68]

This is not an interpretation based on hindsight. On the contrary: Many contemporaries from the educated middle class saw a connection between the new militarism and imperialism of the 1890s and the young generation's attempt to find new goals for the future.[69] The first to anticipate such a development seems to have been the historian Heinrich von Sybel in his famous comment after the capitulation of Paris in the Franco-Prussian War:

My eyes continue to look at the special newspaper, and the tears flow down my cheeks. What do we deserve God's mercy for to be allowed to experience such great and powerful events? And how shall we live afterwards? What has been the content of all wishes and actions for twenty years has now been given to us in such an absolutely beautiful way. Where shall one find a new content for the future life at my age?[70]

For publicly active people for whom the political fight was of essential importance, this might have been an immediate problem. But the vast majority were happy to settle back into a more comfortable civilian life, drawing self-confidence from pride in the new Imperial Germany and from their past as soldiers in combat: They identified with the image of the role of the warrior without having to endure any longer its reality of hardship, dangers, and boredom. In contrast to Sybel, most contemporaries stressed the fact that imperialism was particularly popular with the next generation. Thus, Gerhard Ritter said more as a witness of the time than as a historian:

The younger generation strived beyond those borders of Germany's international power politics. Whoever remembers the Wilhelmine epoch from his own experience (like the author) can clearly see how the then new catchwords of striving for "world power" and "sea power" were received as a salvation from the eternal backward-oriented pathos of traditional patriotism.[71]

Less-conservative persons also equated youth and imperialism. Thus, Friedrich Naumann asked whether it was "Byzantinism, if our whole

---

68 This is not to deny that it was also difficult for the veterans to maintain a backward-looking militarism over time. If the veterans wanted to maintain the level of nationalist enthusiasm, they gradually had to celebrate nation and army in the present as well as in the past. But for the reservists this problem was far more urgent.

69 See also Nipperdey, "Jugend und Politik," 92–3, 113–14.

70 Heinrich von Sybel in a letter to H. Baumgarten (Jan. 27, 1871), quoted from Julius Heyderhoff and Paul Wentzcke, eds., *Deutscher Liberalismus im Zeitalter Bismarcks: Eine politische Briefsammlung*, 2 vols. (Bonn, 1925-6; reprint, Osnabrück, 1967), 1:494.

71 Ritter, *Staatskunst und Kriegshandwerk*, 126–7.

youth identifies with the concept of a fleet?"[72] and Max Weber said in his famous inaugural lecture in Freiburg that "the unification of Germany was just a youthful prank which the nation committed in her old days and which she should have left off because of the costs involved, if it was the end and not the starting point for German world politics."[73]

The extreme nationalists, who moved toward a "national opposition" in their criticism of what they perceived as a cowardly policy of the German government, also regarded themselves as a young movement breaking with old traditions, inhibitions, and complacency. Eduard von Liebert wrote about "the youth, which is enthusiastic about colonial expansion,"[74] and the army officer and social Darwinist Friedrich von Bernhardi quoted Goethe's *Faust I* to support his view:

Law and rights are continuously inherited like an eternal sickness. They are dragged along from generation to generation and move from one place to the other. Reason turns into nonsense, a blessing into a pain; Woe that you are a grandson! Unfortunately nobody ever speaks of the right which is born with us.[75]

Within the Pan-German League the younger generation also was more radical than the veterans of the Franco-Prussian War, and for the later leader Heinrich Class the differences of opinion were mainly expressions of generational conflicts.[76] As he stated in his autobiography, he turned away from the ideals of his parents and adopted the more radical stance of the younger generation. "We, the young, were progressive: we were purely nationalistic; we were not interested in a tolerance which spared the enemies of the *Volk* and the state."[77] Whereas the older generation wanted to remain loyal to the emperor and the government, the "young pushed toward establishing a 'national opposition.'"[78] Their conviction was that Germany was in deep danger and needed the forceful, uncompromising, absolutely loyal support of people who were prepared for any sacrifice, and they styl-

72 Friedrich Naumann, *Demokratie und Kaisertum* (Berlin, 1900), 182.

73 Max-Weber-Gesamtausgabe, vol. 1, pt. 4: *Landarbeiterfrage, Nationalstaat und Volkswirtschaftspolitik: Schriften und Reden 1892–1899,* ed. Wolfgang J. Mommsen and Rita Aldenhoff (Tübingen, 1993), 571.

74 E. von Liebert, *Aus einem bewegten Leben: Erinnerungen* (Munich, 1925), 137.

75 Friedrich von Bernhardi, *Deutschland und der nächste Krieg* (Berlin, 1913), 28. The poet Max Hoffmann expressed the same idea with the words, "Not backwards! No, ahead! To hell with the fatalistic complaint: undistinguished descendants" (Max Hoffmann, *Irdische Lieder* [Grossenhain, 1891], 14).

76 Roger Chickering, *We Men Who Feel Most German: A Cultural Study of the Pan-German League, 1886–1914* (Boston, 1984), 104–5.

77 Heinrich Class, *Wider den Storm: Vom Werden und Wachsen der nationalen Opposition im alten Reich* (Leipzig, 1932), 17.

78 Ibid., 45, 61.

ized themselves as the true warriors, much superior to those whose half-hearted activities still drew on the past to prove their worth.

Scholars have occasionally studied generational conflicts and their relation to militarism during the period between the two world wars.[79] The quotations cited here and the new catchword at the turn of the century, "Battle of the parties for the youth,"[80] showed that all political groups had the same problem of integrating the young generation – a problem that was of particular importance because the percentage of young people within the whole population was exceptionally high at the time, particularly in the urban centers.[81] The militaristic Jungdeutschlandbund with its 750,000 members in 1914[82] and militaristic tendencies within the youth movement itself were further evidence of the fact that this generational conflict was closely connected with attitudes toward war.[83] A young man who did not seriously question military values in general was very likely to be more militaristic than his father. The generational background shaped the attitude toward imperialism and the striving for world power.

CONCLUSION

In evaluating the political role of the reservists' and veterans' associations in Imperial Germany, we observe that their struggle against the organized and politicized working classes is the most obvious fact. The associations were instrumentalized to weaken the Social Democrats and maintain a patriarchal attitude among the common people. Instead of being taught to become independent-minded – critical citizens who tried to represent their own convictions and interests – the common people were taught to put their trust in the state and its official representatives. It is impossible to assess with any precision the effects of the associations' policies, but it seems reasonable that the attempt to manipulate their members must have had

79 Robert Wohl, *The Generation of 1914* (Cambridge, Mass., 1979); Hans Mommsen, "Generationskonflikt und Jugendrevolte in der Weimarer Republik," in Thomas Koebner et al., *"Mit uns zieht die neue Zeit": Der Mythos Jugend* (Frankfurt am Main, 1985), 50ff.; and Detlef J. K. Peukert, *Die Weimarer Republik* (Frankfurt am Main, 1987), 91–110, with references to further literature.
80 Nipperdey, "Jugend und Politik," 87ff.
81 Klaus Tenfelde, "Demographische Aspekte des Generationenkonflikts seit dem Ende des 19. Jahrhunderts: Deutschland, England und Frankreich," in Dieter Dowe, ed., *Jugendprotest und Generationenkonflikt in Europa im 20. Jahrhundert: Deutschland, England, Frankreich und Italien im Vergleich* (Bonn, 1986), 18, 26.
82 Peter D. Stachura, *The German Youth Movement, 1900–1945: An Interpretative and Documentary History* (London, 1981), 69ff., 77ff.
83 Joachim Wolschke-Bulmahn, "Kriegsspiel und Naturgenuss – Zur Funktionalisierung der bürgerlichen Jugendbewegung für militärische Ziele," *Jahrbuch des Archivs der deutschen Jugendbewegung* 16 (1986–7).

quite a strong impact. Thus, the veterans' and reservists' associations played their part in educating obedient subjects and weakening the political party that was most critical of military matters.

Less apparent but at least equally important was the more informal influence of the veterans' and reservists' associations on its members. From the beginning and without any kind of manipulation from "above," these organizations of the common people celebrated the army, the state, and the monarchy because they were proud of the alleged results of the wars in which they had fought. Although the members did not always draw practical political conclusions from their celebrations of the status quo, these celebrations obviously promoted the acceptance of a conservative state marked by political and social inequalities.

Most important, one should note how crucial changes of attitude, which prepared "the road to total war," could occur in a period of peace. The radicalization of militarism in the German Empire was not a direct result of the experiences in the wars against Denmark, Austria, and France but resulted from the way in which a society dealt with these memories. At first sight, the glorification of a war and one's own role in it might appear somewhat childish, yet innocent. But by stylizing the past to gain an advantage for the present, the veterans put pressure on the following generation to prove its own worth. Those who did not break with the militarist and nationalist attitudes were pushed into radicalizing them. They developed modern versions of these ideologies by integrating up-to-date pseudotheories like social Darwinism or even racism and *völkisch* ideas of turning the nation into a homogeneous community. This process contributed not only to creating a completely unrealistic picture of a future war but also to the desire to become a soldier in combat.

Mobilizing Philanthropy in the Service of War

The Female Rituals of Care in the New Germany, 1871–1914

JEAN H. QUATAERT

There is something daunting about researching the place of war in German statecraft. For most of the twentieth century, historians of different political persuasions and for different purposes have analyzed the subject in depth from a variety of perspectives. Indeed, the accumulated research has established a chilling picture of the ways in which the German war machinery and militaristic values and mentalities dominated the heart of the German polity. This is particularly salient – so the argument goes – in understanding the political culture of Imperial Germany, Bismarck's peculiar political construction that constitutionally insulated the military apparatus from essentially all civilian control and accountability. Nicolaus Sombart captures well the main outline of the argument when he writes:

The [Second] Reich as a political entity cannot be likened to any other state existing in Europe at the time. It was not a 'nation-state,' nor a clear-cut monarchy. . . . It was dominated by its strongest member – Prussia – a quasi-absolutist military monarchy, that amazing soldier-state which . . . had built up its power through warfare and robbery and which was made unique by the overwhelming role played by the army as a determining factor in shaping society in its own image. . . . The spirit and pattern of military organization were imposed on all inhabitants of the empire, regardless of class or region, and in spite of the existence of quite different traditions, most notably in the south-west of Germany. . . . The upper classes were permeated by the values of the Prussian officer corps, and the rest of the population was subjected to military discipline and standards through compulsory military service. . . . The dominant social values were martial and, thus, in a very emphatic sense, male. . . . This discriminated against at least 51 percent of the population: women. "La femme n'existe pas!"[1]

1 Nicolaus Sombart, "The Kaiser in His Epoch: Some Reflexions on Wilhelmine Society, Sexuality, and Culture," in John C. G. Röhl and Nicolaus Sombart, eds., *Kaiser Wilhelm II: New Interpretations* (Cambridge, 1982), 290.

Embedded in the analysis, however, are a number of assertions that are open to question. Sombart's account assumes, rather than demonstrates, the spread of military values from the state's war-making institutions into society. But exactly how does this internalization occur, in what contexts, among what segments of the population, and to what extent? His argument rests as well on a limited understanding of the workings of power – here seen solely in their institutional garb. But power, as Foucault persuasively reminds us, is an extremely complex phenomenon, embedded and contested in a range of discursive and ritualistic encounters.[2] In addition, Sombart's line of analysis is too simplistic and belies the real concerns of this "hegemonic" militaristic state with German "public opinion" after June 28, 1914. As war loomed on the horizon, officials betrayed an obsessive preoccupation with popular behavior that reflected deep uncertainty over the nature and extent of loyalty and national identification, at least until the orders for mobilization were issued on August 2, 1914.[3] And, finally, the operating assumptions of the narrative dismiss any further consideration of women, as if women were irrelevant – as agents and subjects – in the nationalist effort to instill a broad willingness to fight and sacrifice for the nation.

My contributions to the debate on German militarism reflect a new way of thinking about nationalism and the struggles over constructing a German national identity. They link nationalism, militarism, and state forma-

2 Michel Foucault, "Body/Power," in Colin Gordon, ed., *Power/Knowledge: Selected Interviews and Other Writings 1972–1977 by Michel Foucault* (Brighton, 1980).

3 This fear is clearly reflected in the detailed coverage of popular sentiment and behavior by the conservative *Neue Preussische Kreuz-Zeitung* (hereafter *KZ*) after the assassination of Archduke Francis Ferdinand in late June 1914. See also Belinda Davis, "Reconsidering Habermas, Gender, and the Public Sphere: The Case of Wilhelmine Germany," in Geoff Eley, ed., *Society, Culture, and the State in Germany, 1870–1930* (Ann Arbor, Mich., 1995). Throughout this study I use the *KZ* in good measure to capture what I call the "official nationalist" agenda (see text following) because of the paper's continually close (but not necessarily always harmonious) association with the house of Hohenzollern and sympathy for the princes and other royalty throughout the states of Germany, its consistent support for the institutional autonomy of the military vis-à-vis the elected representative institutions, and its constant coverage of the world of Berlin "high society" – men and women of the court, aristocrats, high military officers, and government officials who joined together in leisure, philanthropic, and political associations. What comes through the pages of the paper between the founding of the Second Empire and its demise at the end of World War I is the ongoing effort (which in my view is the hallmark of official nationalism in Imperial Germany) to integrate the older royalist with newer nationalist worlds through programmatic and institutional means (written programs and propaganda, associations and organizations) as well as public ceremonies and rituals. This does not imply that so-called nationalist agents spoke with one voice, worked in harmony, or necessarily always supported the government or even the royal houses; there were serious conflicts over the ongoing need to recreate a nationalist identity "from above" as well as to struggle with alternative visions of nationhood emerging "from below."

tion into a highly promising interpretive matrix. To be clear, I am not rejecting the prevailing interpretation among German historians of the significance of war institutions and mentalities in the German polity. Rather, I seek to reexamine the mechanisms of power whereby nationalists after 1871 sought to create meaningful identifications with the nation – to orchestrate dispositions among the citizenry that were designed to transform the state into a nation as an ideal worth fighting and dying for. This approach is strengthened by gender analysis – by bringing women and men into the history of war, which, in the nineteenth-century world of citizen armies, conscription, and civilian involvement in war work, must be seen as a highly gendered phenomenon – and by the demonstration of the essential connections between the assumed opposite poles of wartime and peacetime.[4] My analysis anchors the German case in a historical continuum of nationalist experience that promises to unravel several of the most problematic questions of our contemporary age: How does war as an acceptable policy option become part of the popular consciousness? How central to the nationalist agenda is the willingness to wage war?

Political authority in Imperial Germany reflected an unequal and unstable balance of social and institutional power continually reinforced by the power of ceremonies and the ceremonies of power.[5] Viewed from the geographic and political center — from Berlin and from the Hohenzollern dynasty, respectively – institutional power mirrored a genuine hierarchy. Indisputably, although not immutably, the emperor stood above the princes, Prussia was more powerful than the other German states in the federal structure, and the key institution of the new democratic age of universal manhood suffrage – the Reichstag – operated under severe political constraints. An elaborate system of ceremonies worked simultaneously to reinforce and mask these power hierarchies. Central to the whole structure of power was the Prussian (and later imperial) army and its elaborate public rituals, parades, ceremonies, and commemorative festivities. (By the late 1890s Germany's military might included a technologically up-to-date and

4 Jean Bethke Elshtain, *Women and War* (New York, 1987); Jean Bethke Elshtain and Sheila Tobias, eds., *Women, Militarism, and War: Essays in History, Politics, and Social Theory* (Savage, Md., 1990); Margaret Randolph Higonnet et al., eds., *Behind the Lines: Gender and the Two World Wars* (New Haven, Conn., 1987).
5 For the importance of power in ceremonies and rituals, see, among others, Clifford Geertz, "Centers, Kings, and Charisma: Reflections on the Symbolics of Power," in Sean Wilentz, ed., *Rites of Power: Symbolism, Ritual, and Politics Since the Middle Ages* (Philadelphia, 1985); David Cannadine and Simon Price, eds., *Rituals of Royalty: Power and Ceremonial in Traditional Societies* (Cambridge, 1987); and David Kertzer, *Ritual, Politics, and Power* (New Haven, Conn., 1988).

costly blue-water navy.) And, enveloping these military institutions and practices was a political culture that made war service and sacrifice central values in the state. Embedded in the language of war, its categories and canons were communicated to an ever-widening reading public through the printed word and through elaborate forms of public display.[6] With varying shifts in emphasis, this culture worked to affirm the legitimacy of war as an essential component of statecraft; it established various contexts within which war could and should take place according to religious or secular criteria; and it included the willingness to defend against internal as well as external enemies. It continually created its own history – a story that justified war and struggle, building on and, in turn, keeping alive memories of victories (and defeats), of important battles and tactics as well as heroes and heroines. The war ideology was gendered from the start and over time embraced evolving notions about the proper roles that men and women were to play in wartime and, by extension, in public life in peacetime as well. In short, it became a powerful ingredient that shaped the German identity.

The key place of the army in Prussian and later German life originated in the absolutist right of military command (*Kommandogewalt*), that part of the Prussian and later imperial German constitutions that perpetuated the supreme military authority of the king and emperor independent of political control.[7] That right remained powerful into the age of nationalism and mass democracy and was one of the key pillars of conservative rule. Boldly put, if ceremonies and ideological trappings failed to ensure or instill loyalty, conservative authorities always had ready recourse to the naked power of the army!

The army's place in Imperial Germany as an independent "state within the state" was in no way foreordained. Military autonomy represented a victory of royalist and conservative forces against more liberal and demo-

---

6 The interaction between word and ritual comes through clearly in the pages of the *KZ* with the continual slippage between editorial commentary and so-called objective journalistic accounts. Lead articles editorialized on the importance of war in modern-day life. Here, nationalists sought to persuade by entering the public arena and making their political case through verbal argument. Other "news" accounts described in great detail for the reading public a military ceremony or a cultural event, such as a concert, in which military personnel played a prominent role. The particular ceremony, then, had a snowball effect beyond the actual viewing public. The ceremony itself, the placards, announcements, and images used in its name, along with the orchestrated description of it in the press worked simultaneously to reinforce identification with the shared institution and its values of precision, discipline, and order.

7 Elisabeth Fehrenbach, "Images of Kaiserdom: German Attitudes Toward Kaiser Wilhelm II," in Röhl and Sombart, eds., *Kaiser Wilhelm II*, 270.

cratic groups that through much of the nineteenth century struggled over the very nature of the relationship between state and army. Germany's war culture – and its powerful conservative face – was forged in the center of this large patriotic battle.

The nationalist forces unleashed by the French Revolution and the Napoleonic wars brought into question the relationship between the individual subject-citizen and the state. War, defeat, conquest, and liberation undermined the established authority throughout central Europe – and forced its reconstitution along new lines. French military successes and occupations opened a battle over reform options in which the military played the central role. A strong army was the necessary guarantor of state sovereignty; both reformers and reactionaries could agree on this point. But in the new age of nationalist awakening, the army appeared strong to the extent that its soldiers identified with the state. Domestic conflict quickly focused on the nature, extent, and meaning of popular involvement, as conservative and royalist groups emerged to contain the democratic potential of nationalist mobilization for state formation and military authority.[8] Advocates of a people's army vied with those favoring a royal army, and calls for constitutional guarantees were challenged by appeals for traditional social hierarchies and estates. Once the Congress of Vienna renewed the legitimacy of the dynastic states in central Europe, these fissures structured the politics in each of these countries for more than half a century.

Wars, too, no longer were distinct events but were integrated directly into the life of the state. And wars required women's participation – or at least that was the dominant reading of the Wars of Liberation, which gave Germany's emerging war culture a powerful gender component – a duality of "men in arms" and women turning in "gold for iron" (as the slogan had it in 1813), offering material goods for the war effort as well as providing a range of care and support for the men in war and later the disabled and poor veterans in peacetime. This culture had its female representative, Queen Luise, wife of Friedrich Wilhelm III, king of Prussia during the tumultuous revolutionary decades. Although she died in 1810, three years before the popular victory at Leipzig assuring "German" liberation, she nonetheless became the guarantor of victory, symbol of unity,

---

8 For these conflicts during and after the revolutionary decades see, among others, Thomas Nipperdey, *Deutsche Geschichte 1800–1866: Bürgerwelt und starker Staat* (Munich, 1983), 11–102. See also James J. Sheehan, *German History, 1770–1866* (Oxford, 1989), 235–323; Gerhard Ritter, *The Sword and the Scepter: The Problem of Militarism in Germany,* vol. 1: *The Prussian Tradition, 1740–1890,* trans. Heinz Norden (Coral Gables, Fla., 1969); and Eckhard Trox, *Militärischer Konservativismus: Kriegervereine und "Militärpartei" in Preussen zwischen 1815 und 1848/49* (Stuttgart, 1990).

and martyr to the fatherland. Her name, or so legend had it, inspired the volunteer citizen-soldiers in 1813. Over the course of the nineteenth century, her biographers created a female image that in various guises blended royalist authority and nationalist commitment.[9] Constructed as a loyal wife and mother, yet fiercely political and patriotic (she stood up to Napoleon, after all), Luise came to embody national strength and unity in the face of political humiliation and dismemberment as well as ongoing state concerns for its loyal children – heroic soldiers, poor veterans, soldiers' wives and orphans, and the deserving poor. The highest honor acknowledging women's multiple sacrifices in the Wars of Liberation, a small golden cross, bore her name, the Order of Luise; it was redesigned in 1850 to recognize patriotic women's work for the "fatherland" in 1848–9; and it reemerged in 1865 as a statement by the dynasty, in a society obsessed by rank and titles, acknowledging nationalist women's ongoing and varied contributions to the (imperial) German nation-state in war and peace. In the fluid and uncertain political terrain of the nineteenth century, dynastic forces sought to dominate the war culture by controlling the public rituals defining patriotic service.

The institutional expression of this emerging sphere of care and patriotic work, marked with honor by the Order of Luise, was the *Frauenverein* or women's association. The earliest association emerged in 1813, part of the state-directed efforts to mobilize women for war work and, later, service for needy military personnel. In the *Vormärz* (pre-1848 Germany), a wide range of similar philanthropic groups began to appear in urban centers; some were distinctly local and autonomous, catering to specific social needs, whereas others were state-directed from the start, linking philanthropic activities and patriotic service. The Patriotic Institute of Women's Associations (Das patriotische Institut der Frauenvereine), founded in 1817 by Dutchess Marie Pawlowna of Weimar, provided a compelling model of wide-ranging female service: caring for the sick, training nurses, educating abandoned female youth, and establishing disciplined workhouses. From this civilian side of life, these voluntary philanthropic social activities (as

---

9 I have read a range of biographies and sketches of Queen Luise, the first one published at her death in 1810 and subsequent ones emerging throughout the "long" nineteenth century. It is beyond the scope of this chapter to describe her place in the nationalist discourse over time; but the use of her person is key for understanding how Germany's gendered war culture became incorporated into the ongoing struggle over German national identity. Among other references, see *Luise Auguste Wilhelmine Amalie, Königen von Preussen: Ein Denkmal* (Berlin, 1810); *Luise Königin von Preussen: Dem deutschen Volke gewidmet* (Berlin, 1849); Bernard Rogge, *Königin Luise: Zur hundertjährigen Wiederkehr ihres Todestages* (Liegnitz, 1910); "Hundert Jahre Luisenorden – Zum 3. August 1914," *KZ*, Beilage zu Nr. 358, Aug. 2, 1914.

Paragraph 24 of the Institute's statutes proclaimed) were expected to promote the "strength" and "security" of the state.[10]

The gender component of the war culture was essential to the state's
purposes. Resting on an implicit interdependency of gender symbols, it
worked to structure the appropriate service that men and women would
render the state in times of war as well as peace. In part these gender norms
paralleled, drew on, and yet differed from the bourgeois "world of domes-
ticity" that also appeared at the same time – what historians have labeled a
gender-role ideology that prescribed a proper organization of social life in
the evolving new industrial world of the nineteenth century and provided
a new vocabulary to describe it.[11] Chronologically overlapping, both gender norms rested on a symmetry in which the parts to be played by men
and women were seen as complementary, although they were neither
equally powerful nor especially valued. These ontologically distinct gender
notions intertwined in certain contexts. To the extent that the monarchy
appropriated (or was given) bourgeois gender norms for its public persona
(for example, in the description of Queen Luise as an ideal German wife
and mother or the elevation of her granddaughter Luise, duchess of Baden,
as the model German woman doing her duties – loyal, self-sacrificing,
ministering), royalty gained added legitimacy in the eyes of a receptive
public.[12] But differences are equally instructive, and the gender component

10 One of the oldest and most influential women's associations throughout the century was the Prussian Women's and Young Ladies' Association, formed to honor the bravery of patriotic soldiers
from the victorious battles of Gross-Beeren and Dennewitz in 1813. Its archives are found in the
Geheimes Staatsarchiv Preussischer Kulturbesitz (hereafter GSPK), I, HA, Rep. 89, Nrs. 15607–8:
Acta betr. den Preussischen Frauen- und Jungfrauen-Verein, 1818–1916. I deal with the work of this
group in the following paragraphs. For the Patriotic Institute, see Natalie von Milde, *Marie Pawlowna: Ein Gedenkblatt zum 9. November 1904* (Hamburg, 1904), 41–51, which reproduces the statutes
of the association. For an analysis of the emerging network of women's associations as expressions
of bourgeois self-identity and autonomy, consult Gisele Mettele, "Bürgerliche Frauen und das Vereinswesen im Vormärz: Zum Beispiel in Köln," *Jahrbuch zur Liberalismus-Forschung* 5 (1993): 23–45.
11 For a particularly clear and early formulation, see Karin Hausen, "Family and Role Divisions: The
Polarisation of Sexual Stereotypes of Work and Family Life," in Richard J. Evans and W. R. Lee,
eds., *The German Family* (London, 1981), 51–83. Also consult Ute Frevert, *Women in German History: From Bourgeois Emancipation to Sexual Liberation* (Oxford, 1989).
12 By the time of Imperial Germany, female monarchical figures were held up as ideal German wom-
en by nationalist biographers and agents. The symbol of the monarchy was fluid and, in part, became a projection of the values of the particular group imagining its place in the German community. I saw this clearly in the documents of the Baden Red Cross auxiliary service. At one of the
association's festivals, the speaker stressed the shared values that created a meaningful identification
between the group and the royalty: "the example of doing one's duties puts our circle in close touch
with the circle of the Duchess" (General Landesstaatsarchiv Baden [hereafter GLA, Baden], Abt. 69
[Geheimes Kabinett der Grossherzogin Luise], Nr. 1144: Der Helferinnenbund beim Roten Kreuz,
1908–1911, Festversammlung der Helferinnen vom Rothen Kreuz, Nov. 5, 1908). Also consult
the many biographies of the German royal houses, e.g., Friedrich Hindenlang, *Grossherzogin Luise
von Baden: Der Lebenstag einer fürstlichen Menschenfreundin* (Karlsruhe, 1925); and Heinrich Bingemer,
Eine deutsche Fürstin, Grossherzogin Luise von Baden und ihr Haus: Fest-Schrift (Obernburg, 1912).

of the war ideology functioned in an entirely different arena, that is, openly and at the center of political life. It insinuated itself into the trappings of dynastic authority, easily personified by the rule of the *Landesvater*, the male head of state, and the *Landesmutter*, the female head of state. Above all, it became an essential ingredient of nineteenth-century dynastic rituals of philanthropy that intimately linked together the life situation of veterans and poor people. These ceremonies went back at least to the time of Queen Luise. Her entry into cities and towns, so her biographers are quick to tell us, were occasions for "the inhabitants to feed a considerable number of poor [*Stadtarmen*], invalids, and soldiers' widows."[13] These rituals and ceremonies became part of the way in which central European dynasties sought to establish legitimacy and reinforce loyalty to their states, made all the more problematic by the challenges of the French Revolution and the redrawing of the European map during the revolutionary decades.[14] Increasingly, to celebrate the memory of battles, it became customary to give alms to the poor; or on the queen's birthday, a special public meal was prepared for veterans. Local philanthropic organizations arranged their yearly festivals to mark a royal life-cycle event – a marriage or the birth of an heir. To the extent that these dynastic rituals of rule were transformed into official nationalist creed and ceremony to meet the needs of mass politics (and here I agree with Benedict Anderson that nationalism relegitimized dynastic rule),[15] this war culture functioned to reinforce a particular understanding of the wider national community. And societal interest in war was given an added impetus by German unification through war and by the fact that the Franco-German war was seen as the first political event that all Germans had in common.

In conservative, dynastic designs, the gender war culture operated by evoking a dual conception of the state and, through its words, rituals, and symbols, worked to transform the state into an institution inspiring loyalty – into a nation. The state was above all a war-making machine (a masculine identity), but it also was a caring institution (a feminine identity) – caring for its soldiers at war, its veterans and the disabled, the soldiers' widows and orphans as well as for its needy population in general. And the continuities of dynastic rule in Germany (unlike the case of republican France or the Unit-

---

13 Description of her return to Königsberg in Jan. 1808, found in *Luise Auguste,* 202–3.
14 Sheehan makes the compelling point that during the revolutionary decades, 60 percent of the population in Central Europe changed rulers. Sheehan, *German History,* 251.
15 Benedict Anderson, *Imagined Communities: Reflections on the Origin and Spread of Nationalism* (London, 1983; reprint, London, 1991), 83–6.

ed States)[16] meant that the king and queen (the emperor and empress and the various royal dynasties at the state level) could readily symbolize the distinct functions of the new nation-state after 1871.

In practical terms, in the aftermath of the Franco-Prussian War, the female sphere of care supported and authorized the emergence of a coordinated infrastructure of institutionalized civilian preparedness outside the usual military machinery.[17] The institutions themselves included a wide variety of organizations. The most prominent women's organizations included the Vaterländische Frauenvereine (Patriotic Women's Associations) in Prussia, the separate Frauenverein in Baden, the Alice Verein in Hesse, the Albert Verein in Saxony, and the aforementioned Patriotic Institute in Weimar. There also was the German Red Cross (Deutsche Pflegeverein vom Rothen Kreuz), an organization that operated throughout Germany but was run centrally from Berlin. There were national charitable foundations for war invalids operating on the federal, state, and local levels; groups supporting nursing training hospitals (such as the Kaiserin Augusta Stiftung and the Frauen-Lazareth-Verein in Berlin); and those involved in running sanitariums such as the Heilanstalt für deutsche Invalide in Saxony and the Luisenheilanstalt in Heidelberg. There also were cooperatives for voluntary medical care in war (Genossenschaft Freiwillige Krankenpflege im Krieg) and women's groups that offered charity to needy veterans. Working with the established medical profession – civilian doctors as well as the army medical corps – these associations promoted the training of medical assistants in Germany – nursing sisters and lay nurses, nurses' aides, male orderlies, and scores of voluntary personnel, such as medical crews and well-bred women versed in preventive health measures. To these ends the associations expanded the scope of continuing education and supported a whole range of course offerings in medical science, disease prevention, sanitation, and social hygiene. Costs were underwritten by the local "pri-

---

16 For works that raise interesting comparative issues about the nature of the "public" in distinct political settings, see Joan B. Landes, *Women and the Public Sphere in the Age of the French Revolution* (Ithaca, N.Y., 1988); and Mary P. Ryan, *Women in Public: Between Banners and Ballots, 1825–1880* (Baltimore, 1990).

17 From 1878 on, with passage of a new law on military medical care (*Kriegssanitätsordnung*), many of the formal associations in the infrastructure were placed under military authority. For the role of these associations in military preparations for war, see *KZ*, Beilage zu Nr. 161, Apr. 5, 1888, as well as *KZ*, Nr. 286, June 22, 1892, and Nr. 295, June 28, 1892. Also, the archival documents on the Women's Patriotic Associations are revealing. In the annual reports, the leadership was asked to account for monies spent on war preparation (*Kriegsbereitschaft*). GSPK, H. Rep. 89, Nr. 15611, Bd. III, Bl. 197–9, particularly, reports of the Vaterländischer Frauen-Zweig Verein Lähn. Also, GLA, Baden, Abt. 69, Nr. 887–94: Berichte der Abt. III des Frauenvereins und Antworten, 1890–1922.

vate" organizations in the main, although, demonstrating official involvement, the states regularly offered participants reduced rates on public transportation to attend the classes. And the organizations raised money to build new wings in hospitals and buy the latest in medical technology, and also underwrote cures for poor people as well as needy families of non-commissioned officers.[18]

These philanthropic organizations were a highly visible presence in the German body politic; indeed, their institutional and financial successes depended on public support, so they were determined to keep themselves in the public limelight as much as possible. During natural disasters, such as floods, fires, or outbreaks of cholera, the organizations mobilized their members swiftly and efficiently, evoking a discipline that found its natural counterpart in the army: They published crisp appeals for help in the newspapers, set up strings of locations to receive money and materiel, offered dispatches on the state of affairs and the nature of the cleanup, and kept in close contact by telegraph. The analogy to the military was not coincidental, for even the female leadership consistently employed military metaphors. In a particularly nasty flood of areas along the North Sea in 1888, for example, reports by the district women's association had the beleaguered city of Posen "bombarded" by rising waters and praised "our troops," the columns of women who offered welcome relief – as they would in the case of war.[19] It was part of the politics of this infrastructure that they "performed" their skills before an appreciative audience, and thus they continually arranged public exhibitions. A typical presentation in the genre took place in Leipzig in February 1892, in conjunction with an exhibition of Red Cross activities. The local branch associations demonstrated, to the awe of the public, their ability to feed 3,000 troops on short notice (*Armeespeisung*); other groups regularly displayed on parade grounds usually reserved for military maneuvers their competency to provide logistical and medical support in war. These annual enactments – in Berlin at least – took place in front of the royal family and many local onlookers.[20] The organizations within the infrastructure arranged annual patriotic festi-

18 For these civilian and military medical-training arrangements that were a central part of the infrastructure's activities, see, in particular, GLA Baden, Abt. 456 (XIV. Armeekorps), F. 113 (Sanitätsamt), Nr. 13, Vereine zur Pflege im Felde verwundeter und erkranker Krieger, 1875–1914; Nr. 17, Schriftwechsel über Vereinswesen, Sammlungen in militärärztlichen Kreisen; Nr. 26, Akte betreffend Bestimmungen über Lazarethgehilfe. And also ibid., Abt. 69 (Geheimes Kabinett), Nr. 1094, Die Luisenheilanstalt in Heidelberg betr., 1897–1914, and also Nr. 1143, Die Einrichtung einer Pflegerinnen-Station in Badenweilen betr., 1888.
19 *KZ*: Nr. 75, Mar. 28, 1888; Nr. 90, Apr. 9, 1888; Nr. 131, May 4, 1888.
20 *KZ*, Nr. 53, Feb. 2, 1892; for one example of the Berlin display by the Freiwillige Krankenträger-Kolonne des Kreises Teltow, see also *KZ*, Beilage zu Nr. 445, Sept. 24, 1889.

vals and celebrations and sponsored bazaars, lotteries, and massive fund-raising drives into the remotest corners of Germany. This wide-ranging patriotic structure was so totally integrated into Germany's philanthropic and continuing educational life that it is easy to miss its intimate connections to war. And, because it seemed so innocent, cloaked as it was in the language of humanitarian aid and impartiality, with its claims to scientific advancement and medical progress as well as its emphasis on nursing and other expert medical training, it could be *integrative* at a time when nationalism was increasingly divisive, and considerable argument also existed over the nature of what I have called the "caring state."[21]

This infrastructure – the institutional and ritual world of war-ready patriotic Germans in peacetime – had its own nationalist message, distinct from the voices of the national groups (*Nationale Verbände*), the subject of much excellent research by historians interested in the German radical right. The patriotic infrastructure attracted large numbers of members, considerably more than the national associations at their height.[22] To give several examples: In 1913, there were 1,647 branch associations of the Prussian Women's Patriotic Associations alone, with a total membership of 557,000. One source in 1904 estimated that 16.2 percent of the total female population in Prussia belonged to the women's associations, while a 1909 newspaper report, quoting official statistics, claimed that in Baden more than 15 percent of all women over 25 years of age had joined the state's *Frauenverein*.[23] These philanthropic organizations formed a dense, integrated institutional network throughout Germany, in large cities, medium-size towns, as well as remote rural communities.

Other differences separated patriotic and radical nationalists. The war-readiness infrastructure represented a set of patriotic beliefs and involvements that cannot be understood apart from the way war and peace func-

---

21 Eley makes the important point of just how divisive nationalism was in Imperial Germany. It hardly functioned to integrate diverse peoples despite its own rhetoric of unity and community. My research corroborates this important insight. See Geoff Eley, *Reshaping the German Right: Radical Nationalism and Political Change After Bismarck* (Ann Arbor, Mich., 1980), 202.

22 Eley, *Reshaping the German Right*, app. 3, which contains the membership of important nationalist pressure groups. The largest was the Navy League, which in 1913 had nearly 332,000 members; but the Pan German League at its height (1901) had around 22,000 members and the Colonial Society enlisted about 42,000 members, to mention but several prominent radical associations. See also Roger Chickering, *We Men Who Feel Most German: A Cultural Study of the Pan-German League, 1886–1914* (London, 1984).

23 *KZ*, Nr. 248, May 30, 1913, "Mitgliederversammlung der Vaterländischen Frauen-Vereine." See also Ute Daniel, "Die Vaterländischen Frauenvereine in Westfalen," in Karl Teppe, ed., *Westfälische Forschungen* (Münster, 1989), 171; and GLA Baden, Abt. 69 (Geheimes Kabinett), Nr. 951b, Das 50-Jährige Jubiläum des Badischen Frauenverein am 16. und 17. Juni 1909. Clipping of *Deutscher Reichsanzeiger*, June 19, 1909.

tioned as a continuum in this nineteenth-century political world. People wrote and talked about "war" and "peace" as distinct and separate moments in time, to be sure, but, in reality, each concept did its best "work" by implying the other. For example, when the emperor was hailed as the "peace kaiser" in 1913 as part of the celebration of the twenty-fifth anniversary of his ascension to the throne (and the one-hundredth anniversary of the Battle of Leipzig, as well), the image worked primarily because it implied that Germany was militarily strong – strong enough to deter war or conclude another victorious peace in the case of war.[24] And this war/peace continuum became the circular authorization for the wide-ranging philanthropic and educational activities in the name of patriotism – used particularly effectively by patriotic women. Women in peacetime justified their philanthropic work by its future usefulness in war. They also referred to their historic wartime contributions (drawing on accounts of women's heroic acts from the Wars of Liberation onward but stressing, particularly, the "glorious" months of the Franco-German war[25]) in defending their increasingly prominent role in municipal reform work. In 1881, in a typical expression of the argument, the Women's Patriotic Association acknowledged that its tasks "in war [were to] serve the people under arms and in peace to soothe misery and need, when and where they unexpectedly may break out."[26] Arguing similarly, the Baden Executive Committee of the *Frauenverein* in 1889 capped its case for permission to arrange a lottery to help pay for the construction of a new mother house (headquarters) to train nurses in Karlsruhe by claiming that "the end goal of our whole undertaking is to train and keep in readiness the largest possible numbers of nurses in case of war."[27] In the interim, the nurses would work in all manner of medical facilities throughout the state. The connection between war- and peacetime activities was the fundamental justification for the work of these broad-based and varied voluntary philanthropic associations in Imperial Germany. It was the way in which their members thought and talked about their work and described their contributions to national life in pamphlets, books, reports, and newspaper accounts.

24 *KZ*, Nr. 44, Jan. 27, 1913, "Ein Wort an deutsche Frauen zum Kaisers Geburtstag." For a helpful analysis of the meanings of dual thinking, see David Maybury-Lewis and Uri Almagor, eds., *The Attraction of Opposites: Thought and Society in the Dualistic Mode* (Ann Arbor, Mich., 1989).
25 See the collection GLA Baden, Abt. 69, Nr. 1174: Erinnerungensgaben an Krankenpflegerinnen und Krankenschwestern die im Krieg 1870/71 die Verwundeten gepflegt haben, zum Jan. 18, 1911.
26 *KZ*, Nr. 181, Aug. 5, 1881, among many other possible references.
27 GLA Baden, Abt. 69., Nr. 1158 Bau des Ludwig-Wilhelm-Hospitals in der Kaiserallee in Karlsruhe durch den Frauenverein, 1889–1890: Bitte um Genehmigung der Veranstaltung einer Lotterie, May 1889.

A final distinguishing characteristic of the infrastructure concerns its clientele. This patriotic world brought together a diverse group of privileged people in German society – a social mix that transcends the standard class categories that have shaped much of the interpretation of German nationalism. The story of German nationalism has been written in class terms – as a movement of the bourgeoisie in opposition to the particularist decentralizing dynastic forces of the courts; determined at another point to acquire a viable national market; persuaded, still later, by educational and professional advantages as well as by economic interests, to champion a place for Germany in the sun. Even the literature on the radical right anchors the supporters decisively among the bourgeoisie, in political spaces opened up by the failure of liberal notables to make the transition to mass politics.[28] But this world of patriotic medical service and ceremony drew on a much more complex group that had its own traditions, institutions, and cultural forms. It grew out of the particular way royalist rituals of rule, which underpinned state patriotism, made the difficult transition to the new political world of mass politics and public opinion – and continued to be refashioned, redesigned, and reinvented in the ongoing struggle to control understandings of the German nation and its people. After 1871 these rituals and ceremonies, programmatic appeals, and significant institution-building in the public arena were orchestrated by what I call, borrowing from Anderson, official nationalists: an amalgam of old conservative and royalist forces as well as newer professional and moneyed groups.[29] They were the members of the Hohenzollern house itself; high military officers and their wives; and the men and women of aristocratic circles and of the dynastic courts, of high civil service at the Reich and state levels and of the free professions (particularly clergy) – privileged and powerful people who came together in a festive world of nationalist celebrations and philanthropic sacrifices of their own making. Whatever material differences divided the groups in the formal sphere of electoral politics, here in this "political" world, masked as private and voluntary activities, they hobnobbed together for common purposes – running a charitable institution (an orphanage, sanitarium, old-age home, or tuberculosis asylum), attending concerts, holding bazaars, dedicating a hospital, participating in a parade, or unveiling a war monument. In these

---

28 A number of key works reflect the prevailing interpretation. See, among others, Jürgen Kocka, ed., *Bürger und Bürgerlichkeit im 19. Jahrhundert* (Göttingen, 1987), esp. Hans-Ulrich Wehler, "Wie bürgerlich war das Deutsche Kaiserreich?" 243–80. See also Lothar Gall, *Bürgertum in Deutschland* (Berlin, 1989); and Lutz Niethammer et al., *Bürgerliche Gesellschaft in Deutschland* (Frankfurt am Main, 1990).
29 Anderson, *Imagined Communities*, 86.

ritual and institutional spaces they affirmed their shared commitments to a
militarily strong Germany anchored in the monarchy.[30]

Members of the infrastructure are not hard to identify. Take as a typical
example the composition of the Prussian Women's and Young Ladies' Association (Preussischer Frauen- und Jungfrauen-Verein), an old patriotic
organization that was involved in caring for veterans nearly continuously
from 1814 until 1916. Its executive committee in 1889 (the group then had
around 282 dues-paying members) consisted of the wives of four high military officers, a baroness, a countess, two additional noblewomen, and the
wives of a court preacher, a member of a consistory, and a high government official. Its public arm – the women (*Recherche-Damen*) who personally visited veterans' homes to investigate requests for support – included
wives of professionals (men with doctorates) and a number of leisured un-
married women.[31] This particular social mix also characterized the patriotic elites in Württemberg and Baden, the more "liberal" south German
states in which the power and traditions of the nobility were less pronounced than in Prussia. Subsumed under the umbrella of the dynastic
pair, south German aristocrats, state officials, and professionals, like their
counterparts in Prussia, joined to run the formal philanthropic associations
in the infrastructure as well as the multitude of ad hoc committees fulfilling
specific tasks, such as organizing a bazaar or planning a charity concert.[32]

This elite patriotic world sought all manner of publicity and public attention. Its institutional and ritual activities constituted an influential
sphere of political life in Imperial Germany that is best described as a "female public," a notion that would not be totally unfamiliar to the historic
actors themselves. The concept of a "female public" captures the various

---

30 My argument closely follows the interpretation of Stig Förster, who recognizes the dual face of militarism in Imperial Germany as I recognize the multiple faces of nationalism. This ritualized world
was a place of elite creation/re-creation, giving rise to an official nationalist creed. This does not
imply that material conflicts among the elites were unimportant, only that this ceremonial world
was one space that bridged these economic and political differences at times. See Stig Förster, "Alter und neuer Militarismus im Kaiserreich: Heeresrüstungspolitik und Dispositionen zum Kriege
zwischen Status-quo Sicherung und imperialistischer Expansion 1890–1913," in Jost Dülffer and
Karl Holl, eds., *Bereit zum Krieg: Kriegsmentalität im wilhelminischen Deutschland 1890–1914* (Göttingen, 1986), 122–45.
31 For the Prussian women's association leadership, see GSPK, Nr. 15607, Bl. 145–50: *Sechs-
undzwanzigster Jahresbericht des Preussischen Frauen-und Jungfrauenvereins* (for the year 1889).
32 For details on Württemberg, although in a slightly earlier era, see Carola Lipp, ed., *Schimpfende
Weiber und patriotische Jungfrauen: Frauen im Vormärz und in der Revolution 1848/49* (Moos, 1986),
225. The archival collections of the Duchess Luise contain numerous documents detailing the social background – even religious affiliations – of members of the philanthropic associations. Among
possible examples see GLA, Baden, Abt. 69, Nr. 1133–4, Der Helferinnenbund beim Roten
Kreuz, 1908–1918; as well as the collection on local women's associations (*Lokale Frauenvereine*)
throughout the state of Baden in the German imperial period.

levels of meaning and space that were opened up by wide-ranging patriotic activities, including its gender symbols and imagery – spaces, however,
that often went beyond the intent of the nationalist agents. The patriotic
infrastructure definitely was part of the "public": an effort by quasi-private
(philanthropic) associations to shape public opinion through words and rituals. This was a public that was not distinct from or in opposition to "the
state" but rather represented sets of institutions and practices designed to
conjure up a particular understanding of the state.[33] It also was "female"
because it was anchored and justified in the female side of the gender war
culture, with its stress on multiple services to the state in peacetime in
preparation for future wars. Symbolic authority for these patriotic associations rested with an official protectress who, in nearly all cases, was a
prominent woman member of the royal family – the empress herself in
many instances or the Princess Maria, wife of the nephew of Wilhelm I,
the first emperor – or other princesses or duchesses, such as Luise of
Baden, if the organizations were more locally based. In short, authority
was anchored in the female person of the state. These associations did no
business without a highly ritualized exchange (through a series of
telegrams that were printed in the press or personal visits, when the royal
patron was herself present) acknowledging the importance of the female
protector to their work. These ties were so politically important that in
1889 Empress Auguste (wife of Wilhelm I and patron of the German Red
Cross and the Women's Patriotic Associations, among many other organizations), who was advancing in age, publicly brought in Auguste Viktoria,
Wilhelm II's wife, to share jointly her patronage responsibilities, ensuring
continuity and ongoing identification with the state after her death. A
telling discussion appeared in the *Kreuz-Zeitung* three years after she died
about the proper placement of a monument in her name. The editorial

---

33 The theoretical work of Jürgen Habermas, particularly *The Structural Transformation of the Public
Sphere: An Inquiry into a Category of Bourgeois Society,* trans. Thomas Burger (Cambridge, Mass.,
1992), has stimulated a lively debate among historians on the nature of the "public" in the transition
to a modern industrial world of state activism and intervention. My analysis parts company with
Habermas, particularly in his focus on the autonomy of the emerging "bourgeois" public sphere independent of the state. He misses the extent to which collective "private" activities were state-
directed or state-constituting in central Europe in the first two-thirds of the nineteenth century.
Moreover, this will be an argument of mine as I work this material into a larger, more detailed study
than is possible here. I also part company with feminist scholars who see this institutional world as
enclosing women in the private domain of the philanthropic associations. See, particularly, Sabine
Rumpel-Nienstedt, "'Thäterinnen der Liebe' – Frauen in Wohltätigkeitsvereinen," in Lipp,
Schimpfende Weiber, 206–31. In Rumpel-Nienstedt's analysis, only men saw their place in associational life as part of a public sphere, whereas for women, the association was a "concealed cover," a
public in which women could tread without leaving their private world (218). A fundamental difference of view divides my approach from this interpretation.

comment praised the decision of the prize committee to locate it smack in the center of Berlin at the opera house on Unter den Linden: "the work of this noble Queen was right in the center of public philanthropy (*öffentliche Wohlfahrt*), so her monument must be placed at the focal point of public life [*in den Brennpunkt des öffentlichen Lebens*], in the center of the capital."[34]

The infrastructure was female in more concrete ways as well – ways that were not fully anticipated by official nationalists. It was a space in which elite women felt comfortable out in public, working in municipal poor relief as they did in large numbers, although mostly as volunteers. Here they obtained access to practical training in health care and sanitation and gained impressive organizational and administrative skills. In these settings, they could affirm their patriotism (women were restricted from party membership until 1908) and their willingness to sacrifice for the nation. Such service of care also affirmed their understanding of themselves as women, nurturing and aiding the sick and the needy, but also as privileged women, whose wealth and status no longer were unearned but, rather, justified by the philanthropic and social service itself. They were hardly confined to the inner corridors of the club, and dynastic rituals of rule ensured public recognition of their multiple contributions to society. Baden, for example, designed a medal – the Friedrich–Luise Medal – for state service. The backgrounds of nominees were carefully investigated, and there were many women among the recipients. In 1907 the mayor of Mannheim proposed for the honor the wife of a local lawyer, Frau Dr. Martha Kahn, for her efforts in "founding, organizing, and developing" a reformatory in the nearby village of Neckerau. He wrote glowingly of her "rich service," which practically single-handedly sustained the whole project. Of the required 10,000 marks for the building, she alone raised 8,000 and contributed 1,500 from her own pocket. In a "particularly energetic" fashion, she oversaw the actual construction of the house, working closely with the architect; she negotiated with several Baden firms to obtain free of charge the kitchen stove, the bathtubs, and the toilets. In keeping with the values of her station, she saw to it that the young inmates obtained "regular work" at a local company making waterproof clothing. And she was the institute's treasurer. If this were not enough, Frau Kahn served on the executive committee of the Mannheim *Frauenverein* for Section 7 (overseeing the training of domestics); the district committee for the protection of children, youths, and prisoners; and the legal-aid society for women and girls. In short, her well-known and influential place in Mannheim's municipal

---

34 *KZ*, Nr. 79, Feb. 16, 1893.

welfare structure made her an excellent candidate for special recognition, a public model for others. State officials agreed.[35]

The spaces that opened up for women in voluntary philanthropic work after 1871 were filled at the start by the privileged elites fresh from their war experiences in the Wars of Unification. These patriotic volunteers continued to represent the largest group of women in municipal poor relief and charity work throughout the entire imperial period.[36] But they were not the only ones. Reform feminists, too, entered this space starting in the 1880s – women who had more radical understandings of what the rituals of care might offer for women's own educational and economic growth and personal advancement. And many moderate (bourgeois) feminist associations – from the Lette Verein to Lina Morgenstern's people's kitchens to Helene Lange's educational reform group – found among the female nobility willing patrons and supporters, thereby gaining not only financial rewards but also recognition and legitimacy through the female public's extensive networks.[37] Indeed, possibilities were opening up to redefine the national community in ways beyond the vision of the official nationalist agents.

Never alone in the large nationalist debates, the conservative patriots nevertheless communicated effective nationalist messages through their philanthropic causes. Their broad impact reflected both the depth and strength of their institutional ties as well as the continued power of dynastic rituals reinvigorated by nationalist ceremony. Institutionally, this infrastructure represented a model of associational life that brought elite men and women together for common "humanitarian" purposes, even if the main institutional lines divided by gender. There were separate women's and men's organizations in the structure, although men regularly functioned as secretaries and treasurers of the *Frauenvereine* and women sat on the central committees of the state and federal organizations coordinating the voluntary civilian war service. Among the men and women there were overlapping functions, and rivalry and tensions certainly were not absent from their relationships. But in this nationalist community, the gender division of labor was pronounced and deliberate. Only men trained as volun-

---

35 GLA, Baden, Abt. 69, Nr. 875, Die Verleihung des Friedrich-Luisen Medailles betr.
36 I develop this point in detail in the earlier paper I presented at the first comparative conference on "total war." See Jean H. Quataert, "German Patriotic Women's Work in War and Peace Time, 1864–90," in Stig Förster and Jörg Nagler, eds., *On the Road to Total War: The American Civil War and the German Wars of Unification, 1861–1871* (New York, 1997), 449–77.
37 Reading the "Berliner Zuschauer" section of the *KZ* over the years reveals the extent to which moderate feminist reform groups participated in the ritual exchange with the queen and other royal figures.

teer military medics (*Sanitätskolonne*); and women alone composed the volunteer female auxiliary service (*Helferinnen* and *Helfschwestern*) of the Red Cross, a training that included the latest in midwifery, infant care, and tuberculosis prevention, in addition to front-line and home-front hospital service.[38] The major gender distinction, however, showed up in the local arena. It was women who were on the front lines of daily municipal care, making the "compassionate" commitments of the larger patriotic infrastructure and, by extension, the German state, tangible and visible to the public. The whole edifice – its male and female parts – was symbolically united under the protection of a female head of state, who embodied care and public responsibility; legitimacy for the infrastructure's social work derived from growing acknowledgment that this state indeed provided support and security for its citizens within its borders – and would defend those borders to the death when necessary.

The cumulative effect of philanthropic and patriotic work was not only the ostensible goal of offering impartial "humanitarian" service in case of war – and the press made clear after August 2, 1914, that this coordinated infrastructure was effectively mobilized for the war effort, according to long-standing mobilization plans.[39] In the first days of war, its activities were reported in the conservative press under the telling rubric *Liebesdienst* or labor of love. This work in peacetime had served to instill identification with a caring state that made war in its name that much more possible. Simultaneously, the very rituals of care reinforced power hierarchies and inequalities while they affirmed as well the notions of community and solidarity.

I can illustrate the complex workings of power through ritual in a typical case of German women's patriotic work: the feeding of veterans undertaken annually by the Prussian Women's and Young Ladies' Association to

38 Among other works detailing the activities of the associations in the infrastructure, see GSPK, Civil-Cabinet, I, HA, Rep. 89, Nr. 15609, Bd. I, Bl. 100: *Bericht uber die zwölfte General-Versammlung des Vaterländischen Frauen-Vereins am 24 März 1878,* and similar publications in the archival collection for later years. See also GLA, Baden, Abt. 233 (Staatsministerium), Nr. 2848, Badische Frauenverein, 1866–1919. In addition, consult Kreisverband Ulm e.V. and Ortsverein Ulm, *Hundert Jahre Rotes Kreuz Ulm* (Ulm, 1986), 18–19, 36; and *125 Jahre Rotes Kreuz 1863–1988: Vom Württembergischen Sanitätsverein zum DRK-Landesverband Baden-Württemberg* (Stuttgart, 1988), 12ff.
39 The women's associations affiliated with the Red Cross were incorporated into the army's detailed mobilization calendar, which laid out the orders day by day. Their voluntary war work was overseen by the army (medical officers in the Federal Ministry of War) as well as by officials in charge of voluntary medical service. For a graphic day-by-day mobilization plan and the women's important place within it, see GLA, Baden, Abt. 69, Nr. 1117: Mitteilungen des Badischen Landesvereins vom Roten Kreuz, 1906–1910, particularly the "Übersichtsplan zur Kriegstätigkeit der Badischen Frauen und Männerhilfsvereine vom Roten Kreuz," Dec. 3, 1906, and the "Musterpläne für den Übergang zur Kriegstätigkeit," 1909.

coincide initially with the dates of Napoleonic battles (Gross-Beeren and Dennewitz, August 23 and September 6) and later Königgratz (July 3) from the Wars of Unification. In the Imperial German era, the ritual meal commemorated the victorious entry of Prussian troops into Berlin in 1871 (celebrated every June 18). The association's long and continuous presence in Berlin's political life expressed the workings of the gender war culture, which placed women at the home front in the forefront of ministering to men-in-arms. At the time of the founding of Imperial Germany, the association was under the protectorship of the Princess Friedrich Carl; its members, as indicated, represented a typical social profile of official nationalists drawn from women in military, aristocratic, civil service, and professional circles.

The discourse around veterans was an ideal segue for conservatives into the nationalist age: it forced them to speak the language of community, of equality of sacrifice ("the bullet knew no rank"), and also of responsibility and care.[40] And the ritual meal – reported yearly in great detail in newspapers such as the *Neue Preussische Kreuz-Zeitung* – worked to promote solidarity and integration. Its compelling power was anchored partly in the rituals of everyday life – a meal prepared by women (food is necessary for physical survival, after all) – enjoyed together with like-minded fellows.[41] And the gender dynamics powerfully worked their complex effects – demonstrating the significance of gender symbols and polarities for the whole nationalist enterprise and their centrality to the war culture. On the one hand, because women orchestrated it, the festival had an aura of "naturalness," helping to re-create, in essence, the sense of a large family, reinforced by the mingling of the ages at the meal. The meal was attended by older and younger women – women who were someone's mother, wife, or daughter. Indeed, it reinforced the parallel nationalist effort to define the state as a large family, ensuring the physical as well as emotional well-being of its members. The festival thus affirmed community and fellowship through sharing food and song – and the German readers of the daily papers knew the patriotic songs and hymns and could imagine themselves

40 The place of veterans in Imperial Germany required the old conservative groups, from royalty to military generals to aristocratic women, who had been active in the Wars of Unification, to debate issues of state responsibilities, private responses, and women's place in the structure of care that needed to be organized for war heroes and their families. For a particularly interesting formulation of conservative views, see the appeal of Marie Simon "An die deutschen Frauen," *KZ*, Beilage zu Nr. 272, Nov. 21, 1871.
41 For the importance of food rituals in creating solidarities and expressing ethnic or other differences, see the works by the anthropologist Mary Douglas: *Implicit Meanings: Essays in Anthropology* (London, 1975); *In the Active Voice* (London, 1982); and *Food in the Social Order: Studies of Food and Festivities in Three American Communities* (New York, 1984).

singing along simultaneously. On the other hand, the gender dynamics were more complex. Gender served to mask other forms of hierarchy and dominance. Relations of power cut both horizontally (upper-class women in Germany undoubtedly had less power than men of their class) and vertically. These well-off, privileged women who, one imagines, ate better than the food they served the veterans, reproduced the power hierarchy in German society, eliciting deference in forms of address and indebtedness. Not only was the food a gift, but the less privileged soldiers received other gifts of cigars and champagne, donated by local industrialists or other people who had more power and money. And the presence of a few key generals and prominent members of the Prussian government unmistakably reinforced this power hierarchy, should the more subtle workings of gender be missed. Thus, the ceremony simultaneously affirmed community while underscoring deference, hierarchy, and social inequality. It helped to legitimize the conservative power hierarchy by evoking memories of the glorious victories of the nation through strength and affirming the nation's indebtedness to those who served its needs. Finally, this annual ritual was part of the nationalists' wider, more elaborate calendar of events that organized the year in an orderly fashion around recurring patriotic events – parades and life-cycle celebrations of the royal families or ruler-heroines, such as Queen Luise. In these contexts, as in the feeding of veterans, prayers, speeches, and numerous salutes were offered regularly to the king (as head of the army in war and peace) as well as to the queen and her ranks of patriotic women for their roles in ministering to the needy in war- and peacetime. In this way, powerful nationalist messages were given to participants and those readers throughout Germany who could easily envision themselves as part of the ceremony.

The envisioning of a national community also developed directly out of the very institutional networking promoted by the growth of the infrastructure itself. I can illustrate this important change in consciousness by the experiences of a local women's association in Lähn, a town on the Bober River in a poor, remote agricultural district in Silesia. Archival sources have preserved yearly reports of the association's presidents over forty-seven years.[42] The local branch was run throughout the period by three powerful and articulate aristocratic women (with only a one-year interruption in leadership): Marie von Haugwitz, 1870–83; Marie von L'Estocq, 1883–1901; and her daughter, the Countess Fanny Pfeil,

42 GSPK, Civil-Cabinet, I, HA, Rep. 89, Nr. 15609–13, 1867–1919: Acta betr. den Vaterländischen Frauen-Verein und seine Zweig-Vereine.

1902–18. This unique source – their letters are handwritten and deeply personal while also self-serving for the supplicants are out for money – nonetheless demonstrates the subtle processes whereby nationalist identification grew in the context of traditional loyalty and ties to the monarchy.

The Women's Association in Lähn was founded in July 1870 – in war – to care for wounded soldiers; immediately after the war, its first president exercised the old subject right to petition the king/emperor for an immediate financial subvention – and continued to do so, as did her successors, for the next forty-six years. The tone of the requests was remarkably intimate while simultaneously deferential. Haugwitz, for example, expressed real joy at the prospect of the emperor becoming a grandfather; wrote despondently of the painful memory of the assassination attempt on his life in 1878 and related her organization's needs and sorrow to his own, which, she said, deeply touched all loyal children of the realm (*Landeskinder*); and even sent him a collection of sermons of a deceased pastor "because he so prayed for Your Majesty" over the years, for the prosperity and well-being of the royal house.[43] Other letters and reports made equally clear that the Women's Patriotic Association, as part of the privileged social elite, drew sustenance from its ties to the royal couple and the house of Hohenzollern.[44] Indeed, in the debates in 1880 concerning the restructuring of Germany's poor-relief system, key voices in the military and government favored *patriotic* women's increasing voluntary participation, seeking to capitalize on their conservative, loyal, and monarchical sensibilities.[45] Duchess Fanny Pfeil made no bones about her politics (although she was, after all, petitioning for money from a special royal fund). She consistently represented her dedication to "throne" and "fatherland" – to shared Christian values – and to duty and stability as a dam against social misery, "dissatisfactions," and growing political disharmony.[46] In the process, however, the very notion of the "fatherland" took on new meaning, as local communities like Lähn through their patriotic networks came to empathize with the plight of more distant Germans in the realm. Mobilized when misery

43 Ibid., Bl. 108–9, Jan. 3, 1879; Bl. 115–16, May 18, 1880.
44 On the death of Augusta, a large number of branches of the Prussian Women's Patriotic Association sent condolences to the royal house on black-rimmed stationery. Ibid., Nr. 15610, Bl. 54, Jan. 9, 1890 (Hamburg); Bl. 55 (Loest); Bl. 56, Jan. 14, 1890 (Elbing); Bl. 60, Feb. 7, 1890 (Wiesenburg), among others. In addition, on the hundredth anniversary of the birth of Queen Luise the Executive Committee of the national Women's Patriotic Association sent special greetings to the king/emperor acknowledging the shared interest in her memory. Nr. 15609, Bl. 79–80, Mar. 10, 1876.
45 *KZ*, Nr. 279, Nov. 27; Nr. 280, Nov. 28; 1. Beilage zu Nr 281, Nov. 30, 1880: Conferenz von Armenpflegern.
46 GSPK, Nr. 15611, Bl. 189–90 (1902), 197–9 (1903), 209–11 (1904).

struck elsewhere and recipients of support when it appeared at home, they were able to envision a larger community – "from all parts of the father-land" (*aus allen teilen des Vaterlands*)[47] – joined together in common Christ-ian values of charity and neighborly help. And this new imagination was powerfully reinforced by the growing ability of national headquarters and district organizations to funnel money downward. Members of the infra-structure simultaneously acquired a wider vision of their community while working locally for concrete reforms, which changed the very complexion of the state. The efforts of Lähn presidents bore fruit: They scraped mon-ey together to support three charity sisters who nursed, fed, and fêted the poor and sick, and they renovated an old town hospital that had been founded in 1585. Indeed, the physical landscape in the town was trans-formed as new tasks became part of municipal life: The hospital expanded and buildings took on new functions, housing a nursery school and an old-age home administered by the patriotic association. In 1916, in the middle of war, the Lähn branch sought additional money for major renovation of its hospital, old-age home, and parish hall to accommodate growing num-bers of wounded soldiers. Money was pledged, and the financial commit-ments made in the name of the royalty were honored after 1918.[48] But just as the Württemberg lieutenant-general prophetically said to the emperor in early November 1918: "The army will march home peacefully and in good order under its leaders and Commanding Generals but not under the Command of Your Majesty"[49]; so, too, the patriotic identification with the state – which had become institutionally more complex through the very workings of the patriotic infrastructure – continued long after the formal removal of its *Landesmutter*.

47 Ibid., Nr. 15611, Bl. 155 (1898).
48 Ibid., Nr. 15612 Bl. 198–9, June 8, 1916; and also Nr. 15613, a discussion from Mar. 22, 1918, through Apr. 30, 1919, concerning funding of a training institute for nurses (the Kaiser Wilhelm-Schule Deutscher Krankenpflegerinnen) in recognition of women's significant sacrifices in the war.
49 Quoted by Wilhelm Deist, "Kaiser Wilhelm II in the Context of His Military and Naval En-tourage," in Röhl and Sombart, eds., *Kaiser Wilhelm II,* 187.

PART THREE

Memory and Anticipation: War and Culture

The American Debate over Modern War, 1871–1914

JOHN WHITECLAY CHAMBERS II

"What shall we say of the Great War of Europe, ever threatening, ever impending and which never comes?" an American peace leader asked in 1913. "We shall say that it will never come. Humanly speaking it is impossible."[1] Because World War I erupted less than a year after David Starr Jordan, the president of Stanford University, made these remarks, they have often been quoted to demonstrate the naïveté of prewar peace advocates. Yet they were not all so naïve as might appear from this comment. For Jordan had concluded: "Not in the physical sense, of course, for with weak, reckless, and godless men nothing evil is impossible."

What Jordan was really implying was that war among the major powers might be rendered impossible if the elites and the general public recognized that it would be economically catastrophic and that modern weaponry and mass armies had made modern warfare militarily and politically disastrous as well as inhumane.[2] Jordan was not the only American to make such a prediction, but many others disagreed. In the years before World War I, there was much uncertainty and debate over the evolving nature of modern war, a debate with important ramifications for U.S. foreign policy toward Europe and Asia.

To what degree did Americans at the years around the turn of the century anticipate the kind of modern, industrialized war that would after World War I come to be known as "total" war?[3] In contrast to several broad

---

1 David Starr Jordan, "The Impossible War," *Independent* 74 (Feb. 27, 1913): 467.
2 Ibid., 467–8.
3 On the historical evolution of the term "total war" and its problematic nature, see the introductory essay to this book by Roger Chickering. My own view is that modern "total" war on the scale of the two world wars of the twentieth century involved an expansion of the nature of war in several dimensions. Mass national mobilization for war and the use of much more destructive weapons by industrialized nation-states contributed to the expansion of the geographical area of warfare, of the

studies on British and other European voices prophesying modern war,[4] the American public discussion of the future of war has not received adequate attention.[5] However, the evolution of modern warfare in its technological, organizational, and doctrinal characteristics has received considerable attention, particularly from military historians. There the traditional paradigm has viewed the emergence of modern war as driven largely by the political construction of national mass armies of citizen-soldiers and the rapid technological developments in weaponry. Accompanying late nineteenth-century industrialization and clashing rivalries of contending

duration of sustained warfare, and of the war aims to "total victory" (i.e., unconditional surrender and total subjugation of major states), and these, together with the new weapons technology, led to greatly increased casualties as the definition of combatants was expanded particularly through aerial bombardment to include entire civilian populations.

4 See Peter Paret, ed., *Makers of Modern Strategy: From Machiavelli to the Nuclear Age* (Princeton, N.J., 1986), for an analysis of the views of the military and military intellectuals. The classic treatment of relevant imaginative war literature is I. F. Clarke, *Voices Prophesying War: Future Wars, 1763–3749*, 2d ed. (Oxford, 1992), originally published in 1966 under the title *Voices Prophesying War, 1763–1984*. Clarke's study mainly is of European literary fiction predicting future wars. The year of 3749 in the second edition refers to the beginning of the end of civilization in Walter Miller's *A Canticle for Leibowitz*, published in 1959. For what was seen as the most frightening aspect of modern warfare, aerial bombardment of cities, see Robert Wohl, *A Passion for Wings: Aviation and the Western Imagination, 1908–1918* (New Haven, Conn., 1994); and Robert Wohl, "The Prophets of Air War," *MHQ: The Quarterly Journal of Military History* 7 (winter 1995): 81–91.

5 There have been some studies of the views on war of particular sectors of American society in the late nineteenth and early twentieth centuries, e.g., in the military, Russell F. Weigley, *The American Way of War: A History of United States Military Strategy and Policy* (New York, 1973); James L. Abrahamson, *America Arms for a New Century: The Making of a Great Military Power* (New York, 1981); Perry D. Jamieson, *Crossing the Deadly Ground: United States Army Tactics, 1865–1899* (Tuscaloosa, Ala., 1994); Kenneth J. Hagan, *This People's Navy: The Making of American Sea Power* (New York, 1991); and in the peace movement, David S. Patterson, *Toward a Warless World: The Travail of the American Peace Movement, 1887–1914* (Bloomington, Ind., 1976); C. Roland Marchand, *The American Peace Movement and Social Reform, 1898–1918* (Princeton, N.J., 1973); and John Whiteclay Chambers II, ed., *The Eagle and the Dove: The American Peace Movement and U.S. Foreign Policy, 1900–1922*, 2d ed. (Syracuse, N.Y., 1991).

With regard to general attitudes of Americans in that period toward war, the primary scholarly treatment is contained in Thomas C. Leonard, *Above the Battle: War-Making in America from Appomattox to Versailles* (New York, 1978). However, despite a number of valuable insights in the book, Leonard's account is overstated and sometimes erroneous, such as his contention that the new weaponry was seen as making war less bloody (his sources here are representative of only one side, the minor side, of the debate); he also completely neglects the issue of the economic impact of modern war, which was more widely discussed in the periodical literature than the new weaponry. Leonard's view on the subject is restricted by the limited number of his sources. David Leroy Axeen, "Romantics and Civilizers: American Attitudes Toward War, 1898–1902," Ph.d. diss., Yale University, 1969, explores a narrow time frame and employs a reductionist taxonomy. An imaginative and highly speculative psychological interpretation is put forward in Michael C. C. Adams, *The Great Adventure: Male Desire and the Coming of World War I* (Bloomington, Ind., 1990); a more extensive treatment of dominant American myths about violence, including war, is offered by Richard Sklotkin, *Gunfighter Nation: The Myth of the Frontier in Twentieth-Century America* (New York, 1992). None of these works offers an adequate understanding of the dominant views of war prevalent in American society between 1865 and 1914.

nation-states, modern "total" war is, in retrospect, frequently portrayed as inevitable.[6] But did contemporaries view it as inevitable?

It is worthwhile to examine the degree to which such developments may have been influenced by predominant cultural attitudes as much as by weapons technology. To ask some different questions: What were the public conceptualizations of the future of war and warfare? Did cultural assumptions and expectations help to channel technological, political, and military developments in particular directions? Such an examination might indicate whether there were alternatives to seemingly inevitable developments. Were there other conceptualizations and counterpressures that emphasized restraint rather than promotion of the material and organizational means for waging modern "total" war? Did the American public see such mass warfare as the warfare of the future, and did such views influence U.S. foreign and military policy?

The attitudes toward and interpretations of developments in warfare put forward in America's mainstream magazines represented an important part of the public dialog about the future of war. So great were the changes in technology, society, and world affairs in the late nineteenth and early twentieth centuries, however, that commentators differed widely on their meanings. After the Franco-Prussian War of 1870–1, many nations adopted variations of the mass conscript army based on universal military training. Beginning particularly in the 1870s, science and industry produced a chilling array of deadly new weapons. Among these were high-powered repeating rifles, machine guns, rapid-firing artillery, and high explosives. By the turn of the century entirely new weapons systems were being developed – steel-plated, big-gun battleships, submarines, dirigibles, and fixed-wing airplanes.

Examining attitudes toward war in mainstream magazines in the United States between 1871 and 1914, this chapter explores predominant attitudes and the public debate on the meaning of developments in weaponry, organization, and the nature and place of war in the modern world. The focus is on war as a phenomenon and also predictions about the future of war. Caught in a whirl of change, contemporaries debated many questions: Were social and economic developments leading to an end to war between modern industrialized nations? Or were they intensifying it? Had the causes of war changed in modern times? What was the evolving nature of

---

6 See, e.g., Theodore Ropp, *War in the Modern World* (New York, 1959); and, more recently, Richard A. Preston, Alex Roland, and Sydney F. Wise, *Men in Arms: A History of Warfare and Its Interrelationships with Western Society,* 5th ed. (Fort Worth, Tex., 1991).

warfare? What would it be like in the future? What would it mean to the United States?

This exploratory chapter is based on an examination of more than 300 articles on war in more than two-dozen public-interest periodicals published in the United States.[7] These include the "Big Five" popular illustrated monthly journals of the late nineteenth century, namely, *Atlantic, Century, Harper's, The Nation,* and *Scribner's;* monthly review and public opinion journals, such as *North American Review, Review of Reviews, Forum, Literary Digest,* and *World's Work;* and inexpensive, mass-circulation magazines that began in the new century, such as *Cosmopolitan, McClure's,* and *Munsey's.* Although paid circulation exceeded one million in some cases, the readership of all these periodicals, including the last group, was largely upper- and middle-class.[8]

Most articles about war in these periodicals were written by authorities in fields dealing with issues of peace and war (scientists, social scientists, international lawyers, peace leaders, ethicists, social reformers, diplomats, and military officers). Some were written by journalists. Quite naturally, such articles appeared more frequently in times of war or other major international crises. But what is surprising is how much they became a regular part of the offerings of these magazines, especially in the period between the Anglo-American war scare over Venezuela in 1895 and the outbreak of World War I in 1914.[9] The frequency of articles on war and peace reinforces the idea that modern war was an important public issue in

7　This chapter is suggestive rather than definitive. A more comprehensive analysis of American attitudes toward war during the period would include a survey of newspapers, novels, sermons, speeches, school textbooks, art, music, photography, and film, as well as evidence from various ethnic, racial, and regional cultures in America.

8　The American periodicals examined in this survey, 1871–1914, include the following: *Arena, Atlantic Monthly, Century, Cosmopolitan, Everybody's Magazine, Forum, Harper's Monthly, Harper's Weekly, Independent, International Socialist Review, Leslie's Weekly, Lippincott's Magazine, Literary Digest, Littell's Living Age, McClure's, Munsey's Magazine, The Nation, New Englander, North American Review, Outlook, Popular Science Monthly, Review of Reviews, Saturday Evening Post, Scientific American, Scribner's,* and *The World's Work.* Articles in some more specialized periodicals also were obtained through references in the standard guides to periodical literature, *Poole's Guide* and *The Reader's Guide.* Because the focus was on the public discourse, professional military journals and the periodicals of particular organizations, such as the peace societies, were excluded from this survey. For detailed information on mainstream magazines, such as dates of publication, ownership, editorship, editorial positions, and circulation, see Frank Luther Mott, *A History of American Magazines,* 5 vols. (Cambridge, Mass., 1938–68); and Alan Nourie and Barbara Nourie, eds., *American Mass-Market Magazines* (New York, 1990).

9　After a brief flurry of attention during the Franco-Prussian War of 1870–1, the editors' concern with war and warfare (aside from continuing interest in the American Civil War) resumed only with the crisis with Britain over Venezuela in 1895. However, from 1895 through 1914 there was more or less a continual stream of articles on war and peace, averaging perhaps at least one article every few months, with more in times of international concern, such as the Hague peace conferences of 1899 and 1907, and during actual war. Among the conflicts that produced a major number of articles on the nature of war were the Spanish-American War of 1898, the Philippine-American War of the United States in this period, the latter part of which was a time of modernization and reform known as the Progressive Era.[10]

Of course, any examination of American attitudes toward war in the late nineteenth century must recognize the continuing importance of the Civil War in memory and in myth. Its political meaning was debated and its battles were refought in the pages of the nation's magazines and many other forums.[11] Although in retrospect it can be argued that the Civil War was the first modern "total" war – given the strategies, tactics, logistics, administration, and ideological elements – it was not seen as a harbinger of the nature of the future of modern war. Pitting Americans against Americans, it seemed an aberration.[12] Yet it served as a point of reference and comparison for many American commentators on subsequent developments in weaponry, strategy, and tactics.[13]

1899–1902, the Boer War (or South African War) of 1899–1902, the Russo-Japanese War of 1904–5, and the Balkan Wars of 1912–13.

10 On the Progressive Era, see John Whiteclay Chambers II, *The Tyranny of Change: America in the Progressive Era, 1890–1920*, 2d ed. (New York, 1992); John Milton Cooper Jr., *Pivotal Decades: The United States, 1900–1920* (New York, 1990); and Arthur S. Link and Richard L. McCormick, *Progressivism* (Arlington Heights, Ill., 1983). On the relationship between progressivism and foreign policy, see Chambers, ed., *Eagle and the Dove.*

11 See Edmund Wilson, *Patriotic Gore* (New York, 1966); Leonard, *Above the Battle*, 1–40; and the popular series of Northern and Southern memoirs published in *Century* magazine between November 1884 and November 1887 and reprinted in Robert U. Johnson and Clarence C. Buel, eds., *Battles and Leaders of the Civil War*, 4 vols. (New York. 1887–8).

12 On the paradox of the limited lessons learned from the Civil War as the first modern war, see Edward Hagerman, *The American Civil War and the Origins of Modern Warfare* (Bloomington, Ind., 1988); and Jay Luvaas, *The Military Legacy of the Civil War* (Chicago, 1959). For the difficulty even in developing new tactics, see Jamieson, *Crossing Deadly Ground.*

13 One of the most prescient was former Confederate cavalry General Fitzhugh Lee, who correctly concluded by 1895 that the new longer-range weapons would greatly enhance the effectiveness of defensive forces, particularly if the troops were well entrenched. Each entrenched soldier with a new rifle, he said, could kill or disable twenty-five charging soldiers within fifteen minutes (firing 150 times and hitting one man in every six shots). Fired on with the new rifles and artillery, every man in Pickett's charge across 1,800 yards would have been a casualty, and the attack never would have reached the Union lines. Given that and the firepower of the new "automatic machine gun" (the Maxim fired 650 shots a minute; the latest Gatling gun, 1,800 per minute), Lee concluded – incorrectly, it turned out – that "no commanding general is likely to order a direct assault on an enemy occupying strong defensive lines." Rather, defensive battles would be at a premium and armies would maneuver at night and prepare for attack at dawn. With modern artillery, which had a range of five miles, McClellan could have shelled and destroyed Richmond from his positions on the peninsula. Fitzhugh Lee accurately forecast that, given these rates of fire and the mass armies, one of the primary problems of future wars would be supply. Immense ammunition trains would be needed to supply the bullets and shells, and expanded medical departments would replenish the ranks by restoring the wounded to the battle lines as rapidly as possible. See Fitzhugh Lee, "The Future of War," *Century* 28 (July 1895): 422–4. See also the review of Spenser Wilkinson's *War and Policy* (New York, 1900) in *The Nation* 72 (Mar. 14, 1901): 217–19, in which the American reviewer took the British author to task for ignoring developments in the Civil War in his emphasis on recent changes in means of war, ignoring the use of field entrenchments, the superiority of the bullet over the bayonet, and the fact that despite the Union's naval blockade only hard fighting on land defeated the South.

Between the Civil War and the Spanish-American War, the United States was not engaged in any wars of national mobilization. Certainly the U.S. Army engaged in conquering and policing Indians in the West, and after the Spanish-American War, it conquered insurgent Filipinos during the Philippine Insurrection of 1899–1902 and joined in 1900 a multinational military expedition to Beijing during the Boxer Rebellion in China. In this age of imperialism, European nations were engaged in numerous colonial wars. Discussion of warfare was frequently bifurcated between two different categories of war. These were "major" wars between industrialized nations and "colonial" wars (labeled "little wars" by Europeans) in which Western forces conquered non-Western, often stateless, peoples.

At the turn of the century, Americans joined Europeans in conceiving of the world as divided between the "civilized" nations and the others – whose people were labeled, with varying degrees of severity, "less civilized" or "uncivilized" peoples, or "barbarians" and "savages." Justifying the use of force against anti-American insurgents in the Philippines, Theodore Roosevelt asserted in 1899 that "In the long run civilized man finds he can keep the peace only by subduing his barbarian neighbor; for the barbarian will yield only to force."[14] However, the bloody antiguerrilla campaign waged by the U.S. Army from 1899 to 1902 to crush the Philippine Insurrection led to a major public outcry against "atrocities," the destruction of crops and villages, and the forced relocation of thousands of civilians.[15]

Against peoples considered "uncivilized," Western nations were willing to use military means that they were reluctant to use against one another. This distinction was not new, going back at least to the Crusades, when the crossbow could be used against Muslims but not against fellow Christians. Much later, in 1718, an Englishman had patented a breech-loading gun that could fire two different shapes of bullets: the standard round bullets, to be used against Europeans, and square bullets – which would leave large, gaping wounds – for use against Turks. In the 1890s the British Army developed an equally destructive projectile, the dum-dum bullet, which flattened on impact, for use against ferocious native warriors. The U.S. Army

---

14 Theodore Roosevelt, "Expansion and Peace," *Independent* 51 (Dec. 21, 1899): 3401–5. Even many who disagreed with Roosevelt's belligerence concurred with the occasional need for military force against "barbarism," such as in the Peking [Beijing] Relief Expedition of 1900; see Thomas F. Millard, "A Comparison of the Armies in China," *Scribner's* 29 (Jan. 1901): 78; and W. P. Trent, "War and Civilization," *Sewanee Review* 8 (Oct. 1900): 385–98.

15 For example, the editorial "The Seamy Side of War," *Independent* 54 (Apr. 17, 1902): 939–40; the editorial "The Pesky Anti-Imperialist," *The Nation* 74 (May 8, 1902): 360–1; and Felix Adler, "The Philippine War: Two Ethical Questions," *Forum* 33 (June 1902): 387–99.

adopted a large .45 caliber bullet for use against Moro insurgents in the Philippines. Although an effective machine gun was developed in the 1880s, European and American armies were slow to use it in their major forces. However, the Europeans adopted it rapidly for their colonial wars, for it enabled small numbers of soldiers to inflict casualties on large numbers of native warriors – in the Sudan, Nigeria, Rhodesia, Tanganyika, Zanzibar, and elsewhere.[16] The ruthlessness of colonial warfare, with its lack of restraints, would return to haunt Europe in the slaughter of World War I.

The main focus of the discussion of war in American periodicals in the years between 1871 and 1914 was not on colonial warfare but on war between modern industrial nations. Because the United States rather quickly in the twentieth century rejected the idea of a vast overseas colonial empire, Americans focused instead on relationships among the major powers. The debate over war was embedded in the larger concerns of the Progressive Era. Among these was the degree to which changing circumstances in the world, particularly the economic and military rivalry and expansionism of the major European powers and Japan, affected the United States. Were its traditional defenses and policy of nonengagement in European affairs still appropriate?

The overriding debate about war was largely over whether or not modern society had evolved beyond war and what kind of military establishment was best for the United States. At the turn of the century the debate over these issues, at least among internationally oriented Americans, can be seen as divided between two large and amorphous groupings in the interested public.

Peace-oriented *internationalists*, for example, included "business pacifists" (more accurately "business internationalists" because these conservative corporate leaders and their allies, such as Andrew Carnegie and Elihu Root, were not pacifists and indeed supported a strong military as well as international legal alternatives to the use of armed force). The others were "liberal pacifists" (more accurately "progressive peace advocates," for, although these liberal reformers, such as William Jennings Bryan and Hamilton Holt, advocated dramatic arms reductions, they did not suggest complete abolition of military forces). There were a few "absolute pacifists,"

16 See, e.g., Edward M. Spiers, "The Use of the Dumdum Bullet in Colonial Warfare," *Journal of Imperial and Commonwealth History* 4 (Oct. 1975): 3–14; John Ellis, *The Social History of the Machine Gun* (New York, 1975); and Robert L. O'Connell, *Of Arms and Men: A History of War, Weapons, and Aggression* (New York, 1989), 231–5.

some of whom, such as Jane Addams and Oswald Garrison Villard, had considerable influence. There also were "socialist internationalists," such as Eugene V. Debs, who advocated a worker-based international order freed from "capitalist wars."[17]

In opposition, belligerent nationalists also represented a spectrum of thought. Among the most numerous, particularly in the South and Midwest, were traditional, rural *isolationists,* such as House Speaker Champ Clark of Missouri, who saw armed conflict simply as an inevitable if sporadic consequence of international relations and who emphasized moderate-size forces for hemispheric defense and continued nonengagement in European or Asian wars.[18] More vociferous in the turn-of-the-century debate were the bellicose *nationalists,* derisively labeled "jingoes" for their overtly militant expansionism.[19] They included political conservatives such as Admiral Alfred Thayer Mahan and Senator Henry Cabot Lodge of Massachusetts, as well as centrist progressives like Senator Albert Beveridge of Indiana and Governor Theodore Roosevelt of New York.[20] At its most extreme, jingoism, as espoused by a few quasi-militarists (including, occasionally, Roosevelt), celebrated war not simply as an instru-

17 For more on these various groups, see Patterson, *Toward a Warless World;* Marchand, *American Peace Movement;* Sondra Herman, *Eleven Against War: Studies in American Internationalist Thought, 1898–1921* (Stanford, Calif., 1969); Warren F. Kuehl, *Seeking World Order: The United States and International Organization* (Nashville, Tenn., 1969); Charles Chatfield, *The American Peace Movement: Ideals and Activism* (New York, 1992); Thomas J. Knock, *To End All Wars: Woodrow Wilson and the Quest for a New World Order* (New York, 1992); Harriet Hyman Alonso, *Peace as a Women's Issue: A History of the U.S. Movement for World Peace and Women's Rights* (Syracuse, N.Y., 1993); and Chambers, ed., *Eagle and the Dove.*

18 John Milton Cooper Jr., *The Vanity of Power: American Isolationism and the First World War* (Westport, Conn., 1969).

19 "Jingoes" was a derogatory sobriquet applied to bellicose editors and blustering politicians who championed imperialist and other belligerent, ultranationalist foreign and military policies in the late nineteenth and early twentieth centuries. First used in England in 1878, the term came from a chauvinistic music-hall song in London. G. W. Hunt, *Song* (Chorus) 1878: "We don't want to fight, yet by Jingo! if we do. We've got the ships, we've got the men, and got the money too." Quoted in "Jingo," *Oxford English Dictionary,* 2d ed., 20 vols. (Oxford, 1989), 8:242. American editors applied the term in the late 1890s in the Venezuelan Crisis and the Spanish-American War, e.g.: "National Insanity," *The Nation* 62 (Feb. 13, 1896): 132–3; W. D. Le Sueur, "War and Civilization," *Popular Science Monthly* 48 (Apr. 1896): 758; and E. L. Godkin, "The Absurdity of War," *Century* 31 (Jan. 1897): 468–70. Goldwin Smith, "War as a Moral Medicine," *Atlantic Monthly* 86 (Dec. 1900): 735–8, linked jingoism and "the revived love of war" with a new emphasis on the physical over the moral, including the rise of violent games, such as prize fights and football, and the idealization of the "strenuous life."

20 William C. Widenor, *Henry Cabot Lodge and the Search for an American Foreign Policy* (Berkeley, Calif., 1980); William E. Leuchtenburg, "Progressivism and Imperialism: The Progressive Movement and American Foreign Policy, 1898–1916," *Mississippi Valley Historical Review* 34 (Dec. 1952): 497–8; but see also Gerald Markowitz, "Progressivism and Imperialism: A Return to First Principles," *Historian* 37 (Feb. 1975): 274ff.

ment of foreign policy but as a positive benefit to society through the encouragement of martial virtues and national unity and prowess.[21]

In the debate over the causes and consequences of modern war there were major shifts in the two decades prior to World War I. These centered on the relationship of modern society to war. Beginning with the sudden threat of war with Britain in 1895 over a border dispute in Venezuela and then with actual war with Spain over Cuba in 1898, mainstream American periodicals were filled with discussion about "old" and "new" causes of war, and particularly about the role of the new sensationalist mass media in rousing public opinion for war.

Given the optimism encouraged by the rapid growth of industry and international trade, and the dominant theory of social Darwinism, some Americans believed that modern society had evolved to a higher commercial and moral level at which wasteful wars of an older era would be replaced by more rational, nonviolent interaction under evolving systems of international law and commerce.[22] *Current History* magazine pointed out in 1895 that the United States had arbitrated its disputes with foreign nations no fewer than thirty times in the preceding half-century. In the early 1890s it seemed to a number of optimistic American commentators that war might be abolished within a generation.[23]

This assumption was quickly refuted in the 1890s in light of popular enthusiasm for war with England over Venezuela and with Spain over Cuba. Among those particularly appalled by the wars and war scare were conservatives suspicious of what they saw as corrupting and demagogic elements

---

21 For an analysis of Theodore Roosevelt's conception of war and the martial virtues, see John P. Mallan, "Roosevelt, Brooks Adams, and Lea: The Warrior Critique of the Business Civilization," *American Quarterly* 8 (fall 1956): 216–30; and Howard K. Beale, *Theodore Roosevelt and the Rise of America to World Power* (Baltimore, 1956).

22 For example, William Graham Sumner, "War," *Yale Review* n.s. 1 (Oct. 1911): 1–21. Several scientists denied that fighting was innate in men or that warfare was characteristic of "primitive" tribes. See Nathaniel S. Shaler, "The Natural History of War," *International Quarterly* 8 (Sept. 1903): 17–30. Shaler, a prolific writer on the subject, was a Harvard geologist and a respected Civil War veteran. See also Franklin Smith, "Peace as a Factor in Social and Political Reform," *Popular Science Monthly* 53 (June 1898): 225–40; and Alexander F. Chamberlain, "'Fairness' in Love and War," *Journal of American Folk-Lore* 20 (Jan.–Mar. 1907): 1–15.

23 *Cyclopedic Review of Current History* 5, no. 4 (1895): 860. Rev. Harry C. Vrooman observed that "we meet on every hand a marked revival of the cry of peace" in "The Abolition of War: A Symposium," *Arena* 11 (Dec. 1894): 118. The article provided a bibliography that included a score of magazines.

in mass democracy, particularly the mass media. (By contrast, radicals and reformers looked to the public and popular democracy as barriers to wars that they believed were caused by special interests, such as big business.)

The new, chauvinistic urban daily newspapers were accused of playing on people's sympathy and outrage by means of scare headlines and dispatches that were sometimes mere rumors and sometimes fabricated falsehoods. The motives of the so-called "cheap press," the causes of what one hostile editor called "the screaming of our great American Press Eagle," were seen to be a drive for higher circulations and profits and an aping of European-style imperialism. As one critic in *The Nation,* a leading conservative, anti-imperialist magazine, explained in 1909: "[I]t is not statesmen who make wars, in modern times, not soldiers, not monarchs or Presidents, but hysterical public opinion, an inflamed and foolish national pride, a reckless press."[24]

"The time is ripe for the interference of the United States in the affairs of Cuba," cried the martial John Brisben Walker in his *Cosmopolitan* magazine in 1895. *McClure's, Munsey's,* and *Collier's* also were dedicated to the Spanish-American War long before it began.[25] Summarizing current books, magazines, and newspapers in April 1897, the *Bookman* concluded that, "the growing interest in whatever relates to battle makes the explosion seem inevitable."[26] When the war did occur in the summer of 1898, American newspapers, illustrated weekly and monthly magazines, and even the staid quarterly reviews gave major coverage to it, most of them emphasizing the chivalric qualities of America's warriors.[27]

24 "How Wars Are Made," *The Nation* 88 (Apr. 29, 1909): 431. For other critiques of the "jingo" press, see, e.g., "Canada as Hostage," *North American Review* 162 (Jan. 1896): 119; Nathaniel S. Shaler, "The Natural History of Warfare," *North American Review* 162 (Mar. 1896): 328–40; Rev. William Croswell Doane, "Follies and Horrors of War," *North American Review* 162 (Feb. 1896): 190–4; "The Enemy," *The Nation* 88 (Dec. 21, 1899): 462–3; "Working up a War" (on war scare with Japan), *The Nation* 85 (July 11, 1907): 26; Sumner, "War," 24; and "Lying for the Sake of War," *The Nation* 98 (May 14, 1914): 561. Paradoxically, a few peace advocates believed that the press and public opinion could be mobilized against war. H. Havelock Ellis, "War Against War," *Atlantic Monthly* 107 (June 1911): 751–61.
25 See, e.g., "A Word About Ourselves," *Collier's* 21 (1898): 2, which heralded the conflict as "a chivalric war" on behalf of civilization; Theodore Roosevelt, "Admiral Dewey," *McClure's* 13 (1899): 483; and Vaughan Kester, "Transformation of Citizen into Soldier," *Cosmopolitan* 25 (June 1898): 151.
26 John Brisben Walker, editorial, *Cosmopolitan* 19 (Aug. 1895): 470; and "A Brief History of Our Late War with Spain," *Cosmopolitan* 24 (Nov. 1897): 53–61; "The Drift Toward War," *Bookman* 3 (Apr. 1896): 153. See also *Harper's Weekly* 40 (Aug. 1895): 1115; and Hannis Taylor, "Review of the Cuban Question in its Economic, Political, and Diplomatic Aspects," *North American Review* 165 (Nov. 1897): 610–35.
27 For examples of the coverage that emphasized the chivalric nature of the war in Cuba, see "The Nobler Side of War," *Century* 56 (Sept. 1898): 795–6; "The New Chivalry," *Harper's Weekly* 42 (Sept. 3, 1898): 859; and Oscar King Davis, "Dewey's Capture of Manila," *McClure's* 13 (1899): 172. An

Commentators were soon making distinctions between the "old" and "new" causes of war. Before the nineteenth century, it was argued, absolute monarchs employed professional armies to go to war for personal honor or dynastic or territorial ambitions. But by the late nineteenth century, monarchic or dynastic interests were not seen as separable from those of the nation. Whether in constitutional monarchies or parliamentary democracies, widespread suffrage and the extensive interests involved, plus the mobilization of mass armies, meant that war had to be justified to the public. The passions of militant nationalism were correctly seen as an essential part of modern war. The greatest disappointment to critics of modern war was that parliamentary government was not immune to bellicose nationalism and military adventurism.[28]

Before World War I few Americans except the socialists focused on economic reasons for war – on industrial capitalism and international finance.[29] Conservative periodicals argued that business and commerce worked on the whole for peace.[30] Business had been opposed to war during the crisis with Britain in 1895 and initially to war with Spain in 1898.[31] But beginning in the 1890s, a few articles in mainstream magazines saw industry's drive for overseas markets (and to a lesser extent for sources of raw materials) becoming, in combination with jingoistic nationalism, an important new factor for war.[32] In addition, many noted the growing system of defensive alliances in Europe and the increasing military buildup there.[33]

assessment of the coverage is in Richard Harding Davis, "Our War Correspondents in Cuba and Porto [sic] Rico," *Harper's Monthly* 98 (May 1899): 938–48.

28 See, e.g., Ernst Richard, "Constitutional Safeguards Against War," *Outlook* 84 (Sept. 1, 1906): 29–32.

29 On the socialist position even before 1914, see George D. Herron, "War and Peace Under Capitalism," *International Socialist Review* 9 (Dec. 1908): 431–43; "Barbarous Mexico and Capitalist America," ibid. 11 (Apr. 1911): 637; W. G. Henry, "Patriots and Parasites," ibid. 12 (Sept. 1911): 166–8; William E. Bohn, "International Notes: The Working Class and a War Scare," ibid. 12 (Sept. 1911): 182–3; and Mary E. Marcy, "Whose War Is This?" ibid. 14 (June 1914): 729–31. Ira W. Howerth of the University of Chicago, "War and Social Economy," *International Journal of Ethics* 17 (Oct. 1906): 70–8, declared that war's "object today is usually commercial: It is waged for markets." For a similar assertion in the mainstream press, see W. Leighton Grane, "Public Opinion and War," *Living Age* 279 (Oct. 11, 1913): 101–7.

30 Shaler, "The Natural History of Warfare," 338.

31 "The Pocket vs. Patriotism," *The Nation* 62 (Feb. 6, 1896): 112–13. See also Theodore Roosevelt to Brooks Adams, Mar. 21, 1898, in Elting E. Morison, ed., *Letters of Theodore Roosevelt*, 8 vols. (Cambridge, Mass., 1951–4), 1:797–8.

32 Edward van Dyke Robinson, "War and Economics in History and Theory," *Political Science Quarterly* 40 (Dec. 1900): 581–624. See also Shaler, "Natural History of Warfare," 338–40. However, Shaler believed that business would realize that war was economically wasteful and unprofitable and would use its influence against bellicose nationalism and for peaceful trade.

33 Emile de Laveleye, "Mutterings of War in Europe," *Forum* 8 (Oct. 1889): 117–25, summarizing his predictive book, *The Actual Causes of War in Europe*.

Although American socialists echoed their European colleagues' condemnation of these developments, it was not until the eve of World War I that some mainstream journals began to focus on the growing armament industry in the United States. They also asserted that it might be deliberately stimulating war scares in order to sell more munitions and weapons.[34] These developments, it was argued, might draw the United States into foreign wars.

In contrast to such views, some bellicose nationalists in the United States sought to counter this denigration of arms buildups and war. Although particular wars were justified on their own merits, "jingoes" argued that war was an ancient and enduring institution, and some of them stated that it was often useful, moral, and even beneficial. In the face of an evil use of force, "peace at any price" would be immoral, declared naval officer Mahan in 1897; and war then would be the lesser evil or in fact the proper and righteous choice.[35] In an attempt to gain public support for increased armaments and the credible threat or use of military force, a few people were willing to go beyond emphasizing war's occasional necessity and to emphasize publicly that it had positive values.

"War is one of the great agencies by which human progress is effected," Admiral Stephen B. Luce, head of the U.S. Naval War College, asserted flatly in 1891. "So, in the economy of nature, or the providence of God, war is sent, not necessarily for the punishment of sins, nor yet for national aggrandizement; but, rather, for the forming of national character, the shaping of a people's destiny, and the spreading of civilization. . . . The Truth is that war is an ordinance of God."[36] As evidence of progress through warfare, Luce cited the abolition of slavery through the Civil War.[37] Luce, Mahan, and Theodore Roosevelt justified war as an instrument of policy for a great nation. But theirs also was in part an aristocratic-warrior critique of a materialistic business society that they believed had grown soft and selfish and had

---

34 See, e.g., Frederick Lynch, "Peace and War in 1913," *Yale Review* 3 (Jan. 1914): 284.
35 Alfred T. Mahan, "A Twentieth Century Outlook," *Harper's Monthly* 95 (Sept. 1897): 521–33; and "The Use of Force," *Outlook* 64 (Feb. 17, 1900): 386–7. Amos S. Hershey, in "What Justifies Intervention in War?" *Review of Reviews* 31 (Feb. 1905): 199–201, asserted that non-interference was becoming accepted as the general rule in international law and that war could "only be justified on high moral or political grounds," such as great crimes against humanity or essential and permanent national or international interests.
36 Rear-Admiral Stephen B. Luce, "The Benefits of War," *North American Review* 153 (Dec. 1891): 672–83.
37 Ibid. See also Charles Morris, "War as a Factor in Civilization," *Popular Science Monthly* 47 (Oct. 1895): 823–34; see also H. M. A., "The Warlike Spirit," *Harper's Weekly* 41 (Aug. 28, 1897): 858, who reminded readers that "the spirit that prompted the Crusades also built the great cathedrals"; and Alfred T. Mahan, "The Place of Force in International Relations," *North American Review* 195 (Jan. 1912): 28–39.

lost its "manly vigor."[38] Roosevelt and others repeated these views during the Spanish-American War, the Philippine Insurrection, and even London's conquest of the Boers in the South African War, a British action that was very unpopular among Americans.[39]

"Militarism," a term coined in the mid-nineteenth century, denoted the dangers of the glorification of martial characteristics and the predominance of military adventurism.[40] It was used against jingoism in the United States by the widespread peace movement and the clergy, as well as by socialists and representatives of farmers and laborers. At the turn of the century, the argument was primarily against emphasis on martial virtues and military expansion. But around the era of World War I, it also incorporated a resistance to proposals for universal military training. The "militarists" were charged with seeking to curtail American individualism, discipline the work force, and use universal military training and a large army and navy to

---

38 Theodore Roosevelt, "The Strenuous Life," a speech before The Hamilton Club, Chicago, Apr. 10, 1899; reprinted in Roosevelt, *The Works of Theodore Roosevelt*, 26 vols. (New York, 1906–10), 20:1–23. For differing responses to Roosevelt's advocacy of "the strenuous life," see the criticism in the editorial "Civilization vs. Barbarism," *The Nation* 68 (June 1, 1899): 410–11; E. L. G. (Godkin), "War as a Means of Peace," *The Nation* 71 (Nov. 1, 1900): 344–5; J. N. Larned, "The Peace-Teaching of History," *Atlantic Monthly* 101 (Jan. 1908): 114–21; and the support in J. I. C. Clarke, "The Brotherhood of Strenuosity," *Cosmopolitan* 32 (Mar. 1902): 569–70. Concerning the development of a peaceful alternative to the martial use of the "creative energies" of young men (and women) acting together under government's direction for the betterment of society, see Charles William Eliot, "Destructive and Constructive Energies of our Government Compared," *Atlantic Monthly* 83 (Jan. 1899): 1–19; G. Lowes Dickinson, "Peace or War?" *Living Age* 255 (Dec. 14, 1907): 668–74, which argued for channeling energies into an "industrial army"; and, most important, the famous essay by the Harvard philosopher William James, *The Moral Equivalent of War* (New York, 1910). In opposition to James's position, see Bernard Iddings Bell, "War," *Atlantic Monthly* 112 (Nov. 1913): 625–8, who argued for the martial virtues of war, stating that "there is only one moral equivalent of war, and that one is war itself."

On the critique of the corrosive materialism of the "pacifist business society," see Theodore Roosevelt, speech before the Naval War College, June 1897, excerpted as "Need of a Navy," *Review of Reviews* 17 (Feb. 1898): 206–7; Roosevelt, "Machine Politics in New York," *Century* 33 (Nov. 1886): 74–82; Alfred T. Mahan, *The Interest of America in Sea Power* (Boston, 1898), 121, 240, 267; and Brooks Adams, "War and Economic Competition," *Scribner's* 31 (Mar. 1902): 344–52. For a general analysis of this martial, anticommercial view, see Mallan, "Roosevelt, Brooks Adams, and Lea," 216–30.

39 Roosevelt's condemnation of the timidity of big business and finance in its opposition to war with Spain and his own belief in the war's righteousness is forcefully expressed in a letter to Paul Dana, editor of the New York *Sun*, Apr. 18, 1898, reprinted in Morison, ed., *Letters of Theodore Roosevelt*, 2:816–17. For a positive view of war, even during the unpopular Boer War, as building national unity over rampant materialism and self-gratification, see Max Nordau, "Philosophy and Morals of War," *North American Review* 169 (Dec. 1899): 784–97; for similar views about the United States in the Philippines, see F. Spencer Baldwin, "The United States and the Philippines: Some Gains from Expansion," *Arena* 22 (Nov. 1899): 570–5.

40 On the evolution of the term and concept, see Volker R. Berghahn, *Militarism: The History of an International Debate, 1861–1979* (Cambridge, 1984); for concerns about it at the turn of the century in Europe and America, see John R. Gillis, ed., *The Militarization of the Western World* (New Brunswick, N.J., 1989), 13–46.

serve expanding corporate interests overseas, once again demonstrating a
fear about efforts to end U.S. military isolationism – that is, nonengagement in Europe and Asia.[41]

Around 1910 a major new impetus to avoiding modern industrial war
came in a debate over whether the interdependent character of the emerging international economy would make war economically disastrous
among all industrialized nations, even for the nation that started the war.
War had become, in the words of the British author Norman Angell, "the
great illusion." Angell argued that the outbreak of war would immediately
disrupt essential patterns of international trade and finance that had greatly
expanded since the 1880s, causing severe economic losses to all nations involved. Angell and his influential political and economic champions in
Britain and the United States urged elites in the industrialized nations to
avoid war and costly arms buildups.[42] Although his examples often were
simplistic and lifted out of historical context, Angell was a persuasive
writer and a dynamic personality. His writings, appealing as they did to traditional concepts of free trade and liberal internationalism, generated much
support for the peace and disarmament movement in the Anglo-American
nations.[43]

41 For warnings about the dangers of militarism in the United States in this period, see Edward
    Berwick, "American Militarism," *Century*, 47 (Dec. 1893): 316–17; A. B. Ronne, "The Spirit of
    Militarism," *Popular Science Monthly* 47 (June 1895): 234–9; Emile Zola, "War," *North American Re-
    view* 170 (Apr. 1900): 449–63, in which the great French novelist warned against the development
    of militarism in the United States as a result of the Spanish War; E. H. Crosby, "The Military Idea
    of Manliness," *Independent* 53 (Apr. 18, 1901): 873–4; Charles E. Jefferson, "Some Fallacies of Mil-
    itarism," ibid. 64 (Feb. 27, 1908): 457–60; Lucia Ames Mead, "Some Fallacies of Captain Mahan,"
    Arena 40 (Aug.–Sept. 1908); 163–70; Rev. Charles Edward Jefferson, "The Delusion of Mili-
    tarism," *Atlantic Monthly* 103 (Mar. 1909): 379–88; "The Ignorance of Valor," *Outlook* 98 (June 3,
    1911): 240–4; V. L. Kellogg, "Eugenics and Militarism," *Atlantic Monthly* 112 (July 1913): 99–108;
    and see also "German [Friedrich von Bernhardi's] View of the Next War," *Literary Digest* 44 (May 4,
    1912): 926. The *International Socialist Review* carried numerous articles on this subject; see, e.g., the
    issues of Apr. 1907, Jan. 1910, May 1911, and Oct. 1913.
42 Norman Angell, *The Great Illusion: A Study of the Relation of Military Power in Nations to Their Eco-
    nomic and Social Advantage* (London, 1910; New York, 1911; originally published in 1909 as *Europe's
    Optical Illusion*). The effusive praise of one journal was fairly typical: "Nothing has ever been put in
    the same space so well calculated to get plain men thinking usefully on the subjects of expenditure
    on armaments, scares, and wars." "The Economics of War," *Living Age* 265 (June 25, 1910): 812–15.
    In the United States, Angell's champions included Nicholas Murray Butler, president of Columbia
    University, and David Starr Jordan, president of Stanford University.
43 See Louis Bisceglia, "Norman Angell," in Harold Josephson, ed., *Biographical Dictionary of Modern
    Peace Leaders* (Westport, Conn., 1985), 27–31. However, in a noted debate published in a leading
    American periodical, Admiral Mahan contended that Angell had ignored moral reasons for war.
    Nations went to war for justice and national honor, Mahan declared, more than for simply eco-
    nomic reasons. Alfred T. Mahan, "The Great Illusion," *North American Review* 195 (Mar. 1912):
    319–32; Norman Angell, "'The Great Illusion': A Reply to Rear-Admiral A. T. Mahan," ibid. 195
    (June 1912): 754–72; also published in expanded form as *The Great Illusion – A Reply to Rear Admi-
    ral A. T. Mahan* (New York, 1912).

Despite the work of writers like Angell, and because of prevailing military doctrine, such views were not incorporated into actual policy-planning for war by general staffs in Europe and the United States. Because the dominant military doctrine was for a short, highly mobilized war, such as the Franco-Prussian War, little thought was given in military-planning circles on either side of the Atlantic to preparing for the kind of stalemated, long, highly mobilized war involving the attrition of masses of men and material that would, in fact, characterize the industrialized modern warfare of World War I.[44]

PREDICTIONS OF THE NATURE OF MODERN WARFARE

In the period between 1871 and 1914, the growth of mass armies and the development of new weapons – for use on land and sea, and eventually from the air – led to increased speculation in American periodicals about the evolving nature of modern war, particularly the horrors of industrialized mass warfare.

The fundamental developments were organizational and technological. In land warfare the U.S. Civil War and the Franco-Prussian War were fought by enormous armies of citizen-soldiers impassioned by a spirit of nationalism. Railroads moved and supplied them. The Franco-Prussian War of 1870–1 was presented by American periodicals as evidence of dramatic organizational and attitudinal changes in warfare. The press's initial support of the Prussian cause – portraying the war as provoked by an imperialistic Napoleon III seeking to impede German unification – was tempered when the Germans bombarded Paris with long-range artillery. Otherwise, assessing the changing form of warfare, the press noted that the new breech-loading rifles and artillery caused high casualties against forces charging *en masse* across open terrain in the face of such defensive fire (up to 90 percent of some of the German units were hit). Yet American periodicals most frequently stressed the fact that the mass armies of Germany were composed of citizen-soldier reservists from all ranks of society and that their fighting spirit came from their belief in their cause – the defense

44 Jack Snyder, *The Ideology of the Offensive: Military Decision-Making and the Disaster of 1914* (Ithaca, N.Y., 1984); Steven E. Miller, ed., *Military Strategy and the Origins of the First World War* (Princeton, N.J., 1985); Paret, ed., *Makers of Modern Strategy*, chaps. 11, 15, 18. Privately, if not publicly, a number of military writers and planners before 1914 had assumed that if a major European war could not be brought to a swift conclusion, it would create vast destruction and topple political institutions. However, the planners refused to examine that assumption and opted for seeking a quick victory. See Michael Geyer, "German Strategy in the Age of Machine Warfare, 1914–1945," in Paret, ed., *Makers of Modern Strategy*, 530–2.

of German nationalism. That nationalism sustained them despite the casualty rate.[45]

Until World War I, most Americans believed that their tradition of wartime armies composed primarily of volunteer citizen-soldiers remained an adequate response to such developments. But professional officers, such as Generals Emory Upton and Leonard Wood, and their civilian allies, such as former president Theodore Roosevelt, argued increasingly for expanded prewar military training. In the late nineteenth century this assertion was based on the need, because of the increased lethality of the fire-swept battlefield, to obtain the most disciplined fire action and to bring the soldier to a most efficient state – or, as one author put it, "to convert the individual into as much of a machine as possible." Another writer declared simply that under modern war conditions, "the soldier must become like a machine-made good."[46] Later, in the Progressive Era, the emphasis was placed on the inequity and social and economic disruption as well as the military inefficiency caused by the volunteer system. Although they failed to achieve their goal of universal military training, the conscriptionists' arguments did ultimately contribute to the adoption of a selective wartime draft when the United States entered World War I in 1917.[47]

Technologically, the effectiveness of weaponry was given a major boost in the 1880s and 1890s, particularly through the increased range and rapidity of small-arms and artillery fire. New artillery shells containing up to fifty pounds of nitrocellulose, the new high explosive replacing gunpowder as a bursting charge, could rain down jagged shreds of steel shrapnel on enemy positions at distances of more than 3,000 yards. New infantry rifles with magazines holding five to eleven cartridges (so-called "repeating rifles") could be fired at a rate of one shot per second, and the higher velocity of the bullet propelled accuracy to more than 2,000 feet. A reliable machine gun was invented in the mid-1880s. A new smokeless powder replaced the old black powder that had clouded the battlefield. The longer range of artillery and high-velocity rifles extended the "killing zone" to a

45 See, e.g. "Culture and War," *The Nation* 11 (Sept. 8, 1870): 151–2; "A French View of the Prussians," ibid. 12 (Mar. 30, 1871): 214; J. K. Hosmer, "The Giant in the Spiked Helmet," *Atlantic Monthly* 27 (Apr. 1871): 433–46; and F. J. L., "Germany and France as Military Powers," *Old and New* 7 (Apr. 1873): 491–6.
46 "Modern Soldiering," *Review of Reviews* 17 (May 1898): 591; and A. Maurice Low, "Amateurs in War," *Forum* 26 (Oct. 1898): 157–66. See also Capt. James Parker, "Costliness of the Volunteer System," *Review of Reviews* 17 (June 1898): 719.
47 John Whiteclay Chambers II, *To Raise an Army: The Draft Comes to Modern America* (New York, 1987).

depth of up to several miles, and their rapidity meant that the field could be swept with fire.[48]

While military authorities debated whether the new weapons would tactically aid the defense or the offense, public discussion revolved around the horrors of the new warfare and whether the developments would make war shorter and more decisive than before or longer and bloodier. Would the new weapons lead to a more horrible form of warfare, with a higher number of casualties? Would they also bring war directly to civilians?

By the 1890s American periodicals began publishing articles about whether the new rapid-firing weapons would increase or decrease the number of casualties on the battlefield. Some concluded that both sides would be annihilated and that this result might work for peace by making war too destructive to be a useful policy. A number of those involved in developing the new weapons, such as the Maine-born Maxim brothers (Hiram, who invented a machine gun, and Hudson, who developed a high explosive), claimed that they were helping to limit war as well as to improve national defense by increasing the destructiveness of weapons.[49] Many military figures argued that the new weapons and mass organization would produce higher casualties in the short run but less loss of life in the long run because wars would be shorter than previously.[50]

A number of writers contended that modern weapons and modern warfare meant fewer battle deaths than in previous wars. There were several aspects to this. One was a philosophical argument that the more deadly war became, the more ways people would seek to avoid it, or that when it came, they would find mechanisms such as entrenchments to escape the increased volume of fire. As historian Edward van Dyke Robinson put it in 1900, "[R]ecent evidence confirms the maxim that the more deadly the weapons, the less the slaughter."[51] Another argument was that the smaller-size bullets of modern high-velocity rifles would inflict proportionately fewer fatal wounds than the musket balls and other projectiles fired by previous infantry weapons. In the Spanish-American War, 99 of every 118

---

48 For excellent summaries, see Michael Howard, "Men Against Fire: The Doctrine of the Offensive in 1914," in Paret, ed., *Makers of Modern Strategy,* 510–26; and O'Connell, *Of Arms and Men,* 189–240.

49 Robert H. Thurston, "The Border-land of Science," *North American Review* 150 (Jan. 1890): 67–79; Nikola Tesla, "The Problem of Increasing Human Energy," *Century* 60 (June, 1900): 175–211; and Hudson Maxim, "The Warfare of the Future," *Science* 28 (Dec. 11, 1908): 820–31.

50 Henry L. Abbott, "War Under New Conditions," *Forum* 9 (Mar. 1890): 13–23; Capt. E. L. Zalinski, "The Future of Warfare," *North American Review* 151 (Dec. 1890): 688–700.

51 Edward van Dyke Robinson, "War and Economics in History and in Theory," *Political Science Quarterly* 15 (Dec. 1900): 581–624.

American soldiers who had been hit by a bullet had completely recovered. The percentage of combat fatalities in the Philippine Insurrection and the Boer war was nowhere near as high as the casualty rates in the Crimean War or the U.S. Civil War.[52]

Others argued that the effectiveness of weapons was reduced in actual battle conditions because real war introduced factors – fatigue, nervousness, mistakes – that reduced soldiers' effectiveness. Furthermore, tactical formations would disperse. Most important, many writers argued that the percentage of those killed and wounded would be diminished because of the predicted shortness of campaigns and recent improvements in medical diagnosis and treatment, particularly of disease, which in the past had been the main threat to soldiers.[53]

Concern about the destructiveness of modern rapid-firing weapons and high explosives, in addition to the escalating costs of the industrial arms race, led to a number of international conferences – at Geneva, Brussels, and the Hague – that attempted to limit armaments and restrict the violence of modern warfare.[54] Some commentators in American periodicals believed that significant progress was being made at the turn of the century on restraining warfare, a belief that encouraged American internationalists in their support of an expanded American role overseas.[55] The specific results of the conferences were rather limited. The ethics of modern war, as agreed on by 1900, permitted the use of rapid-firing guns, hot shot, and guns of vast range – the object of which, it was argued, was not to kill for the sake of killing but to render aggression ineffective and resistance useless. However, restrictions had been placed on explosive bullets, which were likened to poisoned arrows and held to be uncivilized. The Geneva Convention mandated the neutralization of battlefield hospitals, ambulances, medical service, and chapels, acknowledging the Red Cross and Red Crescent insignia as emblems of neutrality. Consequently, the wounded and prisoners were treated better.

Although there were attempts to distinguish between combatants and noncombatants, it often was a fine line, and many commentators feared that civilians would suffer greatly in industrialized warfare. Even by inter-

---

52 "The Risks of War," *Scientific American* 82 (Jan. 27, 1900): 51.
53 "Is War Growing More Murderous?" *Review of Reviews* 10 (Dec. 1894): 676–7. On modern medicine's reducing the fatalities from disease in war, see "The Hell of War," *Review of Reviews* 37 (Apr. 1908): 497–8, a plea to improve the performance of the U.S. Army Medical Corps.
54 For a recent overview, see the essays in Michael Howard, George J. Andreopoulos, and Mark R. Shulman, eds., *The Laws of War: Constraints on Warfare in the Western World* (New Haven, Conn., 1994).
55 See, e.g., Samuel J. Barrows, "The Ethics of Modern Warfare," *Forum* 25 (July 1898): 555–68.

national agreement, unarmed citizens obtained immunity only by refraining from participation in battle and only to the extent that the exigencies of war permitted. Because uniforms distinguished soldiers from civilians, irregular troops, not in uniform and not acting under central authority, would be treated as brigands. The Prussian Army refused to recognize the French *francs-tireurs* in 1870–1 as regular troops (and indeed the Prussian military feared that the French resistance might expand into a major guerrilla war). Whereas the international conferences agreed to prohibit the deliberate propagation of contagious diseases and the poisoning of food, water, or wells in an enemy country, cutting off food or water supplies in a siege or blockade remained a legitimate strategy, as it had since earliest times.

The theory and practice of siegecraft, however, were not in accord. In theory, civilians in a fortified city were noncombatants and presumed immune from attack. Encouraged by the Brussels Conference of 1876, ethicists contended that any bombardment of such a city should be directed only against the defensive works and not against the civilian structures and population. In practice, however, the Germans had bombarded the entire city of Strasbourg for two days in 1870, causing extensive damage to public buildings and housing in the city. The Brussels Conference laid down the rule that only fortified places were allowed to be besieged and that open and unfortified towns should not be bombarded. Again, in practice, it was recognized that it might be impossible for besieging forces to reduce fortifications without firing into the city itself. Consequently, the Brussels conferees agreed that the commander of the attacking forces should, for the sake of humanity, give prior notice of the bombardment and allow the noncombatants to leave.[56]

Part of the impetus for restricting armaments and warfare had come from what proved in World War I to be one of the most accurate predictions of the effect of modern weapons and mass armies on war between industrialized nations. This was the prediction of total war made by Jean de Bloch, a leading Russian industrialist and philanthropist who was a conservative opponent of modern war. In a six-volume work, *The Future of War in Its Technical, Economic, and Political Relations*, published in 1898 in Russia and in 1899 in England and the United States, Bloch accurately predicted the consequences of modern warfare between industrial nations.[57] Bloch de-

56 Ibid.
57 Jean de Bloch, *The Future of War in Its Technical, Economic, and Political Relations*, 6 vols. (St. Petersburg, 1898), English trans. R. C. Long and published with a prefatory conversation with W. T. Stead in London and New York in 1899. Bloch also wrote a number of other works, translated into

clared that the war of the future would not be a frontier skirmish or a punitive expedition but rather a massive conflict in which fully armed, major
industrial powers would pit themselves and all their resources against each
other in a life-or-death struggle.

The changing nature of war, Bloch argued, resulted from the development of nationalism and weaponry. The increased range and rapidity of
guns plus the unwieldiness of mass armies was shifting the natural advantage in warfare to the defensive side. Indeed, it would now be virtually impossible to defeat a well-entrenched army. Decisive battles, even military
victories, were things of the past. Rather, armies would become dead-
locked on the battlefield. The outcome would be determined by the economy, civilian morale, and political will. In such a war of national attrition,
the result might well be economic collapse and social and political revolution. So monstrous and uncontrollable had war become that Bloch sought
to persuade the ruling classes of Europe that the preservation of the old order rested on the prevention of major war.

Bloch's theories were widely publicized between 1899 and 1902, first
because they led, through the appeal of the Russian czar, to the Hague
Peace Conference of 1899 and then because the Boer War seemed to confirm Bloch's predictions about the effectiveness of defensive positions that
could be held with modern weapons and that were the result of intensive
war nationalism.[58] However, Bloch's international renown did not long
survive his death in 1902, and in the United States his ideas received mixed
reviews at best, applauded by the peace movement but assailed by the "jingoes."[59] Many Americans simply may have ignored his gloomy predictions
because, at least in regard to the western hemisphere, they conflicted with
the swift and complete victory of the United States in the war with Spain.
One American reviewer rejected Bloch's main argument that the costs of
modern war in lives and financial resources would ultimately bankrupt the
economy and result in social revolution. For as historian Edward van Dyke
Robinson pointed out, Bloch had neglected to show that the economic
cost of war had increased more rapidly than the resources of industrial na-

English by R. C. Long, including *Is War Now Impossible?* (London, 1899); *Modern Weapons and Modern War* (London, 1900); and *Work of the Peace Societies: How to Widen Their Programme* (Chatham,
1901). See Peter van den Dungen, *A Bibliography of the Pacifist Writings of Jean de Bloch* (London,
1977).

58 "Monsieur de Bloch on the Boer War," *Outlook* 69 (Nov. 2, 1901): 520–1.

59 Edwin D. Mead, "Jean de Bloch and 'The Future of War,'" *New England Magazine* n.s. 28 (May
1903): 298–309; "The Art of War" (review of Jean de Bloch, *The Future of War*), *Outlook* 76 (Feb.
20, 1904): 470–3.

tions.[60] Even many of those who believed that Bloch's apocalyptic vision of modern industrial war might be accurate did not necessarily think that it applied to the United States or meant the end of armies. As the editor of *Harper's Weekly* explained in 1902 in an editorial titled "The Passing of Great Wars," "armies may still do police duty, as ours has done in the Philippines. It may take one more great war, or attempt at a great war, to determine whether their powers are to be limited to that."[61]

The Russo-Japanese War of 1904–5 provided the first thorough test of modern weapons and equipment since the general reorganization and rearmament of forces following the Franco-Prussian War of 1870–1.[62] After two important Japanese naval victories, the Japanese army fought through Manchuria and besieged the Russian base at Port Arthur in the first of a series of battles that with modern rifles, machine guns, artillery, extensive entrenchments, and barbed-wire entanglements foreshadowed the Western Front in World War I. After several months of fighting, the Japanese army took the port but sustained 58,000 casualties (killed or wounded). A subsequent battle at Mukden (now Shenyang), in which both armies numbered about 300,000 each, was the largest battle in history until World War I. The Japanese final offensive included a two-week attack on a front extending nearly fifty miles. The Russians, having sustained more than 50,000 casualties, abandoned the city. The Japanese lost more than 40,000 soldiers. Exhausted militarily and financially, both sides sought an end to the war in a settlement that was negotiated by President Theodore Roosevelt.

American periodicals gave much coverage to the war and to interpreting its lessons for the future of warfare.[63] *Scribner's* Thomas F. Millard, one of the reporters now called "war correspondents," provided some of the most

---

60 Edward van Dyke Robinson, review of the sixth volume, *Is War Now Possible?*, of Jean de Bloch, *The Future of War: In its Technical, Economic, and Political Relations*, trans. R. C. Long (New York, 1899), in *Political Science Quarterly* 45 (June 1901): 338–41.

61 Editorial, "The Passing of Great Wars," *Harper's Weekly* 46 (Aug. 30, 1902): 1193.

62 The Russo-Turkish War of 1877–8 had been fought with tactics and equipment predating the "lessons" of the Franco-Prussian War, and the Spanish-American War had been too brief and Madrid's forces in Cuba too demoralized to contribute much new information about land operations. The inequality of forces and equipment and the Boers' almost total lack of military organization limited the "lessons" of the South African War.

63 Coverage occurred despite the restrictions Japan imposed on war correspondents. On Japanese censorship, see George Kennan, "Japan at War," *Outlook* 77 (June 18, 1904): 401–7. Kennan, a former vice president of the American Red Cross, had first become a war correspondent during the Spanish-American War. See also Henry W. Nevinson, "The End of the War Correspondent?" reprinted from *The Nation* in *Living Age* 268 (Mar. 11, 1911): 625–8. There was considerable sympathy for Japan in the United States and against expanding Russian imperialism; see N. J. Bacon, "After the War – What?" *Booklover's Magazine* 5 (Jan. 1905): 5–13.

accurate insights into the changing nature of modern war.[64] Most dramatic was the expansion of the battlefront, which had grown so large – up to nearly fifty miles in length around Mukden – that reporters coined the term "fighting front" (a term that would be applied extensively in World War I) to describe it.[65] Modern field telegraph and telephone systems allowed commanders to keep in touch with an army so widely distributed. Furthermore, in Manchuria battles lasted continually for ten days or even two weeks. It was not that the same troops fought all the time; rather, different units were involved in a series of actions, but they were in one general area under one command and had the same general objective.

The Russo-Japanese War demonstrated that the rapid-firing weapons consumed enormous quantities of ammunition during prolonged battles. Although each Russian soldier carried into action 120 rounds of rifle ammunition, this supply seldom lasted through a day's serious fighting. At Liao-Yang, some Russian regiments expended more than 800 rounds per man, meaning that the most active shooters fired 1,500 rounds in the battle. Russian artillery battery limbers carried only 150 rounds per gun, but some batteries fired more than 600 rounds per weapon. "More ammunition has been used in a single day in Manchuria," Millard reported, "than was required to fight the [entire] Spanish-American War."[66]

The shape of the fire-swept battlefield began to emerge in Manchuria. Both armies employed the new, revised "extended-order tactics," as opposed to old close-order formations, so that advancing soldiers would present as dispersed a target as possible. But the space between soldiers could not be too extended or there could be no control over impact of the advancing forces. On the new battlefield, direct assaults on established positions took days or weeks. Troops pushed forward slowly, entrenching themselves and protected, as they advanced, by fire from their own artillery against the enemy, until they were near enough to rush across lines for an effective assault. Most advances were made at night. When attacks were made in daylight, it often took hours to advance a few hundred yards, as soldiers crawled from cover to cover. Even then, only rarely could strong

---

64 Thomas F. Millard, "New Features of War: As Illustrated in the East," *Scribner's* 37 (Jan. 1905): 60–9. Millard was with the Russian army in Manchuria during most of the war and was allowed in the battle zones. His initial sympathy for the Russians did not deter his recognition of the superior adaptation of modern techniques by the Japanese forces.

65 "In using the term 'fighting front,'" Millard explained, "I do not mean that the armies were engaged simultaneously or even occasionally along every mile of the front, because they came into collision only at certain points. However, tactically speaking, they were in contact along the whole front because any advance by one would immediately collide with the other." Ibid., 61.

66 Ibid., 63.

positions be taken by frontal assaults until a successful flanking movement had rendered them untenable. However, Millard reported ominously that both armies acted on the theory that "where sacrifice of human life is necessary to secure decisive results it should be made without hesitation."[67]

Manchuria showed that some of the "lessons" of the Boer War needed to be modified. This conflict between farmer-guerrillas and British troops had suggested a trend toward greater personal initiative by individual soldiers with modern weapons. But Millard reported that the Manchurian experience of mass armies indicated that "a large part of modern war is on too great a scale to give much opportunity for individual initiative."[68] Troops on the battlefront rarely saw one another in Manchuria because of long-range weapons, drably colored uniforms, entrenchments, and smokeless powder.[69]

Artillery, which had taken on new importance in the Franco-Prussian War, became even more important in the Russo-Japanese War, where it had longer range (up to four miles), increased rapidity of fire, and improved projectiles. Gunners now used indirect fire (high-angled, arching fire that fell on the enemy from above) rather than direct, line-of-sight fire. Although high-explosive shells were more effective in destroying cover, it was the shrapnel shells with their jagged, searing fragments that were most feared by the soldiers.[70]

It was mainly in the underestimation of the machine gun that observers in Manchuria erred in their judgment about the future tactical direction of war. "The small calibre machine gun is apparently of little use on the battlefield, and its practical utility is confined, so far as land operations are concerned, to fixed fortifications," Millard stated. "The weakness of the small machine gun in the field is that its range is only equal to that of the infantry rifle, which places field artillery beyond its reach, and when its fire is able to reach infantry the infantry fire can also reach it . . . its effectiveness over the magazine rifle is open to doubt."[71]

The specter of future mass horror revealed itself to some observers in the Russo-Japanese War, among them Joseph Conrad, whose concern

---

67 Ibid.   68 Ibid., 64.
69 The old dispute about the bayonet remained unsettled. Jean de Bloch had argued, as did observers of the Boer War, that with the advent of the long-range rifle, the bayonet had become passé. But the Russo-Japanese War showed that, despite the range of weapons, it was still possible for troops to come into physical contact with the enemy. Enough use was made of the bayonet in Manchuria to justify its retention, although the instances of its use were too insignificant to throw much light on its future. For cavalry, rifles replaced the lance and the saber, and although cavalry was not used in engagements, it did play a role in security and reconnaissance.
70 Ibid., 65.   71 Ibid., 67.

with the conflict between Western and non-Western culture and with isolation and moral deterioration in modern life had filled his novels *The Heart
of Darkness* and *Nostromo*. In 1905, chilled by the slaughter in Manchuria,
Conrad wrote of the war for *The North American Review*.[72] To him, the description of the war in the cold, silent print of newspapers and books was
only "a pale and gray reflection of its terrible and monotonous phases of
pain, death, sickness" as reflected from thousands of miles away through a
veil of inadequate words. What had to be reproduced, he said, was beyond
the previous common experience of war and beyond people's imagination,
lulled by contemporary liberal humanitarianism. Only direct vision of the
fact of death or the stimulus of great art that portrayed it could awaken
people to the recognition of the horror of modern war. As Conrad put it:

> An overworked horse falling before our windows, a man writhing under a cart-
> wheel in the street, awaken more genuine emotion, more horror, pity, and indig-
> nation than the stream of reports, appalling in their monotony, of tens of thou-
> sands of decaying bodies tainting the air of the Manchurian plains, of other tens of
> thousands of maimed bodies groaning in ditches, crawling on the frozen ground,
> filling the field hospitals; of the hundreds of thousands of survivors no less pathet-
> ic, and even more tragic in being left alive by fate to the pitiable exhaustion of
> their pitiful toil.[73]

In both armies, Conrad told American magazine readers, many men were
driven beyond the bounds of sanity by the stress of moral and physical misery. Great numbers of soldiers and officers went mad, as if by way of
protest against the peculiar sanity of a state of war – most among the Russians because the Japanese had the tonic of success in what Conrad called
"this nerve-destroying contest, which, for endless, arduous toil of killing,
surpasses all the wars of history."[74]

  Four years later, one of the most accurate predictions of the nature of
the World War I battlefield came from Alfred von Schlieffen, the former
chief of the German General Staff. Schlieffen's 1909 report had been publicly endorsed by Kaiser Wilhelm II and subsequently was widely reprinted
in magazines and discussed in Europe and America.[75] Drawing on the
lessons of the Russo-Japanese War as well as other developments, Schlief-

---

72 Joseph Conrad, "Autocracy and War," *North American Review* 181 (July 1905): 33–55. The main
   point of the article was Conrad's hope that the defeat would lead to revolution in Russia and the
   overthrow of the czarist autocracy.
73 Ibid., 34.   74 Ibid., 36.
75 (General Count Alfred von Schlieffen), "War at the Present Day," reprinted from *Deutsche Revue*, via
   National Review in *Living Age* 260 (Mar. 6, 1909): 579–88. For a discussion of von Schlieffen's report, see, e.g., "The Present Aspects and Prospects of War," *Review of Reviews* 39 (Apr. 1909):
   500–2, which reprinted excerpts from the *Deutsche Revue* as well as a commentary on the piece
   from the February 1909 issue of the *Fortnightly Review* (London).

fen declared that the problem for future war was how attacking forces could avoid destruction by withering fire from the new rapid-firing weapons. Recognizing the importance of the use of protective cover, Schlieffen foresaw some of the development of trench warfare. Advancing infantry, widely dispersed in a single line, would rush forward from cover to cover while trying to suppress enemy fire with their own rifles and their supporting artillery. But the infantry would eventually reach open ground, which, if narrow, would be crossed quickly. But if the area to be covered were extensive, then, Schlieffen declared, "the only course for the advancing force to take would be to dig their own shelter, as in siege operations, and to work their way forward, from trench to trench, when possible, under cover of darkness." The final assault, he predicted, would be a widely dispersed bayonet charge.[76]

In terms of the battlefield of the future involving armies of a million men or more and covering many miles, Schlieffen accurately foresaw that no matter how extensive they were, nothing would be visible in the vast space. Were it not for the deafening thunder of the artillery and dim flashes of fire, little would indicate that a battle was in progress. From time to time, here and there, a thin line of infantry would seem to leap forward and as suddenly disappear. To Schlieffen, the Russo-Japanese War showed that a frontal attack might be successful in spite of difficulties but that the advantages of such an operation were insignificant because although the enemy might be driven back, he would not be destroyed. His forces would soon recover and take up fresh positions, and the campaign would continue.

Recognizing the new nature of the battlefield, Schlieffen, like most other contemporary military commanders and theorists, rejected the idea of a long war of attrition and instead argued that it was essential to achieve quick results. A war of attrition would be impossible when the existence of a nation depended on the unbroken course of its trade and industry. A quick military decision was necessary so that the halted wheels of trade and industry could be set back into motion. As Schlieffen put it: "Tactics of exhaustion are not practical where the support of millions demands the expenditure of billions."[77]

---

76 (Von Schlieffen), "War at the Present Day," *Living Age*, 580. Whereas in the previous two centuries the firing line had been composed of troops drawn up in close order, with ten to fifteen men per yard of front, in the Russo-Japanese War circumstances forced the armies to reduce the ratio to three men or fewer per yard.

77 Ibid., 584. In conclusion, von Schlieffen claimed that the other powers in Europe were combining to attack Germany and Austria and that only the military preparation of Germany had prevented such an assault.

In contrast to generals like Schlieffen, who asserted that modern war could be won quickly and decisively, a number of writers in the early years of the twentieth century emphasized its horrors. One who proved particularly prescient of the Western Front was a German schoolteacher, Wilhelm Lamszus. His book, *The Human Slaughterhouse,* was suppressed in Germany within three months of its publication in 1909. It was soon translated into English. German censorship stimulated news reports, and excerpts from the book were published in American newspapers and magazines. Modern war was stripped of its glory, as Lamszus focused on the impact of high explosives and machine-gun fire on the human body. In his novel, a young soldier arrives at the front, where he finds a field filled with stiffened corpses. When his regiment is ordered to charge a wooded area defended by machine guns, the men rush forward in spurts, their ranks hit by a hail of lead. They cannot see the enemy. They drop to the ground, listening to a deadly buzz coming from the woods. "The wood, the green wood, is murdering us from afar before a single human face comes in view," thinks the young man. "We are not even charging men. Machines are trained on us. Why, we are only charging machines. And the machine triumphs deep into our very flesh. And the machine is draining the lifeblood from our veins and lapping it up in bucketfuls. Those who have been hit are already lying mown down in swathes behind us and are writhing from their wounds. And yet men are racing up behind us in hundreds – young, healthy human flesh for the machines to butcher." Later, as soldiers launch a night attack across a minefield, giant explosions hurtle men and earth skyward, filling the air and scattering the ground with shards of flesh, fragments of human beings, dismembered hands and feet.[78] Such descriptions were widely publicized by the peace movement, and they reinforced American isolationism.

WAR AT SEA AND IN THE AIR

The navy and the vast oceans were traditionally viewed as America's first line of defense, but beginning in the 1890s a naval arms race among the Great Powers posed a possible threat to U.S. security. Then-Captain Mahan emphasized the need for an offensively oriented, modern-armed, high-seas fleet of battleships instead of America's long-term reliance on

---

78 "A Peace Book Supprest [*sic*] by the Kaiser," *Literary Digest* 46 (June 14, 1913): 1332–3. However, like many other prewar opponents of Wilhelmine militarism, Lamszus supported the decision for war in 1914, arguing publicly that the war would forge a new citizen and a new nation.

coastal defense and raiding of enemy commerce. American periodicals actively discussed the major new naval developments, including the construction of new steel warships with long-range guns and high-explosive shells and what they might mean for naval warfare and the safety of the United States.[79]

Those who supported isolationism and hemispheric defense, strong in rural America in the South and Midwest, argued that new weapons technology could provide an effective seaboard defense against naval blockades or any attempted invasion of the United States.[80] They emphasized longer range and more accurate coastal artillery, electric underwater mines, and self-propelled torpedoes fired by fast torpedo boats and later by submarines. Mahan and his allies, particularly on the coasts, belittled such a defensive orientation and instead emphasized the ever-increasing size and strength of an offensive battle fleet made more powerful by developments in propulsion, armament, and armor. Mahan argued that a solely defensive naval war would mean defeat.[81]

The U.S. naval victories in the Spanish-American War, together with the accelerated naval race among the major powers, contributed to the success of the offensively oriented "big navy" advocates and the construction of an American battle fleet that by 1900 was the third largest in the world. Periodicals frequently contained illustrations of the new battleships, portraying them not simply as weapons of national defense but also as symbols of American technological achievement, national power, and greatness.[82] In regard to the anticipation of modern total war, however, most periodicals focused on Mahan's idea that the battle fleet served as a deterrent in peacetime and as a force for victory in war by achieving what he called decisive "command of the seas."

Mahan's view of the nature of modern naval war seemed validated by the decisive naval victories in the Spanish-American War and the Russo-

79 Because the purpose of this chapter is to examine the degree to which the debate over modern weapons and warfare anticipated the "total" war of the twentieth century, the discussion of naval warfare here is necessarily circumscribed. For more on this subject, see Hagan, *This People's Navy*; Richard D. Challener, *Admirals, Generals and American Foreign Policy, 1898–1914* (Princeton, N.J., 1973); Ronald Spector, *Professors of War: The Naval War College and the Modern American Navy* (Newport, R.I., 1977); John Hattendorf, "Technology and Strategy: A Study in the Professional Thought of the U.S. Navy, 1900–1916," *Naval War College Review* 24 (Nov. 1971): 25–48; and Mark Shulman, *Navalism and the Emerging American Seapower, 1882–1893* (Annapolis, Md., 1995).
80 J. W. Miller, "Rumors of War and Resultant Duties," *Forum* 21 (Apr. 1896): 237–46.
81 Alfred T. Mahan, "Current Fallacies upon Naval Subjects," *Harper's Monthly* 97 (June 1898): 42–53.
82 See, e.g., the illustrations of naval warships in "Types of Modern Warships: The Tremendous Fighting Powers of the Ironclad Monsters of the Sea, and the Types that Naval Science has Specialized – Battleships and Cruisers of the American and Foreign Navies," *Munsey's Magazine* 16 (Oct. 1896): 52–66.

Japanese War.[83] However, the enormous casualties from high-explosive, armor-piercing shells and shrapnel shells in the latter conflict emphasized the cost in human life of the new naval warfare.[84] The horrors were vividly portrayed.[85] Few American periodicals foresaw the kind of naval warfare that would actually emerge in World War I – stalemated battle fleets, long-distance, extensive commerce raiding by submarines, and blockades aimed at starving entire civilian populations and halting munitions shipments.[86]

War in the air, however, captured the most soaring imaginations. Developments came swiftly: Count Ferdinand von Zeppelin built the first rigid airship in 1900; the Wright Brothers mastered controlled flight with a fixed-wing aircraft in 1903. The Wrights sold their first planes to the military in 1909, the year Louis Blériot crossed the English Channel in a "flying machine." Developments such as these inspired H. G. Wells, a noted British science fiction writer, to turn his attention to air warfare. In an article in *The North American Review* in 1901 (later published as a book, *The War in the Air,* in 1908), Wells foresaw vast fleets of aircraft that would rain high explosives on great cities and carry war to the ends of the earth. The result, he predicted, would be extensive death and destruction, and the collapse of trade and commerce, even civilization.[87] It was not only fantasy writers such as Wells who foresaw the dangers of war from the skies. In the half-dozen years before World War I, American periodicals carried many articles about the future military use of dirigibles and fixed-wing aircraft –

83 Ira Nelson Hollis, "The Navy in the War with Spain," *Atlantic Monthly* 82 (Nov. 1898): 612–16; H. W. Wilson, "The Naval Lessons of the War, *Harper's Monthly* 98 (Jan. 1899): 288–97; Alfred T. Mahan, "The War on the Sea and Its Lessons," *McClure's* 12 (1899): 357. Some critics attacked the army and navy bureaucracies for unduly limiting the development of new weaponry; see, e.g., John Brisben Walker, "The Importance of Mechanical Devices in Warfare," *Cosmopolitan* 25 (July 1898): 343–4. On the Japanese naval victories at Port Arthur (Lüshun) and Tsushima Straits, see Exubitor, "Japan's Object-Lessons in Naval Warfare," reprinted from the British journal *Fortnightly Review,* but with additions, in *Living Age* 242 (July 1, 1904): 1–12; Alfred T. Mahan, "Some Reflections upon the Far Eastern War," reprinted from the *National Review* in *Living Age* 250 (July 14, 1906): 67–81. In contrast, a few "small navy" advocates emphasized the effectiveness of the use of torpedo boats and floating mines at Port Arthur; see "A Brilliant Campaign," *The Nation* 79 (Dec. 22, 1904): 496–7.

84 George Kennan, "The Destruction of the Baltic Fleet," *Outlook* 80 (July 29, 1905): 811–19.

85 Ibid., and Paul Briere, "Highest of All Explosives: Work of the Terrible Shimose, as Shown in the Wrecked Russian Battle-ships," *Cosmopolitan* 39 (Sept. 1905): 469–72.

86 Similarly, American naval planners did not foresee the kind of submarine warfare and blockade that would be employed in World War I. See the analysis in Weigley, *American Way of War,* 167–91; see also Hagan, *This People's Navy,* 252–8. For discussion of the naval lessons of the Russo-Japanese War, see Exubitor, "Japan's Object-Lessons"; and also Mahan, "Some Reflections." For an example of the coastal-defense advocates' emphasis on the role of floating mines and torpedo boats against battleships, see "A Brilliant Campaign."

87 H. G. Wells, "Anticipations; An Experiment in Prophecy: War," *North American Review* 173 (Sept. 1901): 401–12; and H. G. Wells, *The War in the Air* (London, 1908).

from aerial reconnaissance and attack on land and sea forces to the bombing of cities. By 1911 the press reported that the military staffs of every European country were developing air forces.[88]

Science generated completely new weapons systems so rapidly that speculation was widespread about even more fantastic weapons of destruction. Developments in electricity led writers and inventors to suggest that small gunboats might carry enormous recoilless electric guns, guns firing 2,000-pound shells into battle fleets or seaport cities.[89] Wells speculated about the use of a devastating "heat ray" and poison gas (lethal "black smoke," as he called it) in his novel of a Martian invasion of England. *The War of the Worlds* was published in London in 1898 and serialized the following year in the United States in *Cosmopolitan* magazine and several newspapers.[90]

In a similarly fantastic, if eerily prescient, speculation written in 1913, Wells warned of the development and use of an "atomic bomb," a term as a well as a concept that he originated, drawing on the work in nuclear physics of Albert Einstein and Ernest Rutherford. In *The World Set Free,* published in 1914, Wells grimly described the results of future "atomic" war:

By the spring of 1959 from nearly two hundred centres, and every week added to their number, roared the unquenchable crimson conflagrations of the atomic bombs; the flimsy fabric of the world's credit had vanished, industry was completely disorganized, and every city, every thickly populated area, was starving or trembled on the edge of starvation. Most of the capital cities of the world were burning; millions of people had already perished, and over great areas government was at an end.[91]

Some science fiction writers, like Jules Verne and Albert Robida, stressed possible new weapons of mass destruction not simply for sensational purposes but also in the hope that even the threat of these death-dealing ma-

---

88 See F. N. Maude, "Can Science Abolish War?" reprinted from *Contemporary Review* in *Living Age* 257 (May 16, 1908): 387–92. Only partially in jest, an American periodical reprinted a report from Paris in which a Frenchman, Monsieur Prier, envisioned a future conflict with England in which the British would send from London at breakfast time five hundred warplanes that would destroy Paris at lunch and return in time for their pilots to dress for dinner in Piccadilly that evening ("Killing No Murder," *Living Age* 269 [May 27, 1911]: 555–9). By contrast, the explosives inventor Hudson Maxim, while championing the role of aircraft against naval vessels, declared that they would not do much damage to cities because dynamite required confined places to cause wide destruction. Were it to be dropped into broad city streets, the main force would be blown upward (Hudson Maxim, "The Warfare of the Future," *Science* 28 [Dec. 11, 1908]: 820–31).
89 Maude, "Can Science Abolish War?" 391.
90 On the adaptation and serialization of Wells's book in the United States in 1899, see David Y. Hughes, "The War of the Worlds in the Yellow Press," *Journalism Quarterly* 43 (1966): 639–46.
91 H. G. Wells, *The World Set Free: A Story of Mankind* (New York, 1914), 152.

chines might cause enlightened societies to abandon war and arms races.[92]
A number of commentators in American periodicals felt the same way.[93]

In 1914, at the very outset of World War I, American periodicals still
published debates about the nature, direction, and costs of modern war. A
French general was quoted as saying that it was not clear whether the war
in Europe would be like the Franco-Prussian War, in which brief battles
were fought at infrequent intervals while the armies remained in the field
and economic costs were exacted, or like the Russo-Japanese War and the
Balkan Wars of 1912–13, where the fighting continued nearly every day
and the battles lasted as long as two weeks. "The art of killing is always surpassed by progress in the art of defense," the French general asserted.[94]

Even some who thought wars would become shorter than in the past
predicted that they would be more devastating. In 1914 an American periodical quoted a French physician, Dr. E. Helme, who claimed that although war now lasted only a matter of one or two years instead of seven,
thirty, or a hundred years as in some earlier conflicts, modern war had become more intense, exhausting combatants more readily.[95] Comparing the
Franco-Prussian and the Russo-Japanese wars, Helme agreed that the
shorter battles of 1870 rendered more casualties per day of battle, but in
the Manchurian campaign the overall number of battle deaths was much
larger. Furthermore, counter to popular opinion, Helme reported an increasing proportion of mortal to nonmortal wounds.[96] He also rejected as
a "troublesome legend" the story that modern bullets, being smaller and
moving faster, inflicted less serious wounds. It was true that slight wounds
could be healed more quickly, but modern projectiles – rifle bullets and
shrapnel shells – could cause extreme wounds,[97] particularly as artillery
shells exploded into red-hot fragments that seared the flesh. Shell wounds

---

92 John Trowbridge, "Science and War," *The Nation* 77 (Nov. 5, 1903): 359; Albert Robida, *La Guerre
   au vingtieme siècle* (Paris, 1887), which appeared in 1883 in the French periodical *La Caricature*; Jules
   Verne, *Twenty Thousand Leagues Under the Sea* (Paris, 1870), and *The Clipper of the Clouds* (London,
   1891).
93 Maude, "Can Science Abolish War?" 387–92.
94 Analysis by a French general named Percin in *La Science et la Vie*, reprinted in "How Much It Costs
   to Kill a Man in Battle," *Scientific American* 111 (Aug. 29, 1914): 147. The cost had increased enormously. Percin predicted that improved hygienic methods would be more important in reducing
   losses in war than the more effective forms of defense.
95 Dr. E. Helme in *Le Temps*, reprinted as "The Other Side of War," *Scientific American Supplement* 78
   (Aug. 5, 1914): 150–1.
96 In 1870–1, the Prussian Army lost ten killed to every fifty-eight wounded; in 1904–5, the Japanese
   Army lost ten killed to every thirty-seven wounded. Ibid.
97 Because of their high velocity, modern rifle bullets were much more prone to ricochet off obstacles
   or to tumble in flight, and when they did enter broadside, they left a long, gaping wound. Also,
   when high-velocity bullets hit bone, the bone splinters ripped through the body so terribly that
   some observers believed the damage was caused by exploding bullets. Ibid.

in the 1870 war amounted to 91 per thousand wounded, but there were 176 per thousand in the Manchurian campaign and nearly 400 per thousand in the Balkan War of 1912–13.[98] Helme had identified a trend: Artillery fire would be a major cause of battle deaths in World War I.

PREDICTIONS OF THE IMPACT OF MODERN WAR ON THE
HOME FRONT

American periodicals seldom discussed the impact of modern war on what, beginning in World War I, would be called "the home front." This was because few commentators foresaw the duration of extended, fully mobilized industrial war. Magazines did, however, print occasional pieces on modern war as a burden on the taxpayers, a detriment to the stock market, and a drag on the economy.

Some articles discussed economic issues raised by the Russo-Japanese War and a subsequent war scare in the Balkans in 1908, both of which provided some harbingers of the costs and disruptions of modern war. But such discussions were mainly centered on finance. They addressed in particular the enormous monetary costs of waging modern conflict, a factor caused by the amount of munitions and other supplies required for massive armies with rapid-firing weapons. "The cost of modern warfare has increased by such tremendous bounds that it becomes quite as important to study national budgets and balance sheets as to know the fighting strength of armies and the effectiveness of naval equipment," wrote Frank Vanderlip, vice president of National City Bank, who had been assistant secretary of the Treasury during the Spanish-American War.[99]

Finance ministers had as much influence on military events as ministers of war, Vanderlip declared. When the United States easily raised the $350 million needed to launch the war with Spain, "the display of irresistible financial strength at the beginning of the war played as important a part in ending the struggle as did naval blockades and land investitures [by the army]."[100] After the Russo-Japanese War, Jacob H. Schiff, head of the New York investment banking firm of Kuhn, Loeb, and Co., said that

98 Ibid.
99 Frank A. Vanderlip, "The Cost of War to Russia and Japan," *The World's Work* 7 (Apr. 1904): 464–50.
100 Ibid., 464. Vanderlip added that the South African War cost Great Britain $1.2 billion. Even what he called a second-rate war cost England $2 million a day in field operations, and despite London's strong financial position, its bonds dropped from 103 to 86, a $500 million loss to holders of British government securities. At the beginning of the Russo-Japanese War, when Vanderlip wrote the account, Russia was in the stronger financial situation because its bonds were held mainly in

were it not for strong financial support from American and British investors, who purchased every Japanese war loan, nothing could have averted the financial and economic ruin of Japan at a comparatively early stage in the war.[101]

With the growing fear of a major European war in the first decade of the twentieth century, some American commentators speculated about its possible economic impact on the United States. The brief war scare in the Balkans in October 1908 led *Harper's Weekly* to assess stock market reactions to recent wars and war scares.[102] The effect on the market depended less on the war or war scare than on other conditions affecting the value of stocks and the availability of money, declared economist Howard Schenck Mott. These in turn were linked to the larger direction of, and confidence in, the economy.[103] The status of trade and corporate earnings usually was more powerful in the ultimate effect on the markets than the demands made by war. Mott concluded that a major war in Europe would have a stimulating effect on the U.S. economy in 1908:

Our financial and industrial situation could not be better than it is today. . . . While such a war would involve a destruction of wealth and increase the demand for loanable capital, it would also increase the demand for breadstuffs and that for the manufactured goods of the United States. The effect on our trade and industry, and ultimately on our stock market as well, would doubtless be stimulating. The revival of trade that seems to be coming in the United States, however, would be more wholesome without the raw intoxicant of outside demand for our products created by the necessities of war.[104]

By contrast, others, often citing the work of the British peace advocate Norman Angell, argued that a general European war would be economi-

France, which had $1.4 billion of them. (France had offered its capital in exchange for Russia's military alliance against Germany.) Vanderlip predicted that Russian war bonds would also be bought by investors in Belgium, Germany, and Holland. Because France already owned so much Russian debt, it would have to purchase war bonds to prevent an overwhelming defeat and collapse of Russia and thus default on its debt. In addition, Russia had gold stocks. By contrast, Japan could market her bonds only in Britain, which had provided the capital for Tokyo's development and had established a formal Anglo-Japanese defense alliance in Asia in 1902.

101 Jacob H. Schiff, "Japan After the War," *North American Review* 183 (Aug. 1906): 161–8. Schiff argued that given Russian autocracy and the oppression of minorities, Japan was fighting not only for its own cause but also for that of the civilized world.

102 Howard Schenck Mott, "Finance: War Scares and Their Effects," *Harper's Weekly* 52 (Oct. 24, 1908): 28.

103 "In fact, in every case of war, it is the destruction of wealth and the demands on capital which powerfully influence the markets. The explanation lies in the fact that the larger the demand for capital the higher the interest rates rise, and the higher the interest rates rise, the lower the relative return from security investments" (Ibid.).

104 Ibid.

cally disastrous to more than just the financial community. It would mean stock market crashes, the end of dividends on securities, income losses for large and small investors, the recall of international credits, and offers of enormous war loans. This soon would be followed by the closure of factories and mills (because the production and trade of raw materials would be curtailed), cutting off of food supplies, strikes, riots by those facing starvation, and conscription of thousands of men for the armed forces. After a few years at war, industry would cease to advance the standard of living, and old machinery would wear out without replacement. The *Review of Reviews* in 1909 quoted one speaker on the rural Chautauqua lecture circuit as warning that "a prolonged and expensive war between great powers would mean simply that the work of the past century in raising the standard of living would be lost."[105]

Socialists had been asserting this for some time, and by early 1914 a few mainstream periodicals carried articles warning of the adverse impact on the working classes. In March of that year the *Atlantic Monthly* ran a long essay by Alvin S. Johnson, an economist at Cornell University, asserting that the gains for the working class in modern war were few, whereas the costs of war to the working class were mounting.[106] Common soldiers no longer were allowed to loot, nor were they given parcels of the enemy's land as was done in the past. In modern war, they fought because they felt it to be their patriotic duty; they also acted within a framework that gave substantial protections to private property, even the property of the enemy. Furthermore, modern war resulted in higher casualties among soldiers and greater hardships for noncombatants. Among the working population at home, the costs of future wars, Johnson predicted, would be higher than in the past. These costs would include high wartime taxes as well as commercial and industrial dislocation and a resulting loss of income for workers and their families.

The reason the burden of modern war was greater on the working classes than it previously had been was that modern nations were increas-

---

105 Quoting Charles A. Conant in the *Chautauquan* in "What a War between the Great Powers Would Mean," *Review of Reviews* 39 (May 1909): 613–14; see also L. H. Baekeland, "Introductory Address," *Science* 28 (Dec. 11, 1908): 817–20, noting that it cost a warring nation about $1 million a day to keep an army in the field and that the results for the victor also were disastrous. He gave as an example the financial crisis in Germany after its victory in the Franco-Prussian War and the then current poverty of Japan after its militarily successful wars in 1895 and 1905. For statistics on the dramatically increasing amount of munitions fired by land and naval forces in modern wars (such as the Franco-Prussian War and Spanish-American War) in contrast to earlier wars, and the enormous financial costs involved, see "The Cost of War," *Scientific American Supplement* 49 (Feb. 3, 1900): 20158.
106 Alvin S. Johnson, "War and the Interests of Labor," *Atlantic Monthly* 113 (Mar. 1914): 344–53.

ingly urbanized. In addition, few industrial nations were economically self-sufficient, and Johnson predicted that there would be a painful period of readjustment as war cut off peacetime flows of agricultural and industrial commerce. Furthermore, mass armies would be compensated from among urban industrial workers, whose wives and children would then have to seek employment. Wartime spending by the government would lead to inflation, which in turn would erode workers' purchasing power. And the outbreak of war would reduce the gains labor had made in the reforms of the Progressive era. There would be a political and economic decline in the state's ability to aid the poor and working classes. War would distract public attention from reform, and its influence would be "inevitably reactionary."[107] It was not only the socialists who believed that modern war would be disastrous to reform and to economic prosperity. Most social welfare progressives, trade unionists, and agrarian reformers held such a view as part of their suspicion of European-style militarism and imperialism.

CONCLUSION

Given all this debate, to what extent did Americans between 1871 and 1914 anticipate modern "total" war? They assessed in various ways the new developments in weaponry, military organization, and tactics, and also the highly volatile mixture of intense national pride and expanding international rivalries; but how accurately did they foresee what would actually happen in modern war? Did they anticipate the type of massive, long-term, military, economic, and psychological mobilization of 1914–18? Did they envision the bloody stalemate on the Western Front? Did they anticipate the horrors of World War I – on land, on sea, and from the air? Most important, what effect did their views of modern warfare have on U.S. foreign and military policy? What impact did they have on the relationship of the United States to World War I?

In all except the nature of the battlefield, most pre-World War I predictions about the future of war were extraordinarily inaccurate or incomplete. Few guessed correctly about the full nature of the war of 1914–18 – the global conflict, the long war of attrition, the sustained mobilization of a war economy for years, and the ramifications that the mobilization, eco-

---

107 Ibid., 351. For similar sentiments expressed in the leading American socialist journal, see Anton Pannekoek, trans. William E. Bohn, "War Against War," *International Socialist Review* 13 (Feb. 1913): 89–93; Vincent St. John, "The Working Class and War," ibid. 15 (Aug. 1914): 112–18.

nomic disruption, and mass death might have on a nation's social, cultural, and political institutions.

Few American magazines had prophesied the economic nature of modern war as it would actually develop in 1914–18. The most accurate prediction about modern war leading to prolonged national economic mobilization, military stalemate, and, for some nations, revolution and political collapse had been put forward in 1899 by Jean de Bloch, the Russian industrialist and conservative peace advocate. But Bloch's pessimistic warnings were greeted with mixed reactions in the United States and then rather rapidly forgotten. The forecast in 1909 of the English writer Norman Angell that a major war would lead to immediate collapse of commerce and finance continued to receive attention for several years before the onset of the world war. But Angell's anticipations proved erroneous, for he underestimated the flexibility of international trade and finance and the economic capabilities of the modern state.

Predictions by American socialists, trade unionists, and social-welfare progressives that war would terminate reform and impoverish the working classes were undermined at first by the surging economic demand in 1914-17 for American goods and commodities. Although there were divisions among the unions, the reformers, and the socialists in 1917 over whether the United States should enter the war, the most influential members of these groups supported President Woodrow Wilson's crusade to make the world "safe for democracy." They predicted that an expanded wartime progressive state would bolster democracy at home and abroad.[108]

Much of the focus of the discussion of modern war in American magazines in the pre-1914 era was on the impact of modern weapons on warfare – the nature of the battlefield of the future and the horrors of modern war. After considerable disagreement and speculation in the last third of the nineteenth century, American periodicals in the early twentieth century began to suggest that the new weapons would increase the horror of war. This was demonstrated most graphically by the Russo-Japanese War of 1904–5.

Speculation about the future of modern war in mainstream periodicals, however, suggested more about American society and thought than about any inherent quality of modern "total" war. To an important degree, atti-

---

108 In fact, although U.S. belligerency was accompanied by some progressive reforms and increased unionization, the war, and more especially the postwar period, led to a curtailment of reform and increasingly to reactionary and repressive measures. Economic hardship also was caused by the postwar inflation and depression. See Chambers, *Tyranny of Change,* 233–73.

tudes toward the meaning of the new weaponry, the mass armies, and the future of warfare were shaped by conceptions about the direction of society, the thrust of international relations, and the destiny of the United States. New developments in weapons and warfare were filtered through lenses designed to look at other issues and were made to conform to expectations about those subjects.

As evaluation was often shaped by pre-existing policy, peace-oriented *internationalists* hoped that the terrifying aspects of modern weaponry and the high costs of modern conflict might deter nations from going to war. These internationalists, such as Jane Addams, Andrew Carnegie, and William Jennings Bryan, worked to curtail the arms race and restrict the use of certain new weapons through the Hague Conferences of 1899 and 1908 and through an expanded international peace movement. They also sought ways to resolve international disputes through alternative, nonviolent means: mediation and arbitration, "cooling-off" agreements, international law, a world court, a league to enforce peace, even a form of world government.[109] Socialists argued against war and militarism as exploiters of the working classes and urged instead a solidarity of workers across national borders.

Conversely, bellicose *nationalists* continued to view armaments and war as legitimate and even inevitable aspects of international relations. They argued that technological and organizational developments could mean more rapid and decisive use of military and naval force. As part of their policy for a modernized and expanded army and navy, advocates such as Mahan and Roosevelt asserted that such forces would enhance the ability of the United States to act as a great power and would deter other nations from using military force against it.

Isolationists, such as House Speaker Champ Clark of Missouri, continued to emphasize the traditional U.S. foreign policy of nonengagement, of avoiding political or military involvement in Europe, to which many isolationists added Asia as well. Emphasizing the need to protect the United States and its hegemony in the western hemisphere, isolationists responded to military developments and predictions about the future of warfare as reinforcing their belief in the need to avoid the New World's becoming mired in the wars of the Old World. Afraid of European and Asian mili-

---

109 Calvin D. Davis, *The United States and the First Hague Peace Conference* (Ithaca, N.Y., 1962), and Calvin D. Davis, *The United States and the Second Hague Peace Conference: American Diplomacy and International Organization, 1899–1914* (Durham, N.C., 1976); for contemporary analysis, see Waldo L. Cook, "Ten Years of War and the Hague Treaty," *International Journal of Ethics* 16 (Jan. 1906): 158–71; "The Prevention of War" and "The Amelioration of War," both in *Outlook* 87 (Apr. 13, 1907): 828–9; and G. Lowes Dickinson, "Peace or War?" *Living Age* 255 (Dec. 14, 1907): 668–74.

tarism and mass warfare, these Americans supported some of the efforts by peace-oriented internationalists to limit arms races, but they remained suspicious about any international cooperation that might limit the ability of the United States to act unilaterally in its own interest. Isolationists also supported some expansion and modernization of the armed forces, particularly the navy, but not to the extent recommended by bellicose nationalists, and with the aim of defending the western hemisphere rather than involving the United States actively overseas.

Enough disagreement existed in American magazines about the potential impact of the new weapons and the future of war that people fit such information into radically different attitudes toward war and foreign affairs. It was not clear, for example, whether future battles would be long or short, or whether the new, smaller bullets and the more effective medical departments would mean fewer fatalities. Furthermore, speculation about future weapons of destruction and their impact on warfare – from the flying machine and the dirigible to possible fantastic long-range electric- or heat-ray guns or even "atomic" bombs – gave an unreal quality to aspects of the debate, a blend of scientific fact and fiction. Before the world war shattered Victorian illusions, the prevailing faith in the positive direction of science and society served as a powerful antidote to fears that awesome weaponry and intense nationalism might destroy the nations that claimed to be the apex of "civilization."

Few realized that what would happen in modern "total" war was that the unrestrained violence of colonial wars on the periphery of Western "civilization" would arrive at the core. (One of those who did was H. G. Wells, who in 1878 predicted for Europe the kind of annihilation that Europeans had recently inflicted on the Tasmanians.[110]) In 1914–18, the savagery of the colonial wars was brought home to Europe. Not just defense workers, but entire civilian populations came to be seen as quasi-combatants, helping to sustain the war effort. Civilians and civilian installations then became legitimate targets. The goal became total victory – complete conquest and in some cases destruction of the enemy nation. The means escalated to meet the goal, particularly in the face of fierce enemy resistance and high casualties.

In the colonial wars, Western industrial technology and military organization had usually proved victorious and with limited Western casualties

---

110 Wells's 1898 novel *The War of the Worlds*, whose cataclysmic vision of destruction visited on England by invaders from another world (the planet Mars), was inspired in part by the utter destruction of the native Tasmanians by their British conquerors. See Wells's reminiscence quoted in Clarke, *Voices Prophesying War*, 84.

compared to indigenous peoples. Such victories might have inured even normally sensitive individuals to the value of human life. This could be one of the meanings of Mark Twain's 1889 fable about a Connecticut Yankee who became a time traveler to King Arthur's court; his visit ended when he slaughtered 25,000 attacking medieval knights, killing them with high-explosive mines, electrified fences, and Gatling machine guns.[111] There had been considerable debate in American magazines about the morality of the U.S. Army's anti-guerrilla warfare in the Philippines in 1899–1902, but that conflict was over quickly and had been seen as too distant to have much impact on American views about modern war.

What happened in 1914–18 in Europe is that the ends of total victory and the means of modern weaponry and large-scale mobilization became linked to produce a war of bloody attrition. This contributed to a degeneration of the rules of war and to the development of more brutal forms of warfare against combatant and noncombatant populations (a distinction that became increasingly blurred). These new methods included the use of long-range bombardment, poison gas, and naval blockades against food imports as well as munitions, the torpedoing of ships (including passenger vessels) without warning, and the aerial bombing of military facilities and sometimes of cities (and in the Ottoman Empire, genocide – the mass murder of Armenians). The full horror of such warfare would not reach Europe until World War II, but it was foreshadowed in World War I.

The views of modern war in mainstream American periodicals in the four decades before World War I, when combined with other aspects of public debate, resulted in reinforcing the conviction of the majority of Americans that the United States should remain uninvolved in wars in Europe and Asia. The new weaponry and mass armies of those nations made them more dangerous. The growing militarism on the continent at the turn of the century led many to reassert their belief in American exceptionalism. Rural America, especially the South and the Midwest, clung to isolationism; the urban East divided between supporting a bellicose nationalism and a peace-oriented internationalism.

The outbreak of World War I in 1914 and the first three years of that conflict, with its high casualties and the use of the brutal new forms of warfare, strengthened support for avoiding U.S. military entanglement in

111 Mark Twain, *A Connecticut Yankee in King Arthur's Court* (New York, 1889), 392–402. It is not clear whether Twain intended this episode as such a lesson; it could also be interpreted simply as another of his "tall tales." See John C. Gerber, *Mark Twain* (Boston, 1988), 123–4. For an interpretation of the novel and the destruction of the knights by the well-armed American visitor as an indictment of imperialism by Twain, see Andrew Jay Hoffman, *Twain's Heroes: Twain's Worlds* (Philadelphia, 1988), 136–41.

Europe – through isolationism or some form of mediation to end war. At the same time, however, these developments also encouraged backing for a modernized and expanded U.S. Navy as well as improvement of the army and military reserves, primarily to maintain U.S. security in the western hemisphere.[112]

The American policy of nonengagement in European wars, reinforced by the journalism of the late nineteenth and early twentieth centuries, helped keep the United States out of World War I for nearly three years. In 1914 President Wilson declared the United States to be neutral. In 1916 this public sentiment caused President Wilson, when he ran for re-election, to make an implicit, if rather disingenuous, pledge to continue to keep the country out of the war. At the same time, however, Wilson supported "reasonable preparedness," an expanded army and navy, and the establishment of a business-government mobilization advisory council. Thus the president sought to appeal to different groups. He would seek to keep the United States out of the fighting and would try to mediate an end to the war and possibly prevent future wars through international law enforced by a League of Nations. But he would also strengthen the nation's defenses with the new weapons, the large-scale, pretrained reserve forces, and the mechanisms for industrial mobilization that were the basis of modern war.[113]

After his re-election, when in response to a new German submarine campaign Wilson broke with his nonengagement policy and took a highly divided nation into war in 1917, most Americans thought the U.S. role would continue to be primarily economic supplier to the Allies. Only a few realized from the beginning that the declaration of war would mean the commitment of sizable American ground forces to the horrors of the Western Front. In fact, massive numbers of "doughboys" joined the fighting only in the last few months before the armistice in November 1918. However, American ethnocentrism fostered the belief in the United States that the American soldiers had shown the Allies how to fight and had played a key role in winning the war. In the post-World War I era, disillusionment with the war and its consequences, together with fears that new forms of warfare, such as aerial bombing, would lead to massive civilian and military casualties, contributed once again to debates over the meaning for U.S. military and foreign policy of the nature of modern "total" war.

112 John P. Finnegan, *Against a Specter of a Dragon: The Campaign for Military Preparedness, 1914–1917* (Westport, Conn., 1974); David S. Patterson, "Woodrow Wilson and the Mediation Movement," *The Historian* 33 (Aug. 1971): 535–56.
113 Chambers, *To Raise an Army*, 65–71, 103–24; Knock, *To End All Wars*, 75–9.

12

Whose War? Whose Nation?

Tensions in the Memory of the Franco-German War of 1870–1871

ALFRED KELLY

In 1910 an East Prussian pastor named C. Mozeik, seeking to bridge the gap to his working-class flock, sat down for seventy hours of interviews with one of his elderly parishioners. Identified only as Frau Hoffmann, she was a sixty-nine-year-old former maid and factory worker chosen for her rough-and-ready intelligence, good sense, and long-term perspective on village life, customs, and attitudes. When asked about common topics of conversation, Frau Hoffman told her pastor: "Sometimes at home we just die laughing when my husband comes home drunk and starts talking about Paris and the French war, even though he wasn't there. But he's heard war stories so often from veterans that when he's drunk he thinks he himself was in the war, and then he tells his stories."[1]

Falsely believing that one is a war veteran may be the most extreme form of memorializing a war. Yet there can be no doubt that the memory of the "Great and Glorious War of 1870–1" was a central part of national identity in the German Reich. No matter that more than 97 percent of the German population had not gone to France in 1870–1 — years later, nearly all Germans would "remember" the war.

When, at the end of 1898, the *Berliner Illustrierte Zeitung* surveyed its readers' views about the most significant people and events of the outgoing century, the people and events of 1870–1 figured prominently: Readers chose the Franco-German War and its consequences as the most significant historical event, Kaiser Wilhelm I as the most important man, and Helmuth von Moltke as the greatest thinker (!) of the century. Other superla-

---

1 Alfred Kelly, ed. and trans., *The German Worker: Working-Class Autobiographies from the Age of Industrialization* (Berkeley, Calif., 1987), 356.

tives were reserved for the Napoleonic Wars: Napoleon I was said to be both the greatest field marshal (edging out Moltke, who was more a "thinker") *and* the greatest miscreant; the Battle of Nations at Leipzig the most important battle (Sedan was second), for Leipzig ended the unhappiest period, the French occupation; and Queen Luise, the "Prussian Madonna," was the greatest woman. Clearly, the roughly 7,000 respondents saw the history of their nation largely as a heroic struggle against the French. Incidentally, the last question of the survey asked about hopes for the twentieth century. "World peace" was the most frequent response.[2]

Even poorly educated Germans were relatively well informed about the Franco-German War and the birth of the empire. A now-obscure survey illustrates the point nicely. In 1903 a young physician named Ernst Rodenwaldt received permission to test the educational level of 174 working-class army recruits in Silesia. These healthy men were to set the norms for use in testing for "defectives." Among the 167 questions that Rodenwaldt asked each man in individual oral exams were the following:[3]

Question	Percent answering correctly
Who waged war in 1870?	79.9
Who ruled France at the time?	41.4
Do you know someone who was in the war?	80.5 (yes)
Have you heard any stories about the war?	64.9 (yes)
Who won the war of 1870/71?	98.3
Name some battles in the war.	63.8 (84.5)[a]
Name some generals in the war.	60.3 (75.9)[a]
What did Germany become as a result of the war?	67.2
What did France have to cede to Germany?	58.0
How much money did France have to pay Germany?	32.2
What is Alsace-Lorraine?	28.2[b]
Name a city in Alsace-Lorraine.	51.1
When is Sedan Day?	71.3
When was the crowning of the Kaiser?	47.1
Where was the crowning of the Kaiser?	44.3

2 Friedrich Luft, ed., *Facsimile Querschnitt durch die Berliner Illustrierte* (Munich, 1965), 46–9. The paper's readership probably was largely working class and petty bourgeois, although the respondents may have been more educated than average; on the *Berliner Illustrierte,* see Hartwig Gebhardt, "Illustrierte Zeitschriften in Deutschland am Ende des 19. Jahrhunderts," *Buchhandelsgeschichte* (1983): B45–B46.
3 Ernst Rodenwaldt, "Aufnahme des geistigen Inventars Gesunder als Massstab für Defektprüfungen bei Kranken," Ph.D. diss., University of Halle, 1904, 13, 18–19, 30, 32–6; it should be noted that 23 percent of the men actually were Poles, who were probably less well informed about German history than were German nationals; compared with a statistical cross-section of the male working class in the Reich, the group also was weighted a bit in favor of the urban, unskilled, and Catholic; overall, German working-class males in 1903 probably were somewhat better informed than the data suggest.

Have you heard of Bismarck?	100.0 (yes)
What is the name of the first German kaiser?	66.1
By way of comparison:	
What is the name of the current Reich chancellor?	24.1
What is twelve times thirteen?	51.7
Name works by Goethe.	3.4

[a] Percentages in parentheses include those who mixed some wrong names in with the correct ones.

[b] "Reichsland" was the only acceptable answer.

Rodenwaldt was appalled by the recruits' ignorance, although we should note that he accepted as correct only the most precise answers. In contrast to Rodenwaldt, the historian is struck by how much these young men *did* know about the major events of their parents' generation, at least in comparison with the other areas tested. Barely half of the recruits could multiply two two-digit numbers, and yet the vast majority of them could name some battles from the Franco-German War. Three times as many could name generals from the war as could name the current chancellor; and nearly *ten* times as many knew the exact size of the war indemnity as could name a single work by Goethe, the nation's most famous writer. When asked to quote at least one verse from a poem or song, almost 90 percent could do so. The four most frequently cited works were "Heil Dir im Siegerkranz," "Deutschland, Deutschland über alles," "Ich hatt' einen Kameraden," and "Ich bin ein Preusse" – all but the second being popular 1870 songs.[4]

We should not be surprised by these results. On both public and private levels, imperial Germany was steeped in images of the nation's founding war. Sedan Day, celebrating the great victory and the capture of Napoleon III on September 2, 1870, was the major (although unofficial) national holiday. It functioned rather like the American Memorial Day, Independence Day, and Veterans' Day commemorations all rolled into one. The day was marked by parades, band and choral music, flag waving, banquets, children's games and declamations, and stylized rhetoric from local dignitaries. Every town had its 1870 war monument (often mass-produced and ordered from a mail-order catalog) and its victory oak. The great museums were filled with war paintings; during the heyday of the huge panoramas in the 1880s, literally millions flocked to the eerily lit giant rotundas to see "realistic" wide-angle battle scenes. In the schools the readers and history texts served up a steady diet of war heroism. Nor was there any escaping

4 Ibid., 30.

1870 images in the private realm. Popular illustrated histories, collections of poetry, novels, plays, even puppet shows kept the memory alive, as did the intimate objects and rituals of everyday life – postcards, playing cards, chocolate wrappers, placemats, handkerchiefs, tool bags, parlor games, and boys' toy soldiers (complete with instructions for setting up "real-life" battles).

Embedded in these images were six common themes that, taken together, we may call the myth of 1870:

1. Wicked France, personified by Louis Napoleon and the Empress Eugenie, was jealous of Prussia after 1866 and sought a pretext for war. In July 1870 France awoke Germany from an innocent and peaceful sleep, thrusting an unwanted war upon the unsuspecting and unworldly German people.
2. In the immediate sense, the war was caused by French Ambassador Benedetti's insolent demand that King Wilhelm renounce forever any Hohenzollern claim to the Spanish throne. The personal affront to the king's honor at Ems (made all the worse because he was an elderly, dignified military officer on vacation) was a slap in the face for *all* Germans. The king *was* the nation; he was a people's king; his virtues were the nation's virtues; his honor the nation's honor. He was the *Heldengreis* (heroic old man). Likewise, Benedetti's insolence, disingenuousness, and cynicism were the faults of the French people as a whole.
3. In a larger sense, the war was a resumption of the Wars of Liberation; it was 1813 all over again. France was the "hereditary foe" and personal continuity in the struggle was key. There was another Napoleon to be defeated, and the son of the martyred Queen Luise and the heroic King Friedrich Wilhelm III could finally put France in its place. Wilhelm's much publicized and illustrated visit to his parents' tomb, where he sought wisdom, strength, and guidance for the coming ordeal, was a great symbolic link to 1813–15. Significantly, he chose the same day as this visit, the sixtieth anniversary of his mother's death, to renew the Iron Cross, which had been instituted by his father on his mother's birthday in 1813.
4. As befitted the renewal of a great national struggle, the nation rose up in a united, spontaneous, voluntary effort to defend its honor. This was not a cabinet war but a people's war, fought by a huge people's army that cut across regional and class lines. The people were in arms. Reservists, *Landwehr* (militia) men, and volunteers left field, shop, classroom, and hearth to flood the recruiting depots. Schoolboys sneaked onto the troop trains; children collected their pennies for *Liebesgaben* (literally, love gifts) for the troops; and women and girls folded bandages, prepared dressings for wounds, and staffed refreshment stations as the singing and praying heroes rode off to the field of honor. Old differences were forgotten as the whole nation closed up shop and bonded in a sacred union. In the words of one popular school textbook:

A storm of enthusiasm went through the German land. Once again, the classrooms and the professorial chairs emptied, plowshares and shops were abandoned, and from the grand country houses and tiny cottages everyone rushed to the colors to serve in the same army and fight for the same goal. In every square and street one heard the clatter of arms and the sounds of war, and in quiet chambers clasped hands were raised in prayer. The people and the army congregated in the houses of God for a universal day of prayer to implore the Almighty for His help; with faith in God and their hearts steeled for battle, the warriors flocked around their banners. The fiery iron horses drew thousands westwards; and from the cars there echoed "Lieb Vaterland, magst ruhig sein, fest steht und treu die Wacht am Rhein." At every station the soldiers were received with loud cheers; men and women surged forward to offer them refreshments. In a fortnight, nearly a half-million soldiers stood ready to meet the enemy, while just as many waited in reserve.[5]

5.   The Germans were churchgoing, pious, earnest, hardworking, humble, and spiritual. Their approach to war was epitomized by the days of national prayer and repentance held during the mobilization and by the traditional German Christmas celebrated in the field. The French, by contrast, were thought to be irreligious, cynical, pampered, materialistic, and arrogant. Their approach to war was epitomized by their unleashing of the barbaric Turkos (North African troops) against solid German family men and by their shooting at German Christmas trees. France and everything it stood for was a moral threat to Germans, who, in their innocence, were always tempted by wicked French imports – from atheism to salacious frocks. By defeating France, Germans turned back the moral threat to their character. They purified themselves as they shed the enemy's and their own blood. "Welch eine Wendung durch Gottes Führung" (What a turnaround through God's leadership) – the famous words at the end of King Wilhelm's telegram announcing the victory at Sedan – would become the byword of the war.

6.   In a series of dramatic battles culminating at Sedan, the people's army fought heroically. Those who died always died a "hero's death" on the "field of honor," with comforting thoughts of country, family, and victory easing their last moments. The great majority returned home in triumph to a hero's welcome and the eternal gratitude of the nation. Those who had been especially heroic received the coveted Iron Cross.

Such was the myth of 1870. What are we to make of it? Walt Whitman once remarked of the American Civil War that the real war would never get into the books – it was too terrible to describe and impossible to imagine vicariously. More broadly, we might argue that a real war never enters the public memory at all. Real war endures only in the fragile preserve of the private memories of the small and diminishing fraction of the population who were combat veterans. Eventually, we may speculate, these private memories come more and more to resemble the generic public memory. Once the veterans have died out, the public images – the myth of the war, if you will – complete their victory, save for a rear-guard action of a

5 Cited by Alfred Kelly, "The Franco-Prussian War and Unification in German History Schoolbooks," in Walter Pape, ed., *1870/71–1989/90: German Unifications and the Change of Literary Discourse* (Berlin, 1993), 48–9.

few historians. As the title of this chapter suggests, I believe that the myth
of 1870 had a problematic existence from the beginning. Of course, war
myths had always been problematic, but by 1870 the clash between the reality of war and its institutionalized memory was more jarring. In the past
the usual categories of patriotism, heroism, individual bravery, and adventure had been under attack, but at least they had not been blatantly refuted
by the technology and organization of war. In 1870 Europeans confronted
mass industrial war for the first time, getting a taste of World War I.
Against the terrible, impersonal, long-range fire of the breach-loading
chassepot (*Schassepopo,* as the Germans dubbed it), bravery and heroism either had to be redefined or the reality of war simply suppressed.[6]

Until the Napoleonic period there had been no pretense that the whole
nation could be in arms in a grand gesture of national self-definition. Soldiers were merely agents of the crown and war a misfortune for the civilians who happened to get in the way. Even in the so-called Wars of Liberation from France, the idea that the patriotic nation was in arms appealed
only to a few young intellectuals. There *was* no German nation to be in
arms and little popular sense that a nation might be made; and in the aftermath of the war there was no centralized authority or symbol of national
striving and little technology to distribute images to a rural society. Only
later, in 1870, when they were emotionally linked to a new war, would the
Wars of Liberation be popularly redefined in terms of romantic patriotism.

In suggesting that a clash between the myth and reality of 1870 existed
from the start, I do not aim simply to debunk the myth and proclaim the
reality. That would imply – incorrectly, in my view – that the myth was
entirely false and foisted on an unsuspecting public as a hegemonic tool to
hold the nation together. I do accept the now-commonplace thesis that
national identity is not an organic given but a relatively recent social construct – a cluster of "invented traditions," in Eric Hobsbawm's phrase.[7]
What I wish to insist on here is that national myths must partake of real
experience and that they must be fashioned and sustained at all levels of
society. The myth of 1870 does have some truth to it, but it is not the
kind of truth that emerges from sustained empirical analysis. It is, rather,
an overgeneralization and exaggeration of striking vignettes, unrepresentative anecdotes, and sentimental genre scenes. None of the particular images are false. Many railroad-carloads of men did sing "Die Wacht am
Rhein," some women did stay up late making dressings for wounds, and a

6 Paul Horn, *Die Deutsche Soldatensprache* (Giessen, 1899), 140.
7 See Eric Hobsbawm and Terence Ranger, eds., *The Invention of Tradition* (Cambridge, 1983), chap. 7.

few *Landwehr* men did receive an Iron Cross and get hugged by comely wives on their return. But taken together, the images of 1870 are a myth in that they are a distortion of reality. They are, as it were, "feuilletonized" truth – the impressionistic truth of the newspaper feuilleton, at once comforting and titillating.

Obviously, a detailed examination of the multifaceted myth of 1870 would go far beyond the scope of this chapter. What I would like to do instead is ask three manageable questions about key elements of the myth: First, was there really a "people in arms"? Second, who got the Iron Cross and why? And third, what benefits did the people's army receive? In subjecting the myth of 1870 to these three "reality checks," I hope to locate and explain the origin of some of the fault lines in national identity. These fault lines may run between private feelings and public discourse (especially for veterans), between men and women, Protestants and Catholics, young and old, or between regions or social classes. Mapping these fault lines, which we can only begin to do here, will highlight the strengths and weaknesses of the national community and suggest how it might come apart under stress. More specifically, these three "reality checks" on the myth of 1870 will help us locate the psychological and institutional bases of militarism and gauge its strength and depth.

WAS THERE REALLY A "PEOPLE IN ARMS"?

The total population of the German states that went to war in 1870–1 was about 39,355,000.[8] According to official statistics, a total of 1,494,412 men were in the military at some time during the war. Of these, 1,146,355 actually crossed the border into France and were, at least technically, on the campaign.[9] The immediate mobilization of July 1870 amounted to only about 627,000 men,[10] with an average strength in France in August (the month of the greatest fighting) of 780,723.[11] At any one time there were never more than 1 million men in France.[12]

---

8 Wolfgang Köllmann, ed., *Quellen zur Bevölkerungs-, Sozial- und Wirtschaftsstatistik Deutschlands 1815–1875*, vol. 1: *Quellen zur Bevölkerungsstatistik Deutschlands 1815–1875*, ed. Antje Kraus (Boppard am Rhein, 1980), 330; I have averaged the figures for 1870 and 1871.

9 Kriegsgeschichtliche Abteilung des grossen Generalstabs, ed., *Der deutsch-französische Krieg 1870–71*, 5 vols. (Berlin, 1874–81), 5:865.

10 Ottomar Freiherr Osten-Sacken und von Rhein, *Preussens Heer von seinen Anfängen bis zur Gegenwart*, vol. 3: *Das preussisch-deutsche Heer bis zur Gegenwart* (Berlin, 1914), 181.

11 Ernst Engel, *Die Verluste der deutschen Armeen an Offizieren und Mannschaften im Kriege gegen Frankreich 1870 und 1871* (Berlin, 1872), 282.

12 Ibid., 283.

Thus, about 3.8 percent of the German population served in the army at some time during the war and 2.9 percent actually went to France. During the July mobilization, when men "rushed to the colors," according to the romantic myth, 1.6 percent were in the army; during the great fighting of August the number was 2.0 percent. There was some regional variation. For example, Schleswig-Holstein, Hannover, and Hesse-Nassau, all of which had come under Prussian administration only in 1866, had mobilized significantly smaller percentages.[13] Writing in the *Pall Mall Gazette* on October 8, 1870, Friedrich Engels bluntly called the "people in arms" a fraud.[14]

A more nuanced picture emerges when the numbers who served are compared with the actual pool of military-age men. The North German Bund followed the Prussian "3–4–5 system." Starting at age twenty, one was liable for three years of active duty, followed by four years in the reserves, followed by five years in the *Landwehr*. Other states had similar systems.[15] At any given time there were thus twelve *Jahrgänge* (age cohorts), ages 20–31 inclusively, who *in theory* were of military age. But because the standing army was set at about 1 percent of the population, there were far too many men in each *Jahrgang*, even considering the large numbers who failed the physical exam. During the war there were about 3,717,000 men ages 20–31 in Germany.[16] That would mean that 40.2 percent of the military-age men were in the army at some time during the war, and that 30.8 percent crossed the French border. However, in many districts there weren't enough men in the reserves and the five *Jahrgänge* of *Landwehr*, so authorities dipped another four years (that is, through 35-year-olds) into the pool.[17] Because there were roughly 1,100,000 men in those four older *Jahrgänge*, the total pool of military-age men would have been as much as 4,817,000. Revising our earlier percentages, then, we would have 31.0 percent of military-age men in the army and only 23.8 percent crossing the French border. These figures are not exact, but they do provide a good general picture. No matter how the accounting is done, the conclusion is

---

13 Gustaf Lehmann, *Die Mobilmachung von 1870/71* (Berlin, 1905), 30.
14 Friedrich Engels, *Der deutsch-französische Krieg 1870/71: Sechzig Artikel aus der "Pall Mall Gazette"* (Berlin, 1957), 177. Engels claimed that in the 1860s only 12 percent of Prussian men passed through the army, but his own figures actually yield a rate of 27.4 percent.
15 Baden's was the same as that of the North German Bund; Bavaria had 3-3-5 starting at age 21, and Württemberg had 3-4-5 starting at age 21; see Gerald F. Talbot, *Analysis of the Organization of the Prussian Army* (London, 1871), 69–73.
16 Brian R. Mitchell, *European Historical Statistics, 1750–1970* (New York, 1976), 37; a bit of extrapolation is necessary given the way the age groups are broken down in the statistics.
17 Lehmann, *Die Mobilmachung,* 275–8.

inescapable: A large majority of Germany's young men *did not* fight in the "people's army" during the "Great and Glorious War of 1870/71." They stayed home.

On the whole, there was little enthusiasm among the older reservists and *Landwehr* men, who were supposed to be the real core of the people in arms. As Carl Rückert, author of perhaps the finest memoir of the war, recalls, "Most of them didn't understand the political significance of the war. They considered this war, like every other, a terrible misfortune."[18] Thousands of men showed up late for the mobilization because they were sick, they were working somewhere else, or they had moved away.[19] Actual evasion, however, was difficult and relatively rare. Men who were really serious about evading service had probably emigrated. In Prussia between 1862 and 1871, 39,913 young men were suspected of leaving to avoid military service. Significantly, emigration of young men had risen sharply in Schleswig-Holstein, Hannover, and Hesse-Nassau after their incorporation into Prussia in 1866. In Baden, too, the introduction of a Prussian-style conscription had spurred emigration.[20] Many men who might have caused trouble in 1870 were watching the war from afar in places like Milwaukee and St. Louis.

But what about all the volunteers, the heroes of poetry, popular illustrated histories, and schoolbooks? There even were touching stories of tottering veterans of the Wars of Liberation showing up in their ancient uniforms.[21] In fact, it was extremely difficult to volunteer if one had no prior military experience. Those few who tried usually were rebuffed or shunted from regiment to regiment. Most officers considered a raw recruit too much trouble to take on a campaign. Karl Zeitz, a genuine volunteer, recalled that when he finally talked his way into a regiment, he encountered hostility from the noncommissioned officers and disbelief from the reservist he replaced: "The man stared at me as though he just could not believe his good luck. He apparently thought that I was insane and that my madness might show itself at any moment, destroying his beau-tiful dream

---

18 Carl Christian Rückert, *Mit dem Tornister: Ungeschminkte Feldzugs-Erinnerungen eines Infanteristen aus dem Jahre 1870,* 2d ed. (Frankfurt am Main, 1912), 13.
19 Lehmann, *Die Mobilmachung,* 46–8.
20 On these issues, see Wilhelm Mönckmeier, *Die deutsche überseeische Auswanderung: Ein Beitrag zur deutschen Wanderungsgeschichte* (Jena, 1912), 54–5, 83–4; Eugen von Philippovich, ed., *Auswanderung und Auswanderungspolitik in Deutschland* (Leipzig, 1912), 149; T. Bödiker, "Die Auswanderung und die Einwanderung des preussischen Staates," *Zeitschrift des Königlich Preussischen Statistischen Bureaus* 13 (1873): 10–11; Mack Walker, *Germany and the Emigration, 1816–1885* (Cambridge, Mass., 1964), 180.
21 Ferdinand Schmidt, *Der Franzosenkrieg 1870–1871,* 2 vols. (Berlin, [1870-2]), 1:191–215.

of being set free."[22] Other volunteers had similar troubles, and, once enlisted, they were often treated with contempt by the other men.[23]

The numbers here are slippery. Gustaf Lehmann's official study of the mobilization counted only 1,164 newly enlisted volunteers for the North German Bund.[24] But the situation is complicated by the ambiguity of the term "volunteer." In Prussia after 1814 there had been a provision that allowed young men of the educated classes to fulfil their compulsory military service by "volunteering" for only one year. They were then freed from active duty with the opportunity, if they qualified, to become officers in the reserve. This system, which was eventually adopted by the other states, was designed to protect the educated classes, while still acculturating them to the military. These so-called one-year volunteers really were volunteers in name only; their military service actually was just as compulsory as that of the masses of draftees. Thus, when war broke out in 1870, there already were one-year volunteers in the army, and more would come in during the coming months. Just how many is unclear. Lehmann puts the number at 8,977,[25] though a later scholar insists there were 16,182.[26] Even if we accept the higher estimate, we must note that most of these men were not volunteers in the usual sense, that few of them got into the real fighting, and that, in any case, they numbered only slightly over 1 percent of the total.[27] A glance at the numbers of university students in the war confirms that there was no great rush of educated men to volunteer. Of the 13,765 students who had matriculated for the summer 1870 semester at Germany's 20 universities, only 2,745 (19.9 percent) were combatants. Another 914

22 Karl Zeitz, *Kriegserinnerungen eines Feldzugsfreiwilligen aus den Jahren 1870 und 1871* (Altenburg, 1891), 29.

23 Ibid., 60; see also Rückert, *Mit dem Tornister,* 8; Hugo Ehrenberg, *Feldzugs-Erinnerungen eines Fünfunddreissigers 1870/71* (Rathenow, 1891), 3; Paul Güssfeldt, *Meine Kriegserlebnisse im deutsch-französischen Feldzug, nebst autobiographischen Mitteilungen aus den Jahren 1868/69 und 1906/07* (Berlin, 1907), 24–6; A. Dressel, *Mit dem Kaiser Alexander-Garde-Grenadieren in und um Le Bourget, 1870–1871* (Berlin, 1912), 27–9.

24 Lehmann, *Die Mobilmachung,* 287–8; Gerhard Ritter accepts the same number; see his *The Sword and the Scepter: The Problem of Militarism in Germany,* vol. 1: *The Prussian Tradition, 1740–1890,* trans. Heinz Norden (Coral Gables, Fla., 1969), 155, 269.

25 Lehmann, *Die Mobilmachung,* 281–6.

26 Johannes Wilke, "Die deutschen Kriegsfreiwilligen von 1870/71," *Zeitschrift für Heereskunde* 37 (1973): 5.

27 One-year volunteers were awarded about 0.8 percent of the Iron Crosses, even though they were disproportionately at the level of *Gefreiter* or above; this suggests that the lower figure, used by Lehmann, is probably more accurate. See Königlich General-Ordens-Kommission, ed., *Königlich Preussische Ordens-Liste (1877)* (Berlin, 1877), pt. 3. Thousands of educated young people did volunteer to work in field hospitals, but most of them were sent home quickly because they were in the way or couldn't stand the hardships; see Adolf Held, "Bemerkungen über die freiwilligen Krankenpfleger im Kriege von 1870," *Preussische Jahrbücher* 27 (1871): 121–44, 251–73.

were medics, for a total of 3,659, or 26.6 percent. In other words, almost three-fourths of German university students stayed home![28] If anything, their participation rate was *lower* than average, particularly in comparison with their age cohorts. In retrospect, the number of one-year volunteers appeared huge because they wrote a disproportionate number of books about the war.

The concept of a "people in arms" was not exactly a fraud, as Engels claimed. There were, after all, nearly 1.5 million men in uniform. That already was enough to make War Minister von Roon uneasy. He considered a people's army dangerously democratic and was loath to dip deeply into the pool of *Landwehr* men when the war unexpectedly dragged on after Sedan.[29] Still, the number of real combat veterans would have been quite small, for the major fighting was early in the war and was handled, as von Roon wished, mostly by the active-duty soldiers and the younger reservists. To the men already in the field, the replacements were just *Schwamm* (literally, sponge or fungus).[30] Few *Landwehr* men got to France soon enough to do much fighting. In August, the most dangerous month, there were only 115 *Landwehr* infantry casualties, compared with 52,437 for the standing army. Overall, there were 3,084 *Landwehr* casualties for the whole war (only about 2.6 percent of the total). Despite his sentimental appeal as a citizen-soldier, a *Landwehrmann* was more likely to get venereal disease than to get wounded.[31] Indeed, for the majority of veterans the major war experience would have been illness. More than 475,400 men were sick enough on the campaign to be confined to field hospitals – a vast pool of candidates susceptible to memory readjustment to fit a more glamorous image of the campaign.[32] It is impossible to know for sure, but a good guess would be that no more than 400,000 to 500,000 men saw sig-

---

28 Ludwig Bauer, ed., *Der Deutschen Hochschulen Antheil am Kampfe gegen Frankreich* (Leipzig, 1873), 477; Bauer got his data from the rector's office of each university; overall statistics actually show a smaller drop (12.4 percent) in matriculation between the winter semesters of 1869–70 and 1870–1 (for students studying Catholic theology, it was only 6.2 percent); however, between 1870–1 and 1871–2 there was an increase of 2,971 students; see Wolfram Fischer, Jochen Krengel, and Jutta Wietog, *Sozialgeschichtliches Arbeitsbuch*, vol. 1: *Materialien zur Statistik des Deutschen Bundes 1815–1870* (Munich, 1982), 230.

29 See Manfred Messerschmidt, "Die Reorganisation der preussisch-deutschen Armee nach dem Kriege," in Rainer Riemerschneider, ed., *La Guerre de 1870/71 et ses Conséquences* (Bonn, 1990), 396–407.

30 Horn, *Die deutsche Soldatensprache*, 36.

31 Militär-Medizinal-Abteilung des Königlich Preussischen Kriegsministeriums, ed., *Sanitäts-Bericht über die Deutschen Heere im Kriege gegen Frankreich 1870/71*, 6 vols. (Berlin, 1884–6), 2:10–11; *Der deutsch-französische Krieg 1870–71*, 5:875.

32 *Sanitäts-Bericht*, 2:4–5.

nificant action during the war. In other words, roughly 1 percent of the population (diminishing to perhaps 0.3 percent by 1914) had first-hand knowledge of what a modern battle was like – not much of a check on a fertile popular imagination.

WHO GOT THE IRON CROSS AND WHY?

The Iron Cross was one of the great symbols of 1870. Its roots in the Wars of Liberation, its sentimental link to Wilhelm's parents, its religious overtones, and the democratic pretense that it was to be awarded without regard to rank gave it special appeal.[33] Every veteran got his little commemorative medal (*Pflaume* or plum, the soldiers called it) just for showing up. But to have the Iron Cross – that was the real honor. Of course, one did not want to appear *too* eager. Excessive desire for an Iron Cross, *Kreuzschmerzen* (literally, backache) in soldiers' slang or the obvious making of lists of candidates after a battle were considered bad form.[34] During the Empire the Iron Cross was widely visible as a national symbol, decorating countless war monuments and appearing on the royal banners of both Prussia and the Reich.

In reading the popular fiction on the war and perusing the ubiquitous illustrations, one gets the impression that *every* returning reservist and *Landwehrmann* had won an Iron Cross. *Gartenlaube,* by far the most popular magazine in 1871, never left out the Iron Cross in its "typical" genre pictures. One striking scene depicts a grandfather getting out his old Iron Cross from 1813–15 when he sees that of his returning grandson. Only now, with the unity of the Reich, says the old man, does his cross achieve its true meaning. "Long live the Kaiser, long live the Rhine!" he concludes as he invites his grandson to parade to the local tavern to show off the family decorations.[35] Friedrich Hofmann's play *Drei Kämpfer* (Three Fighters), written for Sedan Day in 1873, also celebrates the generational bond of grandfather and grandson getting crosses. The middle generation had kept the faith during dark times, and standing by is a fourth generation, "the

33 On the Iron Cross, see Kurt Bauch, *Das Eiserne Kreuz 1813/1939* (Berlin, 1941); Oskar Höcker, *Das Eiserne Kreuz und seine Wiedergeburt: Ein vaterländisches Erinnerungsblatt für das deutsche Volk an die ruhmreichen Jahre 1813 und 1870* (Leipzig, n.d.); Werner Otto Hütte, "Die Geschichte des Eisernen Kreuzes und seine Bedeutung für das preussische und deutsche Auszeichnungswesen von 1813 bis zur Gegenwart," Ph.D. diss., University of Bonn, 1968; L. Schneider, *Das Buch vom Eisernen Kreuze* (Berlin, 1872).
34 See Horn, *Die deutsche Soldatensprache*, 52; Josef Christ, ed., *Kriegserinnerungen eines Veteranen von 1870–71* (Trier, 1910), 45; on the medals, see L. Schneider, *Die Kriegsdenkmünze für den Feldzug 1870–71* (Berlin, 1872).
35 *Gartenlaube* (1871): 444–5.

Kaiser's future soldier," ready to keep the memory alive and defend the new nation.[36]

Such was the feuilletonized truth of the Iron Cross. Like all feuilletonized truth, it is impressionistic and anecdotal; it only implies that the cases are typical. But underneath lurks a statistical truth that many veterans suspected but for which they had no hard evidence. That truth was that only a tiny percentage of common soldiers earned an Iron Cross. According to the official figures of the Prussian Decorations Commission, 47,102 Iron Crosses were awarded for service in the Franco-German War. (Technically, even after the founding of the Empire in January 1871, Wilhelm gave out all crosses in his capacity as king of Prussia; soldiers from all the German state armies were equally eligible.)[37] There were two types of combat Iron Crosses, a relatively small group (1,295) of first-class crosses and a large group (41,702) of second-class crosses. Noncombatants received the remainder of the crosses. A glance at the list of first-class cross recipients reveals that this cross was essentially an award for senior officers. Overall, officers got about 90 percent of the first-class crosses, noncommissioned officers most of the rest, with only a handful going to common soldiers.[38] What really concerns us here, and is central to the myth of 1870, is the second-class cross. To my knowledge, the Decorations Commission never published a statistical breakdown of who got those 41,702 second-class crosses. Taking a random sample of 3,326 from the list, I got the following breakdown: Officers – 30.7 percent; noncommissioned officers – 41.2 percent; common soldiers – 28.1 percent, with *Gefreite* (roughly, lance corporals) getting 12.0 percent and the rest of the common soldiers (i.e., more than 80 percent of the army!) getting a mere 16.1 percent.[39] What this means in round numbers is that half of the officers, a quarter of the noncommissioned officers, and less than 1 percent of the common soldiers below *Gefreiter* got Iron Crosses. Because the *Landwehr* did not get into much fighting, the common *Landwehrmann* below *Gefreiter* with an Iron Cross was roughly one in ten thousand among returning veterans!

Returning for a moment to the sentimental generational bond to the Wars of Liberation, we can easily see that a grandfather/grandson combi-

---

36 Cited by Klaus Sauer and German Werth, *Lorbeer und Palme: Patriotismus in deutschen Festspielen* (Munich, 1971), 87–8.
37 Other states gave awards too, but these awards received little attention; see Waldemar Hesse Edlen von Hessenthal and Georg Schreiber, *Die tragbaren Ehrenzeichen des Deutschen Reiches* (Berlin, 1940), 38, 62, 109, 170, 342, 358, 362, 408, 435, 459–60, 501, 505.
38 *Königlich Preussische Ordens-Liste,* 6–45.
39 Ibid., 47–1105; I sampled two pages of every 25; I am grateful to Dennis Showalter of Colorado College for helping me to sort out the more obscure rank designations of the various state armies.

nation of Iron Cross bearers among common soldiers would have been an extreme rarity. For the fiftieth anniversary of the Battle of Nations in 1863, only about 18 percent of the 1813–15 veterans were still alive.[40] Eight years later, the ranks of these old men no doubt had thinned considerably. Men in their eighties were rare at this time; in fact, there were only 66,000 men over eighty in all of the Reich in 1871.[41] Now, in 1813–15 only 5,928 Iron Crosses had been awarded to noncommissioned officers and common soldiers (there is no breakdown beyond that).[42] Assume for the sake of argument that 500 of these men were still alive in 1871, and that each one had three grandsons. As we've seen, even assuming that these 1,500 grandsons were of the right age to have been in the war, most of them would *not* in fact have been veterans. And of those who were, only a handful would have received an Iron Cross, as grandpa had. Thus, our *Gartenlaube* illustrator had uncovered an extraordinarily rare event – or he had simply invented the whole thing.

Right from the beginning there were rumors of favoritism in the awarding of Iron Crosses. Indeed, Wilhelm's largesse in handing out crosses to superannuated generals and aristocratic camp followers (*Schlachtenbummler* in the inimitable original) was a minor scandal. "Generals von Boyen and von Treskow," wrote the Crown Prince in his diary, "have received the First Class of the Iron Cross, without anything so far having come to our knowledge of their actual doings in the face of the enemy."[43] Likewise, the painter Bleibtreu complained that the headquarters at Versailles was filled with men like the cowardly Duke of Koburg, who were collecting Iron Crosses without ever seeing the enemy.[44] Even Bismarck was disgusted and accused the king of handing out crosses to everyone in his entourage – though Bismarck didn't turn down *his* crosses.[45] His banker, Gerson Bleichröder, who helped arrange both the war finances and the French indemnity, also got a cross – "as if he'd risked his own blood like the brave men of Wörth and Sedan," in the words of one critic.[46] The satirical mag-

---

40 Theodor Troschke, "Das Eiserne Kreuz," *Jahrbuch für die Deutsche Armee und Marine* (1871): 7; Schneider, *Das Buch vom Eisernen Kreuze,* 138; another estimate has about 10 percent of all 1813–15 Iron Cross bearers alive in 1861, but because many were officers and career men, they probably were older than the average veteran and thus more had died; see Höcker, *Das Eiserne Kreuz,* 44.

41 Mitchell, *European Historical Statistics,* 37.

42 Schneider, *Das Buch vom Eisernen Kreuze,* 136.

43 A. R. Allinson, ed. and trans., *The War Diary of Emperor Frederick III, 1870–1871* (London, 1927), 177.

44 Ernst Feder, ed., *Bismarcks grosses Spiel: Die geheimen Tagebücher Ludwig Bambergers* (Frankfurt am Main, 1932), 218–19.

45 Hütte, *Die Geschichte des Eisernen Kreuzes,* 171.

46 Rudolph Meyer, *Politische Gründer und die Corruption in Deutschland* (Leipzig, 1877), 75.

azine *Kladderadatsch* ran a picture of Bleichröder's cross as a scissors for clipping stock-dividend coupons.[47] Carl Vogt, the old forty-eighter, scoffed that all those petty princes living in comfort at Versailles were "at most threatened by historical shelling."[48]

Wilhelm's prestige was far too great to be tarnished by this petty corruption. What really embittered the average soldier was not favoritism to dukes (it was their nature to get favors) but rather the conviction that the officers were collecting the lion's share of the crosses while the little man was left unrecognized for his sacrifices. No one begrudged a brave officer his cross, but there was a widespread belief that many undeserving officers got their crosses through connections. As one former supply official recalled, supply officers seemed always to get their crosses and then promptly report sick and go home.[49] Carl Rückert, a one-year volunteer, admitted to getting his Iron Cross through the influence of a highly placed noblewoman, the recommendation of his superior officer having gone unheeded. The common wisdom, he said, was summed up in the popular ditty that ended, "Ein Zehntel von dem Orden/Such gröblich vor dem Feind/Neun Zehntel von dem Orden/Such höflich bei dem Freund."[50] ("Seek one-tenth of the decorations roughly from the enemy/seek nine-tenths of the decorations politely through a friend.") The figure nine-tenths had a nice ring to it and was frequently batted about. On the day of the *Einzug* (the entry of troops) in Berlin (June 17, 1871), the social-democratic paper *Volksstaat* claimed that officers had received 90 percent of the Iron Crosses and common soldiers only 10 percent.[51] Of course, as we've seen, this was true only of the relatively rare first-class cross. Another variation on the story was that 90 percent of the officers had gotten crosses.[52] None of the percentages really meant anything – they merely represented an uncomfortable feeling that something in one's private experience did not jibe with the public images.[53] If it was a people's army, why were the people were not getting their due? Whose war was it? Whose nation was it?

Not far below the surface here lurks class resentment – one of the flies in the ointment of national unity. If officers were favored, then the upper

---

47 Ibid., 75–6.   48 Carl Vogt, *Politische Briefe an Friedrich Kolb* (Biel, 1870), 42.
49 Hermann Freyer, *Erlebnisse eines Feldbeamten im deutsch-französischen Kriege 1870–71: Nach seinen Erinnerungen niedergeschrieben* (Darmstadt, 1910), 129.
50 Rückert, *Mit dem Tornister,* 177.
51 Reinhard Höhn, *Sozialismus und Heer,* vol. 2: *Die Auseinandersetzung der Sozialdemokratie mit dem Moltkeschen Heer,* 2d ed. (Bad Harzburg, 1961), 322.
52 Troschke tries to debunk these stories but provides no statistics of his own; see his "Das Eiserne Kreuz," 25–6.
53 The belief that most crosses went to officers persisted for years; see, e.g., Comite zur Abwehr antisemitischer Angriffe in Berlin, ed., *Die Juden als Soldaten* (Berlin, 1896), viii.

classes were favored. One can read through thousands of names of Iron Cross recipients without finding a single "von" who was not an officer. Noncombatant crosses also went disproportionately to the middle and upper classes – physicians, wealthy benefactors of the wounded, paymasters, and officials of the railroad, telegraph, postal, and supply systems.[54] Similarly, the list of some 3,150 women who got the service cross for women (mostly in recognition of collecting *Liebesgaben,* staffing refreshment stations, and nursing the wounded) contains almost exclusively upper-middle-class and aristocratic women.[55] Of course, it hardly could have been otherwise; a working woman or peasant wife would have lacked the money, leisure time, and connections to perform voluntary service. Quite simply, if you were part of the class of people who gave out the awards, then you were more likely to get an award.

Despite appearances, more than just blatant favoritism is at work here. The Iron Cross was an *honor,* and honor had always been the prerogative of the upper classes. Built into the very notion that all ranks were eligible for the Iron Cross was a peculiarly modern attempt to democratize honor. The problem is that it was easier to democratize war than honor, as illustrated in Ernst Wichert's play *Iron Cross* (1871), which was about two old veterans of the Battle of Leipzig. One is a noble estate owner, the other his overseer. They live in a state of tension because back in 1813 the estate owner, then an officer, had accepted the Iron Cross that his overseer, then a common soldier, had actually earned in battle. Now, in 1870, each has a son in France. There is a repeat of the incident of 1813 between the sons, only this time the noble officer goes in front of the whole regiment and turns over the Iron Cross to the common soldier, who truly deserves it. In the eyes of the old estate owner, the Iron Cross actually ennobles the overseer's son, so the latter is now a fit husband for his daughter. Here, the little man is allowed to have his honor (unlike in 1813), but honor moves him into the upper classes.[56]

On the stage, justice, if not democracy, may triumph. In the army, ancient class ideas about honor persisted despite the new technology of war and were sustained by the politics of careerism – all at the expense of the little man. During an intimate conversation, Hermann Tiemann, a one-year volunteer, once complained to an officer about the many Iron Crosses going to undeserving officers and their orderlies, many of whom had been at the rear. He received this stunningly candid reply:

54 *Königlich Preussische Ordens-Liste,* 1117–254.
55 See L. Schneider, *Das Verdienst Kreuz für Frauen* (Berlin, 1872); the list identifies the husband's occupation.
56 See Albert Lindner, "Der deutsche Krieg und die deutsche Bühne," *Deutsche Warte* 1 (1871): 69.

Yes, but good Lord, what can you do? True distinction in the face of the enemy is rarely possible with the contemporary style of warfare because there is no more hand-to-hand combat, and mostly the fighting occurs at a distance. So, in addition to the officers, they prefer to give the Iron Cross to the men who intend to remain in the army, the non-commissioned officers and the re-enlistees, because the decoration may be useful to them in their later life. That's of less importance to the other soldiers.[57]

The statistics in the Prussian War Ministry's official medical report on the war confirm that soldiers rarely got wounded facing the enemy at close quarters. Of the 98,233 treated wounds, bullets or artillery shells had caused 98.1 percent. The *chassepot,* which was deadly at up to 1,500 meters, had done the most damage. The *mitrailleuse,* a primitive machine gun, accounted for perhaps 5 percent, and shell fragments for between 8 and 18 percent. Of the remaining 1.9 percent, 0.6 percent had resulted from slashes or abrasions and 1.3 percent from stabs, of which 0.7 percent were from bayonets.[58] These latter types of wounds would have been inflicted in the occasional cavalry charges or in house-to-house fighting in villages. Basically, on the battlefield the enemy was distant, anonymous, and largely invisible. The common soldier had little idea where he was, what he was doing, or what role he was playing in the larger plan.

It would be too much to say that the Iron Cross was a fraud. Many men *were* brave under fire, and *some* of them were recognized. But the cross was tainted by class prejudice, army politics, and the profound changes on the battlefield effected by the industrialization of war. The idea of the "field of honor," where one faced his foe and risked dying a "hero's death," lived on in public ceremony, which was usually orchestrated and attended by those who had never been in battle. While many veterans surely knew that the reality of the Iron Cross didn't always match the Sedan Day rhetoric or the inscriptions on monuments, they must have had little incentive to set the record straight. How could they do so without implicitly demeaning their own and their comrades' achievements? Debunking of Sedan Day rhetoric, which was de rigueur among Social Democrats and other radicals, never really called into question the ideas of honor and heroism represented by the Iron Cross. The complaint merely was that the big shots were trying to steal the show from the men who had carried the burden – a continuation of the old lament that the wrong people were getting the crosses. Over time, the public myth would simply overwhelm private doubts, which lacked both psychological and institutional support. Memory would

---

57 Hermann Tiemann, *Vor fünfundzwanzig Jahren: Feldzugserinnerungen eines Kriegsfreiwilligen: Dem deutschen Volk erzählt,* 2d ed. (Braunschweig, 1904), 44.
58 *Sanitäts-Bericht,* 2:83.

become hazy, fragmented, and anecdotal. Eventually, with few left to dispute it, the truth of the feuilleton would be the only truth about the Iron Cross. In the end it is a lot easier if everyone is a hero.

In June 1871 there were local celebrations in cities and towns across Germany for the return of the victorious troops. A cartoon of the time shows a returning soldier being crowned with a laurel wreath by a smiling local dignitary in a public ceremony. Later in the day the same portly, top-hatted gentleman, this time scowling, shows up at the soldier's apartment and evicts the family for failure to pay the rent. Promised that he would be taken care of, that it was his war, his victory, and implicitly, his nation, he ends up with nothing. The cartoon strikes a particularly raw nerve, not only because of the jarring contrast between public and private reality but also because of the popular perception that the state was immensely rich and could afford to be generous to the people's army. After all, five billion francs of indemnity was to flow into the coffers – a virtually unimaginable sum. In theory, it was enough to give every soldier who'd crossed the French border about 1,200 thaler – more than six years' wages for the average laborer! But how much of that money would really go to the veterans, and how would it be disbursed? The answers to those questions would embitter many veterans and raise serious doubts about whose victory it had been.[59]

In the midst of the victory celebrations, the newly elected Reichstag got down to the serious business of debating veterans' benefits. Technically, there were three separate debates, one on the pension law as such, one on a loan program to help reservists and *Landwehr* men re-establish themselves, and a third on the Kaiser's request for 4 million thaler to divide as dotations among a small but unspecified number of generals and high officials. Debate on the pension bill quickly focused on the relationship between honor and material rewards. War Minister von Roon, introducing the government's draft, told the Reichstag that treating the veterans well was a matter of national honor. That may have sounded promising to those who wished for generous benefits, but von Roon went on to say that those who had lost their limbs in the war had already increased their honor.[60] Did this mean that they did not need material benefits or that

59 The cartoon appeared in *Reichs-Fackel*, June 22, 1871; on the bitterness of veterans, see, e.g., Rückert, *Mit dem Tornister*, 176.
60 *Stenographische Berichte über die Verhandlungen des deutschen Reichstages,* I. Legislatur-Period. I. Session 1871 – vol. 2 (Berlin, 1871), 674; for the entire pension debate, see 673–80, 1017–88, 1141–64, 1170.

honor was somehow above mundane discussions of money? Not exactly.
The provisions of the bill, which eventually passed largely unchanged,
heavily favored the officers over the common soldiers, suggesting that
honor was a confused and illogical justification of class privileges. For example, in addition to their generous regular pensions, officers who were
invalids received 100–250 thaler per year, plus another 200 thaler if they
were amputees. By contrast, common soldiers who were invalids started
with a base of no pension at all (unless they were career men) and got between 24 and 120 thaler annually, depending on the degree of incapacity.
If they could prove that they had been incapacitated in the war, they got
an additional 24 thaler, with an extra 72 thaler if they were amputees.
Widows of common soldiers fared no better. Whereas officers' widows
got an annual pension of 300–500 thaler plus 50 thaler for each child up
to age seventeen, the widows of common soldiers got only 60 thaler plus
42 thaler per child up to age fifteen. Of the 13,288,000-thaler estimated
annual cost (to be taken from the indemnity), the government proposed to
spend 27.3 percent of it on officers' benefits, even though the accompanying casualty estimates were that officers comprised only 4 percent of the
casualties.[61]

   These benefits were somewhat more generous than the Prussian benefits
for the veterans of 1866, but they still seemed paltry for common soldiers.
Carl Rückert claimed that the whole victory celebration was empty, even
for the healthy men, because of the state's stinginess.[62] A bitter article in
the *Social-Demokrat* advised war invalids to become hurdy-gurdy men on
the streets. Then they could at least collect a few pennies playing "Heil Dir
im Siegerkranz" – or "Allons enfants de la patrie," if so inclined.[63] Even the
Kaiser recognized that the benefits were inadequate and directed the
Crown Prince to set up the Kaiser Wilhelm Foundation for Invalids, to be
funded by voluntary contributions. "State aid alone, even when it can be

---

61 See the *Reichs-Gesetzblatt* (1871): 278, 285, 291–2, 297–8; for the entire law, see 275–302; for an
   explanation of the many complexities of the law, see "Das Reichs-Militär-Pensiongesetz vom 27.
   Juni 1871 und die Kaiser-Wilhelm-Invalidenstiftung," *Annalen des deutschen Reiches* 4 (1871):
   1001–42. Eventually, some 70,000 veterans were certified as invalids for at least a short period. The
   largest number at any given time was 57,775 in 1877; the breakdown was 53,755 noncommissioned
   officers and regular soldiers, 3,386 commissioned officers, 305 medical officers, and 329 officials;
   see Arthur Krocker, "Die staatlich-militärische und die internationale Krankenpflege," in Julius von
   Pflugk-Harttung, ed., *Krieg und Sieg 1870–1871*, 2 vols. (Berlin, 1895-6), 1:390; for a guide to later pension legislation, see August Glock, *Systematische Zusammenstellung des gesammten geltenden
   Reichsrechtes* (Berlin, 1894), 114–17.
62 Rückert, *Mit dem Tornister*, 176.
63 Ursula E. Koch, *Berliner Presse und europäisches Geschehen 1871: eine Untersuchung über die Rezeption
   der grossen Ereignisse im 1. Halbjahr 1871 in der politischen Tageszeitungen der deutschen Reichshauptstadt*
   (Berlin, 1978), 350; see also Höhn, *Sozialismus und Heer*, 2:319–38.

relatively generous," said the Crown Prince, "is not capable of supporting the great number of invalids and survivors. This aid provides only the absolute necessities, is unavoidably tailored to general norms, and cannot meet the needs of the individual."[64]

Whether the state could afford to be more generous remained an open question. (In fact, the state never even spent the yearly sum originally estimated.[65]) The Reichstag debate was not really about the total amount of money, the deputies having rejected a motion to refer that issue to a commission for study.[66] Instead, they went directly to a plenary debate, which centered on the question of whether the proposed money was divided fairly. Captain von Plötz, speaking for the government's draft as the Royal Prussian Federal Commissioner, defended the greater benefits for officers by pointing to their higher casualty rates. He drew this provocative conclusion:

That [the higher casualty rate for officers] proves, gentlemen, that the officer has a much greater sense of honor than the common soldier (murmurs, great commotion. Oh! Oh! from the floor) and makes every possible effort to overcome the illness that he probably already feels coming on. Gentlemen, factual proofs are available. I can offer as further proof the experiences I had in the military field hospitals while recovering from my illness caused by a wound. These hospitals were not overfilled with unwounded officers, but they were frequently overfilled with unwounded common soldiers.[67]

When War Minister von Roon later appeared, he acknowledged that Plötz should have chosen his words more carefully, but he called it a "naked fact" that officers had a greater "capital of sense of honor."[68] Several deputies countered that it was the officers' duties that put them in greater danger, but no one pointed out that von Roon's own argument proved exactly the opposite of what he intended: If being wounded or killed was evidence of honor, and honor was what entitled one or one's survivors to higher benefits, then common soldiers who had been wounded or killed were entitled to higher benefits. The only people under discussion were the (presumably honorable) casualties; comparing wounded officers with unwounded common soldiers, as von Roon did, was irrelevant.

64 "Das Reichs-Militair-Pensiongesetz," 1036.
65 In the peak year of 1877, the sum was 22,880,501 marks, or 7,626,834 thaler; see Krocker, "Die staatlich-militärische und die internationale Krankenpflege," 390. In 1873 the government had set up a fund of 187,000,000 thaler, the annual interest from which was to be used for invalids' and survivors' benefits; see Gerhard Stoltenberg, *Der deutsche Reichstag, 1871–1873* (Düsseldorf, 1955), 168–71.
66 *Stenographische Berichte,* 680.   67 Ibid., 1061.
68 Ibid., 1062.

Looking back, one suspects that neither von Roon nor anyone else knew what they meant by honor. Invoking it merely confused an argument that actually was about whether the edifying rhetoric of the people in arms would be translated into material rewards. Bad logic aside, no manipulation of the casualty figures could make officers appear *seven times* braver than common soldiers, the per-capita spending ratio estimated by the government. Speaking in favor of an amendment to extend benefits for the orphans of common soldiers to age seventeen, Deputy Ludwig urged his colleagues to put aside their class interests and vote for what was fair: "I ask you: When the war began, did anyone in any quarter make the kind of distinctions that are being instituted now, after peace has been concluded? ... At that time everyone was said to be equal!"[69] The amendment was rejected, and on June 13, 1871, the whole pension law passed the Reichstag "almost without dissent."[70]

On the same day the deputies took up the two other emotion-laden bills – on dotations to generals and on loans to returning reservists and *Landwehr* men to help them re-establish themselves. The latter proposal was popular and had been the subject of several petitions to the Reichstag. The *Allgemeine Zeitung* had proposed on March 24, 1871, that *every* returning veteran be compensated for business and work losses with an average of 100 thaler, to be taken from the indemnity.[71] That proposal would have used up roughly 10 percent of the indemnity and had no chance of being enacted. Bismarck opposed *any* compensation for reservists and *Landwehr* men, but when it became clear that Wilhelm's request for dotation money was in trouble without some help also going to the rank and file, he reversed himself. The 4 million thaler for the dotations would be "matched" by 4 million for the reserves and the *Landwehr*. Striking a decidedly different tone than von Roon's, Bismarck told the Reichstag that there was no reason to make distinctions among the ranks, because officers and men had withstood the dangers and battles "with equal devotion" (no mention of honor though). With only 4 million thaler at stake and the Kaiser's pet project on the line, he could afford to be generous. The bill passed without opposition. Eventually, some 300,000 men got small low-interest loans (wage earners were excluded because they had lost no business).[72]

69 Ibid. 70 Ibid., 1170.

71 "Kriegsentschädigung und Entschädigung der Krieger," *Ausserordentliche Beilage zur Allgemeinen Zeitung*, no. 83, Mar. 24, 1871.

72 See *Stenographische Berichte*, 861–77, 1170–5, 1189–91, 1203; Bismarck quoted on 1171; see also Höhn, *Sozialismus und Heer*, 2:300–2; Koch, *Berliner Presse*, 351–5; and Harold Müller, "Hungerpfennig und Ehrengabe: Die Auseinandersetzung um das Unterstützungs- und das Dotationsgesetz 1871/72," *Militär Geschichte* 14 (1975): 553–60.

Although sweetened by the accompanying loan program, the dotations provoked significant opposition. To socialists, progressives, and some in the Catholic Center Party, huge outright gifts to a few generals smacked of class privilege and royal absolutism. In his introduction of the draft legislation, Bismarck anticipated these objections by claiming that every man had a chance to rise to general, and if he himself didn't make it, then he at least had hope for his son.[73] Given the aristocratic domination of the higher officer corps in 1871, Bismarck must have known that this was a highly dubious justification. He concluded his remarks by appealing to the deputies' affection and esteem for the Kaiser and by simply asking for a special favor for the old man: "Forget for a moment your role as delegates who appropriate money and think about satisfying this heart-felt need of His Majesty the Kaiser. Give him the satisfaction that he has richly earned by his devotion to, and courage for, Germany."[74]

What seemed most troubling to the opposition was the signal that dotations would send about the nature of the war that had just been fought and the kind of nation that had been born in that war. Only under an absolutist state, they argued, did the king, as supreme military leader, distribute war booty to his generals. Generals were now supposed to be state officials doing their civic duty at the head of a people's army. The thanks of the nation should be enough; material reward would merely demean their achievements, and, not incidentally, encourage them to promote war. Granted, Prussia had given dotations in 1815 and 1866, but those were not precedents. It was a new nation and a new army, and the people were now opposed to any special privileges for *their* war. Deputy Schröder suggested that monuments, not cash, could honor the bond between generals and the little man:

Gentlemen, the common soldier who stands under the monument of General Werder and says, "I was there too in the great *Landwehr* battle at Belfort" – he shares totally in the full, undiminished glory of this hero. (shouts of Bravo! from the left) But gentlemen, he can't share in the money; the gleam of the gold doesn't extend beyond the moneybox of the man who possesses it.[75]

That was well put, but the dotation bill passed with a "large majority."[76] The generals got their money.

So, despite the cheers and banquets in June 1871, the common soldier had little to show for his sacrifices. But the war invalids didn't go away;

---

73 *Stenographische Berichte,* 1176; for the whole debate, see 1191–201, 1203–12, 1775–81.
74 Ibid., 1176.   75 Ibid., 1205.
76 Ibid., 1212.

they lived on as a constant reminder of the unfulfilled promises to the people in arms. Every Sedan Day down to World War I, there were complaints that the celebration was empty unless more money was spent on veterans. Thirty-five years after the war, the *Schwäbische Tagwacht* bitterly recalled Captain Plötz's contention that officers had a greater sense of honor.[77] The remark still stung. In 1912 the same paper claimed that 230,000 of the 450,000 surviving 1870 veterans were living in poverty and that the Deutscher Kriegerbund (German Veterans' Association) was overwhelmed with 25,000 yearly requests for support.[78] Such was the underside of the myth of the "Great and Glorious War of 1870–1."

CONCLUSIONS

Given the tensions within the myth of 1870, how could it have originated and then sustained itself for so long? This is a highly complex and far-reaching question, but I would like to venture a few tentative answers.

The average soldier, who was literate but poorly educated, had little role in originating the myth. He lacked the historical and cultural knowledge to locate the war within a larger context, but, most important, his actual experience of the war was highly fragmented. Usually he had no precise idea of where he was or what was going on. For example, the great decisive battles west of Metz were spread over dozens of square miles. Only later did a soldier learn that he had participated in a "glorious victory" at Gravelotte, with the final charge led by Moltke himself. Most likely, he'd never seen Moltke and didn't even know (until he'd been told) that he had "won" and was a "hero." To achieve a larger meaning for what he had done, to have a story of his part in the war, the soldier had to integrate his narrow experience into the larger narrative constructed by his leaders. They had looked down on the whole scene from a hill, fit their broad perspective of what had happened into the whole campaign, and then released versions of that to the public, including the common soldiers. In effect, the leaders defined what had "really happened." They wrote the first draft of a key chapter of national history. Their version was not wrong and was not designed to deceive anyone – it was not in itself a myth. But it was a "privileged narrative" in every sense of the term. By its very distance from the action (both physically and in terms of social class), the war lent itself to romantic glorification, unchecked by the confusion and gore at the micro-level. From above, a modern battle could still appear as a visual drama whose

---

77 *Schwäbische Tagwacht*, May 25, 1906.   78 Ibid., July 27, 1912.

outcome seemed to depend on the collective possession of certain traditional virtues. Here, I believe, is the origin of the war myth, not in the outright attempt to manipulate. From the outset it was at odds with the experience of the individual soldier, but it was something he would need if he were to live comfortably with his terrible experience.

On its way to the public, this original view of the war was filtered through the second-hand experiences of reporters and illustrators − educated, patriotic men who were looking for good stories and pictures. Reporters were kept away from the actual fighting, coming on the scene only after − sometimes days after − the battles. By that time, they had already been told by their contacts at headquarters what had happened. Completely at the mercy of headquarters for information, access, and protection, they had little choice but to fit their physical observations into the official version, which, as we've seen, was not conducive to an unglamorous "worm's eye" view of the action. Fortunately for those looking for drama, the physical remains of battle − the unburied men and horses, the broken and abandoned equipment − gave the appearance that there had been more combat at close quarters than there really had been. What had happened was that as the German lines advanced they had moved among French bodies and equipment lying in positions where the French had *formerly* been. As the battle continued, German bodies and equipment fell in among the French bodies and equipment, as though the clash of arms and death had occurred at close range. Actually, both armies had been firing at each other over long distances. Illustrators and painters, who also arrived late, got the same impression. It is no wonder that they took some of the colorful, atypical (though sometimes true) anecdotes about combat and generalized them. This is what I have called the feuilletonized truth, which was, appropriately, well suited to fill the pages of illustrated newspapers and magazines. Given the limitations of photography in 1870, there could be no action photos against which to check these impressions. (Of course, nothing prevented photographing German dead on the battlefields of 1870–1, but such photos − if they exist − were never seen by the public.) The illustrators and painters, relying on the information of leaders, on deceptive, after-the-fact visual inspections, and on traditional tropes of what war was "supposed" to look like, determined the public's visual impressions of the war. They had no competition.

Glory, heroism, and unity institutionalize and ritualize better than gore, confusion, and divisiveness. No one would donate money for a statue that did not represent vigilance and heroism, especially for a victorious war. One can scarcely imagine a monument to "the man who stayed home in

1870," or to a soldier with typhus, lying in misery on a wretched straw pallet. Yet those experiences were in fact more typical than heroic deeds. Oppositional memories are fated to remain private and isolated or limited to intimate conversation. They never find their way into stone, bronze, schoolbooks, panoramas, or Sedan Day rhetoric.

The number of knowledgeable veterans in a position to challenge the war myth was small to begin with and diminished over time. Moreover, these veterans had little interest in challenging the myth, for to do so would have undercut their own self-esteem as well as their moral authority over the younger generation. Called on by fate to be the heroes of the founding generation, they had to rise to the occasion and adjust their memories, or at least their public actions, to a version of the war created largely by noncombatants. Those who had missed the war had much to prove. As Martin Doerry and Thomas Rohkrämer have argued, the attempt to live up to the glorious legacy of 1870–1 may account for the aggressive bluster of many in the Wilhelmine generation.[79] "Weit vom Streite macht alle Kriegsleute" ("Far from battle, all are warriors"), says the old German proverb.

The war myth of the heroic people in arms was the richest source for the rituals of national solidarity in a young nation divided by class, religion, region, dialect, and history. Although the myth was a creation of the upper classes and served their interests, it was not simply imposed from above. It survived only because it dovetailed with the private needs of veterans, their friends, and their families. Like Frau Hoffmann's husband, *everybody* could participate.

Finally, the myth did *not anticipate* anything. It was strictly retrospective. All the glory was in the past, and Germany was now free of French military domination. The danger was not that the myth directly encouraged war but rather that it kept alive an image of war that was already obsolete in 1870. Tragically, by 1914 the ugly lessons of 1870 survived only in the dim recesses of the memories of a tiny percentage of the population. Most had never even known those lessons, for they were not "Great and Glorious."

---

79 See Martin Doerry, *Übergangsmenschen: Die Mentalität der Wilhelminer und die Krise des Kaiserreichs* (Weinheim, 1986); and Thomas Rohkrämer, *Der Militarismus der "Kleinen Leute": Die Kriegervereine im Deutschen Kaiserreich (1871–1914)* (Munich, 1990).

13

War Preparations and National Identity in Imperial Germany

VOLKER R. BERGHAHN

This chapter addresses the questions of how far a link can be established between the armaments policies of the Bismarckian empire of 1871 and efforts to create a unified nation, and how far the identification with that nation was reflected in Imperial Germany's preparations for war. It is concerned with the impact of what has been called *Rüstungsnationalismus* (arms-based nationalism) on society and politics before 1914.[1]

Although the liberals of central Europe had worked quite hard in the decades prior to the founding of the German Empire to generate a German national consciousness based on a common language, historical and cultural experiences, and geography, they still were far from having achieved widespread popular identification with a German nation-state when Otto von Bismarck succeeded in uniting Germany under Prussian leadership in 1871. However one may judge his achievements, no one was more aware than the first Reich chancellor himself that much still had to be done to bring about a solid identification with the new Reich among the 40 million people who now lived within its borders.

His efforts to generate a sense of national unity were not aided by the fact that the new order had been founded as a union of federal princes, created in a deliberate attempt to preserve a monarchical system of government at the top and an oligarchical power structure in society at large.[2] In considering the origins of the Bismarckian empire, one should bear in mind this constitutional starting point, and we should not be misled by the fact that the first Reich chancellor also introduced universal manhood suf-

---

1 See Volker R. Berghahn, "Militär, industrielle Kriegführung und Nationalismus," *Neue Politische Literatur* 1 (1981): 20–41.

2 Quoted in Elmar M. Hucko, ed., *The Democratic Tradition: Four German Constitutions* (New York, 1987), 121.

frage for elections to the Reichstag, the new national parliament. As Theodore S. Hamerow and others have shown, he was not a believer in representative and democratic forms of government and had ulterior motives when he introduced a seemingly revolutionary measure into German political practice.[3]

However, the introduction of universal manhood suffrage clearly had the effect of facilitating popular participation in politics. Eligible voters began to go to the polls in growing numbers.[4] In 1871 turnout totaled 50.7 percent and during the next 14 years hovered around the 60 percent mark; but it soon rose to more than 70 percent after 1877 and reached its peak in 1912, at a remarkable 84.5 percent. At first glance, it therefore appears that universal manhood suffrage was increasingly seen by voters as an opportunity to identify with the larger nation. This identification was even more pronounced because the individual federal states retained restricted suffrage systems, such as the Prussian *Dreiklassenwahlrecht* (three-class voting system), that excluded large sections of the population from equal representation in the diets. A second glance at this problem later in this chapter will reveal that the link between the vote in national elections and identification with the national whole was quite strictly limited.[5]

At the same time, even if the Reichstag elections made voters aware of a world beyond the parish water pump, localism and regionalism remained very strong.[6] Many people continued to see themselves as Bavarians, Prussians, or Hessians first and Germans second. Parochialism reigned, and politics, at least up to the 1890s, largely remained in the hands of informal groups of notables. Parties, as Sigmund Neumann put it more than sixty years ago, were *Honoratiorenparteien* (parties of dignitaries).[7] It took some time for deputies to become full-blown professional politicians and for Berlin to emerge as a central reference point for politics. Heinrich Best has collected more detailed information on the social profile of Reichstag deputies and has found that, although major sociological change did occur, it remained incomplete and unfolded in segmented fashion.[8] Thus, the trend

---

3 Theodore S. Hamerow, "The Origins of Mass Politics in Germany, 1866–1867," in Immanuel Geiss and Bernd-Jürgen Wendt, eds., *Deutschland in der Weltpolitik des 19.und 20.Jahrhunderts* (Düsseldorf, 1973), 105–20.

4 Margaret L. Anderson, "Voter, Junker, *Landrat*, Priest: The Old Authorities and the New Franchise in Imperial Germany," *American Historical Review* 98, no. 5 (Dec. 1993): 1448–74.

5 See, e.g., Stanley Suval, *Electoral Politics in Wilhelmine Germany* (Chapel Hill, N.C., 1985).

6 See, e.g., David Blackbourn, *Class, Religion, and Local Politics in Wilhelmine Germany* (New Haven, Conn., 1980).

7 Sigmund Neumann, *Die Deutschen Parteien* (Berlin, 1932).

8 Heinrich Best, "Politische Modernisierung und parlamentarische Führungsgruppen in Deutschland 1867–1918," *Historical Social Research* 13, no. 1 (1988): 5–74.

toward professionalization was much more prevalent in the Social Democratic Party (Sozialdemokratische Partei Deutschlands or SPD) than elsewhere. The percentage of farmers and men from small towns among the deputies remained higher than might have been expected from the percentage of the total population living in urban centers.

The re-election of such incumbent parliamentary representatives reflected deeper mentalities and attitudes among the electorate. Local and regional cultures and traditions proved very durable in the face of the unifying pull not only of Bismarck's politics but also of industrialization, urbanization, and administrative centralization that proceeded at a rapid pace in the final decades of the nineteenth century.[9] Centripetal forces proved particularly powerful in the early 1870s. The founding of the *Kaiserreich* promoted an economic boom and a massive effort under the leadership of the liberal majority in the Reichstag to unify the legal systems of central Europe and to initiate legislation on a wide range of issues. Above all, the *Gründerboom* (economic boom of the early 1870s) generated plenty of optimism that the federal states and their populations – separated as they were by customs, history, and dialect – would slowly grow together.[10]

Bismarck, anxious to support this process while preserving the basic conservative-monarchical structure of the Reich constitution, even geared his foreign policy toward this task. Working hard to overcome his reputation of being a politician of violence, which was acquired during three wars in the 1860s, he presented the new Reich to the outside world as a satiated power. He posed as the honest broker among the other great powers and, whenever possible, tried to deflect to the periphery of Europe international conflicts that threatened to upset his policy of internal consolidation.[11] However, the alternative of pursuing an aggressive foreign policy as a way of integrating divergent political forces at home and of weakening his opponents was never far from the surface. Bismarck tested this alternative for the first time in 1875 when the threat of another war with France loomed on the horizon. At that point the German military, alarmed by the quick French recovery from the defeat five years earlier, began to prepare for a preventive war. This and the ratification of a French armaments bill in March 1875 triggered the so-called "War in Sight" crisis.[12] The hostile re-

---

9 See Hans-Ulrich Wehler, *The German Empire, 1871–1918,* trans. Kim Traynor (Leamington Spa, 1985); Blackbourn, *Class, Religion, and Local Politics.*
10 See Volker R. Berghahn, *Imperial Germany, 1870–1914* (Oxford, 1994), 190ff.
11 See Wolfgang J. Mommsen, *Grossmachtstellung und Weltpolitik: Die Aussenpolitik des Deutschen Reiches 1870 bis 1914* (Frankfurt am Main, 1993), 17ff.
12 See ibid., 22ff.

sponses of Britain and Russia led Bismarck to abandon this attempt at a
more vigorous foreign policy.

The Reich chancellor now resumed his diplomacy of caution and international mediation, which he pursued over the next decade. It was only in
1884–5, a year of national elections, in his desire to create a stable, pro-
government majority in parliament that he yielded to a rising clamor by
certain special-interest groups and their press organs for colonies.[13] Indeed,
Bismarck himself engaged in agitation for the acquisition of overseas territories. It was not that he had ever been enthusiastic about the dream of a
large empire in Africa and Asia; rather, he not only accepted its presumed
commercial benefits but also recognized the integrating force behind the
idea of a Greater Germany. Two years later, in 1887, he once again used an
alleged external threat, this time from Russia, to step up land armaments,
and, as before, German war preparations contributed to an upsurge in patriotism and national identification among sections of the population.[14]

However, it would be quite wrong to overlook the fact that other sections
of the population and their political spokesmen remained deeply suspicious
of Bismarck's use of military and nationalist agitation for the purpose of politically integrating a culturally diverse society. No less important, divisions
over foreign policy tended to overlap with another rift that the first Reich
chancellor had caused when he started his campaign against alleged domestic *Reichsfeinde* (enemies of the Reich). At first it was the German Catholics
who were cast into this role during the Kulturkampf.[15] By the late 1870s
they had been replaced by the Social Democrats. Culminating in the antisocialist laws of 1878–90, the working-class movement was purposely
turned into an enemy of the Reich and proscribed.[16]

This brief survey of the Bismarckian period from the perspective of national integration shows that by the time the first Reich chancellor was dismissed in 1890, a number of policies had been introduced that tried to link
armaments and colonial and naval agitation with the creation of a German
identity was a way of overcoming regionalism and localism. What they had
in common was an underlying strategy of integrating parts of the population by ostracizing others, by promoting a sense of national self vis-à-vis
the unpatriotic "other," and by excluding the "fellows without a fatherland," as the Social Democrats were decried, from the national consensus.

Beyond the Catholics and the working-class movement there existed
minorities whose experiences also are relevant to the general theme of this

---

13 See Wehler, *German Empire*, 170ff.   14 See Mommsen, *Grossmachtstellung*, 77ff.
15 See, e.g., Ellen Evans, *The German Center Party, 1870–1933: A Study in Political Catholicism* (Car-
   bondale, Ill., 1981).
16 See, e.g., Willy L. Guttsman, *The German Social Democratic Party, 1875–1933* (London, 1981).

book and in particular to the theme of this chapter. Their situation within the larger society raises the question of how far the majority was prepared to permit their integration, a process not to be confused with assimilation; or, to put it differently, how far the majority tried to ostracize the minority. Integration, in short, implies acceptance of diversity and difference on the part of the majority. Assimilation, by contrast, relates to the willingness of minorities to merge with the majority.[17] The two concepts are thus complementary and offer an indirect segue into the questions of national identity formation and who is considered part of the fatherland.

Seen from this perspective, it quickly becomes clear that minorities in Imperial Germany came to be used as part of a wider effort to define "Germanness." The Poles who migrated from the eastern provinces to work in the Ruhr mines present a good case in point.[18] When this ethnic minority arrived in the Ruhr region in larger numbers, ultimately amounting to some 400,000, politicians and the native majority around them confronted them with a stark choice: Germanization or ghettoization. Pressure to become German mounted during the 1880s, with the Prussian government interfering in the schooling of Polish children and the public use of the Polish language. What initially was merely a Polish quest to be allowed to preserve their cultural identity thus became increasingly politicized because of the Germanization policies of the government. In the end, being a German citizen meant, from the perspective of the majority, rejection of one's non-German ethnic culture and absorption by the German majority culture that was being forged. The experience of the Jewish minority of Imperial Germany also fits this pattern. However much they may have wanted to, Jews were less and less able to live as German citizens of the Jewish faith, that is, to assume political rights and obligations but to retain their ethnic traditions. The options were either to abandon their identity as members of a distinct cultural group or to exist outside the national consensus as pariahs and scapegoats.

With the latter increasingly being the case and anti-Semitism rising, the flip side of the minority experience became more visible[19]: The treatment of Germany's minorities helped to define who was German and by what criteria. Even more significant, from the 1890s onward, if not before, biology, genes, and the "blood tie" entered the discourse of what it meant to be

17 This differentiation has been elaborated on with reference to the Jewish minority in Germany in Marion Berghahn, *Continental Britons: German-Jewish Refugees from Nazi Germany* (Oxford, 1984), 22ff.
18 See, e.g., Christoph Klessmann, *Polnische Bergarbeiter im Ruhrgebiet 1870–1945* (Göttingen, 1978).
19 Robert Gutteridge, *Open Thy Mouth for the Dumb! The German Evangelical Church and the Jews, 1879–1950* (New York, 1976); Peter J. Pulzer, *The Rise of Political Anti-Semitism in Germany and Austria* (New York, 1964); Uri Tal, *Christians and Jews in Germany, 1870–1914* (Ithaca, N.Y., 1974).

German. Anti-Slavism and anti-Semitism became ways of defining the "other," the person who was deemed never to be able to become part of the national consensus by virtue of his or her genetic makeup. How firmly this vision of German identity had established itself by the 1910s is probably best reflected in the *Reichs- und Staatsbürgergesetz* (citizenship law) of July 23, 1913.[20] Whereas anyone in France or Britain born on national soil acquired the country's citizenship (*ius solis*), the German Empire now officially adopted the *ius sanguinis* principle, which enshrined in law precisely those biological notions of Germanness that had been emerging in the debates on national identity in the previous decades. Although the citizenship rights of those Jews and Poles living in Germany before the promulgation of this law were not affected by it, it became immensely more difficult for foreigners trying to settle in Germany – and most of them before 1914 were of Jewish or Slav extraction – to gain citizenship and with it civic protection and rights.

But what was the German identity that was being defined here vis-à-vis the "other"? Above all, had it taken firmer root by, say, the turn of the century? It is certainly true that industrialization, urbanization, and bureaucratization created a greater *awareness* of the Reich and its capital, Berlin, in the provinces. Germany's diplomacy in the concert of the great powers had similar effects. But the question remains whether awareness may be equated with identification. There were, of course, people who saw themselves as German before anything else. But regionalism remained strong and was in part fueled by the fact that its advocates increasingly defined themselves in terms of their opposition to the center. No less seriously, industrialization and urbanization produced new centrifugal forces that divided German society more sharply along new lines of class, gender, and religion. One of the hallmarks of imperial German history as it unfolded toward the turn of the century was its growing fragmentation and pluralization in social and cultural terms.[21] To some extent this was an inevitable consequence of explosive population growth. The 40 million people who lived in Germany at the time of the founding of the Reich had grown to no less than 65 million by 1914, excluding some 3 million who had meanwhile emigrated overseas.

However, society was, of course, not fragmented into 65 million lonely individuals. A number of lines separated or unified them all. It did make a difference whether a person was male or female, a Bavarian or a Berliner,

20 See Rogers Brubaker, *Citizenship and Nationhood in France and Germany* (Cambridge, Mass., 1992).
21 See Berghahn, *Imperial Germany*.

young or elderly, Jewish or Protestant. Associational life provides an inkling of this growing diversity, but also of the numerical balances.[22] Ultimately, by 1914 there was hardly a field of human activity that could not be pursued collectively within the framework of some private organization. In this sense, pre-1914 Germany was everything but a uniform society that was highly regimented from the top. Historians have meanwhile abandoned that stereotype. Instead, pre-1914 Germany is viewed as having been more colorful and culturally richer than had been assumed.[23] But diversification was accompanied by another development that cut across the pluralizing trend: polarization. Feminist historians have argued that this polarization occurred along the gender line and that gender identities began to overwhelm all other societal divisions. Although there may have been an increase in tensions between the sexes before 1914, the evidence adduced so far is not particularly strong.[24] As regards traditional divisions along denominational lines between Catholics and Protestants, it appears that they softened after the end of the Kulturkampf. If the behavior of Catholic voters is any guide, it must be concluded against Thomas Nipperdey's work[25] that – certain regional "lags" notwithstanding – class in the long run proved more important in the attitudes of Catholic industrial workers than denomination.[26]

The same weakening process can be observed in regard to regionalism. Research on the Ruhr area has postulated that regional traditions were very powerful in shaping the structures of Imperial Germany at large. It is assumed that men and women living in the Ruhr area had common bonds on the level of how they interpreted the world around them. They saw these bonds as a way of setting themselves apart from the inhabitants of other regions in the country. Manfred Brepohl even went so far as to argue that "the people of the Ruhr area regard themselves as 'us' because they feel the same, judge in similar categories, and believe that – a lack of structures and a blurring of borderlines notwithstanding – there exists a spatially identifiable sense of togetherness."[27] Yet however striking regional differences may have been to the traveler in a Germany that was, after all, a fed-

---

22 Ibid., 221ff.
23 Geoff Eley, David Blackbourn, and Richard Evans first directed my attention to this issue.
24 Ute Frevert, *Women in German History: From Bourgeois Emancipation to Sexual Liberation,* trans. Stuart McKinnon-Evans (Oxford, 1989).
25 See Thomas Nipperdey, "Religion und Gesellschaft: Deutschland um 1900," *Historische Zeitschrift* 246, no. 3 (1988): 612.
26 Walter Tormin, *Geschichte der deutschen Parteien seit 1848* (Stuttgart, 1967), 283ff.
27 Manfred Brepohl, *Der Aufbau des Ruhrvolkes im Zuge der Ost-West-Wanderung* (Recklinghausen, 1948).

eral state, in the long term class lines came more powerfully into play. Language provides a good yardstick in this respect. For the outsider the Baden or Saxon dialect may be lacking in class specificity. However, for natives the differences in vocabulary, gesticulation, and intonation are easily discernible. Hamburgians recognize immediately whether a fellow citizen grew up in the working-class quarter of Barmbeck or in grand-bourgeois Pöseldorf. Karl Rohe has defined the culture of the Ruhr region as "essentially a culture of the 'little people.'" And these were primarily those millions of industrial workers who formed the backbone of the Ruhr population.[28]

By the time of Bismarck's dismissal, many politicians were well aware that less progress had been made toward welding the nation together than had been hoped for twenty years earlier. If anything, society seemed to be moving not just in the direction of greater diversity but also of greater polarity at the same time, with class increasingly becoming the most important impulse behind the fissures opening up in German society and politics. The question is how political leaders reacted to this perceived trend. In this respect the late 1890s represent the first dramatic period of the Wilhelmine era in which the question of national identity and armaments loomed large. Although it took Wilhelm II quite a few years to revamp his government according to his designs of Personal Rule, by 1897 he had succeeded in appointing a number of loyal and politically shrewd men, with Bernhard von Bülow and Alfred Tirpitz most prominent among them.[29]

Throughout their terms of office and beyond in their memoirs, both men never ceased to bemoan the disunity of German society.[30] To some extent the target of their criticism was the persistence of regionalism and parochialism. Tirpitz in particular regretted that most Germans, living in remote, landlocked areas, lacked the outward-looking traditions of the coastal populations along the North Sea. They had no understanding, he believed, that the country had meanwhile become a major industrial and commercial nation that was vitally dependent on the seas for its economic survival and prosperity. This is what needed to be changed. Bavarians had to become just as supportive of Wilhelmine *Weltpolitik* (global policy) and the quest for overseas possessions and trade as the people of Hamburg and

28 Karl Rohe, "Regionalkultur, regionale Identität und Regionalismus im Ruhrgebiet," in Werner Lipp, ed., *Industriegesellschaft und Regionalkultur: Untersuchungen für Europa* (Berlin, 1984), 137.
29 See John C. G. Röhl, *Germany Without Bismarck: The Crisis of Government in the Second Reich, 1890–1900* (London, 1967).
30 See, e.g., Bernhard von Bülow, *Deutsche Politik* (Berlin, 1916); Admiral von Tirpitz, *Erinnerungen* (Leipzig, 1919).

Bremen. But there also was the aspect of class that, in Tirpitz's view, similarly disunited the nation. It was Bülow, the foreign secretary and from 1900 Reich chancellor, who became the most vocal advocate of what he saw as a panacea: The best means of combating the Social Democrats and their alleged promotion of class conflict, Bülow asserted, was to adopt "a courageous and generous policy that knows how to uphold the joy in the present character of [our] national life, a policy that mobilizes national energies; a policy attracting the numerous and ever-growing *Mittelstand* (middle class) that in its overwhelming majority firmly supports the monarchy and the state . . . ; a policy that appeals to the best patriotic sentiments. The national aspect must be moved into the limelight time and again so that the national idea will never cease to move, integrate and divide [!] the parties."[31]

This strategy, so neatly summed up by this quotation, at this point even went beyond the middle classes and included the hope that parts of the working class could be wooed away from the Social Democrats. This is why he added: "We must unswervingly fight for the souls of our workers; [we] must try to attract them again to the state, to the monarchy [and] keep the non–Social Democratic workers away from Social Democracy."[32] He continued: "If we fight Social Democracy, it is not in order to hit the worker but to remove him from Social Democratic entanglements and accustom him to the idea of the state." This means that Bülow's approach at the turn of the century to create a German national identity was still inclusive. But it soon became clear that the industrial working class could not be won over. On the contrary, it supported the Social Democrats in ever-larger numbers. Bülow then abandoned his strategy of comprehensive integration in favor of a policy of polarization that drew a clear line between the political forces loyal to the Bismarckian order and the fellows without a fatherland on the left.

For Tirpitz, the leading naval officer and political strategist in the Kaiser's government, the creation of "great national tasks" and the pursuit of *Weltpolitik* had never been as vague as it was in Bülow's speeches. For him, the policies adopted in the late 1890s had a hard core: naval armaments that he clearly expected would enhance identification with the nation and secure it for the future thanks to the economic and emotional benefits that could be reaped from "a great overseas policy" backed up by

31 Bernhard von Bülow, in Philip Zorn and Herrmann von Berger, eds., *Deutschland unter Kaiser Wilhelm II,* 3 vols. (Berlin, 1914), 1:97.
32 Ibid., 95–6.

naval power.[33] This is why he thought it best to try to exploit the presumed rallying potential not of a hazy *Weltpolitik* but of naval armaments as the foundation of an expansionist German foreign policy. The foreign policy dimensions of his plan and his desire to outbuild and defeat Britain as the premier power of the period have been described many times. But, just like Bülow, he also was motivated by domestic considerations. His most famous dictum to this effect has been cited frequently. As he put it in 1895, "In my view Germany will quickly sink back from its great power position in the coming century if we do not promote our general maritime interests energetically, systematically and without delay – to no small extent also because the great new national task and the economic benefits to come with it offer a strong palliative against educated and uneducated Social Democrats."[34]

No less important, this is not the only remark we have from Tirpitz about the linkage between naval armaments and the generation of national consciousness. In a statement relating to a memorandum by Admiral von Knorr from November 1895,[35] he took the view that promoting Germany's maritime interests would "forge at the same time the best means against uneducated and educated Social Democracy." And in a letter to his friend, Captain von Maltzan, in August 1895 he had written that the navy was "called on to make an essential contribution to the solution of the social question."[36]

For a number of years after the turn of the century, *Weltpolitik* and navalism, with its supposedly integrating benefits at home, remained the broad strategy of Wilhelm II and his advisers. It was a carefully calculated policy that tried to steer a middle course between those political forces that had embarked on the Tirpitz Plan with some reluctance and naval enthusiasts who believed that the armaments buildup was not large enough. Both positions came to be reflected in the policies of the Navy League. On the one hand, there was the Bavarian wing under the leadership of von Würtzburg, who admonished Tirpitz not to go too fast because the consciousness-raising efforts of the League in southern Germany fell on less fertile ground than in other parts of the country; on the other, there were the radicals who pushed for naval increases that even Tirpitz believed would overthrow his financial calculations and engage the Reich prema-

33 See Volker R. Berghahn, *Der Tirpitz-Plan: Genesis und Verfall einer innenpolitischen Krisenstrategie unter Wilhelm II.* (Düsseldorf, 1971).
34 Von Tirpitz, *Erinnerungen*, 52.   35 Quoted in Berghahn, *Tirpitz-Plan*, 91n.
36 Quoted in ibid., 146.

turely in a costly and dangerous naval arms race with Britain, the external target of his program of battleship building.[37]

In short, for the moment the role of armaments as an instrument of re-inforcing popular identification with the German nation-state remained inclusive, extending even to industrial workers who were not yet confirmed Social Democrats. Nor was the Tirpitzean navy at this early stage designed as a preparation for war in the strict sense.[38] Only in the long term, from about 1920 onward, when the formidable force of 60 large battleships would be available, did the naval secretary expect it to be ready for use in war – a war against the Royal Navy, then the largest fleet in the world. Until that point had been reached, Tirpitz hoped to avoid international crises that might test the strength of an as yet incomplete imperial navy. Not to alarm the British and not to draw them into a preventive strike, a "Copenhagen" became a major concern in the early years, even if it meant toning down naval agitation at home and thus the navy's effectiveness as an instrument of national integration.[39] It was a tightrope walk that required considerable political skills both at home and abroad.

If the Tirpitzean navy did not represent a preparation for immediate war in the power-political sense, it nevertheless anticipated later notions of total war in its strategic meaning. From the start it was conceived as a fleet of capital ships that would be sent into an all-out, do-or-die battle in a confined space, the North Sea. The German navy abandoned the earlier strategic doctrine of cruiser warfare around the globe. It was to be kept in one place as a concentrated force, ready for the *rangierte Entscheidungs-schlacht,* the decisive encounter in home waters.[40] In this respect Tirpitz emulated the army, which under Alfred von Schlieffen's leadership had adopted the doctrine of a battle of annihilation in its plans for land warfare.

The idea of naval expansion as a preparation for war in the *longer* term and as an *inclusive* instrument of national integration was abandoned around 1905–6. Thenceforth, the building of battleships and, from about 1910 onward, the renewed buildup of Germany's land forces came to be geared to the waging of an early war (whose character, because of the aforementioned German strategic doctrine, was bound to be total).[41] At

---

37 See Geoff Eley, *Reshaping the German Right: Radical Nationalism and Political Change After Bismarck* (New Haven, Conn., 1980), 261ff.
38 See Berghahn, *Tirpitz-Plan,* 157ff.
39 See Jonathan Steinberg, "The Copenhagen Complex," *Journal of Contemporary History* 3 (1966): 23–46. The terms refer to the preventive strike against the Danish navy in 1807.
40 See Berghahn, *Tirpitz-Plan,* 45ff.
41 See Volker R. Berghahn, *Germany and the Approach of War in 1914* (New York, 1973), 116ff.

the same time, armaments assumed a divisive role in German politics and society. No less important, as opposition to stepped-up military expenditure grew, the preparation for war was deliberately used by the government and its organized supporters to polarize and thus to integrate only those who were prepared to give nationalist agitation their unqualified support.

The remainder of this chapter focuses on the reasons for this momentous strategic shift, which resulted in armaments becoming a preparation for an *early* war and national identity coming to be defined in terms of confrontation with those Germans who refused to support a heightened *Rüstungsnationalismus*. Both policies were increasingly deployed as complements to one another.

In analyzing this shift, it must be remembered that sections of the naval officer corps had never been happy with Tirpitz's notion that battleship building was more important than immediate preparedness for war.[42] However, in the early years of the twentieth century, the navy secretary succeeded in silencing this criticism. Its spokesmen, many of whom worked in the Admiralty Staff and were hence concerned with the development of operations plans against various potential enemies, were painfully aware of the weaknesses of the front-line navy. But in line with the basic design of his long-term program, Tirpitz refused to provide adequate resources for improvements. Then, from about 1904–5 onward, Germany's international position began to deteriorate. There was, to begin with, the conclusion of the Anglo-French Entente Cordiale. The Kaiser's attempt to test the strength of this Entente by unleashing the First Moroccan Crisis was a miserable failure.[43] London stood firmly by Paris and also supported France against Germany during the Algeciras Conference, from which Berlin emerged virtually empty-handed. Worse, Britain, meanwhile also alarmed by Tirpitz's naval buildup, began its policy of containment, raising the specter of an early confrontation with the Royal Navy.

One of the Kaiser's first reactions to the Reich's growing international isolation was to establish a commission under the chairmanship of Admiral August von Heeringen with the mandate to make recommendations on how "our readiness for war might be increased."[44] The report that Heeringen submitted in December 1904 began by stating that "the expansion of our fleet has so far been based on the assumption that peace could be preserved until its completion." In the meantime, however, the outbreak of an

42 See Michael Epkenhans, *Die wilhelminische Flottenrüstung 1908–1914* (Munich, 1991), 313ff.
43 See Eugene N. Anderson, *The First Moroccan Crisis, 1904–1906* (New York, 1928); Heiner Raulff, *Zwischen Machtpolitik und Imperialismus: Die deutsche Frankreichpolitik 1904–6* (Düsseldorf, 1976).
44 See Berghahn, *Approach of War*, 64.

early war had become a distinct possibility. In view of this, the Reich had no choice but to put "its preparedness for war . . . above all other considerations." Henceforth, the question of what might happen in the more distant future would have to be subordinated to the consideration of how a genuine gain in naval strength might be achieved "in the period immediately ahead of us." It was, Heeringen added, ten times more preferable to accept additional financial burdens in peacetime than "to be surprised by a war in a state of insufficient readiness." If the navy were defeated in such circumstances, "History and the nation will make the *military* authorities responsible for the deficiencies in military preparedness," and no excuses or attempts to shift the blame would be accepted by the country.

Only a few months later the chief of the Admiralty Staff, Wilhelm Büchsel, produced a memorandum concerning "the conduct of war against England" that pushed the argument even further.[45] Büchsel argued that a conflict with Britain would cut Germany off from the sea and seriously disrupt its economic life. There might be "a financial and social crisis whose consequences would be incalculable." For this reason France should be confronted with the choice between Britain and Germany. If Paris sided with London, war against Britain would be the next step, not least because it would provide the government with an opportunity to "employ" those workers whom the British blockade had thrown out of their jobs and to feed them "hopefully on foreign soil and at other people's expense." That Büchsel was not the only officer contemplating immediate war at this point is evidenced by a letter that the chief of the Naval Cabinet, Admiral Georg Alexander von Müller, wrote during the same month.[46] He suggested that the German response to British aggressiveness and opposition to Berlin's naval expansionism be the unleashing of a "world war that will take our armies to India and Egypt." If, he added, London were told of Germany's determination, perhaps the British would go along with Tirpitz's naval buildup, "which we need to protect ourselves against a political rape of our commerce."

However revealing these documents may be of the mind-set of key people in the German executive, indicating that Berlin's decision in July 1914 to strike "preventively" had deeper intellectual roots, it was the Kaiser who finally linked the question of an early foreign war with the struggle against social democracy and a policy of exclusion at home.[47] His statement there-

45 Ibid., 65.   46 Ibid., 65–6.
47 See Wolfgang J. Mommsen, "The Topos of Inevitable War in Germany in the Decade Before 1914," in Volker R. Berghahn and Martin Kitchen, eds., *Germany in the Age of Total War: Essays in Honor of Francis L. Carsten,* Am. ed. (Totowa, N.J., 1981), 23–45.

fore must be seen against the background of the failure of his earlier policy of inclusion. The Reichstag elections of 1903 had increased the socialist vote from 2.1 million in 1898 to 3 million. The socialists had gained a total of 81 seats, and it was merely the vagaries of the electoral system that prevented them from gaining more, commensurate with their percentage rate of 20.4.[48] That Wilhelm's foreign and naval policy had done little to win over the country's workers was demonstrated to the monarch when he visited the imperial naval shipyards at Kiel in June 1904.[49] Instead of showing their gratitude for his having enhanced their job security, the assembled workers greeted the Kaiser with icy silence.

After this, Wilhelm and some of his advisers became convinced that something had to be done to curb the "fellows without a fatherland." By 1905, with international tensions rising and talk about an early war reaching its first peak, it was almost a matter of course for the Kaiser to combine the two ideas sequentially. In an apparent reference to Heeringen and Büchsel, he believed that sending "a single man abroad" would spell "extreme danger to the life and property of the citizens" because of "our socialists."[50] The first step therefore was to destroy the working-class movement, "if necessary by means of a bloodbath, and then a foreign war, but not beforehand and not *à tempo.*"

The significance of this statement, made by no lesser person than the monarch who, under the Reich constitution, was the ultimate decision-maker in matters of war and peace and the use of the military in a civil war, lies in the fact that both the time scale of the preparations for war and of the concentration of military action abroad and at home had become telescoped. No less important, the idea that Germany was being encircled by its external as well as internal enemies became an obsession in government circles that now was no longer confined to Heeringen, Büchsel, and an excitable emperor. By 1910, if not before, the army leadership had likewise convinced itself that not just Britain but also Russia and France were ganging up against Germany and its only reliable ally, Austria-Hungary.[51] After years of passivity in which the army refused to augment its size in order to avoid an influx of "unreliable elements" into both the rank-and-file (that is, of social democratic workers) and the officer corps (that is, reserve officers of bourgeois background), even the archconservatives in the Prussian War Ministry and the Military Cabinet began to change their mind.[52] Like the chief of the General Staff, they now argued for increased military expendi-

48 See Tormin, *Geschichte der deutschen Parteien,* 283ff.   49 See Berghahn, *Tirpitz-Plan,* 480.
50 Quoted in Bernhard von Bülow, *Denkwürdigkeiten,* 4 vols. (Berlin, 1930), 2:198.
51 See Berghahn, *Approach of War,* 116ff.   52 Ibid., 16ff.

tures, thus abandoning their earlier concerns about the force's political reliability if faced with mass demonstrations, strikes, or rebellions by industrial workers.

This revision of previous policies culminated in the ratification of two army bills in 1912 and 1913. It was accompanied by massive nationalist agitation and a growing feeling on the part of the leadership that even these war preparations might fail to prevent a major conflagration on the European continent.[53] Although it remains a matter of dispute as to whether the notorious War Council of December 12, 1912, had any tangible consequences, its course nevertheless is very telling of the military mind-set at this time.[54] Moltke wanted war as soon as possible; Tirpitz argued for a deferral by 18 months until the widening of the Kiel Canal for the passage of dreadnoughts had been completed. The other significant point to emerge from the meeting was the decision to encourage anti-Russian sentiment in the German population and to step up nationalist agitation, stressing the defensive character of the German response to the alleged encirclement and rallying people against an external aggressor.

By the spring of 1914 the sense that a war was imminent had become so strong that both Vienna and Berlin seriously discussed this possibility. On February 24, 1914, Moltke forwarded to the German Foreign Office a memorandum in which he raised the threat posed to the Reich by Russia's recent rearmament measures.[55] Franz Conrad von Hötzendorf, his Austrian counterpart, was driven by similar fears. On March 3, 1914, he told Colonel Josef Metzger, the head of the Operations Department of the Austrian General Staff, that he was more often wondering "if one should wait until France and Russia were prepared to invade us jointly or if it were more desirable to settle the inevitable conflict at an earlier date."[56] He added that "the Slav question [in the Balkans] was [also] becoming more and more difficult for us." At a meeting in Karlsbad in mid-May 1914 the two generals then had an opportunity to reinforce each other in their conviction that time was running out. Moltke was certain that "to wait any longer meant a diminishing of our chances; as far as manpower is concerned, one cannot enter into a competition with Russia." When Moltke saw Foreign Secretary Gottlieb von Jagow after his return to Berlin, the latter recorded the following about the thinking of the chief of the General Staff: "The prospects of the future seriously worried him. Russia will have

---

53 See Fritz Fischer, *Krieg der Illusionen: Die deutsche Politik von 1911 bis 1914* (Düsseldorf, 1969), 269ff., 542ff.
54 Ibid., 232ff.   55 Ibid., 576ff.
56 Ibid., 579–80.

completed its armaments in 2 or 3 years' time. The military superiority of
our enemies would be so great then that he did not know how we might
cope with them. Now we would still be more or less a match for them. In
his view there was no alternative to waging a preventive war in order to defeat the enemy as long as we could still more or less pass the test. The chief
of the General Staff left it at my discretion to gear our policy to an early
unleashing of a war."[57]

These statements must be related to Germany's domestic development.
Just as in the international field, the situation at home had also gone from
bad to worse for the Hohenzollern monarchy and the political forces loyal
to it. Because of vastly increased expenditure, first on the navy and later on
the army, state finances were in complete disarray.[58] The attempt to cover
these expenditures through higher taxes triggered major conflicts. Not
only the Social Democrats were in rebellion against higher indirect taxes,
but also the Catholic Center Party, worried about losing its working-class
voters, began to abandon its earlier support for navalism and colonialism.[59]
When its deputies criticized the army's brutal campaign against the native
Herero populations of German Southwest Africa, the Kaiser, with a deeply ingrained Protestant-Prussian suspicion of "ultramontanism," remarked
that the Catholics had once again fallen on "their democratic front paws."[60]
Shortly thereafter they were ousted from the government coalition – a
move that enabled Bülow, having won the "Hottentot elections" of 1907,
to form his "bloc" of liberals and conservatives.[61]

However, this alliance, too, fell apart less than two years later over another finance bill. Popular dissatisfaction with the way the fiscal burdens of
increased armaments had once again been put primarily on the shoulders
of the poorer classes led to strike movements and demonstrations against
the inequalities of the existing monarchical order, particularly the restrictive three-class suffrage in Prussia. And during the 1912 Reichstag elections, popular feelings came through very clearly at the polls: The SPD –
though perhaps not a revolutionary force in German politics, certainly the
most radical critic of government policy – gained a total of 4.25 million
votes (34.8 percent of the total) and 110 seats (27.7 percent).[62] The socialists were now the largest party in Parliament, and it had become com-
mensurately more difficult to find government-loyal majorities for the pas-

57 Ibid., 584.
58 See Peter-Christian Witt, *Die Finanzpolitik des Deutschen Reiches von 1903 bis 1913* (Lübeck, 1970).
59 See Berghahn, *Tirpitz-Plan,* 479ff., 490ff.   60 Quoted in ibid.
61 See George D. Crothers, *The German Elections of 1907* (New York, 1941); Theodor Eschenburg,
   *Das Kaiserreich am Scheideweg: Bassermann, Bülow und der Block, nach veröffentlichten Papieren aus dem
   Nachlass Ernst Bassermanns* (Berlin, 1929).
62 Tormin, *Geschichte der deutschen Parteien,* 283ff.

sage of vital legislation. Thenceforth, the Kaiser and his military and political advisers felt besieged and encircled not merely by the other great powers but also by those who demanded political, constitutional, and socioeconomic change at home. It was a feeling shared by all who believed that the fatherland was under threat from an "internal enemy" as well.

Their reaction to these developments was not to try to broaden the basis of their support, as Bülow had labored to do at the turn of the century, when he argued for an inclusive German nationalism and identity. Rather, they deliberately polarized the situation with the aim of excluding all those who demanded constitutional change and a greater say for the Reichstag in foreign and domestic affairs. It is important to remember that these latter forces were highly heterogeneous and must be seen as part of the pluralization that German society experienced after the turn of the century under the continued impact of industrialization, urbanization, and secularization. Indeed, it seems possible to argue that all efforts of creating a unified nation notwithstanding, Germany's cohesiveness as a nation had become more fragile – not merely because of the persistence of regional consciousness but also by virtue of a further differentiation of its system of social stratification and economic inequality.

In light of these developments, the promotion of a polarizing and heightened *Rüstungsnationalismus* appeared to be the best way forward to assure a greater measure of national solidarity. The strategy was to integrate parts of the population by ostracizing others and to generate a feeling of "them" and "us" toward not merely the outside world but also the critics of vigorous war preparations. Nor is it surprising, given the previously mentioned attitudes toward minorities, that "them" would ultimately come to include not merely Social Democrats and Progressives but also Jews, Poles, and other groups that, though desirous to integrate themselves as citizens, were reluctant to give up their own cultural identity, not least because the strength of regional cultures made it rather difficult to define a Germanized national identity in the first place.

How far the idea of an early war had become conflated with that of an exclusionary nationalism by 1913 may be determined from a memorandum that the retired Bavarian General Konstantin von Gebsattel circulated, with the encouragement of the leadership of the Pan-German League, to prominent political figures, including Crown Prince Wilhelm, the Kaiser's son.[63] The latter then showed it to his father, who forwarded it to Reich

---

63 Text in Immanuel Geiss and Hartmut Pogge von Strandmann, *Die Erforderlichkeit des Unmöglichen* (Frankfurt am Main, 1965), 32ff.

Chancellor Theobald von Bethmann Hollweg for a response. Fundamentally the document conformed to the Kaiser's 1905 idea of clamping down on domestic dissent before embarking on a settling of accounts with Germany's presumed foreign enemies. With this sequence in mind, Gebsattel suggested the launching of a *Staatsstreich*, a violent coup against critics of the existing order in general and the Social Democrats in particular. He aimed to impose a state of siege in order to abolish universal suffrage in the Reich. To him it was unacceptable that "the blind, led by agitators, make the decisions all by themselves." A halt had to be called to a situation in which "the masses decide on the well-being of those educated and propertied parts of the population that are more closely tied to the state by virtue of their achievements and interests."

Gebsattel's strategy also included the introduction of censorship, especially of the Social Democratic and, significantly enough, the "Jewish" press. Here he clearly played on the widely held view that Jews dominated the formation of newspaper opinion and, in line with anti-Semitic prejudice, had a pernicious influence on the German mind. This is why Gebsattel also proposed to use this era of violence for a more general solution of the "Jewish Question," as he put it. The Jews were to be treated as aliens; taxes levied on them were to be twice as high as those of *Germanen*. Jews were to be removed from positions in the public sector and be barred from acquiring landed property. A mixing of the "Jewish and Germanic races" was to be made more difficult. Because Gebsattel expected these anti-Semitic measures to lead to Jewish emigration from Germany, "the bulk of Jewish property" was to be taken over by the state.

It is to Bethmann's credit that he argued his case mainly on grounds of the impracticality and dangers of Gebsattel's proposals and poured cold water over them. In particular he warned that unleashing a period of strife and reactionary policies at home would give the country's foreign enemies a welcome opportunity to intervene. He also pointed to the losses that Pan-German anti-Semitism would bring to the national economy. Wilhelm II, in his subsequent reply to his son, largely fell into line with the chancellor's argument.[64] And yet the correspondence is very revealing of the state of mind of the Hohenzollern court. Bethmann knew that feelings there were strong enough to require a refutation not on principle but on grounds of tactics and timing.

Nine months later, at the end of July 1914, the point of decision had been reached. In the wake of the Sarajevo assassinations, Moltke pressed

---

64 Ibid., 37ff.

for a major war against France and Russia.[65] It is typical that, for a brief moment, the military leadership thought of arresting the Social Democratic leadership before proclaiming a general mobilization. Horrified by the idea of waging a civil war at the same time that the government faced a foreign war, Bethmann persuaded the "red-baiters in uniform" to desist, while his aides entered into negotiations with moderates in the SPD.[66] Arguing that the Russian steamroller and czarist autocracy were about to invade and destroy Germany and its cultural achievements, including those of the working-class movement, he convinced the socialist leadership to support the imperial government in its defensive response to foreign aggression.

It is now generally accepted that Bethmann hoodwinked the Social Democrats and their followers into this support. In fact, it was the Reich government, pushed by the military, that first escalated the July Crisis and later refused to de-escalate it, although it was in the best position to do so. But by portraying the now inevitable war as a defensive response to Russian aggression, Bethmann achieved a political effect that the *Rüstungsnationalismus* of the previous years had failed to deliver. The impact of the war preparations had been to polarize the country into "patriots" and fellows without a fatherland. The pull of an allegedly defensive *war* itself was so powerful as to force all Germans into a new national identity – that is, one created by military conflict and the expectation of early victory. If the effect of war preparations on Wilhelmine politics and society had been increasingly divisive, the deployment of the military instrument that had been created exerted an overwhelming pressure that, with a few exceptions, silenced the monarchy's critics of the previous years.

It is important to stress this connection between preparation for war, war itself, and national identity because it points to a neglected aspect of the July Crisis of 1914. The general assumption, still to be found in most history books, is that the mass of the population joined up enthusiastically. It may well be that generations of historians have copied from one another for too long. Recent research suggests that patriotism was more pensive and subdued.[67] After all, only a few days earlier a number of major German cities had seen peace demonstrations warning the Austro-Hungarian government not to wage war on Serbia. Following the work of Volker Ullrich on Hamburg it may well be worth our while to take a close look at the

65 Fischer, *Krieg*, 704ff.   66 Ibid., 699.
67 See Volker Ullrich, *Kriegsalltag: Hamburg im Ersten Weltkrieg* (Cologne, 1982); Michael Stöcker, *Augusterlebnis 1914 in Darmstadt* (Darmstadt, 1994).

faces that appear on those well-known photographs of August 1914. It is perhaps also relevant to reconstruct the tremendous psychological pressure that the tense situation exerted on people. No doubt, the patriotic appeal to participate in a defensive war was difficult to escape. It affected ordinary workers as well as middle-class Jews. Nor did many people realize what total industrialized warfare would look like. But it seems that we have barely begun to understand the sociopsychological predicament of those millions of Germans who only a few days earlier had faced a deliberately divided nation and had found it difficult to identify with the political and social order for which the Hohenzollern monarchy stood.

National solidarity created by war rather than by war preparations did not last long. As the prospect of an early victory receded into the distance, the former divisions reappeared. Once again they were deliberately highlighted to integrate some sections of the population while ostracizing others. The Wilhelmine experience thus raises the question of whether anything more than a superficial national identity ever existed in Germany, if it had to rely so heavily on *Rüstungsnationalismus* and exclusion. All too many citizens were given little choice but to retain older identities, such as locality or denomination, or to develop new ones, like that of class. Or, to put it differently and in terms of a "grassroots" perspective, older modes of popular identification proved quite resilient and hence point to the force of nationalism. The same applies to new modes of identification to be found, for example, in the working-class movement and relating to transitional and transsystemic imagined communities. We have barely begun to understand the implications of these realities for the development of Wilhelmine political culture and its peculiarities. However, it certainly opens up opportunities for comparative history. It will be interesting to see what differences and/or similarities emerge between the German and the American experiences in the rest of this book.

14

Military Imagination in the United States, 1815–1917

DAVID F. TRASK

During the Cold War, two dominant modes of analysis and interpretation influenced U.S. historians who studied national security behavior. Both approaches were reactions to the sustained Russian-American antagonism that marked the era from 1945 to 1990. The first to appear, the "power realism" popularized by the work of Hans Morgenthau and George F. Kennan, assigned virtue to the United States and vice to the Soviet Union, but its emphasis was on the interaction of nations as the appropriate focus of scholars interested in international behavior – that is, it stressed "external causation." Assuming a high degree of rationality in the behavior of the Soviet Union, the chief complaint of the power realists was that U.S. foreign policy was too moralistic and idealistic. It required a strong dose of realism to preserve the national interest. The second mode, which became popular during the Vietnam conflict, found expression in the work of the "New Left revisionists," among them William Appleman Williams and Gabriel Kolko. They argued that the United States, far from being idealistic, was a consciously counterrevolutionary nation, whereas the Soviet Union represented the wave of the future. The United States must therefore abandon its backward outlook and support the goals of international revolution. Otherwise it would suffer eclipse. The internal workings of nations, especially the class struggle, provided a focus for their research and writing. The New Left viewed reform as a "stalking horse" for reaction rather than as a posture distinct from either revolution or reaction.

After the Cold War, a third, much less publicized but active approach, which has been labeled "eclectic," appears much more credible than either power realism or New Left revisionism. This mode assumes that both "realism" and "idealism" in varieties of mixes may influence public opinion and policy makers. The eclectics manifest caution in drawing sharp dialectical distinctions between the principal antagonists on the world stage, recognizing that both internal national peculiarities and external power realities affect decisions in one or another mix. Historians do not need to choose between realism and idealism or between domestic and external causation when treating the international behavior of nations. They do not have to assign either special virtue or special vice to their protagonists. Evidence can be examined with all possibilities in mind. Historians can eventually draw conclusions about description and causation after applying empirical tests.

Ideology has a place in the practice of history. It is a legitimate basis for (1) choosing a topic or (2) evaluating the pragmatic or ethical qualities of historical behavior. It has no place in the canons of scholarship, specifically the tests of authenticity and credibility. Now that the Cold War has ended, historians who might have been unduly influenced by the ideological conflict of earlier years might re-evaluate their approaches, recognizing the potential of the more restrained but more acceptable stance of the eclectics. It is a difficult change to make. Many may be called to the task, but perhaps few of the past generation will be chosen to undertake it.

This chapter is consciously eclectic in the hope that it improves on prior treatments of its subject, but it is also intended to offer historical insight of use to both present and future policy makers. The obsolete views of the realists and the New Left are all too likely to lead responsible authority into egregious error. Historians bear at least some of the responsibility for the prolongation of the Cold War well past reasonable justification.

The notion of 1914 as one of the great dividing lines in the history of the United States now seems indisputable, a conception that probably strikes most European and Asian scholars as painfully obvious but is only now gaining general currency among American historians. That year marked the end of the traditional military imagination that had become regnant during the nineteenth century. After the "guns of August" a radically different pattern soon emerged. What were the components of the traditional pattern that prevailed between 1815 and 1914 and what changes were made thereafter?[1]

The international balance of power in Eurasia has always been the principal determinant of national security behavior in the United States, although

---

1 This chapter treats the background to a previously published essay on the role of Woodrow Wilson in the intervention of 1917. The argument presented here is briefly outlined in David F. Trask, "The American Presidency, National Security, and Intervention from McKinley to Wilson," *Revue internationale d'histoire militaire*, no. 69 (1990): 290–316.

it was by no means the only influence.[2] After the nation firmly established its independence, a task that was accomplished during the tumultuous years between 1775 and 1815, a stable balance of power in Eurasia underwrote the national security of the United States. When that stability dissolved during the early years of the twentieth century, external dangers posed threats to the vital interests of the United States for the first time since the earliest years of the republic, a sudden change that led to fundamental alterations of national security policy and the thinking associated with it.[3]

Throughout its existence the United States has benefited from striking geographic advantages that have made it difficult for Eurasian powers to undertake military operations against it. The nation is distant from Eurasia, and great oceanic reaches or icebound wastelands separate the New World from the Old. An invasion of North America from either eastern or western Eurasia would be a difficult proposition at best. Given the extraordinary logistical requirements associated with such an attack and the distinct possibility that strong neighbors at home might seize opportunities to aggrandize, the great powers of Eurasia were understandably reluctant to seek imperial domains in the New World. They concentrated instead on the Eurasian rimlands, seizing empires in Africa and Asia. The only armed force capable of attacking the United States across its protective oceanic moats was the Royal Navy, but Great Britain's preoccupation with continental rivals such as Austria, France, Germany, and Russia dictated avoidance of serious difficulties with the United States, a lesson learned painfully between 1775 and 1815. Periodic Anglo-American disputes arose, but all were settled amicably.

The enduring Eurasian balance between 1815 and 1914 conferred on the United States one of the rarest of political gifts, a century of "free security."[4] For one hundred years Eurasian powers never gained a real opportunity to threaten the United States. Moreover, no other nation in the New World developed sufficiently to compromise its national security. Americans enjoyed security from external aggression without having to

---

2 When this chapter was presented at Augsburg it occasioned a certain amount of controversy because it challenged established views, specifically those of the New Left. The observations expressed in the introductory paragraphs are designed to clarify the author's approach to his subject.

3 The term "national security policy" as used here refers to the political goals of the nation and the means of obtaining them, that is, strategy, including military, economic, psychological, and other means. Sometimes the term "grand strategy" is used to refer to the mix of political ends ("policy") and political means ("strategy"). The terms "military thinking" or "military thought" are used broadly. They encompass the term "military imagination," which can mean many things. For a comprehensive treatment of the changing balance of power, see Ludwig Dehio, *The Precarious Balance: Four Centuries of the European Power Struggle* (New York, 1962).

4 C. Vann Woodward coined this felicitous term.

pay for it. During the nineteenth century they were permitted to concentrate almost all of their attention on domestic matters.

Two cardinal policies established themselves as free security manifested itself after the Napoleonic wars:

1. One policy, which controlled diplomacy, was *political isolation* from the affairs of Eurasia. American statesmen studiously avoided sustained involvement in Eurasian politics, preferring to concentrate on the internal agenda of the new nation, which included perfection of the federal system, settlement of the western lands, and economic development. This posture did not preclude cultural contacts or economic exchanges with other nations, but it took the United States out of world politics.
2. A second policy, which governed the management of the armed forces, was *passive defense*. The United States did not require a strong military establishment in order to deter potential aggressors. The oceans did that. No nation in Eurasia developed sufficient power to overcome the geographic bulwarks of the United States. Although Great Britain dominated trade and investment in Latin America, the United States gradually if insensibly gained *de facto* hegemony in the Americas, a position that it did not exploit extensively. Domestic preoccupations minimized the American role in Latin America as well as in Eurasia.[5]

A brief description of the American armed forces during the era of free security illustrates the passivity of the country's defense policy. To begin with, the army was remarkably small in number. As late as the "little war" with Spain in 1898, the regular army included only 28,000 men, the size of a single American division during World War I. The navy also was modest in size, a shadow by comparison with those of France, Germany, Great Britain, and Russia. When Spain went to war with the United States to avoid the loss of Cuba, its leaders assumed that the American fleet could not overcome the defenses of Spanish holdings in the Caribbean Sea and the western Pacific Ocean.

Neither the army nor the navy attained the professional standards of their Eurasian counterparts despite the efforts of some reform-minded officers. Many Americans persisted in the notion that the militia, citizens prepared to bear arms in the event of a national emergency, could frustrate aggressors. Backwardness also characterized adaptation to the new technology of warfare. John H. Parker, an army officer who had commanded a battery of Gatling guns at Santiago de Cuba in 1898, failed to elicit support for his proposals to develop machine guns. His advocacy led only to a derisive nickname – "Machine Gun" Parker. Proponents of modern naval gun-

---

5 Although discussions of security matters during the nineteenth century do not always advance this view, the evidence in such works often confirms it. See, e.g., the outstanding work by Edward M. Coffman, *The Old Army: A Portrait of the American Army in Peacetime, 1784–1898* (New York, 1986).

nery, such as William S. Sims, were equally unsuccessful in efforts to maintain parity with other navies.

Of even greater significance was the lack of interest in fighting wars. This neglect seemed reasonable because the armed forces never contemplated warfare with powerful Eurasian enemies. There was no threat. The only gesture toward external enemies was an emphasis on coastal defense. The army developed elaborate coastal artillery, and the navy built ships mostly to protect the seaboard. During the nineteenth century the prime responsibility of the army was to police the moving western frontier. After 1898 it busied itself with the administration of the modest empire acquired from Spain in 1898 and also with the Panama Canal, leased from Panama in 1903. The navy devoted most of its energy to small squadrons located in European, Latin American, and Asiatic waters to protect the nation's limited international trade. These were peacetime missions. They reflected the persistent American assumption that peace was a natural and normal state of affairs and that war was unusual and transient.

American military thought was largely derivative or backward before 1914. Like their European counterparts, American military intellectuals and educational institutions studied Napoleonic warfare and the reason for the vogue of Jomini, although Clausewitz was unread and unremarked. The Napoleonic emphasis on the strategic offensive seemed irrelevant to many officers. Their principal concern was the strategic *defense* of the homeland, either to deter or repel seaborne invaders.

What other influences affected military thought besides the lack of credible enemies? Some have mentioned the compatibility of a pervasive democratic ideology with the national security paradigm of political isolation and passive defense. Democracy stresses peaceful resolution of conflicts by majority rule. In the American case it also demands anti–imperialism and anti–militarism, both legacies of the colonial and revolutionary experiences. During the nineteenth century the absence of external enemies helped strengthen the national commitment to democracy and to a pervasive rejection of militarism and imperialism, political diseases flourishing in Eurasia that Americans sought to avoid. The United States conveniently ignored or rationalized the plainly imperialistic character of what was called the winning of the West. Annexationist policies led to the acquisition of all the territory between the Mississippi River and the Pacific Coast – by peaceful means in the cases of France, Great Britain, Russia, and Spain and by military conquest in the case of Mexico.[6]

---

6 The best general analysis of American expansion during the nineteenth century is by Richard van Alstyne, *The Rising American Empire* (New York, 1960).

Other scholars have noted the American obsession with economic development, a route to the acquisition of large personal fortunes. Although
Americans always condoned measurable governmental intervention in the
economy, a profound embrace of private enterprise became possible in
great part because of free security. The nation did not need extensive centralization or regimentation to guarantee effective national defense. Economic development on capitalist lines presupposed a stable political environment. As in the case of free security and democracy, private enterprise
and free security reinforced each other.

So far, no mention has been made of the Civil War (1861–5). During
this brief period internal turmoil posed a threat to national security far
greater than any that came from abroad. Everyone knows that at this moment both the Union and the Confederacy fielded huge armies and navies.
These forces ultimately attained considerable professional proficiency, a reflection of their total commitment to the fight. The Civil War was perhaps
the most sanguinary of the conflicts that occurred between Waterloo and
the First Battle of the Marne. The limited wars of Europe pale in comparison with the all-out struggle between the North and the South over the
questions of national supremacy and slavery.[7]

Nevertheless, the Civil War had remarkably little effect on future national security policies. When the conflict ended, the armed forces almost
immediately reverted to their prewar size and character. The use of the
military during the period of Reconstruction (1865–77), when the Southern states were slowly restored to full status in the Union, derived from
prewar experience with domestic policing rather than the late war. The
history of the armed forces between 1865 and 1917 gives little indication
that the nation had passed through a great civil conflict.

The imposing internal threat, however difficult to overcome, immediately disappeared after the surrender of General Robert E. Lee at Appomattox, and the external threat, if temporarily enhanced during the war,
did not appear different after 1865 than before 1861. Surely the American
Civil War was one aspect of nationalist manifestations throughout the
world that stimulated considerable international instability from 1848 to
1871. In the end, however, the Eurasian balance of power, although tested,
remained in place and endured for more than another generation. The resolution of domestic conflict in the United States and the strengthening of
the Union have something in common with unification in Italy and Ger-

---

7 For an impressive one-volume history of the Civil War, see James M. McPherson, *Battle Cry of Freedom: The Civil War Era* (New York, 1989).

many and with the modernization of Japan. The fact, remains, however, that the Civil War had no lasting effect on the army and navy. Once dealt with, the internal crisis disappeared, and no one expected another of such magnitude. The national security apparatus returned to the familiar task of policing the West. Generals such as Philip Sheridan, George Custer, and Nelson Miles easily reverted to Indian fighting, taking on the Sioux and Apaches over the plains and mountains of the West as their predecessors had the Seminoles and Cherokees of the eastern forest. They drew on expertise in guerrilla warfare gained during previous Indian wars rather than on their memories of Shiloh, Gettysburg, and Spotsylvania.

The nation never grasped the significance of the Civil War as a military portent – as a technical foretaste of a new kind of warfare – however much it might have affected its later political, social, economic, and intellectual behavior. General Edward Porter Alexander, a Confederate artilleryman, expressed the primal military lessons of the war simply and cogently. "When the South entered upon war with a power so immensely her superior . . . she could entertain but one single hope of final success. That was, that the desperation of her resistance would finally exact from her adversary such a price in blood & treasure as to exhaust the enthusiasm of its population for the objects of the war." His mordant conclusion was: "we could not hope to *conquer* her [the Union]. Our one chance was to wear her out."[8] The technology of warfare, deeply affected by a half-century and more of industrialization, not only enhanced the lethality of the battlefield but also vastly strengthened the defense and burdened the offense. Attrition rather than maneuver became the key to victory in a necessarily protracted conflict. Could the superior force retain its morale and domestic support long enough to gain victory by exhausting its antagonist? General Ulysses S. Grant proved that attrition could succeed when maneuver failed. Ferdinand Foch, the ultimate victor in the Great War of 1914–18, did not attain success until he grasped the lesson that Grant had learned in the fires of Cold Harbor, Spotsylvania, and Wilderness.

The Civil War provided a glimpse of what lay ahead during World War I, when protracted and general destructive warfare akin to that of 1861–5 decimated a generation of Europeans and wrought unmatched destruction of property. The Union vastly outweighed the Confederacy in human and material resources, but the southerners mounted an inspired strategic defense, drawing on the industrial technology to prolong the conflict beyond

---

8 Gary Gallagher, ed., *Fighting for the Confederacy: The Personal Recollections of General Edward Porter Alexander* (Chapel Hill, N.C., 1989), 415.

any reasonable length in the hope of destroying the will of the Union to persevere. If before or after suffering defeat in conventional warfare General Lee and other Southern leaders had been prepared to engage in guerrilla warfare, a means by which the South could husband scarce resources and wear out the enemy, the war might have ended differently.[9]

Certainly the battles of the Civil War became fodder for intensive analysis at institutions of military education, such as the academies at West Point and Annapolis, and new officer training schools, such as the Naval War College at Newport and the Command and Army Staff College at Fort Leavenworth. However, the curriculum did not stress General Alexander's irrefutable observations about the primacy of the defense and the need to win by attrition. The schools insisted on offensive mobility and maneuver as the means of forcing a decision. In any event, whatever the content of military education, fighting wars never received priority in military and naval thought between Appomattox and the First Battle of the Marne. The armed forces prepared for peace rather than war, emphasizing coastal defense, administration of the western territories, and naval presence in distant waters to show the flag.[10]

In 1898 the United States suddenly acquired a modest insular empire, a by-product of the war with Spain. Historians are divided over the meaning of this event: Did it represent an experiment in the type of imperialism then prevalent among the great Eurasian powers? Whatever the meaning of the new empire in the Caribbean Sea and the western Pacific Ocean, it did not engender fundamental changes in the armed forces, nor did it lead to the militarization of society. The tasks of protecting and administering the new empire did not represent basic changes in the missions of the armed forces. Substantively it proved similar to the stewardship of the moving frontier across the nineteenth century. It was an exercise in peacetime responsibility of considerable importance that provided useful experience for a generation of officers, but it did not markedly alter the national embrace of essentially passive defense, still deemed sufficient to guarantee security from external dangers.[11]

9 A book of great interest is Herman M. Hattaway and Archer Jones, *How the North Won: A Military History of the Civil War* (Urbana, Ill., 1983).

10 The army's preoccupation with Indian affairs in the West is best chronicled in Robert M. Utley, *Frontier Regulars: The United States Army and the Indian, 1866–1891* (New York, 1973). See also Utley's chapter in this book (Chapter 17).

11 Two modern accounts are by David F. Trask, *The War with Spain in 1898* (New York, 1981), and Graham A. Cosmas, *An Army for Empire: The United States Army in the Spanish-American War* (Columbia, Mo., 1971). A recent study in wartime diplomacy is by John L. Offner, *An Unwanted War: The Diplomacy of the United States and Spain over Cuba, 1895–1898* (Chapel Hill, N.C., 1992).

Between 1880 and 1914, particularly after the war with Spain, a notable interest in reform of the armed forces, especially a preoccupation with professionalization, affected a goodly number of ambitious younger career soldiers and sailors. Participants in this movement looked to Eurasian armed forces, notably Great Britain's Royal Navy and Germany's Wilhelmian army, for new models to guide reform, including reorganization of the war and navy departments. Among other things, the reformers studied fighting wars to a much greater extent than had officers of earlier years, a significant harbinger of things to come, but little resulted from it at the time. Although the army established a general staff in 1903, it bore no resemblance to the German counterpart or to others in Europe. The navy finally received a chief of naval operations in 1915, but like the army's changes, this departure meant little at the time. The behavior of the executive and legislative branches of government in dealing with national security remained easily identifiable with that of the latter nineteenth century, although some success was attained in efforts to enlarge the battle fleet.[12]

Any comparison of the American services with those of the other great powers as of 1914 regarding armament, equipment, organization, size, strategy, tactics, and training reveals their commitment to the traditional peacetime missions. It also reflects backwardness and weakness in the ability to wage war against powerful opponents. This generalization is all the more cogent if we compare the American armed forces with those of the belligerents at the beginning of 1917. Although various forward-thinking officers and civilians interested in national defense during the generation before World War I predicted the difficulties that might stem from a disintegration of the Eurasian balance of power, advocates of far-reaching changes in national security policy attracted little attention. They failed to stimulate the manifold reform required to strengthen the armed forces so that they could wage war on reasonable terms with any of the great powers.[13]

Much attention has been given to the notion of an "American way" of fighting wars, especially in the writings of the leading American military historian Russell F. Weigley, and properly so. But this aspect of the American military imagination should not obscure the dominance of the old national security paradigm described earlier among responsible statesmen and their military advisers. This fact mirrored the prevailing conviction that the

---

12 A fine account of the reform movement is to be found in James L. Abrahamson, *American Arms for a New Century: The Making of a Great Power* (New York, 1981).

13 For information on the state of the armed forces when the United States intervened in World War I, see David F. Trask, *The AEF and Coalition Warmaking, 1917–1918* (Lawrence, Kans., 1993), 1–28.

United States need not concern itself with the troubles of the Old World or maintain powerful armed forces. However much the Americans decried the militarism and imperialism they observed in Eurasia, they showed no inclination to do anything about it. They refused to abandon their traditional commitments to political isolation and passive defense.[14]

Such was the prevailing situation in the United States when World War I began, and, even after a year or so of bloodshed, few Americans suspected that a revolutionary change in national security policies impended. Nevertheless, President Woodrow Wilson proved capable of making a sound estimate of the European conflict and of initiating unexampled alterations in national security policy. Despite thirty years and more of modern scholarship, which has clarified the evolution of Wilson's statecraft from 1914 to 1917, all too many textbooks and popular histories preserve the myth that the United States intervened in World War I because Germany refused to forgo unrestricted submarine warfare (attack without warning) against peaceful maritime commerce on the high seas. Thankfully, very few still echo another venerable misinterpretation, the contention that American entanglement in the economies of the Allied powers explains the intervention of 1917. Neither Germany's unrestricted submarine warfare nor the expansion of American trade with the Allies mandated intervention against the Central Powers. Wilson did not decide his course on either of these grounds.[15]

The president's commitment to traditional neutrality when the war began reflects the dominance of political isolation and passive defense as late as 1914. There was no instant recognition that general warfare in western Eurasia – that is, a war over the hegemony of the region – might eventually pose unprecedented threats to vital national interests and aspirations. Little in public opinion or in the activities of the federal government during the first months of warfare suggested that the nation might intervene in the European struggle. This was understandable because at the beginning, it was waged with the conviction that the war, although violent, would be

14 For Russell F. Weigley's views, see his influential work, *The American Way of War: A History of United States Military Strategy and Policy* (New York, 1973).
15 For the leading work on the United States and the submarine controversy, see Ernest R. May, *The World War and American Isolation, 1914–1917* (Chicago, 1966). Charles C. Tansill helped publicize the economic motive in *America Goes to War* (Boston, 1938). For a more detailed exposition of my views on Wilson's policy, see David F. Trask, "Woodrow Wilson and the Reconciliation of Force and Diplomacy," *Naval War College Review* 27 (Jan.–Feb. 1975): 23–31, and "Woodrow Wilson and International Statecraft: A Modern Assessment," *Naval War College Review* 36 (Mar.–Apr. 1983): 57–68.

short. The short-war illusion prevailed in Washington as in the capitals of the belligerents. Soon the demand for American goods stimulated the economy without altering the presumption that the United States would maintain neutrality. Even the controversy over the rights of neutrals and noncombatants on the high seas, which stemmed from German submarine depredations, did not decisively modify the public mood.

Nevertheless Wilson was remarkably quick to recognize the possible consequences of protracted total war in western Eurasia. It was evident that instability in the Old World would stunt the emergence of democratic institutions everywhere, a development that many Americans deemed more or less ordained by history and even by God. Another was less obvious: Wilson sensed that total war, an extended struggle to the death with extraordinarily destructive modern armaments, would be ruinous to all the belligerents, regardless of who won. The toll on the victorious would be comparable to that on the vanquished. There could be no victory in the conventional sense at the conclusion of a struggle that attained the lethality and destructiveness that new military technology made possible. A third insight also helped the president decide the nation's national security policy: He saw that instability in the international balance of power would sooner or later implicate the United States in warfare, particularly if it should create a threat of hegemony at either or both extremities of Eurasia. Only the acquisition of such hegemony could generate the resources required to overwhelm the strong defensive capabilities of the United States, in which case the republic might have to wage a desperate struggle for survival.

Wilson shared the enduring American hatred of war as a means of resolving political tensions. Although he was no pacifist, he was deeply committed to peaceful resolution of conflict through the workings of the democratic process. Violence was acceptable only as a last resort. Nevertheless, Wilson quickly learned that he could neither influence the behavior of the great powers nor guarantee the vital interests of the United States if he failed to undertake a vast alteration in national security policies.[16]

One possible adjustment to the danger was to mount an active hemispheric defense, a shift from passivity but one that presumed continuing in-

---

16 For an arresting treatment of Wilson's views on the relations between force and diplomacy, see Frederick S. Calhoun, *Power and Principle: Armed Intervention in Wilsonian Foreign Policy* (Kent, Ohio, 1986). This work completes the tendency to reinterpret Wilson's statecraft as having realistic as well as idealistic aspects. The critical views of the "power realists," often conservative in outlook, are summarized in Lloyd E. Ambrosius, *Wilsonian Statecraft: Theory and Practice of Liberal Internationalism During World War I* (Wilmington, Del., 1991).

sulation from aggression without tremendous changes. Discussions within the Wilsonian circle concerning the prevailing inter-American system could have led to this course, but events buried any such possibility.[17]

Only a few months after the beginning of the war, Wilson decided to depart from strict neutrality; he undertook a sustained secret attempt to mediate the European conflict. Far too little attention has been paid to this effort, whereas too much attention has been given to the more public and dramatic controversy over submarine warfare. Edward M. House, the president's most trusted confidant, made his most important contribution to the administration by serving as the president's intermediary on behalf of American mediation, maintaining contacts with both sets of belligerents by means of visits to Europe, confidential contacts in New York City, and extensive correspondence.

The American effort to mediate the war, despite its impracticality, led quickly to the most important changes in national security policies in the nation's history. The decisions to intervene in World War II and later to wage the Cold War, however difficult, were easier to make than Wilson's decision to abandon political isolation. Moreover, the decisions of 1941 and 1947 represented an extension of Wilson's support of powerful intervention in Eurasia.

The president's repudiation of political isolation in favor of political intervention in Eurasian affairs began without public support or knowledge. Wilson's effort to mediate the war secretly continued until late in 1916. In December, after his narrow re-election, Wilson abandoned his secretive approach and asked all the belligerents to state their war aims publicly, hoping to uncover a political formula acceptable to both coalitions that would lead to mediation.

The failure of the belligerents to accept mediation of the Eurasian conflict forced Wilson to take further steps. At first he had lacked a comprehensive conception of the international political reforms that would have to follow the war. In 1915, however, he committed himself to the creation of new international institutions to manage the peace – that is, he decided to advocate international political arrangements designed to maintain a stable balance of power but also intended to encourage gradual but far-reaching reforms that would do away with the underlying causes of war and foster democracy in Eurasia. The initiative of 1915 expanded over time into the concept of the League of Nations. This organization would

---

17 For Wilson's Latin American policy, see Mark T. Gilderhus, *Pan-American Visions: Woodrow Wilson in the Western Hemisphere, 1913–1921* (Tucson, Ariz., 1986).

guarantee to all peoples the democratic principle of self-determination. It would also keep the peace, relying on collective security, a scheme designed to correct the impermanence and inequity of traditional balance-of-power politics as practiced by Metternich and Bismarck. International reform would flow from long-term international cooperation through the operations of various organizations set up to manage such concerns as public health, labor, and international trade.

The president once referred to his plan as simply an extension of the Monroe Doctrine to the entire world, an attempt to render intervention palatable to his countrymen and also to underline the importance of self-determination and international cooperation as essential elements in a world without war. For Wilson, the Great War had become a war to end all wars. He recognized that warfare had become impossibly destructive. He also sensed that because of the primacy of defense, armed forces could not force a decision quickly enough to avoid unacceptable losses to all parties to the conflict. War had become obsolete because it no longer could assure a successful victory. The appeal of the league lay in its obvious compatibility with democratic theory and practice – self-determination, majority rule, respect for minorities, and so forth.

Wilson's innovations in national security policy did not end with his commitment to active and sustained intervention in the politics of Eurasia. In 1916 he adopted a new conception of national defense, one that was as significant as his turn to intervention. He took this step largely because he came to recognize that his efforts to mediate the Great War had foundered in great part because the American armed forces were too weak to lend credibility to his diplomacy. Two of the most significant pieces of national security legislation in the nation's history, both adopted in 1916, began the process of abandoning passive defense. The Wilsonian conversion to preparedness in 1916 was embodied in the National Defense Act, which envisioned a radically improved army, and in the Naval Act, which for the first time obligated the nation to build a navy second to none. These measures represented a definitive rejection of the idea that the United States and its neighbors in the Americas were secure from danger regardless of the politics of Eurasia and could depend for protection principally on the isolated insular position of the United States. Unstable international politics dictated the shift from passive to *active* defense.[18]

---

18 Most students of the preparedness movement see its causation as stemming from domestic political influences rather than from the external pressures noted here. Both elements obviously played a part. See John P. Finnegan, *Against the Specter of a Dragon: The Campaign for American Military Preparedness, 1914–1917* (Westport, Conn., 1974).

Well before the United States intervened on the side of the Allies, Wilson committed himself to a revolutionary revision of the nation's cardinal national security policies. His secret attempt to mediate the war and his conversion to huge, powerful, and highly professional armed forces dedicated largely to the mission of fighting wars add up to revolutionary change. Early in 1917, when Germany resumed unrestricted submarine warfare, Wilson finally acknowledged the improbability of imposing mediation on the belligerents. He went to war because he realized that only by armed intervention could he hope to dictate a desirable peace settlement to both coalitions. The submarine issue determined the timing of the American entry, but it did not cause it.[19]

Although the nation subverted the Wilsonian revolution during the interwar years, beginning with the refusal of the Congress to endorse the Treaty of Versailles, the experiences of World War II and the Cold War eventually formed a broad national consensus in support of dynamic intervention in Eurasian affairs and active defense policies based on credible capability to fight wars – that is, the ability to challenge the strongest military formations in Eurasia. The new national security paradigm, first conceived during World War I – political intervention in Eurasia and active defense – finally gained public acceptance, confirming the wisdom of Woodrow Wilson.[20]

The old national security paradigm – political isolation and passive defense – was peculiarly compatible with the nation's insular location and distance from Eurasia during the nineteenth century. It also comported with democratic ideology, much more easily adopted by insular countries with strong naval forces than by continental nations in Eurasia with powerful land forces. The presence of dangerous antagonists on one's borders makes it difficult to survive without active diplomacy supported by military and naval strength. Sustained international crises surely encourage authoritarian government and its proclivity for militarism and imperialism, a lesson that Americans learned at a terrible price during the sustained violence of the

19 For a detailed interpretation of these matters, see David F. Trask, *The United States in the Supreme War Council: American War Aims and Inter-Allied Strategy, 1917–1918* (Middletown, Conn., 1961), chap. 1, and David F. Trask, *Captains and Cabinets: Anglo-American Naval Relations, 1917–1918* (Columbia, Mo., 1972), chap. 1.

20 For a negative assessment of Wilson, emphasizing his presumed lack of realism in the sense of post-World War II historians who adopted the views of Morgenthau and Kennan, see Ambrosius, *Wilsonian Statecraft*. The New Left revisionist school generally portrays the United States as a counterrevolutionary power. It has not devoted much attention to World War I, but see N. Gordon Levin Jr., *Woodrow Wilson and World Politics: America's Response to War and Revolution* (New York, 1968). For a middle-ground analysis favorable to Wilson, see the various works by Arthur S. Link, the leading student of the wartime president.

years from 1914 to 1945 and the deep commitment to the deterrence of the Soviet Union and its allies between 1945 and 1990. Wilson's support of a strong army and a great navy reflected the fact that the United States possessed the capabilities of a continental land power as well as an insular naval power and could behave in both capacities to counter hegemonic enterprises originating from Eurasia.[21]

Any examination of the American military imagination must consider the sharp change in requirements for national security that occurred at the time of World War I. Only then did fighting wars become a primary concern of the American defense establishment, military and civil. The peacetime missions that dominated during the long century after Napoleon lost their centrality during the "second thirty years' war" that devastated large regions of Eurasia between 1914 and 1945. The best proof of its destructiveness is the length of its aftermath, the Cold War, extending to the last decade of the twentieth century. American contributions to the intellectual arsenal of war have gained international significance and acceptance only during the past fifty years, after the nation finally accepted a major role in the maintenance of the international balance. Before then, military thought in the United States appeared relevant only to affairs in the western hemisphere. After 1914, when the United States was perforce required to think and act as a leading land power involved in world politics, its military activities attracted much attention elsewhere as well as at home.[22]

The American people have never felt fully comfortable with the new national security paradigm. The recent practice of forming coalitions composed of other naval powers and land powers threatened by dangerous neighbors and of controlling or neutralizing the Afro-Asian rimlands – a task formerly undertaken by Great Britain – ameliorates to a measurable degree the requirements of active diplomacy and defense, a luxury not granted to Eurasian continental powers. When an opportunity to relax from the rigors of world politics occurs, neo-isolationist sentiments quickly emerge in one guise or another, be it in the views of a George McGovern or a Ronald Reagan. Because a recognizable balance of power now

---

21 This view of the differing circumstances of land powers and sea powers is well treated in Clark Reynolds, *Command of the Sea: The History and Strategy of Maritime Empires* (New York, 1973).

22 The conception of a second "Thirty Years' War" first came to my attention just after World War II in the work of the émigré scholar Sigmund Neumann, who discussed the subject in *The Future in Perspective* (New York, 1946). This broad view of war in the twentieth century still is not firmly established in the United States, perhaps because America's brief experience in World War I has obscured its significance and its connection to World War II. The later struggle can be viewed as a second violent episode in the same extended war. American preoccupation with World War II has inadvertently kept many historians of national security affairs from developing an international vision of organized violence in the twentieth century.

exists, it discourages real or presumed hegemonic enterprises such as those of 1914, 1939, 1941, or 1947. It does not appear likely, however, that international conditions in the foreseeable future will alter to the extent of permitting a return to anything remotely resembling the isolation and passivity of earlier years. Much may change, but American entanglement in Eurasian affairs is likely to continue at a significant level.

15

Dreams and Nightmares

German Military Leadership and the Images of Future Warfare, 1871–1914

STIG FÖRSTER

A SHORT-WAR ILLUSION?

In August 1914 the generals of continental Europe's great powers led their armies into huge offensives in order to win a decisive strategic advantage over their opponents with one mighty blow. By mid-September, however, all these offensives had failed disastrously. What followed were four years of seemingly endless catastrophic warfare that, particularly since 1916, had turned into something akin to total war.[1] When that war was over there were no real victors, at least as far as Europe was concerned. France and Great Britain, to be sure, could celebrate military victory. But almost like the losers, they had suffered catastrophic economic, financial, and demographic losses. Moreover, in the following decade they had to face political and social unrest as a result of the war effort, and their standings as world powers were mortally damaged. One thing was clear: After the "Great War" Europe would never be the same.

Why did that catastrophe happen? Why were Europe's military leaders, who prior to 1914 regarded themselves as the best professionals in the world, unable to prevent the disaster of a long war? These are questions that from the fall of 1914 up to the present day have been hotly debated among soldiers and historians. Particularly in Germany – a country that had to fight on several fronts against superior numbers and against the superior resources of its enemies, that was supported only by weak allies and faced a damaging naval blockade, and that therefore was bound to lose a war of at-

---

1 The question of "How total was World War I?" will be addressed in the next book in this series. See Roger Chickering and Stig Förster, eds., *Great War, Total War: Combat and Mobilization on the Western Front, 1914–1918* (forthcoming).

trition – the debate on whether there was a chance to win a rapid military victory and thus avoid being bled to death gained special importance.

Immediately after the Battle of the Marne, which ended all German dreams of a rapid victory on the western front, arguments erupted as to whether an incompetent military leadership had bungled an excellent chance to annihilate the French army. The former chief of the General Staff, Helmuth von Moltke the Younger, who had lost his position as a result of the Marne defeat, staged a fruitless defense of his actions in August and September. He blamed the lack of support by the Kaiser and hinted that the German offensive was eventually bound to fail against superior numbers.[2] But this was to no avail. After the war, critics lambasted Moltke for having squandered certain victory. The official German publication on the campaigns of World War I blamed Moltke for having ordered a retreat when the army had already won the battle.[3] Even fiercer was the attack by Germany's last military leader during the war, Wilhelm Groener, who criticized Moltke for having changed important parts of the otherwise "ingenious" strategic plan of his predecessor, Count Alfred von Schlieffen. These changes, along with Moltke's bungling in 1914, allegedly destroyed an otherwise infallible recipe for victory.[4] In other words, a rapid victory to avoid the disasters of a drawn-out war would have been possible had it not been for Moltke's incompetence.

This bemoaning of a "missed chance" by disappointed officers and nationalists led historians to look deeper into Germany's strategic planning before 1914. In particular, the Schlieffen Plan, which during the 1920s and 1930s had become legendary, fascinated historians. Gerhard Ritter was not only the first to publish all the relevant documents but also to analyze thoroughly the significance of that strategic plan. In contrast to Groener and all the other creators of the Schlieffen legend, however, Ritter rigorously criticized Schlieffen's operational planning and the willingness of the Younger Moltke as well as of Germany's politicians to go along with such a risky and unbalanced strategy. Ritter therefore concluded that the disaster of August and September 1914 came about because Germany's military and

2 Helmuth von Moltke, "Betrachtungen und Erinnerungen" (Nov. 1914), in Eliza von Moltke, ed., *Generaloberst Helmuth von Moltke: Erinnerungen, Briefe, Dokumente, 1877–1916* (Stuttgart, 1922), 8–28.
3 Reichsarchiv, ed., *Der Weltkrieg 1914 bis 1918,* 12 vols. (Berlin, 1925–1939), 4:508–43, esp. 542.
4 Wilhelm Groener, *Das Testament des Grafen Schlieffen* (Berlin, 1930). In a private note from 1935 Groener emphasized that Schlieffen would never have agreed to the changes that Moltke, the deputy Stein, and Ludendorff made to the original plan, namely, their idea to weaken the offensive right wing of the German army on the western front in order to reinforce the defenses in the south. Bundesarchiv-Militärarchiv (hereafter BA-MA, Freiburg), Freiburg im Breisgau, N-46, Groener papers, no. 51: "Zum Schlieffenplan."

political leadership followed Schlieffen's hazardous short-war strategy. According to Ritter, therefore, it was precisely the weaknesses of the Schlieffen Plan itself that led to its failure in 1914 and that made the long war, which it sought to prevent, a certainty.[5] Thus the notion of the "short-war illusion," according to which the German military leadership single-mindedly planned for a short war of annihilation that would destroy the French army within a couple of weeks, began to dominate historiographical thinking about the military origins of World War I. Generations of historians accepted the arguments of Ritter's influential book.[6] L. L. Farrar even made *The Short War Illusion* the title of his study of the campaigns of the summer and fall of 1914. But he took few pains to investigate more deeply the origins of that notion. Like Ritter, he simply accepted that concept as reality without digging deeper into the social and political background of the alleged short-war ideology and without asking whether there were alternatives.[7] A few historians doubted whether it was really that simple. Lothar Burchardt, for instance, clearly demonstrated that apart from Schlieffen himself, most German military leaders were afraid that a strategy of annihilation and short war might not work.[8] Still, most of Burchardt's colleagues accepted his other arguments about Germany's lack of preparation for extended warfare, as they tended to fit better into the generally accepted picture. Even Jack Snyder, who wrote an excellent analysis of the "ideology of the offensive" in Europe, largely used Burchardt's findings in that way. Snyder came to the conclusion that for French, German, and Russian generals alike, the "unlikely had to be the necessary," meaning that to them there was no alternative to short war.[9] This European dimension was recently taken up by Dieter Storz, who like Snyder claimed that

5 Gerhard Ritter, *Der Schlieffenplan: Kritik eines Mythos* (Munich, 1956). For details of Ritter's criticism, see the following passages in this chapter.

6 As examples, see Jehuda Wallach, *Das Dogma der Vernichtungsschlacht: Die Lehren von Clausewitz und Schlieffen und ihre Wirkungen in zwei Weltkriegen* (Frankfurt am Main, 1967); Gunther E. Rothenberg, "Moltke, Schlieffen, and the Doctrine of Strategic Envelopment," in Peter Paret, ed., *Makers of Modern Strategy from Machiavelli to the Nuclear Age* (Princeton, N.J., 1986), 296–325; Detlef Bald, "Zum Kriegsbild der militärischen Führung im Kaiserreich," in Jost Dülffer and Karl Holl, eds., *Bereit zum Krieg: Kriegsmentalitäten im wilhelminischen Deutschland 1890–1914* (Göttingen, 1986), 146–59. Many others could be cited here. In a recent article, Jost Dülffer argues that at least the army leadership hoped for a short war. But Dülffer also points out that many contemporaries felt uneasy about taking a brief and victorious war for granted. Jost Dülffer, "Kriegserwartung und Kriegsbild vor 1914," in Wolfgang Michalka, ed., *Der erste Weltkrieg: Wirkung, Wahrnehmung, Analyse* (Munich, 1994), 778–98, esp. 778–9, 794.

7 L. L. Farrar, *The Short-War Illusion: German Policy, Strategy, and Domestic Affairs August–December 1914* (Oxford, 1973).

8 Lothar Burchardt, *Friedenswirtschaft und Kriegsvorsorge: Deutschlands wirtschafiliche Rüstungsbestrebungen vor 1914* (Boppard am Rhein, 1968), and subsequent passages in this chapter.

9 Jack Snyder, *The Ideology of the Offensive: Military Decision-Making and the Disasters of 1914* (Ithaca, N.Y., 1984), 9–31, 41–54, 155, 164.

military leaders all over Europe rejected the idea of defensive warfare out of fear of a long war.[10]

With respect to the role of the German army's leadership, in particular the General Staff, many historians went even further. The well-known episodes of warmongering by the General Staff, which at virtually every large-scale international crisis since 1871 demanded that the political leaders wage pre-emptive war against France and Russia, have always been of historiographical interest.[11] But it was the role of the Younger Moltke, who from 1911 pressed increasingly for war and who at the height of the July Crisis in 1914 forced the German government "to press the button," that gained most attention. Several historians interpreted Moltke's aggressive stance as the result of his increasing fear that the Schlieffen Plan might be invalidated by the military buildup. As Germany was about to lose the arms race, the argument goes, Moltke looked for an opportunity to carry out the strategic plans of the General Staff before it was too late. The Schlieffen Plan therefore developed from a recipe for victory into a major cause of war. Under these circumstances the short-war illusion not only made it easier for politicians and generals to resort to arms but in itself forced them to unleash a war that proved uncontrollable.[12]

This argument appears to be rather convincing. Indeed, I myself pursued a similar line when I analyzed the Schlieffen Plan and its influence on German armament policy.[13] Yet I always felt doubts about whether Germany's military leadership after 1906 really did pin all its hopes on such a clearly flawed strategy. Were they indeed stuck in a short-war illusion and misled by undue optimism about the feasibility of a strategy for rapid victory? After all, my subsequent studies on the Elder Moltke showed that up to the 1890s such optimistic notions did not exist in the General Staff.[14]

---

10 Dieter Storz, *Kriegsbild und Rüstung vor 1914: Europäische Landstreitkräfte vor dem Ersten Weltkrieg* (Herford, 1992), 372.

11 See, e.g., Karl-Ernst Jeismann, *Das Problem des Präventivkrieges im europäischen Staatensystem, mit besonderem Blick auf die Bismarckzeit* (Munich, 1959), and Albrecht Moritz, *Das Problem des Präventivkrieges in der deutschen Politik während der ersten Marokkokrise* (Bern, 1974).

12 See, e.g., Fritz Fischer, *Krieg der Illusionen: Die deutsche Politik von 1911 bis 1914*, 2d ed. (Düsseldorf, 1969), 565–84; Adolf Gasser, "Deutschlands Entschluss zum Präventivkrieg 1913–14," in Marc Sieber, ed., *Discordia concors: Festschrift für Edgar Bonjour zu seimem 70. Geburtstag am 21. August 1968* (Basel, 1968), 171–224; Adolf Gasser, "Der deutsche Hegemonialkrieg von 1914," in Immanuel Geiss and Bernd-Jürgen Wendt, eds., *Deutschland in der Weltpolitik des 19. und 20. Jahrhunderts: Festschrift für Fritz Fischer zum 65. Geburtstag* (Düsseldorf, 1973), 307–40; John G. C. Röhl, "Die Generalprobe: Zur Geschichte und Bedeutung des 'Kriegsrats' vom 8. Dezember 1912," in Dirk Stegmann, Bernd-Jürgen Wendt, and Peter Christian Witt, eds., *Industrielle Gesellschaft und politisches System: Beiträge zur politischen Sozialgeschichte: Festschrift für Fritz Fischer zum 70. Geburtstag* (Bonn, 1978), 357–73; James Joll, *The Origins of the First World War* (London, 1984), 81–4.

13 Stig Förster, *Der doppelte Militarismus: Die deutsche Heeresrüstungspolitik zwischen Status-quo-Sicherung und Aggression 1890–1913* (Stuttgart, 1985), 158–65.

14 Stig Förster, "Facing 'People's War': Moltke the Elder and Germany's Military Options After 1871," *Journal of Strategic Studies* 10 (1987): 209–30; Stig Förster, "Helmuth von Moltke und das Problem

At that time, visions about future warfare had been very pessimistic and, as events were to demonstrate, rather realistic. In his last speech in the Reichstag, on May 14, 1890, Moltke had warned the public that any major war would bring catastrophe to Europe:

The age of cabinet war is behind us – all we have now is people's war. . . . Gentlemen, if the war that has been hanging over our heads now for more than ten years like the Sword of Damocles – if this war breaks out, then its duration and its end will be unforeseeable. The greatest powers of Europe, armed as never before, will be going into battle with each other; not one of them can be crushed so completely in one or two campaigns that it will admit defeat, be compelled to conclude peace under hard terms, and will not come back, even if it is a year later, to renew the struggle. Gentlemen, it may be a war of seven years' or of thirty years' duration – and woe to him who sets Europe alight, who first puts the fuse to the powder keg![15]

Moltke was not the only one to warn of disaster. In 1887 the military analyst Friedrich Engels had written of a

world war of never before seen extension and intensity, if the system of mutual outbidding in armament, carried to the extreme, finally bears its natural fruits. . . eight to ten million soldiers will slaughter each other and strip Europe as bare as no swarm of locusts has ever done before. The devastation of the Thirty Years' War condensed in three to four years and spread all over the continent; famine, epidemics, general barbarization of armies and the masses, provoked by sheer desperation; utter chaos in our trade, industry, and commerce, ending in general bankruptcy; collapse of the old states and their traditional wisdom in such a way that the crowns will roll in the gutter by the dozens and there will be nobody to pick them up; absolute impossibility to foresee how all this will end and who will be victors in that struggle; only one result was absolutely certain: general exhaustion and the creation of circumstances for the final victory of the working class.[16]

Other warnings came from the Polish banker Ivan Bloch, who in his monumental analysis rather correctly predicted the disastrous nature of a major war in Europe.[17] Should the German generals, who subsequently were in charge, really have ignored such warnings, especially when they came from the admired war hero Moltke the Elder? Should these professionals really have understood less about the nature of future warfare than "amateurs" such as Engels and Bloch? This seems to be rather unlikely, and it therefore will be the task of this chapter to investigate the validity of the

des industrialisierten Volkskriegs im 19. Jahrhundert," in Roland G. Foerster, ed., *Generalfeldmarschall von Moltke: Bedeutung und Wirkung* (Munich, 1991), 103–16; Stig Förster, *Moltke: Vom Kabinettskrieg zum Volkskrieg: Eine Werkauswahl* (Bonn, 1992).

15 *Stenographische Berichte über die Verhandlungen des Reichstages 1890–1* (Berlin, 1892), 114:76–7.

16 Karl Marx and Friedrich Engels, *Werke*, ed. Institut für Marxismus-Leninismus beim Zentralkomitee der Sozialistische Einheitspartei Deutschlands, 39 vols. (Berlin, 1958–68), 21:350–54.

17 Johann von Bloch, *Der Krieg*, 6 vols. (Berlin, 1899).

"short-war illusion," particularly for the thinking of the German General Staff, which was solely responsible for operational planning.

The underlying question of this analysis has to be what the General Staff and other leading officers between 1871 and 1914 thought about the nature of warfare in their time. As shown previously, the Elder Moltke was convinced that a "people's war" was the order of the day. Others, like his disciple Colmar von der Goltz, fully agreed with him and spoke of an "age of people's war" that determined the character of future warfare.[18] Clearly many German officers were shell-shocked by the experience of the second half of the Franco-Prussian War, when staunch French resistance had demonstrated that even the most brilliant victories over a regular army were not sufficient to force the enemy nation quickly into submission.[19] As the threat of war on two fronts – against France and Russia – steadily increased, the problem of people's war gained an increasingly dangerous significance.

In 1937, when discussing Erich Ludendorff's book *Der totale Krieg*,[20] General Groener wrote: "In my opinion total war developed out of universal conscription and was intensified by the improvements in technology."[21] Conscription and technology were the two main ingredients of an industrialized people's war since the mid-nineteenth century. They had determined the nature of the American Civil War and the Franco-Prussian War, and they were to dominate German military thinking between 1871 and 1914.[22] But did they convince the German generals that total war was looming?

THE UNWINNABLE GAME, 1871–1895

In his interesting article, "German Grand Strategy," Dennis E. Showalter recently traced the origins of the blitzkrieg concept. He came to the conclusion that the idea of short, sharp campaigns using maximal force to

---

18 Colmar von der Goltz, *Das Volk in Waffen*, 2d ed. (Berlin, 1883), 17.

19 In his book on the leader of French republican resistance against the German invaders, Goltz made it clear how impressed he was by the power of "people's war," that is, the arming of a whole nation and its fight against all odds. See Colmar von der Goltz, *Léon Gambetta und seine Armeen* (Berlin, 1877). Goltz's overenthusiastic hailing of the archenemy, however, did not sit well with conservatives in the War Ministry and the Kaiser's entourage. He was severely reprimanded and his career almost came to an end, but a sympathetic Moltke protected Goltz. Friedrich Freiherr von der Goltz and Wolfgang Foerster, eds., *Generalfeldmarschall Colmar Freiherr von der Goltz: Denkwürdigkeiten* (Berlin, 1929), 105.

20 Erich Ludendorff, *Der totale Krieg* (Munich, 1935).

21 Wilhelm Groener, "Ludendorffs *Totaler Krieg*," unpublished manuscript, BA-MA, Freiburg, N-46, Groener papers, no. 60.

22 See the introduction to Stig Förster and Jörg Nagler, eds., *On the Road to Total War: The American Civil War and the German Wars of Unification, 1861–1871* (New York, 1997).

achieve limited strategic and political aims within a limited period of time had always been at the core of the Prussian and later on the German tradition of strategic thinking: "The German heritage, properly understood, is a heritage of total force applied in limited ways for limited objectives."[23] Indeed, situated in the middle of Europe, hemmed in by at least three great powers (France, Austria, and Russia), and possessing rather limited manpower and material resources, Prussia since the days of Frederick the Great had never been in a position to afford protracted warfare.[24] Hence, a quick campaign to punish the enemy without demanding too much of him in subsequent peace negotiations became the ideal of the Prussian mode of warfare.

It was the Elder Moltke who modernized and perfected that system. Making practical use of an otherwise rather narrow-minded understanding of Clausewitz's analysis *On War,* Moltke made the principle of annihilation the centerpiece of his strategy.[25] In the campaigns of 1866 and 1870 he went for a rapid and, as far as possible, complete destruction of the main body of the enemy's regular army. The battles of Sadowa and even more so of Sedan were the hallmarks of this strategy. All this fit neatly into Bismarck's policy of limited war aims (at least against Austria) and therefore was a strategy for modern "cabinet war," as Moltke later put it.[26]

But one of the decisive preconditions for Moltke's victories was numerical superiority. Moltke was lucky in the fact that in the 1860s only Prussia had a system of more or less universal conscription. Hence, Prussia (and in 1870 its German allies, which in the meantime had introduced conscription as well) possessed the "stronger battalions" against Austria and imperial France. It was only a question of using this force efficiently enough to crush a weaker enemy in one decisive blow. Under these circumstances conscription worked as a tool to shorten campaigns.

A second factor that helped Moltke was the fact that the Western world experienced at that time the dawning of industrialized warfare. Most important of all, the logistical problem of transporting and supplying mass armies efficiently and rapidly could be solved by making use of the new rail-

---

23 Dennis E. Showalter, "German Grand Strategy: A Contradiction in Terms?" *Militärgeschichtliche Mitteilungen* 48 (1990): 66.

24 Prussia survived the Seven Years' War only with financial support from Britain and sheer luck. See Gerhard Ritter, *Staatskunst und Kriegshandwerk: Das Problem des "Militarismus" in Deutschland,* 4 vols. (Munich, 1954–68), 1:44–9, and Theodor Schieder, *Friedrich der Grosse: Ein Königtum der Widersprüche* (Frankfurt am Main, 1983), 170–223.

25 Carl von Clausewitz, *On War,* ed. and trans. Michael Howard and Peter Paret (Princeton, N.J., 1976), esp. books 1 and 8.

26 Helmuth von Moltke, "Über den angeblichen Kriegsrath in den Kriegen König Wilhelms I" (1880–81), in Förster, ed., *Moltke,* 129–37.

roads. Nobody understood this better than Moltke. Progress in weapons technology (breech-loading rifles at Sadowa and modernized field artillery in 1870) also came to the aid of Prussia's armies.[27] Improvements in fire-power, on the other hand, also meant a strengthening of the tactical defense against the offense. Drawing from experience in the war against Denmark, Moltke himself concluded wisely and early enough that attacks across open fields against well-covered bodies of infantry armed with breech-loading rifles had become suicidal. But in his time Moltke was still able to devise an offensive strategy that would force the enemy on the tactical offense by outflanking him. After the failure of such an attack and after the enemy had suffered severe losses, the Prussians would successfully counterattack and thereby continue their strategic advance.[28]

All in all, Moltke was the man to adapt the Prussian mode of warfare to the period of industrialized cabinet war: short, aggressive campaigns of annihilation based on conscription and a skillful use of modern technology. The results not only were shining victories on the battlefield but also, perhaps more important, were brief wars that saved Prussia from economic, social, and political upheavals as well as from the intervention of hitherto neutral powers. The short-war concept had become reality most brilliantly in 1866.

But after the battle of Sedan that concept came to a sudden end. As Germany's political and military leaders overstretched the limitations of their war aims, they forced the new republican regime in France to continue fighting. Gambetta and Freynicet organized a *levée en masse* by introducing full-scale conscription and waged a people's war against the invaders. In consequence, the war dragged on for another six months, during which twelve more battles were fought and the German armies reached the limits of their capabilities while struggling against the superior, albeit under-trained, numbers of their foes. Moreover, the Germans had to dispatch 100,000 men to protect their lines of communication against French guerrillas. The Germans themselves resorted to atrocities and began a systematic campaign against civilians. Just as in the American Civil War, the demon of industrialized people's war began to raise its ugly head. At the height of the crisis, in winter 1871, Moltke shifted away from the now obviously defunct Prussian mode of warfare and proposed to wage something like total war against the enemy. Using conscription to the fullest extent while giv-

---

27 Dennis E. Showalter, *Railroads and Rifles: Soldiers, Technology, and the Unification of Germany* (Hamden, Conn., 1976). On logistics, see also Martin van Creveld, *Supplying War: Logistics from Wallenstein to Patton* (Cambridge, 1977), 75–108.
28 Helmuth von Moltke, "Bemerkungen über den Einfluss der verbesserten Feuerwaffen auf die Taktik" (1865), in Förster, ed., *Moltke*, 147–63.

ing absolute control over all operations to the military leadership, he wanted to crush France completely. Thus was born the idea of a war of annihilation instead of merely a campaign of annihilation. It is important to note that Bismarck prevented Moltke from carrying out his plans precisely because he feared a further prolongation of the war that might lead to serious disruptions at home and to the intervention of third powers. The year 1871 therefore marked the beginning of the problems facing Germany in any future war: Could a long war be avoided, and how should one react if this danger became reality?[29]

If anything, these problems were bound to be much more serious after 1871. First of all, there was the danger, which after 1890 became reality, that the newly created Reich would face not just one great power in any future war. It was highly unlikely that France would always remain isolated. In terms of strategy and foreign policy, Russia was its natural ally. A war on two fronts, however, would complicate the situation to such a degree that victory might become impossible. The best hope was certainly to smash one of the two enemies first and very quickly in order to deal with the other one later. But was rapid victory still possible in the age of a people's war, when whole nations would be called to arms? Second, very soon after the end of the Franco-Prussian War the French rearmament program started a continental arms race that by far surpassed all previous proportions. Particularly in France, Germany, and Russia the numbers of soldiers under arms increased as continental armies based recruitment on conscription. At the same time (until 1890) arms technology, the railroad system, and fortresses were improved. In this process Germany lost its military advantage against the looming combination of France and Russia. From the German General Staff's point of view, the prospects for the future were bleak indeed.

Until his retirement Moltke attempted twice to solve this problem by demanding a pre-emptive strike. In 1875 he proposed to attack France before it was fully rearmed. In 1887, just before he left office, Moltke and his deputy, Count Alfred von Waldersee (soon to be his successor), asked for pre-emptive war against the growing might of Russia. On both occasions a horrified Bismarck refused.[30]

Moltke did not protest these decisions. The reason was that he had become increasingly uncertain about the feasibility of victory, even after a surprise attack. A careful analysis of his strategic plans after 1871 demon-

---

29 For a detailed analysis of the Prussian leadership's politics during the Franco-Prussian War, see Stig Förster, "The Prussian Triangle of Leadership in the Face of a People's War: A Reassessment of the Conflict Between Bismarck and Moltke, 1870–71," in Förster and Nagler, eds., *On the Road to Total War*, 115–40.

30 For details, see Förster, "Facing People's War," 218–20.

strates that he found it impossible to solve the vexing question of how to achieve rapid and decisive victory in the age of people's war, especially in a war on two fronts. As early as April 27, 1871, Moltke drafted a memorandum on a war against France and Russia, which he already regarded as a likely future scenario. Certainly it would be the best solution if one could defeat the enemies one by one. But, Moltke went on, Germany "could not hope to rid itself quickly of one enemy by a rapid and successful offensive, leaving itself free to deal with the other enemy. We have only just experienced how difficult it is to bring to a close even the most victorious war against France."[31] In the subsequent two decades Moltke worked hard to find a solution. But no matter whether he intended to start a war with an offensive against France or whether (toward the end) he preferred to begin with an attack on Russia, Moltke always came to the same conclusion: Rapid victory over one of the enemies had become impossible.[32]

In his operational plans, Moltke cited the arms race, the French fortress construction program, and the sheer size of Russia as reasons why a rapid and complete victory against one side had become impossible. It is true that the ongoing improvement in firepower gave the tactical defense more and more advantage over the offense. This factor, combined with the growing size of the armies, which made it increasingly difficult to outflank them, especially when they were partially protected by mighty fortresses and entrenchments, left little room for a successful offensive. Even if most generals in Europe deluded themselves with the firm belief that attack was still the best way to fight, it was clear that the situation had become difficult.[33] But as important as these problems were, there was more to it. Warfare's character itself had changed. The experience of the second half of the Franco-Prussian War had demonstrated to the German officers that it was no longer sufficient to smash the enemy's field army. In the age of a people's war, they would have to deal with whole nations that were ready to fight to the last. As Moltke had already indicated in his memorandum of April 27, 1871, this was the main reason why rapid victory and a short-war scenario had become unlikely. And Moltke was not the only one who came to that conclusion. In his influential book *Das Volk in Waffen*, Goltz set out to explain to the general public the military situation and the future of warfare. He certainly did his best to paint an optimistic picture. For in-

---

31 Memorandum, Apr. 27, 1871, reprinted in Förster, *Moltke,* 598–609.
32 For a complete edition of Moltke's operational plans after 1871, see Oberstleutnant a. D. Ferdinand von Schmerfeld, ed., *Graf Moltke: Die Aufmarschpläne 1871–1890* (Berlin, 1929). For an analysis, see Förster, "Facing People's War," 220–2.
33 Storz, *Kriegsbild,* 25–32.

stance, he argued that modern firepower would make wars less bloody and also help to shorten wars, as overall losses of about 10 percent would be sufficient to destroy the fighting power of an army.[34] But this was more a red herring than the true outcome of his analysis. In fact, his book was more a plea to prepare for extended warfare, huge battles, and a war of annihilation than an advocacy for the feasibility of rapid and decisive campaigns.

He began his arguments by pointing out that since 1871 limited warfare had become impossible. Mass armies and the ever-increasing arms race stood against the idea of cabinet war. Moreover, in the age of a people's war whole nations would fight to the very end, mobilizing all their resources. The outcome would be decided by sheer exhaustion. Even on the tactical level, brief and decisive offensive campaigns had become unlikely, as improved fortresses and the increased use of field fortifications even by the attacker slowed down the advance.[35] Goltz wrote that "*it is certain that any war in the future must lose much of the element of mobility that characterized to a large extent our last campaigns.*"[36]

Because under these circumstances war had on all levels become a struggle for the nation's very existence, Goltz demanded that his readers draw radical conclusions. To prepare for such a war was of the utmost importance:

War still serves policy to achieve the latter's aims. But even for limited objectives it has to strive for the complete subjugation of the enemy. This leads necessarily to the decisive use of all means, intellectual as well as material, to subdue the enemy. Even in peacetime it is therefore fully justified to get the existing resources ready for use in the calamity of war.[37]

Conscription was the best way to achieve "the full amalgamation of military and civilian life."[38] Goltz justified this militarization of society with the need to prepare for the possibility of a war of annihilation, as Moltke had demanded in the winter of 1871. Because the enemy under strong leadership might not be ready to accept defeat quickly, a complete occupation of his territory and putting pressure on the civilian population for years could become the only way to achieve final victory.[39]

There was little in Goltz's book that pointed in the direction of a short-war illusion. Far to the contrary, in advocating militarization and a war of annihilation he seemed to head toward total war, that is to say, a war in

34 Goltz, *Volk,* 10–11.
36 Ibid., 146, original emphasis.
38 Ibid., 8.

35 Ibid., 2–17, 138–47.
37 Ibid., 7.
39 Ibid., 415–20.

which all human and material resources are mobilized under the firm leadership of the generals in order to subjugate the enemy once and for all. Indeed, Goltz demanded that the officer corps be given a distinct position in
society and that the military leadership, in case of war, act independently of
the civilian politicians.[40] This was more than just an advocacy of militarism
because it was to serve the aim of total victory.

Still, Goltz did not fully grasp the implications of his plea for total mobilization. In his chapter on supplying war he dealt only with the problem
of how to provide enough food for the field army. The difficulty of feeding the civilian population under the impact of prolonged mass warfare did
not occur to him. Similarly, he treated the problem of supplying ammunition only from a logistical point of view. He did not address the difficulties
of maintaining and increasing industrial production in wartime.[41] Clearly,
Goltz had little understanding of how to run a war economy, a vital part of
total warfare.

Nevertheless, Goltz's book, which appeared under several imprints until
1914, strongly hinted at the need to prepare the general public for a huge
war that might take years. But how could Germany win such a war, especially if it had to fight on two fronts? Goltz's answer was the unlimited use
of force, which pointed in the direction of total warfare. Such a strategy,
however, could not bring rapid results and would therefore threaten Germany not only with a deadly struggle against the superior resources of the
enemies but also confront its economic, social, and political fabric with the
possibility of collapse. It was before this background that Engels, Moltke,
and Bloch developed the horrific scenarios mentioned here. Under these
circumstances, German strategy faced an unwinnable situation.

Some people grew desperate about this problem. Toward the end of his
life Moltke the Elder, who knew better than anybody else that in case of
war victory was impossible, publicly suggested a policy to avoid war altogether. Strong governments should keep the warmongering chauvinists in
all countries under control. Powerful armaments, he hoped, would help
deter any potential aggressor. In other words, Moltke advocated a rather
modern policy of deterrence and abandoned any hopes that a pre-emptive
strike or a strategy to achieve rapid victory were possible.[42] By the 1890s
the general strategic situation and the changed character of modern warfare left no room for the short-war illusion. After almost twenty years of
economic depression that had shattered many hopes of a brilliant future

---

40 Ibid., 44–9, 125–31.   41 Ibid., 386–403.
42 Most prominent, of course, was Moltke's speech in the Reichstag on May 14, 1890. On this and
   other comments that pointed in the same direction, see Förster, "Facing People's War," 222–6.

following German unification,[43] such pessimism was perhaps part of a widespread negative mood. But it was certainly based on detailed knowledge of the facts. It is also true that some irresponsible officers, such as Moltke's successor Waldersee, still toyed with the idea of starting a war regardless of the consequences.[44] But they stood no chance for the moment, given that the Kaiser and the government feared the risks involved. Again, it is also true that more and more generals and politicians, such as general, admiral, and then chancellor Leo von Caprivi, increasingly regarded war as inevitable.[45] But they shied away from the idea of starting it themselves. War had ceased to be an attractive means of policy-making.

How desperate the situation really was became clear once again when in August 1895 the quartermaster of the General Staff, Major General Friedrich Köpke, wrote a memorandum on the chances of a German offensive against France. Köpke pointed out that a rapid and successful campaign had become impossible against the belt of fortresses in eastern France. Moreover, in a war on two fronts Germany could not expect to use numerical superiority against the French. Because any risky operation was doomed to failure and could even lead to disaster, only limited objectives could be reached: "Even with the most offensive spirit . . . nothing more can be achieved than a tedious and bloody crawling forward step by step here and there by way of an ordinary attack in siege style – in order to slowly win some advantages." One had to be content with the fact that "only a sum of partial and small successes" was achievable. Köpke continued:

> In any case, there are sufficient indications that future warfare will look different from the campaign in 1870–1. We cannot expect rapid and decisive victories. Army and nation will have to get used to that thought early on in order to avoid alarming pessimism right at the beginning of the war that could become a great danger for the outcome. Positional warfare in general, the struggle surrounding

43 See Hans Rosenberg, *Grosse Depression und Bismarckzeit: Wirtschaftsablauf, Gesellschaft und Politik in Mitteleuropa* (Berlin, 1967).
44 Waldersee perhaps was a special case. Throughout his career he repeatedly demanded the use of force against the external enemy and the "enemy within." See John C. G. Röhl, *Wilhelm II: Die Jugend des Kaisers 1859–1888* (Munich, 1993), 601–28.
45 See, e.g., Caprivi's memorandum to the Kaiser of Aug. 27, 1891, in Reichsarchiv, ed., *Der Weltkrieg 1914 bis 1918,* 2 vols., supplement to vol. 1: *Kriegsrüstung und Kriegswirtschaft* (Berlin, 1930), 45–50 (hereafter *Kriegsrüstung,* supplements). Here and in his public and secret speeches to justify the armament program of 1892, Chancellor Caprivi expressed his view that war would come anyway and that one should be prepared for it. This not only was propaganda to force his army bill through but also the beginning of a widespread syndrome in Wilhelmine Germany that helped to make war a self-fulfilling prophecy. Cf. Wolfgang J. Mommsen, "The Topos of Inevitable War in Germany in the Decade before 1914," in Volker R. Berghahn and Martin Kitchen, eds., *Germany in the Age of Total War: Essays in Honour of F. L. Carsten* (London, 1981), 23–44. On Caprivi and the army bill of 1892, see Förster, *Militarismus,* 36–57.

long fronts of field fortifications, the siege of large fortresses, must be carried out victoriously. Otherwise we will not be able to achieve success against the French. Hopefully we will then not lack in the necessary intellectual and material preparations and we will, at the decisive moment, be well trained and equipped for this form of fighting.[46]

This clearly was a nightmare scenario because it meant nothing less than a war that could drag on for a very long time and would not end in anything like a shining victory. Instead, Köpke proposed to prepare the army and the general public for the fact that a second Sedan was not in the cards. Clearly, to him the game was unwinnable.

SCHLIEFFEN'S PASSING SHOT, 1891–1912

It is said that the then chief of the General Staff, General Alfred von Schlieffen, found Köpke's arguments on the effects of a frontal offensive against France's fortified border very convincing.[47] But Schlieffen was not prepared to accept them as a verdict that ruled out any possibility of a decisive offensive and a brief, victorious campaign. Instead, throughout his tenure as the head of the General Staff, Schlieffen worked vigorously to find an alternative. As early as the spring of 1891, very much to the anger of his predecessors Moltke and Waldersee, the new man in charge showed signs that he intended to abandon their cherished project of attacking Russia first in case of war.[48] Schlieffen did not believe that anything like a rapid victory was possible in the vast eastern European theater, where the Russian armies could easily withdraw into the interior of their huge country, escaping from German (and Austrian) attempts to encircle and smash them. A weak infrastructure and new Russian fortresses near the border made things even more complicated. Schlieffen therefore was convinced that only the French could be beaten in a short and decisive campaign.[49]

46 This document was lost during the partial destruction of the army archives in Potsdam during World War II. Here I quote from an unpublished manuscript written in the research department of that archive (Kriegsgeschichtliche Forschungsanstalt des Heeres), that survived in the East German military archive. See Dr. Dieckmann, "Der Schlieffenplan," unpublished and unfinished manuscript, Bundesarchiv-Militärarchiv, Abteilung Potsdam (hereafter BA-MA, Potsdam), Bestand Kriegsgeschichtliche Forschungsanstalt des Heeres, W-10, 50220, 53–7.
47 Ibid., 57–8.
48 On the day of his death (Apr. 24, 1891), Moltke expressed his apprehension about Schlieffen's intentions and complained to Waldersee that the Kaiser did not consult him anymore on strategic matters. Moltke was clearly disappointed to be left out in the cold. But his criticism of Schlieffen's new ideas also may have stemmed from his insights into the impossibility of devising a strategy for rapid victory. See Heinrich-Otto Meisner, ed., *Denkwürdigkeiten des General-Feldmarschalls Alfred Grafen Waldersee*, 3 vols. (Berlin, 1923), 2:205.
49 Ritter, *Schlieffenplan*, 19–20.

There is no need to recount in detail here the development of the Schlieffen Plan. Gerhard Ritter has given us an excellent analysis of this story.[50] It will suffice to remember the main facts: In August 1892 Schlieffen decided to shift to the west the emphasis of a strategy for a war on two fronts. But Köpke convinced him that an offensive against the French belt of fortresses would be futile. Hence, on August 2, 1897, Schlieffen for the first time came up with the idea of avoiding these obstacles by attacking along the northern front, thereby breaking the neutrality of Luxembourg and, above all, Belgium. This was supposed to become his passing shot that would solve the strategic dilemma. But it took seven more years before Schlieffen finally decided that this would be the only way. In 1904–5 he surprised his subordinates with the outlines of what would later become his famous plan: The larger part of the German army was to assemble on the right flank, march through Belgium and the southern Netherlands, and outflank the French army to the south. Fourteen years of hard thinking on Germany's strategic dilemma culminated in Schlieffen's *Grosse Denkschrift*, which he handed over to his successor, the Younger Moltke, in January 1906.[51] The old man proposed to go on a breathtaking adventure. Two-thirds of the German army ($33\frac{1}{2}$ corps) were to make up the offensive right wing in the west, while far weaker forces were to take up defensive positions along the Vosgue Mountains and the Upper Rhine. Just one corps was entrusted with the task of defending East Prussia against the expected Russian onslaught. Even the reserve corps and the *Landsturm* were to support the advancing right wing. Schlieffen bet everything on one move.

The main idea of the Schlieffen Plan was to march the offensive right wing through the Low Countries, envelop Paris, and then take the mass of the French army at the rear. The purpose was complete and rapid annihilation. Under no circumstances were the French to be allowed to escape into the interior, as this would lead "to an endless war." Schlieffen made it clear: "The French army must be annihilated."[52]

He therefore intended to reduce the whole campaign to just one huge battle, a Sedan of gigantic proportion. Toward this end he was prepared to break the neutrality of Belgium and the Netherlands, thereby allowing the risk that Britain, whose army he did not take very seriously, might join the war.[53] He also allowed the risk of a French invasion of Alsace and was pre-

---

50 Ibid., 20–45.

51 The original of Schlieffen's memorandum and later additions are printed in ibid., 145–95.

52 Ibid., 157.

53 He intended to deal with any British intervention by either smashing their troops or locking them up (together with the Belgians) in Antwerp. Ibid., 154, 175–6.

pared to let them advance even as far as the Black Forest.[54] Schlieffen
avoided talk about the possible fate of East Prussia, but his intention almost
to denude the eastern front of troops, in addition to later remarks, demonstrate that he was ready to accept the temporary loss of that province.[55]

Nothing was to distract the Germans from the single-minded idea of
destroying the French army in one go. But this in itself was an extremely
difficult and risky task. Everything depended on a very tight time schedule.
Roads, bridges, and railroads had to be taken quickly and intact so that the
advancing right wing would always be ahead of French countermeasures.
Seemingly learning from the Russo-Japanese War, Schlieffen emphasized:
"Never must the offensive be allowed to come to a standstill, as happened
during the war in East Asia."[56]

Breaking with Prussian military tradition, he therefore pre-planned
every move in detail. He intended to leave nothing to chance, as if Clausewitz had not devoted a whole chapter of his *On War* to the impact of friction. Clearly, however, even Schlieffen himself was not entirely convinced
that such a method of planning a campaign would work. His language was
full of "ifs," "whens," and "hopefuls."[57] But perhaps worst of all was the fact
that Schlieffen's plan demanded a numerical superiority in the west that the
German army neither in 1906 nor in 1914 ever possessed. Indeed, when
Schlieffen wrote his *Denkschrift*, eight corps in his calculation simply did
not exist.[58] All in all, Gerhard Ritter was completely right when he stated
that the Schlieffen Plan was anything but a safe recipe for victory: "It was
an audacious, even more than an audacious adventure that depended on
many coincidences of luck."[59]

Why then, one might ask, did the chief of the General Staff propose to
embark on such a dangerous adventure? Why indeed did he singlemindedly-
ly insist on a plan that contained so many obvious flaws? Was he just a se-
nile idiot, as a well-known military historian suggested to me?[60] I believe
that such an explanation would be too simple. After all, not only were the
principles of the Schlieffen Plan accepted by Imperial Germany's political
leadership, but Schlieffen's successor also did not dare to abandon this

54 Ibid., 157–60.
55 See Schlieffen's memorandum, Dec. 28, 1912, ibid., 185–6.
56 Ibid., 156.   57 Ibid., 146–55.
58 Wallach, *Das Dogma der Vernichtungsschlacht*, 94. It may well be, however, that this was also Schlieffen's way of telling his successor to force through his long-cherished demand for the full realization
   of universal conscription. See Förster, *Militarismus*, 164–5.
59 Ritter, *Schlieffenplan*, 68.
60 My friend and colleague asked not to be quoted by name.

scheme and left it largely intact. It therefore is important to understand Schlieffen's reasoning that formed the basis for his plan.

Wilhelm Groener was absolutely right when he noted that, above all, the old field marshal wanted to avoid a war of attrition by all means. According to Groener, Schlieffen was fully aware that Germany stood no chance of winning such a contest.[61] Indeed, Schlieffen abhorred scenarios such as those envisaged by the late Helmuth von Moltke or by General Köpke. He was convinced that Germany could not afford to fight a prolonged war on two fronts against the superior numbers of the Franco-Russian alliance. Unless a decisive victory against one of the two enemies could be achieved quickly, the German armies would be squeezed to death by their opponents.[62] This geostrategic argument found support among the military community at the time.[63]

As time went on, however, Schlieffen found other arguments that to his mind made a war of attrition an unacceptable option. Perhaps under the influence of Ivan Bloch's ideas about future warfare, Schlieffen turned to economic reasoning. In 1905 he commented on a war game:

The [economic] machine with its thousands of wheels, through which millions find their living, cannot stand still for long. One cannot move from position to position in battles of twelve days' length for one or two years, until the belligerents are completely exhausted and worn out, both beg for peace, and both accept the status quo. We must attempt to overthrow the enemy quickly, and annihilate him. . . .[64]

In 1909 Schlieffen, who continued to contemplate his strategic plan until well after his retirement, wrote in an article for the *Deutsche Revue*: "[Long] wars are impossible at a time when the existence of a nation is founded upon the uninterrupted progress of commerce and industry. . . . A strategy of attrition will not do if the maintenance of millions of people requires billions." Schlieffen went on to express his fear that a major war, lasting years, would bring to collapse not only the economic and financial system but indeed the entire social and political fabric of Imperial Ger-

---

61 Wilhelm Groener, "Über den Schlieffenplan" (1935), BA-MA, Freiburg, N-46, Groener papers, no. 51.

62 Ritter, *Schlieffenplan*, 37–8; Snyder, *Ideology*, 139.

63 In an anonymous article on "Der Burenkrieg und die europäische Kriegskunst," the *Militärwochenblatt* argued in 1900 that in spite of the recent experience in southern Africa, German military doctrine had to insist on the priority of the offensive because Germany's geostrategic position did not allow the army to remain on the defensive. Quoted in Storz, *Kriegsbild*, 55.

64 Quoted in Snyder, *Ideology*, 108.

many. Such a disaster might eventually lead to revolution and confound the worst fears "about the red ghost that lurks in the background."[65]

There can be no doubt that the Schlieffen Plan was to a large extent based on the wish to avoid major domestic trouble, which a clear-sighted Schlieffen knew would become unavoidable in a long war. Here was a conservative militarist strategy that aimed at preserving the very fabric of Imperial Germany's class society even under the strains of a large war in Europe.[66] One of Schlieffen's aims, therefore, was to make a successful war possible in spite of the Elder Moltke's and Engels's predictions that in the age of industrialized people's war a major conflict between the great powers could destroy European civilization as one knew it. In other words, the Schlieffen Plan was a highly risky strategy that its conservative creator regarded as the only way to prevent the economic, social, and political catastrophes of a lengthy war. It was a desperate gamble. It is against this background that Schlieffen never even attempted to insist on long-term economic and financial preparations for extended warfare or to fend off the consequences of a British naval blockade.[67] The next war had to be short, or all was lost anyway.

Certainly there was still more behind the Schlieffen Plan. The "demigods" inside the General Staff simply could not afford to accept Moltke's verdict that war had ceased to be a viable option of policy. Otherwise, not only they but also the whole army would lose their elevated position in German society, which was based on the promise that the "true knighthood" of the officer corps would save the fatherland from any emergency.[68] This had been one of the main reasons, after all, why Köpke's proposal to prepare the army and the nation publicly for a long war was rejected. Another problem was the fact that the General Staff was not in charge of overall war planning. In fact, its sole task was operational planning. Hence, in the polycratic chaos of Wilhelmine bureaucracy, Schlieffen could turn his mind exclusively to preparing for a campaign, not for an entire war. Under these circumstances his strategic plan remained limited to the problem of defeating France and did not discuss the larger issue of winning a whole war against France, Russia, and possibly Britain. Many of the contemporary and subsequent misunderstandings of Schlieffen's planning

---

65 Graf Alfred von Schlieffen, "Der Krieg der Gegenwart," quoted in Generalfeldmarschall Graf Alfred von Schlieffen, *Gesammelte Schriften,* 2 vols. (Berlin, 1913), 1:11–22.

66 Förster, *Militarismus,* 163–5.   67 Burchardt, *Friedenswirtschaft,* 38–47.

68 In his popular book, Goltz insisted on the special social position of the officer corps precisely on those grounds. Like most of his comrades, he also demanded a free hand for the military vis-à-vis the politicians in case of war. See Goltz, *Volk,* 44–9, 125–31. On the social reasoning behind the Schlieffen Plan, see Snyder, *Ideology,* 122–4.

stemmed from ignoring this background to it. The Schlieffen Plan was much less a recipe to win a war than an operational plan to win a campaign.[69] Nevertheless, Schlieffen clearly hoped that a decisive victory over France would discourage Russia and Britain from continuing the war. There were precious few arguments, however, that supported such optimism. Why indeed should even France give up fighting when in 1870 it continued to do so after Sedan?

The desperate gamble of the Schlieffen Plan was not just a contingency for the unlikely outbreak of war. What made it so dangerous was the fact that it was based on the firm belief that war would come sooner or later anyway. Schlieffen lived in an environment where political and military leaders were increasingly convinced of the inevitability of war.[70] Schlieffen himself was one of the staunchest supporters of the notion that Germany was surrounded by irreconcilable enemies who waited only for the best opportunity to attack. In his article of 1909 he expressed almost paranoid views about the sinister intentions of the Triple Entente.[71] From these considerations it took very little indeed to conclude that rather than wait for an attack under unfavorable circumstances, Germany should seize the initiative and undertake a pre-emptive strike. Indeed, Schlieffen is reputed to have demanded such action during the First Moroccan Crisis.[72] Moreover, the tightly knit Schlieffen Plan, combined with a fatalistic view of the possibilities of avoiding war altogether, was almost an invitation to the General Staff to demand action before the enemies' armament was too strong to keep the plan viable. Professional worst-case thinking could thus turn war into a self-fulfilling prophecy.[73] Indeed, as will be shown here, after 1911 the General Staff became a hotbed of warmongers.

All in all, it can be safely stated that the Schlieffen Plan made no sense. But the reasoning behind it can be explained. In a nutshell, it was an old general's dream to prevent a nightmare. Employing total force, Schlieffen hoped to win a brief and decisive campaign in order to avoid the calamities of a lengthy war. He continued to dream until his end: In his last memorandum of December 28, 1912, the day before his death, he radicalized his

---

69 I am very much indebted to Gerhard Papke for this insight.

70 See the excellent article by Mommsen, "Topos of Inevitable War," 46–62.

71 Schlieffen, "Krieg," 20–2.

72 Groener alleged that Schlieffen already in 1904 demanded an attack against France, while Russia was fighting its war against Japan. Groener, "Über den Schlieffenplan." Schlieffen's aggressive stance during the Moroccan crisis is analyzed by Heiner Raulff, *Zwischen Machtpolitik und Imperialismus: Die deutsche Frankreichpolitik 1904–6* (Düsseldorf, 1976), 78–9. Others have staunchly denied that Schlieffen ever demanded pre-emptive war. See, e.g., Ritter, *Staatskunst*, 2:133, 240–1.

73 Förster, *Militarismus*, 162.

considerations even further. Now he gave up the defensive idea that war was inevitable because of the machinations of Germany's enemies. Having adopted the imperialistic frenzy of the Agadir Crisis, he now declared war necessary in order to break Britain's world-power status. The way to this end was to smash France and the British Expeditionary Force according to the plan of 1905. Russia was to be ignored, even if this meant the loss of East Prussia. In the West, maximum force was to be employed. Even heavy artillery was to advance with the offensive right wing in order to threaten Belgian fortresses. After breaking into northern France, these weapons would find a nice target in the industrial city of Lille.[74]

THE PASSING SHOT GOES WIDE, 1906–1914

On January 1, 1906, Helmuth von Moltke, the nephew of the victor of Sedan, took over as the new chief of the General Staff. The Kaiser trusted in him and had helped him to assume full control against the resistance of Schlieffen, who was very unhappy about his retirement. Moltke was an unimaginative man with a tendency to fatalism, and he was not even sure that he wanted to inherit the enormous burden of stepping into the shoes of his famous uncle. But he certainly was no weakling, as some of his critics later described him. As a precondition to accepting the job he even managed to convince Wilhelm II to refrain from further interference in the annual *Kaisermanöver*.[75]

Moltke was not the man, however, to devise a radically new strategy of his own. He stuck to his predecessor's grand design and did not dare to abandon the Schlieffen Plan in spite of its obvious shortcomings. Instead, he tried to convince himself and others that there was no alternative to at least trying to go for a rapid campaign against France against all odds.[76] Still, Moltke clearly was uneasy about certain details of the Schlieffen Plan. From 1908 onward he therefore began to undertake significant changes in detail. He shifted troops from the offensive right wing to the south in order

74 See original text in Ritter, *Schlieffenplan*, 181–90.
75 See Moltke's letters to his wife in early 1905. Moltke, *Erinnerungen*, 304–20. For a fair assessment of Moltke's personality, see Arden Bucholz, *Moltke, Schlieffen, and Prussian War Planning* (Oxford, 1991), 214–26.
76 In 1913 he even abandoned working on the alternative plan for an offensive against Russia. See Ritter, *Schlieffenplan*, 31–5. After his dismissal he emphasized again that there was no alternative to the Schlieffen Plan as the only way to avoid drawn-out trench warfare in the west. Moltke, "Betrachtungen," 16–17. Most officers in the General Staff supported that view. Not only Groener regarded the Schlieffen Plan as "brilliant" but, after the war, even Ludendorff wrote that the plan presented Germany with the best chance to win victory. Erich Ludendorff, *Kriegführung und Politik*, 2d ed. (Berlin, 1922), 69–74.

to strengthen the defense of Alsace Lorraine. Moreover, Moltke abandoned Schlieffen's original idea not only to break the neutrality of Belgium but also to march through the southern Netherlands. As this significantly narrowed the road for the German offensive and emphasized the need to take the Belgian lines of communication intact, Moltke had to think of ways to keep the rapid advance of a huge army through Belgium possible. In cooperation with Colonel Erich Ludendorff, he therefore worked out a plan for a surprise coup on Liège that was to take place before the mobilized army was fully assembled.[77]

It is futile to speculate as to whether or not these changes did indeed weaken the otherwise "ingenious" Schlieffen Plan to such an extent as to cause its failure in 1914. After all, this plan was flawed anyway. For our purpose it is more interesting to look into the reasons behind the changes. In a memorandum on the Schlieffen Plan, Moltke justified his decision not to break the neutrality of the Netherlands with the need to keep this country viable as a "wind pipe" for German commerce in case Britain should join France and impose a naval blockade.[78] This was a clear indication that Moltke was afraid that the war in the west might take longer and Germany would therefore require an outlet to keep its economy going while the fighting went on. It might also well be that the expectation of a longer war was the reason behind Moltke's decision to shift troops south in order not to yield too much territory against a French offensive there. After all, the important industrial Saar region had to be protected if Germany were to support and supply an extended war effort.[79]

Moltke indeed was very pessimistic about Germany's prospects in a major war. Already in January 1905 – the Schlieffen Plan was not yet completed – Moltke told the Kaiser, on the offer to become Schlieffen's successor, that even a war against France alone would present a grim scenario:

We will not anymore, as in earlier times, be faced with a hostile army that we can engage with superiority but with a nation in arms. It will be a people's war that cannot be won in one decisive battle but will turn into a long and tedious struggle

---

77 The consequence of this intended *coup de main* was to radicalize the political impact of the Schlieffen Plan insofar as to force the hand of Germany's leadership in any major international crisis. The German army had to begin its attack before the Belgians were ready, which narrowed the time for the politicians to find a peaceful way out of the crisis. This is precisely what happened at the height of the July Crisis in 1914. In addition, the surprise attack on Liège strengthened even further the element of luck on which the Schlieffen Plan hinged anyway. Indeed, only the incompetence of the Belgian defenders enabled the German troops to obtain their objectives in August 1914. See Burchardt, *Friedenswirtschaft*, 48–50, and Snyder, *Ideology*, 150–3.

78 Moltke's memorandum (probably 1911), in Ritter, *Schlieffenplan*, 178–80.

79 At least this was Ludendorff's argument to justify Moltke's changes to the Schlieffen Plan. Ludendorff, *Kriegführung*, 71.

with a country that will not give up before the strength of its entire people has been broken. Our own people too will be utterly exhausted, even if we should be victorious.[80]

This did not look like a "short-war illusion." Quite to the contrary: The Younger Moltke entered office holding views on the prospects of future warfare that were very much like those his uncle had held toward the end of his life.

It remained that way until summer 1914 – in spite of the Schlieffen Plan! Moltke's views might have vacillated from time to time, and for tactical reasons he occasionally promised the politicians a short campaign. But generally he became increasingly convinced that the next war would take at least two years. Especially after 1912, when the continental arms race heated up as never before and made it increasingly unlikely that Germany could quickly overpower the ever-growing French and Russian armies, Moltke became more and more pessimistic. He now believed that a long war on both fronts against France and Russia was the most likely scenario. In this conviction Moltke did not stand alone, as many prominent officers in and outside the General Staff held similar views.[81] Schlieffen and his disciples were rather isolated. In fact, it appears that in the overall period from 1871 to 1914 Schlieffen's self-imposed optimism about the possibility of a short and victorious campaign to prevent a war from becoming a nasty and almost endless affair was the exception to the otherwise grim predictions of most military thinkers.

In an analysis of France's operative intentions in a war against Germany, the Third Department of the General Staff noted in May 1910 that a rapid and complete victory over the French army was extremely unlikely. The annihilation of an army of two million men in the first onslaught was next to impossible. The French therefore would have the opportunity to withdraw into the interior of their country and continue the war. In other words, the Schlieffen Plan would not work.[82] On November 1, 1912, Moltke and Ludendorff wrote to the War Ministry warning them that large

---

80 Moltke reported this conversation in a letter to his wife, Eliza, on January 29, 1905. Moltke, *Erinnerungen,* 308. It should be noted that in his conversation with the Kaiser, Moltke used this argument to convince Wilhelm II to abandon his personal command in army maneuvers. Still, it is interesting to see that Moltke referred to the notion of a long war against France. Moreover, as subsequent developments demonstrated, Moltke stuck to this scenario.

81 See Burchardt, *Friedenswirtschaft,* 20–7. Once again it should be pointed out here that Burchardt put much effort into demonstrating convincingly that, apart from Schlieffen and his followers, few German generals held a short-war illusion. But most historians have ignored this aspect of his findings.

82 Grosser Generalstab, 3. Abteilung, May 1910 (revised Nov. 11, 1912, and Apr. 1914): "Aufmarsch und operative Absichten der Franzosen in einem zukünftigen deutsch-französischen Kriege," BA-MA, Freiburg, PH3/256 (Generalstabakten).

amounts of ammunition had to be stockpiled in order to prepare for a lengthy conflict. The German army would not be strong enough to defeat the enemies quickly:

We will have to be ready to fight a lengthy campaign with numerous hard, lengthy battles until we defeat *one* of our enemies; the strain and consumption of resources increases when we have to win in several theaters in the west and in the east, one after another, and when before that we will have to fight with inferiority against superiority. The need for a great deal of ammunition over a long period of time is absolutely critical.[83]

What made matters worse was the fact that at the time of Moltke's take-over from Schlieffen a war on three fronts became increasingly likely. The naval arms race, the Entente Cordial, and the First Moroccan Crisis drove Britain into the arms of France. The intended breach of Belgium's neutrality, moreover, made it all but certain that Germany would have to fight three great powers in the case of war. The immediate problem here was the fact that the German fleet could never hope to defeat the Royal Navy. A British naval blockade therefore could become a deadly threat to Germany's economic ability to sustain the lengthy war effort that the generals increasingly expected.[84] It also was clear that Britain's overall resources in manpower, finances, and industrial production would make the task for the German army to win a rapid victory more difficult, especially as Haldane's army reform promised to provide the allies with even more valuable troops in the defense of France.

Against this background the navy leadership protested that there was no reason to harbor any short-war illusions. Admiral von Tirpitz warned the home secretary, Count Arthur von Posadowsky-Wehner, that a nonchalant attitude toward the dangers of a long war was unacceptable. On January 28, 1907, Tirpitz sent him an analysis by the navy department of Germany's provisions with foodstuffs that had the following to say about the possible duration of a potential war:

It cannot be said why the war should last only nine months, especially when several powers and various theaters are involved; a longer period is certainly not im-

---

83 Quoted in Dr. Dieckmann, "Die Vorbereitungen für die Versorgung des deutschen Heeres mit Munition vor Ausbruch des Weltkrieges" (1939), BA-MA, Potsdam, Bestand Kriegsgeschichtliche Forschungsanstalt des Heeres, W-10/50777, 37–8. This unpublished manuscript is of particular interest not only because it contains quotations from subsequently destroyed sources but it also constitutes the first chapter of the never-completed second volume of *Kriegsrüstung und Kriegswirtschaft*. This material contains a letter from the Kriegsgeschichtliche Forschungsanstalt to General Sieger from September 21, 1939, spreading the news that work on the second volume had to be stopped because of the outbreak of war.
84 Burchardt, *Friedenswirtschaft*, 55–7.

probable. In order not to hang on to any illusions, a longer duration of warfare, perhaps one-and-a-half years, a period of time in which the impact of the war will become fully felt – provides the basis of this analysis.[85]

The memorandum went on to warn of serious social disturbances resulting from a shortage of food, unemployment, and severe problems in industrial production due to a lack of raw materials.

Moltke and other prominent army officers clearly were not alone in fearing that a long war might be unavoidable and that such a people's war would have dire consequences. Such views, moreover, were not expressed only behind closed doors. As shown previously, leading officers, such as the Elder Moltke and Goltz, publicly warned of the danger of a prolonged people's war. Prominent civilians took up these warnings and protested against undue optimism.[86] The military historian and journalist Hans Del-brück wrote time and again that the next war would be not only terrible but also very lengthy.[87] On December 5, 1904, the leader of the Social Democrats, August Bebel, gave a speech in the Reichstag that predicted utter disaster in case of war. Obviously referring to Engels, Bloch, and the Elder Moltke, he warned of the catastrophe of the inevitably long duration of such a war, culminating in collapse and revolution.[88]

Professionals might have publicly refuted such warnings by "amateurs." But some of the most prominent officers were themselves convinced that there was no room for short-war illusions. This became very clear at the moment of decision. On July 28, 1914, Moltke wrote a secret letter that, on the next day, was handed over to Chancellor Bethmann Hollweg. In it he talked about Austria-Hungary's "just cause" against "murderous" Serbia. He criticized the "sinister machinations" of Russia that might trigger a war. But he also talked of this war as a "world war." He warned of "the mutual tearing to pieces by Europe's civilized nations (*Kulturstaaten*)." And finally he wrote that only a last-minute miracle could prevent a war "that will destroy civilization in almost all of Europe for decades to come." Still, he de-

---

85 Tirpitz to Posadowsky-Wehner, Jan. 28, 1907, and "Untersuchung des Reichsmarineamts," in *Kriegsrüstung*, supplements, 219.

86 It would make much sense to investigate the impact of these warnings. It seems to me that the myth of the short-war illusion is just as wrong with regard to the general public as it is to the military leadership.

87 See Arden Bucholz, *Hans Delbrück and the German Establishment: War Images in Conflict* (Iowa City, Iowa, 1985), 73–6.

88 *Stenographische Berichte über die Verhandlungen des Reichstages 1903–1905* (Berlin, 1906), 201:3353–64. It may well be that Bebel's warnings influenced Schlieffen's planning and especially his justification in "Der Krieg der Gegenwart."

manded of the chancellor that he engage as quickly as possible.[89] Another leading German officer held similar views. On the news of the declaration of war, retired Field Marshal Goltz told his son: "This is going to be a long and very difficult war. Right now I cannot see how we will obtain peace with Russia and England."[90] All this demonstrates that Schlieffen's parting shot had gone wide. By July 1914 at the latest, the general in charge as well as other leading military figures were convinced that there was no hope of a short war. Gone were the days of Schlieffen's optimism.

Still, Moltke and the General Staff did hang on to the operational principle of the Schlieffen Plan. But from what has been shown here, it appears that Moltke and his subordinates had given this plan a different meaning: They no longer believed it to be a foolproof recipe for a short war but rather intended to use it as an opening shot to provide Germany with a major strategic advantage in the expected long war against three great powers. This promised to be the only hope of military survival in a catastrophic people's war. Thus the Schlieffen Plan was no longer the basis of a short-war illusion, as historians generally interpreted it, but a desperate operational plan for the opening campaign of a long war. This also explains why Moltke, Ludendorff, and others clung to the Schlieffen Plan in spite of their insights into the nature of a future war. They believed they had every reason to stick to it by all means, even if doing so meant turning the topos of inevitable war into a self-fulfilling prophecy.

GOING FOR BROKE, 1906–1914

In theory, Germany's political and military leaders had two alternatives to the hazardous strategy of entering what would likely be a long people's war with a less-than-convincing first-strike scenario. A first strike aimed to deprive one of the enemies of most of its offensive capability in one mighty blow, thereby providing a strategic advantage for the continuation of the war against the others.

---

89 Helmuth von Moltke, "Zur Beurteilung der politischen Lage," July 28, 1914. Secret memorandum for the chancellor (copy), BA-MA, Freiburg, N-46, Groener papers, no. 40: Correspondence with the Reichsarchiv. This document was already reprinted in Moltke, *Erinnerungen,* 3–7, but without reference to its secret character and without mention of the added note by von Fabeck that this letter was handed over to Bethmann Hollweg on July 29. Historians have usually quoted this letter as proof of Moltke's warmongering during the July Crisis. Correct as this interpretation is, it ignores the fact that Moltke had a pretty clear idea about the consequences of that war. After all, it is hard to explain why someone should demand war if he has such grim ideas about its probable results.

90 Goltz and Foerster, eds., *Denkwürdigkeiten,* 345–6.

1. The German authorities could have prepared state, economy, and society for a long war against superior enemies. By mobilizing all human and material resources immediately, Germany would have gained some advantage over its less prepared enemies and thereby have won perhaps sufficient ground to survive a war of attrition. This would have meant nothing less than preparations for total war long before 1914.

2. Germany's leadership could have pursued a policy of *détente* in order to avoid war altogether, perhaps according to those lines that the Elder Moltke had suggested in 1890. The basis for such a turnaround in German foreign policy after 1905–6 had to be clear warnings by the General Staff to the political leadership and the Kaiser not only that there was no hope for a short war but also that, even with the help of the Schlieffen Plan, Germany stood very little chance of winning against the combined forces of France, Great Britain, and Russia. The generals otherwise would have had to resign themselves to being nothing more than tools of a policy of deterrence.

Neither of these two alternatives was of course seriously pursued. The reasons for this and the consequences for the activities of the General Staff will now have to be briefly explained.

Perhaps the most obvious field of preparation for total war was the mobilization of human resources, namely of manpower for the armed forces. In spite of the fact, however, that universal compulsory service was enshrined in the constitution, conscription was never fully implemented after 1871. Thousands of young men were not drafted. From the 1890s until his retirement, Schlieffen demanded time and again that this inequity be rectified, especially given his fear that not enough troops might be available to carry out his operational plan.[91] But over the years the political leadership, the War Ministry, and the Reichstag agreed to only very moderate increases in the army. The Younger Moltke for a long time did almost nothing to continue Schlieffen's fight for the full implementation of conscription. Only after 1911, when international tensions and the continental arms race became increasingly ominous and influenced by the more vigorous Erich Ludendorff, did the chief of the General Staff begin to concentrate on the question of large army increases. On December 21, 1912, he finally sent to the chancellor and to the war minister a memorandum demanding imme-

---

91 Even in his memorandum of December 1905 (quoted in Ritter, *Schlieffenplan,* 155.), Schlieffen emphasized the urgent need to implement conscription fully:

> We invented universal conscription and the nation in arms and demonstrated to the other nations the necessity to introduce this institution. But after we brought our sworn enemies to increase their armies endlessly, we relented in our own endeavors. We still rely on our large numbers of inhabitants, on the mass of people that we have at our disposal. But these masses are not trained and equipped to the same extent as those who are more capable.

diate action. He spoke of the aggressive intentions of the Triple Entente and expressed his fears that Germany might lose the arms race, depriving the army of any chance of victory. Only full conscription could help. This would allow for a further increase in the army's strength to not less than 300,000 men.[92] In the spring of 1913 a huge army bill was indeed introduced and passed by Parliament. (It was the last before the war.) But the General Staff got far less than half of what it had demanded. Thus, when war broke out a year later, tens of thousands of able-bodied men had not been trained and could not be drafted.

Preparing for the full mobilization of Germany's human resources, at least in terms of conscription for the army, had foundered on several obstacles. Conservatives in the military establishment, especially within the War Ministry, stood against full conscription because they feared for the social coherence and political reliability of the army if too many socialist workers were drafted into its ranks and too many liberals were appointed officers. The naval buildup required too many financial resources. Domestic politics prevented a thorough financial reform, which would have made sufficient funds available. Until 1911 the Reichstag was not ready to agree to full conscription. The political leadership felt no inclination to fight against such opposition to thoroughgoing army reform, and when it did after 1911, it was all too ready to compromise.[93] Not even the General Staff itself had consistently pressed that issue. Clearly, even in the field of armament policy Imperial Germany was unable to prepare for total war. Far from it!

The evidence in every other respect, too, demonstrates that neither the political leadership nor the generals had any idea of the requirements of total warfare. Consequently, very few preparations were made. This is particularly true for the field of economics. Before 1900, as has been shown previously, not even Goltz, who otherwise demanded the militarization and mobilization of civilian society for the purpose of people's war, understood the necessities of economic preparations. He did not contemplate the problems of supplying sufficient foodstuffs for the civilians nor of obtaining raw materials for industry. Until 1906 this was the typical attitude of civilian and military authorities alike. In the General Staff Schlieffen was clearly afraid of the economic consequences of a long war. But this was precisely one of the reasons why he desperately planned for a short war.

92 Moltke to Bethmann Hollweg and von Heeringen, Dec. 21, 1912, in *Kriegsrüstung*, supplements, 158–74.
93 For a full investigation of Germany's armament policy, see Förster, *Militarismus*.

Consequently, he had little interest in economic preparations for a war of attrition.[94] In a meeting in the summer of 1906 representatives of various ministries echoed Schlieffen's optimism by concluding that long-term economic preparations for a protracted war were not necessary.[95] Tirpitz and the Navy Department were the first to protest such undue optimism when in January 1907 they warned of dire consequences if Germany were unprepared for fighting a longer war.[96] Moltke took up this point. On February 12, 1907, he wrote to the war ministry that something had to be done to get the financial markets ready for war. Moreover, he expressed his concern that no provisions had been made to secure the alimentation of the civilian population in case of war. This could lead to unrest and thus seriously hamper the war effort: "The interests of the people, however, cannot be separated anymore from those of the army. They mutually influence each other."[97]

Other officials supported this view, but little was done.[98] On May 14, 1914, Moltke therefore wrote to the home secretary, Clemens von Delbrück, and reminded him of the importance of economic preparations for the war. To supply the home front was a decisive precondition for the success of the army. Even military victories were useless if the economy collapsed: "A perhaps lengthy war on two fronts can only be sustained by an economically strong people." Moltke demanded of Delbrück that he do everything in his power to organize the economic mobilization for war.[99] But it was already too late because the war broke out only two-and-a-half months later.

Because of Lothar Burchardt's excellent investigation, the lack of economic preparations in Imperial Germany now is a well-established fact. Burchardt also explains the reasons for the failure of the German authorities to react to the economic dangers of war. The administrative chaos within the polycratic system of government made sure that no department accepted responsibility – not even the Navy Department or the General Staff. The financial deadlock prevented decisive action in this field, too. Most important of all was that nobody, not even Moltke, grasped the full

94 In his notes from 1935 on the Schlieffen Plan, Groener stressed this point. BA-MA, Freiburg, N-46, Groener papers, no. 51: Zum Schlieffenplan.

95 Burchardt, *Friedenswirtschaft*, 16.

96 Tirpitz to Home Secretary Count Posadowsky-Wehner, Jan. 28, 1907, and memorandum from the Imperial Navy Department, in *Kriegsrüstung*, supplements, 218–23.

97 Moltke to the War Ministry, Feb. 12, 1907, ibid., 224.

98 See, e.g., the memorandum by the Geheime Finanzrat Dr. Meydenbauer to the Prussian minister of finance, Dr. Lentze, Apr. 23, 1914, ibid., 274–87.

99 Moltke to Delbrück, May 14, 1914, ibid., 287–91.

implications to the economy of a war, and nobody had any idea of how a modern war economy might be organized.[100] The concept of total warfare simply did not yet exist! Instead, even pessimists such as Moltke harbored vague ideas about a long people's war, the dangers of a naval blockade, and the necessity of accumulating sufficient foodstuffs. But nobody ever mentioned the possibility of a government-controlled war economy along the lines of Ludendorff's *Kriegssozialismus* (wartime social policy) after 1916.[101] Typical of this is an incident that Groener reported in his reflections on the Schlieffen Plan. According to him, in February 1914 the General Staff demanded the purchase of Argentina's complete grain harvest. The grain was to be stored in ships on the Rhine to be ready for distribution in case of war. But the Imperial Finance Department rejected the idea because of its enormous costs.[102] Nobody suggested, however, the much more promising measure of increasing agricultural production in Germany itself by applying tight governmental control.

A similar case for the lack of preparation can be made in regard to provisions with ammunition for the army. Having been pressed by Ludendorff, Moltke discovered only in late 1908 that the army had just enough ammunition to fight a few battles. Neither stockpiles nor provisions for wartime ammunition production were sufficient to sustain even a war that lasted only a few months. In January 1909 Moltke wrote to the War Ministry demanding action. But again very little was done, largely due to the lack of finances. When the war broke out, 20 to 50 percent of the needed ammunition reserves for most weapons had not been stockpiled. The industrial capacities were so low that the full ammunition requirements of the army could not be produced in only eight weeks, as the General Staff had demanded, but in six months! Once again administrative chaos, the chronic shortage of funds, and the slow pace of civilian and military bu-

---

100 Burchardt, *Friedenswirtschaft*, 242–50.

101 After the war Ludendorff himself argued that nobody at the time understood the economic requirements of modern large-scale warfare: "Of course, nowadays the interrelations of things in the economic sector, too, are clearer than before. Only the events could bring about a full understanding" (Ludendorff, *Kriegführung*, 60).

102 BA-MA, Freiburg, N-46, Groener papers, no. 51: Zum Schlieffenplan. To date I have been unable to find any reference to this incident in the official government documents. It is interesting to speculate, however, as to what made the General Staff think of such a measure in February 1914. Being stored on the Rhine River, the grain could not have lasted much longer than six to eight months. After that, the government would have had to sell the grain on the open market, thereby provoking an outcry by the powerful agricultural lobby because of the collapse of grain prices. Such a measure made sense only if war was to be expected by the summer of 1914. But in February of that year Archduke Franz Ferdinand and his wife were still very much alive. If Groener did not make up this story, one might well ask whether the General Staff by that time already knew something that historians have so far failed to find out retrospectively.

reaucracy (including the General Staff) prevented the implementation of decisive measures.[103]

All this indicates that preparing for total war was no option in Imperial Germany before August 1914. Even if the General Staff held pessimistic (and quite realistic) views about the probability of a long war, they neither had any idea about its full implications nor did they get the funds to prepare for it, and they certainly had no clout to ensure the full mobilization of state, economy, and society. Jack Snyder may therefore be right in arguing that, under these circumstances, all the General Staff could do was to concentrate on its own immediate concern: planning for the campaign of the first couple of weeks in a war.[104] To emphasize again, however: This did not mean that the General Staff was convinced that the Schlieffen Plan was a recipe for a short war. But neither did Moltke and the other leading army officers opt for the other alternative either, to demand that war be avoided altogether. Quite to the contrary: Moltke is well known to have been one the prime warmongers in Imperial Germany. He continued the tradition of all his predecessors of demanding a pre-emptive strike at every opportunity. At the height of the Second Moroccan Crisis, when the German government began to retreat before British and French threats, he wrote to his wife:

I am getting sick and tired of the unfortunate Morocco business. It certainly is a sign of laudable endurance to permanently sit like a cat on hot bricks, but it is not pleasant. If we again slip away from this affair with our tail between our legs, and if we cannot bring ourselves to put forward a determined claim that we are prepared to force through with the sword, I shall despair of the future of the German Empire. I shall then resign. But before handing in my resignation I shall propose to abolish the army and place ourselves under Japanese protection; we shall then be in a position to make money without interference and to develop into ninnies.[105]

But he did nothing except continue "to sit on hot bricks." On December 8, 1912, at the infamous war council, or *Kriegsrat*, a hysterical Kaiser assembled his military advisers on the news that Britain's Foreign Secretary, Lord Grey, had told the German ambassador to London of His Majesty's Government's firm intention not to stand idly by while Germany overran France. Wilhelm II demanded an immediate declaration of war as the only suitable answer. Moltke concurred. Seeing a chance to get off the bricks,

103 The unpublished chapter of the second volume of *Kriegsrüstung* provides an excellent analysis of the ammunication problem. BA-MA, Potsdam, Bestand Kriegsgeschichtliche Forschungsanstalt des Heeres, W-10/50777, Dr. Dieckmann, "Die Vorbereitungen für die Versorgung des deutschen Heeres mit Munition vor Ausbruch des Weltkrieges" (1939).
104 Snyder, *Ideology,* 154.
105 Moltke to his wife, Eliza, Aug. 19, 1911, in Moltke, *Erinnerungen,* 362.

he exclaimed: "I believe a war to be inevitable, and the earlier, the better." War was not declared, however, as a horrified Tirpitz, afraid for the safety of his unfinished fleet, managed to convince the Kaiser to wait at least another one-and-a-half years.[106]

In the meantime, Moltke became more and more anxious to get into action. In March 1914 he explained to a surprised Foreign Secretary Gottlieb von Jagow that war had to come very soon, otherwise all was lost:

The prospects of the future seriously worried him. Russia will have completed her armaments in 2 to 3 years. The military superiority of our enemies would be so great then that he did not know how he might cope with them. In his view there was no alternative to waging a preventive war in order to defeat the enemy as long as we could still more or less pass the test. The chief of the General Staff left it at my discretion to gear our policy to an early unleashing of a war.[107]

Four months later, Archduke Franz Ferdinand was assassinated in Sarajevo. Moltke now had his chance. He would not allow it to slip away.

Toward the end of the July Crisis, Moltke indeed became one of the major warmongers. On July 29 the clearly horrified Bavarian military plenipotentiary in Berlin reported back to Munich that the chief of the General Staff pressed for war.[108] In fact, on the same day, Bethmann Hollweg received Moltke's letter, which spoke of a world war and the destruction of European civilization for decades to come. In this letter Moltke nevertheless demanded that the chancellor move forward and soon.[109] If these were veiled hints, Moltke on July 30 finally came clean. In a meeting with Bethmann Hollweg and the war minister, he insisted on immediate action because he saw no alternative to war.[110]

---

106 Quoted in Walter Görlitz, ed., *Der Kaiser . . . Aufzeichnungen des Chefs des Marinekabinetts Admiral Georg Alexander von Müller über die Ära Wilhelms II* (Berlin, 1965), 124–5. See my interpretation of the War Council (Kriegsrat) in *Militarismus*, 252–5.

107 Jagow's report on his conversation with Moltke is quoted in Volker R. Berghahn, *Germany and the Approach of War in 1914* (London, 1973), 172.

108 The Bavarian military plenipotentiary in Berlin, von Wenninger, to the War Ministry, Munich, July 29, 1914, Bayerisches Hauptstaatsarchiv-Kriegsarchiv, Munich, Abt. IV, KA, Bayerischer Militärbevollmächtiger, vol. 1.

109 Helmuth von Moltke, "Zur Beurteilung der politischen Lage," July 28, 1914, BA-MA, Freiburg, N-46, Groener papers, no. 40: Correspondence with the Reichsarchiv. For a good analysis of the General Staff's role in the July Crisis, see Joll, *Origins*, 81–4.

110 Holger Afflerbach, *Falkenhayn: Politisches Denken und Handeln im Kaiserreich* (Munich, 1994), 158–9. In his account of the July Crisis Afflerbach quotes at length from Falkenhayn's most interesting diary. Strangely, the war minister, who was even more of a warmonger, expressed several times his disappointment about Moltke's alleged uneven stance in that matter. At least according to this document, Moltke hesitated to go to war too quickly. It may well be that Afflerbach is correct to explain this stance by Moltke's apprehensions about the reliability of the Austro-Hungarian leadership. It also is possible that Moltke was for a brief moment reluctant to press for a war, about the outcome of which he had made such gloomy predictions. But all this did not prevent him from ultimately demanding war.

All this looks crazy, and it would be hard to believe if it were not so well documented. But Moltke had not gone mad, and he did not even stand alone when clamoring for war. He simply perpetuated the stance of all his predecessors. Even his uncle had warned against the dangers of a major war only after his retirement. His contemporaries, such as Goltz and Friedrich von Bernhardi, were just as eager for war as the chief of the General Staff himself.[111] Still, it requires special explanation why someone like Moltke, who was clearly pessimistic about the prospects of a war, would demand exactly that, "the earlier, the better."

First of all, to restrict themselves to the role as agents of a policy of deterrence to avoid war altogether was out of question for Germany's leading army officers. As has been said previously in connection with Schlieffen's planning, the "demigods," especially within the General Staff, were not prepared to give up their elevated position in German society. But to admit that they were at the end of their tether and saw no way to win the next war would have meant nothing less. Moltke in particular had to fulfill the high expectations the Kaiser had of the bearer of such a famous name, and he had to promise that under his guidance the General Staff would always be ready to do the job again.[112] But as his conversation with Jagow demonstrates, he became increasingly afraid that Germany might lose the arms race against France and Russia. He had failed to press through his demands for a full implementation of conscription, and there was little hope that he would succeed in the future. At some point, perhaps in two to three years, the German army would simply no longer be strong enough even to try to put the Schlieffen Plan into practice. From then on a defensive war of attrition would be the only military option left, entailing certain defeat. Hence, Moltke was determined to go for broke, as long as there was a glimmer of hope.

But even so, he was very skeptical about the outcome. It appears that the best he hoped for was a successful beginning to the war, providing Germany with a chance at least not to lose an otherwise lengthy and terribly destructive conflict. That this war would come anyway was a foregone conclusion to him. Like Schlieffen and many others, Moltke was con-

---

111 See, e.g., Friedrich von Bernhardi, *Deutschland und der nächste Krieg,* 2d ed. (Stuttgart, 1912).
112 According to Moltke's own report, Wilhelm II went berserk when, on Aug. 1, 1914, the chief of the General Staff hinted that he could not perform miracles. The Kaiser had asked him to drop the impending offensive against France and march against Russia instead. Moltke refused on the grounds that everything was ready to carry out the Schlieffen Plan and that to wheel around the whole army toward the east would create utter chaos. An outraged Wilhelm II retorted: "Your uncle would have given me a different answer!" From this moment on, Moltke's self-confidence was broken. Moltke, "Betrachtungen," 19–21.

vinced of the inevitability of war, if only because of the aggressive designs of Germany's sworn enemies. The paranoia of encirclement, which was widespread in Germany at the time, combined with professional worst-case thinking and led to an almost self-centered view of the world.[113] Moreover, Moltke, like many other officers not just in Germany, held strong views of cultural pessimism and social Darwinism. To largely conservative officers, the advancement of modern industrial society, as represented for instance in the progress of the Social Democratic Party, meant nothing less than the impending decline of civilization. Against that development only a war could purify the nation and give it a chance to prove itself in the eternal struggle of the survival of the fittest.[114] From this point of view, war still was a desirable option, even if its duration and its outcome could not be predicted.

After his dismissal, Moltke justified the war he had helped to bring about with fatalistic arguments based on social Darwinism. To him this war had been necessary according to the plan of world history:

> It demonstrates how the epochs of civilization follow one another in a progressive manner, how each nation has to fulfill its preordained role in the development of the world, and how this development follows an upward-pointing line.
>
> Thus the German nation also has to fulfill its role in civilization. The fulfillment of such a task, however, is not carried out without conflicts, as time and again opposition has to be overcome; it can only be done through war. Assuming that Germany would be annihilated in a war, it would mean the destruction of German intellectual life, on which the further spiritual development of mankind depends, and of German culture; the whole development of mankind would be set back in the most disastrous way. . . .
>
> We live in a colossal time.
>
> War will cause new developments in history and its result will determine the course that the whole world will take in the next centuries.[115]

Clearly, Moltke tried to console himself with the comfortable argument that war was only natural in the course of world history. Hence, he had not hesitated to unleash it, even though he did not know how to win it. In an uncertain world that he and his comrades no longer understood, resorting to arms was perhaps the only thing they thought they were able to rely on. Maybe, with luck, something good would come of it. But when Moltke

---

113　On worst-case thinking, military professionalism, and self-centeredness, see Dieter Senghass, *Rüstung und Militarismus* (Frankfurt am Main, 1972), and Morris Janowitz, *The Professional Soldier: A Social and Political Portrait* (New York, 1960).

114　On social Darwinism among the European officer corps, see Storz, *Kriegsbild,* 79–91.

115　Moltke, "Betrachtungen," 13–14.

wrote those lines, the war had already gotten out of hand. Soon his worst expectations would come true. Moreover, this was going to be not just a huge people's war but the beginning of total warfare, something nobody had predicted. Thus, all dreams turned into nightmares, which then happened to become reality.

16

"A Calamity to Civilization"

Theodore Roosevelt and the Danger of War in Europe

RAIMUND LAMMERSDORF

At first glance, Theodore Roosevelt's attitude toward war and his approach to foreign policy seem to have been contradictory. He was the most prominent militarist in American history, but during his presidency he kept the United States out of war.[1] He was a firm believer in military virtues, yet he earned the Nobel Peace Prize for his efforts in ending the Russo-Japanese War. He was a brilliant politician, but still he got himself involved in European power politics although doing so could only have harmed his domestic political position.

The historiography on Roosevelt's foreign-policy thinking offers two different answers to the puzzle: The currently predominant school of thought projects him as a strong, heroic figure who was motivated by altruistic and moralistic goals. Scholars who hold to this view celebrate Roosevelt as an omnipresent and omniscient genius of diplomacy who single-handedly forced the Kaiser into submission and became the peacemaker of Europe.[2] Other scholars prefer to view his diplomacy in the context of economic imperialism and dismiss his jingoism as mere rhetoric. For them, Roosevelt is a skillful and pragmatic strategist who competed with the European powers for new markets.[3]

The interpretation offered here takes a more critical view of Roosevelt's capacity as a diplomat and concentrates on his personal ideology as the key

---

1 John Milton Cooper Jr., *The Warrior and the Priest: Woodrow Wilson and Theodore Roosevelt* (Cambridge, Mass., 1983), 12.

2 Essays of the major Roosevelt champions are collected in Natalie A. Naylor, ed., *Theodore Roosevelt: Many-Sided American* (Interlaken, N.Y., 1992); for an overview of the literature, see John Allen Gable, "The Man in the Arena of History: The Historiography of Theodore Roosevelt," in ibid., 613–43.

3 E.g., Ragnhild Fiebig-von Hase, *Lateinamerika als Konfliktherd der Deutsch-Amerikanischen Beziehungen 1890–1903: Vom Beginn der Panamerikapolitik bis zur Venezuelakrise von 1902/03* (Göttingen, 1986); cf. Holger H. Herwig, *Germany's Vision of Empire in Venezuela, 1871–1914* (Princeton, N.J., 1986).

to his foreign-policy program.[4] Economic reasoning played only a marginal role in Roosevelt's discussions of foreign policy. Instead, there is an abundance of sources in which he explains his views on war and foreign relations, the roles of nations in the international system, and the foreign-policy goals for America in terms of his racial ideology. These statements provide the material for an attempt at an intellectual history of American foreign policy at the beginning of the twentieth century.

It is hard to ignore the ideological element in Roosevelt's public and private life. Whatever one may think about his sometimes racist, often bigoted beliefs, he was not a hypocrite. To many contemporary observers he may have seemed naïve in his rough righteousness; to the political bosses of his time, his puritan honesty appeared outright dangerous. But nobody questioned his sincerity. What is more, his meteoric rise to political prominence and power would have been impossible without the unwavering self-confidence that resulted from his firm internal belief system. In the confines of this ideology, which was well within the mainstream of white male elitist thinking, he acted rationally and predictably, with force and political success. This philosophy served him well not only in his approach to domestic politics but also during his brief forays into the uncharted territory of international relations. Ultimately, it was ideology more than power politics or economic interests that determined his attitude toward the rivalries between the European powers and the dangers of war in Europe.

At the core of Roosevelt's weltanschauung was a racial interpretation of the world. He combined Darwinism with the teachings of Lamarck and divided humanity into different races whose characteristics determined their position in the world. It is important to note that during the Progressive Era the term "race" did not carry an exclusively biological meaning but could signify any group of people who shared certain characteristics, such as language, nationality, ethnicity, or color of skin. This made possible a far-reaching taxonomy of world races that met the scientific standards of the late nineteenth century because it acknowledged humanity's submission to the laws of nature. This racial worldview helped Roosevelt and contemporary Americans interpret world developments and justify America's outward thrust.[5]

---

4 See Raimund Lammersdorf, *Anfänge einer Weltmacht: Theodore Roosevelt und die transatlantischen Beziehungen der USA 1901–1909* (Berlin, 1994).
5 See definition no. 3 of "race" in *The Century Dictionary and Cyclopedia*, 12 vols. (New York, 1911), 8:4926; Thomas G. Dyer, *Theodore Roosevelt and the Idea of Race* (Baton Rouge, La., 1980), 29–30; Howard K. Beale, *Theodore Roosevelt and the Rise of America to World Power* (Baltimore, 1956), 26–34.

According to Roosevelt, all races went through three evolutionary stages, beginning with primitivism, the lowest level, at which native Americans and Africans endured a miserable existence. But each race could rise to the next-higher level, namely, barbarism, the stage of the organized warrior society, as achieved by the Turks or the Russians. The third and final step was civilized society, created by the western European Protestant nations, including the "English-speaking races" as they had spread over the globe.

But Roosevelt did not believe only in the upward mobility of a race. Any highly developed civilization was in constant danger of degeneration. This fear was the driving force behind Roosevelt's political and personal behavior. While he saw the American race as "the greatest branch of the English-speaking race,"[6] he always believed in the constant necessity for vigilance against degeneration. Decadence and the subsequent decline of a race could be averted only if a healthy balance was maintained between barbaric and civilized values. "Unless we keep the barbarian virtues, gaining the civilized ones will be of little avail."[7]

Next to the improvement of civilized society it therefore was necessary to keep the fighting edge. As a politician and writer, Roosevelt worked for political and social reform. To these tasks he added personal perfection through the "strenuous life." He was an avid hunter and rider, played tennis, learned boxing and jiujitsu, worked as a farmer and cowboy, and reveled in strenuous marches through Washington's forested hinterlands. He demanded military training for all American men to keep them healthy and forceful, instill and maintain in them the fighting spirit so important for a healthy civilized race, and provide the United States with great military power. For women, he considered the health risks that pregnancy and childbirth posed as being comparable to the dangers a soldier confronted in combat. Birth control, then, was not only dishonorable but socially irresponsible because it meant racial suicide.

The highest and noblest achievement a man could possibly attain, Roosevelt believed, was to participate in war. Throughout his early life he clamored for a chance to prove his masculinity and his barbaric qualities in combat. Already in 1886 he offered to raise a cavalry regiment of cowboys to fight Mexico, in 1892 he hoped for a war against Chile, and during the Venezuelan Crisis of 1896 he was disgusted and disappointed with the lack

6 Theodore Roosevelt (hereafter TR) to Henry White, Mar. 30, 1896, Elting E. Morison et al., eds., *The Letters of Theodore Roosevelt* (Cambridge, Mass., 1950), 1:523 (hereafter *TR Letters*).
7 Edward Wagenknecht, *The Seven Worlds of Theodore Roosevelt* (New York, 1958), 260.

of fighting spirit in the business community.[8] He finally got his chance in the Spanish-American War in 1898. Although severely handicapped by myopia and in spite of his advanced age and his responsibilities toward his wife and many children, he gave up his position as assistant secretary of the navy to fight in Cuba. With characteristic bravado he went into battle, stormed Kettle Hill, and returned a hero. As much as he was pleased with his exploits (which not quite incidentally proved rather helpful in his political campaigns), he regretted that he had not been injured or killed in battle. This supreme honor had eluded him. When one of his sons fell in World War I, Roosevelt's grief was sincere, but so was his pride and envy that his son "had his crowded hour, of a life that was not only glorious but very happy; he had got his man; he had rendered service."[9]

But Roosevelt was not just a bespectacled "Rambo" with a barely concealed death wish. He was intelligent enough to transcend the extravagant individualistic aspects of his philosophy and put combat and war into a larger perspective. He acknowledged, if reluctantly, that war was not an end in itself or a generally acceptable way to achieve personal self-fulfillment. He always asserted that only righteous war was justified. "War is a dreadful thing, and unjust war is a crime against humanity." Nevertheless, he insisted that "it is such a crime because it is unjust, not because it is war."[10] Equally ambivalent were his pronouncements on the meaning of peace: "As a civilized people we desire peace, but the only peace worth having is obtained by instant readiness to fight when wronged – not by unwillingness or inability to fight at all."[11] Deep down he may have believed in war for its own sake because the "victories of peace are great; but the victories of war are greater."[12] Yet intellectually and politically he realized that this belief was immoral and unacceptable.

Roosevelt's definition of a "just war" further clarifies his understanding of foreign relations. Put into an interracial perspective, war was a means by which righteousness was established between the races. Any race, when wronged, had the duty to defend itself and to fight for its rights. But war was particularly justified when it helped to further the cause of civilization, the triumph of civilized over primitive races. In the Darwinian fight for the survival of the fittest, imperialistic expansion was a necessity and a moral

8 Cooper, *Warrior and the Priest*, 35–6; TR to the editors of the *Harvard Crimson,* Jan. 2, 1896; TR to Henry Cabot Lodge, Jan. 2; TR to Frederick C. Selous, Feb. 7, 1900, in *TR Letters,* 1:505–7, 2:1175; see Beale, *Rise of America,* 48–54.
9 Wagenknecht, *Seven Worlds,* 250.
10 TR, "Citizenship in a Republic," address delivered at the Sorbonne, Paris, Apr. 23, 1910, in TR, *The Works of Theodore Roosevelt,* 20 vols. (New York, 1925), 15:357 (hereafter *TR Works*).
11 Henry Cabot Lodge, introduction to TR, "Hero Tales from American History," in *TR Works,* 9:xxi.
12 Wagenknecht, *Seven Worlds,* 248.

duty for any superior race. Therefore, "every expansion of civilization makes for peace. In other words, every expansion of a great civilized power means a victory for law, order, and righteousness."[13]

Thus the two elements of race and war became the fundamental principles on which Roosevelt's understanding of U.S. foreign relations and the powers' diplomacy was based. The relative position of a nation in international politics was determined by its racial characteristics. Just war as a means of extending a race's influence was limited only to the most civilized nations. They had the right and the moral duty to overcome the lesser races and to expand their healthy, civilizing influence.

It goes without saying that Roosevelt put the American race at the top of his list of nations. He defined it as one of the English-speaking races with strong roots in Great Britain. However, frontier experience, westward expansion, and a republican form of government had helped Americans to evolve and divest themselves of the less admirable British qualities. The first settlers looking for liberty and independence had provided the foundation. Each non-English group that followed in their footsteps had lost most of its national characteristics in a few generations and assumed the unifying American nationality. Through this continual immigration and assimilation, the existence and development of the American race had been guaranteed.[14]

Still, the continuing growth of the American people and the United States' superior position in the world necessitated further expansion. Of that Roosevelt was certain. The United States as a civilized nation had the right and the duty to extend its rule over the western hemisphere according to the Monroe Doctrine, eventually displacing the remaining European colonial powers. He remained unclear on how this expansion would be realized – whether the United States would take colonies, displace European trade, or create an informal empire.

A steady American foreign policy was needed to implement this expansionist mission. Roosevelt's "big stick" diplomacy, often mistaken for haphazard imperialism, provided a pragmatic policy to safeguard American interests in the most effective way. Its central element was a strong navy to supply the necessary power to enforce American policies against weaker nations in the Caribbean.

But more important, it would strengthen American sovereignty in the international system. With the development of faster and more powerful navies to the east and the west of the United States, the oceans no longer

13 Ibid., 258.
14 TR to William Archer, Aug. 31, 1899, in *TR Letters*, 2:1063–4.

sufficed as barriers against violations of American security interests. Roosevelt therefore wanted a fleet that was strong enough to dissuade America's potential enemies from any military adventures in the western hemisphere. This new navy was not meant as a deterrent against an actual enemy. Instead, its mere existence would guide potential adversaries, in particular Germany and Japan, away from contemplating policies that would threaten American interests and lead to enmity and war. America should simply show itself ready to defend its interests by force if necessary while avoiding any aggressive behavior and keeping friendly with potential adversaries. Unnecessary conflicts between civilized nations and the United States could thus be avoided. In the end America would even be able, where desirable, to cooperate with other powers on an equal footing.[15]

Most likely were cooperative agreements with races that were closely related to the American people. The obvious candidate was Great Britain because both nations supposedly shared a common racial background. But they arrived at close political cooperation only after several decades of hostility. Before 1898 Roosevelt had been adamant in defending American interests against British imperialism, especially in the first Venezuelan Crisis, when he advocated war to crush British attempts to violate the Monroe Doctrine.[16] Obviously, racial affinity did not preclude imperialist competition. Roosevelt's and the American public's attitude changed when London provided vital support to the United States during the Spanish-American War and gave up its remaining interests in the Caribbean. From then on Roosevelt became a staunch supporter of Anglo-American friendship.[17]

As for the United States, the main duty of the European civilized powers was to expand civilization, if necessary by force of war. Accordingly, Roosevelt gave staunch moral support for Great Britain's war against the Boers in South Africa. The Boers' stubborn resistance against the stronger British troops should have evoked much sympathy in the United States. Here was a pioneering people, similar to the American frontiersmen, who defended their liberties against the oppressor, Great Britain. But the Boers found support only among American Democrats and Irish and German immigrants. Republicans such as Roosevelt, John Hay, and Alfred Thayer

15 See, e.g., TR to Henry Cabot Lodge, Mar. 27, 1901; TR to George von Lengerke Meyer, Apr. 12, 1901; TR to Hermann Speck von Sternburg, July 20, 1900; TR to Arthur H. Lee, July 25, 1900; TR to Cecil Arthur Spring Rice, Nov. 19, 1900, in *TR Letters*, 2:1358, 1362, 1422–3, 1428, 3:31–2, 52.
16 Beale, *Rise of America*, 48–54.
17 Bradford Perkins, *The Great Rapprochement* (New York, 1968); Alexander E. Campbell, *Great Britain and the United States, 1895–1903* (London, 1960).

Mahan stood with Great Britain. Their Anglophilia had developed into a new ideology that equated racial affinity with political agreement.

Roosevelt deplored this fight between two civilizations, but sometimes these confrontations were unavoidable. This war in particular, he believed, showed the tragic aspects of human evolution. "International law, and above all interracial law, [is] still in a fluid condition, and two nations with violently conflicting interests may each be entirely right from its own standpoint."[18]

Roosevelt himself had Dutch ancestors and admired the Boers for their stamina both in fighting against the British and in conquering the land. But he was convinced that the advancement of civilization depended on British predominance in South Africa, just as the United States had to rule over the western hemisphere. Once the English-speaking race in all its branches had established the largest possible dominion, victory for civilization was guaranteed.[19] Because the British had the better claim, it was in the Boers' interest as a civilized race to lose the war. It was their mistake that they did not see their inferior position. John Hay even maintained that it was the responsibility of the Boers themselves that women and children had to suffer in British concentration camps – the Boers should have given up the fight and submitted to British leadership. Eventually both races would intermingle and experience the same development as the United States.[20]

This war, Roosevelt thought, also was an important challenge for Great Britain. The empire had shown an alarming tendency toward weakness and decadence. The Boer war, as Roosevelt's friend Cecil Spring Rice put it, could help to overcome the "fatness and luxury and boasting and the general sleek Jewishness of London." Roosevelt agreed that "there are ugly forces at play in all our Western civilization, and it may be that in a few centuries it may have gone down utterly." But there was still hope "that the healthy tissue will gradually eat out the unhealthy." And a war was perfectly suited to such a process.[21]

There was no danger of decadence among the German people. Roosevelt felt a strong kinship with the Germans because he believed that the

18 TR to Spring Rice, Aug. 13, 1897, in *TR Letters,* 1:644–5.
19 TR to Henry White, Mar. 30, 1896, in *TR Letters,* 1:523.
20 TR to John St. Loe Strachey, Jan. 27, 1900; TR to Frederick C. Selous, Feb. 7, 1900; TR to Spring Rice, July 3, 1901, in *TR Letters,* 2:1144–6, 1175–7, 3:109; Beale, *Rise of America,* 96–100; Stuart Anderson, "Racial Anglo-Saxonism and the American Response to the Boer War," *Diplomatic History* 2 (1978): 219–36.
21 Spring Rice to TR, Jan. 18, 1900, Theodore Roosevelt papers, Library of Congress Manuscript Division, Washington, D.C. (hereafter LC TR papers), microfilm reel 4; TR to Spring Rice, Jan. 27, 1900; Mar. 12, 1900, in *TR Letters,* 2:1147–8, 1216–17.

"German is of our blood, our principles and our ideas." This, according to Roosevelt, explained why German immigrants to the United States assimilated so quickly and readily embraced American republican virtues. They never constituted an alien element but were a healthy addition to the American race.[22]

The Germans' militaristic character only added to their attractiveness for Roosevelt. Along with many Americans, he admired the seemingly harmonious relationship between a strong military spirit and the highly developed German culture.[23] Germans clearly had advanced to the highest level of racial perfection. What was still missing in the Reich was a republican form of government. This is what pushed the German race just below the English-speaking races, in Roosevelt's assessment.

At least the German emperor realized his duty to spread civilization. Roosevelt generally supported Germany's imperial ambitions. The only problem was the direction German foreign policy took. German imperialists were demanding coaling stations close to the future transisthmian canal in the Caribbean. Bismarck himself had called the Monroe Doctrine "quite an extraordinary insolence." Judging from the rhetoric German expansionists used, from their disdain for U.S. security interests to maneuvers of the German fleet in Latin American waters, it seemed as if the Germans were focusing their imperialist ambition on Latin America.[24] Instead of misdirecting their expansionist policy, Roosevelt believed, the Germans should look toward the east. There Asiatic Russia threatened the development of European civilization. It was the German emperor's task to protect Europe from the Slavic hordes. According to Roosevelt, Kaiser Wilhelm should have defeated Russia, conquered the Baltic provinces, freed Finland, and turned Poland into a buffer state, even if that would have meant defeating France first. "It has always seemed to me that the Germans showed shortsightedness in not making some alliance that will enable them to crush Russia."[25]

Roosevelt's task as president was to turn the Kaiser away from a policy that could lead to a confrontation with the United States. Although he conceded that the Germans had every right to expand in Latin America,

22 TR to Spring Rice, Aug. 11, 1899; TR to William Archer, Aug. 31, 1899; TR to Louis Viereck, Sept. 1, 1900; TR to H. White, Nov. 23, 1900, in *TR Letters,* 2:1049–50, 1063–4, 1396–7, 1436–7.
23 Dyer, *Theodore Roosevelt,* 2–3; TR, *An Autobiography* (1913; reprinted: New York, 1985), 23.
24 Alfred Vagts, *Deutschland und die Vereinigten Staaten in der Weltpolitik* (New York, 1935), 2:1471–3, 1704–5; Herwig, *Germany's Vision,* 175–208; Fiebig-von Hase, *Konfliktherd,* 1:428–71.
25 TR to Spring Rice, Aug. 5, 1896; Aug. 13, 1897; Aug. 11, 1899, in *TR Letters,* 1:555, 645–6; 2:1051–2.

he also maintained America's right to uphold the Monroe Doctrine and to oppose German imperialism in the western hemisphere. To resolve this conflict of interests between two civilized nations, he resorted to the carrot-and-stick approach of his "big stick" diplomacy. From the start of his presidency Roosevelt tried to stay on friendly terms with the Germans. He encouraged closer ties with Berlin and welcomed all attempts at fostering a better relationship between the two nations. At the same time, he advocated the expansion of the American fleet. As a result, he made the Germans feel that they had more to gain from American friendship than from a confrontation. "I should adopt [that course]," Roosevelt asserted, "without in the least feeling that the Germans who advocated German colonial expansion were doing anything save what was right and proper from the standpoint of their own people."[26] Roosevelt's deterrence was not meant as a containment of a German threat that did not yet exist. It was a means of staking American claims, clarifying American policy to the Germans, and avoiding an unnecessary confrontation between civilized nations, and thus creating peaceful and friendly German-American relations.

Although Roosevelt could find full support in the United States for his policy in the western hemisphere, foreign relations in Europe had not played a major role during his first term. The American people limited the president's diplomatic activities to traditional areas of interest: upholding the Monroe Doctrine, building up the navy to protect the United States from aggression, and pursuing the open door policy in China. Except for the Monroe Doctrine, even these limited goals were highly contested political issues. Roosevelt often complained about the restraints that the democratic decision-making process put on his ability to consider "great and far-reaching policies – especially foreign policies." A republic's liberal institutions, he believed, gave far too much influence to the "stay-at-home" and "peace-at-any-price people," to anti-imperialists who "screamed with anguish over the loss of a couple of thousand men in the field; a sentiment of preposterous and unreasoning mawkishness."[27]

From a domestic perspective, then, Roosevelt could do no better than to keep his involvement in international affairs to the necessary minimum. Even in terms of its foreign relations, the United States had no direct interest in European affairs. Still, when in the summer of 1905 tensions grew between Germany, France, and Great Britain, the president, especially after

26 TR to Spring Rice, Aug. 13, 1897; TR to John D. Long, Sept. 30, 1897; TR to Francis C. Moore, Feb. 5, Feb. 9, 1898; TR to Charles A. Moore, Feb. 14, in *TR Letters,* 1:645, 695, 768–9, 771–2; TR to William W. Kimball, Jan. 9, 1900, in *TR Letters,* 2:1130–1.
27 TR to Spring Rice, Dec. 27, 1904, in *TR Letters,* 4:1083–5.

his efforts at peacemaking between Russia and Japan, felt called on in his capacity as a neutral party to stop the possible outbreak of a war in Europe.

Based on the information Roosevelt received from British, German, and French sources in 1904 and 1905, Europe seemed to be on the brink of war. The British diplomat and presidential friend Spring Rice wrote the president from St. Petersburg, describing the cooperation between Russia and Germany against the democratic powers. According to Spring Rice, the war that the czar waged against Japan was only the beginning of a much larger battle. It was the first step of "common action of the two great military despotisms – Germany and Russia – on the common ground of spoliation." "The Emperor of the West turns his back on the Emperor of the East, and lays his hand on the little peoples of the West, while his brother is free to gobble the East. . . . The dream here, clearly, is common action against England (America being wicked and succulent, but unfortunately distant)."[28]

But Roosevelt was not convinced: "I cannot believe that there will be such a continental coalition against England." He thought that Spring Rice was "an alarmist." The real danger was that both England and America were "unmilitary . . . yet both rich and aggressive." Rather than being threatened from outside, "the spirit of mere materialism and shortsighted vanity and folly" was weakening each race from within.[29] "England . . . is pretty flabby, and I am afraid to trust either the farsightedness or the tenacity of purpose of her statesmen; or indeed of her people."[30]

As for Germany, Roosevelt's initial misgivings about German expansionist dreams in Latin America had been revived during the early years of his presidency by the Anglo-German intervention in Venezuela in 1902–3. However, the affair ended on a positive note and was not as dangerous as he himself portrayed it during World War I or as later historians would have it.[31] But even if Roosevelt was no longer afraid about German attempts to violate the Monroe Doctrine, the erratic and difficult behavior that the

28 Parenthetical remark in the original; Spring Rice to TR, Jan. 20, 1904, LC TR papers, reel 40; ca. mid-Feb. 1904, Stephen Gwynn, ed., *The Letters and Friendships of Sir Cecil Spring Rice: A Record* (London, 1929), 1:394–7; see also Spring Rice to Lodge, Feb. 19, 1904, Massachusetts Historical Society, Henry Cabot Lodge papers, box 88.

29 TR to Spring Rice, Mar. 19, 1904, in *TR Letters,* 4:761; TR to Sternburg, July 19, 1904, LC TR papers, reel 334.

30 TR to G. v. L. Meyer, Dec. 26, 1904, in *TR Letters,* 4:1080.

31 For a critical evaluation of the crisis, see Herwig, *Germany's Vision;* Lammersdorf, *Anfänge einer Weltmacht,* 54–96; Nancy Mitchell, "The Height of the German Challenge: The Venezuela Blockade, 1902–3," *Diplomatic History* 20 (1996): 185–210; and two publications supporting Roosevelt's story: Fiebig-von Hase, *Konfliktherd,* and Edmund Morris, "'A Few Pregnant Days': Theodore Roosevelt and the Venezuela Crisis of 1902," *Theodore Roosevelt Association Journal* 15 (1989): 2–13.

German government displayed during this affair did not inspire confidence in the peaceful intentions and overall capability of its diplomacy.

Following his policy of wooing a potential enemy, the focus of Roosevelt's friendly overtures was the German Kaiser. He wrongly believed that Wilhelm alone was responsible for his empire's foreign policy. For the president, only the somewhat difficult personality of the Kaiser could explain the strange course of Germany. Dealing with Germany meant getting along with the emperor and controlling his temper. The president spoke softly with Wilhelm, coaxing him on a course of German–American friendship.[32]

Roosevelt was far more successful than he had intended. Inspired by his friendly remarks to German diplomats, the German foreign office began thinking that they could use the president's obvious German sympathies and turn him into a pawn of the empire's *Weltpolitik* (global policy). They matched his friendliness with a concerted friendship campaign that included, among other things, the visit of the emperor's brother Prince Heinrich to the United States, the donation of a statue of Friedrich II, and the endowment of the Theodore Roosevelt chair at the Friedrich Wilhelm University in Berlin. Roosevelt's profuse gratitude and his many statements, such as "The only man I understand and who understands me is the Kaiser," confirmed and strengthened the belief among German diplomats that the inexperienced and naïve president would cooperate with Germany in areas of common interest.[33]

The first tangible result of this diplomacy was close cooperation in China. To Roosevelt's surprise, the German emperor was enthusiastically supportive of the president's campaign for the open door. On this point Roosevelt gladly complied with Berlin's request for a policy of Chinese neutralization during the Russo-Japanese war and secured a pledge by the powers for the integrity of China. Although not wholly convinced that Germany was acting out of unselfishness, Roosevelt was glad for the opportunity to gain a positive statement from Germany on the open door and "to nail the matter with the Kaiser."[34]

In fact, Germany's interests in China were not aimed against the open door. Rather, in the highly complex and complicated conceptualization of German foreign policy, China was only one piece in a giant game of *Weltpolitik*. Chancellor Bülow and the German foreign office wanted to gain

---

32 See Lammersdorf, *Anfänge einer Weltmacht,* 34–43.
33 Sternburg to Auswärtiges Amt, Sept. 27, 1904, Johannes Lepsius et al., eds., *Die Grosse Politik der europäischen Kabinette 1871–1914,* 40 vols. (Berlin, 1922–7), 19, pt. 2: 541–2.
34 John Hay diary, Jan. 9, 1905, LC John Hay papers, box 1.

the status of a world power for the German Empire – that is, domination over Europe and at least equality with the British empire. At the same time they were haunted by the specter of a quadruple alliance between the Russo-French and the Anglo-Japanese alliances that would crush the German Empire under its might. German diplomats were trapped in the paranoid vision of a "belated" empire that was being deprived of its right to share in the partition of the world and whose ambition was continually thwarted by those already established as colonial powers. In every contested region, German politicians were jealously guarding what they saw as their right to participate in the development of new colonies. In the case of China, bringing in Roosevelt and the American open door policy would call the four powers' game while avoiding a confrontation with Germany.

Luckily, the U.S. president repeatedly professed his willingness "to walk hand-in-hand with Germany in East Asia."[35] And Roosevelt's prompt support for Germany's neutralization policy in China created the impression (which soon became a conviction) among German diplomats that the president shared Germany's suspicions of French and British evil intentions. There was ample reason to believe that President Roosevelt would continue to cooperate with Germany against the schemes of the other powers. America's interest in the open door could be combined with Germany's defense against British and French supremacy outside of Asia.[36]

German diplomats did not hesitate to call on Roosevelt's help during the Moroccan Crisis of 1905–6. At that time France, together with Spain and supported by Great Britain, intended to introduce internal reforms in Morocco – most important the establishment of a police force and a bank – that would eventually draw the country into the French North African empire. The German government protested this attempt to violate Morocco's sovereignty and demanded an international agreement on the reforms and equal access to the country.[37]

The Berlin foreign office's real aim behind the defense of the open door in Morocco was to disrupt the Entente Cordiale. By challenging France's claim to Morocco and by threatening war if their demands for an international conference on Morocco's future were not met, the Germans put Britain's loyalty to France to the test. Berlin was certain that Great Britain would not risk a war with Germany over France's North African interests.

35 Sternburg to AA, Aug. 11, 1904, in *Grosse Politik,* 19, pt. 2:535–6.
36 See, e.g., Bülow to Wilhelm II, Dec. 26, 1904; Holstein memorandum, Dec. 29, 1904; Bülow to Sternburg, Mar. 23, 1905, in *Grosse Politik,* 19, pt. 2:400–3, 551–6, 585–7.
37 For the Moroccan Crisis, see Eugene N. Anderson, *The First Moroccan Crisis, 1904–1906* (Chicago, 1930).

If the challenge was strong enough, the British would back off from their promises to France. The Entente would thus be destroyed, and Germany's *Weltpolitik* of dividing the powers and achieving hegemony over Europe would have achieved an important victory.[38]

Roosevelt was to play a central role in this scheme. Out of principle, so the Germans believed, the president had to support Germany's policy of the open door in Morocco. He should put pressure on the British to refrain from backing France's imperialist ambitions in North Africa. Combined with Germany's war threats, Roosevelt's intervention would help to persuade the British that the Entente with France was against their own best interests.

To convince Roosevelt, who at first seemed very reluctant to get involved in purely European matters, Chancellor Bülow sent a barrage of memoranda to Washington. The German government meant to supply Roosevelt with conclusive evidence both of the evil intentions of the Entente and of the righteousness and altruism of German foreign policy in Morocco.[39] Through no fault of their own, they argued, the situation in Europe had become exceedingly dangerous. Germany had to insist on the freedom of Morocco, not merely because of its own economic interests in North Africa but in order to protect those of all nations. It was not just Morocco that was threatened. If the Entente powers were not resisted, they would continue to carve up the world among themselves, finally realizing the goal of a quadruple alliance and subduing all other powers with their combined strength. This is why Germany had to insist on the open door and the sultan's sovereignty in Morocco and protect it with military force if necessary.

But, the German ambassador told the president, if Roosevelt would "give England a confidential hint as to [his] attitude in the question, it would greatly add to a peaceful solution."[40] Once the British government would realize that the United States had found out about the Entente's secret plan and opposed it, London would withdraw all support for France, and a war no longer would be necessary. The president would score another triumph as the world's peacemaker and "would render the peace of the world another great service, without encountering any risk."[41] However, should Roosevelt not support Germany in its fight for the open door in

---

38 Lammersdorf, *Anfänge einer Weltmacht,* 195–222.

39 See Sternburg's many letters to TR, May–July 1905, LC TR papers, reels 54–5.

40 Sternburg to TR, Apr. 13, 1905, LC TR papers, reel 53.

41 Bülow to Sternburg, no. 129, June 9, 1905, Politisches Archiv des Auswärtigen Amtes, Bonn, Botschaftsakten Washington, 4 A 1c, vol.2; Sternburg memorandum, June 11, 1905, LC TR papers, reel 55.

Morocco and leave the German government alone in its altruistic campaign for international justice, "we would have to choose between the possibility of a conflict with France or any compensations that France would offer to avoid this conflict."[42]

German diplomats were never in doubt that Roosevelt would appreciate Germany's service to all nations and that he shared their conception of war as a natural instrument of foreign policy. For them, threatening war was the appropriate way of dealing with other powers and of forging or destroying alliances. They readily assumed that all other powers, including the United States, shared this concept.

Of course, Roosevelt never accepted the German interpretation of the international situation. He rejected the phantasm of a quadruple alliance, he never saw the connection between the open door and Morocco, and he certainly did not feel that any American interests were involved. Most of all, he was alarmed at the callousness with which the Germans planned and threatened war.

Because all diplomatic notes from Berlin appeared to come from the emperor, Roosevelt interpreted German diplomacy as the result of Wilhelm's personality. At first the Kaiser's messages were just annoying and made Roosevelt "wish to Heaven our excellent friend, the Kaiser, was not so jumpy and did not have so many pipe dreams."[43] Reacting to the abundance of messages from Berlin, he complained: "The Kaiser has become a monomaniac about getting into communication with me every time he drinks three pen'orth [pennies worth] of conspiracy against his life and power."

But Roosevelt became increasingly concerned that a real danger of war in Europe would result from the Kaiser's paranoid vision and a similar British fear of a continental coalition as outlined by Spring Rice. There was a certain irony in the situation. "It's as funny a case as I have ever seen of mutual distrust and fear bringing two peoples to the verge of war."[44] Tensions between the two countries, Roosevelt concluded, were unnecessary and dangerous because they could escalate to war. "Each Nation is working itself up to a condition of desperate hatred of each other from sheer fear of each other." If Roosevelt could use his close contacts with all sides for a better understanding between Germany, France, and Great Britain he would gladly lend a hand.[45] Therefore, he continued to stay in close touch

42 Bülow to Sternburg, no. 98, May 10, 1905, in *Grosse Politik*, 19, pt. 2:620–2.
43 William H. Taft to Sternburg, Apr. 5, 1905, LC TR papers, reel 337; TR to Taft, Apr. 8, in *TR Letters*, 4:1159.
44 TR to Hay, Mar. 30, Apr. 2, 1905, in *TR Letters*, 5:1150, 1157.
45 TR to Taft, Apr. 20, 1905, in *TR Letters*, 4:1161–2, 1165.

with the Germans and remained as friendly and as courteous as possible. He believed that soon his friendly relations with the emperor might become useful for maintaining the peace in Europe.

While he conferred with the German ambassador, he also looked elsewhere for a rational explanation for the emperor's "pipe dreams." He received it from French ambassador Jean-Jules Jusserand, who had become a close friend of the president's soon after arriving in Washington. Jusserand had helped Roosevelt understand the political implications of the Russo-Japanese war for Europe and found him supportive of the Entente Cordiale. It was only natural for the president to turn to the French ambassador once the Kaiser began his attack on the Entente.

Jusserand was able to unravel the Germans' twisted logic for the president. He pleased Roosevelt by agreeing that the Kaiser did not want war but could cause it through his reckless speeches and actions.[46] It was not too difficult for Jusserand to refute the German complaint that France was closing access to Morocco. Roosevelt was soon ready to acknowledge France's role as civilizing agent, rejected Germany's demand for a conference, and privately supported the expansion of French domination in North Africa.[47] When the German memoranda to the president became more belligerent in tone, a concerned Roosevelt showed them to Jusserand. The French ambassador not only received valuable information for his own government, but together with Roosevelt he composed the replies.[48]

This close cooperation with France pulled Roosevelt even deeper into the European imbroglio. At first, he protested that he could not get himself involved in foreign affairs because it was already hard enough "to keep this nation on an even keel. . . . I certainly do not intend to go into peacemaking as a regular business."[49] But the continuing European crisis in the summer of 1905, the repeated German warnings that France was provoking war, and Jusserand's alarming reports of German war threats against the French convinced him that he should use whatever influence he had to halt the escalation.

Positioned as a disinterested neutral between the rivaling powers, he could try to manipulate the Kaiser through flattery while he was able to talk reasonably with the French. In contrast to the Germans, they had al-

---

46 Jean Jules Jusserand to Théophile Delcassé, no. 37, Apr. 1, 1905, Commission de Publication des Documents Relatifs aux Origines de la Guerre de 1914, eds., *Documents Diplomatiques Français (1871–1914),* 2d series (1901–11), (Paris, 1935–46), 2, pt. 6:276–7.
47 Jusserand to Delcassé, no. 113, Nov. 16, 1904, Archives Diplomatiques, Ministère des Affaires Etrangères, Paris, N.S. Etats-Unis 3.
48 Jusserand to Rouvier, no. 105, June 26, 1905, *Documents Diplomatiques Français,* 2, pt. 7:156–7.
49 TR to Spring Rice, Nov. 1, 1905, in *TR Letters,* 5:61–4.

ways been far more open to a sober and intelligent assessment of the world situation. Unhampered by paranoia, they would listen to Roosevelt's sensible suggestions. When Roosevelt finally changed his course and supported Germany's demand for a conference on Morocco, he did so not because he had become convinced that the Kaiser was right. He assured Jusserand that the German interpretation of world politics was based on "rather incoherent hypotheses." He knew that the emperor's policy was intended as an attack on the Entente. But Wilhelm's motives were now beside the point. The real questions were, How serious were the emperor's threats, and how could an unnecessary war between civilized nations be avoided?

In what seems to be a curious reversal of his position on war, and believing that honor and righteousness were more important than peace, he now urged France to give up its opposition to the German demands and make concessions to the emperor's vanity. But in Roosevelt's view it was no longer a matter of defending French honor. He believed that the French government could yield to Germany without giving up its interests because it was already clear that the Germans would be isolated at the conference and would be unable to achieve their goals. In this instance, France would not dishonorably give in to pressure but through clever concessions would gain a political victory for itself and for civilization. Because the emperor was clearly acting irrationally, carelessly risking war and the destruction of Europe, it was up to the rational French to act in the interest of "the welfare of the world at this time."[50]

Roosevelt's involvement in European power politics ended with the conference. He had done his duty and believed that he had helped prevent the outbreak of war between France and Germany.[51] In this endeavor he had not been concerned about American political, strategic, or economic interests. Roosevelt's fear of war in Europe and his involvement in old world politics were motivated by a sincere and disinterested desire to assist in the achievement of a higher goal: the safety and advancement of human civilization. The civilized nations of Europe, whose destiny was to spread their culture and dominance over a barbarous world, were barely saved from committing the greatest folly of all: fighting among themselves while the world needed to be saved. Righteous war against a weaker, less civilized power provided for the improvement of man and race. It was natural and

50 Jusserand to Rouvier, no. 82, June 15, 1905, and Jusserand to Rouvier, no. 91, June 18, 1905, *Documents Diplomatiques Français,* 2, pt. 7:68–70; TR to Sternburg, June 23, 1905, in *TR Letters,* 4:1251; Sternburg to AA, No. 129, June 24, in *Grosse Politik,* 20, pt. 2:466–7.
51 On the details of U.S. participation at the conference, see Lammersdorf, *Anfänge einer Weltmacht,* 192–282, 311–54.

unavoidable. But conflict between civilized races was tragic and deplorable because it weakened civilization as a whole. Looking back on the crisis, Roosevelt reflected: "I should have felt such a war to be a real calamity to civilization; and . . . I felt that a new conflict might result in what would literally be a world conflagration."[52]

Today, this motivation for foreign policy is likely to be dismissed as mere rhetoric meant to camouflage Roosevelt's "real" political and economic interests or a policy of imperialism. Taking Roosevelt at his words, so the argument goes, could lead to a historicist and therefore incorrect or at least incomplete understanding of his policies.

Certainly, Roosevelt's worldview has to be condemned as racist and imperialist. To his credit, he was not a rabid extremist for racial purity. He believed in the upward mobility of any race, condemned the lynching of southern African Americans, and even invited Booker T. Washington to the White House. But he had no regard for the sovereign rights of peoples whom he considered inferior. He first supported, then presided over the vicious and brutal suppression of the Philippine struggle for independence, and he considered colonial oppression a God-given duty for self-styled civilized nations.

But as distasteful and unconvincing as this ideology appears today, it does not make it any less important for an understanding of Roosevelt's actions. Just because in the present-day Western view racial interpretations of the world situation are considered irrational, it does not follow that they carried no meaning for Roosevelt and his contemporaries. Rationality, after all, is a historical construct with different meanings at different times and in different cultures. Although historians have to avoid a historicist reading of sources, an approach that is too heavily based on today's supposedly more rational construction of meaning may be just as imbalanced.

The prevailing American attitude toward foreign policy at the time of Roosevelt's presidency left enough room for ideology as its basis. There was no need for realpolitik in the sense of European power politics because the United States' hegemonic position in the western hemisphere could not be challenged. For the same reason, it does not make sense to speak about balance of power in America. The United States could not through its existence or policies provoke any external dangers that might threaten its political freedom of action. Given this almost idyllic geopolitical position, the American polity could afford the luxury of neglecting foreign relations. After all, the Spanish-American War as policy remained an excep-

52 TR to Whitelaw Reid, Apr. 28, 1906; TR to Jusserand, Apr. 25, 1906, in *TR Letters*, 5:236, 221.

tion and there was always a strong anti-imperialist tendency. The foreign policy elite could convince the American people to support naval armaments only after the navy's role had been confined to protecting American security. It would not be used to pursue European-style foreign policy. As *The Nation* had written twenty years earlier, it was still true that "the people of the United States want as little of foreign policy as possible."[53]

It is not surprising, then, that Roosevelt's day-to-day interest in diplomacy was very limited. And the more remote an interest was, the simpler a policy concept could be. Roosevelt did not need a more complex idea of American foreign policy toward Europe than what he had developed in his racial philosophy. It was unnecessary for him to learn more about European developments because they were not his concern as the American president. He readily admitted that he did not really know what was going on in Europe. And he did not care until the signs of an impending war became so obvious that he felt it his personal duty to intervene – not in his capacity as leader of the United States, but as a bystander with a small chance to help. His involvement was not in the direct interests of the United States but sprang from a feeling of personal responsibility.

Roosevelt's involvement in European power politics was exceptional and remained a secret during the remainder of his presidency. His concern about war in Europe did not establish a more activist American foreign policy. But his policy fairly represented the attitude of the United States toward the Europeans during the first decade of the twentieth century. No immediate American political interests would have been touched by a European war. Americans did not yet think that a war would have a direct impact on the economic or security interests of the United States. Of course, America would not remain unaffected by a conflict in Europe. But only a minority saw the need for taking a position in favor of any party in a conflict.

The three years of neutrality after war broke out in 1914 gave proof to America's aloofness. In 1917 the historic change from neutrality to engagement on the part of the Allies was possible only after repeated German provocations and after a majority of Americans began to feel that the war had gained two significant qualities: It had become a question of vital American interests – freedom of the seas, trade interests in Europe, protection of American lives – and a fight of the civilized and democratic powers against despotism and barbarism. Germany no longer was considered to be a civilized power. The war in Europe was a righteous war to further the

---

53 *The Nation* 36 (Mar. 22, 1883): 249.

advancement of civilization. It no longer was a calamity but a heroic duty for all civilized races.

In this crucial aspect, Roosevelt's ideology of American racial superiority and his reluctant diplomacy reflect commonly shared American beliefs. His involvement in Europe may have been singular and atypical in its activism and willingness to intervene in affairs outside the western hemisphere. There also was no direct link between his support for France or his suspicions of German aims in Latin America during his presidency and the declaration of war in 1917. Yet his worldview was just one variant reading of the recurrent dogma of American superiority. Racial rationalizations slowly decreased in importance. But the need to base any activist foreign policy, especially when committing the United States to armed intervention, on America's perceived exceptional qualities as a civilized power – be they racial, philosophical, or political – remained.

PART FOUR

The Experience of War

17

Total War on the American Indian Frontier

ROBERT M. UTLEY

According to conventional wisdom in the United States and elsewhere around the world, the term "genocide" describes the treatment of American Indians by the dominant race and its government. The genocidal creed arises from the guilt Americans have come to feel over the centuries-long ordeal of the native Americans. It has gained constant reinforcement from motion pictures, television, and popular literature, such as the immensely popular and influential polemic of Dee Brown, *Bury My Heart at Wounded Knee*.[1] It also has been encouraged by the tribal activism that began in the 1960s with the Red Power movement; "Custer Died for Your Sins," proclaimed one bumper sticker. Today, a large segment of both Indian and white populations perceive this experience as having been genocidal.

However fashionable, the formulation in the conventional understanding of the word is nonsense. The dictionary definition of "genocide" is "the deliberate and systematic extermination of a national, racial, political, or cultural group." In the public mind, genocide is equated with the Holocaust – the intentional obliteration of a people by means of mass physical annihilation. No more than a tiny portion of the white population of the United States, mainly in the West, ever advocated such a measure. No government official ever seriously proposed it. The occasional rhetoric of generals such as William T. Sherman and Philip H. Sheridan was just that: angry reactions to particular events involving particular Indian groups.[2] They

1 Dee Brown, *Bury My Heart at Wounded Knee: An Indian History of the American West* (New York, 1970). Presented as history and popularly read as history, the book has progressed through innumerable editions and is still in print. Millions of copies have been sold. Whatever its faults as history, this book surpasses all other influences of the past quarter-century in shaping American beliefs about the morality of white treatment of Indians.

2 Sherman, angrily reacting to the Fetterman Massacre of December 1866: "We must act with vindictive earnestness against the Sioux, even to their extermination, men, women, and children" (Senate Executive Document no. 13, 40th Congress, 1st session, 27). Sheridan's flippant remark, "The only good Indians I ever saw were dead," is more an expression of bad taste than proposed policy. Paul Andrew Hutton, *Phil Sheridan and His Army* (Lincoln, Neb., 1985), 180–1.

never pushed the agenda implied by the rhetoric. If the federal government ever set a genocidal objective, moreover, it failed spectacularly in its implementation. Today, the Indian population is twice that of a century ago.

Extinction by disease cannot be termed genocide. Between 1492 and the end of the nineteenth century, European disease may have reduced the North American Indian population by as much as 90 percent. The smallpox epidemic on the upper Missouri River in 1837, for example, all but wiped out the Mandan and Arikara tribes. Most tribes sustained periodic losses of catastrophic proportions from the ravages of sudden epidemics. The white man caused such epidemics, of course, but not as a measure of deliberate genocidal intent.[3]

In one sense the concept of genocide is relevant: cultural genocide. Although the U.S. government did not set forth to obliterate a people, it did attempt to obliterate their culture. Indeed, after roughly 1880 "civilization" of the Indian was the centerpiece of federal Indian policy. It aimed at transforming the Indians in every respect save skin color into imitation white people. Some theorists even foresaw, although ambivalently, eventual assimilation of Indians into the white race.

The civilization program rested on the almost universal assumption of white reformers and officials that Indian culture contained nothing worth preserving, that the white civilization of Victorian America represented the peak of cultural achievement. Indian agents often employed coercion and intimidation to advance their policies, but rarely violence. Indeed, cultural genocide could not have commanded more benevolent motives: What greater gift from one people to another than their own culture?[4]

The objectives and programs of cultural genocide dominated U.S. policy until Franklin D. Roosevelt's "Indian New Deal" of the 1930s. Only then did the government concede value in Indian culture and the Indians' right to recapture and nurture traditional ways. Today Indian culture, identity, and pride are vibrantly alive.

Indian culture today, however, is not the same as it was in the pre-reservation years of freedom. No Indian now living personifies that culture. This is testimony hardly to the success of the government's misguided civilization program but rather to the collapse of such foundation blocks of the old life as war and the hunt, from which the central institu-

3 For a survey of the literature on this important subject, see Henry F. Dobyns, *Native American Historical Demography: A Critical Bibliography* (Bloomington, Ind., 1976).
4 The magisterial work on U.S. Indian policy is Francis Paul Prucha, *The Great Father: The United States Government and the Indians,* 2 vols. (Lincoln, Neb., 1984); see also Robert M. Utley, *Indian Frontier of the American West, 1846–1890* (Albuquerque, N.M., 1984), chap. 8: "The Vision of the Reformers."

tions of society, government, economy, and religion drew content and meaning.

However suitable in scholarly discourse, cultural genocide is not a concept to be loosely tossed about in popular media. In the twentieth century the word "genocide" has become so freighted in the public mind with explicit meaning that it should be used only for such lethal atrocities as the Holocaust or Serbian "ethnic cleansing." Applying it to the experience of the American Indians, however deep and just their grievances, grossly falsifies history.

Nor was the U.S. Army's adoption of total war genocide, either in intent or result. As waged against the American Indians, total war contained both a military dimension and a moral dimension. Militarily, how well did it work, and was it the best strategy? Morally, how to rationalize the suffering and death of the enemy's noncombatant population? In rudimentary form, these questions prefigured questions that would trouble Americans in the great foreign conflicts of the twentieth century.

TOTAL WAR AS MILITARY DOCTRINE

Total war – warring on entire enemy populations – finds ample precedent in America's frontier experience. The military historian Russell Weigley has pointed out how different the colonial Indian wars were from the formal and not very destructive warfare of the European pattern. In King Philip's War of 1675–6, for example, the Indians almost wiped out the New England settlements, and in response the colonists all but wiped out the Indians. "The logic of a contest for survival was always implicit in the Indian wars," Weigley writes, "as it never was in the eighteenth century wars wherein European powers competed for possession of fortresses and countries, but always shared an awareness of their common participation in one civilization, Voltaire's 'Republic of Europe.'"[5]

Examples of total war recur periodically through subsequent centuries of Indian conflict, notably in the Seminole wars, but it remained for Generals Sherman and Sheridan to sanctify it as deliberate policy. With the march across Georgia and the wasting of the Shenandoah Valley as models, they set forth in the two decades after the Civil War to find the enemy in his winter camps, kill or drive him from his lodges, destroy his ponies, food, and shelter, and hound him mercilessly across a frigid landscape until he gave up. If women and children fell victim to such methods, it was re-

5 Russell F. Weigley, *The American Way of War: A History of United States Military Strategy and Policy* (New York, 1973), 19.

grettable but justified because it resolved the issue quickly and decisively, and thus more humanely.[6]

To avoid judging by a double standard, it should be noted that the Indian style of warfare also was total war. Indians carried women and children into captivity; more often they killed enemy noncombatants the same as enemy fighting men. Indian villages and stock herds lay vulnerable to pillage and destruction that caused suffering or death among all who escaped the battlefield with their lives.

"Doctrine" is too formal a term to apply to total war as conducted by either side. For the U.S. Army, it was a body of thought that simply evolved into the practice of certain commanders. In truth, the U.S. Army never had a prescribed doctrine of Indian warfare. That background is important to evaluating not only total war but other practices of which it was an outgrowth.

The American regular army was almost entirely a product of the frontier. Frontier needs prompted its creation. Except for two foreign wars and one civil war, frontier needs fixed its principal mission and employment for a century. Frontier needs dictated the periodic expansions of the regular army in the nineteenth century.[7] Frontier needs underlay Secretary of War John C. Calhoun's "expansible army" plan of 1820, which, although never adopted, contained assumptions that shaped military policy until 1917.[8]

For a century, the regulars worked the frontier West. They explored and mapped it. They laid out roads and telegraph lines and aided significantly in the advance of the railroads. They campaigned against Indians. They guarded travel routes and protected settlers. By offering security or at least its appearance, together with a market for labor and produce, they encouraged further settlement. As enlistments expired, some men stayed to help people the frontier.

Citizen-soldiers contributed, though less significantly. From King Philip's War to the final clash at Wounded Knee in 1890, colonial and state

6 I have discussed total war in *Frontier Regulars: The United States Army and the Indian, 1866–1890* (New York, 1973), chap. 3; and in more detail in *Contribution of the Frontier to the American Military Tradition*, Harmon Memorial Lectures in Military History, no. 19 (Colorado Springs, Colo., 1977).

7 The First and Second Dragoons in 1832 and 1836, the Regiment of Mounted Riflemen in 1846, the First and Second Cavalry and the Ninth and Tenth Infantry in 1855. The Army Act of 1866 expanded the regular army to meet both frontier and Reconstruction duty, but the reduction of 1869, as Reconstruction needs diminished, left a net gain of four cavalry regiments (Seventh to Tenth) and six infantry regiments (Twentieth to Twenty-fifth) that reflected frontier needs. (All mounted regiments were restyled cavalry in 1861 and a Sixth Cavalry was added in response to Civil War needs.)

8 Walter Millis, *Arms and Men: A Study in American Military History*, Mentor edition (New York, 1956), 73. Calhoun's plan was an attempt to reconcile the differing needs of war and peace. The frontier, of course, made a peacetime army necessary. See also Russell F. Weigley, *Towards an American Army: Military Thought from Washington to Marshall* (New York, 1962), chap. 3.

militia, territorial and national volunteers, rangers, and "minute companies," spontaneously formed home guards, and other less admirable aggre-
gations of fighting men supplemented or altogether supplanted the regulars
on the frontier. Often, indeed, the two worked at dramatic cross-purposes.

Experienced army officers recognized their foe as a master of guerrilla
warfare. Their writings abound in admiring descriptions of his cunning,
stealth, horsemanship, agility, endurance, and skill with weapons. His tactics featured hit and run, cover and concealment, mobility, and exploita-
tion of the natural environment for military advantage. The feats of individual fighters took precedence over the maneuvers of organized forces.
They usually avoided open combat or any combat unless with small risk
and overwhelming advantage or unless unavoidable.

The basic offensive maneuver was the war expedition. Five to thirty
men took the field under any leader with the prestige to enlist them. He
"commanded" only to the extent that his followers chose to obey. In combat every man was his own commander. Taboos and rituals influenced
every action. The successful war expedition returned home with plunder,
captives, trophies, combat honors, and no casualties.

This style of fighting differed fundamentally from those of the British,
the Mexicans, the Confederates, and the Spanish in the conventional wars
of the nineteenth century. Despite nearly continuous preoccupation with
the frontier, however, military leaders never formalized a doctrine of Indian and frontier employment. No military school or training program, no
tactics manual, and little professional literature provided guidance on how
to fight or deal with Indians.[9]

---

9 Apparently, Dennis Hart Mahan included in one of his West Point courses a brief discussion of Indian-fighting tactics, although this can scarcely be regarded as institutionalizing techniques of unconventional warfare. This lecture is noted in William B. Skelton, "Army Officers' Attitudes Toward
Indians, 1840–1860," *Pacific Northwest Quarterly* 67 (1976): 114, 121, citing Thomas E. Griess, "Dennis Hart Mahan: West Point Professor and Advocate of Military Professionalism," Ph.D. diss., Duke
University, 1968, 306–7.

Had Lieutenant Colonel Upton responded to General Sherman's belief that the British experience in India held lessons for the U.S. military frontier, Upton's *Armies of Asia and Europe* (New York,
1878) might have ventured into the doctrine of unconventional war. In fact, Upton did see parallels
between India and the U.S. frontier. He admired the organization, discipline, and record of native
troops led by British officers. He likened the native peoples with whom the British dealt to the
American Indians in their disposition to fight one another more than their colonial overlords, and he
attributed British success to a policy of mingling in their quarrels and playing off one group against
another. He declared the British Indian army worthy of U.S. imitation. But except for rotation of
officers between staff and line, scarcely a reform of special frontier application, he failed to spell out
particulars (75–80). Continuing to Europe, Upton forgot about India in his enchantment with the
Prussian war machine, and he finally concluded (97) that the United States must look to the armies
of Europe for its models. See in this connection Weigley, *Towards an American Army,* 105–6. Captain
Arthur L. Wagner's *The Service of Security and Information,* first published in 1893, contained a short
chapter on Indian scouting, but it seems almost an afterthought to the substance of the book.

The explanation for this failure is found in the tendency of military leaders to look on Indian warfare as a fleeting bother. Today's conflict or tomorrow's would be the last, and to develop a special system for it hardly seemed worthwhile. Lieutenant Henry W. Halleck implied as much in his *Elements of Military Art and Science,* published in 1846, and the thought lay at the heart of Emory Upton's attempted redefinition of the army's role in the late 1870s.[10] In 1876 General Winfield Scott Hancock informed a congressional committee that the Indian mission merited no consideration in determining the army's proper strength, organization, and composition.[11]

The attitude of the generals drew on two motives. First was a desire to place the army on a more enduring basis than that afforded by Indian warfare. Second, and probably more controlling, was a genuine concern for national defense. Even though the staff was not organized to plan for conventional war (or for any other kind, for that matter), strategists worried about what they would do if foreign war broke out. The army they designed, therefore, fit their ideas about the next conventional war rather than the present unconventional war.

Lacking an institutionalized body of doctrine for unconventional war, the army waged conventional war against the Indians. Organization, composition, command and staff, strategy and tactics, weapons, and the system of military education were all conventional. They did not change fundamentally for foreign conflict or the Civil War, which called into service separate volunteer armies without materially altering the regular establishment.[12]

The central aim of the army in the West was to protect white settlers and travelers. This meant keeping the Indians away from white settlements and travel routes. The basic strategy for accomplishing the objective rested on a system of forts. Most were not truly fortified but rather collections of barracks, quarters, and utility structures from which units operated.

---

10 Weigley, *American Way of War,* 84–5. Stephen E. Ambrose, *Upton and the Army* (Baton Rouge, La., 1964), 106.

11 House Miscellaneous Document no. 56, 45th Congress, 2d session, 5.

12 This thesis contradicts the theories of Emory Upton and the more recent scholar of American military policy, Samuel P. Huntington. They believed the army had never been ready for real war because it had been structured chiefly to fight Indians. However, a close scrutiny of the defining features of the military system reveals them to have been shaped by an assessment of conventional needs and hardly at all by perceived frontier needs. On the outbreak of the Civil War, e.g., these features were expanded but not fundamentally altered. Ambrose, *Upton and the Army,* 106. Samuel P. Huntington, "Equilibrium and Disequilibrium in American Military Policy," *Political Science Quarterly* 76 (Dec. 1961): 490.

Offensive operations took the form of war expeditions conducted in a very different manner from the Indian war expedition. Columns of infantry and cavalry locked to ponderous supply trains sought out the Indians in their villages or, better yet, tried to bring their fighting men into open combat on the battlefield. The ideal was to entice them into assaulting fixed defenses or into standing against a mounted charge by cavalry or bayonet charge by infantry.

The total war of Sherman and Sheridan merely refined this approach to account for their Civil War experience. They had severely undermined the Confederate will to resist, they felt, by making Georgia howl and by so devastating the Shenandoah Valley that a crow flying over it had to carry its provisions. Against the Indians, the purpose now was not only to kill the enemy but also to destroy food, clothing, shelter, and transportation and cast everyone destitute on a hostile land to endure climatic extremes and psychological stress. Ideally, this would be accomplished in winter, when the quarry holed up in some remote valley to sit out the bad months. Weak stock, snow and cold, and dwindling food supplies hampered mobility and dulled watchfulness. If a village could be surprised and attacked, its inhabitants cut down or scattered across a frozen wilderness, lodges and provisions destroyed, and ponies either captured or slaughtered, the will to resist would collapse and the enemy would give up.

So ran the reasoning. And it succeeded often enough to prevent serious challenge or a search for an alternative strategy. As elaborated into the Sherman-Sheridan concept of total war, the conventional tactics of the Scott, Casey, and Upton manuals sometimes worked by routing an adversary who had foolishly decided to stand and fight on the white man's terms, by smashing a village whose occupants had grown careless, or by wearing out a quarry with persistent campaigning that made surrender preferable to constant fatigue and insecurity.

A classic application of the Sherman-Sheridan concept occurred two years before they came west, in the winter of 1863–4. Operating under the command of Brigadier General James H. Carleton, Colonel Christopher Carson – the celebrated Kit Carson of mountain-man fame – led a force of New Mexico and California volunteers against the Navajos. In five separate sweeps through northwestern New Mexico he seized their stock, destroyed their crops and orchards, and kept them constantly on the run and increasingly demoralized. By the end of 1863 these incursions into the Navajo homeland had killed seventy-eight people and wounded forty – hardly a genocidal toll. But the devastation had been appalling and the psychological effect decisive. By March 1864, 6,000 people, half the tribe, had surrendered; and by the end of the year more than 8,000 had been uprooted and exiled to the opposite side of the territory.[13]

General Sheridan himself, with the hearty backing of Sherman, oversaw the next significant exercise in total war. The campaign of 1868–9 against the southern Plains tribes began at the onset of winter and featured an innovation that would become a hallmark of Sheridan's strategy. By launching three columns to converge on the theater of war from three directions, he hoped to treble the chances of finding and striking the enemy. His principal striking arm, the Seventh Cavalry led by Lieutenant Colonel George A. Custer, tracked a Cheyenne raiding party through the snow to the winter village of Black Kettle, on the Washita River in the Indian Territory (present-day Oklahoma). Custer launched a surprise attack at dawn on November 27, 1868, struck down more than one hundred people and drove out the rest, burned the village, and slaughtered the pony herd. He kept up the pressure all winter until the Cheyennes, exhausted and destitute, gave up and settled on the reservation.[14]

Using similar methods, Sheridan scored another victory in the Red River War of 1874–5. Because the Cheyennes, Comanches, and Kiowas bolted from their reservations in the Indian Territory in summer, the campaign began then. Again it featured converging columns, this time five from as many directions. On September 28, 1874, Colonel Ranald S. Mackenzie and the Fourth Cavalry fell on a combined camp of the tribes in the Palo Duro Canyon of the Texas panhandle. In a repeat of the Washita, he drove out the Indians, destroyed their tepees, and slaughtered their pony herd. The decisive operation, however, occurred in the winter, when Colonel Nelson A. Miles and the Fifth Infantry kept the enemy so tired, hungry, and demoralized that by spring all had surrendered. The Red River War ended hostilities with the tribes of the southern Plains.[15]

Again in 1876 Sheridan organized a winter campaign of three converging columns against the Sioux and Cheyennes of the northern Plains. This operation, however, did not get underway until spring and ended with the reverse of Brigadier General George Crook at the Battle of the Rosebud on June 17 and Custer's disaster on the Little Bighorn a week later. Success came only with the following winter. On November 25, 1876, Col-

13 I have dealt with this operation in *Frontiersmen in Blue: The United States Army and the Indian, 1846–65* (New York, 1967), 237–47.

14 Hutton, *Phil Sheridan's Army*, chaps. 2–5. I have dealt with this campaign in *Frontier Regulars*, chap. 10.

15 Hutton, *Phil Sheridan's Army*, chap. 11; Utley, *Frontier Regulars*, chap. 13.

onel Mackenzie smashed a Cheyenne village in a canyon of the Powder River, and throughout the winter Colonel Miles and his footsoldiers campaigned so relentlessly that by spring the disheartened Indians had given up.[16]

Such successes lulled military leaders into a complacent reliance on old ways. For the thoughtful observer, however, experience yielded ample evidence of the flaws in the system. It should have prompted an institutional examination of its underlying assumptions.

For one, the framework of forts itself contained serious drawbacks. They tended to be placed less for strategic reasons than in response to the demands of pioneer communities for protection and local markets. Freed of political pressures, Sherman and Sheridan doubtless would have maintained fewer forts in different locations. Also, forts encouraged further westward movement and the need for still more forts.

The truly fatal defects, however, lay in comparative capabilities of mobility and logistics. Indians lived off the land, unencumbered by heavy equipment, free of vulnerable supply lines. War parties moved swiftly, silently, and nearly invisibly across terrain they knew intimately. Villages shifted often because groups were nomadic or seminomadic.

By contrast, soldiers struggled under the weight of individual equipment and could never get far from slow-moving supply trains bearing essential rations and forage. Most offensives, operating across vast distances deficient in water, grass, and fuel, merely broke down the grain-fed cavalry horses and ended with the troops devoting as much effort to keeping themselves supplied as to chasing Indians. As one officer recorded, "We traveled through the country, broke down our men, killed our horses, and returned as ignorant of the whereabouts of Mr. Sanico [a Comanche chief] as when we started."[17]

The prime illustration of the flaws of conventional war is the offensive of 1865 against the northern Plains Indians, a failure so complete that no general could gloss it over. Brigadier General Patrick Edward Connor launched three heavy columns into the Powder River country. The Sioux and Cheyennes easily avoided them until bad weather wiped out horse and mule herds weakened by starvation and almost did the same to soldiers in similar condition. Then, with the advantages all in their favor, the Indians pounced. At the close of the season the armies dissolved, thoroughly beat-

16 Hutton, *Phil Sheridan's Army*, chaps. 13, 14; Utley, *Frontier Regulars*, chap. 14 and 15. I have dealt with Custer's Washita and Little Bighorn campaigns in *Cavalier in Buckskin: George Armstrong Custer and the Western Military Frontier* (Norman, Okla., 1988).
17 Joseph H. Parks, *General Edmund Kirby Smith* (Baton Rouge, La., 1954), 89–90.

en not by Indians but by terrain, distance, weather, logistics, morale, and the miscalculations of the generals.[18]

Another vivid example occurred after the Custer disaster at Little Bighorn in 1876. So disheartened were officers that they resisted further operations until overwhelmingly reinforced. When Generals Terry and Crook finally moved early in August 1876, their columns were so unwieldy that they stood hardly any chance of overtaking the quarry. Rain turned the plains drained by the Yellowstone River and its tributaries to mud. The generals quarreled. The troops suffered. The supply services – drawing on steamboats as well as wagons and mules – could barely keep up with demand. The Indians had long since scattered and left the zone of operations. In September a column under Crook blundered into some of them, but men and animals were so weak, hungry, and dispirited that they had little heart for a fight.[19]

That the army as an institution never elaborated a doctrine of Indian warfare does not mean that it contained no officers capable of breaking free of conventional thought. The most original thinker was General Crook. Despite his sorry performance in the Sioux War of 1876, he pointed the way. Few followed.

Crook pioneered two innovations: He achieved mobility through reliance on pack mules instead of supply wagons, and he pitted Indians against Indians. In Oregon in 1866–8, he mobilized Shoshones against Paiutes. In the Tonto Basin of Arizona in 1872–3, he enlisted Pimas and Maricopas against Apaches. In Wyoming and Montana in 1876, he employed Crows and Shoshones against the Sioux and Cheyennes.

In these last operations, Crook did not form the auxiliaries into military units but brought them along under their own leaders and let them fight as custom dictated. That had its drawbacks, for the allies did pretty much as they pleased with infuriating disregard of Crook's wishes.

In the second Arizona tour, however, Crook took the ultimate step. He sent brother against brother, Chiricahua Apache against Chiricahua Apache. Crook's scouts had all the skills of the enemy and knew how they thought, where they were likely to be, and what they could be expected to do. This practice, moreover, severely damaged the enemy's morale. As Crook put it, "To polish a diamond there is nothing like its own dust. It is the same with these fellows. Nothing breaks them up like turning their own people against them."[20]

18 Utley, *Frontiersmen in Blue*, chap. 15.   19 Utley, *Frontier Regulars*, 267–71.
20 Charles F. Lummis, *General Crook and the Apache Wars* (Flagstaff, Ariz., 1966), 17. I have dealt with Crook in *Frontier Regulars*, 53–5, 177–81, 192–8, and chap. 19. See also Robert M. Utley, "Crook

Crook organized his Apaches in company-size units commanded by carefully selected regular officers. Able officers, versed in Indian culture and adept at leading Indians, were critical to success. Admiring their skills, the artist Frederic Remington termed them less "Indian fighters" than "Indian thinkers."[21] The loyalty and reliability of the scouts caused constant worry. With one exception, however, the Cibicu affair of 1881, they justified Crook's faith.

The Apache scouts, combined with a logistical system founded on mules rather than on wagons, gained Crook repeated successes until his last campaign, when he failed. Many, including General Sheridan, distrusted Crook's scouts and wanted to give the regulars greater visibility. Succeeding Crook, Brigadier General Nelson A. Miles shifted the focus of publicity to regulars but finally, and discreetly, had to fall back on Crook's methods, which ultimately brought him the success denied Crook.

A close study of the record of the Indian-fighting army leads to the conclusion that it failed on two scores:

First, conventional methods usually failed unless the Indians abandoned their conventional methods. The successes the army pointed to occurred when the Indians violated their own precept to avoid surprise by remaining ever watchful and aware of the enemy's location or when the Indians abandoned their own guerrilla-style practices to engage the whites in open combat. At Horseshoe Bend in 1814, at the Bluewater in 1855, at the Washita in 1868, at Summit Springs in 1869, at Palo Duro Canyon in 1874, and at Bear Paw Mountain in 1877, the Indians allowed themselves to be caught napping. At Solomon's Fork in 1857 the Indians played into the army's hands by dropping their aversion to open combat and holding firm to receive a cavalry charge. At the Wagon Box and Hayfield battles in 1867, they went a step further and charged fortified positions. The results of all these engagements were less victories for the army than defeats for the Indians.

Second, as Upton recognized, although for the wrong reason, the frontier not only failed as a training ground for orthodox wars, it also positively spoiled the army for orthodox wars, as became painfully evident in 1812, 1846, 1861, and 1898. Scattered across the continent in little border forts, units rarely operated or assembled for practice and instruction in more than battalion strength. The company was the basic unit, and it defined the so-

and Miles: Fighting and Feuding on the Indian Frontier," *Military History Quarterly* 2 (autumn 1989): 81–91.

21 "How an Apache War Was Won," in Harold McCracken, ed., *Frederic Remington's Own West* (New York, 1961), 49.

cial and professional horizons of most line officers. Growing old in grade, with energies and ambitions dulled by boredom and isolation, the officer corps reflected General Richard S. Ewell's observation that on the frontier an officer "learned all there was to know about commanding forty dragoons and forgot everything else."[22]

Had the nation's strategists understood the lessons of General Crook's experience, they would have recognized that the frontier army was a conventional military force trying to control, by conventional military methods, a people who did not behave like conventional enemies and, indeed, quite often were not enemies at all. The strategists would have recognized that the situation usually did not call for warfare but merely for policing; that is, offending individuals needed to be separated from the innocent and punished. The strategists would have recognized that the conventional force was unable to do this and that, as a result, punishment often fell, when it fell at all, on guilty and innocent alike.

Had the strategists acted on such understandings, the army might have played a more significant role in the westward movement – and one less vulnerable to criticism. An Indian auxiliary force might have been developed that could differentiate between guilty and innocent and, using the Indians' own fighting style, contend with the guilty. Indian units were indeed developed, but never on a scale and with a continuity to permit the full effect to be demonstrated. Such an Indian force would have differed markedly from the reservation police. It would have been larger, better equipped, and less influenced by the vagaries of the patronage politics that afflicted the Indian Bureau. Above all, it would have been led by a cadre of carefully chosen officers imbued with a sense of mission and experienced in Indian relations – Remington's "Indian thinkers." How different might have been the history of the westward movement had such a force been created and employed in place of the regular army line? How vastly more substantial might have been the contribution of the frontier army to twentieth-century traditions of unconventional warfare?

TOTAL WAR AS MORAL DILEMMA

Total war raised disturbing moral questions for a society steeped in the sentimental and romantic Victorian code of nineteenth-century America. Total war subjected women, children, and old people to death or cruel suffering. Surprise attacks on Indian villages, the centerpiece of the strategy,

---

22 Quoted in Huntington, "Equilibrium and Disequilibrium," 499.

inevitably struck down noncombatants. They were rarely killed deliberately but fell simply because they were there and in the line of fire. In the smoke and dust and tumult of battle, distinctions were difficult, especially when men and women wore similar clothing. The destruction of property, food, and transportation, followed by weeks of fearful flight to avoid the soldiers, forced women and children to endure terrible hardship.

Adding to the moral dilemma was the ever-present question of whether the enemy really was an enemy. Campaign after campaign exposed the fallacy of neat classifications of peaceful and hostile. Indians changed from friend to foe to neutral with bewildering rapidity, and one could hardly ever be distinguished from another. The common response was to declare all Indians on a reservation peaceful and all off it hostile. This seldom worked because hostile Indians might be within the safe zone and peaceful Indians outside it. Further complicating the problem was that both types were often mixed together in the same group. Thus the army suffered the torments of warring on people who some said were peaceful and others said were hostile but who in truth could almost never be neatly categorized as either.

Custer's Washita campaign of 1868 is an illuminating example. Extolled in western and military circles for a brilliant victory, Custer drew the abuse of humanitarians, who castigated him for attacking a peace chief and slaughtering women and children. Black Kettle and his fellow chiefs genuinely wanted and sought peace. But their young men favored war; a war party had returned from a raid on Kansas settlements the night before the battle, and the village contained four white captives. Was it peaceful or hostile? Yet Custer saw himself compared with the merciless Colonel Chivington and the Washita with Sand Creek. Although Sherman and Sheridan rose to his defense in life as in death, Custer would forever after be judged by many as an indiscriminate butcher of innocent, peaceful Indians.[23]

The humanitarian community of the East made no allowances for the ambiguities and complexities of Indian warfare. From such former antislavery leaders as Wendell Phillips and William Lloyd Garrison, the army felt the sting of rhetoric sharpened in the long war against the slavocracy. "I only know the names of three savages upon the Plains," Phillips declared in 1870, "Colonel Baker, General Custer, and at the head of all, General Sheridan." Baker's assault on a Piegan village in 1870 inspired a verse that typified the humanitarian stereotype of the army:

23 Utley, *Cavalier in Buckskin,* chap. 4.

Women and babes shrieking awoke
To perish 'mid the battle smoke,
Murdered, or turned out there to die
Beneath the stern, gray, wintry sky.[24]

Officers bitterly resented this portrayal. Not only did it stain their public image, but it also contained enough truth to shake their moral sensibilities. The officer corps subscribed to a Sir Walter Scott code of chivalry that
exalted womanhood. Although perhaps not embracing Indian womanhood, it nevertheless held in contempt the mistreatment of women. In an
attack on an Indian village, most officers tried hard to spare women and
children. Even Wounded Knee, which took the lives of at least sixty-two
noncombatants, discloses extraordinary efforts to avoid harming them.[25]

Military attitudes toward Indians reflected the army's dual mission of
police and war. Soldiers who had witnessed the plunder, rape, torture, and
mutilation of Indian hostilities readily saw the adversary as a savage beast.
Yet between conflicts troops and Indians mingled with enough familiarity
to reveal dimensions of Indian character that a white man could find fascinating and even admirable, and to disclose some of the injustice, deceit,
fraud, and cruelty the Indian endured from government officials and frontier citizens.

Ambivalence, therefore, marked the military view of Indians – fear, distrust, loathing, contempt, and condescension on the one hand; curiosity,
admiration, sympathy, and even friendship on the other. Most officers who
wrote for publication, and their wives too, recognized no inconsistency in
characterizing Indians as ferocious wild animals bereft of human emotion
and in the same pages describing their customs and individual personalities
in sympathetic if patronizing terms.

A veteran of Apache service exposed this ambivalence. "Exasperated,
our senses blunted by Indian atrocities, we hunted and killed them as we
hunted and killed wolves." Yet after serving with Apache scouts, he con-
fessed: "My feelings toward them began to change. That ill-defined impression that they were something a little better than animals but not quite
human; . . . the feeling that there could be no possible ground upon which
we could meet as man to man, passed away."[26]

Against the familiar picture of cavalry storming through a village cutting
down fleeing Indians, the army could point to a long and creditable record

24 Robert Winston Mardock, *The Reformers and the American Indian* (Columbia, Mo., 1971), 69.
25 Robert M. Utley, *The Last Days of the Sioux Nation* (New Haven, Conn., 1963), chap. 12.
26 Britton Davis, *The Truth About Geronimo* (New Haven, Conn., 1929), 50, 111.

as defender of the Indian. Generals Oliver O. Howard and George Crook battled against the deportation of the Chiricahua Apaches to Florida after the surrender of Geronimo in 1886. General Nelson A. Miles advocated the cause of Chief Joseph after the Nez Perce surrender of 1877. General John Pope eloquently if verbosely assailed the inequities of federal Indian policy for more than three decades. The performance of Indian agents of such officers as Adna R. Chaffee, Ezra P. Ewers, and George M. Randall revealed the army in a conspicuously humanitarian stance. "Oh where is my friend Randall – the captain with the big mustache which he always pulled?" an Apache chief asked about a former agent. "When he promised a thing he did it."[27]

Such self-congratulation, however, could not drown the question that haunted contemporaries and still haunts Americans of all races: What of the morality of the strategy of total war? What of the morality of seeking and destroying Indian villages where women and children would suffer death or injury?

That question is not to be asked of the Indian wars alone. The frontier army does not deserve to be singled out for special condemnation. Sherman's strategy for the conquest of the Indians was as moral, or as immoral, as his march across Georgia during the Civil War or as the leveling of cities from ground and air in World War II and Vietnam. The ethical questions implicit in the style of war against the Indians are not unique to the frontier army, as modern generations would like to think, but recur through the entire sweep of the nation's military history and tradition.

The frontier army was not, as it saw itself, the heroic vanguard of civilization, crushing the "savages" and opening the West to settlers. Still less was it the barbaric band of butchers, eternally waging unjust war against unoffending Indians, that is depicted in the humanitarian literature of the nineteenth century and the atonement literature of the twentieth. Instead, the frontier army was merely one of the historical forces that conquered the Indian – and not the most significant one at that.

That the Indians lost the Indian wars did not mean that the army won them. The army won occasional successes because the Indians dropped their guard, or a commander adopted Indian methods, or a commander

---

27 John G. Bourke, *On the Border with Crook* (New York, 1891), 436; William H. Carter, *The Life of Lieutenant General Chaffee* (Chicago, 1917), chap. 12; Martin F. Schmitt, ed., *General George Crook: His Autobiography* (Norman, Okla., 1946), 289–300; Herbert Welsh, *The Apache Prisoners at Fort Marion, St. Augustine, Florida* (Philadelphia, 1887); Alvin Josephy, *The Nez Perce Indians and the Opening of the Northwest* (New Haven, Conn., 1965), 634; Richard N. Ellis, *General Pope and U.S. Indian Policy* (Albuquerque, N.M., 1970).

wore down his foe. But every tribe succumbed to larger powers than the purely military: economic, diplomatic, political, psychological, and even cultural (compulsory acculturation).

The economic was the most decisive. Travelers, settlers, railroads, and technology destroyed the Indian's subsistence base. Whites wiped out the buffalo and other wild game, stripped the grasslands of forage, cut down the stands of timber, and finally, herding the tribes onto reservations, appropriated the Indian land base.

The role of the army was therefore simply to hasten a process ordained by other forces. A more thoughtful approach might have hastened the process, or made it more humane, but it would not have fundamentally changed it.

18

"The Fellows Can Just Starve"

On Wars of "Pacification" in the African Colonies of Imperial Germany and the Concept of "Total War"

TRUTZ VON TROTHA

War is the collective and organized use of three basic forms of domination (*Aktionsmacht*): material harm, absolute violence, and total violence.[1] The destruction of the enemy's material resources is one of the most evident elements of war, and in many especially modern cases it captures the imagination of later generations long after the dead have been forgotten.[2] The essence of war is the use of absolute violence. It means killing the adversary. In war, absolute violence goes along with total violence, which brings together the glorification of violence, the indifference toward the suffering of the victims, and the mechanization of violence.

As part of its collective and organized character, war is directed against collectivities. It destroys or appropriates the material resources of the adversaries, limits or destroys their political autonomy,[3] or harms the enemy physically and materially to such a degree that the whole society of the en-

---

1 For the concepts of "domination" (*Aktionsmacht*), "absolute violence," and "total violence," see Heinrich Popitz, *Phänomene der Macht* (Tübingen, 1992), 24–5, 44–5, 56, 66–7.
2 Contrary to the annihilation of people, in most cases the destruction of the material world is never absolute, thus keeping alive the relationship between past, present, and future. It is the ruins that remind us – and that are the basis of the archeologist's contribution to society's memory and contribute to the establishment of an abstract relationship to past wars, which is part of our relationship to the material world. Of course, this is much more pronounced in modern non-oral and secularized societies that place so much emphasis on "data-creating power" (*datensetzende Macht*) based on technology; for the concept of data-creating power, see ibid., 32.
3 Inasmuch as the political power or even the political autonomy of the enemy itself is challenged in all wars, Clausewitz's famous observation is sociologically correct, namely, that war is "the continuation of political intercourse with the use of other means" ("eine Fortsetzung des politischen Verkehrs, eine Durchführung desselben mit anderen Mitteln"); Carl von Clausewitz, *Vom Kriege: Hinterlassenes Werk des Generals Carl von Clausewitz* (1832; reprinted: Frankfurt am Main, 1980); see John Keegan's excellent, but with respect to this observation misleading, critique in *A History of Warfare* (London, 1993), 3ff.

415

emy collapses or the enemy ceases to exist (in the case of genocide). The combination of total violence, collective organization, and the violent confrontation of collectivities themselves involves the strict distinction between "the internal and external group ('we' and 'they') and a related separation of the internal and external morals."[4] In war, people follow two types of moral codes, one that applies to the members of one's own group and one that is valid for the confrontation with members of the "enemy" group. Thus war articulates most sharply a basic feature of society that always draws a line between members and nonmembers, between the "internal and external morals." And to take up sociologically a military truism: War is an interactive process and has a history. The course and character of war are shaped by the process, which confronts actors and sociocultural orders. Typically, war is a particularly dynamic phenomenon that highlights the element of speed as a fundamental feature of domination.[5]

Collective mobilization and organization of violence, material harm, the killing of the enemy, the glorification of violence, the indifference toward the suffering of the victims, as long as they belong to the enemy, and the use of a technology of violence, process, and interaction are thus the basic elements of the phenomenon we usually call "war." These elements are part of the wars of slash-and-burn agriculturalists or tribal societies as well as of chiefdoms and wars between the industrial nation-states of the twentieth century. The differences between various types of war are to be found in the forms that these different elements acquire, in the meaning these elements of war have for different cultures and social orders, and the goals for which wars are waged.

This chapter is divided into three sections. On the basis of observations about total war in "polycephalous societies"[6] and chiefdoms, the first section presents a general concept of "total war" and looks at the particular

4 Wilhelm E. Mühlmann, "Krieg und Frieden: Ein Leitfaden," in Wilhelm Bernsdorf, ed., *Wörterbuch der Soziologie,* 3 vols. (Frankfurt am Main, 1972), 2:475–6; Wilhelm Bernsdorf, *Krieg und Frieden: Ein Leitfaden der politischen Ethnologie: Mit Berücksichtigung völkerkundlichen und geschichtlichen Stoffes* (Heidelberg, 1940), 39ff.

5 Trutz von Trotha, *Koloniale Herrschaft: Zur soziologischen Theorie der Staatsentstehung am Beispiel des "Schutzgebietes Togo"* (Tübingen, 1994), 70–5. In this study I do not analyze those forms of war that are characteristic to many hunter-and-gatherer societies and slash-and-burn agriculturalists and that are marked by extreme ritualizations of violent confrontations between warring groups. In addition, for many periods the dynamics of war were rather limited in the European Middle Ages, of which the Hundred Years' War is an example.

6 Rüdiger Schott prefers the term "polycephalous" for societies that in social anthropology are usually called "acephalous" (stateless) societies; see Rüdiger Schott, "Qui juge dans les sociétés sans juges. Les limites du pouvoir et de l'autorité dans les sociétés acéphales," contribution to the conference, "Le Juge: Approches anthropologiques d'une figure d'autorité," 4e Colloque franco-allemand des anthropologues du droit, Paris, Nov. 24–6, 1994.

features of total war between industrialized societies. The second section addresses the colonial wars of Imperial Germany in Africa. It studies the bloody struggles and wars of the years 1904 to 1908 in Southwest and East Africa and the violent pacification process in Togo, which more or less came to an end at the turn of the century. The general thesis of the study is that German colonial wars in Africa were not total wars. They instead were variants on wars that might be called "wars of pacification." The chapter distinguishes between two types of wars of pacification: the "limited" and "unlimited" (or genocidal) wars of pacification. In the third and last section, I compare the characteristics of wars of pacification with those of total war.

I

Total war is not an invention of the industrial age. On the contrary, it was practiced by many comparatively egalitarian societies and chiefdoms, at least in Melanesia and the Americas if we take the following peculiarities as being characteristic of total war: War tends to involve all members of the society engaging in warfare and at the same time is directed without distinction against all members of the "hostile" society. In my opinion, these two characteristics are the most important in distinguishing total war from other forms of war.[7] Nevertheless, I include four further features that per-

---

7 Criticizing the "master narrative" of "total war," Roger Chickering underscores in his essay in this book (Chapter 1) that there might be a confusion of the "rhetoric with the reality of war," which overlooks the "powerful restraints, both material and moral, under which soldiers and politicians" led so-called total wars. He is of course right when he states that "the everyday life of most participants, men, women, and children, was a great deal more 'normal' than the extravagant terms of total war would suggest," because even in total wars the involvement of total populations seems to be rather limited. But in comparing different forms of war I would argue that Chickering misses, conceptually and empirically, some important elements of total war. First, and contrary to Chickering's observations, many times war in polycephalous societies involves almost all members of society, even tearing down that basic cultural and institutional barrier that usually separates men and women with respect to fighting and war. Second, total war tends toward an all-out involvement of the members of a society, either as victims of enemy attacks or as agents in the war machinery composing not only the fighting personnel but also the many who contribute to keeping the war machinery going. Certainly, within states there always are organizational limits to the active involvement of all the members of a society. But one should neither miss the extraordinary organizational capacities of modern bureaucratic state power that were demonstrated in the two world wars of the twentieth century nor underestimate the ideological dimension characteristic of total war fueled by the call for total engagement of all members of society and for their support (e.g., Erich Ludendorff, *Der totale Krieg* [Munich, 1988]; Carl Schmitt, "Totaler Feind, totaler Krieg, totaler Staat," *Völkerbund und Völkerrecht* 4 [1937/38]: 139–45). In "pure" total war, people are confronted with the demand either to be victorious or to perish, for which Goebbels's infamous address in the Berlin sports arena on February 18, 1943, is one of the most articulate examples. Third, maybe apart from "primitive" total war, no war of urban civilizations probably ever started as a total war. Total war typically is the outcome of a

haps are also found in other forms of war and yet are radicalized in such a way that they give rise to their own particular type of war that is total war.

The radicalized indifference toward the suffering of the victims and the strict delineation between inner and outer morality is expressed in the cruelty with which opponents are murdered. Because of the strict ethnocentric opposition between "us" and "them," the opponent tends morally to be no longer considered a member of the human race. Total war typically is a "holy" war. It has a religious or an ideological basis. Total war is aimed at the complete destruction of the opponent or his merciless expulsion from the area inhabited or laid claim to by his opponent. In anthropology, the ethnic tribes of east and northeast New Guinea are particularly well known for this type of practice.[8]

Total war in stateless societies can result in the destruction of villages and the expulsion of entire societies – and we shall probably never know exactly how many societies and cultures have been annihilated in the course of history.[9] By comparison with the total war of industrialized nation-states, it does, however, have clear limitations that make it appear more closely related to the "limited wars" that have been prevalent throughout the history of humankind.

The total war of industrialized societies is unlimited. This lack of limitation refers to the quantitative size of the population that can be mobilized on the one hand and to the number of people on the "enemy" side who are affected by the war on the other. The distinction between soldier and

process of "totalization." In this process, pure total war remains a utopia but is a vision that gives total war its specific dynamic and draws more and more people and material resources into it: Total war is a maelstrom.

I would, however, join Chickering in stressing the fact that, probably with the exception of primitive total war, war is always characterized by the coexistence of "normal" life and war, not only with respect to the people at home but also with regard to the men at the front. A society at war, even under the conditions of total war, is still a society with all its conflicts, ambitions, and pursuits that might be called "mundane" from the perspective of the soldier at the front. I would even suggest that to fight a war, this mundane world has to be preserved up to a certain degree that is, of course, very much dependent on the respective culture. But I would add that a central feature of total war is its destruction of this mundane world. It is exactly this dynamic that is the very problem of total war. By destroying mundanity, total war undermines the conditions of its very existence. Thus, for example, a hundred years' war probably could not be fought as a total war.

8 Peter Hanser, *Krieg und Recht: Wesen und Ursachen kollektiver Gewaltanwendung in den Stammesgesellschaften Neuguineas* (Berlin, 1985); concerning the Tauade, a particularly severe case, see Christopher Robert Hallpike, *Bloodshed and Vengeance in the Papuan Mountains* (Oxford, 1977); for further examples in other areas of the world, see Harry Holbert Turney-High, *Primitive War: Its Practice and Concepts* (Columbia, S.C., 1971); and Mühlmann, "Krieg und Frieden."

9 I shall not address the question of the extent to which total war in stateless societies, which in fact is a product of the confrontation of stateless societies and organized states, is due to the so-called tribal zone; R. Brian Ferguson and Neal L. Whitehead, eds., *War in the Tribal Zone: Expanding States and Indigenous Warfare* (Santa Fe, N.M., 1992).

civilian is lost.[10] Everyone becomes a part of the "war machine." Everyone becomes a target of absolute violence. In a specific sense, war becomes a territorial war as it basically involves all people in a specific area, both as soldiers "in the field" and as victims on the "home front."[11]

The incomparable degree of mobilization in the total war of an industrialized society is partly due to the banal fact that nation-states include remarkably large numbers of people. However, what is more important is the fact that industrialized nation-states have a historically unique organizational power over the people in their territory, whereby they become known as "the masses" and, in the case of total war, simply "human material."[12] This power of organization includes the industrialization of the organization of military resources, the extreme division of labor in war management, and, above all, the comprehensive militarization of a society at war. The degree of integration of centralized power in an industrial society is reflected in the comprehensive militarization of society.[13]

Initially, the industrialized organization of war involved technology that overshadowed everything that humankind had known up to the revolution in weapons technology during the last third of the nineteenth century. Since the first atomic bomb was dropped, industrialized warfare has threatened the world with a "war of total annihilation" in which a "new way of killing, human behavior of a new kind" has evolved, as Heinrich Popitz so rightly emphasizes.[14]

Total war in the industrial age is a war of systematic innovation of lethal technologies; the process of innovation is akin to a competition to come up with weapons technologies. In this sense total war in an industrial society is a war of science, especially natural sciences and engineering. Total war in an industrialized nation-state also is a war of irreconcilable ideologies. These ideologies are immediately incorporated into the aims of war,

---

10 Chickering is right when he observes that "the distinction between the home and fighting fronts never disappeared entirely." But I would nevertheless argue the comparative relevance of his observation on the basis of my remarks made in note 7 to this chapter.

11 See Hans J. Morgenthau, *Macht und Frieden: Grundlegung einer Theorie der internationalen Politik*, trans. Gottfried-Karl Kindermann and Dieter G. Wilke (American ed., 1948; reprint, Gütersloh, 1963), 212, 308; Bertrand de Jouvenel, *Über die Staatsgewalt: Die Naturgeschichte ihres Wachstums* (Freiburg im Breisgau, 1972), 182.

12 Jouvenel, *Über die Staatsgewalt*, 13–20.

13 For the concept of the "integration of power," see Popitz, *Phänomene der Macht*, 233–60. I should add that the militarization of society includes even peace, insofar as (e.g., unlike war in the Middle Ages) the preparation for war is an important part of society (e.g. in the form of the arms industry). In this respect, however, attention should be drawn to the basic differences between liberal democracies and totalitarian dictatorships with regard to the degree of militarization of society and its limitations, which also are to be seen in various types of total war in industrialized nation-states.

14 Ibid., 74.

the way war is waged, the sum total in which violence is glorified, and the indifference toward the suffering of the victims is legitimized.[15]

II

The history of colonization is the history of wars. Imperial Germany alone waged thirteen wars between 1884 and 1908 simply to subdue its African colonies and keep them under control. This figure includes only the more important confrontations. The more or less comprehensive "punitive expeditions" amount to hundreds.[16] We shall never know how many people died as a result of these wars and "punitive expeditions" and their immediate or long-term consequences. The number of African dead can only be guessed at and must amount to hundreds of thousands.[17]

In the following consideration and observation of these wars I shall limit myself to three points of view: (1) I shall place these wars in the context of general features of violence and of its monopolization by foreign conquerors within a process of state building in particular, and investigate war first and foremost where its violent side appears in one of its most awful forms – massacre; (2) I shall relate the wars to the "colonial situation," that is, to a specific structure and culture of domination; and (3) I shall consider the wars in the context of the historical process of colonial conquest and armed African opposition.

The colonial conquest and suppression of armed opposition took place

---

15 These ideologies are important distinguishing features of the types of total wars in industrialized civilization. Particularly noteworthy is the distinction between the "war of total world domination" of National Socialism and the "war of total defense" of liberal democracies.

16 In German West Africa between 1891 and 1897 more than sixty large-scale "punitive expeditions" were sent out by the Germans; Horst Gründer, *Geschichte der deutschen Kolonien* (Paderborn, 1985), 154. Between 1895 and 1899 the official record of the police troops in the small and, from the military point of view, comparatively problem-free country of Togo lists seventeen "marches," "expeditions," "military," and "punitive expeditions"; Peter Sebald, *Togo 1884–1914: Eine Geschichte der deutschen "Musterkolonie" auf der Grundlage amtlicher Quellen* (Berlin, 1988), 172–3.

17 Death records were more accurate for the temporary victors in these armed confrontations. Regarding purely military personnel (i.e., without taking into account the "police troops"), by 1918, 7,200 officers, noncommissioned officers, and soldiers had died. But here again African soldiers made up the greater part of the army, and their numbers were only estimated. In the wars of Southwest Africa, 1,849 German officers and soldiers lost their lives, many of them due to sickness and other injuries that were not a direct result of war. From the beginning of April to the end of September 1905, for example, 132 officers, noncommissioned officers, and soldiers lost their lives in the war against the Nama. During the same period, 139 officers, noncommissioned officers, and soldiers died of disease, mainly typhoid, and 13 others died as a result of other accidents; L. H. Gann and Peter Duignan, *The Rulers of German Africa, 1884–1914* (Stanford, Calif., 1977), 126, table 15; Kriegsgeschichtliche Abteilung II. des Grossen Generalstabes, ed., *Die Kämpfe der deutschen Truppen in Südwestafrika: Auf Grund amtlichen Materials bearbeitet*, vol. 5: *Der Hottentottenkrieg: Die Kämpfe gegen Cornelius und Morenga bis zum September 1905; das Ende Hendrik Witboois und seines Stammes* (Berlin, 1907), 187; see also Jon M. Bridgman, *The Revolt of the Hereros* (Berkeley, Calif., 1981), 164.

within the framework of the idea of occidental state power, which, in the eyes of the conquerors, was to be established, carried out, and maintained in its essential features, that is, in the form of a modern territorial state.[18] The colonial wars of conquest were not satisfied with the control of trade, terms of tribute, and other economic and political considerations. The despotic and armed intruders did not undertake conquest in order to expel the inhabitants in accordance with the old, familiar pattern of territorial expansion. Nor did they consider the area a source of slaves that could be plundered with impunity and without risk of dangerous and expensive opposition – although when confrontations became more intense, an increasing number among the conquerors called for the destruction and expulsion of Africans in certain areas.[19]

The writing of history therefore has introduced the concept of the "pacification phase" as the first phase of colonial conquest. It is a term that was chosen based on the end result and is accordingly somewhat euphemistic and suppresses two underlying facts: Typically, pacification took place as a violent incursion, that is, as a form of violent conquest. Massacre also is a characteristic feature of the pacification process.[20] Pacification establishes the threshold of violence if those who are to be subjugated do not accept the imposition and decide instead on armed resistance. Pacification as conquest is based on violence, and as a check on violence it finds itself faced with the fact that in order to curb violence, the use or at least the threat of violence is a prerequisite.

Accordingly, colonial pacification was the bloody proof of the conquerors' superiority. It introduced the destructive use of power, generally in the form of massacres. Bloodbaths commonly are a part of pacification. A look at pacification in apparently "unproblematic" Togo, where, just as elsewhere, massacre played a part, is useful here.

18 I shall not go into the colonial political debate of the period and the reasons why European states and the German government in particular got involved in colonial conquest. I am solely concerned with the fact that from the start of the "establishment of the German protectorate," the subheading of a semiofficial book on Togo, the broad view of order taken by administrators and officers was based on the model of the occidental state, which the theoreticians of the colonial administration attempted to modify over time according to their experience. The most well-known attempt in this respect is Lord Lugard's idea of "indirect rule"; Georg Trierenberg, *Togo, die Aufrichtung der deutschen Schutzherrschaft und die Erschliessung des Landes* (Berlin, 1910); Frederick John Dealtry Lugard, *The Dual Mandate in British Tropical Africa* (Edinburgh, 1922; reprint, London, 1965).

19 In addition to the chief of staff, Count Alfred von Schlieffen, the commander-in-chief of the German troops in Southwest Africa with dictatorial powers, General Lothar von Trotha, was one of this number. But Trotha's political (and belated) failure, because the Herero and Nama paid for it by being almost completely wiped out, is a reflection of the perspective in which the colonial wars took place, wars that were aimed not at annihilating or driving away the people in the colonies but at subjugating them to the state rule of foreign conquerors; Uwe Timm, *Morenga: Ein Roman* (Cologne, 1985), 29–30.

20 Trotha, *Koloniale Herrschaft*, 37–44.

Three factors combine to give massacre a systematic place in the process of pacification: the economy of violence, the limited power of the conquerors, and the necessity of threat to establish state rule:

Violence is an extremely economical means of rule in the face of scant resources.[21] Violence is very convincing. It is simple and obvious. There are no communication problems. The "language of violence" needs no translation – and this applies particularly to a world in which the colonial conquerors could make themselves understood in their meetings with Africans only when they were accompanied and assisted by interpreters.[22] In the language of violence, conquerors can express themselves directly and may also know that they have been understood.

Superior violence convinces without the need for external legitimation.[23] It justifies itself by its very matter-of-factness and superiority. Death is dumb, the survivor accepts his "inevitable fate," the victor asks no questions but rather issues orders. "The mortal danger of domination [is], as a rule, the most reliable guarantee of its continuing existence."[24] No power structure renounces the threat of death. All gamble on the fear of the ruled of being killed if resistance is offered. The ruled are never free of this fear. The "prius" of fear corresponds with the "prius" of violence mentioned by Jacob Burckhardt.[25] Wherever this fear has been overcome and resistance is risked, the conqueror subsequently shows that he can teach the people renewed fear.

Violence is never limited to the physical injury of people. It always has an effect on the psyche, as well. Superior power humiliates the vanquished. Violence is a psychological weapon; the more punitive it is in character, the greater harm it causes. The proof of superior power is a ceremony of degradation.[26] Superior violence thus may break the "will" of the conquered – and did just that in the colonies.[27]

---

21 For this and the following observations, see Trotha, *Koloniale Herrschaft*, 39–44.
22 On the role of interpreters, see ibid., 186–205.
23 Trotha, *Koloniale Herrschaft*, 39–40; Trutz von Trotha, "'Streng, aber gerecht' – 'hart, aber tüchtig': Über Formen von Basislegitimität und ihre Ausprägungen am Beginn staatlicher Herrschaft," in Wilhelm J. G. Möhlig and Trutz von Trotha, eds., *Legitimation von Herrschaft und Recht / La légitimation du pouvoir et du droit* (Cologne, 1994), 75–7.
24 Popitz, *Phänomene der Macht*, 54; see also Niccolò Machiavelli, *Der Fürst* (Italian ed., 1532; reprinted, Stuttgart, 1961), 100–3.
25 Jacob Burckhardt, *Weltgeschichtliche Betrachtungen: Historisch-kritische Gesamtausgabe: Mit einer Einleitung und textkritischem Anhang von Rudolf Stadelmann* (n.p., n.d.; 1905/1868–73), 57.
26 Harold Garfinkel, "Bedingungen für den Erfolg von Degradierungszeremonien," in Klaus Lüderssen and Fritz Sack, eds., *Seminar: Abweichendes Verhalten III: Die gesellschaftliche Reaktion auf Kriminalität*, vol. 2: *Strafprozess und Strafvollzug* (Frankfurt am Main, 1976), 31–40.
27 Hendrik Witbooi's death is a particularly tragic example of this; when he lay dying he is purported to have said: "That's enough now. It's over for me. The children can have peace and quiet now" (Kriegsgeschichtliche Abteilung II., ed., *Kämpfe der deutschen Truppen in Südwestafrika*, 180).

It should not be forgotten that violence is very economical in the effects that are most obvious: dead people, destroyed villages, burnt fields, plundered grain stores. Violence destroys human and material resources that make successful defense and resistance possible. Generals record this in their reports, which in their stylistic combination of more or less subliminal bragging and soldierly conciseness stress the instrumental and economical properties of violence. For example, Lieutenant Valentin von Massow wrote in his report about his "punitive expedition" against the Bekpokpam (Konkomba) in Togo in late autumn and winter 1897: "The Maxim machine gun was also put into action here and there. . . . Altogether I have burnt to the ground approximately 40–50 villages, destroyed as many farms as possible, and driven off around 300 cows and 100–200 sheep."[28] Such reports are typical for all colonies in the time of pacification.

The many-sided economy of violence is the more attractive for the conqueror, the fewer the means of domination he has at his disposal. In this respect, the situation for all colonial conquerors was anything other than encouraging. This is particularly true considering the small number of conquerors who even today still cause astonishment and clearly begs Hume's famous question concerning the reasons for the "ease with which the many were governed by the few" – although from the fact that at the beginning of the process of establishing rule, the question of "ease" is debatable.[29] In terms of stingy governments and parliaments in the so-called mother countries, the same is true for financial resources. The conditions for infrastructure and organizational administration in ruling the colonies were particularly poor. For example, Jon Bridgman speculates that the lack of rail connections to transport troops and supplies prolonged the war against the Nama by two years in any case;[30] the comparatively rapid increase in the German contingent in the war against the Herero and Nama in German Southwest Africa shows that the superior organizational power of the colonial conquerors was able to eliminate at least part of the obvious resource problem in the short term. Nevertheless, there were almost 20,000 men in German Southwest Africa by the end of the war.[31]

Doubtlessly, and in comparison with the possibilities of the Africans, the firepower of the weapons and the military organization of this firepower were not "deficient." The colonial conquerors made full use of the technological weapon revolution of the last third of the nineteenth centu-

---

28 Quoted in Sebald, *Togo*, 194.
29 David Hume, "Of the first principles of government," in David Hume, *Essays: Moral, Political and Literary*, ed. Eugene F. Miller (Edinburgh, 1741; reprint, Indianapolis, Ind., 1985), 32.
30 Bridgman, *Revolt*, 141.   31 Ibid., 112.

ry and put into practice the basic rules of military organization and waging war that had been so incomparably perfected by Clausewitz.[32] In approaching total war the European colonial troops were the first to benefit from the revolution in weapons. Although the German General Staff, for example, was for a long time opposed to the introduction of machine guns in the German Army, it approved their use in Africa.[33] The superior military organization and weapons technology were to be used without restriction, even more so when it was not just a case of carrying out some raid for booty and glory. What was intended was to convert the capability of destructive violence into a credible threat of destructive violence that would guarantee not only compliance from the defeated in the long term but also whenever the new rulers expected obedience independently of the direct presence of soldiers ready to shoot. It was meant to be a threat that denied all the external inadequacies of the possibilities of state rule.

Massacre therefore is the point at which the economy of violence, the conquerors' resource problems, and the threat of violence converge, if we take into account two elements that constitute the core of massacre: the mortal danger inherent in every form of political domination (*Todesgefährlichkeit von Herrschaft*) and the collective degradation and uniform objectifying of the defeated and threatened.

Without a doubt, the mortal danger that emanates from the new master and that is intended to pre-empt any resistance is central to massacre. This mortal danger is immediate and expressive of such increased destructive force that even the terrible forces of destruction of familiar armed conflict pale by comparison. The unmitigated cruelty and incalculable destruction should engrave themselves in the minds of the people, which especially in oral cultures are so open and responsive. Despite all the problems of communication, massacre is intended to demonstrate to all that resistance is futile. Massacre should stay in people's minds for generations as a permanent reminder, just like the bombastic and brutal proclamation made by General Lothar von Trotha to the rebellious Nama in spring 1905, when he demanded unconditional submission by reminding them of the annihilation of the Herero.

Massacre is the high point of collective degradation at which defeat in war is aimed. The despicable indifference toward everything the victim is and represents is proved here. People and the things they have created are indiscriminately destroyed in acts of unbridled violence that can only be

32 See Keegan, *Warfare*, 3ff.
33 Daniel R. Headrick, *The Tools of Empire: Technology and European Imperialism in the Nineteenth Century* (New York, 1981), 102.

called "senseless" in that they deny that the victims have any sense or sensitivity. Accordingly, in Lieutenant von Massow's reports mentioned earlier, he writes: "In this instance [a raid into the territory of the Kabiyé and 'Losso' at the beginning of 1898] the Maxim machine gun proved to be excellent. . . . At 1,800–2,000 meters, almost before they knew it, it killed 10 of the astonished natives, who only believe in fetishes, and wounded many more."[34] Thus, massacre is not "pathological." Massacre is the rule in the conquest and pacification of rural societies. But massacre also is the proclamation and condensed expression of rule in the "colonial situation."[35]

Three characteristics of the colonial situation should be stressed: the antagonism between the rulers and the ruled, the absolute sense of superiority of the rulers, and the fear of the ruling minority harbored by the ruled native majority.

The gap that separated the colonial conquerors from the conquered peoples was all-consuming and almost unbridgeable. It was evident in all relations and left the conquerors with no alternative but a complex and conflicting variety of intermediary structures of rule. The "administrative chiefdom" was one of the most important of these.[36] The antagonism between the rulers and the ruled was reflected in the absolute sense of superiority on the part of the rulers, which simultaneously fed and maintained this opposition. This sense of superiority took on many forms: One of the most common was the sense of cultural and racial superiority. It was most often expressed as a mixture of both. Even if this civilizing sense of superiority, exemplified mainly by the Christian missionaries, gave the ruled the chance for education,[37] the racism of the colonial conquerors limited the possibility of getting along with the conquered and engendered apartheid, enslavement, or expulsion. All three varieties were apparent in the German settler colonies in Africa.

The conquerors' sense of superiority was determined by the strict division between internal and external morality. Even the most despicable member of the group of conquerors is one of "us," whereas any member of the out-group, of "them," such as Henrik Witbooi or Morenga, who could command the respect of the conquerors even according to their criteria, at

34 Quoted in Sebald, *Togo*, 199.
35 For the concept of the "colonial situation," see Georges Balandier, "La notion de 'situation coloniale,'" in Georges Balandier, *Sociologie actuelle de l'afrique noire: Dynamique sociale en afrique centrale* (Paris, 1982), 3–38; see also Trotha, *Koloniale Herrschaft*, 146–7, 205–18, 339, 440.
36 Trotha, *Koloniale Herrschaft*, 222–334; see also Kurt Beck, "Stämme im Schatten des Staats: Zur Entstehung administrativer Häuptlingstümer im nördlichen Sudan," *Sociologus* 39 (1989): 19–35.
37 Edward Graham Norris, *Die Umerziehung des Afrikaners: Togo 1895–1938* (Munich, 1993).

best was treated with a mixture of contempt and respect. Among other things, the former was evident in the scandalous treatment under German criminal law of the murder of African men and women and the latter in the treatment of Witbooi – who had a 5,000-mark bounty on his head and would probably have been hanged if he had been caught. The official war report, however, recorded his death as follows: "A quick soldier's death saved the Captain, whose military qualities commanded respect even from his opponents, from the miserable end awaiting him."[38]

Antagonism and a sense of superiority were components of an order of fear from which the conquerors were never free, even in the supposedly "model colony" of Togo. Colonial society was a society without any basic trust and gave rise to numerous precautions, not only on the part of the ruled but also on the part of the conquerors, in order to be prepared for the outbreak of violent conflict. They ranged from the communitarian conventions with which the "colonial society" ensured its unity in the face of the defeated, to the notorious "tropical rages," to the generally suspicious status of the Africans, who, as colonial literature never tired of stressing repeatedly, were not to be trusted.[39]

In the case of massacre, all three characteristics of the colonial situation came pointedly together. The unbridgeable opposition between the rulers and the ruled was, in the collective objectifying that massacre produces, driven to the outer limit of the existential opposition of life and death. The rulers' arrogant presumption of being able to do exactly as they wanted with their subjects came to a head in lethal violence, where this presumption was turned into a desire for complete disposability. The cultural incomprehension of the rulers and the uniform objectifying of the ruled led to an undifferentiated, lethal dehumanization to which young and old, men and women alike, fall victim. The ruler's claim to absolute superiority was ensured by the countless numbers of fleeing, helpless, and suffering people, who were unable to escape the conquerors' merciless weapons. The ever-present threat that confronted the rulers because of their small number changed at the moment of massacre into violent triumph and became the source of the conqueror's high-handed sense of superiority.

In summary, pacification was an imposition. In the process of monopolizing violence, pacification unleashed violence. The violent process of pacification and the elements of the colonial situation came together in the massacre that typically was part and parcel of the process of pacification.

38 Kriegsgeschichtliche Abteilung II., ed., *Kämpfe der deutschen Truppen in Südwestafrika,* 180.
39 Amadon Booker Sadji, *Das Bild des Negro-Afrikaners in der deutschen Kolonialliteratur (1884–1945): Ein Beitrag zur literarischen Imagologie Schwarzafrikas* (Berlin, 1986); see also Trotha, *Koloniale Herrschaft,* 205–18, 440–1.

In contrast to the ideas that have for a long time marked the image of colonial conquest, during the past twenty years the fact has come to the fore that the colonial assumption of power was an ongoing struggle on the part of the conquerors against the most varied forms of resistance on the part of those who had been colonized; armed resistance was one of these for a lengthy period of time.[40] In this respect, even the difference between "primary" and "secondary" resistance, the latter in the form of uprisings and rebellions, appears questionable.[41] Instead, it is rather more appropriate to consider the wars of the Germans against armed resistance movements in the African colonies between 1904 and 1908 within the continuity of a process of pacification under the conditions of the colonial situation, which began in the 1880s with the colonial assumption of power and came to a temporary end only in the middle and second half of the first decade of the twentieth century, after the merciless defeat of the resistance movements.

In this process of submission, the patterns of wars follow the logic of pacification the violence of which asserts itself in connection with the occidental war culture and lends the process of pacification, a tendency toward total war. Clausewitz accurately summarized this logic in his ideas on the "first" and "second" interactions that govern war.[42] These ideas proceed along the lines that violence becomes unlimited, that the use of violence "must be taken to the limit"[43] whenever the opponent does not accept defeat, and that "I (must) fear that he may defeat me, that I . . . (am) therefore no longer my own master, but he is the one who (enforces) his rule on me, as I do on him."[44]

The differences between the pacification processes in Togo and in the colonies of Southwest Africa provide evidence for the tendency toward the totalization of war in the process of pacification when it encountered more or less continuous armed resistance. Although people in Togo by and large gave up the strategies of armed collective resistance after the turn of the century in favor of other forms of opposition, the German conquerors in Southwest and East Africa were faced with armed resistance that was not only aimed at driving the intruders from the country. It was resistance that followed the pattern of guerrilla war, which was no longer completely at a disadvantage as far as weapons technology was concerned, the leaders of which made hardly any military mistakes given their resources; and it con-

---

40 Trotha, *Koloniale Herrschaft,* 79–84, 411–41.
41 Terence O. Ranger, "Initiatives et résistances africaines face au partage et à la conquête," in A. Adu Boahen, ed., *Histoire générale de l'Afrique,* vol. 7: *L'Afrique sous domination coloniale, 1880–1935* (Paris, 1987), 67–85.
42 Von Clausewitz, *Vom Kriege,* 18–20.   43 Ibid., 19.
44 Ibid., 20.

sequently very quickly led to losses hitherto unknown on the German side. The Germans were afraid of losing the war.[45]

However, a comparison of the "limited" war of pacification in Togo and the "unlimited" wars of pacification in Southwest and East Africa indicates an important distinction that is to be found in the socioeconomic and political differences between these colonies. Togo was a trading colony where, after the failure of plantation policy and the political defeat of its supporters, a policy prevailed that was directed toward the native, rural family economy – "the promotion and development of Negro cultures," as the director of the Imperial Colonial Office, State Secretary Bernhard Dernburg, expressed it in one of his major speeches on colonial policy.[46]

However, the situation in the settlers' and plantation colonies in Southwest and East Africa was completely different. There, the insatiable hunger of the settlers and, above all, the plantation owners for land, their constant need for cheap labor, and their relentless racism, which the plantation owners and settlers typically adopted, were the rule of the day. They involved a change in conflicts not only between the rulers and the ruled, but also between the groups of rulers themselves.

Unlike in a trading colony, the conquered in settler and plantation colonies saw themselves confronted with the life-threatening alternatives of slavery or expulsion. Unlike in a trading colony, the network of opposing interests within the group of conquerors was far more varied. In Southwest Africa these opposing interests were to be found in the policy conflicts of the governor, Theodor Leutwein, and in the discord between him and Lothar von Trotha.[47] The interests, ideologies, and behavior of the settlers and plantation owners served to sharpen the antagonism of the colonial situation. The ideological bases of the conquerors' sense of superiority became particularly radicalized. In an unlimited war of pacification, the totalizing tendencies of the logic of the circle of violence and the racist radicalization of the sense of superiority on the part of the members of colonial society came together. The results were a military strategy of massacre and "burnt earth" that exposed the people to starvation, a dehumanization of the opponent that prevailed in the destructive objectifying, and an external morality in which either the rules of internal morality were no

45 For the Maji-Maji war, see G. C. K. Gwassa, "African Methods of Warfare During the Maji-Maji War, 1905–1907," in B. A. Ogot, ed., *War and Society in Africa: Ten Studies* (London, 1972), 140; for German Southwest Africa, see Bridgman, *Revolt,* 80ff.
46 Bernhard Dernburg, "Fragen der Eingeborenenpolitik" (Rede vor der Budgetkommission des Reichstages vom 18. Februar 1908), *Deutsches Kolonialblatt* 18 (1908): 226.
47 Bridgman, *Revolt*; Helmut Bley, *Kolonialherrschaft und Sozialstruktur in Deutsch-Südwestafrika 1894–1914* (Hamburg, 1968).

longer valid or were so compromised that nothing remained of them.[48] Not only the infamous proclamation of General von Trotha to the Herero on October 2, 1904, and the contemporaneous exchange of correspondence with his superior, the chief of the General Staff, Count Alfred von Schlieffen, are proof of this; in much the same way, the people and the whole area of the Maji-Maji uprising were similarly wiped out. Faced with the famine in the East African territories that had been destroyed by the burnt-earth policy, Captain von Wangenheim stated: "That's quite right, the fellows can just starve. We'll make sure that we have enough to eat. If I could, I would even stop them from planting anything. That's the only way to make these fellows tired of war."[49] The unlimited war of pacification in the colonies of land-hungry settlers and slave-owning planters had a genocidal tendency.

How far this genocidal tendency could prevail in colonial wars depended to a great extent on what policy the colonial headquarters in the "mother country" adopted and what kind of metropolitan lines of conflict there were. Under conditions of long-lasting military conflict there was an incisive change in the structural relationship between metropolitan headquarters and colonial government; the colonial government lost a large part of its independence. The "true rulers" of the colonial empire, to use a term coined by Robert Delavignette, that is, the members of the administration in the colonies themselves and, first and foremost the governor, became directly dependent on the political confrontations in the "mother country."[50]

The shift in the balance of power between the colonial administration in Europe and the government in the colony took many forms. Here I shall treat only three: (1) There was a metropolitan politicization of colonial rule; (2) this politicization strengthened the ideological aspect of armed conflict; and (3) the politicization increased the amount of direct intervention from the metropolitan colonial headquarters. In German colonial history all three developments are exemplified both in the role that General von Trotha played vis-à-vis Governor Leutwein in the Southwest African colonies and in the so-called "Hottentot election" in 1907. In this respect it could be said that, in the categories of a political-military "dependency theory," wars of pacification that were long-lasting and escalated were "pe-

48 When the Germans in Southwest Africa spoke of "monkeys," they usually meant the Africans; see Bridgman, *Revolt*, 62.
49 Quoted in Gwassa, *Methods of Warfare*, 140. According to a report in the *Kingonsera Chronicle* of February 1906, Captain von Wangenheim's words were reported by Captain Richter in Songea; Gwassa did not make this very clear; see Karl-Martin Seeberg, *Der Maji-Maji-Krieg gegen die deutsche Kolonialherrschaft: Historische Ursprünge nationaler Identität in Tansania* (Berlin, 1989), 79–80.
50 Robert Delavignette, *Les vrais chefs de l'empire* (Paris, 1939).

ripheralizing processes" of colonial rule. The metropolitan headquarters acquired more decision-making power. The colony was involved in a process of becoming a militarily and politically "peripheralized area."

In brief, the German colonial wars of pacification in Africa were determined by the conquerors' lack of resources, the necessity of a threat that would guarantee their rule, and the logic of pacification organized by the economy of violence and the features of the colonial situation, both of which included massacre. In settler and plantation colonies there was a tendency for the limited war of pacification to develop into an unlimited one. Above all, when there is a long-lasting, armed resistance by the subjugated to the rule of the conquerors, then war becomes peripheralized and the waging of war is more closely linked to the situation of political conflicts in the "mother country." With the political situation in Imperial Germany, the colonial headquarters' increasing decision-making power meant that the way of dealing with armed conflict increasingly depended on the Kaiser's instructions to General von Trotha to suppress the uprisings with all the means at his disposal – and later to inquire into the reasons why the Africans had rebelled.[51]

III

What differences exist between the colonial wars of pacification and the total wars of industrialized nation-states? Where are the tendencies toward the totalization of colonial wars of pacification to be found?

First, the degree of mobilization of the population remained limited on the side of the German conquerors, even when, at the height of the success of the African resistance, there were moves to set up militias with members of the European colonial society.[52] Disregarding the narrower political conflicts, the population in Europe remained untouched by the war. For service in Africa it was possible to limit recruitment to volunteers in Imperial Germany. The picture of the African side was much more complex because the degree of mobilization depended on the political structures – that is, on the one hand, it depended on the degree of centralization of the societies affected and, on the other, on the conflicts existing between the different political units. Nevertheless, in the struggle against the German conquerors, both in Southwest and East Africa, there were not only trans-local and trans-tribal relations, but the pattern of guerrilla

51 Bridgman, *Revolt,* 111.   52 Seeberg, *Maji-Maji,* 65.

warfare entailed that large parts of the population were drawn into the war, and the dividing line between "civilian" and "soldier" disappeared.[53]

Second, the situation is different when the victims are considered. Here, in comparison with the degree of mobilization, the approximation to the features of total war between the German conquerors and the Africans who offered armed resistance tends to be the other way around. The annihilation of the colonial Germans was beyond any realizable goal of African resistance. Even at the height of their military success, the major military aim of the Africans could be no more than to force the Germans to forgo their military conquest and leave the country.[54] In order to attain this end, armed African resistance typically did not indiscriminately attack all whites who lived in the colonies. In Southwest Africa, Witbooi and Morenga limited any extension of the category of victims, which the German strategy of massacre and burnt earth suggested, by repeatedly mentioning and carrying out the practice of sparing women, children, and prisoners of war. Nevertheless, members of European colonial society still were very much at risk and fell victim to African attacks.

With the development of unlimited wars of pacification on the German side, the divisions between the "civil population," soldiers, and prisoners of war became increasingly less distinct, not only from a tactical but also from a moral and strategic point of view. In addition to the numerous massacres that took place in all wars of pacification and the strategy of burnt earth that the Germans used, particularly in the Maji-Maji war, the strategy and policy of General von Trotha, who not only drove the Herero to their deaths after the battle of Waterberg but also developed the idea of an irreconcilable "racial struggle," are once again exemplary.[55]

Third, the degree of mobilization of the affected African and German populations obviously differed a great deal. On the African side, in certain regions and at certain times, large parts of the population were involved. For example, at the height of the Herero and Maji-Maji uprisings, the war involved all the members of the affected societies. For the Africans, resistance had the features of total war in stateless societies. At the same time,

---

53 This caused, for example, the governor of East Africa, Adolf Graf von Götzen, to speak of a "people's war"; ibid., 72.

54 The leader of the Maji-Maji movement, for example, tried to mobilize his supporters in the war against the Germans by means of this military goal; see Gwassa, *Methods of Warfare*, 136.

55 Timm quite rightly and sarcastically commented on the order of Trotha in connection with the notorious proclamation to the Hereros on October 2, 1904, when he revoked the death threat for women and children: "The Prussian Code of Honor: one may not shoot women and children, so one drives them into the desert to die of thirst" (Timm, *Morenga*, 143).

however, the violent resistance of the Africans reflected the lack of interethnic and intertribal organizational power in African societies. Their
resistance could therefore be considered limited from the point of view of
the conquerors, provided that the interethnic and intertribal context did
not reach a level that endangered conquest itself, in that it encompassed the
entire area of conquest at any one time.[56]

On the German side, mobilization was far from being that of total war.
Moreover, in the colonial wars of pacification, there were basic structural
limits to a direct militarization of the society to which the conquerors belonged. Thus, the political context of colonialism, the limits of the pe-
ripheralization process, the limited organizational power of the colonial
rulers, and the war itself, which tested the superior strength of the conquerors – all prevented the process of militarization from being put into
practice.

Fourth, the conquerors brought to bear the occidental, industrially
based technology of war. The superiority of European weapons technology always transformed armed conflict into massacre for the Africans whenever, and this was mostly the case, they were unable to equip themselves
sufficiently with European weapons and did not adopt the tactics of guerrilla warfare.[57] In addition, the technical improvement of logistics (particularly the use of the telegraph) gave the Europeans important tactical advantages.

Nevertheless, the technological side of colonial wars of pacification
should not be overestimated.[58] The supply of the most modern weapons
was largely limited to the European officers and noncommissioned officers.
The Africans in the German colonial armies, by contrast, had to be satis-

---

56 This issue raises highly complex methodological and conceptual problems. If one correctly proceeds from the premise that the Africans constituted a world of great political, cultural, social, and
even economic heterogeneity, then the colonial conquerors' so frequently invoked policy of divide-
et-impera implied that it was still based on the false premise that the opponent had a unified territorial and ideological order. (What is there "to divide" when it is already "divided"?). In other
words, the conqueror conducted a war against "the" Africans, at the same time feeling himself to be
someone who destroyed the entire fighting force of his opponent and, because of the limited interethnic and intertribal relations of his opponent, did not consider himself to be faced with total
war (as two villages or nations can wage a total war against each other). Thus, from the point of
view of mobilization, what developed into total war for individual African societies was understood
by the conqueror to be regionally and ethnically limited conflict; this is the reason why mention was
made of "bands" and uprisings of individual "tribes." Understandably, this means that the concept of
total war came to depend on the different political forms of organization and ideas of government
of the parties involved in the conflict.
57 Killingray points out that the Europeans, especially after the Brussels Conference of 1890, were relatively successful in preventing the Africans from equipping themselves with modern weapons;
David Killingray, "Colonial Warfare in West Africa, 1870–1914," in J. A. de Moors and H. L. Wesseling, eds., *Imperialism and War: Essays on Colonial Wars in Asia and Africa* (Leiden, 1989), 153.
58 Wesseling, "Colonial Wars: An Introduction," in ibid., 5–8.

fied with antiquated guns.[59] Equally important was the military organizational power of the conquerors, who waged their wars with professional armies commanded by highly trained and motivated officers. Above all, neither the Germans nor the Africans were in a position to create "war machines." The more the Africans countered the Germans with the tactics of "bush war," that is, guerrilla war or war with guerrilla-like tactics, the less likely was the outcome of the battle determined by technology. On the contrary, the Germans forced the unconditional surrender of the Africans by using nontechnological tactics, namely, the strategies of burnt earth and hunger. The restricted importance of weapons technology also is documented by the fact that the German losses, as in any traditional war, were to a great extent due not to immediate armed conflict but rather to sanitary and hygienic conditions and fatal diseases.[60]

Accordingly, the wars of pacification were hardly a competition to invent and develop weapons technology. The Germans used the technologies that they had at their disposal and deemed sufficient for victory in a bush war. Specific innovations, which were not even technological in the strictest sense of the word, such as the deployment of a camel troop, were limited. With the important exception of the "Maxim" machine gun, the totalizing tendencies of the war rather were more political and ethical than technical in nature. For example, the Germans used dum-dum bullets in order to terrorize their opponents psychologically.

Clear tendencies toward the totalization of colonial wars are found instead in unlimited wars of pacification. The unlimited war of pacification brings to the fore the total tendency of the war culture of the modern European nation-state, in which war is presented as unrestricted victory, annihilating defeat, decisive battle, and outstanding military leader; Clausewitz's theory of "pure war" has provided excellent examples of these ideas.[61] In the strategy of exposing entire populations to certain death by hunger and thirst, unlimited wars of pacification are radicalized to the limit and take on the genocidal trait of total war. The treatment of the defeated partly resembled genocidal warfare. Men, women, and children were deported, interned in "concentration camps" following the example of the English Boer War, and died there of hunger and diseases due to appalling condi-

---

59 Gann and Duignan, *Rulers,* 119.
60 Ibid.; see also Wesseling, *Colonial Wars,* 7.
61 With this European outlook on war, the colonial conquerors, who had learned how to put these notions into practice while studying at military academies, encountered serious difficulties when they were faced with guerrilla war in Africa. These difficulties not only caused tactical and strategic problems, but also highlighted the different perceptions of time – i.e., war as an ongoing "state of war."

tions in the camps.[62] In Southwest Africa not only the political and social but also the economic structures of the Nama and Herero were destroyed in the interests of an enslaving "worker policy." In the unlimited wars of pacification, the ideological context of war comes to the fore. Ideologies themselves became increasingly and irreconcilably determined by the ideology of "racial war." Both the sense of racial and civilizing superiority and the contempt for the cultures and lifestyles of the Africans were transformed into the conviction that the resistance of the colonized peoples should not only be broken but also that the destruction of peoples, cultures, and social organizations, where armed resistance was rooted, was necessary. The ideologically based complete indifference to the suffering of victims turned into total violence. At the end of the war, just as in Southwest Africa, a policy of controlling the defeated was implemented; its goals were admittedly purely illusory under the conditions of colonial rule, but as Horst Gründer rightly points out, Southwest Africa is the only proof of Hannah Arendt's thesis that the foundations of totalitarianism could be seen to be emergent in the colonial policy of Africa.[63]

However, unlike World War II, where the National Socialist war of destruction became the epitome of modern total war, the ideological totalization of war always remained restricted, even in unlimited wars of pacification. The interests, attitudes, and ideologies, not only on the metropolitan side of colonial policy but also in the colonies themselves, were beset by conflicts. Baron Albrecht von Rechenberg, as governor of East Africa, attempted to overcome the devastation left after the Maji-Maji war with an ambitious political program that had nothing to do with settler and plantation colonies and was intended to make the colony a "country for merchants, Indian traders and native cultures."[64] Also, in Southwest Africa, totalitarian dreams were shattered when they came up against the reality of colonial rule and its economy, which depended on being drip-fed by the imperial budget and that consequently saw itself bound to win over the Africans as independent producers. This was impossible in a forced-labor economy, as Secretary of State Dernburg repeatedly pointed out.

---

62 From a total of just under 1,800 people who were ordered to be interned on an island off the coast of Southwest Africa by the commander of the Southwest African "Defense Troop," within one year there were only 254 survivors. Only 25 of these were considered by the camp administration to be fit to work – in a situation where the colonial conquerors were never particularly scrupulous where the Africans' fitness to work was concerned; see Bridgman, *Revolt*, 165.

63 Gründer, *Deutsche Kolonien*, 124; Hannah Arendt, *Elemente und Ursprünge totaler Herrschaft* (Munich, 1986), 310–57.

64 Quoted in Gründer, *Deutsche Kolonien*, 163.

Wars of pacification are aimed at the conquest of and rule over territories and people. Total wars of conquest, however, are characterized by extreme indifference to the suffering of the people. They are aimed at the conquest of certain areas and, provided they do not immediately wipe out the inhabitants of these areas, they are aimed not to rule over people but rather to enslave them. The colonial wars of Imperial Germany in Africa generally remained within the boundaries of wars of pacification. Where they became unlimited, then elements of a total war of conquest emerged.

19

Was the Philippine-American War
a "Total War"?

GLENN ANTHONY MAY

Starting in February 1899 until roughly April 1902, the United States fought an ugly little war in the Philippines. At the height of the conflict, almost 10,000 U.S. soldiers served on Philippine soil, opposed by no fewer than 100,000 Filipino regulars and irregulars. The conflict resulted in the deaths of 4,234 Americans. On the Filipino side, at least 20,000 soldiers were killed. Civilian casualties, according to some accounts, numbered in the hundreds of thousands.[1] In addition, a massive amount of damage was done to Philippine livestock, agricultural land, homes, churches, and public buildings.

At the time of the war there was widespread criticism of the U.S. Army's policies and actions. Anti-imperialists, opposed to America's acquisition of an overseas empire, deplored the appalling destructiveness of the American campaign, its many acts of torture, the huge loss of life on the Filipino side, and much more; over the years, a number of historians have agreed with their critique.[2] Indeed, there can be little doubt that in that ugly little war U.S. soldiers committed many acts that went well beyond the bounds of generally accepted military practice. But did the U.S. Army's prosecution of that conflict amount to something akin to "total war"? Can we find in that turn-of-the-century war any foreshadowing of or connection to the harsh military practices we tend to associate with World War II? In the pages that follow, I will attempt to answer those questions.

---

1 On the question of civilian mortality, see John M. Gates, "War-Related Deaths in the Philippines," *Pacific Historical Review* 53 (Nov. 1983): 367–78; Glenn Anthony May, "150,000 Missing Filipinos: A Demographic Crisis in Batangas, 1887–1903," *Annales de Démographie Historique* 21 (1985): 215–43.
2 See, e.g., Renato Constantino, with the collaboration of Leticia Constantino, *The Philippines: A Past Revisited*, 5th printing (Manila, 1979), 248–54; Stuart Creighton Miller, *"Benevolent Assimilation": The American Conquest of the Philippines, 1899–1903* (New Haven, Conn., 1982), 176–267.

Two caveats must be stated at the outset. First, it should be obvious that any answers I might provide to the foregoing questions are likely to be directly affected by the way in which I define the key, albeit elusive, term that appears in the title of this chapter – "total war." As Roger Chickering (in his contribution to this book) and Mark E. Neely Jr. (in a recent influential article) have both pointed out, that term has been used to describe several different characteristics of mid-twentieth-century warfare – among others, the complete mobilization of a society's economic resources in order to defeat the enemy, the targeting of the enemy's economic resources as well as his army, and the erosion of the "fragile barriers" separating soldiers from civilians. Both Chickering and Neely see the latter characteristic as especially crucial. What makes warfare "total," Neely argues, is the extent to which the civilian population – as distinct from the army of the enemy – is considered a "legitimate military target."[3] In my own effort to assess the "totality" of the Philippine-American War, I will follow the leads of Chickering and Neely, paying particular attention to the U.S. Army's policies and actions toward noncombatants.

Second, it should be recognized that the approaches adopted by the United States in the Philippine-American War may have been – and almost certainly were – influenced as much by the specificities of that military struggle as by any altered or evolving notions about how to conduct warfare in general. As we shall see, the Philippine-American War was, for much of its duration, an unconventional conflict, pitting an American army of occupation against Filipino guerrillas who depended for their very survival on the assistance (the gathering of military intelligence, the furnishing of food and many other supplies) provided by civilians. In this struggle, resistance to the Americans tended to be greatest in regions where the ties between guerrillas and civilians were strongest, and over time, and perhaps not surprisingly, some American commanders came to recognize that the only way to end the resistance was to sever those ties. To some extent, then, the targeting of civilians was a predictable consequence of counterguerrilla operations in specific regions. Furthermore, America's opponents in this conflict were people of color – that is to say, people whom most U.S. officers and soldiers, reflecting the then-prevalent attitudes of white-skinned Americans of the day, considered to be intellectually and morally inferior to Caucasians.[4] And just possibly, such widespread

3 Mark E. Neely Jr., "Was the Civil War a Total War?" *Civil War History* 37 (Mar. 1991): 5–28; reprinted in Stig Förster and Jörg Nagler, eds., *On the Road to Total War: The American Civil War and the German Wars of Unification, 1861–1871* (New York, 1997).
4 On racism in the conflict, see Miller, *Benevolent Assimilation,* 176–95. Obviously, such ethnocentric/racist notions were not shared by the African-American soldiers who served in the Philippines. On their experience, see Willard B. Gatewood Jr., ed., *"Smoked Yankees" and the Struggle for Empire:*

perceptions of the enemy's "inferiority" made it easier for U.S. commanders to embrace policies that, in a war against a Caucasian enemy, might have been considered inhumane. Still further, the nation-state that the United States destroyed in the war, the Philippine Republic, was a newly minted one – a state that, both because of its newness and because of the American intention to absorb it as a colony, was seen to be lacking in legitimacy. This is precisely why the government of the United States referred to the conflict as the "Philippine Insurrection," the implication being that it was a police action, not a genuine war. Again, the point to be emphasized here is that, because the military struggle in the Philippines was considered different in kind, certain unusually harsh remedies may have been resorted to more easily.

I

The Philippine-American War was the continuation of a struggle for independence that Filipino revolutionaries had launched against Spain. In August 1896 fighting had erupted in the Tagalog-speaking provinces of central Luzon between followers of the Katipunan, a secret society intent on ending colonial rule, and Spanish troops. After scoring some initial victories in the province of Cavite, just south of Manila, the Filipinos were thrashed by the Spaniards, and in December 1897 their leaders – including the commanding general Emilio Aguinaldo – were exiled to Hong Kong. Sporadic resistance to the Spaniards continued in Aguinaldo's absence. Then, in April 1898, following a protracted dispute concerning Cuba, the United States and Spain went to war, and shortly afterward Commodore George Dewey's Asiatic Squadron eliminated Spain's Pacific fleet, thereby isolating the Spaniards in the Philippines and dealing a crippling blow to Spanish power in the archipelago. In mid-May 1898 Aguinaldo returned to the Philippines and again assumed leadership of the revolution. Within a few weeks his forces defeated or captured most of the Spanish troops on the island of Luzon. Aguinaldo issued a declaration of independence and established a government with himself as head; in the meantime, the revolution began to spread to other parts of the archipelago.

But the revolutionaries' success was to prove short-lived because it soon became apparent that the United States, having made quick work of Spain in the Spanish-American War, had no intention of leaving the Philippines to the Filipinos. Although President William McKinley appeared to have no specific designs on the Philippines at the time of Dewey's victory, he

Letters from Negro Soldiers, 1898–1902 (Urbana, Ill., 1971), 237–316; and Willard B. Gatewood Jr., *Black Americans and the White Man's Burden, 1898–1903* (Urbana, Ill., 1975), 261–92.

gradually warmed to the idea of taking the archipelago from Spain. In October 1898 negotiators from Spain and the United States met in Paris to discuss peace terms, and McKinley's instructions to the American delegation required them to demand the Philippines. According to the terms of the peace treaty of December 10, 1898, Spain ceded the archipelago, and President McKinley immediately passed the treaty on to the U.S. Senate for ratification.

As America's intentions became more clear, relations deteriorated between Aguinaldo's troops and the U.S. expeditionary force that had been dispatched by McKinley in May 1898. Discussions took place between representatives of Aguinaldo and Elwell Otis, the American commanding general, but they resolved nothing. Finally, the inevitable collision occurred. On February 4, 1899, two days before the U.S. Senate voted to acquire the Philippines, an American sentry shot and killed a Filipino soldier in Manila. The Philippine-American War had begun.

The war in the Philippines passed through two distinct phases. From February to November 1899, the elite units of the Philippine Army, concentrated in the northern half of the island of Luzon, fought a conventional war against the United States. One set-piece battle followed another, almost all with the same results – one-sided American victories and heavy casualties for the Filipino forces. The second, unconventional phase of the war began in November 1899, once it became clear to Aguinaldo that his army was incapable of defeating the Americans in conventional encounters. Thereafter, throughout the archipelago, the Americans were forced to fight an enemy that engaged in hit-and-run raids on American patrols and American-occupied towns. Once the guerrilla phase of the war had begun, Aguinaldo's authority to direct the Filipino war effort essentially ceased; control of Philippine military operations passed to a score of local commanders, typically men of wealth and political influence in their communities. Aguinaldo was captured by the Americans in March 1901, but the guerrilla warfare continued until mid-1902.[5]

More than 10,000 U.S. soldiers served in the Philippines during the period 1899–1902, and in many respects they were a heterogeneous lot. But one thing that they appeared to have in common was a low opinion of Filipinos, combatants and noncombatants alike. "I have not seen a good look-

---

5 For overviews of the war, see William T. Sexton, *Soldiers in the Sun: An Adventure in Imperialism* (Harrisburg, Pa., 1939); John M. Gates, *Schoolbooks and Krags: The United States Army in the Philippines, 1898–1902* (Westport, Conn., 1973); Miller, *Benevolent Assimilation;* Glenn Anthony May, "Why the United States Won the Philippine-American War, 1899–1902," *Pacific Historical Review* 52 (Nov. 1983): 353–77.

ing native since we have come here," wrote Pvt. Lee Osborn. "They are for a fact the homliest [*sic*] race of people I have ever seen." "They are extremely filthy in their eating," opined another soldier. Comments about the Filipinos' supposed intellectual and cultural backwardness appeared regularly in the correspondence of American fighting men. "They cannot be said to be half-civilized, but must be classified as barbarous," wrote Capt. John Leland Jordan to his mother. Jordan's regimental commander, George S. Anderson, agreed with the assessment: "They rank as barbarous, not much above our better class of Indians." Not only did soldiers apply to the Filipinos the racial stereotypes that contemporary white Americans applied to African Americans, Native Americans, and other non-Caucasians, but they also applied the same racial epithets. Many, if not most, of the soldiers referred to Filipinos either as "niggers" or "gugus" (the latter being a word of indeterminate origin that bears a curious resemblance to "gook").[6]

Such attitudes were not, of course, appreciably different from those that had been expressed by U.S. officers and enlisted men in the Indian Wars. Furthermore, some of them indulged in similar rhetorical excess in prescribing policies to pacify the Filipinos. "The country won't be pacified until the niggers are killed off like the Indians," one soldier told a reporter. Theodore Schwan, a brigadier general, essentially favored the same approach: "The people are by no means civilized. . . . They are in identically the same position as the Indians of our country have been for many years, and in my opinion must be subdued in much the same way, by such convincing conquest as shall make them realize the futility of armed resistance."[7]

Although the rhetoric seemed to suggest that a genocidal approach might be adopted, for most of the conflict nothing of the sort occurred. During the conventional phase, U.S. commanders adopted essentially the same tactics that they had used since the Civil War, directing most of their attention to the task of engaging and eliminating the large Filipino military units that opposed them in central and northern Luzon. Although there is more than a little evidence of atrocious conduct on the part of the U.S. forces – the torching of residences, crops, even entire towns; the torture and execution of civilians and captured enemy soldiers – such actions did

---

6 Russell Roth, *Muddy Glory: America's "Indian Wars" in the Philippines* (West Hanover, Mass., 1981), 42–3, 50, 54; Glenn Anthony May, *Battle for Batangas: A Philippine Province at War* (New Haven, Conn., 1991), 141, 146–7; Miller, *Benevolent Assimilation*, 176–7, 182, 184–5, 188; William Henry Scott, *Ilocano Responses to American Aggression, 1900–1901* (Quezon City, 1986), 26, 133, 146–7; Lewis O. Saum, "The Western Volunteer and the 'New Empire,'" *Pacific Northwest Quarterly* 57 (Jan. 1966): 18–27.

7 Miller, *Benevolent Assimilation*, 179; May, *Battle*, 95, 161.

not appear to occur anywhere near as frequently as they did later in the war. Official U.S. military policy discouraged burning, except in unusual circumstances, and did not condone mistreatment of civilians and captured soldiers. In fact, more than a few of the men responsible for such abuses were punished for their actions.[8]

The unconventional phase of the war posed considerably more formidable problems to the Americans. Now dispersed in hundreds of garrisons around the archipelago, U.S. troops were opposed by an enemy that fought infrequently, inflicted a bit of damage, and then melted into the countryside. The change in the nature of the conflict brought the Americans into much more frequent contact with the noncombatant population. U.S. troops had daily social and commercial interactions with civilians who lived or worked near the posts; they also encountered noncombatants regularly on patrols, as they scoured the provinces in search of the elusive guerrillas.

The Americans did not adopt a single, monolithic approach to coping with this new guerrilla enemy. As Brian Linn has shown, once the guerrilla phase of the war began, the U.S. command (like the Filipino) exercised fairly weak control over the officers who directed operations in the field, allowing them the flexibility to devise policies that were appropriate for the provinces in which they operated. In effect, the guerrilla phase of the Philippine-American War amounted to a collection of small, largely independent and self-contained regional conflicts.[9]

So, for example, in the Fourth District of the Department of Northern Luzon, which included the provinces of Nueva Ecija and Principe, U.S. officers encountered fairly weak resistance, thanks in large measure to the poor leadership exercised by Filipino commanders in the area and ongoing tensions between those military men and local elites. Because of the relatively favorable conditions they found, U.S. officers in the Fourth District received a substantial amount of cooperation from elite Filipinos in the region, were able to establish an effective intelligence network, and did not, as a consequence, have to resort to measures that caused much discomfort to the civilian population. When, however, the local resistance was more deeply entrenched – as in the First District of the Department of Northern Luzon, which included several provinces populated primarily by ethnic Ilocanos – a sterner approach was adopted: mistreatment of prisoners, the

8 On atrocities, see Richard E. Welch Jr., "American Atrocities in the Philippines: The Indictment and the Response," *Pacific Historical Review* 43 (May 1974): 233–53; Miller, *Benevolent Assimilation*, passim.
9 Brian McAllister Linn, *The U.S. Army and Counterinsurgency in the Philippine War, 1899–1902* (Chapel Hill, N.C., 1989), xi, xiii, 163–5.

destruction of crops and personal property, and the use of provost courts to try (and imprison) civilians suspected of aiding the guerrillas. U.S. commanders in the Bikol region of southeastern Luzon likewise resorted to harsh measures – especially the destruction of large amounts of food.[10]

In both northwestern and southeastern Luzon, then, one could find the U.S. Army doing things that, according to the Chickering/Neely formula, might be associated with total warfare because of their impact on civilians. But, however harsh those actions were, they were surely no harsher than the ones committed by troops under Sherman, Sheridan, or Grant during the Civil War.[11] As in the earlier conflict, civilians suffered from food shortages, and some were tortured, arrested, and imprisoned. The fragile barrier separating soldiers from civilians was definitely breached but not, it appears, in radically new ways.

II

Still, there were two theaters of operation that, if conventional wisdom about the Philippine-American War is to be believed, may merit further scrutiny: the island of Samar, located about 300 miles southeast of Manila; and southwestern Luzon, which included the provinces of Batangas, Laguna, and Tayabas. In both places, resistance to the Americans was long-lasting and American casualties were high; in both, according to contemporary anti-imperialist critics and several generations of historians, U.S. commanders adopted policies that were especially harsh on civilians, and U.S. troops were guilty of extraordinarily gruesome conduct.[12] Can we find something akin to total war in either of those campaigns?

Let us start with Samar. The leader of the Filipino resistance on the island of Samar was General Vicente Lukban, a native of Camarines Norte

10 Linn, *U.S. Army*, 29–118; Scott, *Ilocano Responses;* Orlino Ochosa, *The Tinio Brigade: Anti-American Resistance in the Ilocos Provinces, 1899–1901* (Quezon City, 1991); Norman G. Owen, "Winding Down the War in Albay, 1900–1903," *Pacific Historical Review* 48 (Nov. 1979): 557–89. On the guerrilla war in other regions, see, e.g., Ma. Fe. Hernaez Romero, *Negros Occidental between Two Foreign Powers, 1888–1909* (Bacolod City, 1974), 124–214; Caridad Aldecoa-Rodriguez, *Negros Oriental and the Philippine Revolution* (Dumaguete City, 1983); Luis Camara Dery, *From Ibalon to Sorsogon: A History of Sorsogon Province to 1905* (Quezon City, 1991), 146–202. In a recent article John S. Reed makes the case that, in the southern Philippines during the period 1900–1, "illegal acts against noncombatants" were consistently punished by the U.S. Army. See Reed, "External Discipline During Counterinsurgency: A Philippine Case Study, 1900–1901," *Journal of American-East Asian Relations* 4 (spring 1995): 29–48.
11 See Neely, "Was the Civil War a Total War?" 14–28.
12 See Daniel B. Schirmer, *Republic or Empire: American Resistance to the Philippine War* (Cambridge, 1972), 232–9; Richard E. Welch Jr., *Response to Imperialism: The United States and the Philippine-American War* (Chapel Hill, N.C., 1979), 139–41; Constantino, *Past Revisited*, 250–1; Miller, *Benevolent Assimilation*, 196–267; Gates, *Schoolbooks*, 248–57.

(in southeastern Luzon) who had been educated in Manila. Lukban arrived in Samar in December 1898 with a commission from Aguinaldo to bring Samar and the neighboring island of Leyte within the orbit of the Philippine Republic. In the following months, Lukban attempted to do so, forging strong alliances with influential men in several towns and raising money for Aguinaldo's government and war effort. U.S. troops did not arrive in Samar until January 1900, when an expedition under General William Fiobbé landed at Calbayog and Catbalogan and established garrisons there. Lukban offered no resistance to the landings, but not long thereafter his guerrilla forces began harassing the Americans on the island. Samar – mountainous, covered with tropical vegetation, and lacking a decent road system – was an almost ideal place for a guerrilla force to operate, and Lukban's men had a modicum of success. Throughout the guerrilla war, the guerrillas received substantial amounts of supplies from noncombatants in the towns, although, as time passed and Filipino fortunes waned in other theaters, it appears that such civilian support diminished somewhat. Despite repeated efforts by U.S. officers to induce Lukban to surrender, he steadfastly refused to do so.[13]

The lack of success galled U.S. commanders, especially Brigadier General Robert P. Hughes, who had charge of U.S. operations in the region, and in June 1901 he began to increase the pressure on Lukban's forces. Patrols were stepped up. Crops were destroyed. In addition, Hughes sent a battalion to garrison several communities in southern Samar, including the town of Balangiga.[14]

In August 1901 Company C of the Ninth Infantry, commanded by Captain Thomas W. Connell, reached Balangiga. Connell apparently believed that the inhabitants of the town could be trusted, and as a result, the company was poorly prepared for any hostilities. Then, on the morning of September 28, several hundred Samareños boldly attacked the garrison. The Balangiga massacre, as it was called, resulted in the deaths of 48 of the 74 members of Company C. It also led the ranking U.S. Army officer in the Philippines, Adna Chaffee, to take immediate steps to escalate U.S. military operations on Samar. Several additional battalions of infantry were sent to the island, along with approximately 300 Marines. In October 1901

13 John R. M. Taylor, *The Philippine Insurrection Against the United States: A Compilation of Documents with Notes and Introduction,* 5 vols. (Pasay City, 1971–3), 2:426–38; 5:629–716; Brian M. Linn, "The Struggle for Samar," in James C. Bradford, ed., *Crucible of Empire: The Spanish-American War and Its Aftermath* (Annapolis, Md., 1993), 158–82; E. M. Holt, "Resistance in Samar: General Vicente Lukban and the Revolutionary War, 1899–1902," *Kabar Seberang Sulating Maphilindo* 10 (Dec. 1982): 1–14; John N. Schumacher, *Revolutionary Clergy: The Filipino Clergy and the Nationalist Movement, 1850–1903* (Quezon City, 1981), 141–2.
14 Linn, "Struggle," 165–7.

Brigadier General Jacob H. Smith arrived to oversee the pacification of the island.[15]

Smith's direction of the Samar campaign has long been the subject of controversy. Contemporary press accounts labeled him a "monster," and even well-known defenders of the American conquest of the Philippines such as Senator Henry Cabot Lodge denounced Smith's conduct.[16] Whereas J. Franklin Bell, the general who orchestrated U.S. operations in southwestern Luzon, was consistently defended by his superiors and later promoted to the post of chief of staff of the U.S. Army, Smith was court-martialed, convicted, and summarily retired from the service. Yet in reality, the Samar campaign, however harsh, was probably undeserving of the notoriety it received. What differentiated it from all the others was the rhetoric of the general who conducted it, not the actions of the officers and men who served under him. Like the famous U.S. Civil War leader William Tecumseh Sherman, Smith was inclined, in the heat of battle, to make extraordinarily draconian pronouncements about how to fight a war.[17] Although the soldiers in his brigade were guilty of atrocious acts, they never came close to putting into practice the pronouncements of the commander.

From the start, Smith made it clear to his subordinates that he intended to deal severely with the inhabitants of Samar. Toward the end of October 1901 he told Major Littleton W. T. Waller, who commanded the contingent of Marines that had been sent to Samar: "I want no prisoners. I wish you to kill and burn. I want all persons killed who are capable of bearing arms in actual hostilities against the United States." When Waller, stunned by the order, asked Smith to clarify it, the general informed him that he was to consider any person of ten years or older "as being capable of bearing arms." On the next day Smith spoke to Waller again, conveying essentially the same message. "Kill and burn," he said to the major. "The more you kill and burn, the better you will please me. I want no prisoners, do you understand?" Sometime in December, moreover, after Waller had begun to operate against the guerrillas in Samar, Smith sent him a brief handwritten message that read: "The interior of Samar must be made a howling wilderness!"[18]

---

15 Joseph L. Schott, *The Ordeal of Samar* (Indianapolis, 1964), 7–66; Gates, *Schoolbooks,* 248–50; Miller, *Benevolent Assimilation,* 199–204, 219; Linn, "Struggle," 167–8; Holt, "Resistance," 9, 13. Linn points out that there was some confusion over who actually was in charge on Samar. Smith appeared to be, but Hughes constantly interfered.

16 Miller, *Benevolent Assimilation,* 236; Linn, "Struggle," 172; Welch, *Response,* 138–41.

17 On Sherman, see Neely, "Was the Civil War a Total War?" 14–15.

18 Schott, *Ordeal,* 71, 76, 98; Kenneth Ray Young, "Atrocities and War Crimes: The Cases of Major Waller and General Smith," *Leyte-Smith Studies* 12 (1978): 64–77.

Now, those are truly scary words and, had they been carried out to the letter by Smith's brigade, a case could perhaps be made that Brigadier General Jacob H. Smith was the father of "total war." But they were not. True, the campaign on Samar was incredibly destructive. Between October 1901, when Smith assumed command, and February 1902, when Lukban was captured, the Americans destroyed thousands of homes, tons of food, hundreds of cattle, and much additional property. In the meantime, U.S. naval vessels prevented Samareños from receiving supplies from other islands. These policies proved to be so effective that by the end even noncombatants were suffering from severe food shortages.[19]

True too, U.S. troops committed some genuinely awful acts. In December 1901 seven prisoners were shot on the orders of Captain William Wallace. Major Edwin Glenn kidnapped civilians, tortured suspects, and probably was responsible for the death of no fewer than ten Filipinos. Waller, on his part, ordered the shooting of eleven noncombatants who had apparently conspired against the American troops, and at least one other civilian was killed on the orders of one of Waller's subordinates, Lieutenant John Day. But, significantly, when those actions came to the attention of General Chaffee, both Waller and Day were brought before courts-martial on charges of murder, and they managed to avoid conviction only because they were able to show that General Smith had given them such open-ended orders to kill. Those courts-martial, as well as the subsequent trial of Smith, gave a clear signal that the U.S. Army was unwilling to condone the wanton killing of noncombatants.[20]

In summary, then, although Jacob Smith's campaign on Samar was undeniably brutal, it would be difficult to argue that it looked anything like total war. Smith's rhetoric was extraordinary. A massive amount of property was destroyed. Waller and other officers sometimes dealt with noncombatants in appalling ways. But most of the U.S. officers and men who served on Samar did not appear to view the civilian population of the island as legitimate military targets.

III

Somewhat less notorious than the Samar campaign but many times more draconian was the one in southwestern Luzon. That region, located fairly close to Manila, had been a hotbed of anti-Spanish activity during the final

19 Linn, "Struggle," 168–75; Schott, *Ordeal,* 79–147.
20 Ibid., 134–284; Miller, *Benevolent Assimilation,* 225–32; Schumacher, *Revolutionary Clergy,* 143–5;
   Linn, "Struggle," 172; Young, "Atrocities," 64–77.

days of Spanish rule. Several of the leading figures in the revolution of 1896 came from the area, and heavy fighting had taken place in the provinces of Batangas and Laguna between October 1896 and June 1898. Following the liberation of the region from the Spaniards, most of it (everything except a small section of Laguna, which was occupied by U.S. troops in July 1899) had experienced approximately eighteen months of self-rule. Then, in January 1900 the Americans finally entered southwestern Luzon in force, occupying the principal towns without great difficulty but then finding themselves harassed by guerrilla forces. The key players in the Filipino resistance in southwestern Luzon – the leaders of the local armies, the men within the occupied towns who directed the efforts by the noncombatant population to provide money, food, and intelligence to the Filipino fighting men – were members of the indigenous political and economic elites, many of whom also had played prominent roles in the earlier struggle against Spain.[21]

Initially, the American commanders in the region attempted to end the resistance by pursuing the guerrillas ceaselessly, and for about a year they scoured the area, paying particular attention to the outlying barrios and mountainous terrain the Filipino forces were known to frequent. To a certain extent, they succeeded. Hundreds of Filipino troops were killed or captured by scouting parties, and by the beginning of 1901 the local forces were in disarray. Contributing to their difficulties were discouraging developments outside the region: the surrender of Mariano Trias, Aguinaldo's second-in-command, in the nearby province of Cavite in mid-March 1901; Aguinaldo's capture a few days later; and the growth of the Federal Party, an organization led by prominent Manila-based Filipinos who were assisting the Americans in pacifying the archipelago.[22]

But then, starting in April 1901, the resistance in southwestern Luzon experienced a second wind, thanks in large measure to the leadership, policies, and tactics of a remarkable Filipino general named Miguel Malvar, a native of the province of Batangas, who succeeded Trias as the commander of the entire Philippine Army in the southern part of Luzon. From the start, Malvar attempted in a number of ways to strengthen his control over the noncombatants in the region. First of all, he placed great emphasis on gaining the full support of common men and women, individuals whose interests had largely been ignored by Aguinaldo and other leaders of the Philippine government who had consistently concentrated on promoting

---

21 May, *Battle,* 36–127; Elsie Ramos, "Tayabas, 1571–1907," M.A. thesis, University of the Philippines, 1992, 119–88.
22 May, *Battle,* 131–207.

the interests of the indigenous upper class. Second, in a series of circulars, Malvar made it clear to the inhabitants of southwestern Luzon that additional assistance would be needed. Among other things, he required noncombatants to grow specified amounts of rice, corn, sweet potatoes, squash, and other crops to feed the troops, and he ordered the heads of towns to establish arsenals where cartridges could be manufactured and reloaded. Finally, Malvar issued warnings that anyone who provided information to the enemy would be severely punished and that spies would be killed. In the weeks and months that followed, Malvar's lieutenants carried out his orders, extracting large amounts of food from the noncombatants and selectively killing people who collaborated (or even appeared to collaborate) with the Americans.[23]

Malvar's policies had two obvious results: On the one hand, they definitely helped to keep the resistance alive in his area of operations. In some respects, it was even stronger than before, thanks to the elevated level of support that the troops received from lower-class Filipinos in the region. But on the other hand, by doing all that and by continuing to cause trouble for the U.S. troops, Malvar also paved the way for the adoption by the Americans of extremely severe measures in southwestern Luzon and the devastation that followed. The fundamental irony of the situation is one inherent in warfare: The price paid by a dogged, outmanned fighting force is always much higher than that paid by a less committed, outmanned one.

In southwestern Luzon, the first U.S. commander to consider the adoption of a significantly sterner approach was Samuel S. Sumner, the son of a Civil War hero. When Sumner took charge of U.S. operations in southwestern Luzon in April 1901, at about the same time that Malvar began issuing his circulars, he evidently believed that increased military pressure alone might be sufficient to end resistance in the region. So, in May 1901 he launched a major campaign against the guerrillas, assigning about one thousand additional men to temporary duty in Batangas and Laguna, the provinces in which Malvar's forces were especially strong. Those beefed-up forces were ordered to scout constantly in an effort to break the enemy's will to resist. But in the end, Sumner's campaign had little appreciable effect on the guerrillas; its only discernible result was to fill the hospitals with U.S. troops, who were suffering from malaria, dysentery, and various other illnesses.[24]

23 May, *Battle,* 211–22, 239–41.
24 Samuel Sumner to Adjutant General (AG), Department of Southern Luzon (DSL), May 23, 1901, U.S. National Archives (hereafter USNA), Record Group 395 (hereafter RG 395), file 2349; diary entries, May 26–July 3, 1901, Charles Dudley Rhodes Diary, Library of Congress Manuscripts Division.

By mid-June 1901, therefore, Sumner became convinced that such operations were unlikely to produce victory in southwestern Luzon, and he reported as much to his superiors:

The operations of this command demonstrate that a well organized force of considerable strength control this country and are paid and subsisted by the inhabitants. General Malvar exercises supreme command and the country of which Tanauan is the center is governed and controlled by a Colonel Gonzales. . . . While we have found several of his camps and destroyed them, it has been impossible to overtake this force or damage it to any extent. It has been found almost impossible to gain any information owing to fear or sympathy of natives.

To cope with this difficult situation, Sumner advocated new measures. He recommended that even more troops be assigned to southwestern Luzon and that they be permitted to occupy any barrio "as protection against weather or for military purposes" and to destroy any "that are used by the enemy or furnish supplies." Sumner also wanted to arrest all the men in the region, transporting them to U.S. posts and forcing them "to surrender arms or give information." He was even willing to send all the prominent men "out of the country and let it be known that they will be held till the active Insurrectos come in and surrender their arms."[25]

Clearly, Sumner was signifying his willingness to apply an enormous amount of pressure to the noncombatant population. Not only was he endorsing a significant increase of property destruction, but his comments about the detention of noncombatants suggested that he was prepared to depart significantly from previous practice. Since the early days of the unconventional phase of the war, the American forces had conducted frequent "roundups" of civilians in which the male inhabitants of a community were detained and interrogated, and suspected guerrillas and guerrilla supporters were sent to prison.[26] Now, it seems, Sumner was prepared to arrest all the men and pressure them to cooperate and even to exile the leading citizens of the region. Although no one could say that Sumner was advocating anything close to total war, he was, all the same, planning to target the civilian population in distinctive ways.

As it happens, Sumner's recommendations were not implemented. For reasons that are unclear, someone up the chain of command (almost certainly Sumner's immediate superior, Brigadier General James F. Wade) did not believe that the situation in southwestern Luzon warranted the sort of approach that Sumner was advocating. Although some additional troops were assigned to his district, Sumner was not authorized to destroy barrios

---

25 Sumner to AG, DSL, June 18, 1901, USNA, RG 395, file 2349.
26 Linn, *U.S. Army,* 138–9.

that sheltered or supplied the guerrillas, nor to arrest noncombatants without cause, nor to deport them.[27] For the next few months Sumner continued, without much success, to lobby for the adoption of sterner measures
to deal with the guerrilla resistance he faced. Eventually he grew frustrated:
"The amount of country actually controlled by us," he admitted in August
1901, "is about as much as can be covered by the fire from our guns."[28] The
situation had not changed appreciably when Sumner and General Wade
were relieved of command at the end of November 1901 by superiors – in
particular, General Chaffee – who were dissatisfied with the lack of progress in southwestern Luzon. By now, the American command's embarrassment about and growing irritation with the ongoing guerrilla activity in
the region had overcome the scruples anyone might have had about the
means to be used to eliminate it. Chaffee simply wanted that resistance to
end. He chose as Sumner's replacement a feisty brigadier named J. Franklin
Bell, who had a reputation for aggressiveness and ruthlessness. Even before
he set foot in southwestern Luzon, Bell had evidently decided that operations in his areas of responsibility would not be directed only at the military
units of General Malvar. En route to his new command, Bell stopped
briefly in Manila, where he had an opportunity to discuss his new assignment with a U.S. civilian administrator named Bernard Moses. "He is sent
to make peace," Moses noted in his diary, "and he proposes to do it even if
the peace which he establishes must be the peace of desolation. He seemed
to be in a somewhat reflective and subdued frame of mind in the presence
of an undertaking which may bring destruction to a once rich province
and great suffering to a large body of people."[29]

Bell spelled out his approach to warfare in southwestern Luzon in a series of circulars, most of which were issued in December 1901. The key
element was the policy of "concentration," which was intended to shut off
the guerrillas in the field from their sources of supply. He directed commanding officers in Batangas and Laguna to establish "zones" in all towns,
designated areas "within which it may be practicable, with an average-sized
garrison, to exercise supervision over and furnish protection to inhabitants
(who desire to be peaceful) against the depredations of armed insurgents."
Although technically the people of those provinces were not required to
relocate to the zones, Bell made it clear that unless they did so their property would become "liable to confiscation or destruction." Travel outside

27 F. S. West (by command of Sumner) to W. S. McCaskey, July 19, 1901, USNA, RG 395, file 2349;
    Sumner's endorsement (to a report written by Lieut. McNair), July 16, 1901, USNA, RG 395, file
    2348.
28 Sumner to AG, DSL, Aug. 2, 1901, USNA, RG 395, file 5101.
29 Diary entry, Nov. 29, 1901, Diary, vol. 6, Bernard Moses papers, University of California, Berke-
    ley Archives.

the zones by noncombatants was to be strictly regulated: No person could leave a town without a special pass from the commanding officer, and such passes could be given to able-bodied males only in cases of extreme necessity. "Any able-bodied male found by patrols or scouting detachments outside of protected zones without passes will be arrested and confined, or shot if he runs away."[30]

Bell also signaled his intention to strike directly at certain categories of noncombatants who, in his view, were providing the guerrillas with the bulk of their support. Aware that municipal officials had long acted as agents of the guerrillas, he directed station commanders to arrest and bring to trial all municipal presidents and chiefs of police against whom sufficient evidence could be found to demonstrate a connection to Malvar's forces. Wealthy and influential residents of those provinces could be confined and held in custody even if the army merely suspected that they were involved in the resistance:

To arrest anyone believed to be guilty of giving aid or assistance to the insurrection in any way or of giving food or comfort to the enemies of the government, it is not necessary to wait for sufficient evidence to lead to conviction by a court, but those strongly suspected of complicity with the insurrection may be arrested and confined as a military necessity and may be held as prisoners of war [at] the discretion of the station commander until receipt of other orders from higher authority. It will be frequently impossible to obtain evidence against persons of influence as long as they are at liberty, but once confined, evidence is easily obtainable.[31]

In a subsequent directive, Bell went even further, ordering station commanders to arrest all municipal and barrio officials, *principales* (certain categories of people who were entitled to participate in local elections during the Spanish era), members of the police force, and any other members of the community suspected of aiding or sympathizing with the resistance, except for those who had previously demonstrated their loyalty to the United States by guiding American troops to enemy camps, denouncing secret agents of the enemy, or performing other public acts that committed them irrevocably to the side of the Americans. The purpose of this measure was, in Bell's words, "to place the burden of the war on the disloyal and to so discipline them that they will become anxious to aid and assist the government in putting an end to the insurrection and securing the reestablishment of civil government."[32]

Beyond all that, Bell called for a stepped-up campaign against both the guerrillas and the resource base of the region. Having turned most of

---

30 M. F. Davis, comp., *Telegraphic Circulars and General Orders . . . Issued by Brigadier General J. Franklin Bell* (a pamphlet filed in AGO file 415839, USNA, RG94), 1–2, 13–14, 16.
31 Davis, comp., *Telegraphic Circulars,* 4–5.   32 Ibid., 4, 16–17, 21.

Batangas and Laguna into a virtual free-fire zone by concentrating the non-combatants in the towns, Bell was determined to search "each ravine, valley and mountain peak for insurgents and for food, expecting to destroy everything I find outside of towns[;] all able-bodied men will be killed or captured." He also was determined that the troops in his brigade be given the greatest possible latitude: "Subordinate commanders and young officers of experience should not be restrained or discouraged without excellent reason, but should be encouraged to hunt for, pursue, and vigorously operate against armed bodies of insurgents wherever they may be found."[33]

On the surface – and on the level of rhetoric – Bell's approach to warfare may not have seemed as harsh as General Smith's. Although Bell had specifically targeted both the resources and the noncombatants of southwestern Luzon – food and personal property found outside the zones were to be confiscated or destroyed; people found outside the zones were to be captured or killed; the troops were free to make life miserable for wealthy and influential residents of the towns – there were none of the verbal fireworks found in Smith's orders, no references to indiscriminate killing. But several things ensured that Bell's campaign in southwestern Luzon would be infinitely more destructive and more "total" than Smith's in Samar. For one, Bell's orders, unlike Smith's, were actually carried out. For another, the policy of concentration he intended to introduce posed enormous unstated and unacknowledged (but not unknown) health risks to the civilians who were to be confined in the zones. As Bell surely knew, a similar kind of policy had been adopted by European armies in two recent colonial wars – the Cuban war for independence and the Anglo-Boer War – and, in both cases, death rates among the concentrated civilians had reached crisis proportions because of widespread disease. In fact, the *reconcentrado* camps in Cuba had been so severely criticized in the American press that the Spanish commander responsible for introducing them, General Valeriano Weyler, was widely known as "Butcher" Weyler.[34]

Two simple points need to made at this juncture. The first is that an American commander did not have to issue orders specifically calling for the killing of civilians in order to produce many civilian deaths. Merely by

---

33 Ibid., 3; U.S. Senate, Committee on the Philippines, Hearings: Affairs in the Philippine Islands, S. Doc. 331, 57th Congress, 1st session, 1902, 2:1691. For a more complete discussion of Bell's directives – including those concerning "retaliation" against the enemy for "assassination" – see May, *Battle*, 248–54. I choose not to discuss Bell's controversial "retaliation" orders here largely because there is no evidence that they were carried out in Bell's campaign. Still, there can be little doubt that, like Smith's orders to Waller, they had the ring of total war.

34 Thomas Pakenham, *The Boer War* (London, 1979), 493–518, 572; Lewis L. Gould, *The Spanish-American War and President McKinley* (Lawrence, Kans., 1982), 22.

introducing the zones of concentration in Laguna and Batangas, Bell was placing at risk the entire civilian population of those provinces. That risk was widely recognized; any literate American or European alive at the time was aware of it. What such a person also knew was that, in wars against stubborn guerrilla forces in their empires, colonial powers of the day sometimes chose to expose civilians to that risk. In a real sense, in this turn-of-the-century colonial war, the establishment of zones of concentration was the moral/military equivalent of the World War II practice of bombing cities.

The second point, implicit in the first, is that, although Bell's approach may have been distinctive in the context of the Philippine-American War, and although it may have represented a giant step for the U.S. Army in the direction of total war, it was hardly a new development in the history of warfare. Bell's concentration policy was, after all, merely a variation of policies adopted earlier by Weyler and Kitchener. Seen in comparative context, it was nothing more than a well-known extreme measure used by a militarily superior force in wars of a certain kind and a particular historical period – small wars of conquest and pacification against peoples whose claims to statehood were either dismissed or ignored in distant parts of the colonial world.

In January 1902 Bell's brigade began to put his plan into operation. Troops were kept almost constantly in the field, scouring the region for any sign of people, animals, and food supplies and engaging in an orgy of destruction. On a single expedition in southern Batangas in January 1902, U.S. soldiers burned approximately 1,400 tons of rice and *palay,* hundreds of bushels of corn, and at least 6,000 houses, and they killed thousands of animals. Later that month, two other expeditions in the same general area destroyed hundreds more tons of *palay* and hundreds more animals. A similar process of destruction occurred throughout the region.[35] Systematically and ruthlessly, large sections of Batangas and Laguna were being turned into a wilderness, totally lacking in crops, domesticated animals, and human shelter.

In the meantime, civilians were subjected to extremely harsh treatment. In accordance with Bell's directives, hundreds of individuals of wealth and influence were deposited in jail, often in facilities that were inadequate to

---

35 Senate Affairs, 2:1690–92, 1698–9; A. B. Wells to AG, Third Separate Brigade (3SB), Jan. 8, 1902, USNA, RG 395, file 4208; T. J. Wint to AG, 3SB, Feb. 8, 1902, with enclosures, USNA, RG 395, file 4212; H. Hall to AG, Batangas, Jan. 13, 14, and 28, 1902, USNA, RG 395, file 5052; T. J. Wint to Adj., San Pablo Expeditionary Column, Jan. 18, 1902, with enclosures, USNA, RG 395, file 2379; S. Price to Adj., Batangas, Feb. 7., 1902, USNA, RG 395, file 2354; diary entries, Feb. 19–22, 1902, Charles Dudley Rhodes Diary, Library of Congress Manuscripts Division.

accommodate them. Many of them were tortured and beaten, and several died of the beatings received. Some of the worst abuses were committed by native auxiliaries, principally a company of Ilocano Scouts assigned to Bell's brigade, who were under the command of a sadistic second lieutenant named F. B. Hennessy. Macabebe Scouts also raped local women.[36]

Furthermore, and predictably, morbidity and mortality rates escalated among the civilians confined to the zones. Although the U.S. Army steadfastly maintained that conditions in the zones were healthy, the truth was that they were nothing of the sort. In the province of Batangas, mortality during the fourth-month period of concentration soared to an annualized crude death rate of 90 per thousand – close to three times the normal death rate. Throughout the entire region at least 10,000 more civilians died during the period of concentration than would typically have died in times of peace. The principal cause of death was malaria, but large numbers of people also succumbed to measles, dysentery, and various enteric disorders.[37]

Why were death rates so high? To a certain extent the zones of southwestern Luzon exhibited some of the same conditions that had prevailed in Cuba and South Africa – for example, poor sanitary conditions and poor water supplies.[38] But other factors also played a part: One was a shortage of food, especially rice, which resulted from a combination of circumstances – the destructive policies of Bell's brigade, a shortage of human labor (which was needed, of course, to plant and harvest crops) due to military service, and an absence of animal labor due to an ongoing epizootic of rinderpest (cattle plague) that killed most of the water buffaloes. That food shortage caused nutritional deficiencies, and those nutritional deficiencies compromised human immune systems, making them no match for the microparasites they encountered. Furthermore, microparasites – and, in particular, malaria sporozites – were prevalent in the human population in extraordinarily high numbers. That was so in part because the aforementioned rinderpest caused the local anophelines, the vectors of malaria that normally preferred to take their blood meals from cattle, to shift to humans and in part because the policy of concentration, confining large numbers of people in areas that generally housed much smaller

36 May, *Battle*, 257–60, 262. The Macabebes came from the province of Pampanga, the Ilocanos from the Ilocos region. Both spoke a different language from that of the Tagalogs they fought against in southwestern Luzon. In hiring native auxiliaries as "scouts," the U.S. Army in the Philippines was continuing a policy it had adopted with success in the Indian Wars. On that issue, see Robert M. Utley's essay in this book (Chapter 17).
37 Ibid., 263–4, 300; May, "150,000 Filipinos," 236–8.
38 May, *Battle*, 266–7; Pakenham, *Boer War*, 516–17; Gould, *President McKinley*, 22.

populations, vastly increased the possibility of disease transmission from one human host to another.[39]

In light of the complexity of the ecological/epidemiological picture in southwestern Luzon, it would be unfair to blame Bell and his brigade entirely for the substantial increase in mortality that occurred during the period of concentration. Some of the underlying causes of those deaths – the rinderpest epidemic (which actually began in the 1880s) and the shortage of human labor – were obviously beyond General Bell's control. Moreover, given the state of medical knowledge at the time, Bell could not have been expected to understand how *certain* of the actions of his brigade were increasing the health risks of the people confined in the zones; he knew nothing about the curious connection among bovines, anophelines, and humans in the regional landscape. Still, Bell cannot escape at least a measure of responsibility for the demographic catastrophe that occurred. He knew – and, in fact, all of his superiors knew – that merely by introducing the policy of concentration in southwestern Luzon he was exposing the civilian population to grave danger. He knew, in other words, that his policies were breaching the fragile barrier separating soldiers from civilians.

In any case, the predictable result of Bell's harsh campaign was victory. Pursued relentlessly by Bell's brigade, cut off from their civilian supporters, and deprived of food and other supplies, the remaining guerrillas found it impossible to remain in the field. By the end of February, most of Malvar's forces had come in. Malvar himself surrendered on April 16, 1902. By the end of that month, the Filipino resistance in southwestern Luzon had largely been eliminated.

IV

What, then, are we to conclude about the policies and actions of the U.S. Army in the Philippine-American War? In most campaigns, including the much-criticized one in Samar, it appears that although major atrocities were committed and much property was destroyed, the troops did not do much that had not been done in the U.S. Civil War. Noncombatants were targeted to some extent and many of them suffered, but very little of that was especially new. Bell's campaign, on the other hand, was decidedly different. Bell's aim from the start was to subject civilians to an extraordinary – and, in the context of the Philippine-American War, an unprecedented – amount

---

39 For lengthier discussions of this dynamic, see May, *Battle*, 264–7; and Ken De Bevoise, *Agents of Apocalypse: Epidemic Disease in the Colonial Philippines* (Princeton, N.J., 1995), 142–63.

of pressure. Not only did he intend to destroy crops and homes and allow his troops to incarcerate the wealthy and influential people of the region, but he also required hundreds of thousands of people to enter zones of concentration where, if recent history was any guide, large numbers of them could be expected to die. Although he did not have tanks or airplanes at his disposal, Bell was practicing a certain variation of total war.

Yet, to suggest that an early-twentieth-century analog of mid-twentieth-century total war could be observed in an obscure theater of a long-forgotten small war in the Philippines is not to say that the *analog* should necessarily be considered a *direct antecedent* of the later war. One thing that is striking about the Philippine-American War, aside from the destruction it caused and the large number of Filipinos who perished in it, is how quickly all recollection of it appeared to fade from the collective memory of the U.S. Army. In the years following the Philippine conflict, there is no evidence that, in deciding how to fight big wars, any American political or military leaders were influenced in any way by the policies and actions of the U.S. Army during that earlier small war. And, when the barriers between soldiers and civilians began to disappear by midcentury, eroded by new technology and ostensibly new notions about how to fight a war, no one came forward to suggest that the erosion had actually begun in J. Franklin Bell's campaign in southwestern Luzon.

Indeed, the truth of the matter is that, both at the time and in the following decades, the conflict in the Philippines was viewed as something less than a *real* war. It was a colonial war, a minor episode, not a major test on the battlefield against a powerful Western nation-state. Officially, it remained an "insurrection" – a designation that, besides being factually inaccurate (Aguinaldo had established an independent government well before the outbreak of hostilities), was offensive to Filipinos. For all intents and purposes, the Philippine-American War seemed to be forgotten until the 1960s, when the United States found itself embroiled in an unconventional war in faraway Vietnam, and some scholars, government officials, and even a few military men belatedly recognized that there might be lessons to be learned from the turn-of-the-century struggle in the Philippines.[40]

However, all this does not mean that the Philippine-American War was irrelevant to the emergence of total warfare in the twentieth century. For even if policymakers and military men did not remark on (and possibly were not conscious of) the parallels, we, surveying the scene long after the

40 See, e.g., the comments of Roger Hilsman, a State Department official, in "Internal War: The New Communist Tactic," in Franklin Osanka, ed., *Modern Guerrilla Warfare: Fighting Communist Guerrilla Movements, 1941–1961* (New York, 1962), 455–6.

events, can readily imagine that the experience of colonial conflicts like the one in the Philippines *must* have had an impact on the great powers that participated in them – that, if nothing else, it must have prepared them psychologically for the astounding destructiveness that lay ahead. Because colonial wars were fought by states that considered themselves "advanced" against peoples whose cultural difference could be interpreted as "backwardness" and "savagery," they provided the former with much practical experience with dehumanizing an enemy. They also gave the armies of the great powers the opportunity to target civilians in ways that, at the time, would have been unthinkable in conflicts against well-established nationstates.

Colonial wars thus might be seen as practice runs for the world wars that followed. They allowed great powers to breach the fragile barriers between soldiers and civilians without pain or significant penalty. In a sense, what happened over the course of the twentieth century was that incrementally – in Belgium in 1914, in the Spanish Civil War, and on several fronts in World War II – warfare among the great powers took on the characteristics of earlier colonial struggles. Civilians in "advanced" nationstates were now treated as legitimate targets, just as, at an earlier date, "niggers" and "gugus" had sometimes been treated. What came to be called "total war" was colonial warfare writ large.

20

An Army on Vacation?

The German War in China, 1900–1901

SABINE DABRINGHAUS

GERMANY AND THE BOXER WAR

As we look back from the perspective of the twentieth-century experience of total war, we can see that some of the wars conducted by the colonial powers at the overseas peripheries of their empires seem to foreshadow the unlimited conflicts of a later age. One example is the war in China that took place under German supreme command in 1900–1 as a result of the Boxer Rebellion. Although the German action in China occurred on a modest scale when compared with the German colonial wars in Africa and the United States' engagement in the Philippines, German behavior in China displayed some important features of modern total war. The ideological dehumanization of the enemy and the destruction of entire villages during "cleansing operations" and "punitive actions" reminds us of activities of the German military and security forces in the twentieth century. An examination of the German expedition to China can, therefore, provide insights into the mentality that came to underpin total war.

Unlike France, Great Britain, Japan, and Russia, Germany did not take part in the wars of aggression against the Chinese empire until the very end of the nineteenth century. The seizure of Jiaozhou Bay in 1897 by the German navy was an act of limited military significance.[1] It did not result in major bloodshed. The proper "German war in China" was restricted to a brief period of time in the aftermath of the Boxer Rebellion (1900–1). But Germany was not facing China singlehandedly; it was one member of a multinational military force intervening to stop the xenophobic violence

---

1 John E. Schrecker, *Imperialism and Chinese Nationalism: Germany in Shantung* (Cambridge, Mass., 1971). On connections between the missionary movement and German expansion, see Karl Josef Rivinius, *Weltlicher Schutz und Mission: Das deutsche Protektorat über die katholische Mission von Süd-Shantung* (Cologne, 1987), 456–500.

of the Boxer fighters. As far as it is justified to speak of a German war *in* China, this war took place at a time when the allied war *against* China had already been won and the besieged legations in the capital, Beijing, had been liberated. It was conducted behind whatever had existed in the way of a proper military front. However, the German actions did not amount to a war of colonial conquest. In contrast to Russia, which used the suppression of the Boxer movement (*Yihetuan yundong*) as an opportunity to seize China's northeastern provinces (Manchuria), permanent occupation of Chinese territory had never been contemplated by the German government. The German war in China was a punitive operation on an enormous scale but of short duration, ending with the withdrawal of the German expeditionary forces in June 1901.

The Boxer movement was not one of national liberation comparable to the antagonists of the United States in the "Philippine Insurrection." The Boxers stood squarely in the old Chinese tradition of peasant protest that was related to recurrent economic and ecological crises. What distinguished the Boxers from their predecessors was their aggressive resentment of the presence and activities of foreigners in China that would ultimately provoke military intervention on the part of the imperial powers. The Boxers regarded missionaries and foreign officials as the main causes of the deteriorating living conditions in northern China. Those who, from 1898, joined heterodox organizations, such as sects, secret societies, and martial arts groups, believed that they were able to make themselves magically invulnerable against foreign bullets. They wanted to expel or destroy all "foreign devils" (*yang guizi*) and thus restore the old order disrupted by the alien intruders.

The Boxer movement passed through three distinct stages: The first stage began in mid-1898, when natural disasters coincided with an economic crisis to revitalize a traditional movement of peasant protest on the northern Chinese plain. The protest was directed mainly against the growing number of missionary converts. Local officials initially supported the anti-Christian activities. Confronting this growing popular and official resentment, the Germans extended protection to Chinese Christians far beyond the borders of their recently acquired small protectorate on the coast of Shandong province.[2] It therefore was easy for the Boxers to lay all sorts of problems at the door of the assertive invaders. The movement of the *Yi-*

2 Zhu Maoduo, "Deutsche Truppeneinsätze in Shandong nach dem Abschluss des 'Jiaoao-Pachtvertrags,'" in Kuo Heng-yü and Mechthild Leutner, eds., *Deutschland und China: Beiträge des Zweiten Internationalen Symposiums zur Geschichte der deutsch-chinesischen Beziehungen* (Berlin, 1994), 309–32; Ding Mingan, "Deguo yu Yihetuan yundong" [Germany and the Boxer movement], in Zhongguo Yihetuan yanjiuhui [Chinese Society for the Study of the Boxers], ed., *Yihetuan yundong yu jindai zhongguo shehui* [The Boxer movement and modern Chinese society] (Jinan, 1992), 774–85.

hetuan ("Militia United in Righteousness") spread rapidly throughout Shandong, with members attacking missionaries of all nationalities and their Chinese converts.[3]

The second stage was marked by the internationalization of the conflict and the joint military intervention of the foreign powers against the Boxers and their sponsors in the Qing government. The flashpoint was reached when, in May 1900, telegraphic communication between the legations in Beijing and the outside world was disrupted. Gangs of Boxers poured into Beijing and the seaport of Tianjin, attacking anything foreign.[4] Open warfare broke out between foreign forces and Boxer groups that now were massively supported by regular Chinese troops. On June 19 the German minister, Freiherr Clemens von Ketteler, was assassinated on his way to the *Zongli yamen,* the Chinese Office of Foreign Affairs.[5] The following day, the Qing court issued an edict proclaiming war against the foreigners.[6] The famous siege of the legations began. Seven weeks later the embattled foreigners were liberated by an international expeditionary army of about 18,800 men. The Empress Dowager Cixi and her court fled to Xi'an in Shaanxi province, abandoning Beijing to the looting and murderous revenge by the troops of the "civilized nations."[7]

Chinese authority in Beijing and the surrounding countryside had almost completely collapsed. Thus, the third stage began with the intervening forces moving into a power vacuum of which none of them was able

3 Joseph W. Esherick, *The Origins of the Boxer Uprising* (Berkeley, Calif., 1987); Lu Yao, *Yihequan yundong qiyuan tansuo* [The origins of the Yihequan movement] (Jinan, 1990).

4 The official Hua Xuelan noted in his diary that a whole family was killed by the Boxers only because a book titled *Introduction into the Natural Sciences* was found in their house. See Otmar Becker, *Gengzi Riji: Das Tagebuch des Hua Xuelan aus dem Beijing des Boxeraufstandes, mit einer Einführung zum Tagebuch in der chinesischen Tradition* (Hamburg, 1987), 162.

5 On Clemens von Ketteler, see Per Fischer, "Chinas geopferter Freund, Clemens von Ketteler," in Kurt Schleucher, ed., *Deutsche unter anderen Völkern,* vol. 6: *Bis zu des Erdballs letztem Inselriff: Reisen und Missionen* (Darmstadt, 1975), 170–223; Per Fischer, "Clemens von Ketteler: Ein Lebensbild aus amtlichen und privaten deutschen Quellen," in Kuo Heng-yü and Mechthild Leutner, eds., *Deutschland und China: Beiträge des Zweiten Internationalen Symposiums zur Geschichte der Deutsch-Chinesischen Beziehungen (Berlin, 1991)* (Berlin, 1994), 333–58.

6 Edict, Guangxu 26/5/25 [June 21, 1900], in Gugong bowuyuan Ming-Qing dang'anbu [Office of the Imperial Palace, Bureau of Ming-Qing Archives], ed., *Yihetuan dang'an shiliao* [Archival materi-al concerning the Boxers], 2 vols. (Beijing, 1959), 1:162–3. See also Jin Jiarui, "Lun Yihetuan yundong shiqi Cixi de dui wai 'xuan zhan'" [The "declaration of war" by the Empress Dowager Cixi during the Boxer movement], in Jilu shushe bianjibu, ed., *Yihetuan yundong shi taolun wenji* [Collect-ed articles on the history of the Boxer movement] (Jinan, 1982), 343.

7 Zan Bojian, *Yihetuan* [The Boxers], 2 vols. (Beijing, 1953), 1:223; anon., "Lianjun qujing jiwen" [News on the looting by allied troops], in *Qingyi bao* [The China Discussion] 62, Nov. 9, 1900, 7–8; Zhong Fangzhi, "Gengzi jishi" [Notes of the year 1900], in Zhongguo kexueyuan lishi yanjiusuo disansuo [Third Institute of the Research Institute of History, Chinese Academy of Sciences], ed., *Gengzi jishi* [Introductory history of the year 1900] (Beijing, 1959), 34–5; Alfred von Waldersee, telegram, Dagu, Sept. 29, 1900, Bundesarchiv-Militärarchiv, Freiburg im Breisgau (hereafter BA-MA, Freiburg), RM 3/4273.

to take unilateral advantage. The "settlement" of the Boxer crisis was now pursued on two different levels. In the realm of high diplomacy, the powers jointly dictated to the remnants of the Qing government peace terms of extraordinary severity.[8] Even so, the rule of the conservative Qing dynasty was never called into question, and the old instigator of *Yihetuan* violence, the Empress Dowager Cixi, was invited to return to her capital. On a lower level, the powers divided Beijing into zones of occupation[9] where plundering on a gigantic scale was practiced from senior officers and diplomats downward[10] and common soldiers were allowed to exercise their own bloody revenge on the disarmed Chinese population. No German troops were among the victorious foreigners moving into Beijing. The German navy authorities in the Jiaozhou area feared the extension of international warfare into Shandong province and refused to have anything to do with the Boxer crisis in this last stage.[11] Therefore, no German troops were sent from Shandong to the capital to join the allied forces. At the same time, the small number of German naval forces at Tianjin proved technically unable to proceed to Beijing.[12]

German involvement in the Boxer crisis began only with the appointment of Alfred Graf von Waldersee as the commander-in-chief of the Eight Nation International Expedition. In early August Kaiser Wilhelm II had engineered this appointment through vigorous personal pressure. However, Waldersee arrived in Beijing as late as October 18, two months after the military aims of the expedition had been accomplished. He therefore presided only as the nominal head of the allied forces. In fact, with the relief of Beijing, common aims had ceased to exist.[13] The commander-in-chief barely managed to enforce his authority over non-German units, which were divided by pre-existing international rivalries. The foreign occupation thus took on as many different forms as there were occupational forces. The Germans were allotted parts of Beijing for temporary occupation. During the autumn of 1900 German troops poured into Zhili prov-

---

8 Fritz Klein, "Zur China-Politik des deutschen Imperialismus im Jahre 1900," *Zeitschrift für Geschichte* 4 (1960): 817–43.

9 The only satisfactory analysis of the occupation, limited, however, to the American zone is Michael H. Hunt, "The Forgotten Occupation: Beijing, 1900–1901," *Pacific Historical Review* 48, no. 4 (Nov. 1979): 501–29.

10 In the Imperial Palace German officers met the British minister, Sir Claude MacDonald, who supervised the removal of the Chinese treasures. See "Wie man in Beijing plündert," *Vorwärts,* Dec. 7, 1900.

11 Udo Ratenhof, *Die Chinapolitik des Deutschen Reiches 1871 bis 1945: Wirtschaft-Rüstung-Militär* (Boppard am Rhein, 1987), 161.

12 See the report by the commander of SMS Hansa, "Vormarsch nach Beijing, Befreiung und Besetzung der Stadt," Taku Rhede, Sept. 25, 1900, BA-MA, Freiburg, RM 3/3612.

13 "Bericht Pohl über die Einnahme Beijings," BA-MA, Freiburg, RM 5/5614.

ince. By December they numbered 17,150, by far the largest contingent among the 64,000 foreign officers and men stationed in northern China during the third stage of the crisis.[14] Field Marshal Waldersee was left to supervise the punitive operations that foreign troops, most of them German, conducted within the area of occupation.[15] But Waldersee was by no means the inventor of "mopping-up" tactics in China. Organized anti-Boxer "cleansing operations" had been mounted by each of the major powers immediately after the fall of Beijing.[16] Under Waldersee's command, however, "pacification" was implemented with a new degree of thoroughness and enthusiasm and was prolonged up to a time when the other powers had lost interest in the destruction of Chinese villages.

THE EXPERIENCE OF WAR

Allied troops were stationed in Beijing, Tianjin, and the provincial capital of Baoding.[17] The triangular area in between was marked out as a "zone of occupation." Columns radiated out from their three garrisons to comb the countryside for "Boxers" and regular Chinese troops. During the winter, when larger expeditions were impossible, the occupied area was divided into eleven districts, where small units of allied troops had to keep up daily patrols.[18]

However, during the last stage of the Boxer crisis, "Boxers" were difficult to identify among the male population.[19] The notorious Boxer symbols – red scarves and sashes, special banners and spears, and so forth – could easily be hidden and were never, even in the most obvious of cases, reliable indicators of allegiance to antiforeigner sects.[20] Therefore, the German troops tended to act on mere suspicion.[21] If weapons were found in a

14 "Tagebuch Boxeraufstand," Jan. 19, 1901, BA-MA, Freiburg, RM 121/396.
15 A summary list about the expeditions through December 1900 was published by the *Ostasiatischer Lloyd,* Jan. 4, 1901. Between December 1900 and April 1901, 46 other expeditions were organized by Waldersee, 35 of them with German participation only. See William J. Duiker, *Cultures in Collision: The Boxer Rebellion* (San Rafael, Calif., 1978), 186.
16 Rudolf Zabel, *Deutschland in China* (Leipzig, 1902), 165; E. Baron Binder-Krieglstein, *Die Kämpfe des deutschen Expeditionskorps und ihre militärischen Lehren* (Berlin, 1902), 4.
17 On the distribution of allied troops throughout the area of occupation, see *Ostasiatischer Lloyd,* Jan. 11, 1901, 29.
18 "Nachrichten vom Oberbefehlshaber Graf Waldersee," Dec. 12, 1900, BA-MA, Freiburg, RM 121/399. A report concerning this measure also appeared in the *Ostasiatischer Lloyd,* Jan. 11, 1901, 29.
19 *Kölnische Zeitung,* Feb. 27, 1901; Binder-Krieglstein, *Kämpfe des deutschen Expeditionskorps,* 224.
20 *Kölnische Zeitung,* Feb. 27, 1901.
21 "Kriegstagebuch von Hoepfner," Jan. 7, 1901, BA-MA, Freiburg, RM 121/401; Alfred von Waldersee, *Denkwürdigkeiten des General-Feldmarschalls Grafen Alfred von Waldersee,* ed. Heinrich Otto Meisner, 4 vols. (Stuttgart, 1923), 3:60.

village, houses or even the entire village was burned in retribution.[22] All places supposed to be "Boxer villages" were destroyed.[23] The same happened whenever German troops were shot at.[24] Sometimes, villages were destroyed "by mistake."[25] In "lighter" punitive cases villages were thoroughly plundered, and their inhabitants were forced to pay fines.[26] The peasants often tried to evade foreign terror by fleeing into the mountains or cornfields and by hiding their belongings.[27] In spite of the numerical superiority of the foreign troops and their better arms, the former Boxers continued to launch guerrilla attacks. They compelled Waldersee to step up the brutality of his "punitive actions." The "cleansing" of towns and villages extended warfare into purely civilian areas and cost more lives than pitched battles. The county seat of Liangxiang was razed after partisans had disappeared in the streets of the town.[28] In just one month, October 1900, 26 villages between Tianjin and Baoding were burned.[29]

In cases where Chinese were caught carrying weapons, the culprits were invariably put to death.[30] Suspected "Boxers" were handed over to local magistrates for (often capital) punishment. Sometimes local officials themselves were accused of conspiring with the insurgents and were executed. In October 1900, when an allied army occupied the city of Baoding, Ting Yong, the head of the civil administration, cavalry colonel Kui Heng, and

22 *Kölnische Zeitung,* Aug. 25, 1900, and Jan. 6, 1901; *Frankfurter Zeitung,* May 22, 1901; Alfred von Waldersee, telegram, Feb. 25, 1901, BA-MA, Freiburg, RM 121/397; Li Wenhai, Lin Dunkui, and Lin Keguang, eds., *Yihetuan yundong shi shiyao lu* [Notices of the historical events of the Boxer movement] (Jinan, 1986), 450, 453, 455; Kui Shun, memorial, Nov. 27, 1900, in Diyi lishi dang'an guan [First Historical Archives], ed., *Yihetuan dang'an shiliao xubian* [Further compilation of archival materials concerning the Boxers] (Beijing, 1990), 1:861.

23 Heinrich Haslinde, *Tagebuch aus China, 1900–1901* (Munich, 1983), 53.

24 Anon., *Die Tätigkeit der deutschen Pioniere in China 1900/1901,* Mitteilungen des Ingenieur-Komitees no. 45, (Berlin, 1908), 12.

25 E.g., Haslinde, *Tagebuch,* 54.

26 Ibid., 46; Oberkommando für Ostasien, ed., *Deutschland in China, 1900-1901: Bearbeitet von Teilnehmern an der Expedition* (Düsseldorf, 1902), 211–12; "Xuanhua xian xinzhi" [New Chronicle of the Xuanhua disctrict], in *Yihetuan shiliao* [Historical sources on the Yihetuan], 2 vols. (Beijing, 1982), 2:983–4; Li, Lin, and Lin, *Yihetuan yundong,* 462.

27 Haslinde, *Tagebuch,* 44; Alfred Graf von Waldersee, telegram, Oct. 10, 1900, BA-MA, Freiburg, RM 121/399; *Kölnische Zeitung,* May 1, 1901; "War diary of the II. See-Bataillon," Feb. 3/5, 1901, BA-MA, Freiburg, RM 121/402; report "Vormarsch auf Beijing, Einnahme und Besetzung der Stadt," Kommando SMS Hansa, Sept. 25, 1900, BA-MA, Freiburg, RM 3/3612; "Hunnenbrief" (Tianjin, Sept. 21, 1900), *Vorwärts,* Nov. 14, 1900; Zabel, *Deutschland in China,* 222–3.

28 *Kölnische Zeitung,* Nov. 5, 1900. Concerning the destruction of Liangxiang, see "Reise nach China: Kriegsmitteilungen von Teilnehmern," iii. See also Bataillon (July 1900–Mar. 1901), BA-MA, Freiburg, RM 38/86.

29 Li, Lin, and Lin, *Yihetuan yundong,* 459.

30 Major von Mühlenfels, *Die Erlebnisse des II. Bataillons 1. Ostasiatischen Infanterie Regiments in China* (Shanghai, 1902), 89.

regional commander Wang Zhankui were accused of being responsible for anti-Christian and antiforeigner violence and were shot after a brief court-martial.[31]

By and large, the Qing army managed to withdraw from the area of occupation. Governors of neighboring provinces such as Yuan Shikai ordered their troops to avoid any contact with the foreign military.[32] Therefore, only in a few instances was the imperial Chinese army engaged in regular battle.[33] In the rare cases when shattered remnants of the army or larger groups of Boxers were cornered by Waldersee's units, these incidents always resulted in far higher numbers of casualties on the Chinese side than on the foreign side. After a skirmish near Tianjin on August 20, 1900, for example, the Yihetuan left more than 300 dead, while the allied troops sustained only 11 wounded.[34] In another case, German columns in January 1901 marched to the Great Wall in the north of Beijing, where they attacked a Boxer camp, killing more than 150.[35]

Losses and devastation due to foreign invasion first occurred during the allied advance from the sea toward Beijing. Waldersee himself estimated that up to 300,000 civilians were rendered homeless during the course of this one campaign.[36] The total number of victims of German pacification during *stage three* of the Boxer crisis is impossible to determine. Nobody kept complete records of casualties. Sources abound showing that minor skirmishes and the rounding up of individual *Boxernester* often left hundreds of Chinese dead. Apparently the German troops heeded the admonition of their emperor not to bother with taking prisoners.[37] Letters, newspaper reports, and memoirs all coincide with the pictures of towns

31 *Guangxu zhengyao* [Political events during the reign of the Guangxu emperor], ed. Shen Tongsheng, 4 vols. (n.p., n.d.), 3:1548; Liao Yizhong, Li Dezheng, and Zhang Shiru, eds., *Yihetuan yundong shi* [The history of the Boxer movement], (Beijing, 1981), 366; Binder-Krieglstein, *Kämpfe des deutschen Expeditionskorps*, 53; Rudolf Gierhl, *China-Fahrt: Erlebnisse und Eindrücke von der Expedition 1900–1901* (Munich, 1903), 59.

32 Liao, Li, and Zhang, *Yihetuan yundong shi,* 359.

33 Anon., *Tätigkeit der deutschen Pioniere,* 66; *Vossische Zeitung,* Dec. 18, 1900.

34 *Kölnische Zeitung,* Aug. 25, 1900. Chinese sources report of over 350 deaths. See Li, Lin, and Lin, *Yihetuan,* 385.

35 Diary "Der Boxeraufstand" (Jan.–July 1901), BA-MA, Freiburg, RM 121/397; as another example, see Mühlenfels, *Erlebnisse des II. Bataillons,* 56.

36 Waldersee, *Denkwürdigkeiten,* 3:20. See also Haslinde, *Tagebuch,* 31–2; Georg Friederici, *Berittene Infanterie in China und andere Feldzugserinnerungen* (Berlin, 1904), 60–3; Gierhl, *China-Fahrt,* 26; Emil von Lessel, *Böhmen, Frankreich, China (1866–1901): Erinnerungen eines preussischen Offiziers,* Studien zur Geschichte Preussens, no. 34 (Berlin, 1981), 214; "Hunnenbrief" (Aug. 22, 1900), *Vorwärts,* Oct. 20, 1900; "Brief eines amerikanischen Offiziers," *Vorwärts,* Jan. 1, 1901.

37 On the Kaiser's *Hunnenrede,* see Bernd Sösemann, "Die sog. Hunnenrede Wilhelms II: Textkritische und Interpretatorische Bemerkungen zur Ansprache des Kaisers vom 27. Juli 1900 in Bremerhaven," *Historische Zeitschrift* 222 (1976): 350; see also *Kölnische Zeitung,* Nov. 9, 1900.

and villages in ruins, deserted by their inhabitants and stripped of animals, provisions, and anything of value.[38] Because of military destruction and army requisitions, famine struck the local population throughout Zhili province.[39] On Waldersee's orders, women and children were to be spared. Even so, a line between combatants and noncombatants was impossible to draw.

It is obvious that the conflict was conducted with extreme ferocity on both sides. According to Chinese sources, the number of Chinese Christians who lost their lives at the hands of the Boxers may have exceeded 20,000.[40] The powers held China responsible for the deaths of two diplomats and 229 other civilian foreigners, mostly missionaries and their families.[41] Military casualties were somewhat higher. By June 1901, the Germans had lost 300 men.[42] Because living conditions in the garrisons were worse than expected and the army had neglected medical precautions, many more German soldiers fell victim to typhus, malaria, or dysentery than to Chinese spears and bullets. In January 1901, a particularly disastrous month, of the 103 German dead, 99 succumbed to sickness and accidents.

The squalor of life in the military camps and especially the excesses of the German troops in China did not remain unnoticed or uncriticized. Public opinion in the two countries where the Boxer expedition had raised less enthusiasm than elsewhere took a skeptical view of Waldersee's policies: The *Japan Daily Mail* accused the field marshal of carrying out unnecessary expeditions and concluded that "the Germans have been equaled by none for unrelenting mercilessness from first to last."[43] The American government protested German "mass executions" and demanded an immediate cessation of "further bloodshed."[44] In Germany, even the *Kölnische Zeitung,* generally sympathetic toward the China campaign, took exception to Waldersee's "punishing without difference innocent and guilty people."[45]

---

38 The Western stories were confirmed by Chinese sources. See Ren Zhi, "Gengzi shiyi jilu" [Notes about the events during the year 1900], in *Yihetuan shiliao* [Historical sources on the Yihetuan], 2 vols., 1:411.

39 *Ostasiatischer Lloyd,* Dec. 28, 1900; *Frankfurter Zeitung,* May 19, 1900; *Gengzi jishi,* 36.

40 Wu Jingheng, Cai Yuanpei, and Wang Yunwu, eds., *Yihetuan yundong shi* [History of the Boxer movement] (Shanghai, 1916), 78–80.

41 Immanuel C.Y. Hsu, "Late Ch'ing Foreign Relations, 1866–1905," in John K. Fairbank and Liu Kwang-ching, eds., *The Cambridge History of China,* vol. 11: *Late Ch'ing, 1800–1911* (Cambridge, 1980), pt. 2:125.

42 *Kölnische Zeitung,* Jan. 28, 1901, and June 14, 1901. On Dec. 7, 700 soldiers were reported being ill from typhus and dysentery. See the *Frankfurter Zeitung,* Dec. 7, 1900.

43 *Japan Daily Mail,* June 10, 1901.

44 The American statement was discussed in a report of the *Kölnische Zeitung,* "Die Durchführung der Friedensbedingungen," Mar. 2, 1901.

45 *Kölnische Zeitung,* Jan. 1, 1901.

The strongest criticism, however, arose on the left, employing the voice of the common soldier. The *Vorwärts* collected a great number of so-called *Hunnenbriefe* (Hun letters) – army mail sent home by privates to their families. Many of the German soldiers were young volunteers who had been told by the Kaiser that "a magnificent task" awaited them and that they would be fighting against a "crafty, courageous, well-armed enemy."[46] They were deeply disappointed.[47] Opportunities for heroism were rare indeed. Some may have agreed with the war correspondent of the *Kölnische Zeitung:* "Apart from sporadic and unconnected bloody incidents, little in the way of genuine war was to be noticed during our tours through the province. One might have said: an army on vacation."[48] The alleged holiday atmosphere, however, was clouded by rather mundane necessities. A major preoccupation of the expeditionary corps was to ensure its own survival. Because logistics were organized on a somewhat makeshift basis, much time was spent in securing provisions, chasing sheep and chickens, rather than in fighting the enemy.

To the degree that fighting did occur, actual warfare with its nasty counterinsurgency operations flatly contradicted expectations of soldierly exploits. In contrast to official army documents, the letters from the field openly describe the cruel behavior of the German troops. Harrowing pictures are drawn in these letters of the destruction wrought in the Chinese countryside – villages going up in flames; rotting corpses lying about everywhere, polluting the rivers and poisoning the air.[49] Although some of the young volunteers, probably with some journalistic help back home, seem to have painted their experiences in more than vivid colors, Chinese sources often confirm the events. An execution in the German zone of Beijing, for example, is mentioned in material from both sides. Hua Xuelan, a Chinese official who witnessed all the stages of the Boxer movement, described in his diary the capture of more than one hundred "bandits." Their queues were tied together, then the foreign soldiers opened fire on them. The few who survived were set free.[50]

It comes as no surprise that the German military command tried to discredit the reports by some of their soldiers about brutality and atrocities in

---

46 Ernst Johann, ed., *Reden des Kaisers* (Munich, 1966), 90–1. Concerning the Kaiser's war fantasies, see Bernhard Fürst von Bülow, *Denkwürdigkeiten,* 4 vols. (Berlin, 1930), 1:369.
47 "Die Wirren in China: Die Besetzung von Petschili," *Kölnische Zeitung,* Feb. 27, 1901; "Mit den verbündeten Truppen in Petschili," *Kölnische Zeitung,* Apr. 12, 1901; *Frankfurter Zeitung,* Dec. 7, 1900; *The Times,* Dec. 26, 1900; Zabel, *Deutschland in China,* 186.
48 *Kölnische Zeitung,* Apr. 4, 1901.   49 *Vorwärts,* Nov. 30, 1900.
50 Becker, *Gengzi riji,* 140; *Vorwärts,* Nov. 14, 1900; "Bericht Pohl über die Einnahme Pekings," BA-MA, Freiburg, RM 5/5614.

China. Waldersee himself complained about unfounded "horror stories" and condemned "the nonsense spread by many newspapers."[51] The image of the intervention in China as a crusade of "civilization" against "barbarism" was not to be damaged.

REVENGE AND RACIAL THINKING IN THE IDEOLOGY
OF WAR

The great powers were unanimous in their condemnation of the Boxer movement, which they deemed "a terrible crime without parallel in the history of mankind."[52] They all upheld the principle of punishment. The Boxer Protocol of September 1901 (the legal form of the peace settlement) contained a long list of severe demands on the part of the powers. The stipulated indemnity of 450 million *taels* exceeded the annual national budget by four times. All fortifications on the coast of Zhili province had to be destroyed. Also, among the demands were articles envisaging specific punishments for eleven individually named members of the Manchurian court and government. They were held responsible for the involvement of the Qing army in antiforeigner activities and for the extension of the Boxer movement, originally confined to Shandong province, to the entirety of northern China.

In fact, however, *both* sides had gone beyond culturally determined misperceptions and misunderstandings during the third stage of the Boxer crisis. The inconsiderate behavior of European missionaries in northern China and Chinese popular response to their provocations in the form of antiforeigner sects and martial arts groups could, to some extent, be interpreted as the unpremeditated results of a clash of cultures. During the final phase of the confrontation, both the empress dowager and her advisers, as well as the Western governments and military commanders, employed means of deliberate misrepresentation and propagandistic deceit. For Kaiser Wilhelm II, in search of opportunities for German *Weltpolitik,* the assassination of German Minister von Ketteler provided a welcome opportunity for an ideological interpretation of the conflict.[53] In his notorious *Hunnenrede* of July 27, 1900, he admonished the troops on their way to China "to revenge the severe misdeeds" the Chinese had committed.[54] Public opinion not only in Germany blamed the Chinese for "crimes unparalleled

51 Waldersee, *Denkwürdigkeiten,* 3:97.
52 See "Die Gemeinsame Note," *Kölnische Zeitung,* Dec. 26, 1900.
53 See M. Michael, "Zur Entsendung einer deutschen Expeditionstruppe nach China während des Boxeraufstandes," in Kuo Heng-yü, ed., *Von der Kolonialpolitik zur Kooperation: Studien zur Geschichte der deutsch-chinesischen Beziehungen* (Munich, 1986), 143–50.
54 Quoted in Sösemann, "Die sog. Hunnenrede," 349.

in the history of mankind."[55] Therefore, China was to be excluded from the "legal community of civilized nations."[56]

There was no uniform opinion among foreigners on the degree of pressure to be put on the Chinese. The Germans seem to have placed an unusual emphasis on the idea of punishment and to have linked it closely with the demand for *Sühne* (atonement) and revenge. To a large extent, this was for tactical reasons. The German demands for prominence in the Boxer suppression rested almost entirely on the fact that it was the German minister who had been assassinated.[57] The German war in China also was a war of prestige in the circle of the great powers and for domestic acceptance of a flamboyant type of *Weltpolitik*.[58] Because the Germans arrived too late on the scene, the Boxer expedition under Waldersee's command assumed the form of a gigantic police operation in the wake of a successful multinational expeditionary venture in which the Germans had not taken part.

German perceptions and behavior have to been seen not merely as responses to a specific situation but also within the broader framework of contemporary attitudes toward Asia. The European and American invasion of China at the turn of the century was predicated on a variety of ideological assumptions concerning the "Orient" and the "oriental character." Some of these were even shared by the Japanese, who began to insist on their special and superior position in the history of Asia.[59] China was seen as an old, decadent, rotten civilization that had become unable to control its own destiny.[60] The "orientals" and in particular the Chinese were regarded not as innocent "savages" but as cruel and deceitful people with whom relations of trust or even of paternal benevolence were impossible.

Waldersee expressed a basic tenet of imperialist thinking when he wrote that "one can only command the respect of the Asian through force and its ruthless application."[61] Generally, the German commanding officers refused to practice "outdated clemency" toward the "yellow race." In the con-

---

55 *Kölnische Zeitung*, Dec. 26, 1900.

56 *Schlesische Zeitung*, May 9, 1901. In this report China was given a "half-civilized" status because it had at least concluded treaties with the "civilized states."

57 *Kölnische Zeitung*, Jan. 2, 1901.

58 Peter Winzen, *Bülows Weltmachtkonzept: Untersuchungen zur Frühphase seiner Aussenpolitik 1897–1901* (Boppard, 1977), 92. The importance of prestige also was reflected by the fact that the German government even risked a weakening of its navy at home by sending nine ships to East Asia. See Walther Hubatsch, *Der Admiralstab und die obersten Marinebehörden in Deutschland 1848–1945* (Frankfurt am Main, 1958), 107–8.

59 See Stefan Tanaka, *Japan's Orient: Rendering Pasts into History* (Berkeley, Calif., 1993).

60 Waldersee, *Denkwürdigkeiten*, 3:41; Oberkommando für Ostasien, ed., *Deutschland in China*, 6; Binder-Krieglstein, *Kämpfe des deutschen Expeditionskorps*, 64–5.

61 Waldersee, *Denkwürdigkeiten*, 3:28. See also *Vossische Zeitung*, Dec. 18, 1900; Zabel, *Deutschland in China*, 194.

frontation with this "ridiculous, childish people" they preferred "dread, severity and seriousness."[62] Of course, the Western assessments of China and the Chinese were influenced by all sorts of racist ideas, from the "yellow peril" to the stereotype of habitual weakness and lack of discipline (*Zuchtlosigkeit*).[63]

This racism was not without its own contradictions. The contrast between "superior" white man and "inferior" yellow man was partly canceled by the other one between Christians and heathens.[64] The Germans time and again interfered in village disputes on behalf of Chinese Christians. When the French bishop Alphonse Favier (1837–1905) complained about anti-Christian riots in the Kalgan (Zhanjiakou) region of Inner Mongolia, Waldersee even mounted a punitive expedition beyond the occupied area.[65] Only the "heathen" Chinese were considered to stand outside international law.[66] The life of an indigenous Christian was thought to be "worth" many times more than that of his non-Christian neighbor. Chinese Christians often served as spies for the foreign troops and thus placed themselves in a position to wreak revenge on their compatriots.[67] The general attitude of the German soldiers toward the Chinese was one of contempt. They were described as "animals" or as having the "souls of dogs."[68] The soldiers felt themselves to be on a "civilizing mission," introducing their humane, clean lifestyle into the occupied zones.[69] They described "real" China as a world of "human skulls, animal cadavers and corpse-eating dogs."[70]

The allied powers had intervened in China in order to safeguard and enforce international law and a universal "standard of civilization." In dealing with the vanquished Chinese, however, they did not feel themselves bound

62 Binder-Krieglstein, *Kämpfe des deutschen Expeditionskorps*, 93.

63 Sir Robert Hart, *The Beijing Legations: A National Uprising and International Episode* (Shanghai, 1900), 33; Alfred von Müller, *Unsere Marine in China* (Berlin, 1901), 246; Schrecker, *Imperialism and Chinese Nationalism*, 24; Heinz Gollwitzer, *Die Gelbe Gefahr: Geschichte eines Schlagworts* (Göttingen, 1962), 210–18.

64 J. Scheibert, *Der Krieg in China 1900–1901*, 2 vols. (Berlin, 1901), 2:74–5.

65 Waldersee, *Denkwürdigkeiten*, 3:49, 168; Binder-Krieglstein, *Kämpfe des deutschen Expeditionskorps*, 53; Oberkommando für Ostasien, ed., *Deutschland in China*, 212.

66 See the report by the commander of the Kreuzergeschwader Bendemann, "Die militärpolitische Lage in China," Aug. 23, 1900, 6–7, BA-MA, Freiburg, RM 3/4748. For the American side, see Hunt, "Forgotten Occupation," 503.

67 Waldersee, *Denkwürdigkeiten*, 3:49, 77; *Kölnische Zeitung*, Feb. 27, 1901; "Yangyuan xianzhi" [Gazetteer of the district Yangyuan], in *Yihetuan shiliao* [Historical sources on the Yihetuan], 2 vols., 2:986.

68 *Vorwärts*, Nov. 11–14, 1900. See also Waldersee, *Denkwürdigkeiten*, 3:69.

69 "Bericht des Marinekapitäns von Pohl," BA-MA, Freiburg, RM 5/5609. See also Mühlenfels, *Erlebnisse des II. Bataillons*, 50.

70 *Kölnische Zeitung*, Nov. 15, 1900.

to the same principles. Chinese looters were executed straightaway. Foreign plundering in Beijing, by contrast, was not limited to the pillaging of the city during three days after the relief of the legations.[71] As late as in February 1901, newspapers reported how gilded tiles were sold for $10 apiece and how British looters removed statues weighing two tons each from Buddhist temples.[72] Chinese state treasuries were plundered, thousands of documents and files were burned, and official buildings as well as private houses were destroyed.[73] Female family members of killed officials were raped and sent to brothels to service foreign soldiers.[74] Many women preferred to take their own lives. Chinese civilians were indiscriminately rounded up in the streets of Beijing and Tianjin and forced to work in army garrisons without payment.[75] Even so, Vice-Admiral Bendemann, the commander-in-chief of the cruiser squadrons, declared that "the military in China had not been issued regulations concerning the treatment of the enemy and the civilian population other than what was already authorized for warfare in Europe."[76] The reform-oriented press in China did not fail to notice the obvious contradiction between the Eurocentric demand for moral superiority and barbaric Western warfare in China.[77]

The brutalization of German warfare during the Boxer expedition was deeply rooted in popular racial thinking. By dehumanizing the Chinese enemy, soldiers learned to practice methods of total war. A medical language was introduced in calling the military campaigns "cleansing operations." Its dehumanizing function was reflected in terms such as "Ausheben von Boxernestern" (rounding up of nests of Boxers) for the burning of villages. In general, the Boxer expedition was described as a defensive act of the civilized nations against "Asiatic hordes."[78] The Chinese themselves were even blamed for the bloodshed caused by foreign revenge expeditions – had they accepted the peace terms of the powers, the reasoning went, the punitive actions would have ceased immediately.[79]

71 "Bericht Pohl über die Einnahme Pekings," BA-MA, Freiburg, RM 5/5614.
72 *Frankfurter Zeitung*, Feb. 9, 1901; Report "Vormarsch auf Beijing," Sept. 25, 1900, 29, BA-MA, Freiburg, RM 5/5614; Waldersee's notes from Nov. 12, 1900, in his diary, *Denkwürdigkeiten*, 3:47–8. During the spring of 1901 Chinese sources also described looting activities by German troops. See *Yihetuan dang'an shiliao*, 2:1001.
73 Ibid., 2:1012.   74 Zan Bojian, *Yihetuan*, 1:268.
75 *Vorwärts*, Nov. 11, 1900.
76 Chef des Kreuzergeschwaders, "Tagebuch des Boxeraufstandes," Dec. 8, 1900, BA-MA, Freiburg, RM 121/396.
77 Ying Haizong, "Rendao hu yi rendaozhi zei hu" [How humanity harmfully represses humanity], *Qingyi bao* [The China discussion], Oct. 1, 1900, 4:4185.
78 *Kölnische Zeitung*, Oct. 4, 1900. See also *Wiener Fremden-Blatt*, Sept. 23, 1900.
79 Heinrich Wanrows, "4. Kompanie des I. See-Bataillons," Mar. 9, 1901, BA-MA, Freiburg, RM 38/86.

It is of course impossible to overlook the terror against foreigners and Chinese Christians unleashed by the Boxers in spring and summer 1900 and ignore the blatant breach of international law that occurred when the Qing court authorized the assault on the legation quarter in the capital. The bitterness of foreign attitudes and the severity of the response were not totally unwarranted. Yet during the third stage of the crisis, the Waldersee period, the conduct of the forces of "pacification" and especially of the Germans lost all sense of proportion. The repression and atrocities committed served only symbolic rather than instrumental purposes. Given the disintegration of Chinese state authority in Beijing and the surrounding area and the helplessness of the indigenous population, it sounded cynical when the press and the authors of war reminiscences spoke of a "closing of ranks of the civilized powers" against the "scheming, bloodthirsty hyperculture of the Chinese."[80]

During the quarrels about the definitive peace conditions to be forced on the Chinese, the united front of the "civilized powers" disintegrated. A colonial partition of China proper now was out of the question. However, this did not prevent China's international status from dropping to its lowest point in modern history. The Boxer Protocol of September imposed a Carthaginian peace: To the huge financial burdens and the punishment of high officials was added the symbolic humiliation of the Chinese monarchy. The triumphal procession of "barbarian" troops to the sacrosanct Forbidden City, the spacious imperial palace that represented the center of the traditional Chinese world order, meant an unthinkable violation of the idea of cosmic rulership. The foreign powers now placed the Chinese sovereign on the same ceremonial footing with Western heads of state. Their diplomatic representatives were henceforth allowed in the imperial presence and received permission to enter the innermost halls of the palace. In the eyes of his subjects, the monarch thereby lost his (or her) aura of the universal and the sublime. The enforced demystification of the summit of the Chinese state contributed in a very significant way to the terminal weakening of the Qing dynasty and its downfall a few years later, in 1911.

ANTICIPATIONS OF TOTAL WAR

Compared with the huge uprisings that shook China during the nineteenth century (above all with the Taiping Rebellion of 1850–64) and also with colonial wars elsewhere in the world (for example, concurrently in

---

80 *Wiener Fremden-Blatt*, Sept. 23, 1900. See also Müller, *Unsere Marine*, 10; Schlieper [no first name], *Meine Kriegserlebnisse in China* (Minden, 1901), 23–4.

the Philippines), the Boxer Rebellion and its repression, judged by its scale of destruction, was a somewhat minor affair. But for the Germans it provided one of the only opportunities between 1871 and 1914 to experiment with new means of warfare.

Total war implies, among other things, an almost unlimited scope and intensity of military action, a stretching of moral boundaries and international law, a blurring of the line between combatants and noncombatants, and an ideological dynamic that makes possible the exclusion of the enemy from among those who share at least some basic values of a common civilization. The dehumanization of the foe, the justification of brutal punishment and revenge inflicted on the civilian population, and even outright genocide can be the consequences of such a mentality.

It is obvious that the German war in China never assumed the proportions of twentieth-century total wars. It was, in Trutz von Trotha's words, a special kind of "limited war of pacification."[81] In contrast to military interventions in Africa, it was not intended to pave the way for the establishment of colonial rule. During the suppression of the Yihetuan uprising, the Germans and the other foreign powers had finally decided to aim at a more-or-less joint control over the rulers of China, not at political partition and acquisition of Chinese land for colonization. The only *practical* purpose of military pacification was to put pressure on the Chinese officials who were negotiating the peace settlement by causing a Chinese bureaucrat's nightmare: chaos. Anything transcending this tactical goal had to be otherwise explained.

The idea that the violent deaths of Westerners had to be avenged and that China was to be punished for its breach of international law was common among all the foreign powers involved. There were, however, degrees in their insistence on moderation and due process of law. The notion that atrocities ought to be atoned for by counteratrocities did not find general approval. The German case was unique in its extreme obsession with prestige. This had its roots in the personal ambition of Wilhelm II, who saw the Boxer crisis as a godsend for German *Weltpolitik*. The German Boxer expedition was therefore burdened with all sorts of extravagant expectations. They were all the harder to fulfill, as the Germans had missed the opportunities for heroism. The rescue narrative had to be inadequately replaced with a narrative of retribution. In the moral economy of prestige, the humiliation of China was traded, or so it seemed, against international reputation for Germany. But, as the campaign revealed, punitive actions

---

81 See Trutz von Trotha's essay in this book (Chapter 18).

against invisible partisans and against a civilian population whose degree of involvement in antiforeigner activities was almost impossible to determine replaced conventional warfare. Thus, the German war in China became more a war of myth than of tangible achievement. The "pacifying" deeds of German soldiers in the service of the nation and of civilization in general were elevated as high as possible. An astonishing amount of memorial literature leaves the impression that the German troops departed from China with a feeling of satisfaction and the belief that they had restored order and even law.[82]

Although the Boxer involvement had been heavily criticized by the German left, it continued to figure as a proud achievement in the memory of the right. In their view, "the expedition has opened a new page of glory in the history of the German fatherland."[83] Germany had demonstrated "capability in world politics," and the young soldiers had received an opportunity abroad "to feel [like] Germans."[84] Many agreed with Waldersee that German prestige in east Asia had been increased.[85] The literature of reminiscence is replete with stereotypes of "Chineseness," some of which could not possibly have been based on first-hand observation. Antiforeignism seemed deeply rooted in the national culture.[86] Boxer attacks were described as "inhumane warfare of cruel hordes."[87] And, of course, "the yellow peril" was invoked with monotonous frequency.

The real results of the intervention fell far short of the successes of which many Germans were persuading themselves. "Pacification" had basically achieved the exact opposite of what had been intended: Anarchy prevailed on the northern Chinese plain. The occupational power had devastated and plundered the countryside, rendered hundreds of thousands of people homeless, and destroyed their means of livelihood. The invasion had set free economic side effects that canceled any attempt to stabilize northern China. Moreover, the foreign presence had removed or delegitimized and disarmed the local authorities. The main beneficiaries of the ensuing power vacuum were, ironically, exactly those predatory "bandits"

---

82 Oberkommando für Ostasien, ed., *Deutschland in China*, 94.
83 Müller, *Unsere Marine*, 282.
84 "Die Bedeutung des chinesischen Feldzugs für Deutschland," *Die Grenzboten* 59, no. 4 (1900): 105, 107.
85 Waldersee, *Denkwürdigkeiten*, 3:141–2, 151–2; Oberkommando für Ostasien, ed., *Deutschland in China*, 94; Otto Loeffler, *Die China-Expedition, 1900–1901* (Berlin, 1902), 39; Zabel, *Deutschland in China*, 81; "Die Ergebnisse des chinesischen Feldzugs," *Die Grenzboten*, 60, no. 3 (1901): 50.
86 Müller, *Unsere Marine*, 101; anon., "China," *Die Grenzboten* 59, no. 4 (1900): 305.
87 Schlieper, *Meine Kriegserlebnisse*, 23–4.

who were recruited from among former Boxers, dispersed troops, and newly uprooted elements.[88] The province of Zhili became a hotbed of banditry for decades to come. To the degree that Germans became aware of the failure of German pacification, this was explained by the inability of China "to change into a European state."[89] It seemed impossible to influence the totally different character of the Chinese. Even the collateral goals of the expedition were only partly realized: Northern China was hardly suitable as a field for maneuvers, and Germany's modern weapons found few worthy targets.[90] Within the German military, the Boxer expedition touched off a discussion about the establishment of a colonial army. Waldersee recommended it because he objected to the use of undisciplined volunteers and reservists under the strenuous conditions overseas.[91] Indeed, the dissoluteness of young soldiers, who dreamed of proving their heroic manliness and soldierly qualities, was confirmed by a Chinese official in Beijing who thought them more brutal than the navy troops they had replaced in fall 1900.[92]

Because of its obvious limitations, the Boxer war was not a total war *en miniature*. Not all Chinese, only the Yihetuan and their supporters at the Qing court, were officially called enemies. No genocide was planned or systematically practiced. As in colonial wars of conquest, the relationship between the two sides was asymmetrical: A modern, industrialized power fought against a popular protest movement, not against another state and not for domination, but for the restoration of the status quo ante. Ironically, the Boxers themselves practiced a type of warfare that had several points in common with the technical definition of total war. They successfully mobilized the peasant society of the northern China plain. Women became involved in fighting through a special organization, the "Community of the Red Lanterns" (*Hongdeng hui*). In their attitude toward the foreign enemy, Boxers did not distinguish among military or diplomatic representatives, missionaries, or other civilians. They were determined to kill them all. In China, too, there existed a nonwestern concept of total war, going

---

88 Liao, Li, and Zhang, *Yihetuan yundong shi*, 457–63.
89 Zabel, *Deutschland in China*, 60.
90 "Die Besetzung von Petschili," *Kölnische Zeitung*, Feb. 27, 1901.
91 Alfred Graf von Waldersee, "Denkschrift über Erfahrungen in China" (n.d.), BA-MA, Freiburg, N 224/51. See also Bernd F. Schulte, *Die deutsche Armee, 1900–1914: Zwischen Beharren und Verändern* (Düsseldorf, 1977), 169–70; Binder-Krieglstein, *Kämpfe des deutschen Expeditionskorps*, 221–5; anon., "Brauchen wir ein deutsches Kolonialheer?" *Die Grenzboten*, 59, no. 4 (1900): 1–9; Bülow an Auswärtiges Amt, June 22, 1900, in *Die Grosse Politik der Europäischen Kabinette*, 40 vols. (Berlin, 1924), 16:18–20.
92 Becker, *Gengzi riji*, 140.

back at least to the great rebellions of the Taiping and the Nian after the middle of the nineteenth century.[93]

From the perspective of German military experience, the expedition to China opened up a new chapter. The unpreparedness of the army for the specific requirements of quasi-colonial pacification was indicative of the novelty of the challenges faced three decades after the Franco-Prussian War. The confrontation between young German volunteers and northern Chinese peasants reinforced and gave concrete expression to current notions of cultural contempt and racial superiority. In the actual situation in China, preconceived and propagandistically inculcated images of the alien enemy combined with the unpleasant surprises and exasperations of guerrilla warfare to make possible a type of behavior not provided for in manuals of military training. The limited "totalization" of warfare developed from conditions on the spot. Perhaps the most powerful effect of the Boxer intervention derived from the myths that were woven around it by scores of commentators and memorizing participants. In the mainstream literature, the expedition was presented as an undiminished success and a glorious achievement for German arms and the Germanic character. The irritating novelty of a dirty colonial war thus entered the collective consciousness shrouded in the mantle of the white man's presumed triumph.

93 Teng Ssu-yü, *The Nien Army and Their Guerrilla Warfare, 1851–1868* (Paris, 1961).

Index

Müller, Georg Alexander von
(1854–1940), German army officer,
319
Mumm, Reinhard (1873–1932),
German theologian and politician,
135
Munsey's, war articles from, 244, 250

Nama people, 423–4
Napoleon I (1769–1821), French
soldier and emperor, 282
Napoleon III (1808–73), French
politician and emperor, 47, 125,
283
Napoleonic Wars, 19, 23, 221, 235,
282
Nation, The: on foreign policy, 394; war
articles from, 244
National Civil Liberties Union (U.S.),
124
National Committee of Patriotic and
Defense Societies (U.S.), 100
national defense, and navalism, 69
National Guard (U.S.), 72, 75,
139–40, 142, 144–5: cadet corps,
145–6; local units, 140
national identity, 5, 6; construction of,
6; German, 307–8, 312, 314
National Liberal Party (Germany), 168
national security issues, U.S.: changes
in, 341; during Civil War, 332–4;
during Cold War, 327–8; and
international balance of power,
328–30; policies, 330, 340; during
World War I, 336–41
nationalism: divisive and integrative,
227; and German unity, 307; vs.
internationalism, 131–2; Jewish,
114; jingoistic, 248, 251–2; and
modernization, 129; and navalism,
41; and Protestantism, 4; radical,
129; and religion, 129, 130; and
theory of evolution, 206; and
warfare, 3, 248–9, 250, 260, 276,
278; of youth, 179; *see also
armaments nationalism*
nationality, and race, 98

Native Americans: in Civil War, 7,
99–140; culture, 400–1;
dehumanization of, 8; economic
losses, 414; military training, 143;
post-Civil War fighting, 333; race
relations, 118–19; smallpox
epidemic, 400; total war and,
401–14; U.S. Army vs., 246,
401–10; U.S. policy (Indian New
Deal), 400
nativism, *see* Association for National
Service, Guardians of Liberty,
Military Order of the Loyal Legion
of the United States, and National
Committee of Patriotic and Defense
Societies
Naumann, Friedrich (1860–1919),
German clergyman, publicist, and
politician, 212–13
Naval Intelligence Office (U.S.), 66,
68, 101–2
Naval War Board, (U.S.), 67–8
Naval War College (NWC), 59, 66,
67, 68
navalism, 3, 40–6, 266–71: armaments
race, 45–6; and bipartisanship, 67;
dark ages of, 65; gun-boat
diplomacy, 43; modernization,
65–71, 76; and national defense, 69;
and nationalist chauvinism, 45; and
nationalist integration, 41; and
progressivism, 68; propaganda, 45;
secret wireless codes, 79–80;
Wilhelmine, 41–2, 44, 316
Navy Department (U.S.), 69, 76
Navy League (Germany), 70
Nazis/National Socialists, 135
Neeley, Mark E., 19, 438, 443
Neue Preussische Kreuz-Zeitung
(newspaper), 235
Neumann, Sigmund (1904–62),
German political scientist, 308,
341n22
neutrality: and Geneva Convention,
258; U.S., 279, 336–8, 394
New Left, on international revolution,
327

Scott, Winfield (1786–1866),
American army officer, 75
Scribner's (periodical), war articles from,
244
Sedan, Battle of (1870), 36, 125, 285,
349; commemoration of (*Sedantag*),
35, 125–6, 192, 283, 292
Sedition Act (1918; amendment to
Espionage Act of 1917), 97
Seeger, Alan (1888–1916), American
poet, 166
Selbstbehauptung des Krieges, 15
Seton, Ernest Thompson (1860–1946),
American naturalist and writer, 152,
158, 162
Seven Years' War (1756–63), 22
Seward, William H. (1801–72),
American politician, 46–7
Shafter, William Rufus (1835–1906),
American army officer, 100
Sheridan, Philip H. (1831–88),
American army commander, 19–21,
333, 399, 401, 405–6, 409
Sherman Anti-Trust Act (1890), 60
Sherman, William Tecumseh
(1820–91), American army
commander, 19–21, 39, 71, 72,
399, 401, 405–6
short-war concept, 265–6, 345,
348–50, 366–7
Showalter, Dennis E., 348–9
Signal School (U.S.), 72
Sigsbee, Charles Dwight (1845–1923),
American naval officer, 102
Sims, William S. (1858–1936),
American naval officer, 331
Skinner, B. F. (1904–90), American
psychologist, 160
slavery, in wars of pacification, 428
Slovak League, 112
Smith, Jacob H., 445–6
Smith, William, 142
Snyder, Jack, 345–6
social Darwinism, 3, 7, 42–3, 48, 50,
206–9, 249, 375
Social Democratic Party of Canada,
123

Social Democratic Party of Germany
(SPD): censorship of, 324; on class
conflict, 315; enmity against,
193–9; as other, 310;
professionalism in, 309; on taxes,
322; youth organization, 169, 171,
173–5, 184–5
socialists (U.S.): on armament industry,
252; loyalty of, 117; support of
Allies by, 118
Société d'Heracleé, 82
Society for Social Reform (Germany),
169
Sombart, Werner (1863–1941),
German historical economist, 42,
217–18
Souchon, Wilhelm A. T.(1864–1919),
German naval officer, 83n11
South African War, *see* Boer War
South German Association of Young
Catholic Men, 179
South Sea Islands, 46; Samoa as part
of, 29;
Spain: and insurrection in the
Philippines, 439–40, 447; and
limited conscription, 22; and
Moroccan Crisis of 1905–6, 388;
overseas empire of, 46; *see also*
Spanish-American War
Spanish-American War (1898), 39,
108, 116, 249–51, 260, 271, 330,
334, 380: and army modernization,
72–3, 75–6; mobilization, 59; naval
warfare in, 67–8, 267; and peace
movement, 40; and racist
sentiments, 100, 107; veterans, 106,
160; volunteers, 141
SPD, *see* Social Democratic Party of
Germany
sports, and relationship to warfare,
156, 166;
Spring Rice, Cecil (1859–1918),
British diplomat, 383, 386, 390
Steever, Edgar, 146–7
Stern, Fritz, 131
Stimson, Henry L. (1867–1950),
American statesman, 74–5